Comparative Europe[an Politics]
The Story of a Profession

Edited by

Hans Daalder

with contributions by

Erik Allardt; Gabriel A. Almond; Pierre Birnbaum; Jean Blondel;
Hans Daalder (also on Stein Rokkan); Robert A. Dahl;
S. N. Eisenstadt; Peter Gerlich; Ted Robert Gurr; Jack Hayward;
Guy Hermet; Max Kaase (on Rudolf Wildenmann);
Dennis Kavanagh (on S. E. Finer); Gerhard Lehmbruch;
Arend Lijphart; Juan J. Linz; Mogens N. Pedersen; Richard Rose;
Giovanni Sartori; Philippe C. Schmitter; Gordon Smith;
Sidney Verba; Klaus von Beyme (also on Carl Joachim Friedrich);
Harold L. Wilensky; Vincent Wright

PINTER

London and New York

PINTER
A Cassell imprint
Wellington House, 125 Strand, London WC2R 0BB
370 Lexington Avenue, New York, NY 10017–6550

First published in 1997. Reprinted in paperback with minor corrections 1999.

British Library Cataloguing in Publication Data

A catalogue record for this book is available from the British Library

ISBN 1 85567 399 1 (hardback)
     1 85567 607 8 (paperback)

Typeset by Chapter One (London)
Printed and bound by Redwood Books, Trowbridge, Wiltshire

Contents

To Anneke

and to those who accompanied the other contributors
on the long road of European politics

1 Introduction

Hans Daalder

LEIDEN UNIVERSITY

A Leiden workshop and a letter of invitation

This volume contains the intellectual autobiographies of twenty-three scholars who have contributed to the development of the study of comparative European politics since World War II, preceded by companion biographies of four scholars, no longer with us, who exercised a powerful influence in the same field. The book grew out of a workshop entitled 'The intellectual autobiography of comparative European politics' which took place during the Joint Sessions of the European Consortium for Political Research, held at Leiden University from 3 to 8 April 1993.

The rationale of this workshop, and of this volume, is best explained by the following lengthy extract from the letter of invitation sent out in 1992 to potential contributors to this book. In that letter a selection of specialists were asked to join in a new venture, 'an attempt to chronicle the intellectual (auto)biography of the study of comparative [European] politics since the end of World War II'.

The letter proceeded as follows:

> The study of comparative politics has seen many developments in these years. It had to face fargoing political changes in a world clearly not free for democracy: the fall of Weimar Germany and everything which followed, the rise of totalitarian regimes, the demise of colonialism and the arrival of a host of new states which generally turned into autocracies of various kinds. Within what we have learnt to call somewhat loosely the advanced industrial democracies, a more differentiated knowledge and an increased awareness of processes of political change, have made for new theories, typologies and approaches in the comparative analysis of politics. The field has become much more professional, less institutional, often more empirical. It has undoubtedly become a massive corpus of learning.

> At the same time, the field now faces entirely new political developments, including the fall of many totalitarian and autocratic regimes, the paradox of the possible decline of the nation-state as the hitherto largely undisputed unit of analysis in an increasingly interdependent world combined with the resurgence of nationalism, a massive debate on the welfare state often thought to be one of the major achievements of modern politics,

1

prophesies about the decline of representative institutions and party systems, etc. One might argue that the discipline is facing an entirely new world in which many of the existing paradigms must come in for critical discussion.

The letter continued:

> It would seem that the development of comparative politics, [and more] particularly of comparative European politics, has been the work of a particular generation (or should we say possibly a generation or two?), itself still trained by scholars of a pre-war generation, who had to cope with a complex world of political change in a period of strong professionalization of our discipline and an unparalleled growth of knowledge on different countries and societies. It would seem both interesting and important to analyse the intellectual factors which went into the important growth of the field. One way would be the chronicling of the particular intellectual development of some of the most important scholars in the field.
>
> The idea would be to prepare a work ... in which each author would analyse the development of his or her own work. This might start with a description of particular political experiences which were important in your formative years, as well as a review of important books and scholars who influenced you in your student days. The story might then move to particular problems which you wanted to clarify. Often these might find their root in problems of particular societies, clarified by comparative perspectives. Whilst the chapter should not be a detailed *compte rendu* of all your many writings, it should deal with the birth and development of your major contributions to the field. A discussion of persons and institutions which had a strong influence on your work should not be amiss. The chapter could then move on a critical reappraisal, and an exposition of continuing puzzles, hopefully followed by an exposition of what you would regard as the most important work which you feel ought to be done or [that you] would do if there were enough time and resources.

The letter met with a gratifying response. It eventually resulted in this book, which brings together the stories of some of the more prominent architects of the new comparative European politics following World War II.

Europe within the context of a more universal comparative politics

The project opted early for a specific choice: it restricted the scope of the project to the comparative analysis of European democracies. This also determined the list of possible participants. Admittedly, the development of the new comparative politics since the 1940s and 1950s was particularly influenced by other political developments: the rise of totalitarian regimes first, a concern with 'new states', or more generally with 'non-western' politics, later. In fact, for a time 'Europe' seemed to many an enthusiastic innovator a world of staid democracies about which all was known and where little happened. But such sentiments did not last long, for reasons inherent in the new comparative politics itself and because of scholarly developments within Europe.

The persistent concern about 'totalitarianism' naturally made for comparative enquiry into past events: what after all had caused the breakdown of democratic regimes in some European countries and not others? The failure of imposed constitutional regimes in many former European colonies raised the issue of whether alternative models of democracy might have done better; where apart from North America was one to find these but in Europe (the British dominions usually being regarded as mere offshoots of a British system)? The general concern with development posed many questions for which the history of different European countries might provide possible answers, whatever the dangers of historical analogies. There was a rich literature on European countries, and access to sources was relatively easy. Europe provided, moreover, a variety of cases vital for comparative analysis with a generalizing intent, provided one really knew the specific cases that made up Europe, and went beyond the exclusive concentration on a few larger countries only.

At the same time forces at work within Europe led to a new internationalization of political research. Traditionally, the study of European government had tended to be focused heavily on the study of individual countries, generally approached in a largely descriptive manner, and often a prescriptive one as well. The experience of totalitarian dictatorships, of war and occupation, fostered a desire in the post-1945 period to understand developments, for which social sciences might offer more ready answers than law and political philosophy had traditionally provided. It also created a favourable climate for a new internationalization of political studies. This climate was greatly assisted by the generous funding from American foundations, and from governmental programmes like the Fulbright programme and, to a lesser extent, the British Council.

As many a chapter in this volume will show, this resulted in the massive trek of a new postwar generation of younger scholars to the United States particularly. They found there an exhilarating world of scholarship, with all manner of theoretical speculation and rich empirical research. This stood in marked contrast to the paucity of 'modern' social science literature in their own country, and led naturally to a desire to emulate and replicate studies on America with comparable studies at home. At the same time, a confrontation with Anglo-Saxon scholarship also provoked a natural reaction against what were often felt to be too specifically 'British' or 'American' theories, typologies or models, and fostered a desire to develop alternative theories and typologies which were more in line with the understanding of these scholars' own countries. At a minimum, it was widely felt, more countries should be brought on to the map of European comparative politics.

The development of comparative politics writing in and on Europe thus represented a process of growing international exchange, initially consisting largely of 'bilateral' relations between American scholars and experts on single European countries, to develop later into a more genuine 'multilateral' international exchange (for a fuller analysis see Daalder 1987b).

New approaches, new resources

If the new comparative European politics owed much to a growing international exchange and a better understanding of both commonalities and differences in political systems, it also shared in other processes of innovation, subsumed somewhat loosely under the label 'the behavioural revolution' (cf. Dahl 1961b). There was a growing readiness to engage in interdisciplinary or at least multidisciplinary research, and with it, to take over concepts and approaches between different disciplines. The borderline between political science and sociology became often blurred, and there was a marked influence from both economics and cultural anthropology on the new terminology of comparative politics. New research techniques became available, with survey analysis taking a particularly important place. Survey data were increasingly put at the disposal of other scholars, and were stored in newly-established data archives. New statistical tools were developed, applied with increasing ease with the aid of calculators and eventually computers. Aggregate statistics allowed for new types of comparative analysis, as both individual governments and a growing number of international organizations collected increasingly elaborate and standardized data, which were collected in more and more sophisticated data handbooks.

All such factors made for the building of entirely new infrastructures for comparative analysis. Their development owes much to the work of a number of scholars described in the chapters that follow. Given the weight and richness of American scholarship, developments within the USA were particularly important. Thus, the reader will find tributes to the role of particular departments and universities, notably Chicago, Columbia, Yale, Princeton, Stanford, Harvard, Berkeley and Michigan, to the role of American Foundations, and above all to the American Social Science Research Council with its highly influential committees (such as the Committee on Political Behavior, and above all the Committee of Comparative Politics (which under the leadership of Gabriel Almond became so influential that for the academic community the short term 'the Committee' usually suffices).

On a more international level, the chapters that follow underscore the important role of international organizations. One will find ample reference to the importance of UNESCO, the International Social Science Council, the International Political Science Association and the International Sociological Association (which were joint sponsors of the Committee of Political Sociology under the leadership of S.M. Lipset and Stein Rokkan), and, later, of the European Consortium for Political Research, which with its manifold activities now is the most influential organization in the field of the study of comparative European politics. While this volume does not intend to offer a full history of all such organizational efforts, it will testify to the role of individual scholars in such organizations, and to the lasting importance of increasingly dense personal networks which developed with and within them, in both individual and collaborative projects.

The contributors

The letter of invitation quoted at the beginning of this introduction was sent to more authors than eventually contributed to this volume. Some of those written to declined the invitation. Others who had accepted for a variety of reasons did not in the end write the chapter promised. Numbers were limited given the clear indication from publishers that a two-volume book would not really be publishable.

Readers will undoubtedly note that the contributors consist largely of an older generation, generally born before World War II. As the letter of invitation made clear, that choice was deliberate. The project was directed to a pioneering generation. The 'world' of younger scholars was a somewhat different political world, and to the extent that they were the pupils of the generation which established the new comparative European politics, their inclusion would have made for a different book.

Even so, there remains a difference in age: the oldest scholar treated in this book (Carl J. Friedrich) was born in 1901, whereas the youngest contributors were born during World War II. One reason for the age difference lies in the manner in which modern political science came to different countries. While the study of politics was a long-established separate academic discipline in the United States and Great Britain, this was much less true of a number of European countries, where the field really developed only from the 1950s or even later (for reviews, see Andrews (ed.) 1986; Vallès and Newton (eds) 1991). The general process of internationalization of academic research in the field of comparative politics affected some countries much earlier than others. Given that at least one consideration in the selection of contributors was to show the manner in which different countries were brought on to the map of comparative European politics, this made for a choice of authors in particular instances whose major work only began in the 1960s.

A further consideration in the selection of authors was a desire to take account of different approaches and paradigms. Thus, writers on neo-corporatism, the welfare state and internal violence were consciously approached in addition to scholars of political development, comparative institutions or comparative political behaviour, although in the latter case the link between their work and comparative *European* politics was somewhat less obvious. Unhappy circumstances caused two leading international survey analysts of Ann Arbor vintage to bow out, which causes the book to do less justice to important developments in that field than desired (but see Miller 1994).

Two scholars were present at the Leiden workshop in 1993 who have since died: Edward Shils and Rudolf Wildenmann. Edward Shils had intended to write a first chapter for this book, dealing with the state of comparative studies at the eve of World War II, a subject none could have covered better than this great and versatile intellectual who did so much for international social science. Fortunately, Shils has left us a series of volumes of essays in which he gave at least his own intellectual autobiography (see notably Shils 1972). And there is some consolation in the existence of an analysis by Harry Eckstein of the same subject, written as the introductory chapter by him for the path-breaking *Comparative Politics: A Reader* (1963) which he edited with David E. Apter.

Rudolf Wildenmann was one of the founding members of the European Consortium for Political Research, and the originator of its Joint Sessions of Workshops, which since 1973 have been one of the key assets of the study of comparative European politics. Characteristically, he was the first participant to present himself at the registration desk of the Leiden Joint Sessions, but the illness which killed him a few months later forced him to return home prematurely. For the *Intellectual Autobiography* workshop he had drafted a paper dealing with the road he had begun to travel which was to lead him to the summit of German and international political science. He had badly wanted to complete the paper, but could not. Max Kaase gallantly integrated the Wildenmann draft in an arresting description of Wildenmann's scholarly life in Chapter 5, which is thus partly an intellectual autobiography, partly a biography.

One author sadly missing from the volume is Karl W. Deutsch. At the time the volume was planned his health was such that it seemed inappropriate to send him an invitation to contribute, yet untimely to ask someone else to write a chapter on him. Another, happier reason was that Deutsch *had* already written two autobiographical essays, although not specifically on comparative European politics, to which the reader might profitably turn (Deutsch 1980, 1989).

Are there other regrettable omissions? Of course. One could easily draw up a list of prominent scholars in the field of comparative European politics, which would have doubled the number of contributors to this volume. They are missing, either through non-delivery of manuscripts on their part or through the absence of timely action by the editor of this volume, coupled with considerations of length. The book would have been richer if it had included more essays on older authors such as Herman Finer, Karl Loewenstein, Sigmund Neumann, Henry Ehrmann or Otto Kirchheimer. It could have benefited from the inclusion of a greater number of leading French political scientists, most notably Maurice Duverger (even though his contribution to comparative European politics centred on a rather limited period of his academic and political life). The choice of a single author for most individual countries inevitably does injustice to the richness of scholarship within them – not to speak of the absence of any scholar from countries such as Belgium, Sweden or Switzerland. Not only feminists will regret the absence of even one woman political scientist. So does the editor, who did not succeed in persuading those approached to deliver a chapter.

For all such regrets, the book which has finally come out of the project contains a unique chronicle of developments in the field of comparative European politics. It contains some twenty-seven individual life stories of leading scholars, showing how particular experiences in youth turned them towards the study of politics. It describes the particular milieux – personal and academic – in which they developed as scholars, singling out important sources of intellectual inspiration, possibly traumatic political experiences, and individual paths of scholarship. It describes the development of important collaborative ventures and budding organizational initiatives. If offers stories of academic careers, of achievements and doubts, of lessons learned or imparted.

Working with so many authors, of whom even the oldest invariably presented manuscripts on floppy disks, with intensive communication facilitated by fax and e-mail, was an exciting venture. I thank them all.

Given the many cross-references throughout the book, it was decided to amalgamate all chapter bibliographies into one common bibliography at the end of this book.

I gladly acknowledge important editorial and secretarial help from Marlene Posthumus Meyjes-Lumas, Willeke van Staalduinen and Annette Slinger.

2 A founding father of comparative politics: Carl Joachim Friedrich

Klaus von Beyme

Personal background

Carl Joachim Friedrich was the son of a professor of medicine. His mother came from one of the oldest families of Prussian nobility. Friedrich was proud of both: the background of the *Bildungsbürgertum* which made it natural that he became a university professor like his father, and the background of the landed gentry. Until his retirement he ran a farm in New Hampshire. The book about the *New Belief in the Common Man* (1942) in which Friedrich opposed the American ideal of the common man to the ideal of the British gentleman is a homage to life in the country-side and the reconciliation of Friedrich's two souls: American and European, bourgeois and aristocratic.

There was no political science proper when Friedrich studied in Heidelberg in the early Weimar Republic. He did his German dissertation in economics under Alfred Weber (the brother of Max Weber) in 1925. A year later he started teaching at Harvard University. Friedrich stayed in America because of the new field, so underdeveloped in Germany, and because of the splendid conditions for research whereas in Germany prospects were dim in the late Weimar Republic and the Nazi period. He therefore never felt as an émigré and he kept a more positive attitude towards his home country than other German-speaking scholars who had to leave the country. When he met in the early 1940s an old friend of his, Fritz Morstein Marx, and the latter refused to speak German and declared that he would never go back to Germany, Friedrich is reported to have been seriously upset: 'What does that mean? Of course all of us will go back to Germany and help to build up democracy as soon as the war is over.' Morstein Marx went also. He even came back on a permanent basis to the Administrative Academy of Speyer – which was planned to become a kind of German *ENA*.

After the Nazis took over, Friedrich was always preparing the re-education of Europe. He acted as chairman for a 'committee on the instruction of civil servants' and as a director of a 'study group on broadcasting'. After 1940 he published *Controlling Broadcasting in Wartime* and similar contributions to the field. In 1943 he became Director of the School of Overseas Administration. After 1945 Friedrich was the most important adviser to General Clay, heading the military government in Germany. Friedrich had some impact on drafting the constitutions of certain *Länder* in the American zone of occupation. His role in the constitution-making process of the Federal Republic of Germany is not yet completely explored. Friedrich tried to defend the autonomy of the German founding fathers and to prevent Clay from excessive interference (Friedrich 1949). The perceptions of the Germans involved and Clay's views were in retrospect, however, quite different. The Germans felt that the Americans imposed certain principles on them. The Americans wondered rather why Germans exercised little resistance against the views of the military administration (Clay 1950, p.422).

Clay went back to America. Friedrich, however, was fascinated by commuting between America and Germany. In 1954 Friedrich accepted a deal between Harvard University and the German authorities enabling him to teach part-time at Harvard and in Heidelberg. The German question seemed to be settled by the division of the country. Friedrich turned to the unification of Europe. The IPSA group on European Unification was one of the first research groups in the international political science organization. As President of IPSA (1970–73) Friedrich concentrated on building up political science in Europe and contributing to the unification of Europe.

Friedrich was among the very few figures who were represented in the ranking of great men of the discipline in the pre-1945 period, as well as after the war (Somit and Tanenhaus 1964, p.66). This success was mainly due to his work in both political theory and comparative politics. Moreover, most émigrés from the German-speaking countries in American political science remained rather European in outlook. With the exception of Karl W. Deutsch or Heinz Eulau, they rarely worked on the American system. The great figures possessing powerful book-learning who had an impact on American thought, such as Leo Strauss, Eric Voegelin or Hannah Arendt, developed schools of devoted disciples, but they hardly had any relation with American politics. Friedrich, in his *New Belief in the Common Man*, showed, however, a genuine under-standing of American democratic thought and he was interested in demonstrating the American impact on European countries (cf. Friedrich 1967).

On the other hand, Friedrich kept away from over-adaptation. Friedrich wrote his American Ph.D. dissertation on the German thinker Johannes Althusius. Again, he was interested in the intersections of political traditions. Althusius, with his idea that the state is only a 'federation of federations', was one of the few German thinkers quoted in *The Federalist Papers*. Althusius, as a Calvinist exception among German thinkers, was, moreover, an example to show that simplifications of German history of the kind 'From Luther to Hitler' fell short of grasping the whole German tradition. There was a line of thought from Althusius to Kant which Friedrich emphasized against the contemporary anti-German history of ideas which normally dealt with Fichte, Hegel, Schelling, Nietzsche and others who had their intellectual merits but were hardly democratic pluralists. Shortly after the Second World War Friedrich published on this tradition in his book *Inevitable Peace* (1948). Cusanus, Pufendorf, Althusius, Thomasius, Kant, Mohl and others attracted Friedrich's attention in his studies on the *Philosophy of Law in Historical Perspective* (1960).

Friedrich has always amazed his American colleagues by his universality and his reluctance to become a narrow specialist. There is hardly any area of political science in which he did not publish. Even international relations attracted his curiosity in the time of Nazi rule, when he wrote his book *Foreign Policy in the Making* (1938).

For Friedrich however, the history of ideas was not, unlike for his teacher McIlwain, a subject in itself. Friedrich was always interested in the impact of these ideas on contemporary politics. He offered no exclusive historical approach which was satisfied to evaluate theories in their time. He always looked for modern equivalents of classical notions. This was most clearly shown in his book *Constitutional Reason of State. The Survival of the Constitutional Order* (1957). He started with Machiavelli and ended with modern devices for the protection of constitutionality. At the end of the book he compared modern solutions to the problem. Friedrich saw four solutions: (1) the legal solution (the USA, Switzerland); (2) outlawing radical organizations (Germany); (3) the purging from the administration of extremist elements (France); (4) handling the problem within the limits of penal law (Britain). Friedrich favoured the British solution. He objected less to the German concept of 'defensive democracy', however, than other émigrés such as Karl Loewenstein. He also accepted the German measures for stabilizing the parliamentary system in order to protect it from tendencies of erosion under the Weimar regime. His friend Alexander Rüstow, who helped to bring him to Heidelberg, was among those liberal thinkers who already in the late Weimar Republic thought about the introduction of the 'constructive vote of non-confidence'. There existed in Germany the school of *Ordo* Liberalism, centring mostly in Freiburg. Rüstow and Röpke were among its most important thinkers.

Ludwig Erhard, Minister of Economic Affairs under Adenauer, was implementing these ideas through a premature liberalization of the economy. Friedrich shared many of the views of the *Ordo* Liberals though he was never dogmatic on economic matters. But he shared with his friends of the Freiburg school the basic idea that liberalism has to be defended by order.

Comparative studies of constitutionalism and democracy

When I invited authors to contribute articles to a Festschrift for Friedrich's 70th anniversary, I received a written rebuff from one of America's pioneers of the behavioural revolt – another émigré from Germany. The letter concluded: 'I don't care for *Dogmengeschichte*, but Friedrich was a pioneer in comparative politics and generations of political scientists have been educated with his major book. I shall write a chapter on the theory of comparison.' This was a typical error of the scientistic behaviouralists, to confound 'political theory' and 'history of ideas', because the Festschrift had the title *Theory and Politics* (the title was proposed by Karl W. Deutsch; cf. von Beyme, 1971a).

Indeed, Friedrich was appreciated by large numbers in the scientific community mostly because of his contributions to comparative politics, since for most American political scientists the history of ideas was a marginal field, characteristic of a pre-scientific state of affairs. Friedrich was one of the exceptional scholars who linked theoretical and empirical interests. He applied what he called 'descriptive theory' to comparative politics, though even some of his former students dubbed this a *contradictio in adiecto*. Harry Eckstein (1963) called Friedrich's approach to comparative politics an 'antimethodological methodology'. Friedrich had a clear antipathy against rigorous scientism and the behaviouralist orthodoxy which began to establish itself after the war. *Man and his Government* (1963) – one of the most daring attempts to integrate theory and description of systems – was not able to repeat the enormous success which his best-known book on comparative politics had in America before the war. Its first title in 1937 was *Constitutional Government and Politics*. A revised 1946 edition changed the title to *Constitutional Government and Democracy*. But the main notion was still 'constitutional government'. On the one hand this served the purpose to include pre-democratic regimes. On the other hand Friedrich, as a liberal conservative, was far from advocating radical democracy. He was attracted by the American presidential system and American constitutionalism because he estimated precisely the prevalences of checks and balances over the monistic perception of a *volonté générale*. At the same time he refrained from the dogmatism of many scholars of the time, especially in the debate, on the superiority of British parliamentary government at the end of World War II, between Price and Laski in the *Public Administration Review* (1944).

The time of constitution-making after World War II was a time of vehement debates on various *governmental systems*. Friedrich kept aloof from the alternatives: presidential or parliamentary government. At a time when even the American Political Science Association was unwise enough to jump collectively into the political arena and to advocate a more 'responsible party government' according to the British model, Friedrich had a wider range of experiences at his disposition. American debates at that time were concentrated on the alternative of 'American' or 'British' experience. Hardly anyone saw valuable elements on the continent. Even the great comparativists initially did not understand all European systems. In the 1950s Almond still worked with three types: 'British', 'continental' and a 'mixed type', under which he subsumed everything which did not fit, especially Scandinavia and the Benelux countries. Friedrich had at least the Swiss example at his disposition. With Taylor Cole he had worked on his first empirical study *Responsible Bureaucracy. A Study of the Swiss Civil Service* (1932).

After the war Friedrich pondered introducing the *presidential system* into Germany. But there was little possibility of this. Only the Bavarian conservatives in the CSU and some conservative Liberals in the FDP were in favour of such a system. A 'grand coalition' in the parliamentary council stuck to the German tradition of the parliamentary system which dated back to the revolution of 1848–49.

The search for the best governmental system was soon abandoned. It sprang up again in 1958 when de Gaulle introduced a new semi-presidential system in France. But he did not mean to copy American presidentialism but rather the 'Orléanist' system of parliamentary rule. By that time, Friedrich was less concerned with individual European states, but rather with the European community. After thorough examinations of various regimes he advocated in his *Studies of Federalism* (Bowie and Friedrich 1954, p.84) the *Swiss council system* for the budding European political system. The Swiss model seemed to avoid competition in terms of prestige between the various nationalities, since executive leadership is rotating among them. The Swiss system for Friedrich offered a ready solution for the problem of how to provide a functioning ceremonial Head of State, without requiring the discarding of existing heads in the member states.

Friedrich's main thrust in comparative politics was the *safeguard of constitutionalism and democracy*. Friedrich's concept of democracy however, was – as was later Dahl's concept of polyarchy – broader than the notions of the radical democrats after World War II. Friedrich shared the emphasis on constitutionalism in his early years with the constitutional lawyers of his time. Unlike the jurists, however, he avoided constitutional formalism. Friedrich was one of the first comparative scholars who elaborated the great topics of political sociology which were theoretically developed by classical political thinkers from Montesquieu to Tocqueville and Mohl.

Friedrich's problem underlying all the comparative studies was twofold. First, he was concerned with *restriction* on the realization of the people's will by constitutionalism, division of powers, federalism, judicial review. In this respect Friedrich was more American than European. His second question to comparative politics was: which are *typical dangers for democracy*? Having grown up in the Weimar Republic, close to the spirit of liberals such as Alfred Weber and Alexander Rüstow who held their chair in sociology, he was motivated by the question: 'How can the erosion of democracy be avoided?' His hostility towards identity theories of political representation was partly shaped by his refutation of the theories of democracy of Carl Schmitt, who advocated charismatic leadership in the tradition of Max Weber, but soon deteriorated to apologies for the charismatic dictatorship of Hitler.

Friedrich largely deviated from the mainstream of comparative treatises after the war. His *Constitutional Government and Democracy* did not start with representative institutions and parliaments, but with bureaucracy and the military establishment. Police and justice followed. The second part was devoted to constitutionalism, including his favourite topic: federalism. The core of representative government was dealt with only in the third part of the book. His concept of democracy was a rather conservative one. In spite of his interest in Switzerland he distrusted direct democracy. 'The will of people has lost some of its luster as basis of legitimacy and as a ground for securing universal acceptance' (Friedrich 1968, p.556). He did not exclude plebis-citarian elements. Direct popular action can serve to strengthen the democratic element. But he was afraid that mostly the 'dose is too strong', so that it hardly ever serves as a remedy for the shortcomings of representative government.

Friedrich's systematic approach to comparative politics was largely shaped by his personal political experiences: the double legitimacy of elections and referenda and direct election of the president in the Weimar Republic, the abuses of power in the time of the Nazi rule, the attempt to expel the 'devil' of authoritarian rule with the Beelzebub of constitutional dictatorship and military rule in postwar Germany. It is not by chance that the book concludes with a chapter on 'constitutional dictatorship and emergency powers'. On the whole, Friedrich's concept of democracy was not shaped by American optimism and true 'belief in the common man'. Friedrich's belief in the 'common man' remained on the level of the 'history of ideas', written about in a time when he lived in the romantic Arcadian area of Concord. His political experience was rather of 'abuse of powers', and this largely shaped his views on constitutional government and democracy.

Democracy and constitutionalism were in danger through concentration of power. In situations of political crisis the 'constitutional *reason of the state*' had to protect the democratic system. Friedrich (1957) did not share the American hostility towards ideas of the 'reason of the state'. Only after the Vietnam war did he become obsessed with the pathologies of modern politics: violence, betrayal, corruption, secrecy, and propaganda (Friedrich 1972).

The students' rebellion had some impact on Friedrich after he became Emeritus. He worried increasingly about the survival of Western democracy. The substitution of 'bullets for ballots' and 'bombs for arguments' led the old Friedrich (1972, p.232) to more conservative views. The rebellious students were most upset to read: 'Our analysis has, I hope, shown that politics needs all these dubious practices; it cannot be managed without violence, betrayal, corruption, secrecy, and propaganda.' 'Secrecy' was particularly criticized. This was the time when students broke into the Heidelberg Institute in order to uncover Friedrich's alleged relations with the CIA.

Like another émigré from Germany in his time, Hans Morgenthau, who concentrated on international relations, Friedrich always was a realist. He distrusted moralism in politics, and sentimentalist and romantic movements in political life. Unlike Morgenthau he dealt with constitutional orders. 'Law', not moral fundamentalism, was to rule modern democracy. Even in his last book, when defending 'dubious practices' he remained an advocate of 'moderate politics'.

The comparison of non-democratic regimes

A second danger to constitutional government and democracy Friedrich saw lurking from outside. Friedrich developed his views on democracy not only by comparison between the most *similar* cases of democracy. Without direct methodological commitment to a comparison between the most *dissimilar* cases, he contrasted Western democracy with the dangers of competing systems of rule, especially totalitarianism.

Friedrich had little interest in the Third World. But as an adviser to Muñoz Marin in the constitution-making process of Puerto Rico he published on at least one aspect of a Third World country (1959). Third World countries were considered by Friedrich as countries on the road to democracy. He was not interested, as Barrington Moore was, in developing alternative roads of development. His pluralism was restricted to the ideas of the Christian North-Atlantic world. Even today the most frequently quoted book of Friedrich's remains *Totalitarian Dictatorship and Autocracy* (Friedrich and Brzezinski 1956, 1965).

The antithesis to constitutional government in his time was totalitarianism. He was not so obsessed with the Nazi regime as Hannah Arendt was, although the parts on fascist regimes in *Totalitarian Dictatorship and Autocracy* were predominantly his. More than Arendt he was interested in empirical comparisons. But for the integrity of his type of totalitarian dictatorship he had to homogenize developments. He even induced one of his students to write a dissertation on Mussolini's system as a totalitarian dictatorship, although the majority of scholars have always seen fascist Italy as a case apart (Germino 1959).

The sections on communist regimes were written by Brzezinski, who originally had accepted Friedrich's rigid definitions of totalitarianism, but increasingly doubted that they applied to most of the communist countries. He too experienced, especially via contacts with his native country (Poland) after 1956, the fact that there were not only 'islands of seperatedness' in communist systems, but a certain degree of pluralism or even resistance. Friedrich clung to the idea that totalitarianism can never be toppled by resistance from within. He did not elaborate on the consequences for foreign policy. Fortunately the deadlock of atomic power arsenals prevented decision-makers from applying Friedrich's theories to world politics. Friedrich was falsified only after his death. In spite of this falsification the theory of totalitarianism experienced a revival after the collapse of communism, because it was the theory most critical of the communist countries. However, Friedrich never accepted the view developed by Gordon Skilling, Klaus von Beyme and others in the mid-1960s that interest group and élite pluralism theories had to be applied to the studies of communism.

Friedrich's theory was an important asset in political quarrels about communism. His theory of totalitarianism was hailed as being correct. The internal development towards more democracy and constitutionalism was indeed halted. The present writer, and the positivistic mainstream of Sovietologists, have been more optimistic than Friedrich. After the collapse of communism Friedrich became a chief witness for the rotten character of communism *ex tunc*. But the new wave of application of Friedrich's version of totalitarianism overlooked that a second prognosis was wrong: Friedrich thought that totalitarian systems can only be defeated by force from outside. In this respect Friedrich's theories were proved wrong.

Franco's Spain had already caused me to argue with Friedrich. In the early stages this system came close to Friedrich's definition of totalitarianism. But there nevertheless was internal development – not imposed from outside. The *dictadura* turned step by step into a *dictablanda*. Friedrich relativized these events by the argument that Spain is within the Western world and so was under heavy pressure. Also, Spain was not a socialist system. The argument was plausible in the 1970s, but it made his theory still less correct, because it implied that a 'socialist economy' cannot be disrupted from inside. That is precisely what happened! Not only Friedrich was wrong in his prognosis. The forecasts that communism would collapse through ethnic strife (Carrère d'Encausse) or through internal conflict (Amalrik) were also wrong. Communism collapsed mainly because of its incapacity to develop its economy. National strife was rather a consequence of this than the reason for the decline of the system.

Brzezinski did not co-operate on the second edition of their common book. Apparently they had different views on the subject in the meantime. Brzezinski had increasing doubts about the comparability of Nazi and communist dictatorship. He was a more thorough observer of the communist camp and did not overlook certain new developments. In the Festschrift for Friedrich's 70th anniversary Brzezinski wrote on 'Dysfunctional totalitarianism'. He anticipated contradictions between the modernization of society and the rigidity of the political system which Friedrich had never realized (see Brzezinski in von Beyme 1971a, pp.375–89).

Conclusion

Carl Joachim Friedrich was a commuter between his two fatherlands: the USA and Germany. His sense of family, intensive as the ancient Greeks, linked him to Germany and forced him to migrate back and forth in spite of the fact that he ruined his health. Friedrich had no émigré complex and was more optimistic than other émigrés about the necessities of political reconstruction after the war.

Friedrich had many students on both sides of the Atlantic, but he never had 'true disciples' and he left no school. This did not mean, however, that he had no mission and no vision. He was among the first American scholars to study European integration. As early as 1954 he combined institutional approaches with the analysis of certain policy arenas (Bowie and Friedrich 1954). Later he studied, with a group of young German scholars, the social dimensions of European community building. More than in former studies, developments at the grass roots of politics were included, such as international exchange and the *jumelages* between the cities of Europe.

The title of Friedrich's book *Europe as an Emergent Nation* (1969) sounded as though it was promoting an illusion. Actually it was fairly realistic in the details of its analysis and it was more correct in its prognosis than many of the forecasts which have fascinated generations of scholars working on Europe, ranging from Ernst Haas's neofunctional hypothesis to Karl Deutsch's cybernetic games with the formation of contacts in Europe.

Friedrich was a scholar of the nineteenth-century type, a type doomed to disappear. Nobody today would dare to deal with all the political systems in history. In *Man and his Government* (1963) he discovered thirteen types of rule. Moreover, his historical interests always included topics such as 'the arts and politics'. Friedrich was not only a great scholar but also a kind of artist. He was proud of having the right to participate with his cello in the practice sessions of the Boston Symphony Orchestra. In his book *The Age of Baroque* (1952) he discovered fascinating parallel developments in political theory, art, music and literature.

Friedrich was a genuine comparativist. Comparison to him was not restricted to comparisons within one narrow discipline. It was interdisciplinary long before this catchword became a nostalgic slogan of narrow specialists who tried to leave their respective ivory towers.

3 The fusion of history and politics: the case of S.E. Finer*

Dennis Kavanagh

University of Liverpool

The writings of Sammy Finer provide a good part of his own intellectual biography. They are full of comments and asides about the state of the discipline, of how he came to approach the subject he was writing about, and of authors whose work he found useful and less than useful. He filled his pages with his own vibrant personality and strong opinions. In addition, he wrote 'An Idiosyncratic Retrospect' for a special issue of *Government and Opposition* (Finer 1980b), which provided an amusing and opinionated essay on his intellectual development. There is also a Festschrift (Kavanagh and Peele (eds) 1984) and a special issue of *Government and Opposition* (1994), both of which contain essays which comment in part on his life and work.

Sammy Finer's published writings are impressive on several counts, not least because of their range. His studies cover biography, public administration, the military, British pressure groups and political parties. West European trade unions, the political influence of private capital, constitutions, Parliament, studies of Pareto and Siéyès, electoral systems, the influence of ideas on British government in the nineteenth century, as well as the history of government. It sounds like the record of a butterfly, until one reads the work!

Finer once identified ten approaches to comparative government. His own work exemplifies at least five:

1. Typological (e.g. his *Comparative Government*).
2. Group analysis (e.g. his *Anonymous Empire*).
3. Phenomena analysis (e.g. his study of the military in *The Man on Horseback*).
4. Élite theory (e.g. his edition of the writings of Pareto).
5. Historical analysis (e.g. his study of the role of the military in state building in Charles Tilly's *The Formation of National States in Western Europe* and his final work, *The History of Government from the Earliest Times*, published posthumously (Finer 1997)).

* I am grateful, for comments on an earlier version of this paper, to Hugh Berrington and Jack Hayward, both former colleagues of Finer, and to Catherine Jones Finer, his widow.

What he did not perform was:

1. Traditional country-by-country description (e.g. Bryce).
2. Traditional cross-institutional description (e.g. Friedrich and Herman Finer).
3. Functional analysis (e.g. Almond).
4. General systems analysis (e.g. Easton).
5. Profile and scale analysis (e.g. Banks and Textor).

This chapter does not purport to be an appreciation of Sammy Finer's work nor of his place among students of comparative politics. Rather, it tries to assess the intellectual influences on his work, the impact of American political science and the continuities in his research interests and methods. Finally, it discusses the approach he adopted in his major studies.

Influences

Sammy Finer always impressed observers as being intellectually self-contained. He could be generous about others, but he had no gurus, except for his brother. He was not much affected in his work by contemporary events, and he did not so much accept or reject other approaches as use them to sharpen his own thinking about subject matter and methods. That said, it is possible to discern three sets of factors that seem to have shaped his intellectual development and the kind of comparative work that he undertook.

First and foremost as a personal influence must be Herman Finer, an elder brother by eighteen years, but in truth more of a father-figure. Herman was the path-breaker in a poor Romanian Jewish family living in North London (Islington) at the turn of the century. He was the first Finer to go to university and pursue a respectable (academic) career, and the first to overcome anti-Semitic prejudice. His great work *Theory and Practice of Modern Government* was first published in 1932. This, along with Carl Friedrich's *Constitutional Government* (1937), was the first institution-by-institution approach and broke away from the country-by-country approach. Sammy was aged 17 in 1932 and would have grown up aware of Herman's work. Herman was a role model and Sammy's declared early ambition was 'to be like my brother'. Herman was also important in persuading their parents to allow Sammy to concentrate on arts rather than science subjects in the sixth form of his school and not pursue a career in medicine.

To the end of his life Sammy was devoted to his brother and a great defender of *Theory and Practice*. He also acknowledged that Herman shaped his intellectual outlook. From his brother he learnt the following:

1. Politics is not a natural science but it can be a disciplined and systematic study. This is best achieved by looking for patterns of uniformities and regularities across time and space. The comparative approach is the nearest approach to a scientific method.
2. All generalizations are limited. A good grasp of history is essential for understanding the context and antecedents of political institutions – and for testing general

statements. Indeed, Sammy's last and greatest work, *The History of Government from Earliest Times*, is comparative in time as well as space.

3. It is more useful to adopt a problem-oriented approach than to seek some grand theory of politics.

As a young man Sammy Finer admired works which had a comprehensive framework, and a bent for practical application. As a student, he was for a time a Marxist ('everything suddenly became clear'), but this phase passed quickly and left no mark (Finer 1980b, p.348). Then he became a follower of John Maynard Keynes. *The General Theory of Interest, Employment and Money* (1936) provided an answer to mass unemployment and was attractive to politically left-of-centre people such as Sammy and Herman. Another influence on the young Sammy was the work of Pareto, particularly the chapter *Introduction à la science sociale* in the *Manuel*. He was impressed by Pareto's realism and his exposure of so much political and moral theory as 'bunkum', or 'pseudo-scientific rationalisations'. For somebody who disliked normative moral and political theory 'Pareto was a welcome beacon: I felt I was in good company, the theories were indeed all poppycock, as I had surmised' (1980b, p.349).

A final influence was more mundane – circumstances. One says mundane because Finer's work seems to have been relatively untouched by the dramatic events of the 1930s – the Spanish Civil War and the rise of fascism – though he was troubled by the treatment of Jews in Germany in the 1930s and the Cold War after 1945. He turned to studying pressure groups in the mid-1950s when he became bored with the study of local government. A period spent as a visiting professor at Cornell University in 1962 stimulated him to outline a course of lectures which subsequently became *Comparative Government* (1970b). Interest in the military grew out of his study of pressure groups and his own curiosity. He recalled, in 1990, saying to a colleague:

> You know, it is amazing. You could draw a geography of volcanic zones, like Latin America and the Middle East, in which there is one eruption after another of military rebellions and revolutions.

Hence, *The Man on Horseback*. An invitation to Stanford University in the summer of 1970 to join a workshop, convened by Gabriel Almond and Charles Tilly, on European state-making also left a mark. This experience must have played a part in stimulating Finer to turn eventually to the history of government as the major project for his retirement. He claims that the idea of the *History* as a retirement project occurred as he woke up from a midday nap. He suddenly realized that nobody had done such an exercise, starting with Babylon and Egypt down to the present.

When in 1974 he was writing his chapter on the role of the military on state-building he still had no long-term project in mind, but waited for topics to come up. He said, in an interview:

> ... there is no great prospective design for any future books. I believe in the knock-on principle in life. (Hennessy 1974, p.7)

His first book, on Edwin Chadwick, had been suggested by Herman. Later publications, such as *Adversary Politics* (1975b) and *The Changing British Party*

System 1945–79 (1980a), were stimulated by suggestions from friends and publishers. Discontent with the British party and political system was both understandable and widespread in the 1970s. What was original about Finer's advocacy of electoral reform was that it was made not on grounds of fairness but on that of promoting good and consistent – i.e. policy-continuous – government. The study of the party system emerged from his membership of a multinational team which was examining how the parties in Western Europe had changed since 1945.

Herman, with his wide range of intellectual interests and international contacts, would certainly have broadened the young Sammy's horizons. There was little else in Britain to encourage a young comparativist. After all, as a politics student at Oxford in the 1930s he would have studied only Western liberal democracies and relied on country-by-country studies, or the new institution-by-institution studies of his brother and Carl Friedrich's *Constitutional Government* (1937). Herman Finer had gone to Chicago before the war and never returned to live or work in Britain. In Britain in the 1950s political studies – the professional association self-consciously rejected the term political science – were still mostly non-comparative and atheoretical, and they showed little interest in other countries apart from France and the United States. Developments in American political science at the time, particularly the application of social science techniques, found few echoes in Britain. Before 1950 it was not possible to take a degree in politics alone (indeed Sammy had studied politics as part of the politics, philosophy and economics degree) and the few university courses on the subject were usually limited to the study of 'the British Constitution', defined narrowly, along with study of the writings of major political theorists. Academic political science was a small, intimate world, largely centred in Oxford and the London School of Economics. D.N. Chester, the first Chairman of the Political Studies Association in 1950, recalled that

> it was comparatively easy for, say, a modern historian to become a well-accepted teacher of politics quite quickly. All that was needed, in addition to the knowledge of British, American and French history they already possessed, was the reading of a dozen or so standard works and an interest in contemporary affairs. (Chester 1975, p.163)

Finer had very precise and disparaging views about Oxford political scientists:

> They have never understood the distinction between political science and contemporary history – and the establishment is such that Oxford's modern history tutors *don't want to know* of any such distinction. (Letter from Catherine Jones Finer)

He regarded post-war Oxford as increasingly a backwater of UK political science, such as it was – for all its sense of self-assurance.

It is worth noting that Sammy Finer wrote on strictly British topics until *The Man on Horseback*, published in 1962 when he was aged 47. But the early work was distinctive. *The Life and Times of Sir Edwin Chadwick* (1952) was historical in approach. Yet Sammy's interest in model building and teasing out lessons was seen in a later, related piece on the impact of ideas on public policy, 'The Transmission of Benthamite Ideas' (1972). *Backbench Opinion in the House of Commons* (1961), with David Bartholomew and Hugh Berrington, with its use of Early Day Motions as a means of studying the attitudes and behaviour of MPs, was inspired by David Truman's *The Congressional Party*. Sammy lost interest in this work and it was Hugh Berrington who carried it on. Finer's interest in pressure groups was also inspired by American studies, notably David Truman's *The Governmental Process* (1951). Finer held back, however, from accepting the more ambitious claims of group theorists that all social and political life was conducted and mediated through groups, and that all political outcomes were the results of group pressures.

What is interesting for the comparativist is that even in these national studies Finer was still looking for relationships and regularities which could then be tested. In his study of pressure groups *Anonymous Empire* (1958) for example, he presented a number of conditions which affected the likelihood of a group's success in persuading a minister to meet its demands. The means by which Benthamite ideas were transmitted to decision-makers in the nineteenth century were, he suggests, *irradiation, suscitation* and *permeation*. These operated in a cyclical fashion – a favourite Finer term:

IRRADIATION made friends and influenced people. Through them, SUSCITATION proved possible. SUSCITATION led to official appointments and hence PERMEATION. And permeation led to further irradiation and suscitation and so on *da capo*. (Finer 1972, p.11)

The American connection

Finer's relationship with American political science was ambiguous. In his essay on the development of political science in Britain, Jack Hayward (1991, p.96) wrote of the 'Muted Impact of American Political Science'. Sammy was aware of it, but always kept his distance – and Americans, by and large, reciprocated. During his academic career he spent surprising little time in the United States. We have already referred to the year at Cornell in 1962 and time at Palo Alto in 1970. Both of these had an influence on him, although mainly in the nature of consolidating the way that his mind was working.

My impression is that Finer was always alert to new developments in the United States, and would come to terms with them, but in time his interest would cool. He also differed from many American political scientists in that he was not much of a team player, though he was a 'team activator' for encouraging other individual researchers. Except for the collaborative work on backbench opinion in the House of Commons, most of his work was done on his own. He did not need research grants or research assistants but relied on a good library, his formidable memory and his own sharp mind.

One positive American influence was the Social Science Research Seminar on comparative politics held at Northwestern University 1952. This produced a report in 1953 and he attended an IPSA Round Table in Florence in 1954 which discussed it. Finer welcomed its call for a study of 'systematic politics', for study of non-Western as well as Western societies, and for the search for patterns of uniformity and difference. He developed his own comparative course of lectures at Keele along these lines. In 1980 he recalled:

My new outlook took me beyond the mere taxonomy of regimes: it made possible a deeper understanding of the nature of political behaviour as such. It is from this standpoint that the course of lectures emerged which, much later, would become the basis for *Comparative Government*. (Finer 1980b, p.354)

Finer recalled (1980b) that his contribution to the Round Table made a distinction between the approaches of the historian and of the comparativist, something that proved to be the key to understanding his own approach. He claimed that governmental data could be classified, analysed and compared, and that they could be shown to exhibit causal interrelationships. In other words, governmental phenomena were not unique to time and place and circumstances, and they therefore differed from historical data. Catherine Jones Finer, in her recent memoir, forcefully makes the point that for Sammy the job of the scholar, including the historian, was

> to explore and account for *particularities*, whereas it was the business of the comparativist to be on the look-out for *regularities* across the range of reported experience. (Jones Finer 1994, p.582)

He was one of the few scholars to engage in both general *and* specialized study.

Finer was certainly impressed with the ambitious work of Gabriel Almond and other Americans comparing political systems across time and place. The conceptual frameworks and models of others always interested him, until he saw through them! He saw merit in the structural-functional approach and thought that it provided a useful checklist of functions for governments. But he became a passionate critic of the search for a Grand Theory and the systems approach of David Easton. He objected to the way that Easton's approach relegated government and political institutions to the category of a 'black box', which converted inputs from the environment into outputs. State and government were now described as a political system which 'steered' or 'processed' inputs from the environment. As we shall see later, Finer made hay with the careless and inconsistent use of the terms in the systems approach. He was also disturbed by three other features:

1. The scant knowledge of history (and therefore understanding) evident in much of the work.
2. The false claim to innovation. He often claimed 'It's all in Herbert Spencer and Pareto, you know'. More particularly, he complained that 'nowadays "automatically produced" reading lists never go back beyond ten years – as if before ten years ago nothing was'.
3. Above all, the reductionist way in which politics and institutions were made into dependent variables. Mainstream American political science, like Marxism, too easily accepted structural determinism (1980b, p.358).

Yet the state-building group, organized by Charles Tilly in the early 1970s, certainly appealed to him. He carried on with the study of military and state-building and this probably gave him the idea for his *The History of Government from the Earliest Times*. Comparative historical analysis had the advantages that it provided a richer variety of states than provided by the late twentieth century and certain pre-conditions might be elicited which might be applicable to the stages and problems of contemporary state formation.

Continuities

A number of themes recur in Finer's comparative work, indeed from the first books on Chadwick and on public administration. The first is the emphasis on political institutions, notably government and the state. Finer took his discipline and his subject matter seriously. Politics was not a dependent variable and its study could not be reduced to sociology or economics. His friend Ghita Ionescu correctly notes that for Finer, government was the real core of politics (Ionescu 1994, p.601).

A second persisting feature is the importance attached to defining terms. He was an enemy of useless neologisms (he would claim that those he coined were useful!) and semantic confusion. The reader is confronted at an early stage in virtually all his writings with a definition of key concepts. The first page of *Comparative Government* offers a definition of government. The very first sentence of *Adversary Politics* defines the subject: 'Briefly, the adversary system is a stand-up fight between two adversaries for the favour of the lookers-on.' The lobby is defined on page 2 of *Anonymous Empire* and an essay on pressure groups and political participation begins: 'By "political participation", I stipulate: *sharing in the framing or execution of public policies*'. The chapter 'State- and Nation-Building in Europe. The Role of the Military' (1975a, pp.84–90) spends the first seven pages defending the author's conceptualization of the two key variables, the modern state and the military 'format' (basis of service, size, composition and stratification). Finer's 1970 essay on Gabriel Almond's use of political system is subtitled 'a textual critique'. He had many problems with the use of systems and its new vocabulary. There was the boundary problem: where did the political begin and the non-political end? How could an input be transformed into an output, unchanged? The term system was so loosely defined that it was virtually impossible to say that it ever disintegrated or disappeared. 'Overload' was defined in terms of 'critical limits', but there was no empirical test of these critical limits.

A third feature stems from his belief that comparative study would never be scientific in the sense that it would generate laws which were universally valid. The goal should be to make testable generalizations of the 'if x ... then y' category. Finer distrusted General Theory and preferred what he called the 'problem centred' approach. He wrote (1980a, p.362):

> I feel sure, now, that 'answers' are problem-related and problem-conditioned and so for that matters are techniques, and indeed classificatory schemes also. Our building blocks and political studies are neither numbers or sense data. They are mental constructs, that is to say *concepts*.

A good example of his pragmatic approach was his boast that he always wrote his introductory chapter last! He found that the scheme he started with broke up as the material unfolded (Finer 1983, p.14). The purpose of comparison was explanation. This was spelt out most eloquently in the same 1980 essay when he wrote:

> When I reflect on what I have been doing in my work, it seems, at the end of the day, something that I can express variously as: *interpreting*, a body of factual knowledge; or, if you will, making a *pattern* out of it: or, most simply and probably, most comprehensively, making *sense* out of it. (1980a, p.363)

Fourth, there was his growing sense of the importance of history. His concern about much of the political development literature on the new states in the 1960s made him welcome the renewed interest in the state-building experiences of the old European states. He complained that too many theories about political modernization were based on the short time-spans of contemporary 'new' states. But how could one understand the present, without understanding the past? How consistent were these theories with past experience and how well understood were the theories of state- and nation-formation in Europe? Isabel de Madariaga writes that at the end of his life he retreated to 'the more solid data of history' (de Madariaga 1994, p.569).

Fifth, there was Finer's realism, his interest in what can be called the pathologies of politics. Pareto appealed to the iconoclastic side of him as did the élitists who at the turn of the century were concerned to get at 'the truth behind the truth'. His *Anonymous Empire* (1958) owed something to this spirit and was the first work to expose the influence of pressure groups in Britain. Finer also was prepared to question and debunk established wisdom. This was seen in his refutation of what he called 'the folklore' that surrounded the convention of individual ministerial responsibility (Finer 1956). He showed that it was not a convention that ministers should resign and that, in any case, resignation was an ineffective remedy for departmental mismanagement. He was dismissive of the interpretation of the ideas that moved legislation in nineteenth-century Britain offered by the constitutional lawyer A.V. Dicey. In the 1970s he attacked two long-praised features of the British political system, the first-past-the-post electoral system and the two-party system. He advocated the replacement of the first-past-the-post system by a more proportional system, not on grounds of fairness but to encourage better government. The same sense of realism fired his interest in the military as an interest group.

Finer's work

Finer wrote several books and articles which are of enduring interest to students of comparative politics. The most important include, in chronological order, *The Man On Horseback*, *Comparative Government*, 'State and Nation Building in Europe', *Five Constitutions* and *The History of Government from the Earliest Times*. This concluding section provides a brief discussion of each of these works.

The Man on Horseback

Finer's study of the military was stimulated variously by his experience in World War II, his interest in the Middle East and his work on interest groups. He was one of the first to note the prevalence of military governments, in Africa, Latin America, Asia and the Middle East. Indeed, for Finer it was the supreme interest group and yet the widespread form of government by the military was at that time virtually ignored by political scientists. He explained military intervention as a result of two sets of forces. One was the capacity and propensity of the military to intervene and the other was the social conditions in the country in which intervention operated. What appeared to distinguish the differing reactions of states to military pressure was the level of their political culture – mature, developed, low or minimal (1962, pp.78–80). He links the four levels of political culture to the characteristic levels of military intervention (for example, influence, blackmail or outright takeover), to the mode of intervention (e.g. collusion, threats or violence), and to the types of regimes to which intervention gives rise. As is usual with Finer there are scores of case studies of military intervention drawn from around the world to illustrate the claims about levels and modes of intervention.

Rather than expressing surprise and horror at military rule, Finer was surprised that the military did not take power more often, bearing in mind the resources at its disposal. In a revised edition (1988) he was able to divide military regimes according to whether they were pro-Western or pro-Soviet, whether their economic regimes were authoritarian, market, statist-market or socialist. Finer not only rejected mono-causal explanations (part of his distaste for Grand Theory) but in his search for explanation would go on classifying.

Comparative Government

The declared object of *Comparative Government*, was 'to provide a map or chart' of all varieties of government (1970b, p.574). Finer offered a conceptual framework, or typology, which would allow him to classify countries and make comparisons. In his own words, his typology

> (a) covers all the known varieties of governmental forms with (b) the most economical set of distinctions, so as to (c) provide the receiver with what he, at any rate, regards as a satisfactory basis for explaining what forms arise in what given circumstances and, (d) hence, has some power of predicting what vicissitudes or alterations a given form may undergo should circumstances change in named respects. (ibid. pp.39–40)

He differentiated the forms of government on three dimensions: the *participation-exclusion* dimension, or the extent to which the public is involved; the *order-representativeness* dimension, or the extent to which the rulers regarded or disregarded the public; and the *coercion-persuasion* dimension, the basis on which the public complied with the government. His typology of forms of government consisted of liberal, democratic, totalitarian, military, quasi-democracy and façade-democracy. The book was largely taken up with case studies of the five types, drawing on Britain, the United States, France, the USSR and Third World states. He took pride in the ability of his approach to enable him to categorize every single government.

Yet over time Finer became aware of the limitations of his approach. It was essentially subjective, being one person's view of the important criteria for comparison. It was not quantifiable. It was static, failing to show how one country moved from one type to another. It would also become out of date. A decade later he was convinced that he needed to study the evolution of government historically.

In his study of the role of the armed forces (or what he calls its 'format') in state-building Finer distilled massive historical and comparative data as a means of identifying clusters of variables, or what he calls *cycles*. These include, *inter alia*, the economy-technology format, the stratification format, the beliefs format and the extraction-coercion cycle. The analysis proceeds by way of claims about the links between the different cycles and demonstrations of the different ways in which they interacted, and their consequences for state- and nation-building, in France, England and Prussia/Germany. Again, it is an example of his use of case studies and the comparative method as a means of uncovering relationships and generating limited generalizations. Some of the variables also prefigure those which are used in his final great work.

Finer's edited *Five Constitutions* (1979) presented the constitutions of the United States, the Fifth French Republic, the Federal Republic of Germany and the USSR for 1936 and 1977 and includes a substantial introductory commentary by the author. Geraint Parry (1994, p.652) draws attention to the remarkable index which shows Finer's strengths in classifying and presenting material in a tabular fashion. The index arranges the constitutions according to broad topical structures and themes and these are then subdivided. For example, under 'methods of amendment' readers are referred to the parts for each of the five constitutions which deal with this particular topic. Finer had a talent not only for painting on a large canvas but also for being able to distil the essential similarities and differences between cases in a succinct way – on occasion reduced to a one-page table.

The History of Government

Some idea of the vast scope and approach of Finer's *The History of Government from the Earliest Times* has already been conveyed in an unpublished paper which he gave in 1983 (Finer 1983) and in a lecture by Jack Hayward entitled 'Finer's Comparative History of Government' (1995c). Students and friends of Sammy Finer are heavily indebted to Professor Hayward and Sammy's widow, Catherine Jones Finer, for helping to bring this great work to fruition. Finer often expressed astonishment that no similar study has previously been attempted, '... for I can think of no human contrivance that is and has been so pregnant with the potential for the welfare or woe of mankind' (1983, p.3). Hayward quotes Finer's intention 'to write a history of government which will not only be sequential and genetic, but also, in some sense, classificatory and analytical' (1995c, p.3). Finer's *History* is organized around five interrelated themes: state-building; military formats; religious belief systems, social stratification, and time-span. These, together with a typology of political regimes, constitute the structure of the book.

Two trends were evident in American political science in the 1980s. One was the renewed interest in the state ('bringing the state back in'); the second was the revival of interest in history, both to gain a better understanding of the past and to tease out propositions which might illuminate the present. Political scientists (e.g. Rokkan) who resorted to history to study the processes of state- and nation-building often went no further back than late medieval Europe. Finer argued that it was essential to go back even further in time, to the age of city states, national states and empires, if one was to understand the characteristics of states. Finer often referred to history as a databank; in this case he covers a period of 5200 years, from 3200 BC to the end of the twentieth century. His typology of states rests on four dimensions: territory, decision-making personnel, level and nature of control relationships, and decision-implementing personnel. This produces ten types of polity, which can be reduced effectively to six. Hayward appropriately summarizes the work as 'a major achievement in circumscribing complexity to manageable proportions, without indulging in over-simplification' (1995c, pp.16–17).

Conclusion

As a comparativist Sammy Finer was wide-ranging and consistent in his approach. His *The Man on Horseback* dealt with virtually all states existing in 1962 and his *History* deals with all forms of government over a 5000 year span. The consistency is seen in his readiness to derive patterns from his data, usually consisting of case studies. Virtually all his comparative work is marked by typologies, schemes of classification and diagrams. Frameworks and models and relationships were not imposed on data, nor were they an excuse for a data-fishing expedition, but emerged from the material or case studies. Reflecting on the body of the work, my impression is less of development – in methods or insights – but rather of a consistent approach applied to an expanding range of material. He belonged to no school and did not found one, although he still managed to inspire, illuminate and entertain a great many of us. He was an individual scholar operating in an age of teams and organizations. The key to understanding Sammy Finer is that he did what interested him. He was sufficiently informed to be able to pick and choose and not to follow fashion.

4 Europe's comparatist from the Norwegian periphery: Stein Rokkan 1921–1979*

Hans Daalder
LEIDEN UNIVERSITY

The young Rokkan

Stein Rokkan was born on 4 July 1921 in Outer Lofoten, North Norway, truly a child from the periphery of a country that he would himself later describe as one of Europe's seaward peripheries. He grew up in the town of Narvik, where his father was a teacher. Like his son, he was an entrepreneur of many causes, perforce on a smaller regional scale: he later became a newspaper editor. The young Stein probably inherited his voracious reading habits from his father. Fellow pupils of his schooldays tell the story that, when they assembled in a local café to relax, the young Stein would drift off to a table with newspapers and devour these in astounding haste, yet with full knowledge of their content when challenged.

In 1939 Rokkan left Narvik for the University of Oslo (then still the only university in Norway) where he studied philology, with French as a major specialization. He continued his studies after the German invasion of 1940 when in the battle of Narvik his parents' home was badly hit. In 1943 the Germans closed the university. Rokkan left a job at the university library and went into hiding in the Lofoten islands. After the liberation his examination results were so brilliant that the word circulated rapidly throughout the university. The philosopher Arne Naess sought the young Rokkan out and persuaded him to continue his studies in political philosophy which he finished in 1948 with an equally brilliant Master's degree and a thesis on David Hume. He translated works by Bertrand Russell and Harold Laski into Norwegian around this time (for a detailed bibliography of Rokkan's work, see Saelen 1981). He also planned writing an advanced doctoral dissertation in political theory.

* This chapter is a revised version of H. Daalder, 'Stein Rokkan 1921–1979. A Memoir', *European Journal of Political Research*, vol. 7 (1979), pp.337–55, with additions from a memorial address, given at a Journée d'Études à la Mémoire de Stein Rokkan organized at the Fondation Nationale des Sciences Politiques, 27–28 May 1980, not previously published in English. In writing the original paper, I profited greatly from talks with Rokkan's stalwart colleague for over a quarter of a century, Henry Valen, who later published his own memoir with Erik Allardt (Allardt and Valen 1981). Their first sentence (p.11) characterized Rokkan as 'the cosmopolite from the periphery'. This revision benefited greatly from comments by Elizabeth Rokkan, Stein Kuhnle and Derek Urwin.

Arne Naess asked the young Rokkan to become his associate in a UNESCO project entitled 'Democracy'. The project brought Rokkan to Paris as early as 1948–49. In the project, Rokkan served both as an organizer and as a high-level 'clerk' who had to make intellectual and semantic sense of the deliberations and writings of an international group of experts. He became joint editor with Richard McKeon of the book *Democracy in a World of Tensions* (McKeon and Rokkan 1951) which issued from the project. Rokkan's grounding in political philosophy proved to be an important asset to him in future years: he had mastered a body of literature which travels relatively easily across cultures, but also forces a constant awareness of the influence of cultural and linguistic variations. His training in political philosophy must also have given him a strong sensitivity to the need for clear concepts, clarity of reasoning, and tidy schematics. In 1952 he published an article in Norwegian, in which he still looked at the efforts of modern social science with the eye of a political theorist (Rokkan 1952). However, through a combination of circumstances he soon turned towards empirical social research.

During the German occupation, a group of young intellectuals belonging to the resistance, which included Arne Naess, had ardently debated the problems of postwar social reconstruction, and apparently expected a major contribution from modern social science. I once heard Arne Naess express the view that Rokkan was lost to serious scholarship when he exchanged philosophical concepts for numbers and statistics. Yet the great importance Naess and his associates themselves attributed to the promise of social science during the war years must have influenced Rokkan's conversion from political philosophy to social sciences, once he came into contact with them after 1945.

Between 1948 and 1950, Rokkan obtained a Rockefeller fellowship, one of the first of such grants from American foundations to a generation of young European scholars who were to become the backbone of the new comparative politics movement in Europe. Rokkan spent his fellowship at Columbia (largely with Lazarsfeld), and in Chicago. His 1952 article quoted earlier clearly reveals the breadth of his reading in that period. Next to classics in political theory, one encounters a roster of names which were to characterize American social science for decades to come (e.g. T.W. Adorno and his associates of *The Authoritarian Personality*, Kenneth Arrow, Bernard Berelson, Duncan Black, Hadley Cantril, Leon Festinger, Harold Guetzkow, Marie Jahoda, Abraham Kaplan, Harold Lasswell, Paul F. Lazarsfeld, Robert K. Merton, J. von Neumann and O. Morgenstern, Talcott Parsons and Edward Shils).

In 1950–51 Rokkan spent a year at the London School of Economics. There he was strongly influenced by the work of the English sociologist Thomas Marshall who was especially concerned with problems of citizenship, social class and political development (Marshall 1964), and who was later active within UNESCO. Since then his contacts with Britain were always close. During this year he married his Welsh wife, Elizabeth.

In 1951, Rokkan became associated with the newly-founded Institute of Social Research in Oslo, a privately financed research institution which had been established by the son of a rich bulk paper manufacturer, Erik Rinde. Rokkan soon became one of its Directors of Research, which he combined with a *Universitetsstipendium*. The Institute of Social Research became the basis of important projects, both on a national and international level. In 1951 the Institute hosted a First International Working Conference on Social Mobility (the transactions were edited for publication in Rinde and Rokkan 1951). In the same year Rokkan and others established an Organization for Comparative Social Research which brought researchers from a number of countries together for what eventually became a seven-nation study on teachers' attitudes. Somewhat later a few students from the University of Oslo (among them Henry Valen) submitted a grant request to the Norwegian Research Council to finance a study of the Norwegian 1953 general election on the model of the earlier Erie County study in the United States. The Norwegian Research Council did not grant the money, but brought the group into contact with Rokkan at the Institute for Social Research. Thus started the long Rokkan–Valen partnership in the Norwegian programme of electoral research, which would soon propel these scholars into the forefront of international electoral studies.

Finally, Rokkan retained his close involvement with developments at UNESCO from the first days of the Naess Democracy Project. The *International Social Science Bulletin* (later the *International Social Science Journal*) was to become Rokkan's chosen instrument for the launching of ideas for new ventures in international research co-operation and the early publication of conference reports.

Research on Norway: comparative research on a single country

Although Rokkan was involved in international organizational activities and explicit comparative study in the 1950s, his chief concern in that period was with the empirical study of Norwegian politics. Within the Norwegian programme of electoral research, he and Valen carried out surveys and built up extensive ecological files. Rokkan has always acknowledged the inspiration from Ann Arbor: 'I learned my trade as a sociologist and a political scientist from the extraordinary group of survey enthusiasts at Michigan', he wrote in the preface to his volume of collected papers *Citizens, Elections, Parties* (1970): 'Our initial work at the Oslo Institute was largely inspired by visitors from Ann Arbor and a number of us were intensively trained, if not indoctrinated, at the Mecca of empirical research, the Survey Research Center.' Yet from the outset, the Norwegian group insisted on the need to adjust the design of electoral studies to the particular structures which voters faced in different political settings. Norway's multi-party system posed very different alternatives to voters than the looser American two-party system, and historical and regional factors seemed more salient for electoral choice in Norway than in the USA. Rokkan and his colleagues therefore strongly insisted on the need to introduce the contextual variable in the design and interpretation of survey findings and thus applied research strategies in the 1950s which would be hailed as innovative in survey research decades later.

Interest in historical processes of political mobilization also led the Norwegian researchers to supplement survey research with ecological analyses, based on time-series data over a long period. The research efforts of the 1950s therefore laid the groundwork for some of Rokkan's major publications of the early 1960s: his long articles with Valen on 'The Mobilization of the Periphery. Data on Turnout, Membership and Candidate Recruitment in Norway' (Rokkan and Valen 1962b) and the article 'Regional Contrasts in Norwegian Politics' (Rokkan and Valen 1964; cf. also Rokkan 1966b, 1967b).

His attempt to interpret contemporary findings thus started Rokkan on his extensive search for explanations through the persistent effects of earlier processes of mass mobilization. Certain elements in these processes captured his attention in particular: the abandonment of absolute monarchy, the extension of the suffrage, the role of electoral systems (1968c), the gap between the formal extension of voting rights and their actual use, the specific cleavages which were politicized, the manner in which new mass organizations were formed not only as parties but more generally as social movements, and the role of the mass media, whether in reinforcing or cross-cutting political allegiances (cf. Rokkan 1959; Rokkan and Torsvik 1960a).

Rokkan's study of the historical and regional processes of mass mobilization inevitably made him very much aware of the multitude of possible cleavage lines, a theme which was to preoccupy him also in his comparative studies. There are numerous variations in the cleavages schemes which Rokkan was to construct, but from an early date these schemes had in common that they distinguished sharply between economic cleavages on the one hand and cultural cleavages on the other, and sought to differentiate within each of these categories according to the dimension of centre–periphery conflict. Rokkan was sensitive to the fact that older cleavages might persist even when new issues might temporarily hide them. This led him to two important political conclusions: (1) his famous 'freezing proposition', the view that 'the [European] party systems of the 1960s reflect, with few but significant exceptions, the cleavage structures of the 1920s' (Lipset and Rokkan 1967a, p.50); and (2) his early forecast that any threat to Norway's sense of autonomy might again politicize the cleavage lines which had determined Norwegian politics in the late nineteenth century. Long before the EEC referendum of 1972 took place, Rokkan sensed that a move to align Norway to continental Europe might split the parties and the party system along earlier centre–periphery lines. Rokkan, that eminently European scholar from the Norwegian periphery, remained himself ambivalent throughout his life about Norway's association with the European Communities.

Norway, then, provided him with many of the cues for his later comparative analyses of centre-formations and coalitions, of the interactions of institutions and mass mobilization, of geographic diversities, of the varied nature of relevant social cleavages, and of the lasting importance of the prior politicization of certain cleavages for the role played by other cleavages. His Norwegian background was also to influence his perspective in other ways. Compared to Denmark and Sweden, Norway was in fact a 'new nation'. Rokkan remained conscious of this factor, even in his personal reactions (he once volunteered the statement to me that it was rather special for the University of Uppsala to give an honorary degree to someone from Norway!). He might not extend this sentiment towards global dimensions, as his fellow countryman Johan Galtung was to do in his 'structural theory of imperialism' (Galtung 1971), but he was always sensitive to the impact of external factors on internal political life, whether within the Scandinavian context, or in Europe generally. To him statehood was not a natural given. The specific manner in which statehood came was to him a variable of paramount importance.

The organizer of the infrastructure of comparative research

While his work in the 1950s had foreshadowed things to come, the true impact of
Rokkan's organizational activities on behalf of comparative research came in the
1960s. In 1958 he moved to Bergen as Research Director to the Christian Michelsen
Institute. This gave him freedom to engage in new exploits (e.g. Rokkan (ed.) 1962a).
In 1966 he accepted a Chair at the University of Bergen, which led him to establish his
own department. It was deliberately called the Department of Comparative Politics.

Rokkan's record in the 1960s shows a dazzling entrepreneurship. He initiated, he
organized, he was a tireless writer and a conscientious editor. His efforts were
practically always of a collaborative nature. I once counted from an earlier bibliography of his works with how many scholars he wrote joint publications or shared
editorial responsibility. I arrived at almost thirty names among whom there are some
ten Norwegians, one Finn, six Americans, three Frenchmen, one Israeli, one Englishman, one German, and two Italians. Rokkan rarely figured explicitly as senior author,
even though he often did most, if not all, of the writing or editing.

Among the many organizations which Rokkan helped organize or in which he was
particularly active were the following:

1. UNESCO had provided him with his first international contacts. He remained true
   to it and its various offshoots, notably the International Social Science Council (of
   which he was President from 1973 to 1977) and the International Council on Social
   Sciences Documentation. One can document many of Rokkan's activities in detail
   through his reports in the International Social Science Bulletin and its successors. He
   sought and obtained UNESCO support for his effort to publish data guides, of
   which *The International Guide to Electoral Statistics* (Rokkan and Meyriat 1969)
   provided a tantalizing example. He also worked through UNESCO in his effort to
   promote the cause of data archives, having emphasized their potential importance in
   an early publication (Lucci and Rokkan 1957). He edited two major symposium
   volumes in this field: *Data Archives for the Social Sciences* (Rokkan 1966a) and
   Comparing Nations (Merritt and Rokkan 1966). In the same context, he prepared
   two other volumes, *Comparative Research Across Cultures and Nations* (Rokkan
   1968a) and, with Sidney Verba, Jean Viet and Elina Almasy, *Comparative Survey
   Research* (Rokkan 1969b; see also Rokkan *et al.* 1977a). He also wrote the long
   article 'Cross-Cultural, Cross-Societal and Cross-National Research' for the UNESCO
   volume *Main Trends of Research in the Social and Human Sciences* (Rokkan 1970b).
   From 1967, he was President of the Committee on Comparative Research of the
   International Social Science Council, and in this capacity he laid the groundwork for
   some data-anchored summer schools of the early 1970s, and some *Workbooks for
   Training on Comparative Analysis* (Rokkan *et al.* 1977a). And he again turned to
   UNESCO for a global project on nation-building, which was to develop into the two
   volumes *Building States and Nations* (Eisenstadt and Rokkan 1973).

2. For ten years (1960–70), Rokkan was Secretary of the International Committee on
   Political Sociology, which had S.M. Lipset as its Chairman for the same period. The
   Committee was originally affiliated only to the International Sociological
   Association (of which Rokkan was Vice-President from 1966 to 1970). But the

work of the Committee and its members also followed the rhythm of the meetings of the International Political Science Association, and in 1970 the Committee became a joint research committee under both international organizations. At the time Rokkan was asked by both ISA and IPSA to become their President; with difficulty he opted for the latter, serving as President of IPSA from 1970 to 1973.

The Committee on Comparative Political Sociology was essentially a personal network of international scholars who shared Rokkan's desire to analyse macro-historical changes. Rokkan edited or co-edited for the Committee important volumes such as *Party Systems and Voter Alignments. Cross-National Perspectives* (Lipset and Rokkan 1967a), *Quantitative Ecological Analysis* (Dogan and Rokkan 1969) and *Mass Politics. Studies in Political Sociology* (Allardt and Rokkan 1970), the last volume containing a number of selected (sometimes reprinted) papers from four of the Committee conferences. The Committee also provided a stimulus for Richard Rose (who followed Rokkan as Secretary to the Committee in 1970) to undertake his project on the social bases of electoral choice, which resulted in *Electoral Behaviour: A Comparative Handbook* (Rose 1974b). This volume also contains one of the fullest papers on Norwegian politics by Valen and Rokkan entitled 'Conflict Structures and Mass Politics in a European Periphery' (Valen and Rokkan 1974). The book itself is dedicated to Rokkan.

3. A third venture in which Rokkan was a catalyst was a project for a comparative study of the smaller European democracies started in 1961 by Val Lorwin, Rokkan and Hans Daalder, later joined by Robert A. Dahl. The project brought together experts on eleven smaller European countries who shared a desire to bring these countries on to the map of comparative European politics, dominated so largely by the images of the politics of the larger European countries alone. Typically, Rokkan insisted from the outset on a substantial data collection. The outline drawn up asked more questions than anyone (even Rokkan) could answer for his country without engaging in large-scale new research. On the whole, the group members were well-chosen, yet there were unforeseen complications. A fair number of the project group were soon afterwards given substantial academic responsibilities. Though now placed in a strategic position to advance national research along the lines of the SED project, they were also involved in building up new departments which were soon to face the storms in the European universities of the late 1960s. To some degree the project was also a victim of the progress which political science made in the 1960s. Conceived on the basis of the discipline as it stood in the late 1950s, the project might have limited itself to providing largely descriptive treatments of individual countries, embellished by *ad hoc* data. As it was, the standards of research and analysis set before the decade was over surpassed the knowledge, time and immediate resources of the group members. The only full monograph which came out of the planned series of country volumes was a volume by Basil Chubb (1970), who had maintained he could not write the volume because there were too few data on his country.

Lack of detailed analyses on all countries in turn complicated the type of comparative analysis which the project had intended to carry out. The project was to bear some fruit in this direction, for example Robert Dahl and Edward Tufte's

Size and Democracy (1973); Rokkan's 'The Structuring of Mass Politics in the Smaller European Democracies' (Rokkan 1968b), which with his introduction to the volume *Party Systems and Voter Alignments* (Lipset and Rokkan 1967) was to be the stepping stone towards the development of Rokkan's macro-model of Europe (discussed below) and a major section in his *Citizens, Elections, Parties* (1970a); Val Lorwin's seminal article 'Segmented Pluralism. Ideological Cleavages and Political Cohesion in the Smaller European Democracies' (1971); and my own work on the interaction of institutions and party systems (e.g. Daalder 1971a), which eventually was absorbed into the later ECPR project *Recent Changes in European Party Systems* (see the chapters on Wildenmann and by Daalder elsewhere in this volume). There was also considerable overlap between the SED project and the group which Robert Dahl brought together for his volume *Political Oppositions in Western Democracies* (1966). Rokkan contributed another major paper on Norwegian politics to this volume, entitled 'Norway: Numerical Democracy and Corporate Pluralism' (Rokkan 1966c). A leading theme of this paper was the distinction between the electoral-representative channels of 'numerical democracy' and the realities of 'corporate decision-making', elsewhere entitled 'Votes Count, Resources Decide' (Rokkan 1975b). The 1966 paper has had such an impact that it led many to believe that Norwegian structures are unique among European countries, while Rokkan himself was dubbed much against his own wish an early member of the 'Corporatist International' of the 1970s (see the chapters by Gerhard Lehmbruch and Philippe Schmitter in this volume).

4. A drive to forge new links with Scandinavian political science came next. The time sequence: regional activities which only followed successful organizational efforts first undertaken at a global or European scale, is paradoxical only in appearance. Political games within IPSA and ISA fostered the formation of regional groupings. Also, political scientists across Scandinavia became increasingly aware that they had parallel national interests in raising the standing of their discipline *vis-à-vis* other disciplines by joining hands across frontiers, and by disseminating the results of their work to a larger professional public beyond the small attentive publics within their own countries. Significantly, the first outward manifestation of collaboration within Scandinavia was the publication in 1966 of *Scandinavian Political Studies*, published initially as a yearbook, which was the result of a memorandum which Rokkan had submitted to the national political science associations of all Scandinavian countries. Rokkan acted a number of times as editor of this yearbook and he made sure from its very beginning that it would contain a very strong bibliographical component. He also ensured the publication of thorough reviews of political science in each Scandinavian country in the last volume he edited (1977), before the yearbook was converted into a quarterly journal. From 1967, Rokkan was one of the moving spirits behind the organization of joint triennial meetings of the national political science associations in Scandinavia, fortified in 1975 by the establishment of a more formally structured Nordic Political Science Association which also established research groups active between the joint meetings.

5. The European Consortium for Political Research came last. Its establishment (described in greater detail by Jean Blondel elsewhere in this volume) owes at least

as much to others – such as Jean Blondel, Peter de Janosi of the Ford Foundation and Warren Miller of the Inter-University Consortium for Political Research in Ann Arbor – as it does to Stein Rokkan. But it was a matter of course that Rokkan would become its sagacious chairman (1970–76). Some of the greatest innovations in the working of the Consortium also came from others, for example from Rudolf Wildenmann, who launched the annual Joint Sessions, or Blondel and Wildenmann, who spurred the Consortium on to the formation of ECPR research groups. But when it came to the drafting of important policy papers or directing one of the international research groups, Rokkan engaged himself fully. He left a large number of potential research themes which in his view should have priority in future European research efforts. Within the Consortium the European Data Information Service was his favourite activity, and his hand is visible on virtually every page of the more than thirty issues of the *European Political Data Newsletter* he published from Bergen. He continued to attend all Joint Sessions of the ECPR, even after his first heart attack. He chafed at not being allowed to attend the Brussels sessions of April 1979, which honoured its reluctant absentee overlord with the Honorary Presidency – a gesture not only of admiration and affection, but intended to make sure that Rokkan could remain a full partner in the busy exchange of memos and position papers through which he worked and lived.

Looking back on this restless organizational life, one might well ask: was it worth the effort? Rokkan was an indefatigable conference participant: he could attend meetings for longer hours than anyone else in the profession, and he invariably enjoyed them. He came to meetings better prepared than most, always offering thoughtful and thorough papers. He was an inveterate note-taker and he issued numerous reports which often made a conference sound a much more intelligent and fruitful affair than many a participant had thought when attending. At least one function of his many meetings was to provide a forum for the early ventilation of research plans and the frank discussion of methodological problems before projects hardened. Rokkan was himself an ardent collector of ideas and papers. His days were always fuller than those of any other participant: he met people at breakfast, lunch, and dinner, and turned up earlier than anyone else each morning, generally having read a paper or two, or having drafted some important policy document during the night. Conferences to him were above all a tool to carry through existing projects and to launch new ones.

What, then, were the specific contributions which warrant the title of this section, 'The organizer of the infrastructure of comparative research'? One can distinguish the following rubrics:

1. Rokkan always attached great importance to bibliographical tools. His own writings abound with references, and within several projects he made an explicit effort to provide extensive bibliographies (e.g., Eisenstadt and Rokkan 1973 and the bibliographies in *Scandinavian Political Studies*, already mentioned).
2. He set great store in disseminating news about new research efforts, if possible from their very inception: he made the *European Political Data Newsletter* as much a chronicle of new research ventures as a survey of data available for analysis.
3. Rokkan was one of the very first scholars to see the intellectual value (and the possible economies) of data archives, although he was also to warn against the

danger of misuse by those capable only of 'numerological nonsense' (Rokkan 1970a, p.288). For a long time he did not wish to take responsibility for organizing a data archive himself, but he actively encouraged the setting up of such organizations (including the Norwegian Social Science Data Services, whose director he was from 1975 to his death), and sought to promote their mutual co-operation.

4. Rokkan had a particular interest in promoting training activities. He supported the ECPR Essex Summer School but his own interest went more to the comparative scrutiny of actual data than to the methods of data analysis, and he promoted a number of special summer schools with that emphasis under the auspices of the International Social Science Council. He was also an ardent advocate of what he called Data Confrontation Seminars – occasions when scholars would meet for a period of several weeks with comparable data on their own countries, to try out common modes of analysis and test general hypotheses (cf. Rokkan 1969b).

5. Less known is Rokkan's early contribution towards the development of the use of computers by social scientists in Western Europe. His own large data collection on Norwegian politics required mechanical data processing from its beginning. His network of personal contacts made it possible for him to help bring American specialists and advanced software packages to Europe (notably OSIRIS and SPSS). And when it appeared that many centres of social research beyond those of his nearest colleagues in Europe found it difficult to catch up with developments, he supported the setting up within the ECPR of the Computer Applications Group. This was a network of younger software specialists and experts in quantitative analysis, based in such centres as Bergen, Cologne, Geneva, Leiden, Mannheim and Strathclyde, who could provide assistance to any department in need and who published extensive information on new computer programs in a separate section of the *European Political Data Newsletter*. Rokkan himself could be an enthusiast. He delighted in the development of new methods of computer cartography: only a year before his death he organized a meeting of experts in this field in Bergen in the autumn of 1977.

Towards a macro-model of European political developments

Rokkan's most enduring contribution to social science is his attempt to develop what he once termed 'a conceptual map of Europe'. Its roots lay, as we saw, in his work on Norwegian politics. His wish to explain the variance of voting brought him to a study of the processes of initial mass mobilization. Logically, this required an analysis of the institutional and social conditions which prevailed before the processes of mass politicization set in. His singling out of the importance of centre–periphery conflicts made him ask detailed questions on the historical composition of the centre: socially, geographically, institutionally. This caused him to delve deeper into historical processes of state formation and nation-building which in turn cannot be understood without going even further back in history to the conditions the High Middle Ages set for the early builders of modern states.

His comparative work followed the same road. Apart from his early publications on social mobility and teachers' attitudes, one of his earliest comparative papers was concerned with 'Mass Suffrage, Secret Voting and Political Participation' (Rokkan

1961). He developed this theme in two large German-language papers: 'Zur entwicklungssoziologischen Analyse von Parteisystemen' (Rokkan 1965) and his long chapter 'Zur Soziologie der Wahlen und der Massenpolitik', which he contributed to Rene König's *Handbuch der empirischen Sozialforschung* – a paper he extensively reworked with Lars Svåsand for the new 1978 edition of the *Handbuch* (Rokkan and Svåsand 1978). Even an elementary accounting for the differences found in cleavages in European party systems (e.g. the differing role of religion and ethnic factors; the relative size of communists and socialists (and of leftist parties in general) among the working class; the presence in some systems but not in others of conservative mass parties; variations within the non-socialist camp between conservatives, liberals and agrarian movements – let alone the very different strengths of fascist and national-socialist movements in European countries in the 1930s) forced him back to historical explanation. Thus, he tried to map European party systems as the historical result of the interaction of at least four revolutions: the Reformation, the National Revolution, the Industrial Revolution and the International (i.e. Russian) Revolution. In the further elaboration of these schemes other historical refinements were brought in: the manner of institution-building since the High Middle Ages, geopolitical and geoeconomic dimensions, the sequence of steps through which different systems moved from élite politics into the era of mass politics, the historical and regional manner of mass politicization, the specific sequence of dominant cleavages, the pace of developments (political or economic), etc. Rokkan's elaboration of such themes and subthemes in his successive papers is breathtaking (for examples, see Rokkan 1970a, 1970c, 1971a, 1971b, 1975a, 1976a; Rokkan and Urwin 1982, 1983), even though his treatment may bewilder those who do not have his detailed knowledge of the history and the contemporary politics of countries throughout Europe, and who may even fail to understand the *explicanda* in the first place.

Rokkan was far from satisfied with his model-building efforts. He constantly sought to check his analyses against the writings of other scholars. Often he leaned over backwards in trying to fit the terminology and theories of others into his own framework of analysis: witness his attempt to reason in Parsonian terms, his application of the Hirschman 'Exit, Voice and Loyalty' paradigm (Rokkan 1974), his dialogues with the Committee of Comparative Politics of the American Social Science Research Council and other scholars such as Karl W. Deutsch, Samuel P. Huntington, Barrington Moore or Peter Nettl in the 1960s (Rokkan 1969a) and his later *Auseinandersetzungen* with authors like Immanuel Wallerstein or Perry Anderson (Rokkan 1976b). He continuously reworked the specification of variables and constantly demanded the empirical testing of alternative models. In a 1977 fellowship request to the German Marshall Fund Rokkan listed five priorities he had set for future work (cf. Stein Rokkan Committee 1980):

> First of all comparisons of the *mobilization strategies and successes of organizations in the mass market*. Here the task would be to study the degrees of fit between processes of socio-economic change and the mobilization efforts of mass parties and parallel movements ...
>
> Secondly, comparisons of the *structures of the mobilizing networks*: the tie-ins between parties, associations, corporations, the media. Here the task would be to identify dimensions of variation and to review alternative explanations of such variations: degrees of verzuiling, ontzuiling; types of organizational clustering ...

Thirdly, comparisons of *elite recruitment and elite interlinkages across* W. *Europe*. Here the task would be to identify sources of variation in the consequences of mass mobilization for the activation of new strata and the opening up of new channels of advancement ...

Fourthly, comparison of the growth and the differentiation of the *welfare apparatus of the modern state*. This is perhaps the most dynamic field of comparative research right now and the one of greatest importance in evaluating my own model. We can distinguish two sets of approaches in this field: the comparative study of *steps and sequences in the establishment of social services* and the comparative study of public sector growth, whether in terms of specific budgets or in terms of manpower ...

And fifthly, comparisons of *manifestation of disruptions and breakdowns during the recent crises*: inflation, increased industrial unrest, student upheavals, backlash movements against the welfare state, overt violence and terrorism.

Even near the end of his life, Rokkan thus set his goals very high. He was never complacent about past achievements, but would think of new ways to do better. His curiosity remained insatiable. Many an observer of his work has noted that he perhaps never intended his 'modelling' of Europe to be finished, deriving too much pleasure from what he himself called 'his topological-typological approach'.

Much of the efforts of his last years went into the ECPR project on *Economy, Territory, Identity*, that he directed jointly with his gifted and versatile colleague Derek Urwin, who was to bring the project to publication after Rokkan's death (Rokkan and Urwin 1982, 1983).

Stein Rokkan: the man and the scholar

What was it that made Rokkan the singular scholar he was?

His early training in political philosophy must have given him a sense of relevance and cultural sensitivity which saved him from falling to the temptations of technique or temporary theoretical fashions. Rokkan was – to say the least – very open to new theories, new analytical schemes, new research techniques. Yet, he always remained his own man, exploiting the new in his constant quest for explanations of the real problems which concerned him.

Rokkan had uncanny linguistic abilities: even his earliest articles list sources in five languages, including Italian. He not only read but published in foreign languages: while most of his work is in English, he also presented papers in German and later also in French.

Rokkan profited fully from his intimate contacts with American social scientists, with whom he carried on an extensive correspondence and often a public dialogue. He thus drew on the richest sources of scholarship which our profession has, combining in a unique manner the two revolutions which characterized American scholarship in the first two decades after 1945: the behavioural and the comparative politics revolution. (Rokkan's impact in turn on American social science deserves further exploration.) The political development literature was, admittedly, particularly concerned with contemporary processes in the Third World like state-building, national identity, legitimacy, mass participation and distribution. Questions were asked, naturally, about the way such processes had been solved historically in Western Europe. Although

Rokkan, as he once said to me, regarded it as 'somewhat strange to re-think one's own country, as if it were an African state', he took up the challenge. (His own feeling of belonging to a relatively 'new state' may have even given him some empathy.) But he also saw the potentially much greater pay-off for systematic study of such processes in Europe as compared with the Third World – given that the eventual outcomes were known, given the very extensive archival and other sources, given also the high level of scholarship on which one could draw. European political development became therefore his favourite terrain, in response to what he often felt to be the overly general theorizing of American scholars involved with the Third World, or even the world as a whole. Within the comparative politics movement, this stance allowed him to be both an enthusiast and a sceptic.

As a national from a small country Rokkan could look at larger states with none of that strain which often creeps into the mutual perceptions of scholars from larger states – assuming they look over their own borders at all. He could therefore 'place' the larger countries in his analytical scheme with detachment, just as his reading and reasoning told him. And he was naturally aware of the value of studying smaller states on their own merit, without that peculiar attitude of some large nation-scholars who treat small countries as if they have only 'derived' experiences, free to follow their errant ways only because they have no real responsibilities in the realm of world politics.

Being a Scandinavian added to this advantage. The coexistence of five polities, whose inhabitants can converse with each other with little difficulty (assuming Finnish scholars speak Swedish), expands the number of cases available for comparative analysis to Scandinavian scholars much beyond the linguistic threshold of single scholars in other countries. As a native from one of the newer Scandinavian states, Rokkan had a very special eye for the similarities and differences in Northern Europe (see Rokkan 1981).

Rokkan had a unique capacity to absorb the findings of many intellectual disciplines. It is not only that he moved from a study of linguistics and political philosophy towards modern social science. But within the social sciences, he was as much a sociologist as he was a political scientist, combining the best of either, and avoiding the pitfalls of both. He was a better historian than most professional historians. He knew about statistics, he read economics, he became somewhat of a cultural anthropologist, and in later years he became particularly intrigued by geography.

Rokkan relished international contacts: he was a tireless traveller and correspondent, who built up a unique network of contacts. Being a generous circulator of memos and copies of letters, he became a one-man clearing house of information – not only between scholars of one discipline across countries, but also between scholars of different disciplines even in their own country.

Rokkan was undoubtedly a great organizer, but he remained a prolific and impressive writer. It is true that his writings were scattered over the most improbable publications. He did not fulfil his ambition to consolidate them in a new book. Nevertheless, his way of publishing had at least the merit of instantly acquainting a large public with work in progress. It also offered him a chance to work in new material and new theories, without becoming a victim of past achievements.

Rokkan understood politics, but he was anything but a partisan. Even his closest friends had contradictory ideas about his party preferences, and according to his wife he never voted in national or local elections, believing that his professional role demanded that he show no personal political bias or preference. Rokkan shunned controversy and would probably have made a poor politician. He was an avid reader of newspapers and magazines in many languages, retaining the facilities of quick reading and digesting which his schoolmates had noted in Narvik. One might have secret doubts about the possibility of true comparative analysis by the single scholar, given the impossibility of anyone understanding the politics of more than two or three countries really well. Rokkan proved to be the exception to that rule: he really knew Western Europe in all its diversity, through his massive reading of academic and journalistic sources alike.

Rokkan's main contribution to comparative politics, then, was perhaps not that of causal analysis, but putting Europe clearly on the map, in all its complexity, with all the very many problems which need further study. He painted miniatures and large canvasses with equal skill and devotion. His schemata for 'conditioning', 'intervening' and 'dependent' variables may seem complicated. But they contain both a parsimonious (a term dear to him!) and a very rich portrayal of historical and contemporary developments, of individual territories, of groups within them, but also of relations among them. In classifying diversities, he challenged uncritical and parochial assumptions, and sensitized one to factors which need detailed study. He rarely offered final conclusions: he was the agenda-setter par excellence.

Such factors may help to explain the phenomenon that Rokkan was. But they say little about the man himself. Rokkan was not a man who sought the limelight. He had his share of honours in life: his various presidencies of international professional associations, four honorary doctorates (Uppsala, Helsinki, Aarhus and Geneva), membership of various Academies (foreign ones, and just before his death also the Norwegian Academy of Science), prestigious fellowships, offers from leading universities (he had a special link with Yale as visiting professor), a decoration as Knight Commander in the Order of St. Olav. But he was essentially a modest man, who was interested in causes rather than personal recognition. (The only time I have ever seen him flustered was when rival organizational interests got in the way of promoting a cause that to him was in the manifest interest of all.) He had, in fact, the most encompassing – and the least egotistical – mind of anyone I have ever encountered. Rokkan was at his best in private talks or small seminars. He much preferred the small workshop to the large congress or lecture hall. Rokkan was exceedingly generous, at times almost uncritically so. He had a profound interest in people and managed to treat even the most junior arrival in the profession as if he (Rokkan) were there to learn, the young one to impart. And he did learn, as his many references to often obscure papers amply show. In Bergen he surrounded himself with a group he lovingly used to call 'my youngsters'. He set them to work in his many enterprises. They in turn sought fiercely to protect him in the last years of his life and have proved worthy successors in what is still uniquely called the Department of *Comparative* Politics in the University of Bergen.

Rokkan left two offices and a house loaded with books and documents. Fortunately, a Stein Rokkan Committee (1980) in Bergen took up his intellectual inheritance and all his papers are now available for consultation in the State Archive in Bergen, facilitated by an elaborate *Stein Rokkan Archives Catalog* (1995). Stein Rokkan lectures are given both yearly in Bergen and at the Joint Sessions of the ECPR, and there is a two-yearly prize awarded by the International Committee of the Social Sciences to younger scholars who have done important new work in comparative politics. A number of commemorative volumes (Hagtvet 1992; Torsvik 1981) and special issues of journals (e.g. *Zeitschrift für Soziologie* 1980; *Rivista Italiana di Scienza Politica* 1980; *Revue Internationale de Politique Comparée* 1995) have appeared since his death. As we saw, Rokkan constantly reworked his papers and his model of Europe. Three of Rokkan's closest colleagues, Peter Flora, Stein Kuhnle and Derek Urwin, have taken upon themselves the daunting task of collecting and screening Rokkan's dispersed writings on Europe, to arrange and integrate them into one volume entitled *State Formation, Nation-Building and Mass Politics in Europe. The Theory of Stein Rokkan* (Oxford University Press, forthcoming). It should secure Rokkan's legacy for generations.

5 Rudolf Wildenmann: German scholar, institution builder, democrat *

Max Kaase and Rudolf Wildenmann†

WISSENSCHAFTSZENTRUM BERLIN
UNIVERSITY OF MANNHEIM

Foreword (Max Kaase)

In April of 1993, Rudolf Wildenmann travelled to the ECPR workshop in Leiden organized by Hans Daalder to prepare a book on the intellectual autobiographies of European political scientists. Wildenmann carried with him a first draft of a paper describing the complex life circumstances which had brought him into political science, a very personal document indeed. Only a few weeks after his return from Leiden to Mannheim he was taken seriously ill and had to move into the Mannheim University hospital for treatment. Only then was the severity of his condition recognized; he died in the hospital on 14 July 1993.

In many conversations with Max Kaase in the hospital he emphasized how important it was for him to rework and complete his piece for this book. The turn of events prevented him from fulfilling that desire. Since in the draft paper he had already written much about the personal context behind his path into the social sciences, but on the other hand had not yet got on to the details of his academic work and priorities, it seemed meaningful and proper to organize this chapter in two parts: part one as the authentic statement written by Wildenmann in 1993 (edited for publication by Max Kaase), and part two on the role of Wildenmann as a European political scientist, written by Max Kaase.

I. FRAGMENTS OF A BIOGRAPHY (Rudolf Wildenmann)

Coming to Canada as a POW

In early May of 1942 a train of the Canadian Pacific Railway stopped near Banff at the entrance valley to the Rocky Mountains west of Calgary, and approximately 500 German prisoners of war, including myself, stepped out. After passing the gateway to a

* The support of Richard I. Hofferbert in improving the English of the text is gratefully acknowledged.

seemingly large camp (it turned out that altogether there were about 10,000 men), we were welcomed by a small group of 'properly' dressed German soldiers – two Senior Sergeant-Majors of the Army and of the Air Force, and one Non-Commissioned officer from the Navy – all in new uniforms.

It was like a fantastic dream: there were the Rocky Mountains, towering over the valley, men in rags and tatters coming all the way from Africa, drifting snowflakes, soldiers in their best uniforms, big tents heated with special stoves, new clothes, coffee and cake, and the whole camp fenced in with barbed wire and watched by the Canadian Veteran Guard. It was the end of my youth.

My youth in Stuttgart

I was the son of an unskilled worker who was employed in the 1920s with a Jewish export and import company trading eggs all over Europe. My father was a member of the Social Democratic Party and of a Socialist club, enjoying the many mixed blessings of the *petite bourgeoisie*, the red flags on the first of May, and so on.

The family initially lived in the medieval part, later on in a newly-built working-class district in the outskirts of Stuttgart, a southern German town. Since my mother also had to work for a living, I looked after my younger sister most of the time. Occasionally, I went for weekends or school holidays to visit my grandmother in the countryside not far away from my home town. Off and on, I was also permitted to spend whole days or at least afternoons with my foster-mother, an educated German-French widow who was expelled from France after the First World War with her elderly mother and two daughters who had later become private teachers for upper-class children. I was their beloved boy, and they taught me important things: how to cook, how much pleasure and stimulation it was to read good books (I almost devoured whole libraries), how to be tolerant with the broad political and cultural variety of young people who were educated in the study room by the family's two daughters.

So, youth for me at the age of 12 became a wonderful adventure, surrounded as I was both by a sophisticated French-German atmosphere and a solid 'rusticana' basis. But it was also a youth full of poverty, not much of a menu to eat: cheap cheese, potatoes, fish and, on Sundays, sometimes meat with noodles (the region's regular Sunday dish).

Being young in those days also meant getting a distinct flavour of political street battles. At the age of seven or eight, I could observe the 'headquarters' of the Nazi and the Communist parties located in two restaurants just across from my parents' flat. Hence, among my first political experiences how these groups violently fought each other figured prominently.

With the family's move to a new home in 1930, we found ourselves in a tenement house among families who were members of quite a few different political parties: there were Nazis and other right-wing party adherents, communists, social democrats, members of religious parties and of various political sects. There was fractionalization all over the place.

The part of the town the family lived in was well known for the diversity of its people. On top of the hill resided the German headquarter of Rudolf Steiner's anthroposophists, including the first and famous *Waldorf Schule* (originally developed for the employees of the Waldorf-Astoria cigarette company). Further down towards the river was the blue-collar-workers district, and in between one would find some small farmers who grew vegetables in their *Schrebergärten*. Little wonder that the elementary school which I attended also reflected the mixture of classes, religions and cultures which resulted from the transition of medieval Stuttgart into an industrial centre.

Political encounters

I was also very much aware of the encompassing political change which had taken place after January of 1933 when Adolf Hitler had usurped power. Schoolchildren had to learn all the new 'revolutionary' songs, and soon the 'Young Men's Christian Association' (YMCA), of which I had been a member, was, by force, incorporated into the Nazi youth (*Hitler-Jugend*) organization. What first seemed like a very romantic event soon turned into a very unromantic treadmill. My church confirmation was special, too, since the parish priest turned out to be a hard-nosed opposition leader against the Nazis, and it happened more than once that a *Hitler-Jugend* group invaded the seminary and terrorized the 14-year-olds preparing for their confirmation.

Neighbours began to disappear now and then, and rumours said they had been taken to the Heuberg, initially a concentration camp for the working class, later on for the few anti-Nazis of the middle class, and then for the Jews.

After 1933, people in the district became very subdued and timid. All existing parties had been dissolved by the NSDAP, and the social democratic leadership had left the country. The spring *Reichstag* election of 1933 – if one would call it an election at all, with all the oppression involved – put the NSDAP, with 39.9 per cent of the vote, in a strong, though not a majority, position. Many people just went along with the Nazis; the few who opposed them were eventually imprisoned. Emigration for the majority of the people was not a viable option.

My father had lost his job after the small Jewish company he had been working for was taken over by some 'Aryan' people. He could not find new employment because he was said to be *jüdisch verseucht* (infected by Jews). However, in 1939, after the war had begun, he was sent down to the South German border as a farm worker. For the family, this obviously created a difficult situation, and we all had to learn how to cope with our new life.

School and vocational training

The educational system in Weimar Germany favoured middle- and upper-class interests; only well-to-do parents could afford to send their children to schools of higher education (*Realschule* or *Gymnasium*) which in turn were a prerequisite for a university education. Lower-class kids usually took eight years of elementary school and then, if things went well, started a vocational training. This was the road I travelled.

After I had completed elementary school, I tried to find an apprenticeship to become a cook. I did not meet with success, although I had passed all the tests very well; I simply was not tall enough. Finally, I managed to get an apprenticeship as a clerk where I was trained in accounting and how to collect overdue money from customers all over the Stuttgart region. After three years of vocational training and two more years on the job, in 1940 I was finally drafted into the army. Under Rommel's command, I fought Britons and Australians in the desert of North Africa until I was captured by British soldiers. After I was able to leave hospital in Egypt, I was sent to Canada, as a POW, with a two months' 'stopover' in South Africa.

The Canadian experience

So, there I was in May 1942, dressed in a new and warm outfit in a valley of the Rocky Mountains in Canada, full of thoughts and experiences which I had to analyse and to sort out in my mind. The POW camp was in many ways a microcosm of German social and political life. Not least, it offered studies in many fields of science, and it even opened up the opportunity to continue one's formal education. I grabbed this chance with both hands, and at the end of January 1945 I successfully completed my school education (*Abitur*), enabling me at some time in the future to attend a university. Gone were the two-and-a-half years of hard scholarly work, of walking around in the 4 square km yard of the camp, of listening to the bagpipes of the Canadian Guards every morning, of cleaning the camp's houses, of summer days doing light work on farms in the countryside, of going to the movies twice a week, of doing sports, of having good food (the Canadians carefully observed the Geneva Convention of the Red Cross and gave the POWs the same food as their own soldiers received), of playing chess or cards, of smoking cheap, but good, tobacco or cigarettes (the German soldiers could pay for that because their 'salary' was transferred to Canada), and of reading various newspapers or magazines which were made available on a regular basis: the *New York Times*, the *Globe* and *Mail*, the *Christian Science Monitor*, *Esquire* and many other papers and magazines. In addition, news broadcasts from Germany on short wave could be received with radios constructed by German POWs. Only many years later, was I able to appreciate fully the chance of comparing information from Berlin with that from Ottawa or Washington and to arrive at my own conclusions.

One day in January 1945, an instructor from the university in Saskatchewan arrived at the camp carrying some books with him. One of these books was Alfred Weber's *Kulturgeschichte als Kultursoziologie*, in a 1935 edition which had been published in the Netherlands. The lecturer turned out to be a former student of Alfred Weber and had, like around 800 other social scientists, been forced to emigrate from Germany by the Nazis. When I asked him about Alfred Weber's whereabouts, the lecturer replied that as far as he knew Weber was still in Heidelberg, where he had gone in early retirement from his university position under pressure from the Nazis.

Reading Alfred Weber opened up completely new intellectual horizons to me. Therefore, with my *Abitur* in hand, I decided that, once I was back in Germany, I would, if possible, begin my studies in social sciences at the University of Heidelberg with Alfred Weber.

Studying in Heidelberg

In the summer of 1952 I presented myself to my Ph.D committee at the University of Heidelberg to obtain my doctoral degree. Almost six years of life as a student were behind me, ten years after I had arrived in Canada in the POW camp. They had been intensive studies, first in economics, then in other social science disciplines, and I had been exposed to stimulating, first-class scholars in those fields. There was my economics teacher, Erich Preiser; there were my teachers in sociology, Alfred Weber and Alexander Rüstow, in history Georg Kühn, Ernst Forsthoff in public law, and Dolf Sternberger, my *Doktorvater*, in political science.

The book *Kulturgeschichte als Kultursoziologie* by Alfred Weber was discussed in his seminar before being reissued, a wonderful opportunity to return to a work which had left such a deep intellectual mark on me during my time as a POW in Canada. Other writers were also important for me: Sigmund Neumann with his theory on the 'integration parties', Robert Michels with his concept of party oligarchy, Hannah Arendt's studies on totalitarianism, Karl Mannheim and his writings on ideology (a very different concept of 'ideology' from the American one), just to name a few.

The years in Heidelberg had in many ways been unique. There were intellectually challenging lectures and seminars on the one hand, and there was the incipient reconstruction of West Germany after the war on the other. The students had heated debates on Germany's recent history and on the concepts for the new constitution. We had even gone 'on strike' once – a fierce one – because we were prevented from studying abroad. We tried to understand modern economics and did indeed travel abroad many times. And we had marched from Heidelberg to the German–French border to tear down the customs barriers in 1949 in favour of a united Europe. Later on, the group of postwar generation students that had met in Heidelberg became university teachers, high ranking diplomats, chief editors of prominent newspapers or top governmental officers. But this generation who had experienced the war and had seen its consequences also became active in reconstructing a new democratic political life in Germany.

Becoming a social scientist

While still studying in Heidelberg, I had written a small book on factors conducive to economic growth and stability in southern Germany. Then I had studied the new system of political parties in West Germany and had written my dissertation on that topic. Both subjects were inextricably intertwined with my biographical history. I would have loved to continue with my academic work, but this turned out to be infeasible. 'Muddle through', one of my teachers said, 'there is no academic position available'. So I muddled through.

First, I worked for four years as a journalist and as a Bonn correspondent for a weekly paper, where I was responsible for covering domestic affairs. This gave me a thorough knowledge of the political actors who 'made politics', and of the problems involved. Not least, this journalistic work in Bonn provided me with the opportunity for a first move back into academic life: after a brief interlude as a civil servant in a Bonn ministry, I was offered and took the position of director of an institution for political education, dealing with communism and the communist states. From there on it was but a brief step to return fully to a university career: in 1959 I became Assistant Professor with Ferdinand A. Hermens who had just come back from political exile in the US to the University of Cologne. There I obtained my *venia legendi* (*Habilitation*) in political science in 1962. In 1964, I accepted an invitation to become full Professor of Political Science at the University of Mannheim. A dream nourished since my youth had finally come true.

In my scholarly work, I was strongly influenced by the German neoliberalist school, by Schumpeter's book *Capitalism, Socialism and Democracy*, by French writings on the impact of literature on politics, by Karl W. Deutsch, by the (almost monomaniacal) concern of Ferdinand A. Hermens with electoral laws, and by several, mostly English, works on government, like Walter Bagehot's *The English Constitution* and the writings of S.E. Finer. From all this has sprung a special interest in electoral research and a strong impetus to promote international co-operation. But more than anything else, the question of why a country of such high cultural achievements like Germany had turned to totalitarianism has continued to bother me, and with this the question of what can be done in the future to prevent such a catastrophe from happening again. Therefore, the questions of the building of democratic institutions, of how to provide a decent life for all citizens, and of how to resolve violent international conflict have become the major issues of my academic life as a political and social scientist.

II. THE SCHOLAR AND RESEARCHER (Max Kaase)

The dissertation

Nowhere in his writings has Wildenmann expressed the impetus behind his intellectual and personal life better than at the beginning of his dissertation: 'The author is convinced that parliamentary democracy, built on political parties and safeguarded by the appropriate systemic measures, more than any other form of government can ensure the free development of humankind, a qualified political leadership, and a responsible government.' (Wildenmann 1954, p.14; translation M. K.)

It is interesting to observe that the three catchwords in this phrase, humanism, political leadership and consent by the governed – the latter expressed in the concept of responsible government – permeate like a red thread Wildenmann's major works, the dissertation (Wildenmann 1954), the *Habilitationsschrift* (Wildenmann 1963) and the book on *Volksparteien* (Wildenmann 1989). The argument of the dissertation, mostly a study of the four parties of CDU/CSU, SPD, FDP and the BHE (a refugee party), revolves around the question: can the link between the parliamentary party and its voters be maintained when strong party bodies outside of parliament dominate parliamentary parties and in the process create a hierarchy within the parliamentary parties of leaders, executives, experts and backbenchers? (Wildenmann 1954, p.158). The conclusion Wildenmann draws from this observed structural strain is that the parliamentarians do not actually represent the voice of the people but rather that of the party leadership committees (ibid., p.93).

Given his structural-institutional approach to political analysis, Wildenmann addresses the question of why parties become isolated from the will of the people, not least by pointing to the impact of electoral laws on the process by which voting power is transferred into governmental power. His opposition to proportional representation comes from the observation that it leads to multi-party systems, diffuses parliamentary responsibility *vis-à-vis* the voters, obscures the important roles of government and opposition, and does not provide the voters with clear programmatic choices. Thus, parties result that are amalgamated with respect to their parliamentary and extra-parliamentary bodies.

One has to keep in mind that these ideas were written down more than forty years ago. Of course, within that time a great deal of comparative empirical evidence has been assembled which would refine, and in some instances correct, the picture drawn by Wildenmann. Still, he had a grip on problems that continue to plague democratic government. Beyond this, in the concluding part of his dissertation he also briefly addressed two topics which feature more prominently in his *Macht und Konsens* (Wildenmann 1963): the élitist distrust in the democratic capabilities of the average citizen, and the challenge of a *national* concept of democracy through the internationalization of governance.

The *Habilitationsschrift*

Konsens – consensus – in Wildenmann's thinking is predominantly the capacity of the political system for producing through the act of voting a (majority) government. Obviously, this is achieved most easily in a two-party system: 'The danger of manipulated public opinion and decision-making in all constitutional states with multi-party systems becomes a permanent, insoluble problem.' (Wildenmann 1963, p.55; translation M.K.) His emphasis on the functional role of parliamentary opposition as a potential replacement government (which is clearly derived from looking at the United Kingdom) reveals his political science credo: political phenomena can be properly understood only when approached as an interaction between institutional, contextual and individual properties within a polity. In modern social science, one would speak of a multi-level approach.

Wildenmann argued that already during the 1948–49 debates in the Parliamentary Council, which had been given the task of designing a constitution for West Germany, the possibility of establishing a constitutional consensus among citizens had been forgone because the formal rules for the acquisition of power had not been properly designed. As a consequence, the most important political impact citizens might have through the vote – the direct formation of a government – had *de facto* been prevented.

It is doubtful whether the constitutional decision in favour of proportional representation indeed represents distrust by the members of the Parliamentary Council of the political wisdom of the masses, as Wildenmann seemed to suggest. However, there can be no question that this distrust was instrumental in the decision of the Council to avoid submitting the draft of the constitution to a public vote of confidence, against the 1948 London recommendation by the Allied powers. 'Obviously, one of the greatest weaknesses of the continental party systems is their totally undemocratic distrust *vis-à-vis* their peoples; thereby, they create the dangers they set out to avoid: the almost unnoticeable estrangement between the citizenry and the political leadership ...' (ibid., p.71; translation M.K.). It was most probably Wildenmann's belief in the practical political wisdom of the everyday person (a position buffered by more recent research, see Popkin 1991; Zaller 1992) that has triggered his encompassing interest in micro-political sociology, a point to which we shall return later.

The second topic to be addressed – the international dimension of domestic politics – is seen in different facets of Wildenmann's thinking. The first hint at this dimension was in his dissertation (Wildenmann 1954, p.164). It seems to be very much a reflection of the experience in the first half of the century that foreign policy had been misused by the political élites as a safety valve for internal tensions and strain. The international theme was then taken up again, but much more systematically, in his *Habilitationsschrift*, where it occupies more than one-third of the book. Given post-war Germany's integration into a variety of international arrangements and its lack of formal national independence (the 'four powers status'), it does not come as a surprise that the international context got special attention, even if the main analytical thrust of the book is on the domestic dimension of the democratic political process. This emphasis on international politics led Wildenmann to become involved for a while in military strategic research. But, in retrospect, it was the interest in the international dimension of domestic politics that finally brought him into the field of comparative politics in a very special way: as an institution builder aiming at the internation-alization of political science research, another point to which we shall return.

Whereas the explicit consideration of foreign policy in political analysis may not appear breathtaking by today's standards, it was nevertheless something new in German institutional analysis in the 1960s (a brief look at the textbooks on Germany's political system from this period easily verifies the point). Even more remarkable, though, was that Wildenmann pushed these thoughts to a point where he questioned the very identity of democracy and the nation state, a very modern theme indeed: 'A "pax democratica" looks at sovereignty differently from a view concentrated on the nation state, a view wedded to post-absolutist thinking. One even has to raise the question whether the 19th century amalgamation of nation state and democracy will not turn out to be a major hindrance for human rights. Here it is the people, not the states that are "sovereign".' (Wildenmann 1963, pp.14–15; translation M.K.)

The Cologne Election study and beyond

Although in many ways Wildenmann's *Habilitationsschrift*, which he started immediately after he had joined Ferdinand A. Hermens at the University of Cologne in 1959, is a classical example of institutional political science analysis, there are nevertheless interspersed many ideas and thoughts drawn from political sociology. In 1961, Wildenmann put his interest in elections and his bias towards political sociology into practice. At Cologne, he joined forces with Erwin K. Scheuch and Gerhard Baumert to conduct a major study of that year's national election. It was a classic study, in many ways more conceptually advanced than even its widely respected American counterparts. In particular, it testified to the pay-offs of a combined political scientific-sociological approach. It treated the election as a part of an ongoing political/institutional process, including parties, interest groups, and mass media as forces interacting with the voters themselves. From that research focus came the decision to study the crystallization of the vote, on the one hand, in selected *constituencies* based on three-wave panels, and, on the other hand, in three cross-sectional surveys of the *national* voting-age population – equally spaced out over time.

(For details of the study design see Scheuch and Wildenmann 1965; see also Kaase and Klingemann 1994.)

The design alone of that Cologne Election Study of 1961 allows it, more than thirty years later, to measure up to the most recent election studies around the globe. Of course, as is frequently the case with complex research operations, the outcome in terms of measurable products fell way behind the expectations. In particular, the wealth of collected micro- and meso-information was never systematically integrated by Wildenmann or, for that matter, by others, into an encompassing monograph.

His involvement in the Cologne Election study, however, proved decisive for his future work on at least four accounts. First, it gave him the sociological and methodological expertise that made him attractive as a colleague for the group of young and hungry professors which had assembled around that time at the University of Mannheim: M. Rainer Lepsius in sociology, Hans Albert in sociology and theory of science, Martin Irle in social psychology. These three scholars, plus Wildenmann and the contemporary historian Erich Matthias, formed the social science nucleus in Mannheim that quickly developed into one of the leading social science research centres in Germany.

Secondly, Wildenmann's interest in and knowledge about elections, as well as his previous journalistic career, made him an attractive partner for the mass media in analysing elections. In particular, early on he came into contact with the Second German Television Network (ZDF), which had started broadcasting on 1 April 1963. He, jointly with Max Kaase and Uwe Schleth, developed a statistical computerized system of projections and analyses at election night for national and regional (*Länder*) elections (with him being the journalistic anchor man). Even more important, however, was his success in convincing the TV people that truly understanding elections required the ongoing study of public opinion through national surveys. The research group *Forschungsgruppe Wahlen* was established at the University of Mannheim for these purposes; after the general election of 1972, students of Kaase, Schleth and Wildenmann took over and moved the *Forschungsgruppe* out of the university as an independent unit. The most important long-term impact of Wildenmann's activities in this field is probably the fact that, starting in the late 1970s, the ZDF – through the *Forschungsgruppe* – has commissioned monthly national surveys of about one thousand respondents through the *Forschungsgruppe* (since unification, a sample of similar size for the former GDR has been added) which are freely available for secondary analyses through the German academic data archive, the *Zentralarchiv für Empirische Sozialforschung* at the University of Cologne, and which are continually used by German and international researchers in analyses of German political behaviour.

Thirdly, the Cologne Election study provided Wildenmann's first major links with the international community of political sociologists that was developing in the early 1960s (one of the first scholarly documentations of the process is Allardt and Littunen 1964; both Scheuch and Wildenmann attended the conference in Tampere which led to that book).

Fourthly, Wildenmann was well aware of shortcomings in the analysis of the Cologne Election Study data. Readers must be reminded that in those days data were on punched cards. As a consequence, analyses were extremely complicated and time-consuming because they had to rely on counter-sorters and card duplicators, and percentages had to be done on desk calculators or a slide rule. The recollections of the frustrations originating from this situation have accompanied Wildenmann through all of his career; without this background, his continuing interest in computers, social science computer software and methodological questions of social science research cannot be understood.

This keen sense of a need for a well-developed social science infrastructure – a need Wildenmann felt was not accepted in the social sciences, but was taken for granted in the much costlier 'hard' sciences – led him to push for the establishment of a German academic social science research institute. It came into being in 1974 as the *Zentrum für Umfragen, Methoden und Analysen* (ZUMA) and was located in Mannheim.

The international years

Among the windfall profits of Wildenmann's links with the international social science community were various invitations to teach in the United States. He spent the academic year 1969–70 at the State University of New York in Buffalo, where he co-operated specifically with Roberta S. Sigel and Lester W. Milbrath. These contacts triggered his formal association with the State University of New York in Stony Brook as a member of the political science department (1970–73). The most noteworthy result of this affiliation was a collaboration with Edward N. Muller, then a member of that department, which led to a research project on political participation and violence in Germany (Muller 1979). Beyond this, he worked closely with Albert Somit, Joseph Tanenhaus and John C. Wahlke.

In these American years Wildenmann also established an intensive scholarly and personal link with Karl W. Deutsch, who fascinated him because of his cosmopolitism, his cybernetics background (originating from Deutsch's work with Norbert Wiener) and his interest in mathematical approaches to political science (Alker and Deutsch 1973). One outcome of that relationship was a conference on mathematical political analysis held in Mannheim in 1972 which brought together major protagonists from that field (Deutsch and Wildenmann 1976). As it turned out, this variant of political science did not quite live up to its promises in the long haul. Still, Wildenmann (and Deutsch, with his Globus World Model developed at the *Wissenschaftszentrum* in Berlin) continued to believe in its potential. However, other than in general statements of intent and interest, this field never again played a major role in Wildenmann's work.

In the final decade of his university life, Wildenmann returned to two topics dating back to his early academic days: the quality of political leadership, and the nature of party government in modern democracies. Regarding the first topic, he and Uwe Schleth had organized the first nationwide German élite survey in 1968. Together with Werner Kaltefleiter in 1972, and Max Kaase and Ursula Hoffmann-Lange in 1981, he continued these studies (Hoffmann-Lange 1992). Immediately before his death, he submitted a proposal to the German Research Foundation for the first all-German élite study after unification. This study was later taken over and completed by one of Wildenmann's former Mannheim assistants, Wilhelm P. Bürklin of the University of Potsdam.

Regarding the second topic, party government, Wildenmann greatly profited from his 1980–83 leave of absence from the University of Mannheim and his move to the European University Institute in Florence. Resources, time on his hands, and an intellectually stimulating environment permitted him to design the last big project of his career: studies on 'The Future of Party Government'. For Wildenmann, party government was the epitome of modern democracy (Wildenmann 1986, p.3); therefore, thinking about democratic rule automatically meant thinking about political parties. Wildenmann argued that party government is increasingly running into problems such as the recruitment of capable political leaders, the impact of modern mass media on the political process, and the growing permeation of national by international politics (Wildenmann 1986, p.5).

The Future of Party Government project, surprisingly, was Wildenmann's first large *comparative* research project, although in his theoretical thinking he had been comparatively oriented from the start. Still, the project was comparative only in a more restricted sense. It entailed no quantitative or qualitative comparisons for a preselected set of countries, but was either conceptual (Volume 1; see Castles and Wildenmann 1986) or looked empirically at idiosyncratically chosen countries in a case-study mode (Volume 2; see Katz 1987).

If some assessment of that research is tried, then it is probably fair to state that it did not quite fulfil his initially high expectations. There were only two more volumes in the series (one of them an EUI dissertation), and it never reached the phase of the systematic comparative stocktaking at which it had aimed. There was, however, a continuation of the theme for the German case (Wildenmann 1989) when a small working party of political scientists produced papers concerned with special aspects of the party alienation theme. These were synthesized by Wildenmann. This book came into being in the context of a new research institute he had founded shortly before his retirement from the University: the Research Institute for Societal Development. This institute was the finishing mark on Wildenmann's life as an institution builder for social science research.

The institution builder

Wildenmann's personality – an almost unbeatable combination of clear thinking, competence, thrust, enthusiasm, emotionality and love of people – from the beginning of his academic life as a professor made him an attractive choice for important positions inside and outside the science system. Of the many obligations of this kind he took on, the most significant ones probably were the rector's office at the University of Mannheim, which he held three times, a six-year election as senator of the *Deutsche Forschungsgemeinschaft*, and various roles in the science system, politics and the mass media.

A service and research institute for German social science

It was mentioned before that the Cologne Election study was *the* professional experience which convinced Wildenmann of the need for a national academic social science infrastructure. Not least, his visits to the Institute for Social Research (ISR) at the University of Michigan in Ann Arbor (and here most noteworthy were the regular contacts with Warren E. Miller and, as his successor to the post of Director of the Interuniversity Consortium for Social and Political Research (ICSPR), Richard I. Hofferbert) made Wildenmann look at the ISR as an example for an equivalent institution in Germany.

The first step in this direction was a meeting of the most important figures in the German social sciences in Bonn called by the *Deutsche Forschungsgemeinschaft* on Wildenmann's initiative in 1968 on the need for and the feasibility of such an institute. This approach to the problem was typical of Wildenmann's way of dealing with institutional matters. On the one hand, from the beginning of this enterprise he tried to secure the co-operation and support of the empirically-minded social science research community. On the other hand, he early on involved the DFG as that institution in Germany which was generally responsible for the funding of university research and commanded an enormous fund of legitimacy in the science system. Nevertheless, even as DFG senator it took Wildenmann until 1973 to succeed in conveying the point to the relevant bodies of the DFG that an academic social science research institute was necessary and – even more important – that it should not be funded by direct state subsidies, but rather by independent money, that is from the DFG budget. Given the reservations held by many scholars, especially from the hard sciences, against the social sciences to start with, plus the anger about the active role of many social scientists in the student unrest of the late 1960s, even today one may marvel at Wildenmann's ability to convince scientists from all the major disciplines that the social sciences should indeed have such an institute (for his reflections on ZUMA after ten years of its existence, see Wildenmann 1985).

It is only a matter of historical precision to add that the *Zentrum für Umfragen, Methoden und Analysen* (Centre for Surveys, Analyses and Methods) was founded on 1 January 1974, in Mannheim, as a DFG institute, with Wildenmann as Head of the Board and Kaase as its first Director. Much later than expected (i.e. only in 1987), ZUMA moved from the sponsorship of the DFG, with its annual peer reviews, into a newly established academic joint social science institute with institutional federal and state funding, combining the previously independent ZUMA, the *Zentralarchiv für Empirische Sozialforschung* at the University of Cologne, and the *Informationszentrum Sozialwissenschaften* in Bonn under a common umbrella (GESIS – *Gesellschaft Sozialwissenschaftlicher Infrastruktureinrichtungen*/Society of Social Science Infrastructural Institutions).

The European Consortium for Political Research

One of the young researchers involved in the Cologne Election study through Wildenmann had been Jean Blondel. Ever since then they had remained in contact, and so it seemed natural for Blondel to come to Mannheim in 1969 to speak about the idea of setting up a European network of political science institutes and scholars, the organization later known as the European Consortium for Political Research (ECPR). Wildenmann greeted this idea with enthusiasm. He not only made Mannheim University one of the first ECPR members, he on two accounts also assumed, from the beginning, a crucial role in the ECPR's emerging activities. First, he helped greatly in acquiring considerable research funds from the Volkswagen Foundation, resulting in a series of ECPR-sponsored projects (Finer 1980a; Newton 1980; Rose 1980; Rokkan and Urwin 1983; Farneti 1985; Daalder 1987a; Mair 1987). Secondly, and much more importantly, it was Wildenmann who came up with the idea for the Joint Research Sessions, an extremely valuable concept which is now regarded worldwide as the trademark and the most important activity ever launched by the ECPR. True to his belief that the proof is in the pudding, and given his ability to secure financial support, the first Joint Research Session took place in Mannheim in 1973. 'Before then, the ECPR had sponsored individual, separate workshops, and few of them at that. With the Mannheim Joint Sessions, the ECPR came truly alive as an organisation. It provided its members, every year, with a focus as well as an occasion to work collectively. We all owe this opportunity to Rudolf.' (Blondel 1993.) With this involvement in the ECPR, it does not come as a surprise that Wildenmann was Chairman of the ECPR Executive Committee from November 1979 to April 1988 as well as Chair of the ECPR Research Board from April 1977 to September 1979.

The *Forschungsstelle für Gesellschaftliche Entwicklungen*

When Wildenmann spoke of ZUMA, he frequently used the term 'institutionalized altruism' (Wildenmann 1985, p.18) to indicate that he had not fought for it in order just to improve his personal research situation. This reflected his belief that empirical social science, too, is in need of a special kind of research infrastructure analogous to the hard sciences' big machines, spectroscopes, and so on, in order to develop into a full-fledged discipline. This sociotropic attitude did not, of course, preclude his thinking about a research infrastructure specifically tailored to his own research interests and needs. The occasion to build such an infrastructure came when Lothar Späth, then *Ministerpräsident* of Baden-Württemberg, the state in which Mannheim University was located, made Wildenmann a member of his brain trust and entrusted him with the preparation of a series of future-oriented major congresses in Stuttgart to bolster the national and international standing of Baden-Württemberg.

The success of the Späth–Wildenmann co-operation finally opened up the avenue for what Wildenmann had long had in mind: a university-based research institute with its own resources under his direction which was at the same time both science- and policy-oriented. After some preliminary funding in 1986, the new institute, the *Forschungsstelle für Gesellschaftliche Entwicklungen* (FGE – Research Unit for Societal Developments), obtained an independent budget in the framework of the general budget of Mannheim University. This institute permitted Wildenmann to do basic research, but it also served as a basis for developing applications for additional funds in the research money market. In his typical way, he recruited young researchers for projects, but at the same time used his network of established scholars to run workshops on selected topics with the aim of quickly producing edited volumes based on the workshop proceedings. Recurrent themes in those publications were democratic government, the political-institutional future of Europe, and problems of German unification (for an account of the work and publications of the FGE see Kaase 1995). Considering the short time-span involved, it is telling that the FGE was able to produce five volumes in its hardcover series, thirteen volumes in its paperback series, two books outside the series, and two special issues.

From 1991, both his deteriorating health and pressures from the Baden-Württemberg administration forced Wildenmann to think seriously about a successor for directing the FGE, and about establishing a closer link with the Mannheim Faculty of Social Sciences. In the end, for a variety of reasons, both efforts failed. Wildenmann grieved about this until his untimely death. In 1992 Baden-Württemberg decided to curtail substantially the FGE funds. It was finally closed down at the end of 1994.

The great book that Wildenmann had always wanted to write on the development of the Federal Republic of Germany did not come into being; it was not even begun. In a way, it is ironic, leading him back to his academic beginnings, that his last publication was a booklet on electoral research not meant for an academic but for a lay audience (Wildenmann 1992).

The essence of a man's academic life

For those among this book's readers who knew Wildenmann in person, his own account of his personal development in this chapter will be so vivid and typical that one will be able almost to hear him speak in his usual Swabian English. But even for somebody not familiar with the man, a life history shines through which is typical of those of many who lived through World War II at an age when those experiences could leave a major imprint on somebody's life as a person and as a scholar. Wildenmann's quest for and interest in democracy cannot be understood without this experience.

Only the future will tell what impact Wildenmann will have left on the substance of international political science. From time to time, he himself wondered about this and quarrelled with his image of a *Macher*. Unquestionably, he and the great number of scholars, who wrote their dissertations and *habilitations* with him, have become an integral part of the international landscape of political science, be it through research or through their work in improving the conditions under which political scientists can do their research. As Jean Blondel wrote in 1993: 'If a very large number of German political scientists owe to Rudolf Wildenmann the ability to accomplish their destiny, probably the majority of Western European political scientists owe to him the power to exercise their profession on a large platform – a platform which I know he would have wanted even larger and leading to closer co-operation.'

6 A voice from the Chicago school

Gabriel A. Almond

STANFORD UNIVERSITY

Graduate training at the University of Chicago

I recall a walk with Harold Lasswell sometime in 1931, in my senior year at the University of Chicago. We were discussing my prospects for graduate work in political science. Lasswell thought that the Rabbinic background of my family, and my training in biblical studies, would be a plus, something like having a second cultural experience in addition to growing up in Chicago. This was very reassuring to me, the first time any one had told me that being Jewish might have some positive career advantages, or that growing up in Chicago was a cultural experience.

I was an Americanist during my graduate years at the University of Chicago during 1933–38, as were almost all of the graduate students except the International Relationists. While Samuel Harper lectured on nineteenth century Russian history and the Bolshevik Revolution in those years, and we had the occasional foreign visitor such as Harold Laski, or Herman Finer, who lectured on European politics, we had no foreign area studies to speak of, and no dissertations focused on the European area. While we were not parochial, the faculty of the department was entirely American-born, and the dominant accent was midwestern, in Merriam's case quite twangy.

The curricular structure was functional rather than geographical. L.D. White taught a course on comparative public administration, and Gosnell one on comparative political parties. Lasswell's Public Opinion course included a lot of European material. The Ph.D in International Relations was interdisciplinary, and included diplomatic history, as well as international economics, and a Lasswell-given psycho-anthropology of international relations.

One of the research programmes going on during my University of Chicago years – Merriam's *Civic Training* series (1931) – included volumes on the Soviet Union, Britain, France, Germany, Italy. We students were not aware of the battle going on between Charles Merriam and Roberto Michels regarding the latter's contribution on Italy to the *Civic Training* series. Merriam wanted the Italian study to include the story of the fascist effort at controlling what we would now call the socialization processes. Michels, then in process of becoming a fascist himself, and wanting to avoid writing anything critical of fascism, insisted on doing a historical monograph on the rise of Italian nationalism (Karl 1974). Merriam invited Michels to spend a summer teaching in the Chicago summer quarter, when he hoped that Harold Lasswell could prevail on Michels to do a revision of the Italian case study. Nothing came of it, and Michels's manuscript went unpublished.

Thus, though we had no professor of comparative government who taught courses under that label or specialized on Europe during my graduate years, we were exposed to European scholarship and encountered European scholars as lecturers or as fellow students. I wrote my dissertation on *Wealth And Politics in New York City* under the supervision of Harold Lasswell and Harold Gosnell. It was indicative of the mood then prevailing in graduate studies at the University of Chicago that I could select a Marxist theme as the topic of my thesis – the relation between economic and political power as reflected in the changing social composition of the economic and political élites in New York City from the Colonial period until the then (1936) present day.

Bernard Crick (1959) did not get the Chicago School right. We were not 'progressives' and 'Bull Moosers', though Merriam had been such early in his career. The ideology of the Department in my years was a mix of political and administrative reform directed against inefficiency and corruption and opposition to the evils of capitalism, then so manifest in the world depression, large-scale unemployment, and the suppression of the labour movement. The more adventurous students among us were exploring a heady mix of Marx and Freud.

During my graduate years I shared an office with Edward Shils. He introduced me to Max Weber whose methodological writings he was then translating in collaboration with Louis Wirth, and more generally to European sociology. He encouraged me to improve on my college German and French by translating Weber's *Politik als Beruf*, and parts of Pareto's *Les Systèmes Socialistes* (1902–03; 1965).

I spent my dissertation year in New York City in 1935–36 as an SSRC pre-doctoral field fellow, at the time that the 'University in Exile' was getting under way at the New School for Social Research. I believe I was one of the first non-local students to seek them out. Hans Speier was my mentor there. I took a reading course in Max Weber under Albert Salomon's supervision. I used to take the subway out to Spuyten Duyvil one evening a week, where I spent an hour or two trying to construe Weber's complex prose.

More significantly, Hans and Lisa Speier introduced me to Dorothea Kaufmann – my future wife – a young refugee child psychologist from Cologne. I acquired added incentives to improve on my German.

My first teaching assignment at Brooklyn College put me deep in Americana. I taught five sections of American Government for fifteen hours per week. To alleviate the boredom I read almost the whole of the monographic and historical literature on American political institutions. I aspired to break out of the American monotony and introduce a course in comparative political parties, but as a young instructor I could not introduce a new, elective course into the curriculum.

A World War II post-doctoral

My German stood me in good stead at the outbreak of war. Lasswell was widely consulted in the gearing up of the US Government for World War II, particularly by the Department of Justice and the various information services. Two months after Pearl Harbor I was hired as head of the Enemy Section of the Bureau of Intelligence of the

Office of Facts and Figures, the predecessor of the Office of War Information. I had to build up a small staff of specialists on Nazi Germany and Occupied Europe to inform our own propaganda people of morale problems in enemy areas. I hired Herbert Marcuse to report on developments in Germany, and Henry Ehrmann to report on Occupied France. Marcuse, in the aftermath of Stalingrad, wrote a lovely memo on a Goebbels speech on the theme of 'Stimmung und Haltung' (loosely translated as 'mood and behaviour'), a distinction the Nazi Propaganda Minister drew in an effort to downplay the defeatism that was beginning to show among German workers and troops. Marcuse then appealed to me as an ironic Hegelian Marxist. He became a cultural guru much later.

I spent the last few months of the war, and the first months after VE Day in Germany, working for the United States Strategic Bombing Survey (US Air Force), interrogating German Gestapo and other Nazi intelligence personnel in the various internment camps of northern and central Germany about the effects of bombing on German morale. Moving as a small mobile team in the lee of the advancing armies, we were able to interview surviving members of small resistance movements as they met our advancing divisions. Though my official mission was to study the effect of strategic bombing on German morale I was more interested in the extent and the character of oppositional activity in Germany during the last years and months of the war.

The anti-Nazi resistance and European political parties

As I returned to academic life in the fall of 1945, I began a study of resistance movements in the various occupied countries of Europe, and within Germany as well. During my last August days at our headquarters in Bad Nauheim, SHAEF issued a regulation against looting by American troops, including documents among the prohibitions. I had precious copies of my interviews with resistance survivors, and other materials such as leaflets, along with some Gestapo arrest statistics. I took a chance and packed these documents in my footlocker and shipped them home, along with my spoils of war – two fencing foils which I had found in an abandoned Gestapo office, a set of carpenter's files, and a wonderfully long editor's shears, which I took out of a German army supply depot, and which I have been using until the present day.

Hence I was able in 1945–46 to complete a study entitled 'The Resistance and the Political Parties of Western Europe' with some unique in-depth data on the German case, as well as materials on the other European countries. I was particularly interested in the Christian parties of Germany, Italy, France, then led by religious elements with *bona fides* through having kept free of, or having actively opposed, Nazism-Fascism (Almond, 1947, 1948a, 1948b, 1949). These parties, along with the Social Democrats and the Communists, created a brief political *entente cordiale* in some European countries which fell apart with the onset of the Cold War.

The market value of a University of Chicago Ph.D

On my return to Brooklyn College and civilian life in 1945 I was already retooled as a European specialist. But my having taught American Government more than thirty times in the pre-war years at Brooklyn College left me with a sense of being an Americanist as well. Or rather, I could never accept the disciplinary convention that 'comparative government' excluded the American case. In another sense I was a somewhat unusual kind of comparativist. My University of Chicago graduate training meant that I had political sociological and psychological training as well.

When I came out of graduate school in 1938, a University of Chicago Ph.D, particularly of a Lasswellian flavour, was a bit on the flaky side. There was some doubt about our qualifications as specialists on the nuts and bolts of political science – the study of governmental and legal institutions. But within a few years the market demand for the University of Chicago interdisciplinary training – exemplified in the visibility of such Chicago Ph.Ds as V.O. Key Jr., Herman Pritchett, David Truman and Herbert Simon, among others – improved greatly. It resulted in my being hired at the Institute of International Studies at Yale in 1946, and receiving tenure in the Yale Department of Political Science in 1949.

The reigning texts in comparative government as the United States returned to civilian life in the late 1940s were Herman Finer's *Theory and Practice of Modern Government* (1932, 1949) and Carl J. Friedrich's *Constitutional Government and Politics* (1937). American political studies were more 'advanced'. Although as time went on Finer and Friedrich included chapters on such themes as parties and elections, pressure groups, public opinion, and political communication, the analytic treatment was largely historical, legal and philosophical. American studies in the first decades of the twentieth century had begun to be more sociological, psychological, processual and functional. The innovative empirical research on American politics being carried on by such scholars as Charles Merriam, Harold Gosnell, Harold Lasswell, Peter Odegard, Pendleton Herring, Elmer Schattschneider and others during the 1930s had brought to light a complex political infrastructure and process.

Europe in the post-World War II years was primarily preoccupied with rebuilding its economy and social structure. It was threatened and divided by the Cold War. Both conservative and Marxist ideology depreciated research on the political infrastructure. For Marxists pressure groups were reduced to class phenomena – the trade unions were part of the working class, and business, professional and farm groups were the agents of capitalism. For the conservatives – anti-democratic, or distrustful of democracy – such institutions as political parties, to say nothing of pressure groups, were viewed as subversive of the sovereign authoritarian state. In some European countries debate still raged on the question of whether the political realm was plural or monist, whether sovereignty could be divided. In the United States this ideological issue had been settled as early as the founding decades and the *Federalist Papers*.

The great social and political science traditions of the Continental Europe of the late nineteenth and early twentieth centuries – exemplified by Marx and his followers, Freud and his social science interpreters, Pareto, Weber, Durkheim, Mosca, Ostrogorski, Michels, and others – had been thoroughly disrupted by World War II. England's six-year-long World War II burden was a serious but not so thoroughgoing interruption. In Germany, and to a somewhat lesser extent in Italy, much of the academic social science community had gone into exile, primarily to the United States, where it enriched the American academy, particularly in the social sciences.

In the 1940s and 1950s there was a widely shared view that the United States and Britain stood almost alone in the world as trustees for humane civilization, and Britain was exhausted from its six-year-long wartime exertions. The United States had an enormously productive economy. Its universities were in the process of expanding in order to assimilate the millions of GIs returning from the war. For the social scientists and political scientists of those years it was 'great to be alive', with large hopes of discovery, important and profound messages to convey, and large resources to back it all up.

I was four times fortunate to be in that generation of American social scientists. From my University of Chicago background I had a unique methodological product line to sell; chance had placed me at the junction of European and American studies; I was in a strong research setting first at Yale, and then at Princeton; I was already known to the Social Science Research Council then about to embark on its greatest years under Pendleton Herring. The SSRC could draw on the strong commitment to the social sciences by the Rockefeller and Carnegie Corporations under the iconoclastic eyes and in the steady hands of Samuel Willets, Charles Dollard, Frederick Keppel and John Gardner.

The SSRC Committee on Comparative Politics

In 1954 I became the first chairman of the SSRC Committee on Comparative Politics, having been 'seconded' from the Committee on Political Behavior. We were a 'young' committee selected with an eye to escaping from American and European parochialism, and intellectual conservatism. Thus we had a number of specialists on what came to be called 'third world' countries (Lucian Pye on China and South East Asia, James Coleman on Africa, Myron Weiner on India); and Europeanists already researching the European political 'infrastructure' (Sigmund Neumann, LaPalombara and Almond). In what follows I will first treat the work of the Committee on Comparative Politics in which I shared, and then turn to my own work in comparative politics.

The first programme of the new Committee might have been forecast from the personnel of the founding Committee on Political Behavior, which included Pendleton Herring, V.O. Key Jr., David Truman, Avery Leiserson, and Oliver Garceau – all of them students of interest groups, and the democratic process. A grant from the Carnegie Corporation enabled us to embark on a 'retail' grant programme for the study of political groups in foreign countries (1957–58). What we proposed to do was to bring foreign area studies up to 'state of the art', encouraging American area specialists to delve into the political infrastructure of European and other foreign countries. Our funds enabled us to assemble our grantees for the discussion of research plans in advance of fieldwork. A number of political scientists made significant research contributions on the basis of these grants – Henry Ehrmann's study of French interest groups (1957), Joseph LaPalombara's study of Italian interest groups (1964), Linz's study of Spanish authoritarianism (1970a), Myron Weiner's study of Indian pressure groups and political parties (1962), Edward Banfield's study of attitudes towards groups in Southern Italy (1958), S.M. Lipset's *Political Man* (1960), Samuel Beer's study of British collectivism (1965), and the like.

In these early post-World War II years there was much theoretical speculation, and programmatic discussion. The SSRC had sponsored a conference on the state of comparative government studies at Northwestern University in 1952. Out of this had come a report published in the *American Political Science Review* (1953), and Roy C. Macridis's *The Study of Comparative Government* (1955), critiques of the state of the field, and proposals for improvement. My early structural-functional contributions, stimulated by the research programmes and conferences of the Committee, appeared during these years (1956, 1960), Lucian Pye's early contributions to modernization theory also appeared during these years (1962, 1966) as did Henry Ehrmann's comparative study of interest groups (1958) and Edward Shils's *Political Development of the New States* (1960), which had been produced for one of our early conferences.

Another major grant, for the period 1960–63, this time by the Ford Foundation, enabled the Committee to embark on a series of conferences on the general theme of political modernization and development. Lucian Pye assumed the Committee chairmanship in 1963, and directed the programme which eventuated in the nine-volume *Political Development Series* published by Princeton University Press over the period 1963–78. Five of the first six volumes dealt with important aspects and institutions of development – the communications media (Pye (ed.) 1963), bureaucracy (LaPalombara (ed.) 1963), education (Coleman (ed.) 1965), political culture (Pye and Verba (eds) 1965) and political groups and political parties (LaPalombara and Weiner (eds) 1966). A sixth volume compared the developmental experience of two relatively modernized, non-European countries, Japan and Turkey (Ward and Rustow 1964). Finally, three volumes turned to the analysis of development in history. The first of these – *Crises and Sequences in Political Development* – by six of the Committee members (Binder, Coleman, LaPalombara, Pye, Verba and Weiner 1971) argued that developmental patterns – centralized–decentralized, democratic–authoritarian, and the like – could be explained by the way in which different countries had been confronted historically by, and coped with, problems of political centralization and authority, collective political participation, national identity and legitimacy, and economic and social welfare. In the ninth volume, a test of the usefulness of this framework was made by a group of ten historians reviewing European and American experience in terms of these 'crises' (Grew *et al.* 1978). The eighth volume (1976), which I shared in planning with Charles Tilly, drew a number of European and American historians and political scientists into doing original historical research on European state-building in the sixteenth to nineteenth centuries. The book differed from earlier studies which emphasized the development of institutions. Tilly proposed dealing with policy areas as causative, as the so-called independent variables, with differences in institutional development as the dependent ones. One part of the volume treated the interplay of historic strategic and security variables with the formation of armed forces, and associated state agencies; another the interaction of economic development, strategic interests, and the formation of the revenue-collecting institutions of the state. Another part of the volume dealt with different patterns of the recruitment and training of bureaucratic personnel, as they influenced the structure and culture of Western European states.

This was an extraordinary period of intellectual activity over an interval of some two decades. The actual number of scholars participating in Committee activities was 245, 199 of them American and 46 foreign, mostly European (Wood 1971). The topics opened up and stressed by the Committee were on the frontiers of political science research.

Other centres of creativity

But while the Committee's programmes were highly visible and influential both in the United States and abroad, they were only one of the creative centres in comparative politics in the post-World War II decades. The Institute for Social Research and Survey Research Center at the University of Michigan were major catalysts in the diffusion to Europe and elsewhere of survey research-based election studies. Wherever these University of Michigan studies touched they left cadres trained in political sociology, psychology and statistics. Robert Dahl at Yale during the late 1960s and early 1970s carried out his own programme of comparative studies, focused on the theme of 'opposition', producing two important volumes of theoretical analysis and country studies (1966, 1973). Dahl's venture into comparative politics culminated in *Polyarchy* (1971), a major contribution to comparative democratic theory. Samuel Huntington at Harvard anticipated the critique of American political science in its pluralistic 1950s decade, with his studies of the role of the military in politics (1957), his collaborative work with Brzezinski comparing the United States and the USSR (1963), and, most important, his trail-breaking *Political Order in Changing Societies* (1967).

The 'political mobilization' studies also developed quite independently of the work of the Committee on Comparative Politics. This research programme was initiated by Daniel Lerner (1958), Karl Deutsch (1961) and S.M. Lipset (1960, 1994) and was based on aggregate statistical analysis of the influence of industrialization, urbanization, the spread of education and mass communications on political mobilization and democratization.

The creative scholars in comparative politics in the 1960s and 1970s were heavily over-committed. I recall an encounter at the Center for the Advanced Study in the Behavioral Sciences in 1967 with Robert Dahl, Val Lorwin, Hans Daalder and Stein Rokkan, then planning a collaborative study of the 'small democracies' of Europe. European studies tended to be dominated by 'Great Powers' examples and data. Most Europeanists specialized on England, France or Germany. A study of the small European countries – the four Scandinavian ones, Ireland, Belgium and the Netherlands, Austria and Switzerland, with their different combinations of ethnic, linguistic, religious, economic and strategic variables – held out great theoretical promise. The later work on 'consociationalism' and 'neo-corporatism' shows this to have been the case. While I was persuaded of this, it was impossible for the Committee on Comparative Politics, then fully involved in the production of the series described above, to take on an additional project. As Hans Daalder points out in his essay in this volume, the Small Democracies project contributed to important theoretical work by its co-directors and others stimulated by its conferences. That it stopped short of its planned series of country and theoretical studies was attributable to the rapid growth of, and politicization of, universities in Europe during the 1960s and 1970s. Only one country study in this planned series – Ireland, by Basil Chubb (1970) – and one theoretical study – Robert Dahl and Edward Tufte on *Size and Democracy* (1973) – ever appeared. Had the Committee on Comparative Politics agenda been less full we might conceivably have been able to help mobilize the resources that would have been required to bring off this promising programme. Thus there were 'opportunity costs' in the development of the programme of the Committee on Comparative Politics.

Overtones of Max Weber

I welcomed the opportunity to engage in theoretical speculation in the early years of the Committee's activities. Ever since graduate student days I had nurtured Weberian aspirations – to know just about everything there was to know, and to write with apodictic confidence about its meaning. I had completed my study *The Appeals of Communism* in the same year in which the Committee was established. I had no major research commitments at the time, and the beginning of the Committee's activities was an invitation to theorize. The immediate post-World War II generation of social scientists was challenged to encompass the variety of political phenomena which were then emerging. How could one grasp and comprehend this immense and unstable reality? Europe and its great civilization and cultural tradition were in a shambles; it was an open question whether democracy would survive on the European continent. We were the heirs to that civilization. (I recall a visit – or should I say a pilgrimage with another aspiring social scientist in uniform – in the summer of 1945 to visit Marianne Weber. We exchanged a few words about Max Weber, nothing much. She was old and frail and spoke faintly. She appreciated our gift of several packages of 'Lucky Strike' cigarettes, which were then exchangeable for scarce items like coffee.)

Two theoretical papers came out of these early years on the Committee on Comparative Politics. 'Comparative Political Systems' was written as a discussion paper for the first conference of the Committee held at Princeton in the spring of 1955. (As I write about this first gathering sponsored by the Committee, I recall that Stein Rokkan, then a Rockefeller Fellow, attended and took an active part in this first encounter, wearing a heavy loden overcoat. June in Bergen was different from June in Princeton, but Stein didn't seem to notice the heat. Stein was with the Committee from the start, giving as well as receiving.)

The paper I presented was an early formulation of the 'Functional Approach', suggesting that different political systems could be systematically compared according to their structural and cultural characteristics. Structure was defined in Weberian-Parsonian terms, as action, behaviour, with legal and normative aspects treated in so far as they influenced actual behaviour; culture was defined as psychological orientation, again in Weberian-Parsonian terms. The essay simply proceeded to compare four 'sorts' of political systems – (1) the Anglo-American, (2) the continental European 'immobilist' systems, (3) the Scandinavian and Low Country, 'working' multi-party systems, and (4) the totalitarian systems – according to these structural and cultural criteria. It delights me to recall that it was this crude sorting of political systems which Arend Lijphart critiqued in 1968, and which was followed by his trail-breaking democratic studies, beginning with his 'Typologies of Democratic Systems' in 1968 and culminating in his definitive *Democracies* in 1984.

Bringing the rest of the world into comparative politics

In its early effort to break out of the Europe-centredness of comparative politics, the Committee on Comparative Politics sponsored, as its first major work, a comparative study of the developing areas. This was a collaboration between Lucian Pye (South East Asia), Myron Weiner (South Asia), James Coleman (Sub-Saharan Africa),

Dankwart Rustow (the Near East) and George Blanksten (Latin America), James Coleman joining me in the editing of the volume. I wrote the introductory chapter presenting the framework of comparison, and James Coleman wrote a concluding chapter summarizing the findings of the various area studies and presenting a typology of developing systems.

Looking back at this product of the late 1950s I would defend it as the first effort to provide an analytical scheme for political scientists embarking on field research in the developing areas. It codified and combined a number of research traditions. The first of these – the European sociological tradition of Pareto, Durkheim, and Weber – was then being transmitted through the writings of Talcott Parsons. Parsons called his research approach 'the action frame of reference', after Weber's ontological view of the subject matter of the social sciences as *Soziale Handlung* or 'social action'. In my introductory essay to *The Politics of The Developing Areas* I conclude that an empirical theory of comparative politics would consist of observations about the variety and properties of political systems conceived as functional-structural statements of probability. I subsequently realized that what I had sought to produce in the late 1950s to help my colleagues decide what questions to ask when they went into the field to study exotic political systems was a 'comparative political statics'. Some years later, as I suggest below, I confronted the problem of comparative political dynamics.

The systemic and functional concepts which I introduced in *The Politics of The Developing Areas* were drawn from anthropological, sociological and political theory. The system–environment, input–output model came from Parsons and David Easton, the first drawing on biological system models, the second on mechanical ones; the recruitment function came from Pareto and Lasswell, socialization from the psycho-anthropologists (Margaret Mead, Ruth Benedict, Florence and Clyde Kluckhohn, Lasswell and Erik Erikson), communication from the social psychologists (Paul Lazarsfeld, Elihu Katz) and the media people, interest articulation and aggregation from the American political scientists of the 1920s to 1950s (Merriam, Gosnell, V.O. Key, David Truman *et al.*); rule making, rule implementation, rule adjudication, came from separation of powers theory. I review this conceptual history in my Presidential Address to the American Political Science Association (1966).

Rereading this essay, spelling out the various political functions and illustrating them with examples from the modern world of European and American, as well as 'Third World' and primitive societies, my mood varies between pride and embarrassment. My embarrassment arises out of its pedantry, and pretentious lapses. My models, of course, were Weber's *Wirtschaft und Gesellschaft* (1922), and Parsons and Shils's *Toward A Theory of Action* (1951). The input–output-system model which I crafted at that time did indeed combine and codify European sociological theory, and Freudian psycho-anthropological theory, as well as the new primarily American 'political process' approach. This recipe was concocted at the Center for Advanced Study in the Behavioral Sciences, where I spent 1956–57 working with a group of imaginative and playful anthropologists (Evon Vogt, John Roberts, John Whiting and Kimball Romney *et al.*) who helped me think about functions, structures and social systems.

I was aware of some of the shortcomings of this essay as I composed it in the late 1950s, and was made aware of more shortcomings as critics were quick to fault it in subsequent years. The argument that it was a static theory was not really damaging; it was indeed a comparative political statics. The appropriate response was to complement it with a political dynamics. This, indeed, became my main interest in the late 1960s and the early 1970s when the work on *Crisis, Choice, and Change* (1973) was being done.

The structural–functional approach

As I taught comparative politics at the graduate level at Stanford in the 1960s in the revolutionary and counter-cultural mood of the time a more sophisticated functional model began to take shape, taking into account the 'post-modern' and 'deconstructive' mood which swept the discipline of political science in those years. I recognized that one had to distinguish 'system functions' from 'process functions', and both of these from 'policy functions'. The three-level treatment of political functions – system, process, and policy – was foreshadowed in the first Almond and Powell book (1966) and fully elaborated in the second edition entitled *Comparative Politics: System, Process and Policy* (1978). Socialization and recruitment shaped and transformed the culture and structure of the political system; the political process consisted of some five distinctive kinds of activities – the articulation of interests and demands, the aggregation of interests into policy alternatives, the formulation, implementation, and adjudication of policies. The political system interacted with its domestic and international environments through extractive, distributive, regulative, and symbolic outputs. These outputs in turn maintained or transformed the domestic and international structure and culture, producing outcomes feeding back as inputs into the political system, and affecting its structure and culture. The communication function seemed to be important at all three levels, between the levels, and between the political system and its environments as well.

A typology of political systems (e.g. the varieties of democratic and authoritarian regimes) would be conceived as structural–functional equilibrium states, described in these terms. This, in retrospect, was the theory of comparative statics that emerged out of the theoretical speculation of the 1950s and 1960s. I believe much of it survives in the contemporary political science theoretical vocabulary.

Crisis, choice and change

Younger colleagues and I organized a workshop at Stanford in 1968 around the theme of 'Political Development', to survey and evaluate the various approaches to political change then being pursued. As the work proceeded Scott Flanagan and Robert Mundt joined me in editing a series of historical developmental studies which appeared in 1973 under the title of *Crisis, Choice, and Change: Historical Studies of Political Development*. The book consisted of a theory of political dynamics, presented in the introductory and concluding chapters, and eight historical case studies, done in accordance with our approach: a study of the British Reform Act of 1832, done by Bingham Powell, and one of the British Crisis of 1931, done by Dennis Kavanagh; a study of the formation of the French Third Republic by Robert Mundt; one on the formation of the German Weimar Republic by Volker Rittberger; one on the Cardenas

Reforms of Mexico by Wayne Cornelius; a study of the Meiji Restoration in Japan by James White; and one of the Indian crises in the mid-1960s by Thomas Headrick.

What our workshop had discovered in the course of our meetings in these turbulent late 1960s and early 1970s years was that some four distinct approaches to the explanation of political development had emerged – structural–functionalism, social mobilization, rational choice, and leadership 'theory'. The approach of *Crisis, Choice, and Change* was based on the recognition that each of these schools had unique strengths as well as distinct weaknesses and liabilities. It seemed logical that a framework of analysis that integrated these separate approaches might be able to combine their separate strengths while at the same time overcoming their individual deficiencies.

In integrating these distinct approaches we tried to bridge two kinds of dichotomies in the comparative field: (1) the static–dynamic or stability versus change perspective; and (2) the determinacy–choice dichotomy which often assumes the form of a macro versus micro approach. We bridged the first dichotomy by applying different methodologies to different phases of our case studies of historical episodes. System functionalism is appropriate for mapping general system characteristics and explaining system maintenance and stability, and was applied to examining the characteristics of the pre-existing political regime, and broader political system, and the new regime and system characteristics that emerged at the end of the historical episode. The differences that these two mapping exercises identified then became our measure of the amount and kind of development and change that had taken place.

By contrast, the process of change was traced successively through social mobilization, rational choice-coalition, and leadership modes of analysis. The analysis of changes in the external environment – the essence of the social mobilization approach – would explain the changing weights and distributions of different resources such as wealth, political incumbency, coercive resources, and the like. Our workshop soon identified the international environment as crucial in the explanation of most of our developmental episodes, rediscovering the insights of historians such as John Robert Seeley (1888) of Cambridge, and Otto Hintze (1975, tr. Felix Gilbert) of the University of Berlin.

The second dichotomy (determinacy–choice) contrasts (1) analysis at the macro, aggregate data level where most of the independent variables are non-political ones, and the political outcomes which are constrained by these contextual, international security-socio-economic variables, with (2) an analysis at the micro, actor level (individuals, élites or masses), where the independent variables are political, and the data ideally are collected at the individual level and focus on the preferences, resources, choices and actions of individuals and groups, élites and masses.

We presented this as an integrated theory of development, integrated in the sense that each approach is conceptually congruent with the others through a common focus on political resources and utilities. System functionalism, employed to specify the 'before and after' of the developmental episode, specifies the distributions of resources among, and the preferences of, the political actors as these are constrained in the more or less stable original political system and in the more or less stable subsequent system. A new resource distribution, and a changed issue agenda, are the end results of the social mobilization process with the emergence of new groups and élites, or of developments in the international environment, which may enhance or decrease the resources of political groups, or change their political preferences. At the micro level coalition analysis generates the logically possible ruling combinations, again through the analysis of the distribution of resources and utilities among the political actors; and leadership is defined as the capacity to transform utilities or issue orientations through creative ideas, and/or to discover and mobilize new and old political resources. Thus leadership is the creative capacity to broker winning combinations which significantly adapt and transform the politics and public policy of a political system. It is the theoretical integration of these separate methodologies that is the special contribution of the *Crisis, Choice and Change* approach. It is not simply a more comprehensive checklist of causes of political change.

Our historical case studies showed, for example, how important the strong individual leadership of Cardenas was in the development of the PRI in Mexico, and how important the weak leadership of Napoleon III had been in the collapse of the second French empire. The British Reform Act of 1832, and the Meiji Restoration in mid-nineteenth century Japan, illustrated the importance of collective leadership. Coalition analysis illuminated the causes of the weakness of the Weimar Republic, and the origins of the *immobilisme* of the Third Republic. Social mobilization theory, particularly when we recognized the great importance of the international environment in the sense of demonstration effect, flows of capital and trade, warfare and its threat, were indispensable in explaining our cases: catastrophic military defeat in the cases of the Third Republic and the Weimar Republic, demonstration effect in the case of the Meiji Restoration, the combination of industrialization and the stand-down from the continual warfare of the French Revolution and the Napoleonic Era in the case of the British Reform Act of 1832. Finally, it became obvious, as we carried on our historical studies, that structural–functional mapping exercises were essential in our efforts to define the 'from what to what?' of political development.

The appeals of communism

The system-process-policy approach to comparative analysis and political typology, and the crisis-choice-and-change approach to political development, represent the culmination of my theoretical efforts. Some brief discussion of two other comparative undertakings with which I have been identified may be in point. The first post-World War II decade was an American decade of pride, but also of shame. The Cold War precipitated a paranoid mood – McCarthyism – which resulted in the persecution by Congressional and state legislative committees, by the media, as well as by the courts, of thousands of Americans accused of membership of the American Communist Party, or affiliated organizations, or of being subscribers to left-wing journals. The image pressed by the leaders of this persecutory movement was of a far-flung communist conspiracy, headquartered in Moscow, and with branches throughout the world committed to the support of the Soviet Union in its efforts to overthrow capitalism and imperialism by every and all means including espionage and violence. The study (1954) which I began in the early 1950s made the case for a much more complex communist system cleansed of paranoia. varying from country to country, according to the social composition of the membership, and according to rank in the communist power structure, from rank and file to cadre and the like.

In making this study I was driven equally by the desire to demonstrate the usefulness of social science methodology in confronting problems of public policy, and to make out the case for a more realistic and differentiated public policy to deal with the 'communist threat'. We interviewed several hundred former communists in the United States and England, France and Italy, workers and middle-class members, rank-and-filers and higher-ups. We interviewed American psychiatrists who had had party members among their patients. We made content analyses of the communist universe of communication – Lenin's and Stalin's writings and the theoretical journals, as well as its mass media – in order to distinguish between the 'esoteric' and 'exoteric' cultures of the Communist Party.

The Civic Culture

Sidney Verba, in reflecting on our five-year-long collaboration on *The Civic Culture*, has imputed to us an unusual capacity for *Chutzpah*, the Yiddish expression for 'nerve'. This expression may be defined on the one hand as 'risk taking', the willingness to take a chance without which important purposes cannot be achieved. Or it may be defined as 'foolhardiness', overreaching. In Yiddish much depends on the inflection. In Verba's retrospective in *The Civic Culture Revisited* (Almond and Verba, 1980) he locates our effort somewhere in between the sober risk-taking and foolhardy extremes.

Verba and I might not agree on just at what point the line should be drawn. I had in my memory Merriam's Civic Education Series in the 1920s and the 1930s, which, in a way, was an effort to make a comparative political culture study in that pre-survey research era. Interviewing of citizen-respondents was the main method Merriam and Gosnell used in their non-voting studies of the 1920s. I had participated in the survey of German opinion and attitudes done by the Morale Division of the United States Strategic Bombing Survey in the immediate aftermath of World War II. In my study of public opinion and foreign policy in the late 1940s I made substantial use of public opinion data; and in *The Appeals of Communism* study I had employed survey organizations operating in England, France and Italy. It was not a big jump to undertake a cross-national study of political attitudes, using probability sampling, open-ended and structured kinds of questions, and adapting and improving on existing measures and indices of participation, affiliation, civic competence and social trust. *The Civic Culture* (Almond and Verba 1963) ventured into new territory, but it was not very far ahead of the pack.

And by venturing as it did it provided the baseline for the masterful, carefully researched and analysed recent work on political participation done by Sidney Verba and his associates (1995), as well as providing the counterpoint for the deeply troubling recent findings on the decline of American voluntarism reported by Robert Putnam (1993). Perhaps at least some of the errors committed in the conduct of the Civic Culture study (and faithfully recorded and acknowledged in the *Civic Culture Revisited*, 1980) may be granted a degree of absolution under Pareto's apothegm, 'Give me a fruitful error, full of seeds, bursting with its own corrections. You can keep your sterile truth for yourself!'

I have been wonderfully fortunate in my co-authors and collaborators – Bernard C. Cohen, Sidney Verba, Lucian Pye, James Coleman, Bingham Powell, Scott Flanagan,

Robert Mundt, and many others. It will never be possible to separate their ideas from mine. We were an intellectual movement of the second half of the twentieth century, beginning with great élan in the first decades after World War II, and encountering heavy waters in the politicized and rational-choice-economistic later decades. We cannot measure our impact, but we know that we left marks on the history of comparative politics.

I do not neatly fit the 'comparative European' category, the boundaries of this 'comparative autobiography'. I have been a comparativist from the beginning of my career. My research of the 1950s – on the resistance movements of World War II and the communist parties of the 1950s – were purely European, and European-American, in their focus. The work of my maturity – *The Politics of The Developing Areas*, *The Civic Culture* and *Crisis, Choice, and Change* – all sought a broader coverage, the inclusion of the Third World, and the recognition of the persistence of the pre-modern in the modern. More recently, my encounter with the fading of the culture of progress (Almond, Chodorow and Pearce 1980), and the emergence of 'fundamentalist' religious movements throughout the world (Almond, Sivan and Appleby 1995) still finds me an incorrigible comparativist with humanist ambivalences.

7 A brief intellectual autobiography*

Robert A. Dahl

YALE UNIVERSITY

Influences from earlier experiences

In 1946, when I gained a temporary appointment as an instructor at Yale University, I began a life of teaching and writing in political science which, as things turned out, I spent almost entirely at Yale until my retirement in 1986.

Looking back, I can now see that the main focus of my scholarly work was determined as much by my earlier experiences outside academia as by my life within it. Four such experiences now seem to me to have been particularly influential.

One was spending my formative years in very small towns, tiny villages or hamlets really. I was born in 1915 in a town with a population of less than 1000 in Iowa, which was then predominantly an agricultural state. Most of the people in and around my town were farmers. My father was a doctor whose patients were mainly local farmers.

When I was ten we moved to Alaska. Growing up in a small Alaskan town with a population of about five hundred had a powerful impact on me. If you live in a village surrounded by mountains on three sides and the sea on the other, where you are cut off from the rest of the world in winter except for the occasional boat delivering supplies, you come to know the people around you extremely well. Almost every person becomes a highly concrete, very specific individual, with very concrete and specific qualities. In that situation you can learn to respect human beings without romanticizing them either individually or collectively.

I also learned something about the world of manual labour and the workplace. Because every young person was expected to work all summer at whatever job was available, like some of the other youths I worked as a manual labourer on the docks

* In writing these recollections and reflections I have drawn freely on the following: the introduction to *Democracy, Liberty and Equality* (Oslo: Norwegian University Press, 1986), pp.7–24; an interview with Nelson Polsby in Michael A. Baer, Malcolm E.H. Jewell and Lee Sigelman (eds), *Political Science in America. Oral Histories of a Discipline* (Lexington, KY: University Press of Kentucky, 1991), pp.166–78; 'Reflections on *A Preface to Democratic Theory*', *Government and Opposition*, vol. 26, pp.293–301; 'Justifying Democracy', *Society*, vol. 32 (1995) which was drawn from 'El poder de la democracia, Diálogo con Ramon Vargas Machuca', *Claves* December, 1994, pp.44–54; introductions to sections of *Collected Works 1940–1995* (Berkeley: University of California Press, forthcoming).

and on the railroad. For me, as I well knew, this condition was not permanent; but I knew it would be for some of the others. I acquired sympathy, which I have never wholly lost, for working people and their often hard and limiting lives. I know that my writings on economic democracy and the problem of worker ownership and control (e.g. Dahl 1985) originated in those experiences.

Finally, growing up in small towns must have contributed to my lifelong interest in the problem of *scale* in social and political life. My concern with the effects of scale was reflected in the book I wrote with Edward Tufte, *Size and Democracy* (1973), and in *Democracy and Its Critics* (1989), in which it is one of the organizing themes. (It is also a major theme in Dahl 1967, 1983, 1984a, 1994a.)

A second set of experiences that helped to shape my later work was the sharp political and ideological conflict that characterized the decade of the 1930s in Europe and the United States. It was impossible both to be highly interested in politics and to avoid taking positions on critical questions of political ideology, organizations, strategies and tactics. When I wrote my dissertation at Yale during the academic year 1939–40 I entitled it *Socialist Programs and Democratic Politics: An Analysis*. It was nothing less than an attempt to examine all the major socialist proposals from the Utopians down to what in the 1930s were ideas about the possibilities of market socialism, in order to assess their compatibility with a democratic political system. The outbreak of World War II and the disasters of the Allies compelled me, like many others, to confront the prospect of a world in which democracy, where it survived, would be at bay indefinitely against totalitarian aggression, internal and external.

Let me repeat here a comment written in 1986 (Dahl 1986, p.22):

> I wrote my dissertation ... after an extraordinary period of reform in the United States, the New Deal, had ended and World War II had commenced. I began it a few weeks after the signing of the Nazi–Soviet Pact in Moscow, which in turn freed Hitler to undertake his invasion of Poland. I turned to the final chapters during the invasion of Norway, completed them with the defeat and occupation of the Netherlands and Belgium, and was awarded my doctorate at a ceremony that occurred about midway between the British retreat from Dunkerque and the fall of France.

During the time I was writing, it was impossible to predict, except on blind faith, whether democracies would survive, and if so where and in what form, and what economic orders would emerge out of war, victory and defeat. I do not much doubt that these times greatly strengthened my belief that the nature of the economic order – whether capitalist, socialist, or whatever – ought to be subordinate to the primary values of democracy, collective self-determination, democratic liberties, and the intrinsic worth of all human beings. In 1940 I published one article entitled 'On the Theory of Democratic Socialism', which was drawn directly from a chapter in my recently completed Ph.D dissertation. It was published (1940) in *Plan Age*, a journal that ceased publication shortly thereafter, and it remained virtually unread. (It was republished as a chapter in Dahl 1986, pp.25–54.)

A third experience that influenced my later academic work was working in Washington for several years in agencies of the federal government. At Yale my aim, surprising as it now seems to me, was not to become a scholar. On the contrary, I wanted to engage in the far more alluring task of changing American public policies, a possibility that had been dramatically demonstrated during Franklin D. Roosevelt's New Deal. After my first two semesters in the Ph.D programme at Yale in 1936–37 I was given the opportunity to spend the following year as an 'intern' at the National Labor Relations Board in Washington. That year opened up a whole new world to me. When I returned to Yale to complete my graduate work I was fired with enthusiasm for a career in public administration, preferably in Washington. By the time I arrived in Washington in 1940 with my newly minted Ph.D, however, the New Deal period was over and Washington was now focusing on the war in Europe, and soon in the Pacific. Working in government bureaux engaged in economic mobilization for the war effort, I learned a great deal about the possibilities and limits of central economic planning in a democratic system. Later I was to draw heavily, if quite indirectly, on these experiences, most fully perhaps in *Politics, Economics, and Welfare* (1953) written with Charles E. Lindblom; they also inspired 'The Science of Public Administration: Three Problems' (Dahl 1947a), which was my second published article, and the first that I published after joining academia in 1946.

Finally, it is worth mentioning a fourth experience which influenced my later work in important ways, though it is harder to say exactly how. This was my service in the American Army in World War II. Before entering the Army in the winter of 1943, I had already concluded that I did not particularly enjoy being a bureaucrat – though I was still unsure about an alternative. In September of 1944 I arrived in Europe as leader of a small reconnaissance platoon in an infantry regiment that spent the fall and winter fighting in the Vosges Mountains, ending up on VE day in the Austrian Alps. Coming to know my comrades with the intimacy and solidarity that, alas, perhaps men can gain only in combat, my respect for the qualities of 'ordinary' human beings was deepened even further. Ordinary people, I came to understand, have extraordinary capacities, though too often, I fear, these are insufficiently developed.

By the end of 1945, I had been away from academic life for five years and had published only one article (Dahl 1940), before the events I've described crowded out such possibilities. But soon after my return to the United States I sought out my earlier mentors at Yale, who offered me a temporary post, which in due time became permanent.

Books and scholars

Although these experiences external to academia stand out as influencing my later life within it, I find it more difficult to pinpoint the immediate effects of specific books and scholars – perhaps because there were so many. A list would include illustrious contributors to the long history of political, philosophical and economic thought: Plato, Aristotle, Machiavelli, Hobbes, Rousseau, Adam Smith, Mill, Marx . . . An attentive reader of my work would realize, I think, that some of these magnificent writers stimulated in me a continuing, and I would hope fruitful, disagreement and debate. My long-standing criticism of the argument of Plato's *Republic* and Rousseau's *Social Contract* continued on into *Democracy and its Critics*.

Oddly, perhaps, it was not until the 1950s that (as best I can now recall) I became acquainted with several writers who exerted considerable influence on my later thinking. I have particularly in mind Max Weber and (surprisingly late in my education)

Tocqueville. As a younger colleague of Harold Lasswell I also became familiar with, and impressed by, his meticulous effort to introduce greater rigour and precision in the concepts of power, influence, authority, and related terms. My own work on 'power' was directly influenced in some measure by his (Dahl 1957, 1961a, 1963).

Several scholars who may have passed into oblivion seeded ideas that were later to germinate in a good deal of my work. I have just taken down from my shelves the only book I retained from my undergraduate days, a heavily marked copy of Leon Duguit's *Law in the Modern State*, first published in English in 1919, with an introduction by Harold Laski (who with his wife Frida translated it from the French). When I read the book as an undergraduate I doubt whether I quite understood what Duguit was attempting to do. Although I might have re-read the book in graduate school, I have definitely not done so since. Yet my interest in 'pluralism' may have been generated, in part at least, by that book.

I also have beside me as I write Francis W. Coker's *Recent Political Thought*, published in 1934. During my first year in graduate school, 1936–37, I enrolled in Coker's year-long seminar on 'recent political thought', which I believe may have been one of the most important and informative courses I ever took. The book's table of contents probably represents fairly accurately the subjects we would have examined in the seminar. Here are some chapter headings: 'Karl Marx'; 'The Socialist Movement and the Orthodox Followers of Marx: Before the World War'; 'Democratic and Evolutionary Socialists'; 'The Socialists of Soviet Russia'; 'The Anarchists'; 'The Syndicalists'; 'The Guild Socialists'; 'The Attack on Democracy'; 'The Defense of Democracy'; 'The Fascists'; 'The Pluralist Attack on State Sovereignty.'

What I read for that seminar, and no doubt discussed with other students in and out of class, had, I think, at least two long-run consequences. First, as the last chapter title cited from Coker's book suggests, I gained a much better understanding of (legal) pluralism. I could see Duguit in the context of English writers with a pluralist perspective, of whom Coker cited J.N. Figgis, Harold Laski, A.D. Lindsay, and, as sympathetic to it, Ernest Barker and an American, Mary P. Follett (some of whose work I later read and admired). I found legal pluralism attractive and interesting, and probably started down the road toward a 'pluralist' interpretation of democratic politics. Secondly, thanks in part to the works I read for Coker's seminar I became interested in this question: how if at all could a socialist economic system be reconciled with a democratic political system? That question not only became the subject of my rather audacious dissertation (what self-respecting department of political science today would allow a student to undertake a dissertation on such a broad and challenging issue?) but formed an interest that I was to pursue in various articles and books thereafter. (These include Dahl 1947b and 1947c, both of which are reprinted in Dahl 1986, as well as the small book *A Preface to Economic Democracy*, 1985.)

Exploring new ground

Mathematics and statistics

My formal training in mathematics had been wretched, my understanding of statistical theory and methods abysmal. By the mid-1950s I became acutely aware of this gap and

I set about to fill it as conscientiously and systematically as I could. I sat in on courses at Yale in mathematics and statistics – one of them taught by a close friend, James Tobin, who was later to win a Nobel Prize in Economics. During a year at the Center for Advanced Study in the Behavioral Sciences at Palo Alto in 1955–56 I was able to improve my understanding of several aspects of mathematics that seemed most relevant to my interests, thanks in part to guidance from a number of other Fellows in residence that year. These included R. Duncan Luce and Howard Raiffa, the authors of one of the first textbooks on game theory; the mathematical economist Jacob Marschak (who had been one of Kenneth Arrow's mentors at Chicago); Martin Shubik, a mathematical economist; Patrick Suppes, a philosopher and mathematician interested in the theory of measurement; and others. My improved (if still fairly primitive) grasp of mathematical and quantitative arguments helped me to gain some understanding of Arrow's argument in his seminal work, *Social Choice and Individual Values* (1951) – considerably before it had become known among political scientists.[1] That book subsequently had a strong impact on the style and content of *A Preface to Democratic Theory* (1956).

However, I was doubtful (realistically, I think) about the extent of my mathematical competence; in any case I was somewhat sceptical about the ultimate contributions that game theory and rational choice could make to political understanding; and perhaps most important of all, I clearly derived much less satisfaction from attempting to work along those lines than I did from attempting to work along others. So, while I was not at all averse to statistical methods and occasionally employed them, I did not choose to pursue mathematical approaches, which in due time were to eventuate in the proliferation of game-theoretic and rational choice models in political science.

Political behaviour

After World War II the sample survey literally transformed the capacity of social scientists to study, describe, interpret, explain and understand voting, elections, ideology, political attitudes, partisanship, and a host of other phenomena. As surveys accumulated over time, it also became possible to interpret changes, which previously could be accounted for only by armchair speculations or conjectures based on rather gross correlations, with much more powerful tools.

The focus on the attitudes and actions of *individuals* engaged in political life, or, for that matter, unengaged, was sometimes referred to as the study of *political behaviour* in contrast with the earlier focus in political science on political institutions, governments, states, and other collective actors. Along with the study of political behaviour came a heightened concern for empirical rigour, quantitative methods, testable hypotheses, operationally definable terms, and some sympathy with neo-positivist interpretations of empirical 'science', all of which I included under the rough label 'the behavioural approach'. (My knowledge of the philosophy of science was greatly enhanced during this period by Carl Hempel, not only through his writings but also as a by-product of innumerable discussions in which we both participated as friends, neighbours, and fellow members of a daily car-pool.) Although the behavioural approach initially encountered the hostility of many traditional political scientists, it rapidly gained momentum. Despite the fact that my own graduate training had occurred before this important development took place, I was highly sympathetic with it. A period of service on the Committee on Political Behavior of the Social Science Research Council in the 1950s provided an opportunity not only to encourage scholarship in the field but to learn a great deal about research in progress. With the aid of colleagues, research assistants, and graduate students whose training in behavioural methods of research was better than mine had been, I sometimes employed such methods in my own work – notably in *Who Governs?* (1961a).[2] Unlike a few of its most enthusiastic advocates, however, I was also convinced that the behavioural approach, which for some purposes was a huge improvement on the methods of earlier political science, had its own limitations. By 1961, the momentum acquired by the behavioural approach was strong enough, it seemed to me, to make it useful to emphasize not only the contributions of the behavioural approach but its limits as well (see 'The Behavioral Approach in Political Science. Epitaph for a Monument to a Successful Protest', Dahl 1961b).

Comparative politics

Beginning in the late 1950s I made a deliberate effort to acquire a better understanding of comparative politics. Up to then my work had focused mainly on the United States or, if not, it tended to be abstract and theoretical (or, as in *A Preface to Democratic Theory*, it included both types of emphasis). In any case I realized that while I knew American political life, institutions and behaviour tolerably well, I needed to gain more understanding of politics and institutions elsewhere. Partly to overcome this serious deficiency I undertook the collaborative effort that turned into *Political Oppositions in Western Democracies* (1966). Drawing on existing friends and acquaintances and adding new ones I was able to enlist an extraordinary group of scholars. (Other than myself, Samuel H. Barnes, Hans Daalder, Frederick C. Engelmann, Alfred Grosser, Otto Kirchheimer, Val R. Lorwin, Allen Potter, Stein Rokkan and Nils Stjernquist were to contribute to the volume.) Our meetings to discuss chapter drafts, held at the Villa Serbelloni in Bellagio and elsewhere, constituted for me a seminar of unbelievable richness and depth. As that volume neared completion I began to feel that our understanding of oppositions needed to be expanded to include not only non-western democracies like India and Japan, but also oppositional tendencies and movements in non-democratic countries and regions like the Soviet Union, Spain, Latin America, and Africa. Here too I was extremely fortunate in gaining contributions from a remarkably talented group of scholars who readily rose to the challenge that work along these lines would pose. *Regimes and Oppositions* (1973) included chapters on oppositions in the Soviet Union by Frederick Barghoorn, Communist East Europe by H. Gordon Skilling, tropical Africa by William Foltz, Spain by Juan Linz, Latin America by Robert Dix, India by Rajni Kothari, and Japan by Michael Leiserson.

At an early meeting Val Lorwin and Hans Daalder broached the idea of a collaborative book about the politics of the smaller European democracies. They, Stein Rokkan and I formed a team to bring together scholars who would provide chapters on each of the smaller European democracies. One chapter to a democracy soon began to look ridiculously short; from one book our ambitious aim expanded to a dozen books. Once again, the discussions that continued over some years and the preliminary drafts of the contributors provided me with a priceless education – one, I may say, that at that time neither I nor anyone else could have gained elsewhere.

Although the series of books we planned did not appear – except for Chubb 1970 on Ireland and, although not a country study, *Size and Democracy* (1973) which I wrote with Edward Tufte as part of the intended series – our efforts, I believe, gave a significant stimulus to research and writing on, and within, the smaller European democracies. When we began, the lengthy and varied democratic experiences of these countries lay outside the purview of standard political science; indeed, even within the smaller democracies themselves their experiences for the most part had not yet been systematically studied and written about. By the time we abandoned our enterprise, neither was true.

It may be appropriate here to add a personal note. Although I had first come to know Lorwin well during my Washington years, before my undertaking the book on oppositions my acquaintance with Rokkan and Daalder had been slight. Our collaboration resulted in friendships, conversations, and continuing exchanges that proved to be extraordinarily enriching.

Democratic theory

Although I had no specific intention of focusing most of my work on aspects of democratic theory and practice, so, in fact, it turned out.

Since the time of Socrates, political philosophers had dealt directly or indirectly with democratic theory and practice, and most of the great works in western political thought bear on it to some degree. Yet as late as the 1950s, 'democratic theory' was not a recognized focus in political science anywhere, so far as I know. Indeed, the expression 'democratic theory' was, if I recall correctly, virtually non-existent. It may have appeared in the title of a book for the first time when *A Preface to Democratic Theory* was published in 1956. Giovanni Sartori, who was to become a close friend and one of the major architects in building twentieth-century democratic theory, was, I believe, the first to use the term straight out and unadorned as a title for his *Democratic Theory* (1962a), which was based on his translation of *Democrazia e Definizioni* (1957), and appeared in paperback in 1965; Sartori returned to the general subject in his two-volume *The Theory of Democracy Revisited* (1987a). Yet it was several decades before 'democratic theory' came into fairly common usage among political scientists. Although what was within the purview of 'democratic theory' was still not very well defined, there was considerable agreement on certain questions, problems, works, and avenues of research that would surely have to be included.

When we were writing *Politics, Economics, and Welfare* Lindblom and I hit upon the term 'polyarchy' as a useful label. It would, we thought, help to sharpen and clarify the distinction between democratic ideals and democratic realities (a distinction, even so, that many readers seem to find difficult to grasp). In addition, we could more easily discuss representative systems with widely inclusive adult electorates as a special, twentieth-century, historically distinctive type of (non-ideal) democracy.[3]

I continued for some years to fuss with the concept until I reached a formulation in *Polyarchy* (1971) that has pretty much remained unchanged in my work. By then I had concluded that polyarchy – modern, inclusive, large-scale, representative democracy –

could be satisfactorily defined by the presence of seven *political institutions*.[4] One desirable, if not wholly anticipated, characteristic of this definition was that it enabled observers to arrive at reasonable judgements about the extent to which these institutions were in fact present in a given country. It turned out that most countries could be ranked on a scale extending from the most undemocratic or authoritarian countries to the most democratic, the polyarchies.[5] The rankings proved helpful in gaining contemporary and historical perspectives on democracy, and thus in providing answers to the difficult question: what conditions in a country are favourable or unfavourable for developing democracy in its twentieth-century form, embodied in the institutions of polyarchy? (*Polyarchy* is devoted to that task, as is Part V, 'The Limits and Possibilities of Democracy', *Democracy and Its Critics* (1989), pp.213ff.)

But if polyarchy is one historical form of democracy, how precisely are actual systems of polyarchy related to the idea of democracy? In other words, to what extent is polyarchy democratic? To answer that I needed some criteria specifying what a fully democratic system would be. Though I tackled the problem in *Polyarchy* and elsewhere, I finally formulated what seemed to me reasonably satisfactory (though highly demanding) democratic criteria in the essay 'Procedural Democracy' (1979). The argument of that essay, which turned into the chapter 'A Theory of the Democratic Process' in *Democracy and Its Critics*, provided me with the set of criteria I wanted, against which to compare the political institutions of polyarchy. These institutions, I argue, are necessary (though not sufficient) if the criteria are to be applied to a political system on a scale as large as a country (see Table 15.1, 'Polyarchy and the Democratic Process', in Dahl 1989, p.222).

The unbounded universe of democracy: open questions

The relation between polyarchy and democracy is only one question that a reasonably satisfactory theory of democracy would, in my view, seek to provide. Indeed, a democratic theory that is both satisfactory and complete – whatever 'complete' means in this context – may well be impossible. One question leads to another, and that to another, and so on. As I put it in *Democracy and Its Critics*, the universe of democratic theory appears to be finite but unbounded. Consider some of the questions to which we want answers:

1. Although we could begin at many other places, we might as well begin with the unavoidable question: What do we *mean* by democracy? Or to use the approach I just mentioned, what *criteria* would a fully democratic process have to meet?
2. The first question immediately suggests others. To set out criteria is not to show why we should reasonably believe ourselves obligated to uphold them. On what grounds is a democratic process for governing an association justified? Why is a democratic process desirable? What goods, goals, or ends does it serve better than non-democratic systems?
3. Surely the achievement of a democratic political system is not the only value, good, or end against which to judge the desirability of a political system. Are other ends also relevant? If so, what are they? Justice, fairness, equity, equality, happiness, self-fulfilment, moral responsibility, freedom, security, safety, stability, economic

well-being, health, and desirable human qualities like honesty and generosity...?
Are there limits to what we should expect of any political system? If so, what
are they?

4. For what *kinds* of associations is democracy desirable? Surely not all. Even if it can
   be shown convincingly that a democratic process is desirable for governing some
   kinds of associations, what about others? Why is it especially desirable for
   governing a state? If a state, why not international organizations? Families? Trade
   unions? Economic enterprises? Educational institutions? Religious organizations?
   And so on, and on. If only some of these, but not others, why? (Elements for an
   incomplete answer are suggested in Dahl 1970, 1982 and 1985.)

5. Assuming that we have satisfactory answers to the first four questions, what kinds
   of practical, feasible arrangements are required if an association is to be governed
   democratically? As I have already suggested, the size or scale of an association
   appears to matter. I have argued that on the scale of a *country* we cannot meet (or
   perhaps I should say, we cannot best approximate to) democratic criteria without
   the full panoply of the political institutions of polyarchy. Yet very small
   associations, it seems, can satisfy democratic criteria pretty well with arrangements
   that would prove unsatisfactory for very large-scale associations. A committee, a
   town, a club is not a country. In small associations like these, what political
   institutions would best approximate democratic criteria?

6. What conditions or characteristics are favourable to the development of democratic institutions in an association? And conversely, what conditions are adverse?
   Why do democracies develop and become stable? Why do they collapse? Why did
   a democratic system arise in Athens but not Sparta? Early in some countries, later
   in others, not at all (yet) in still others? Why did polyarchy develop in the United
   States but not at the same time in Mexico? Why did polyarchy survive economic
   crisis in New Zealand but not in Argentina? Why did polyarchy expand in the
   twentieth century to many more countries than ever before? What favourable
   conditions made this increase possible? With the rapid increase in democratization
   in recent years, attempts to answer questions like these have become voluminous.
   (One attempt is made in *Democracy and Its Critics*, Chapters 17, 'How Polyarchy
   Developed in Some Countries and Not Others', and 18, 'Why Polyarchy
   Developed in Some Countries and Not Others'.)

7. What will be the consequences for democracy of a greater internationalization of
   politics, society, economics, and cultures? (For a brief discussion, see Dahl 1994a.)

8. Among the conditions that bear on the prospects for polyarchy, and democratic
   systems more generally, the nature of the economic order appears to be crucial. In
   this century, polyarchy has been strongly associated with market-oriented,
   predominantly privately owned economies – capitalist economies. Yet the relation
   between democracy and capitalism raises as many questions as it answers. What
   then is the nature of that relationship? Is a capitalist economic order a necessary
   condition for polyarchy? Is it sufficient? Might it be neither necessary nor
   sufficient? Are there alternative economic orders that would be as – or more –
   compatible? If so, what are they?

9. In order to prevent destructive factionalism, earlier democracies and republics
   generally sought to prevent the formation of other political associations within the
   boundaries of the state. They were, or attempted to be, politically monistic.

Theorists like Rousseau applauded monism, believing that associations *within* a state would develop interests in conflict with one another and with the overall good of the republic, the *public* good. Unlike earlier forms of democracy, however, modern polyarchies seem to foster the existence of numerous relatively autonomous associations capable of influencing public life. Polyarchies are socially and politically pluralistic, not monistic. Indeed, the effective right of citizens to form independent associations, including political parties, is one of the distinguishing elements of polyarchy, a part of its *definition*. The question arises, then: to the extent that polyarchies foster pluralism, what happens to the public good? Indeed, in a pluralistic democratic system, does it make sense to speak of 'the public good'? Can it be identified? Can it be achieved? (For some reflections on these questions, see Dahl 1987, 1995.)

10. It is one thing to specify the conditions that favour democracy. But how can they be brought about? No question is more important, and yet, I hazard to guess, on none are we more badly informed. Is a high level of economic development (whether capitalist or not) necessary? Sufficient? Neither necessary nor sufficient? Can polyarchy develop or survive in countries with distinct and different sub-cultures and identities? Are democracy and polyarchy, which are largely products of European civilization and cultures, feasible and desirable in other cultures – for example in Asian countries where Confucian values remain influential?

11. In so far as the political institutions of polyarchy fall short of meeting democratic criteria, what can be done to achieve greater democratization of polyarchies? What *should* be done?

12. And in so far as polyarchies fall short of meeting *other* criteria – like justice, well-being, or others mentioned in the second question – what can be done to correct the deficiencies? What *should* be done?

These questions (one might think of more) provide a huge, perhaps impossibly huge, agenda for democratic theory. Although many scholars have devoted increasing efforts to answer these questions, as I have also, no one should expect to find definitive answers in our work. The odyssey in search of an adequate democratic theory should, and I feel certain will, go on.

Notes

1. And before I knew Arrow himself, who became a friend during a year in Palo Alto in 1955–56. I think it is just possible that the first presentation by an American political scientist of what later came to be called 'Arrow's Theorem' or 'Arrow's Paradox' was in *A Preface to Democratic Theory* (Chicago: University of Chicago Press, 1956). See fn. 9, pp.42–3. 'This brilliantly developed and quite startling argument', I wrote, 'has, unfortunately, so far been totally ignored by political scientists.' At that time only the original monograph *Social Choice and Individual Values* was available (New Haven: Yale University Press, 1951). In the second edition of his work, which appeared in 1963, his presentation was slightly different and more readily understood. Later, he also provided a summary of his argument in 'Values and Collective Decision-Making', in P. Laslett and G. W. Runciman, eds, *Philosophy, Politics, and Society*, 3rd series (New York: Barnes and Noble, 1967). The

commentaries, which laid out the argument with even greater clarity, were still to come (see e.g. MacKay 1980).

2. I was extraordinarily fortunate in securing assistance in research on New Haven from an unusual group of Yale Ph.D candidates of that time. As I pointed out in the Acknowledgements for *Who Governs?* I was particularly indebted to Nelson Polsby, Raymond Wolfinger and William Flanigan. Others whose research and papers were helpful to me were Rufus Browning, William Foltz, James Guyot, Richard Merritt, Leroy Rieselbach, Bruce Russett and James Toscano. All were graduate students who later went on to careers in political science. A study by William K. Muir, written as a senior essay honours when he was still an undergraduate at Yale, provided useful information for one brief chapter.

3. We didn't invent the term. *The Oxford English Dictionary* had already defined polyarchy as 'the government of a state or city by many; contrasted with *monarchy*'. We were unaware of the fact that a few years before we adopted the term, Ernest Barker had used it in *Greek Political Theory* (p.294). Also unknown to us, in the early seventeenth century Johannes Althusius had contrasted a 'polyarchic magistracy' consisting of 'a number of persons' with a monarchy, and had observed further that a polyarchal magistracy could be either aristocratic or democratic; see *The Politics of Johannes Althusius* (1614), trans. by Frederick S. Carney (Boston: Beacon Press, 1964), p.200.

4. In *Polyarchy. Participation and Opposition* (1971) the eight institutions listed in Table 1.1, p.3, 'Some Requirements for a Democracy Among a Large Number of People', were reduced to seven for the scale applied to 115 countries in Appendices A and B, pp.231ff. See also the list in *Democracy and Its Critics* (1989) on p.221 and in Table 15.1, 'Polyarchy and the Democratic Process', p.222.

5. For *Polyarchy* Mary Frase Williams and Richard Norling provided a ranking of 114 countries on a scale of polyarchy (Appendices A and B, pp.231ff.) In preparation for *Democracy and Its Critics* Michael Coppedge and Wolfgang Reinicke developed a scale which they applied to 168 countries, of which all could be scaled except for eleven anomalies. See their 'A Scale of Polyarchy', in Raymond D. Gastil, ed., *Freedom in the World. Political Rights and Liberties, 1987–1988* (Lanham: University Press of America, 1988), pp.101–25, and 'Measuring Polyarchy', in *Studies in Comparative International Development*, vol. 25 (1990), pp.51–72.

8 From comparative political systems to the analysis of civilizations: the civilizational framework of European politics

S.N. *Eisenstadt*

Hebrew University of Jerusalem

Background: youth and student years

The major lines of my scholarly interests were formed from the early 1940s through the 1950s, under the impact of two sets of influences. The first was the scholarly environment in Jerusalem in the early and mid-1940s – possibly, even earlier, the intellectual environment I encountered while a high-school student in Tel Aviv in 1935–40 – followed by my 'post-doctoral' year, 1947–48, at the London School of Economics. The second set of such influences were the momentous social and political processes through which I lived: the struggle for the establishment of the state of Israel, its establishment in 1948 and the processes of its crystallization and the development of Israeli society; and the events which I observed from far away: the worldwide process of the first waves of democratization and development after the Second World War, with the many ensuing crises and tribulations on the world scene.

The central focus of my interest as it crystallized under these influences has been the problem of human creativity and its limitations, especially as it relates to the social arena, the construction of different social formations (ranging from the so-called micro situations to the more formalized institutional and macro institutional formations), and the problem of charisma and its routinization.

The problem of such creativity, and the closely connected problem of the potential range of human freedom in social contexts, has recently re-emerged in theoretical discussions in the social sciences as the problem of human agency in relation to social structure. This problem was, of course, already central in classical sociological theory. One of the most succinct formulations of it can be found in Marx's famous statement, 'Men make their own history, but they do not make it as they please; they do not make it under circumstances chosen by themselves, but under circumstances directly encountered, given and transmitted from the past.' Similarly, Weber's perpetual concern with charisma and its routinization is, of course, tantamount to this problem.

My own interest in this problem was greatly influenced by my studies with Martin Buber, whose major sociological concern was to identify those situations wherein there exist the greatest chances for human creativity in the social and cultural realm (cf. Eisenstadt 1992a, pp.1–22). It was also greatly influenced by the comparative approach to which I was fortunate to be exposed during my graduate and postgraduate studies in two of its major guises. I was exposed to the Weberian approach first through Buber's teaching and later on at the London School of Economics, especially in the seminars of Edward Shils. During my post-doctoral studies at the London School of Economics I also came face to face with the great tradition of comparative studies represented by Morris Ginsberg and T.H. Marshall and by the then leading group of British anthropologists: Raymond Firth, E.E. Evans Pritchard, M. Fortes, Edmund Leach, Audrey Richards, Max Gluckman and their students.

It is thus not very surprising that I approached some of the major problems of sociological theory, as well as the more general problem of human creativity in the social and cultural realm, mostly through comparative studies, especially comparative political studies.

Directions of research: comparative studies and studies of modernization

This interest developed in two major lines of research: one was broad comparative studies, in which historical and sociological analysis were combined; the second consisted of studies of modernization and development. These two lines have converged in the last decade or two in the comparative study of civilizations and their dynamics. Cutting across them was a continual interest in sociological theory (for a fuller exposition see Eisenstadt 1995, esp. introduction and Ch. 13).

I took the first step in this direction in 1950 when I drew up the overall syllabus of studies and curriculum in the then enlarged Department of Sociology at the Hebrew University. I prepared a new course on comparative political institutions, in which I dealt with tribal, historical and modern political systems alike. In many ways this course served as the starting point or springboard of my ensuing research.

This comparative interest became intensified during the year 1955–56 which I spent at the Center for Advanced Studies in the Behavioral Sciences. I had the good luck to be in constant conversation with D. Aberle, R. Bauer, U. Bronfenbrenner, J.S. Coleman, R.A. Dahl, H. Goldhammer, B.F. Hoselitz, A. Inkeles, M. A. Kaplan, J. March, K. Knorr, S.M. Lipset, D.R. Miller, and D.M. Schneider, with most of whom I developed lifelong friendships. At the same time I developed close relations with Talcott Parsons which continued till his death, and with R.N. Bellah and Neil Smelser.

Comparative analyses and sociological theory: *The Political Systems of Empires*

The first major fruit of these endeavours, after a series of articles, was the book *The Political Systems of Empires* (1963). Its analysis was set in the framework of the then prevalent structural–functional analysis, with a strong Weberian tinge. The central concept employed in the analysis of these regimes was that of free resources. The political systems of these empires (compared with various tribal, patrimonial and certain type of city-state regimes) were characterized by the development and internal reproduction within them of relatively high degrees of free resources – that is, resources not embedded in various ascriptive groups or social sectors and committed to use in such sectors. The rulers were interested in freeing resources from commitments to traditional aristocratic, rural or urban groups and in the development of relatively free groups that could create and reproduce such resources. At the same time, the rulers were also highly interested in controlling these resources themselves.

Thus, the rulers attempted to create and maintain an independent peasantry with small holdings against large encroachments by powerful landowners. By this means they sought both to ensure the peasants' independence and to provide resources for themselves. They also established colonies and settlements of free peasant soldiers, not controlled by the aristocracy, to ensure sufficient military manpower for the state. Parallel orientations developed also in policies aimed at other factions: urban merchants, professional and religious groups.

At the same time I stressed that in contrast to modern political systems, the level of such free resources was limited in these empires because of the coexistence within them of traditional, undifferentiated political activities together with more differentiated, specifically political goals. I have noted especially how the latter were limited by the traditional, ascriptive settings. Moreover, I emphasized that these more differentiated activities were limited not only by various traditional ascriptive groups but also by the rulers themselves, whose legitimation was usually couched in traditional terms.

A central part of the argument of *Political Systems* is the analysis of various organizations, such as bureaucracies that developed within these empires, mostly through the efforts of rulers to implement policies designed to maintain institutional contours and characteristics, for example their specific systemic external and internal boundaries and the balance between free resources and more ascriptive settings.

However, the analysis presented in *Political Systems* in many ways went beyond the thrusts of structural–functionalism prevalent at the time. It did not accept the natural givenness of any social system, in this case of these empires; and it emphasized the central role of institutional entrepreneurs in the construction of such systems. This analysis also went beyond the assumptions of structural-functional analysis by its emphasis on the internal contradictions which develop in any such system; on the processes of change that take place in it and on the importance of internal and external forces giving rise to such changes, and possibly causing the demise of such systems. It also went beyond these assumptions, even if just implicitly, by recognizing the autonomy of cultural visions and in turn, their impact on the promulgation of various goals by both rulers and other groups and on the specific dynamics of the respective empires (see Eisenstadt 1992c, introduction).

The Political Systems of Empires also went beyond the evolutionary assumptions which were prominent in many studies connected with the structural–functional school, especially in the early studies of modernization which developed in the late 1940s and early 1950s. The first criticism held that not all massive social change necessarily leads to differentiation. The second, and more important, one maintained that institutional developments that take place at seemingly similar 'stages' of differentiation may nevertheless lead in different directions. In other words, the institutional responses to the problems arising out of growing structural differentiation (i.e. the patterns of integration) that emerge in different societies at seemingly similar stages of differentiation may vary considerably across societies (see Eisenstadt 1969b). Here again I stressed the central role of various entrepreneurs, élites and their coalitions, the visions they bore and the goals they promulgated, in the crystallization and reproduction of different types of institutional formations.

If the analysis in *The Political Systems of Empires* went beyond the basic assumptions of the structural–functional school in all these ways, it did not go far enough in examining the processes through which the systemic boundaries and institutional formations of these empires were constructed and reconstructed. It did not elaborate on the implications of the ways in which the continuous interweaving of cultural forces, power dimensions, and material resources shape institutional formations and dynamics through the activities of various social actors. In particular, the articulation of the boundaries of collectivities, the regulation of power, the construction of meaning, and those activities that are centred around the construction of trust, were not systematically examined.

These problems, in line with continual re-examination of central problems of sociological theory (see Eisenstadt 1992d), were gradually taken up by me in the comparative study of different institutional arenas, and especially in the study of modernization and development.

Studies of development and modernization: Israeli society and comparative studies

My interest in these problems was rooted in the earlier study of the absorption of immigrants in Israel, the analysis of which I have put from the beginning in a comparative framework (Eisenstadt 1953). Here again my scholarly work went in two major directions. One was the study of several central aspects of Israeli society as it developed and crystallized from the establishment of the state of Israel: above all the process of absorption of immigrants and the more general process of the building of a new state. These culminated in *Israeli Society* (1967), updated and enlarged later in *The Transformation of Israeli Society* (1985a).

One central theme of this book (which built on the work of my colleagues and students as well as my own) was the *problématique* of the building of a new state against the background of, first, the routinization of the charisma of the original pioneering revolutionary vision, and second, the ensuing problems of absorption of immigrants and development. This has spilled over into a general interest in problems of development and modernization.

The first result of these concerns with problems of development was a small collection of essays published in Holland (Eisenstadt 1961). It was, however, in 1962–63, when I served as the first Carnegie Visiting Professor of Political Science at MIT and a Visiting Professor at Harvard, that these interests became fully focused and put in a sharper comparative analytical framework. Here my interaction with the late Dan Lerner and Ithiel Pool, with Lucian Pye and with Myron Weiner, with R.N. Bellah and N.J. Smelser and David McLelland, as well as with other members of the Social Science Research Council Committees on Comparative Politics, especially Gabriel Almond, were particularly important, as were also my contacts with Karl Deutsch, Reinhard Bendix and, above all, R.K. Merton. Another framework of scholarly co-operation on problems of modernization, 'nation and state building' was the Committee on Political Sociology of the International Sociological Association, where in addition to American colleagues (S.M. Lipset, and the late M. Janowitz) I had the very good fortune to become closely involved with the late Stein Rokkan, with whom I had already corresponded earlier, and with Erik Allardt, Hans Daalder, Juan Linz,

Giovanni Sartori and many others with whom I was also fortunate to develop close friendships.

The first fruit of these concerns with modernization in a broader comparative framework was a series of articles, later collected in the first part of *Tradition, Change and Modernity* (1973a), the small book *Modernization, Protest and Change* (1966) and, later on, the two-volume *Building States and Nations* 1973, which Stein Rokkan and I edited, based on a conference sponsored by the International Social Science Council.

In all these works of mine on modernization I started, very much in line with the analytical orientations of *The Political Systems of Empires* and in many articles published in the 1960s (some are reprinted in Eisenstadt 1995), to go beyond what the scholarly community and the wider public discourse perceived as the premises and the paradigm of studies of modernization, and of the studies of convergence of industrial societies.

As is well known, one of the central tenets of these studies was the distinction between 'traditional' and 'modern' as two contrasting types of societies. The differences between traditional and modern societies were couched in most of the studies in terms of the respective range of systemic problems with which they could cope, or of the environments – both internal (social, cultural) and external (technological, economic) – which they could 'master'.

Tradition and traditional societies were perceived as basically very restrictive and limited, whereas modern societies were seen as much more expansive and adaptable to a widening range of internal and external environments and problems. Special emphases were given to the ability to cope with change in general and with economic development and industrialization in particular. Behind these studies was the belief or assumption that mankind is moving in an inevitable, evolutionary manner away from traditional to modern societies. Non-modern 'traditional' societies were accordingly studied in terms of their relative resistance to internal or external forces of modernization. Even though there was a growing recognition of the possible diversity of transitional societies, it was still assumed that such diversity would virtually disappear at the end-stage of modernity. The theory of the convergence of industrial societies most eloquently propounded by Clark Kerr (Kerr *et al.* 1960) argued that ultimately all modern industrial systems would develop similar major institutional features. Behind this loomed a conviction of the inevitability of progress toward modernity, be it political or industrial.

From the early (and especially the mid-) 1960s, the momentum of research and development on the world scene gave rise to far-reaching criticisms of these assumptions. These criticisms arose from a variety of vantage points, and they touched not only on the problem of development and modernization, but also on some very central questions of sociological analysis. Behind much of the debate there also loomed political and ideological differences, sometimes forcefully expressed. The two major foci of these criticisms were the alleged a-historicity and the European-centricity of this initial model of modernization and of the closely connected tradition–modernity dichotomy.

These criticisms were reinforced by the growing recognition that: (1) many of these societies and states did not develop in the direction of modern European nation states; (2) these societies were not necessarily in a 'transitional' phase along an inevitable path to this type of modernity; (3) there was nevertheless some internal 'logic' in their development; and (4) at least part of this logic or pattern derived from the traditions of these societies themselves. This line of criticism of the initial model of modernization stressed the importance of analysing contemporary developments in various societies in terms of their 'unfolding' of the traditional forces inherent in them, rather than their alleged movement toward a fixed end-stage.

The other, in a sense opposite, direction that these criticisms took tended to emphasize the unique historical experience of the modern era. This approach, most clearly apparent in the works of many modern Marxists or semi-Marxists, stressed that the modernization process was not universal or inherent in the nature of every society. Rather, it represented a unique historical situation connected with the various aspects of European expansion, and especially with the expansion of capitalism, and of the consequent establishment of a new international system composed of hegemonic and dependent societies.

From their very beginning (even in the studies of the absorption of immigrants in Israel), my own studies of modernization also went beyond numerous premises of the initial paradigm of studies of modernization. In these studies I already stressed the great variability of modern and developing societies; the possibilities of breakdowns and crises of modernity; the connection between the diversity of such patterns of modernization and the different traditions and historical experience of these societies; and the consequent need to re-examine carefully the relations between tradition and modernity (for details see Eisenstadt 1973a). These points or problems were continually taken up in a series of publications on patrimonialism (1973b), post-traditional societies (1972), and patron–client relations and clientilistic systems (Eisenstadt and Roniger, 1984a).

From comparative institutional to comparative civilizational studies. Re-examination of central problems of sociological theory: culture, social structure and agency

In close relation to these studies of modernization, and cutting across the comparative analysis of political systems (and other institutional arenas: see Eisenstadt 1995, Chs 1, 13), I engaged in a series of researches in this period aiming at the re-examination of central analytical problems in sociological theory.

Of central importance from the point of view of the problems discussed here and the more general problem of human creativity was the re-examination of two central concepts: charisma and centre. Charisma has constituted, of course, a central concept in sociological analysis since Weber. It was the way in which Edward Shils reinterpreted and combined this term with the concept of centre coined by him (cf. Shils 1975, pp.3–17, 256–76) that provided the starting point for the line of analysis which I undertook in that period.

I first examined the analytical dimensions of the concept of centre and centre–periphery relations and applied them in comparative analysis in the Introduction to the paperback edition of *The Political System of Empires* (1969a). This analysis emphasized the importance of centre and centre–periphery relations as a distinct analytical dimension of the institutional format of centralized empires but, in principle, of any society. It emphasized that this dimension is not subsumed under the scope of structural differentiation of the social division of labour.

In this analysis, the centre or centres of a society were conceived as dealing not only with the organizational aspects of the social division of labour; they were also seen as primarily dealing with the connection of these aspects of the social division of labour to the charismatic dimensions of social order. That is to say, the centres of society were connected to the attempts to relate the mundane realities of social life, of institutional formations, to what is conceived by humans as the source of existence, of life and its predicaments.

I had addressed myself earlier to some of the more general principled problems of the nature of the processes through which the charismatic dimensions of human action became interwoven with processes of institution building or with the crystallization of institutional formations in the article 'Charisma and Institution Building' (see my introduction to Eisenstadt 1968a, and 1995, Ch. 7). In this article, I gave several indicators about the nature of the major actors (who are bearers of such charismatic visions) and of the loci in which, and the processes through which, such visions are implemented.

One of the central insights of the essay 'Charisma and Institution Building', following the earlier 'Institutionalization and Change' (Eisenstadt 1964; cf. 1995, Ch. 4) is that change (like conflict) is not exogenous to the construction of social formations but constitutes an inherent component thereof. In the essay 'Charisma and Institution Building', this inherence of change in the process of institution formations, in the very construction of social life, was attributed not only to the inherent systemic contradictions and conflicts it entails, but also to the very nature of the charismatic dimension of human action. It was suggested that the central characteristic of this dimension (the attempt to come close to the very essence of human endeavour, to the essence of being, i.e. to come close to the cosmological visions and conceptions of social order) entails by its very nature both constructive and destructive elements or components.

These theoretical problems have become closely interwoven with shifts in my own work, especially with that from comparative institutional to comparative civilizational analysis in which I frontally analysed the process through which culture and social structure and ecological settings are interwoven in shaping the crystallization, reproduction and change of social formations. In this way, I also attempted to redefine the relations between agency, culture and social structure.

The kernels of such analysis could be found in 'Prestige, Stratification and Center Formation' (1968b, 1995, Ch. 10) and in *Patrons, Clients and Friends* (Eisenstadt and Roniger, 1984a). But it was only in a series of comparative civilizational analyses (especially in the researches on the early state in African perspective and above all on Axial Age Civilizations) that I was able to take up these problems systematically (see Eisenstadt (ed.) 1986; Eisenstadt *et al.* 1988a).

One of the first foci of this analysis was a more detailed look at different types of centres and processes of centre-formation, the beginnings of which were already presented in the analysis of strata formation and patron–client relations. In these studies, my colleagues and I analysed the cultural dimension of social order as it is interwoven into social structures; the roles of different types of social actors, especially the coalition of élites; and influential processes of conflict and change.

We emphasized that these various components of centres (the regulation of power, the constitution of trust and of legitimation) do not always go together and that each component may be articulated within different centres to different degrees, giving rise to different modes of control by the ruling élites. These components may come together in different centres in various combinations, and the relative importance of each component may vary. These differences, in turn, are closely related to the nature of the élite coalitions that predominate in a given centre and society, and to the cultural orientations they articulate. As a result, different centres and societies exhibit diverse structures and dynamics.

The analysis of European civilization in a comparative framework

In the following phases of my work these various analyses have coalesced into a broad programme of comparative study of civilizations, especially the so-called Axial Civilizations. This programme developed in close relation with the revival of interest in comparative civilizational analysis in a Weberian model, one of the most important nuclei of which was the meetings re-examining the Weberian programme organized by Prof. W. Schluchter of Heidelberg (cf.Eisenstadt 1984b, 1985b, 1987d, 1988b).

It is in the framework of this programme that I have analysed some of the specific features of European civilization, politics and dynamics. In this I was to no small extent influenced by my collaboration with Stein Rokkan (see my Stein Rokkan lecture, 1987b, Ch. 1).

The starting point of such analyses are some general characteristics of European civilization, the most important of which is the structural and cultural ideological pluralism that constitutes one of the major components of the European historical experience. The structural pluralism that developed in Europe was characterized above all by a strong combination of low, but continuously increasing levels of structural differentiation with the constantly changing boundaries of different collectivities and frameworks. Parallel to this there developed in Europe a multiplicity of prevalent cultural orientations which developed out of several traditions: the Judaeo-Christian, the Greek and the various tribal ones; and a closely related multiplicity and complexity of ways to resolve the tensions between the transcendental and mundane orders, through either worldly (political and economic) or other-worldly activities. This multiplicity of orientations was rooted in the fact that the European civilization developed out of the continuous interaction between the secondary breakthrough of two major Axial civilizations (the Jewish and the Greek ones) on the one hand, and numerous 'pagan' tribal traditions and society on the other.

The combination of such multiple cultural traditions, with pluralistic structural and political-ecological conditions, explains the fact that in Western and Central Europe there developed, more than in other Christian civilizations, continuous tensions between hierarchy and equality, as the basic dimensions of participation of different sectors of society in the political and religious arenas; and between the strong commitment and autonomous access of different groups and strata to the religious and political orders, on the one hand, and the emphasis on the mediation of such access by the Church or by political powers, on the other. At the same time there developed a strong tendency to define the respective institutional arenas, collectivities or strata as distinct social spaces with relatively sharply defined boundaries.

Another major repercussion of these ideological and structural dimensions is the fact that the mode of change that developed in Western Europe, from at least the late Middle Ages on, was characterized by a relatively high degree of symbolic and ideological articulation of the political struggle and of movements of protest; by a high degree of coalescence of changes in different institutional arenas; and by a very close relationship between such changes and the restructuring of political centres and regimes. Changes within various institutional arenas in Western Europe, such as the economic or the cultural arenas, impinged very intensely on one another and above all on the political sphere. These changes gave rise to a constant process of restructuration of the boundaries of these different arenas, which did not, however, obliterate their respective autonomies.

The various centres and collectivities that developed in Europe did not simply coexist in a sort of adaptive symbiosis. The multiple centres and subcentres, as well as the different collectivities, which developed in Europe tended to become arranged in a complicated but never unified rigid hierarchy. In this no centre was clearly predominant, but many of them aspired not only to actual but also to ideological predominance and hegemony.

All these collectivities and central institutions were legitimized in a variety of terms: in terms of primordial attachments and traditions, and of transcendental criteria, as well as in terms of criteria of civic traditions. The perpetual restructuring of centres and collectivities that took place in Europe was closely connected with the constant oscillation and tension between the sacred, primordial and civil dimensions of the legitimation of these centres and as components of these collectivities. While, for instance, many collectivities were defined mainly in primordial terms, and the Church was seemingly defined mainly in sacred ones, at the same time each collectivity and centre also attempted to arrogate all the other symbols of legitimation to itself.

A major characteristic of the reconstruction of centres and of collectivities in Europe was that the frequent attempts at such reconstruction were closely connected, first with strong ideological struggles, which focused on the relative symbolic importance of the various collectivities and centres; second, with attempts to combine the structuring of the boundaries of these centres and collectivities with the reconstruction of the bases of their legitimation; and third, with a strong consciousness of discontinuity between different stages or periods of their development.

Against the background of these general characteristics that developed from the sixteenth century on, several distinct historical processes took place which constituted the more direct background for the development of the modern European political regimes. The most important of these processes were the formations of the modern states: the absolutist states which later were transformed in the wake of the Great Revolutions into modern constitutional, and later into democratic states, and often into nation states; the development of new state–society relations most fully manifest in the emergence of a distinct type or types of civil society; the concomitant transformation of political processes; the crystallization and constitution of new types of collectivities, and last but certainly not least, the development of capitalist, later industrial–capitalist types of political economy. Of special interest in this context are the processes of construction of new types of collectivities, of collective identity or consciousness that developed within modern European societies in conjunction with the processes of constitution of the new states and of legitimation of the new political regimes.

As in preceding historical periods, the different concrete types of collective identity or consciousness that developed in Europe combined primordial, civil and cultural-religious components or orientations, and continually oscillated between these components. But some far-reaching changes developed in the contents of these components and in their concrete constellations.

Among the most important of such changes was the development of the very strong emphasis on the territorial boundaries as the main loci of the institutionalization of collective identity; of new, above all secular definitions of each of the components of collective identity; the growing importance of the civil and procedural components thereof; and an unceasing tension between such different components. Closely related was the strong tendency to the ideologization of these components of construction of collective identities, and the concomitant tendency to the charismatization of the newly constructed collectivities and centres.

The emphasis on the territorial components of collective identity entailed the development of a very strong connection between the construction of states and that of the major, 'encompassing' collectivities. This connection became epitomized in the tendency to construct what was to be called the 'nation state'. The crystallization of the conceptions of the nation state brought with it the development of a very strong congruence between the cultural and political identities of the territorial population; the promulgation, by the centre, of strong symbolic and affective commitments to the centre; and of a close relationship between the centres and the more primordial dimensions of human existence and of social life.

Within these centres and collectivities there continually developed a high degree of tension between the ideals and premises of hierarchy and equality, especially with regard to access to the centre and the construction of the collective goals as articulated and propagated by the centre. The contestation or confrontation between equality and hierarchy constituted a continual focus of political struggle.

The concrete mode of interweaving the construction of states with that of new types of collective consciousness and boundaries in different European societies was, as Lipset and Rokkan have shown, the outcome of the resolution of the religious cleavages which arose in the Reformation and Counter-Reformation. Such a resolution entailed the reconstruction and redefinition of the components of collective identity in different patterns of primordial, civil, and cultural orientations. Such reconstruction itself constituted a focus of struggle and the mode of reconstruction greatly influenced the development of the constitutional democratic regimes which later developed in these societies.

The development of the modern states and the transformation of the conception of sovereignty, representation and citizenship in Europe were closely related to changes in the very structure of power in society (i.e. the emergence of multiple centres of, above all, economic and political power), and to the development of some nuclei of a distinct type of civil society and of a new type of public arena or sphere. This type of civil society was characterized by several components which developed to different degrees in different European societies. Only in some of them did they come continuously together.

One such component was the relative autonomy of sectors from the state. It was not only autonomy *from* the state that was characteristic of this civil society which started to develop, even if at different tempi, in different European societies. Of no less importance was the autonomous access to the central political arena, and a certain degree of commitment to a common setting. Another crucial characteristic of this new society was the openness of these sectors, that is their not being embedded in more or less closed, ascriptive or corporate settings. A third feature was the existence of a multiplicity, a plurality of such sectors; the existence within such sectors of various associations regulating many of their own activities and preventing what would be later called a shapeless 'mass society'.

Of crucial importance in this context was the development of potentially auto-nomous public arenas, distinct from the state, as well as from any single ascriptive group. It was indeed the constant construction of such public arenas, independent both of any single ascriptive sector and of the state, but possibly rooted in many such sectors and above all having an autonomous access to the central political arena, the state, that constituted the epitome of the new type of civil society that developed in this period in Europe. All these developments built upon the potentialities of the pluralistic dimensions of European civilization, but only from about the eighteenth century did these potentialities crystallize into various combinations in different European societies, giving rise to different types of civil society.

One of the most interesting and central aspects of the political process that developed in modern European societies was the importance within them of social movements oriented to the centre, whose major aim was the reconstruction of the centres of their respective societies. The most important of these movements were the socialist and the national or nationalistic ones.

These two major types of movements developed around the basic poles of the construction of the symbols of collectivity: the modern universalistic or civic components, the older religious ones, and also strong primordial components of collective identity, continuously reconstructed in such modern terms as nationalism and ethnicity. They all entailed the confrontation between universalistic and more particularistic or ascriptive components of legitimation of the modern regimes (Eisenstadt and Azmon 1975, pp.1–19).

These movements certainly were not the only ones that developed in modern European societies, and while their relative importance varied greatly in different societies and periods, the prevalence of such orientations to the centre constituted one of the major characteristics of the modern political process as it developed in Europe. One central aspect of this orientation was the development of ideological politics, most fully epitomized in the ideological distinction between left and right as well as in the continuous emphasis on the reconstruction of collectivities in highly ideological terms.

European small states

One of the most interesting illustrations of the importance of these specific charac-teristics of European politics can be seen in their impact on the structure of political processes in European small states (cf. Eisenstadt 1977, 1987b, pp.41–9, 1993).

The most common problem of small states has been, and still is, how it is possible to maintain a general standard of economic and socio-cultural development which is more or less on the same level as the one prevailing in the respective international system. Out of attempts to maintain such a standard certain problems are generated which were indicated about thirty-five years ago by Simon Kuznets (1958) in a lecture he gave in Jerusalem on the economics of small states. He pointed out that the basic problem of these states is that their internal markets are not large enough to create economic momentum for development. The internal markets of small states are neither large enough nor diversified and complex enough to produce all that a small state needs, nor to consume all that it produces. Hence, the answer is specialization for special external markets, stemming from either the geographical location or the specific features of social and economic structure and cultural traditions. The volume of exports in most of these states is much greater in the overall GNP and economic activity than is the case in large states.

Different small states have developed different strategies for coping with these problems. Switzerland, for instance, has specialized in certain industries and has developed into a monetary centre, thereby gaining international power and reputation. Another possible solution is the fostering of international organizations (such as the Red Cross), and the achievement in this way of a 'central' rather than a marginal international position as well as an internal sense of identity. Whatever the solution, the specialization has created a dependency on, and sensitivity to, changes in international markets, above all because small states cannot directly influence fluctuations in the demand for their products.

These problems exist not only in the economic sphere (a field which has been relatively well explored) but also in the cultural, scientific–technological, and political spheres. Thus, in the scientific sphere, one of the main problems is how entrepreneurship and technological discoveries are possible when the heavy investment in facilities needed for this purpose is not available. Small scientific communities, if they orient themselves to large scientific communities, face the problem of maintaining their autonomy, identity, and distinct areas for explorations. In the educational sphere, small countries are under cross-pressures which could endanger their self-identity, making it necessary for them to emphasize their own tradition, history and internal problems, as opposed to sharing the more universal traditions of the large societies. In the cultural sphere, one of the problems of small countries is how to absorb cultural 'floods' (in terms of quantity) from prestigious international cultures and still maintain their own identity and obtain international recognition.

Whatever the success of any given solution, the type of specialization open to small states and the nature of their dependency may change throughout history. One of the great problems of small states is that they may become so attuned to one type of international market that they collapse entirely if this market changes. A famous classical illustration is that of Venice, which for several centuries was wonderfully adapted to a certain type of international market and of international trade routes. Venice evolved into a very complicated and sophisticated commercial centre which was oriented to this market. At the same time, the Venetian diplomatic service was among the best in the world, and helped Venice to maintain its special position in international trade. But once the Mediterranean was no longer the centre of international trade routes, Venice started to decline: it did not have enough flexibility to change. A basic problem faced above all by the small states is the need for a high degree of flexibility *vis-à-vis* those international markets on which they are dependent.

In the context of these special problems it is possible to analyse and understand some of the specific characteristics of the structure of centres and of centre–periphery relations that have developed in most 'successful' small states, especially in the European small states. These characteristics are evident above all in the political structure.

The most important have been: (1) a high degree of concentration of decision-making powers in the hands of the executive and/or bureaucracy with a comparatively limited scope for open parliamentary conduct of affairs; (2) an emphasis on internal arrangements, on 'allocative/distributive' policies and relations between different sectors, compared to ideological or class distinctions more prevalent in the larger states; (3) a relatively great importance of vertical multifaceted sectors, or at least the continuous cross-cutting among the more vertical segments, as against 'class-conscious' socio-political groupings in the larger states; (4) the combination on the one hand of a comparatively high degree of segregation between external and internal issues in the actual policy-making process, and on the other hand, the concentration of decision-making, both internal and external, in the hands of strong executive and/or bureaucratic organizations.[1]

This pattern of policy execution in the field of foreign relations in various small states has been closely related to a certain pattern in their internal social structure and politics. It is here that some of the specific characteristics of the European small states stand out. With time, many cleavages have developed within all of them. As stressed in the literature on consociationalism, such cleavages have been either ethnic and religious in nature or have followed more 'functional' lines, for example class, economic or regional ones, as found in ethnically or religiously more homogeneous societies such as Sweden, Finland or Austria.

These cleavages and the movements of protest related to them have not necessarily differed from those in larger European societies. But they have been much more varied, and above all much more articulated and intensive in their orientation to the centre than those in other contemporary small states, for instance Singapore.

Given the special institutional density of social relations that tends to develop in such small societies, the impact of the intensive impingement of the periphery on the centres can be very problematic. This calls for the development and use of special institutional mechanisms and arrangements. Of central importance in this respect is the fact that in those European small states which have been successful in maintaining their continuity, a combination of two patterns of political organization and activity has developed, namely the combination of a very strong allocative and co-optational mode of internal political arrangements together with a strong emphasis on more open, principled but symbolic politics, as evident for instance in referendums or even in elections.

Co-optation occurs largely through continuous interaction between the executive, the bureaucracy, the parliamentary commissions and the relevant interest groups, and only rarely in the parliamentary plenum. Even when defined in ideological terms, parties are above all important as channels through which this process of co-optation, allocation and negotiation takes place. 'Open' parliamentary debate and 'real' politics in small countries are much more dissociated than in many larger countries. This formal pattern may take the form of 'classical' consociationalism, *Proporzdemokratie*, or of a semi-corporatist democracy like Sweden in the 1970s (Korpi 1983). The very strong emphasis on the allocative and co-optational aspect of politics means that the other aspect, the symbolic one of parliamentary elections or referendums, is purely illusory. These more symbolic processes can be extremely important when it is necessary to change some of the ground-rules in accordance with which the

Proporzdemokratien, consociational or corporatist democracies function daily. The
ground rules must be changed when the internal or external situation changes
drastically; as possible legitimizers of the ground-rules and of possible changes within
them, these more symbolic types of politics become then of crucial importance.

In so far as a small state is able to develop and maintain these various mechanisms it
can provide enough flexibility in decision-making. The ability to overcome the
profound difficulties created by the existence of vertical segmentation and
intersegmental cleavages is explained by a conscious effort on the part of the political
élites to achieve inter-élite accommodation. This tends to reverse centrifugal forces at
the level of the lower strata of the segments. This inter-élite accommodation is achieved
by a combination of institutional and behavioural arrangements which include
the formation of an 'élite cartel' and a tradition of highly developed bargaining
procedures. From an institutional standpoint accommodation is achieved through
formal or informal proportional representation, which in states with multiple cleavages
creates the need for coalitions on almost all levels of central and local government. To
these institutional and behavioural patterns one should add the continuous attempts of
public policy-makers to segregate major areas of decision-making, in order to allow the
subcultural groups as much autonomy as possible in arranging their own affairs.

These characteristics of the European civilizations, and especially of modern
European political dynamics, are evident not only on the Western but also on the
Eastern European scene. They also throw some light on the recent developments in
Eastern Europe, above all on the breakdown of the Communist regime and on the
tribulations of the post-Communist regimes (see Eisenstadt 1992b).

It would be beyond the scope of this chapter to go in detail into these problems.
Suffice it to point out that the comparative civilizational perspective is indeed of
importance in the analysis of these problems, as it is in that of the vicissitudes of
modernity beyond Europe (see Eisenstadt 1992d, 1987a).

Notes

1. Thus many observers of Switzerland have stressed the difference in the whole pattern of
    consultation in dealing with internal matters on the one hand, and foreign policy on the
    other. This is not peculiar to Switzerland. Another important illustration is Finland, where
    one of the major functions of the President in the political system is foreign policy-making.
    A very interesting case study from this point of view is Czechoslovakia between the two
    World Wars: the great, successful democracy which during that period contrasted with the
    failure of Austria. In Czechoslovakia a pattern developed in which foreign policy, including
    foreign economic policy, was in the hands of the President (whether Masaryk or Beneš) in
    consultation with the Prime Minister. It was not really part of internal politics. The basic
    decisions were taken by the executive. The same is true of other small European states.
      A similar pattern developed, from a historical perspective, in Venice. Venice was an
    oligarchic democracy, but not, however, with respect to foreign matters. It was the Small
    Council (and often only the Doge himself) that dealt with most of these matters, and very
    much in secret. The political processes related to external problems were more open in other
    small (historical) societies, but even in these there were interesting similarities. In classical
    Athens at the time of the Peloponnesian War, for example, part of the foreign policy was
    taken out of the usual democratic process for the sake of survival.

9 Chance, luck and stubbornness

Giovanni Sartori

Columbia University

I was born in Florence, Italy, in 1924. I thus have vivid memories of Fascism, of the war of Abyssinia, of the Spanish Civil War (in which Franco was assisted by Italian soldiers) and, of course, of World War II. It goes without saying that my lifelong concern about democracy – solid rather than advanced democracy – arises out of these 'dark' memories of fascism and Nazism. I will tell, therefore, of fortuitous side-effects.

Italy's war in alliance with Hitler ended in surrender on 8 September 1943. In that year I had expected to be and dreaded being drafted (I was nineteen) and sent to war. But the Italian military machine was, after all, Italian and thus behind schedule. My call to arms came up only in October 1943, and came from the newly installed Fascist puppet regime known as the Republic of Salò. Like most of my peers, I sought escape in hiding. The penalty for deserters was, however, to be shot on the spot; and whoever hid a deserter equally risked his or her life. I thus spent some ten months 'buried' (for I was not allowed even to be seen within the household) in a somewhat hidden room until Florence was liberated from German occupation in August 1944. What does one do in just one sealed room for almost a year? Remembering *de consolatione philosophiae*, that consolation was in philosophy, I read Hegel and the two dominant Italian idealist philosophers of the time: Benedetto Croce and Giovanni Gentile. Aside from consolation, it took me one day to read ten, at most fifteen pages of Hegel. At the end of the day I was definitely exhausted and ready for bed. So, just a handful of books (a great convenience under the circumstances) did the trick of getting me through to the end of the war (in Florence) and of establishing for future consumption my reputation as a philosopher, as well-read in the arcana of philosophy – a reputation that brought me, suddenly and quite unexpectedly, into academe in 1950. Just as I had not intended to become a philosopher, I had not planned either to become a professor. Both happenings just happened.

I earned my doctorate in social and political sciences at the University of Florence in November 1946, and for the next four years I had nothing better to do than to linger on. The country was largely in a shambles and the university had many of its 'barons' (i.e. tenured professors) under purge, suspended or indicted for having been Fascists. Since I was considered an *enfant prodige* (remember, I was supposedly able to understand Hegel) I was immediately appointed assistant to the chair of General

Theory of the State – the equivalent of the German *Staatslehre* – and in fact my assistance went as far as to do almost all the teaching in lieu of my frequently absent professor. His name was Pompeo Biondi. He never was a diligent teacher, but had a wonderfully bright mind. Pompeo (as we called him, for he was a heavy, impressive man who deserved a pompous name) implicitly taught me one thing: that intelligence *cum* ignorance (he had little time and less patience for reading) is preferable to erudition *cum* dullness. But since I could not match his wits, it struck me (second lesson) that I had to have my bibliographies in order. I have always read a lot.

Cursus honorum

Now the story of how it happened that I found – or was authoritatively given – my vocation, my *Beruf*. The year was 1950. At a Faculty meeting the Dean, Maranini, told his unsuspecting colleagues that he had a promising young marvel to propose: Giovanni Spadolini, who was then 25 years old (one year younger than I was), and later became managing editor of the *Corriere della Sera* (the major Italian daily paper), minister, prime minister and president of the Senate, and just missed, by a hair's breadth, the presidency of the Republic. As this record shows, Maranini had indeed picked a winner. But Pompeo (my boss) could not accept the loss of face of not having a candidate of his own. On the spur of the moment he proposed me (as his counter-genius), and the first vacant teaching post that flashed across his mind was History of Modern Philosophy. The deal was struck – both Spadolini *and* Sartori – and I was appointed on the spot '*professore incaricato*' (assistant and/or associate professor: there was no difference at that time). I was unsuspecting and was just informed the next day that I had to teach history of philosophy (as I did for six years, 1950–56).[1] Since then I have believed that *fortuna*, chance, luck, matters a lot in life – certainly not less than *virtù*.

Remember, however, that philosophy was for me a war 'accident'. I was mainly interested in logic, not in philosophers. But logic was not taught in Italian universities and was indeed anathema for both idealistic philosophy and Marxist dialectics (the dominant schools). I had to work my way out. It would take too long to rehearse how a combination of stubbornness but also, again, of fortunate coincidences allowed me to move to political science. Skipping all the many amusing anecdotes,[2] by 1956 I had managed to have political science entered in the statute (the list of recognized and permitted teachings) of the Florence Faculty of Political Sciences, and to switch (always as a *professore incaricato*) to this entirely novel and, for many, suspect academic discipline.

Professionally it was not a clever move. Indeed I was told by all my friends (including Spadolini, by then a sort of twin brother) that it was a very stupid one. In the Italian academic system, in order to become a full professor one had to pass a national competition which selected three winners. Since I was alone and the discipline had little if any recognition, had I been a rational, calculating animal I would have reckoned that the date at which I could expect tenure had to be located around the year 2000 – somewhat too late for me. But at times – another lesson for posterity – one can win without expecting victory. What mattered to me was to study what I liked and to pioneer a new discipline. As for the *cursus honorum*, why not leave it, again, to luck? In fact it turned out that *fortuna* was once more on my side. By 1963 (it took me seven years of waiting, but still much less than my statistics predicted) I was the first and only tenured professor of political science in Italy. To be sure, I had to use a back door: I won a chair in sociology. But once 'enstooled' it was easy for me to return to political science. Against all the odds, I had made it. The next and immediate task was to promote and establish the discipline.[3]

Political science in Italy

I must now take a step back. Why political science? And, further, how did I conceive the discipline and land at comparative politics? In truth, I am only a part-time comparativist. My work can be divided in three slices: (1) straightforward political theory; (2) methodological writings where methodology is understood as the method of *logos*, of thinking, not as a misnomer for research techniques; and (3) comparative politics proper.

The political theory slice is best exemplified by my writings on democracy: the early *Democrazia e Definizioni* (1957, with some ten subsequent reprints), *Democratic Theory* (1962a, 1965), *The Theory of Democracy Revisited* (1987a);[4] and also by *Elementi di Teoria Politica* (1987b, 1990, 1995). The methodological slice is represented, in the main, by the writings collected in the volume *La Politica: Logica e Metodo in Scienze Sociali* (1979) and, in English, by my 'Guidelines for Concept Analysis' in G. Sartori (ed.) *Social Science Concepts: A Systematic Analysis* (1984), but also by my articles on the comparative method, to which I shall come later. Finally, the comparative politics slice is represented by *Parties and Party Systems. A Framework for Analysis* (1976),[5] and recently by *Comparative Constitutional Engineering* (1994a).

While I make fun of myself saying that I am a specialist in everything, in fact there is a strong consistency among my seemingly eclectic wanderings. The backbone of all my work harks back to my philosophical beginning (in which in career terms I have invested much 'lost' time, but with no regret), for a theoretical–analytical awareness underlies my comparative writings just as much as the theoretical and methodological ones. Be that as it may, let me now address my previous questions beginning with: why did I choose to become a political scientist?

Since my student days it had struck me that we had, in Italy, faculties of political sciences in which there was, in fact, no study of politics itself. In our faculties we had a lot of law, a fair amount of history, some economics, statistics, geography, philosophy, but no teaching that enabled students to understand politics. My long-fought battle for introducing political science in the curriculum of faculties that called themselves (with little justification) 'of political sciences' was prompted, then, by what I perceived as a logical point: how can we have political sciences in the plural without a political science in the singular that explains what all the rest is about?

To be sure, I did not discover political science because I had to satisfy a logical requirement. While as a *politologo* I was largely self-taught (I had no teachers), I could and did rely, in my learning by myself, on the international context (the IPSA context), on my entering the path-breaking IPSA Committee of Political Sociology (where I made lifelong outstanding friends: Marty Lipset, Juan Linz, Stein Rokkan, Mattei Dogan, Hans Daalder, S.N. Eisenstadt),[6] and on the initial exposure to

American political science in 1949–50, when I was in the United States with a post-doctoral fellowship.

The next question is: how did I conceive the discipline? In the Italian context this was a relevant question, because my understanding of political science did shape the views of a profession that was nurtured at the Institute of Political Science of the University of Florence and thus, willy-nilly, under my wings. In this respect the development of political science in Italy has been unique, and symmetrically different from the German one. The German *Politische Wissenschaft* came about early on, with one large distribution of chairs which had to be filled – there was no alternative – with lateral entries. Even Voegelin, a scholar whom I personally liked and respected, but who certainly was no political scientist, returned to Germany as a *Politische Wissenschaft* professor in Munich. The converse happened in Italy: the growth was slow and, so to speak, unicentric, spreading out as it were from Florence. So, what did I teach to a selected group of post-doctoral neophytes during the mid-1960s?

My understanding of political science undoubtedly bore an American imprint.[7] In a country in which the expression 'merely empirical' was derogatory – it meant that something had no heuristic value – I claimed that political science differed from political philosophy precisely in that it was an empirical science. But since I had to explain what an Englishman would know by instinct, I also stressed that empirical knowledge had to be, at some point, applied or 'applicable' knowledge (Sartori, 1974, 1979). It was already at this juncture, then, that I parted company with the American behavioural slant. In the United States the discipline forsook the theory–practice connection and went wholesale for the theory–research relationship. Along this route theory became largely atrophied into mere research design, research became a sort of end in itself, the question 'science for what?' was ignored, and little was left, at the end, other than operationalization, quantification and statistical treatment of ever growing masses of data. I have always resisted all of that.

To be sure, I endorsed the notion of a research-based science. But I never was converted to behaviouralism. I have always insisted on a 'theory-rich' discipline monitored by a sound training in logic and method ('methodology'); I never believed in a 'superior' quantified science; and above all, as I have already pointed out, my emphasis has always been on the conversion of theory into practice, and thus on 'operative' (not operational) science. In my view political scientists are, like economists, required to know (at least better than laymen) how problems can be solved, which reforms are likely to work and, in a nutshell, to have 'know-how'. Economists are trained to advise, the American-bred political scientist is not. But why not? That has always been my question (see Sartori 1968c).

So, how do we acquire a practice-oriented knowledge? The test is, of course, pragmatic, that is to say, success in application. If we intervene on something, and if the outcome conforms to the intent, that is, turns out as predicted, then we have an applied or applicable knowledge. But this can be a very costly test. Finding out by trial and error involves a lot of error; and we are not speaking here of laboratory tests but of human beings eventually used as guinea-pigs. We must, I thought, do better than that. And here enters, finally, comparative politics.

I do not remember what came first, whether I stumbled into the importance of comparing at the 1954 IPSA Round Table in Florence, at which comparative politics was indeed the issue (and was hotly debated between the 'Young Turks' led by

Macridis and the senior scholars of the time, especially Carl Friedrich and Karl Loewenstein), or whether the notion that 'comparing is controlling' had already been lingering in my mind in the context of my methodological ruminations. At any rate, I was at the time in charge of a quarterly, *Studi Politici*; in it I quickly published the papers of the IPSA Round Table introduced by a preface of mine. Since then I have argued that comparative politics was the very core of political science, for comparisons were a means, indeed the major method, for controlling our generalizations. Is it the case that working democracies are, and must be, of the Anglo-American or Scandinavian type, as Almond held in the 1950s? Do revolutions arise from relative deprivation? Did Duverger hypothethize valid laws on the influence of electoral systems? These and innumerable similar questions can and should be tested *vis-à-vis* the cases to which they apply, that is, by means of a comparative checking.

This has been the methodological tenet on which I have insisted, since the 1950s, in several essays.[8] And this is actually the underlying backbone of *Parties and Party Systems* and, recently, of *Comparative Constitutional Engineering*. In both works I insistently generalize and test (comparatively). In the first, however, I adopt a structural–functional approach,[9] while the second leans heavily on 'condition analysis'. But both works are, so to speak, thickly comparative: whenever I provide causal explanations and make general assertions, I scan through, and control with, all the polities (as many as I manage to know of) that fall under any given generalization.

The American impact

Thus far I have somewhat pictured myself as a self-propelled scholar performing on his own. I must now correct this one-sided account. While I did influence the development of Italian political science in a unique manner,[10] it is quite evident that had I not been exposed to the science of politics that blossomed after World War II in the United States I would have been an entirely different scholar. After the early grant that brought me to New York in 1949–50 (shopping between Columbia and the New School for Social Research), I returned many times to the United States in the 1960s, first as a Visiting Professor of Government at Harvard (1964–65), and subsequently as a recurrent Visiting Professor of Political Science at Yale between 1966 and 1969. The Yale arrangement (Stein Rokkan, Shlomo Avineri and myself were supposed to rotate for a semester each) broke down in my case with the campus revolution, for under its first assaults I was elected Dean of my Faculty in Florence and had to live through the turbulence of 1969 and its aftermath in *loco*. In 1971–72, pretty much worn out by some three years of battlings (in Italy it was quite rough), I went to Stanford, where I spent a delightful and fruitful year 'on the hill' as a fellow of the Center for Advanced Study in the Behavioral Sciences. Thereafter, in 1976, I somewhat suddenly decided to leave Italy. Early in that year S.E. Finer, a wonderful friend and scholar, tried to get me over to Oxford, where the sudden death of John Plamenatz had opened one of the Chichele professorships; and at exactly the same time Stanford offered me the position that Gabriel Almond was leaving for retirement. Both were very flattering offers. The last I heard about the Chichele chair (which went to Charles Taylor) was that I was one vote short. However, as Sammy Finer was telling me on the phone about my Oxford chances, I told him that Stanford had accepted my demands and that I had in turn accepted the position there; I have never known whether I had lost, or might still have won the Chichele competition.

Why did I leave? Well, I had spent more than a quarter of a century (that is how I put it to myself) as a professor at the University of Florence, and I had the feeling that there was nothing more that I could accomplish there, that my Italian cycle was over. The first wave of my pupils was already well placed across the country, Italian political science had attained sufficient momentum to keep going on its own,[11] and I felt the need to work just for myself. Stanford put all the distance between me and Italy that I needed. But then, out of the blue I received an offer from New York that could not be refused. After three years, in 1979, I left Stanford and became Albert Schweitzer Professor in the Humanities at Columbia University, where (as of 1 July 1994) I am Professor Emeritus.

This quick account suffices to indicate the extent of my exposure to American political science. At Harvard I met, or got to know better, Carl Friedrich, Talcott Parsons, Sam Beer, Sam Huntington, Henry Kissinger; at Yale, Robert Dahl, Harold Lasswell, Karl Deutsch, Charles Lindblom, David Apter, Joe LaPalombara; at Stanford, Gabriel Almond, Marty Lipset, Robert Ward; at Columbia, Robert Merton (I had attended his class in 1950), Zbigniev Brzezinski, Severyn Bialer, and others. One always benefits from the company of good, indeed very good, minds. But reading is, as a rule, more important.

The work that perhaps influenced me more than any other was Dahl's *A Preface to Democratic Theory* (1956). When I read it, I was thunderstruck by Dahl's method, by his systematic analysis of 'conditions' (an exercise that Dahl repeated in the early 1960s, under my ever-admiring eyes, at the Bellagio Rockefeller Center for the volume *Political Oppositions in Western Democracies*, 1966). In earlier days I had been very impressed by Friedrich's *Constitutional Government and Democracy* (1946), a superb achievement (considering that its first draft went back to the late 1930s). Another author to whom I owe innumerable insights is Gabriel Almond. Even though I lament that Almond did not really accomplish the structural–functional programme outlined in *The Politics of The Developing Areas* (1960, a truly masterful essay), in my methodology courses and teaching I have insisted that, among the competing paradigms, models and approaches that have been flooding the discipline, structural functionalism stands out, if properly implemented, as the more fruitful scheme of analysis. Also, and to conclude the section on my intellectual debts (with some unjustice, for I am obliged to be brief), the Princeton Political Development series displays, in my opinion, the very best of what American comparative politics has collectively produced to date.

An assessment

Let me now come to the straightforward question: was my moving to the United States a right move? And what is the balance of the American segment of my academic life?

As my pedigree shows, I knew the United States too well to expect success. My success was in having been offered (just in time!) two prestigious positions. But by the end of the 1970s it was very clear to me that American political science had entered a path that I neither would or could accept: the pattern of excessive specialization (and thus narrowness), excessive quantification and, by the same token, a path leading – in my opinion – to irrelevance and sterility. While sweeping generalizations must allow for many exceptions, still if one compares the *American Political Science Review* of twenty or thirty years ago to the *Review* of the last decade, the difference is striking, or even stunning. And if my methodological caveats and criticisms are correct,[12] then much of what American political science is currently producing must be quite wrong.

On these reflections one might conclude that I arrived in the wrong place at the wrong time. Yet I take a kinder view of myself. While my work has never made a splash on American soil (unsurprisingly), sitting on a reputed chair and starting – in the writing business – with a text in English with an American publisher gives a scholar a strong starting edge. It took me five years to have my first Italian book on democracy translated and published in the United States. Thereafter, however, *Democratic Theory* and *The Theory of Democracy Revisited* have obtained some fifteen translations around the world. My *Parties and Party Systems* has done equally well in the international context. And I expect *Comparative Constitutional Engineering* to perform in a similar manner.[13] So, I cannot complain, and indeed I feel good about my overall balance sheet.

I am not happy, however, about the performance of comparative politics. Since this is the focus that I have been asked to pursue, let me close my brief by quoting the closing statement of a recent article (1991a, p.255) on the comparative theme:

> In the last forty years or so, we have enjoyed moving from one 'revolution' to another: behavioral, paradigmatic, 'critical,' postpositivist, hermeneutic, and so on. But revolutions (in science) just leave us with a new beginning – they have to be followed up and made to bear fruits. We have, instead, just allowed them to fade away, as ever new beginnings hold ever new promises which remain, in turn, ever unfulfilled. In the process the basics have gotten lost ... Yes, our sophistication has grown – but at the expense of an increasingly missing core. As is shown by growing numbers of comparativists (in name) that never compare anything, not even 'implicitly,' thus forsaking standardized labels, common yardsticks and shared parameters. Let us squarely face it: the normal science is not doing well. A field defined by its method – comparing – cannot prosper without a core method. My critique does not imply, to be sure, that good, even excellent, comparative work is no longer under way. But even the current good comparative work underachieves on account of our having lost sight of what comparing *is for*.

Notes

1. My lectures of those years were all mimeographed, but until now unpublished (except for a little sideline book, *Stato e Politica nel Pensiero di Benedetto Croce*, 1966). However, I have proposed to the Florence Faculty to publish, in lieu of a retirement *Festschrift*, one of my monographic courses in the History of Philosophy. Two volumes, *Croce Filosofo Pratico* and *Croce Etico–Politico e Filosofo della Liberta* (some 600 pages, I fear) will thus be published by Il Mulino, Bologna (in 1996).
2. I tell some in 'Dove va la Scienza Politica' (Sartori 1985).
3. At the same time I pursued the general reform, across Italy, of the structure and curriculum of the Faculties of Political Sciences. How this near-miracle occurred (no other Italian Faculty has obtained to date a similarly sweeping reform) is a *golpe*-like story that I cannot yet disclose. It was, in retrospect, great fun.

4. Aside from the above-cited books the theme recurs in many articles: 'Democracy' and 'Representational Systems' (in the *International Encyclopedia of the Social Sciences*, 1968a, 1968b), 'Will Democracy Kill Democracy?' (1975), 'Rethinking Democracy: Bad Polity and Bad Politics' (1991b), 'Democrazia' (another Encyclopedia article, and a long one, 1992), and 'How Far Can Free Government Travel?' (1995).

5. The book (*Parties and Party Systems*, 1976), which was very slow in coming, was preceded by my article 'The Case of Polarized Pluralism' (1966) and also by 'The Typology of Party Systems' (1970b). A further elaboration of the 1976 volume is 'Polarization, Fragmentation, and Competition in Western Democracies' (Sani and Sartori 1983). My notion of 'polarized pluralism' has been much debated, and the polarization variable, as I defined it, has become a standard one.

6. The experience in the Committee of Political Sociology was, for all its core members, a very enriching give-and-take affair. While my work on parties owed a great deal to our meetings on the topic, my piece 'From the Sociology of Politics to Political Sociology' (1969) did, in turn, reorient the approach of the group – or so I believe.

7. The Italian political science tradition is represented by Gaetano Mosca; and it is clearly the case that I discontinued that tradition. Mosca's *Elementi di Scienza Politica,* first published in 1896, is really a text of 'drawing lessons' from history, and in Mosca's time 'science' was a loosely used word. I have also been very critical of his celebrated 'law' of the ruling class (see e.g. Sartori 1987a, pp.145–8).

8. The most quoted one is 'Concept Misformation in Comparative Politics' (1970a). But see, more importantly, 'La Politica Comparata: Premesse e Problemi' (1971, which was the lead article of the first issue of *Rivista Italiana di Scienza Politica*), and 'Comparing and Miscomparing' (1991a, 1994b).

9. In *Parties and Party Systems* (1976) the structural–functional framework is not as evident as it should or would have been, because the work was conceived in two volumes and the functional argument was developed in the second one, which never appeared because my near-final manuscript was stolen. I never had the heart to return to it from scratch.

10. To wit, some ten current political science chairholders (remember that Italy has a chair system) were trained at the so-called 'Florentine School' with fellowships obtained from the Agnelli Foundation. Let me mention their names: Maurizio Cotta (Siena), Stefano Bartolini (European University Institute), Domenico Fisichella (Roma), Leonardo Morlino (Firenze), Adriano Pappalardo (Napoli), Gianfranco Pasquino (Bologna), Giorgio Sola (Genova), Giuliano Urbani (Milano), Giovanna Zincone (Torino). The tenth was Antonio Lombardo, who died in his fifties.

11. The turning point came with the *Rivista Italiana di Scienza Politica* started in 1971 (of which I still am officially the managing editor), that immediately established itself as the journal that declared who was 'in' or else 'out' in Italian political science.

12. See not only my 1984 'Guidelines for Concept Analysis', but, more harshly 'Comparing and Miscomparing' (1991a), and 'Totalitarianism, Model Mania and Learning From Error' (1993).

13. The book came out simultaneously with three publishers: New York University Press (for the United States and Canada), Macmillan in London, and Fondo de Cultura in Mexico City (for Latin America in general). The Italian translation quickly followed (1995) and was a bestseller; Brazilian and Japanese translations are forthcoming. Constitutionalism is by no means a new interest of mine. Indeed the first article that I ever published in the United States was 'Constitutionalism: A Preliminary Discussion' (1962b).

10 Between nations and disciplines: personal experience and intellectual understanding of societies and political regimes

Juan J. Linz

YALE UNIVERSITY

The idea of an intellectual autobiography at the outset was tempting and exciting, but it turned out also to be frustrating. My life and work are too complex to tell within the limits assigned. References to historical, social and political contexts will elude most readers. Too many persons, institutions and circumstances that played a decisive role make only fleeting appearances. The dispersion of my intellectual activities, in spite of a fundamental continuity in my interests and close links between apparently disparate subjects, did not make things easier.

Youth in two countries

I was born in 1926 in Bonn. My father, son of a teacher in Bacharach, was a manufacturer. My mother, who came from a bourgeois aristocratic Spanish family, had an intellectual calling and interest in the arts and the social question. My parents were involved in the cultural and political life in Cologne and Bonn, and their home was full of books and works of art. I remember a collection of prints by Pechstein, paintings by Geiger, furniture of the *Deutsche Werkstätten*, of which little was saved from the Spanish Civil War. Before my birth, the German inflation had bankrupted my family's business and with the depression life had become difficult. When in 1932 my mother received an offer to work at the Centre for Historical Studies and at the National Library in Madrid, she accepted it. I was five years old when I left the Bavarian forest and moved to Madrid to live in an apartment, started school and got immersed in another language. My father, who stayed in Germany, was killed by a drunken driver in 1934.

From my childhood on I have been exposed to different cultures and been aware of politics. The person who helped me with my schoolwork and became a lifelong friend was a stateless (Nansen-passport holder) Estonian who had been a Bolshevik in Switzerland. He had been involved in the negotiations leading to Lenin's trip through Germany, had conveyed German money to Bukharin and had been active in the struggle for Estonian independence. He acquainted me with Nordic culture, besides taking me to an anarchist barber's shop. The Spanish Civil War (1936–39) was a

101

crucial experience of which I have vivid memories: the social and political tensions preceding it, the day it started, the revolutionary terror, the religious persecution. In October 1936 my mother took me to Germany where I became aware of different aspects of Nazism: the *Winterhilfswerk* on the one side, but also, through a connection with Preysing (the anti-Nazi bishop of Berlin), reports on the repressive aspects. I was present at a conversation which my mother told me not to repeat to anybody, but never to forget. I was ten years old but the memory of that time came back when I was writing about Nazi totalitarianism.

In March 1937 we arrived in Salamanca, the capital of Franco's Spain. My mother became active in the Falangist welfare organization. While working with my mother I experienced very personally 'the limited political pluralism of the regime' (about which I would write later), the Fascist hopes for social revolution in a basically reactionary milieu, the poverty, and the human impact of repression. My interest in social problems and politics was kindled at that time. The war also resolved my identity crisis: I was a Spanish kid. When we returned to Madrid I did not go to the nazified German school, nor to a religious private one, for my secondary education but to a public high school with a very socially mixed student body. My interest turned to the humanities. If I had been better in mathematics, I might have become an architect.

Study in Spain and the discovery of sociology

I registered in Law School and the newly founded Faculty of Political Science (1943). Good grades earned me free tuition and I graduated in 1947 as the most outstanding student in political science and in 1948 with one of the four best records in Law School. My mother died a few months before my political science graduation and I had to start working to make a living, while at the same time doing three years of military service at the War College as a translator. I learned much about military thought and civil–military relations (besides, the food at the company mess was welcome on my tight budget). When I came to the United States I intended to work with Hans Speier on the military in politics. In view of my academic success and my economic situation, the Director of the War College decided to present me with the costly academic gown required to attend the Political Science graduation ceremony. This story was to serve me well in breaking the ice in talking about transitions to democracy at the Chilean Centre of Higher Military Studies shortly before the end of the Pinochet regime.

Javier Conde, whose assistant I had been at the University, obtained a fellowship for me at the Institute for Legal Studies, where I started working with him on an anthology of sociological texts. Conde played an important role in my intellectual development. I first met him when I was aged ten at a Christmas party in Berlin where he held a fellowship as a young Spanish academic (close to a professor who had translated Marx). After some hesitation, he came to Franco's Spain, joined the group of Falangist intellectuals and became Professor of *Derecho Político* at the University of Madrid. His broad intellectual outlook, nourished by the German social science tradition (Weber, Freyer, Heller, Schmitt, Smend) impressed me. When, after some years of political ostracism, he was appointed Director of the *Instituto de Estudios Políticos*, I joined him there (in spite of not sharing the politics of the institution). When I mentioned themes associated with *Sozialpolitik* as my interests he disapproved, arguing their limited intellectual import. He led me to read the classics of sociology instead. I began to review sociology books for the journals, published a bibliography of electoral sociology, participated in a seminar on 'indirect powers' (interest groups, the army, etc.) and met foreign visitors. I also worked on pre-legislative studies, a report on agrarian reform, etc. Conde was a controversial and contradictory figure; intellectually alive, doctrinaire on some issues, loyal to the regime but supportive of liberal intellectuals. The relation with him became clouded when, concerned about the political implications of my work, he fired me from the *Instituto* while I was at Columbia, which made my returning to Spain more difficult. Years later we would make up in California where we visited together the ageing Kelsen, with whom he engaged in an hour-long conversation in German.

Conde had helped me to obtain a government fellowship to study sociology in the USA. My aim was to study empirical sociology, away from the German theoretical orientation. Before leaving for the United States, I had my first contact with a democratic country and foreign students thanks to an invitation by the *Conférence Olivaint* – an organization of Catholic *Sciences Po* students – to a camp on the island of Port Cros during the summer of 1949 and 1950. There I presented a paper on democracy, based on Kelsen. Years later, I would find out that Gerhard Lehmbruch and Iring Fetcher were there at the same time.

My encounter with American academic life

My arrival in New York in 1950 was not easy. I came with the first group of students who went abroad with grants from the Spanish government. I had left a position and the security of a job for a nine-month fellowship and the life of a student. Coming from Franco's Spain, 'a nation and regime that was despised by ... almost all the graduate students and faculty' at Columbia, to use the formulation of Lipset (1995), I was only allowed to register as a non-matriculated student. By the start of the second semester Robert Lynd supported me for a fellowship for the next academic year, although I had still to pay tuition from savings from the Spanish fellowship and from summer work with Merton and Goode.

In my intellectual outlook I have always been open-minded, which in practice means eclectic, in my choice of theoretical and methodological approaches. I was fortunate that when I arrived at the sociology department of Columbia I did not, as did many other fellow students, identify with one of the members of the faculty but took courses with all of them. Each one added something to my intellectual development. From Robert K. Merton I learned the importance of middle-range theorizing, the idea of a theoretical respecification of empirical findings and of translating theoretical concepts into empirical indicators. Structural–functionalism became part of my intellectual armoury. From Paul Lazarsfeld, I got my interest in survey research, the concept of an attribute space and the construction of typologies, and from Kingsley Davis the attention to demographic data, the use of census data, and the structural comparison of societies using such data. Robert Lynd made the question 'knowledge for what?' central and the concern with issues of social change in works like those of the late Mannheim. S.M. Lipset, then a more junior faculty member, introduced me to Robert Michels and became a constant mentor and friend in my work in political sociology. Their mark can be found in many of my projects and writings. I have to add Reinhard

Bendix, for whom I served as a research assistant reading works, memoirs, and correspondence of German entrepreneurs and officials in Imperial Germany, which later led to my interest in entrepreneurship and the legitimacy of the economic system.

The classics have been a constant point of reference and influence in my work since I started reading in Spain Weber, Simmel, Mannheim, Lorenz von Stein and Pareto and inter-war German political science, particularly Hermann Heller. Later I would add Marx, de Tocqueville and Clausewitz. Durkheim would not play a comparable role. In the course of time, Parsons, Schumpeter, Rokkan, Dahl and Hirschman were added. Weber would be my lodestar and permanent source of inspiration, ideas and concepts. A seminar I taught on Pareto was a stimulus for my work on regime crises, breakdown and re-equilibration. On Robert Michels, however, I have perhaps only written because like myself he was at the intersection in many problems and life 'circles' (Linz 1966a).

When my fellowships were exhausted, I started working with S.M. Lipset on a 'propositional' inventory on political behaviour, which led to an unpublished co-authored work entitled *Social Bases of Political Diversity in Western Democracies* (1956; for a history of the inventory see Lipset in Chehabi and Stepan 1995, pp.6–8). I moved with Lipset to the Center for Advanced Study in the Behavioral Sciences and later to Berkeley, where I worked for Bendix. At the same time, I was writing my dissertation. Originally, it was to be a sociological study of the Italian and German electorates using survey data to learn the research technique, and learning more about two new democracies. Finally, I limited myself to an exhaustive analysis of the 1953 Adenauer election, using data from the *Institut für Demoskopie* at Allensbach.

Return to Spain and teaching at Columbia University

A grant from the Committee on Comparative Politics of the SSRC allowed me to return to Madrid after defending my thesis at Columbia in May 1958. I travelled to Spain with a stop-over in Paris, where I lived the critical days of the end of the Fourth Republic and the ascent to power of De Gaulle. My grant was to work on interest group politics but actually on the nature of an authoritarian regime. The study of interest groups evolved into a large study of entrepreneurship which I co-authored with Amando de Miguel, who joined me in the United States and became a close collaborator. The book *Los empresarios ante el poder público* (1966b) reflects the times in which it was published: the main conclusions about the support for and role of the official corporative structure of the regime, and of the competing more traditional organizations and the private ones, were placed in the middle rather than at the beginning or in a conclusion, which would have been read and resulted in official objections. The study led also to the publication of a large number of articles and it was replicated in theses on Portuguese, Italian and French entrepreneurs. Unfortunately, there was no chance to integrate those studies in a single comparative monograph.

While in Spain, I went to the meeting of the International Sociological Association in Stresa in 1959 and became a founding member of the Committee of Political Sociology (see Rokkan's history of the Committee in Allardt and Rokkan (eds) 1970, pp.1–20). The CPS provided a unique opportunity to meet, and collaborate and establish long-term friendships with, some of the contributors to this volume, and others no longer among us, including Stein Rokkan, who had a decisive influence on my work (Linz 1992), and Raymond Aron, whom I always admired for his intellectual independence. As a sociologist of politics, I shared many interests with Mattei Dogan. When Richard Rose was elected secretary of the Committee and I served as chairman, our friendship became particularly intense. The CPS was an exciting network of scholars which, together with the Almond Committee on Comparative Politics of the SSRC and the Smaller Democracies group of Stein Rokkan, Robert Dahl, Val Lorwin and Hans Daalder, has shaped comparative politics for decades.

Professional opportunities in Spain were limited, and I did not expect my work on the Franco regime to be published there. At Stresa, Merton and Lazarsfeld offered me a teaching post at Columbia. In January 1961 I went to Morningside Heights to start my American academic career. My return to Columbia was not – as some people sometimes say – an exile, since I could come and go, nor in my mind at the time a case of emigration. I thought that sooner or later I would return to Spain, perhaps to engage in politics after Franco. Why I did not get into politics, in spite of my early interest, is too long a story to tell here. To some extent, it is part of the story of my generation in Spain. In 1968 I taught at the new *Universidad Autónoma* in Madrid and there was talk of offering me an academic position, but nothing concrete emerged until 1992 when I was awarded an honorary degree, and appointed Professor Emeritus at the same time. With the award of the *Premio Príncipe de Asturias* in the Social Sciences in 1983 I cannot say that my work has not been recognized in Spain.

In my years at Columbia (1961–68), I not only enjoyed the interaction with some of my former teachers, but I also taught a joint seminar with Daniel Bell who, from a different perspective, challenged my ideas. Many lunches with Otto Kirchheimer were stimulating and I was asked to take over his seminar after his untimely death. We had planned to teach a joint seminar.

The 1968 crisis caught me at Columbia. The Canadian CBS invited me to a telephone hook-up with Quebec and Paris to discuss the *évènements* with student revolutionary leaders and academics, a long conversation that revealed different sources and perspectives of the turmoil. In all the crises and tension, a gratifying experience was to hear one of the occupants of Columbia say that my analysis of breakdowns of democracy was applicable to that situation. I was opposed to the radical students but ended being less hostile towards them than some of my more liberal colleagues. One of the moving legacies of that event was that one SDS leader, Al Sysmanski, would later dedicate one of his books to 'the National Liberation Front of South Vietnam and Juan J. Linz'!

Already before the 1968 crisis I had accepted a joint appointment in Sociology and Political Science at Yale to the surprise of my friends who, in view of my love for museums, art exhibits, subscriptions to the ballet and the opera (which I have kept), thought I would never leave New York. Early on, I had spent a fruitful year at the Center for Advanced Study in the Behavioral Sciences (1963–64) and a semester as Associate Professor of History at Stanford (1966). In Spain I had been involved (1966–67) in a large study of the Andalusian Social Structure with support of the OECD (cf. Linz 1971).

Authoritarianism and totalitarianism

For a meeting of the CPS I wrote in 1963, 'An Authoritarian Regime: The Case of Spain' (1964, 1970a), in which I argued against the simplistic dichotomy totalitarianism vs. democracy, and the conception of a continuum of non-democratic regimes, treating authoritarian regimes as a distinctive type. The essay was the result of the critical reading of the classics on totalitarianism, the Spanish experience, the fieldwork I had done and work on other non-democratic regimes. The initial work led to other writings: on the élites of the regime (Linz 1972c), the role of business and interest groups (Linz and Miguel 1966b), the opposition 'to and under the regime' (1973c), part of the Dahl project on oppositions, the non-competitive elections (1970b), local élites (1971), the bureaucracy (Linz and Miguel 1968), the evolution of the *Falange* from a fascist party into the de-ideologized *Movimiento-Organización* (1970b) and finally, over twenty years later, the study of the transition to democracy (cf. Diamond *et al.* 1988; Linz and Stepan 1996). I probably should have written a book on the regime, but I was interested in too many other problems (but see Gunther (ed.) 1993, Part I, for a review of my work on Spain).

Many years later I would find that the great Catalan conservative politician Francesc Cambó, in his *Dietari* from 1936–40 (1982), had made practically the same distinction between authoritarian and totalitarian regimes (among which he discussed Germany and Russia). My friend Guy Hermet, in his writings about Spain, would contribute much to the understanding of the regime, as Amando de Miguel did in his *Sociología del Franquismo* (1975).

I want to mention that in my writings I have noted the appeal of the totalitarian utopia – with its mobilized participation, its capacity for radical social change, and the meaning given to politics by ideology, the cultural ambitions, and the manifestations of social solidarity. All these aspects were seen as positive not only by many of those living under totalitarian rule, but more significantly, and disturbingly, even by distinguished intellectuals, writers and artists and politicians (including those living in free societies). Totalitarianism has had a fascination that authoritarian regimes would never have. I do not consider terror as a defining element of totalitarianism (despite its being a likely consequence), and have discussed the terrible repressive dimension of authoritarian regimes, including that of Franco, in an essay on types of regimes and human rights (Linz 1991). However, opponents of a non-democratic regime feel better, and this includes many Poles, fighting a totalitarian regime. While some Spanish colleagues have regarded the characterization of the regime as authoritarian as 'legitimizing' the regime, Mexican scholars have used my characterization of an authoritarian regime to question the democratic character of the long-term rule of the PRI.

A year at the Institute for Advanced Study in Princeton (1973–74) allowed me to write a chapter on totalitarian and authoritarian regimes for the *Handbook of Political Science* of Polsby and Greenstein, a chapter that really is a book on the whole range of non-democratic politics expanding my comparative-theoretical analysis (1975a).

My definition of authoritarian regimes as a type distinct from totalitarianism was quite successful and was used to study a wide range of non-democratic regimes. Some conceptual stretching took place and I realized the need to delimit its application. First, it was clear to me that it was absurd to use the same category to describe the Portuguese regime under Salazar, the first servant of the state, and the regimes of the

Somoza clan, of Trujillo, or of Sese Seko Mobutu, who treated the state as a private property for the benefit of themselves, their family and cronies. The reading of Weber's description of an extreme form of patrimonialism as sultanistic led me to use that term in the *Handbook* and in a forthcoming book with Houchang Chehabi. Later came the crisis or change in communist totalitarian regimes and the efforts of some of those familiar with my work to apply the authoritarian regime idea to some post-Stalinist regimes. Again, I felt that this was conceptual stretching and I came to characterize post-totalitarian regimes as distinct from authoritarian regimes (Linz and Stepan 1996).

While at the Institute, I also wrote 'Some Notes toward a Comparative Study of Fascism in Sociological Historical Perspective' (1976), followed by 'Political Space and Fascism as a Late-Comer' (1980b). These two essays illustrate well the importance of including the largest number of cases possible before accepting generalizations based on fewer cases or a single case and of not limiting oneself to the phenomenon one is studying. (For a better understanding of the founding leaderships of fascist movements, with the help of my wife I collected data on the founders and most important leaders of Communist, Socialist and Christian Democratic parties for comparison (cf. Linz 1976).) In extending the search for the sources of the fascist success I turned to a macro-historical-political-sociological comparative study of European societies – beyond the focus on Italy and Germany. The findings made some of the sociological generalizations, based on theoretical conceptions (like those influenced by Marxism), and the study of single cases, questionable. The stress on fascism as a latecomer where other ideologies had occupied the political space, and its ideological appeal to all sectors of the society in the name of national unity, account for the varied social bases of the movement in the different countries. The simultaneous rejection and partial incorporation of various ideological heritages, the distinctive fascist style and organization forms, added to the space left open, largely account for the success or failure of fascism, and for the heterogeneity of its following.

The breakdown of democracy and the transitions to democracy

At that time I finished the book *The Breakdown of Democratic Regimes. Crisis, Breakdown and Re-equilibration* (1978a). The experience of the breakdown of Spanish democracy and the reading of an essay by Karl Dietrich Bracher (1952) and his monumental *Die Auflösung der Weimarer Republik* (1957) had stimulated my effort to understand the breakdown of democracies. The teaching at Columbia of a seminar on that theme, the writing of a paper outlining my thinking, the organization of a session at the Varna Congress of Sociology (with papers by some of my students), and another conference incorporating more Latin-Americanists organized in collaboration with Alfred Stepan, would lead to the book we co-edited in 1978. The book emphasized the political variables, the actions not only of the anti-democrats but of the incumbent democratic governments and democratic parties, the crucial role of semi-loyal oppositions, the neutral powers (echoes of Carl Schmitt), the semi-loyalty of the different actors, the narrowing of the political arena, but also the possibility of re-equilibration (echoes of Pareto). The analysis encountered some hostility or was ignored for some time, perhaps due to the prevalence of mere sociologized interpretations, particularly Marxist interpretations. Years later, especially in the study of transitions, the emphasis on political processes would become dominant and even one of my critics would be accused of a Linzean approach!

Dirk Berg-Schlosser and his collaborators have pursued my interest in the breakdown, re-equilibration and stability of democracies further, including eighteen countries in their comparative analysis (see Berg-Schlosser and de Meur 1994; Berg-Schlosser and Mitchell (eds) forthcoming). I was moved when they made one of their meetings coincide with the awarding to me an honorary doctorate by the University of Marburg, the university where Michels taught briefly and Ortega y Gasset had studied.

To the question 'Can we learn from the experience of those countries how to assure the stability of consolidated democracies in the future?' my answer would be: yes and no. The theoretical introduction and the case studies tell us much about what led to the breakdown or the survival of democracies in the inter-war years, a knowledge that can be translated into what to do and not to do in crisis situations. It should also be clear, particularly from the case studies, that these events happened in a particular historical time, not likely to be repeated, and that whatever the similarities between those societies and others today, the differences are likely to be great. One of the most encouraging conclusions is that most of the societies included are today so different – in part because of their past experience – that it is highly improbable that in any of them democracy will break down.

The book on *Problems of Democratic Transition and Consolidation*, co-authored with Alfred Stepan (1996), has been the result of long-term interests of both authors, collaboration and friendship over many years. It was already announced as a theme for future research in our preface to *The Breakdown of Democratic Regimes* (1978a): 'High priority for further work ... should now be given: to the analysis of the conditions that lead to the breakdown of authoritarian regimes, to the process of transition from authoritarian to democratic regimes, and especially the political dynamics of the consolidation of postauthoritarian democracies.'

The Portuguese 'liberation by golpe' and the subsequent revolutionary process attracted my interest and I travelled several times to Lisbon to follow the events, interview politicians and watch mass demonstrations, while going to Spain as often as possible since a change of regime appeared likely (1977a, 1981b). For a meeting in Bellagio in 1967 I had written a paper on hypothetical events on the eventuality of Franco's death. From autumn 1976 to January 1978, I followed events day-by-day in Spain: attending the meeting of the *Cortes* approving the Law for Political Reform, being present at party congresses, rallies, street demonstrations, meeting politicians, planning and conducting surveys, studying the election results, giving lectures and interviews in newspapers and on TV, commenting on the first free election in June 1977 on TV (together with the future Prime Minister Leopoldo Calvo Sotelo, and Javier Solana, later Foreign Minister). The result of that fieldwork was not the book I initially intended to write but many publications, a massive study of public opinion and the party system in collaboration with my colleagues from DATA (1980a; Linz *et al.* 1981a, 1986c), an essay on innovative leadership in a transition (1993a), and finally the book with Stepan discussed in the next section.

The Portuguese and the Spanish transitions would be the first I would follow closely; later I worked on the Brazilian, the Korean and the Chilean, and from the look-out point of the *Wissenschaftskolleg* in Berlin (October 1990–August 1991) I followed those in Eastern Europe. Many intellectual exchanges with scholars and political actors, and the teaching of seminars and lectures, contributed to my work on transitions and the consolidation of new democracies. In 1983, as Max Weber Visiting Professor at Heidelberg, I gave lectures on transitions to democracy (that should have resulted in a little book). Stepan and I also taught a joint seminar at Yale and we were involved in the Wilson Center project that resulted in the work edited by O'Donnell, Schmitter and Whitehead (1986).

Problems of democratic transition and consolidation: the book with Stepan

We felt we should write our own book but time passed. We joined again in writing an essay, 'Political Crafting of Democratic Consolidation' (Linz and Stepan 1984), and a contribution to a meeting of the SSRC Committee on Southern Europe. Our long paper for that meeting convinced us even more that we should write the book. My stay at the *Wissenschaftskolleg* in Berlin and a mini-conference at the *Kolleg* gave a further push to our plans. However, geographical distance (Stepan had become Rector of the Central European University) delayed the completion until 1995, punctuated by long days and nights of work when we could meet, in Warsaw, Berlin, Brasilia, Taipei, Paris, Budapest and at my house in Hamden.

There was an initial tension between two conceptions of the book. One was the writing of a tight, elegant, somewhat propositional and theoretical book, with only passing reference to the particular cases, inspired by the model of Dahl's *Polyarchy*. Stepan was more inclined to this style than I was. I, as an incorrigible empiricist, was more ready to incorporate the concrete experiences into the theoretical framework. That became difficult since we had advanced far in the writing of the theoretical chapters. Without much initial planning, the country chapters emerged, first fairly sketchy and focused on a specific problem. Then we started working further on them, travelled to the countries, interviewed élites and scholars, and ended up with long chapters sometimes thick with description. I could not resist introducing a wealth of public opinion data (partly thanks to the help of colleagues like Richard Rose and Marta Lagos). But as we went on getting deeper into the cases, new theoretical problems became salient. We sometimes fitted them into the first theoretical chapters, but more often in the introductory or concluding sections on Southern Europe, the sections on the four countries of the Southern Cone of Latin America, and, particularly, in the third part of the work dealing with Eastern Europe, the USSR and the Baltics. Sometimes we turned to a device I took from Georg Simmel's *Soziologie, Exkurse* on a particular theoretical problem. Each of us brought to the work an intimate knowledge of a number of countries, but in the rewriting and discussions of our draft, new ideas popped up. We should have kept notes on how it happened.

We never seemed able to finish the book. There were many notes left in folders, drafts we ended up not incorporating, problems not covered that our critics will miss. Al fortunately put some limits on my drive to include more themes and more countries. I wish I had written a chapter on the collapse of the GDR and the Unification and the legacies of the past, another on South Korea – its transition I had followed – and one on Bolivia, a country that against many odds, and the expectations of many scholars, has made a successful transition. The theme of failed transitions was left out, but my collaboration with Houchang Chehabi on a book on sultanistic regimes and the papers of several contributors to that volume will partly fill that gap.

At the start of the transition I wrote a paper on time and politics (1986b). One of the issues, raised by the Portuguese and other transitions, was the role of provisional governments and the temptation they feel to delay elections in order to carry out social and political change. The problem of who shall rule in the course of transition and the consequences of one or another choice interested Yossi Shain, another former student, who wrote a paper on interim governments which we expanded into a co-authored essay in a book of case studies we co-edited (Shain and Linz 1995).

Other interests

The work on transitions and consolidations is leading me to think about types of democracies beyond the 22 studied so well by Lijphart (1984). The differences between democratic nation states and multinational democracies (e.g. Linz 1995c), the unitary and federal states, the whole range of parliamentary regimes, constitutional monarchs and presidents of parliamentary republics, are among the themes I wish to explore, as well as the even more complex issue of the quality of democracy.

My growing interest in types of democracies is interfering with another long-term project of a comparative study on religion and politics: patterns in all the religious traditions and all the types of regimes, in modern times. A very Weberian project! I have written a number of essays on religion and politics in Spain and I have been teaching regularly a course on the subject (cf. 1993b, 1995a). The interest in religion relates to my excitement about non-western civilizations which has lured me to Asia. A visit to Ise-Shima, the Yasukuni and the Meiji shrines makes it easier to understand state Shinto.

An important part of my work deals with nationalism. In 1970, Stein Rokkan invited me to a conference in Cérisy-la-Salle on state- and nation-building (Linz 1973a; cf. Eisenstadt and Rokkan 1973), and a year later I attended a meeting on multilingualism in Quebec (Linz 1975b). (Joshua Fishman at the Center for Advanced Study in the Behavorial Sciences had stimulated, early on, my interest in that subject.) This meant that when, in the Spanish transition, the peripheral nationalisms became an important issue, I was ready to study them and in 1979 I wrote a major monograph, *Conflicto en Euskadi* (1986a). Among my papers on nationalism, one entitled 'From Primordialism to Nationalism' (1985b) has received little attention, while I consider it one of my most interesting essays. In addition to papers on multinational Spain (1981d, 1985c, 1989) I recently wrote on state, nation and democracy (cf. 1993c, 1995b), a theme that would become central in the book with Stepan on transitions and consolidations. This trajectory shows the convergence of a mentor and friend (Stein Rokkan) with a real political problem (the Spanish transition from a unitary to a multinational state), institutional support for a large survey study and, with change in Eastern Europe and the former USSR, a timely interest.

I have had a continuing interest in political parties since 1949, when I reviewed works on French electoral geography and met André Siegfried in Madrid. In the 1950s I co-authored 'The Psychology of Voting' (Lipset *et al.* 1954), I also co-authored, with S.M. Lipset, *The Social Bases of Political Diversity in Western Democracies* (1956) and wrote my dissertation *The Social Bases of West German Politics* (1963). Lipset and Rokkan asked me to contribute the chapter 'The Party System of Spain: Past and Future' (1967); there was no present then. This essay led to some misunderstanding since, on the basis of the social structure of Spain and the patterns of political behaviour of Italians, I went out on a limb making a prediction of the vote for different parties in the future. In 1977, Christian Democracy, which in the early 1960s seemed about to become a major force, did not appear on the scene – Vaticanum II had happened in the meantime – although the votes I predicted for it went to a centre party (*Unión de Centro Democrático*) that occupied its space. I have continued working on parties and elections (Linz and Montero 1986c) and wrote an introduction (published in Italian) for Robert Michels's *Sociology of Political Parties* which explored the intellectual-political biography of the classic but also allowed me to think about democracy (1966a). More recently, I helped to organize a conference on political parties and guess that I might continue working on the contradictory expectations of citizens about parties, which explain the criticism of parties and politicians.

My relation to Latin American studies is a strange one. In the early 1960s there was an offer of a grant to become a Latin Americanist, but I was set on working on Spain and Europe. When a new programme was started at Columbia and I was asked to teach in it, I called the seminar Authoritarian Regimes in Hispanic Societies and, with the exception of Spain and Portugal, students knew more about specific countries than I did. I could only provide them with a broader theoretical framework and methodological approaches. Many became the leaders in the field; they contributed to a new perspective that looked at Mexico as an authoritarian regime, and drew me into their network. I ended up writing on Brazil, following events in Uruguay, Brazil and Chile (1973b). My book *The Failure of Presidential Democracy* (1994) reflects that involvement, which also led to an exciting experience working with others on a reform of the Bolivian Constitution, to frequent travels to the region and the direction of many excellent dissertations.

I always had an interest in history and, like the older Schumpeter, sometimes feel that I should perhaps have become an historian (I was for one semester an associate professor of history at Stanford, where I conducted a faculty seminar). Not only is there a historical dimension in my work, but I have written a paper on quantitative sources in Spanish history (1972a), an essay on tradition and modernity in Spain (1977b) and a contribution to a collective history of Spain (1995b) which now I am committed to expanding into a book. Some critics have noted the overly historical, descriptive, chronological, component in some of my theoretical efforts as weakening the more systematic theoretical dimension. I plead guilty but unreformed because I strongly believe in the historicity of macro-political-social phenomena: they take place in a unique historical time that will not be repeated. Even if, as a political scientist or sociologist, one has to abstract, select from the myriad of facts, the first step is to know '*wie es eigentlich gewesen*' (to use the phrase of Leopold von Ranke); chronology matters when one pursues causation; 'latent functions' discovered by the analyst are not 'manifest' when the actors pursued other goals and when there is no proof that their actions were motivated by those inferred functions. A historical sensitivity can keep one honest with reality. One of my rewards has been to serve on the editorial board of history journals. Two leading historians have dedicated books to me.

The excitement of survey research

Survey research has been central to my intellectual work: first, my dissertation on German politics (based on secondary analysis), then a youth survey, which was the first Spanish national sample survey in Spain, in 1959–60, the study of entrepreneurs (1960), a monograph on Andalusian rural élites (1966–67), large-scale public opinion studies in 1977 on the transition to democracy, a study of Basque nationalism in 1979, participation in the 1982 Spanish election study (Linz and Montero 1986c), a youth survey focusing on multilingual and multinational Spain (1985a), a study of economic mentalities (Linz 1988), and the participation in the construction of the questionnaire of the European Values study. The reward was the presidency of WAPOR (World Association for Public Opinion Research) and the Helen Dinnerman prize. It is impossible to summarize how much I have learned from those data, even from conducting interviews, about social structure and politics, about Franco's Spain, democratic transitions and nationalism, nor the pleasure I find when in their research others use questions I designed (often not knowing their history). I see the formulating of a questionnaire as an exercise in what Max Weber meant by *verstehen* since it requires that one places oneself in the mind of all possible social actors – the respondents – and also in what Merton taught me about moving from theoretical concepts to indicators and from 'facts' to theorizing. To move from Parsons or Tocqueville to social reality of Andalusian or Spanish society is an exciting enterprise. My participation in the founding of DATA, a private survey research organization in Madrid, has made possible much of this research, which always requires many collaborators, particularly Manuel Gómez-Reino, Francisco A. Orizo and Darío Vila.

I have had only a limited interest in methodology, although in collaboration with Amando de Miguel I wrote the paper 'Within Nation Differences and Comparisons: The Eight Spains' (1966c), arguing for combining inter- and intra-nation comparisons, and another on the usefulness of combing survey and ecological analysis (1969). I was presenting the paper at a meeting organized by Mattei Dogan when a friend brought me the relevant tables which I had a chance to look at while I was talking. They fitted my argument: in an incident with the police the feeling of being treated equally, rather than better or worse, in seven occupational groups varied with the level of economic development (high, medium or low income per capita) of the province of residence. Economic development clearly contributed to a sense of equality (also to greater salience of universalistic achievement values versus particularism or luck).

Style of work

I have seen the area of my work as located in an attribute space – to use the expression of Paul Lazarsfeld – created by the intersection of two axes with the different arenas and institutions of social life: politics, the economy, religion, the military, culture and language, the intellectuals, with each of the intersections offering the opportunity for *Wechselwirkungen* (mutual interactions) deserving attention. Thus I have worked on business and politics, religion and politics, language and politics – and specifically on nationalism. We would not only deal with types of regimes, totalitarian, post-totalitarian, authoritarian, sultanistic, democratic, and religion in general, but their relation to the different religious traditions: Catholic, Protestant, Islam, Buddhism, Shinto and Hinduism. No one can fill all the boxes, but awareness of that multi-dimensionality seems to me essential to locate our work in comparative perspective.

My dual identity as an American professor and a Spanish citizen and intellectual is reflected in a split scholarly personality and publication record. In America, where interest in Spain *per se* is limited, I became a comparativist although my thinking was stimulated by the case of Spain. On the other hand, doing research in Spain, with Spanish funding, in publications for a Spanish audience, I could indulge in detailed analysis that I could not have published for an international readership. As a result, my Spanish writings are largely unknown to my colleagues in the United States. This makes one aware of the limits to the scholarly community of comparativists imposed by language barriers.

One peculiarity of my work is that I am almost always working and writing simultaneously on several major pieces and projects, largely due to commitments made often as the result of international conferences with editors of collective works (which get postponed as new problems come to the fore). So in the academic year at the Institute for Advanced Study in Princeton, I was finishing revisions of the *Breakdown* book, writing an essay on the comparative study of fascist movements and the book-length chapter on totalitarian and authoritarian regimes – a somewhat stressful way to work, but one in which intersecting themes can be understood better (and which makes it also possible to circumvent the space limitations imposed by different publishing programmes). Something similar has happened with *The Breakdown of Democratic Regimes* (Linz 1978a) and *The Failure of Presidentialism* (Linz and Valenzuela 1994). The central idea of the *Presidentialism* book had emerged as an *Exkars* in the *Breakdown* book, the only section without footnotes because it was written while correcting galleys.

The analysis by Lewis Coser (1965) of the circumstances under which Simmel moved from writing books and scholarly papers to essays for a cultivated audience, makes me think about the format of my writings. I have written few books in English and have not published in refereed journals. Why is this? My papers (at meetings) are too long for the American professional journals (although acceptable to Spanish or Italian journals). Moreover, generally the organizers of the meetings were interested in including them in collective volumes. On the other hand, to write a book on some of the subjects I have worked on would have required including much background material on which I would not have been original, reducing space dealing with a specific aspect, in addition to having to submit a fully edited English text for the customary review process. After all, English is only my third language. How much easier to write a long chapter for collective works at the invitation of editors, friends and colleagues who would take care of the publication process. Some, like the editors of the *Handbook of Political Science*, were willing to include a book-length chapter. I have almost always written with a prior assurance of publication. This format of my work means a dispersion, apparent discontinuity, not pursuing all the aspects I would have wished, but it has served me well. I have to confess that I have written papers for meetings to satisfy my love for travel and to know different cultures. Thus a paper on the sociology of intellectuals in sixteenth- and seventeenth-century Spain – which I look forward to pursuing for other centuries – was the result of the wish to visit Jerusalem and Istanbul (1972b).

My work has often been in collaboration with colleagues, starting with S.M. Lipset, and former students too numerous to mention. My wife Rocío de Terán has played a decisive role in my efforts; as a critical reader, research assistant, editor and translator, and as a co-author in my research on the social history of Spain 1930–80. Without her many of my writings would never have been completed and published. One of the most gratifying activities has been the directing of dissertations – often a prolongation of my own interests – on a wide range of subjects. I have directed some fifty theses, most of them published, covering problems in 29 countries in four continents.

Since I am as excited as ever about my work and do not know exactly where the conjunction between interests and opportunities will take me, it makes no sense to end with a rounded conclusion. I don't mind loose ends. I shall keep working, learning new things, and enjoying it.

11 Amateurs into professionals

Jean Blondel

EUROPEAN UNIVERSITY INSTITUTE

Early years

I find it extremely difficult to write an autobiographical note, having always been disinclined to introspection or to the connection of origins and past events to what happened to me in later life. I am also rather unsure about the importance of most aspects of my career. I really do not know why I came to be interested in politics and political science: certainly my family was not inclined in this direction. I also wonder, and the point has sometimes been raised with me, how much the education I had at a Jesuit school in Paris influenced the way I have looked at problems or organized my life.

For these reasons, I prefer to pass very briefly over my early life and merely note that, after the Jesuits and a time at a *lycée*, I went to the Paris Institute of Political Science, the so-called *Sciences-Po*, which does not entirely deserve its name since it is concerned only to a limited extent with what is conventionally regarded as political science in most parts of the world. I then had two years at St Antony's College, in Oxford, writing a thesis on party organizations in the town of Reading, and a year in Manchester, as a graduate student working on local politics. I was to go back to France to prepare for a teaching career, but I had the good fortune to be appointed in 1958 by S.E. Finer as assistant lecturer at the then University College of North Staffordshire, now the University of Keele. I was 29 when I had my first job. My joy was intense, both to have a job at all and to have a post in a country where the structure of universities was and still is far better than almost anywhere in Europe and where political science was and still is better recognized than in most other European countries.

I will make only two further remarks about my early years. The first is that I had the chance to obtain a scholarship to go to Brazil, in the summer of 1952, when I was at *Sciences-Po*, and undertake a study of electoral behaviour in the northern State of Paraiba. This was a great opportunity, but there was no competition: I was the only candidate for that scholarship, among perhaps the thirty or so students who had been told of the opportunity by Jean Touchard, then Secretary General of *Sciences-Po*. I have tended to conclude, perhaps somewhat unfairly, that this lack of competition showed there was too little curiosity about the world among too many. I unquestionably gained enormously from the visit: I acquired concrete knowledge of Latin America and my interest in the subject has remained large, I believe as a result.

The second remark I wish to make about the period is related. It was often said to me that it was surprising that a Frenchman should have wanted to make a career in Britain. I personally never viewed such a move as exceptional or remarkable: it seemed to me normal to go and work where one would be best able to achieve what one wanted to achieve. I know how much I benefited from the change of environment, a point to which I will return later.

I would like to concentrate here on three aspects of my career and work. The first is the build-up of the Essex Department of Government, and in particular the emphasis on graduate training. I started the Department in 1964, chaired it for four years, and remained a member of it up to 1983. The second aspect relates to the European Consortium of Political Research and to the reasons which led to the setting up of that organization, which I founded with seven Western European colleagues in 1969 and of which I was Executive Director up to 1978. The third aspect concerns my endeavour to develop comparative government on both an empirical and a general basis, although some of my work at Florence has been rather more area-based.

Essex and the 'Americanization' of European political science: the endeavour to bring about systematic training

Two opportunities presented themselves almost simultaneously in 1962. I was offered a fellowship by the American Council of Learned Societies to study in the United States: this award enabled me to spend a year at Yale, which, with Bob Dahl, Bob Lane, Karl Deutsch, Dave Barber, and many others, was then by far the most exciting all-round Political Science Department in America, while Michigan was primarily the 'Mecca' of electoral behaviour analysis. At the same time, I was offered the position of founding Professor of Government at the University of Essex, an institution due to open in 1964. The combination of these two opportunities had a major impact on the part I was able to play in the development of political science in Europe, an occurrence which suggest to me that 'chance' or 'luck' are essential, but that opportunities must also be seized.

The combination of my American fellowship and of the Essex post was crucial. The first position enabled me to see how far superior American political science was to European political science – I said this then, have said it since, and continue to say it now. The second enabled me to believe, partly exaggeratedly but also in part correctly, that I could significantly help to improve the state of the discipline in Europe, as I was given almost complete freedom at Essex to shape and develop the new Department.

There are four characteristics which render American political science superior to European, despite substantial advance in Europe (and the European Consortium for Political Research also has some relevance here). The first of these characteristics is size: the American political science profession is large: the American Political Science Association has about twenty thousand members; Britain, with over a fifth of the population of America, has *less than one-twentieth* of the number of political scientists, judging by the membership of the British Political Studies Association. Yet Britain is one of the European countries in which political science flourishes most. Let us not shame French or Italian readers by mentioning the numbers of their political scientists! Size is obviously critical, as it renders more debates, more currents, more groupings possible.

Second, there is a profound belief in America in the value and role of political science, while in Europe there is often worry and sometimes defeatism about the discipline. The Oakeshottian view according to which there is not much if anything we can do to advise and help politicians does not carry much weight, if any, in the United States. This is most fortunate, not just for Americans but for Europeans as well: had the Oakeshottian approach prevailed in the United States, political science in Europe would not have even the small status it has acquired; yet Oakeshott's influence has been highly detrimental to developments in Europe, as it has led to less respect everywhere about our aims and our findings.

Third, American political science is *scientifically*-orientated. There seems to be no complex about this stand, except in remote corners. Why there is so much soul-searching in Europe about the worth of political science investigations is rather mysterious. That those outside the profession should question whether politics can be analysed scientifically is understandable; but it is not clear why someone who chooses to become a political scientist does not believe that he or she can, by working systematically, increase our general understanding of political life. The discovery of 'laws' of politics may be a distant goal: it should none the less be regarded as an aim to pursue.

Fourth, American political science is based on an immense and universal curiosity, a characteristic which is indeed the basis of science in general. Political scientists have to be appreciably more curious than they typically are. This means that the collection of facts has to come, not just before the exegesis of previous texts – an activity for which I see frankly little place in political science, despite the importance that many still give to it – but also before the development of theory. It is just not true that we need theory to amass the facts; on the contrary, we need the facts to be able to even contemplate what the theory might be about. Both the exegesis of texts and the premature building of theory destroy curiosity: they blind us, or at best they make us, like horses, go along well-prepared paths only. What American political scientists have given all of us is a healthy belief in the need to look around us at all political events. Nothing is unimportant; nothing is irrelevant. Every aspect of politics must be examined.

I do not think that I would have appreciated these four points had I not spent a year in America at the time I did. It was because I had seen these 'virtues' flourish in America that I thought it might be possible to implant them in Europe. It was because I had been appointed to Essex and had been given almost a blank cheque there that I thought and still think that, if one could 'Americanize' European political science – beginning with British political science – real progress could be made and made quickly.

These four characteristics of American political science could be summarized in one word: professionalization. And professionalization could only be acquired in one way: by training. The goal was therefore to use the opportunity given by the founding of the Essex department to introduce political science training. America, and Yale in particular, had shown how this could be done. What was needed was not so much to expand or markedly alter undergraduate courses, but to emphasize graduate work and indeed develop a new form of graduate education in political science in Europe. Yale and other American schools showed that this graduate training had to be based on rigorous and systematic teaching.

My appointment at Essex in 1964 turned out to be at the right place at the right moment in this respect. First, that new university had publicly stated that it wished to give a major emphasis to graduate education. Second, this was a time (the early 1960s) when it was widely believed in Britain that the country lagged behind because it had been run by amateurs; better training was needed, as the Fulton Committee was suggesting for the civil service; the Labour Party was even claiming that it would bring about a 'technical revolution'. Third, as part of the same general movement, the Social Science Research Council was set up in Britain: funding for research and training in political science would be more readily available. Fourth, a mechanism to introduce graduate training was found by transforming the British MA from being a degree obtained by thesis only to one in which coursework prevailed. Essex adopted the idea immediately: by early 1965, the Department of Government was calling for applications to a newly set-up MA in Political Behaviour.

This MA was based on the principle that students had to follow two essential components if they were to be trained to undertake research. One was a course in 'empirical theory' – that is to say the examination of the state of the discipline, a subject then little known outside America. The other component was a methods course, some of which was general and 'philosophical', but much of which was designed to provide a grounding in statistics and mathematics. The aim was to break the resistance against quantitative training, a resistance typically coated in rather spurious high-minded language, but often based on the fear of subjects regarded as difficult and abandoned at too early an age. The debate about the extent to which statistical or mathematical techniques should be applied in given types of inquiries should take place *after* these techniques have been studied and *among* those who have studied these techniques, not by scholars whose understanding of what these techniques can give is at best limited, if not non-existent. Thus the aim of the methods course in the MA was to begin to provide researchers with greater statistical and mathematical skills, a move which was indeed much too slow and is still far from complete.

The Essex MA was a success. It attracted many students from Britain and elsewhere: it manifestly contributed towards giving the Department a sizeable reputation quickly. Thus, while the overall achievements in terms of the professionalization of the discipline were more modest than had been hoped – in particular as far as quantitative training was concerned, even at Essex, let alone elsewhere – a change began to occur. Many realized that such a 'professionalization' was a must. The burden of proof, so to speak, is now reversed: systematic political analysis no longer needs to be justified in a markedly sceptical environment. Those who oppose a systematic approach to political analysis are now on the defensive.

The European Consortium for Political Research: a move towards a unified European profession of political scientists

The success of the Essex Department meant that some foreign students began to be attracted to the MA. This opened a window towards political science abroad. I was beginning to be increasingly involved in what was going on on the Continent: I was asked in 1964 to teach a course on Britain at *Sciences-Po* in Paris, my old Alma Mater, and discovered how little was known of developments in Britain there, while most colleagues in Britain knew little about developments in France. Having participated in the first major study of the German elections in 1961, I had come to know Rudolf Wildenmann, who in 1964 was appointed at Mannheim and began building at that university what was to be unquestionably the most flourishing – and 'Americanized' – German political science department. I had known Hans Daalder at Leiden for some time and had become aware of important developments taking place in the Netherlands. Above all, I had come to know Stein Rokkan when I was at Yale, and began to see him frequently in the various seminars and conferences to which I was increasingly invited.

These acquaintances began to provide the basis of a network; but they also showed how pressing was the need to build links which would be regular and open to all, not sporadic and enjoyed only by a few. Moreover, greater contacts would gradually unite European political science and make it stronger.

The pieces of the jigsaw were coming together. In the second half of the 1960s, Michigan came to play a major part, not just on the American but also on the European scene, thanks especially to Warren Miller, as well as to Don Stokes. Michigan had become the 'Mecca' of electoral behaviour, in large part because of the impact of the *American Voter*, written by the 'Four Musketeers' (Campbell, Converse, Miller and Stokes) and published in 1960 (1960 being a vintage year for political science). Yet electoral analysis could not flourish without a large infrastructure and good training. Warren Miller saw that nothing would achieve such a training better than a programme of yearly summer schools; but summer schools are expensive and need substantial funding: Warren Miller thus invented a wholly new structure based on Michigan but associating others to Michigan, the Inter-university Consortium for Social and Political Research (ICSPR), in which *departments*, not individuals, were involved in a co-operative manner. Thus money could be obtained regularly, as the members were institutions, while scholars across the United States who were quantitatively inclined would become the missionaries of the new structure: they would put pressure on their departments to join and would form all over the country a kind of Michigan fan club.

Warren Miller also extended his work to Europe in order to develop electoral studies: he had built contacts in Sweden in particular, but also in Britain, the Netherlands, Germany and Switzerland, while Phil Converse had links with a French political scientist. A network was created in this way: this was a network to which Stein Rokkan also belonged, as Rokkan was a globe-trotter who, in the manner of a medieval monk, moved from one place of learning to another to 'bring about the word'. Warren Miller's European activities also meant that some European departments were beginning to come under the Michigan umbrella: the ICPR structure was not exclusively American and, although the membership fee was substantial, a few European departments joined especially in order to send some of their staff and students to summer schools.

The situation at the end of the 1960s was therefore becoming ripe for the setting up of a Europe-wide structure. Good fortune was once more to help, in the form of a representative of the Ford Foundation, Peter de Janosi, who was then 'stationed' in London to see how the Foundation could strengthen European social science. Peter de Janosi had heard of Essex's early successes: he visited the institution. The move which led eventually to the setting up of the European Consortium for Political Research (ECPR) in 1970 was started by a conversation I had a year or so earlier with Peter de Janosi at Essex. I argued that an institution was needed to bring European political scientists closer to each other and train them better in the process: to achieve these goals, the Michigan model of co-operation within a Consortium seemed the right solution. Money was needed for such a development, however. Indeed, without the extremely generous grant of the Foundation (over a quarter of a million dollars) the ECPR would never have been born.

Peter de Janosi and the Ford Foundation not only provided the money for the early development of the ECPR: they nursed its preparation. A group of political scientists had to be found who would be the 'Founding Fathers' of the organization. These had to be relatively well-known, be open to a common move towards at least the modernization of European political science, be in charge of departments in which substantial training and research took place, and be geographically spread so as to cover Western Europe reasonably well (Eastern Europe could not of course be involved then in a political science operation). Stein Rokkan and I worked on a preliminary draft of the project. We invited, in order to start the new venture, six other scholars: Norman Chester, then Warden of Nuffield College, Oxford; Richard Rose, of Strathclyde in Glasgow; Rudolf Wildenmann, of Mannheim; Hans Daalder, of Leiden; Serge Hurtig, who subsequently became Secretary General of the Paris Institute of Political Science on the death of Jean Touchard; and Jörgen Westerståhl, of Göteborg, whose department had had close contacts with Michigan and who had directed a large co-operative local government study in Sweden.

European political scientists were not accustomed to working together at the time, however, not even those among them who knew each other a little. There were disagreements about substance, as not all the eight felt equally strongly that there was a need to 'modernize' or 'Americanize' European political science: there were therefore differing views about the main goals of the organization and about the key activities it would have to undertake. There was agreement about the formula of a co-operative Consortium, as the only practical way of achieving results and collecting substantial sums of money, but there were differences about the case of expanding the membership rapidly: the smaller the group, the greater the share each participating institution would receive of the funds which Ford was about to grant.

Thus the Ford Foundation and Peter de Janosi in particular, as well as Marshall Robinson, had to nurse the project during its entire preparatory phase. Both Stein Rokkan and I were in North America during the academic year 1969–70. I was at Carleton University in Ottawa and Stein Rokkan at Yale. This made it easier to progress. The founders gradually came to an agreement which recognized that there had to be diversity: this helped to attract more member-institutions despite what seemed to be an extremely high annual subscription of 1000 US dollars. The key part played by the Ford Foundation justifies entirely the fact that it was in New York City, in the magnificent glass Foundation building, that the European Consortium was born, in the late spring of 1970. Only Americans, with their funds, but also with their skills in research management, could bring together a 'representative' body of European political scientists.

The final agreement included a provisional constitution for the ECPR, which required that a general meeting should take place within three years: the 'Founding

Fathers' would have to submit themselves for election at that point if they wished to remain on the executive committee. Stein Rokkan was to be Chairman and I was to be Executive Director; I would be helped by what was described as 'Central Services', to be located at Essex. The activities of the ECPR were listed: these were to be workshops, summer schools, essentially in data analysis, on the Michigan model, a journal, a data information service, and a regular newsletter. The newsletter was to provide information to members about political science activities in Europe; it would be published by the Central Services at Essex. The data information service was Stein Rokkan's baby. It was to be – and still is – located at Bergen; it has provided extremely useful information not normally disseminated elsewhere. The journal, the *European Journal of Political Research*, was to be a real advance for the European profession. Its beginnings were naturally difficult: yet its first editor, Arend Lijphart, who was then Professor of International Relations at Leiden, succeeded in getting the project off the ground. By the 1980s, the journal had attracted enough scholars from both Europe and America to write major articles that it had become one of the leading outlets for the profession.

The summer schools in data analysis and increasingly the workshops have been the key features of the ECPR. A summer school had taken place at Essex during two successive years, but funds were scarce. A permanent summer school in data analysis was of crucial importance. It was the quickest and indeed the only realistic way to provide the kind of methodological training which was probably even more necessary on the European plane than on the British plane, as only a small number of teachers and students could be subsidized to go to Michigan. The professionalization of the discipline depended on the existence of a regular arrangement for data analysis training: the Consortium provided the solution.

The scheme which was adopted broadly followed the Michigan model, although it was made less demanding, perhaps unfortunately. Warren Miller and his team generously helped the school in the early years with staff and materials. The suggestion was made by some early on that the school might rotate among ECPR institutions, but the base had to be the same if the programme was to flourish. The summer school remained located at Essex. It flourished; it was expensive, but rendered dividends, not only in terms of specific training but because it enabled networks of scholars to be set up.

The most important activity of the ECPR is probably now constituted by the workshops, however. Praise for this development has to go entirely to Rudolf Wildenmann, as it was he who, in 1973, proposed to launch and to finance the first 'Joint Sessions of Workshops'. The idea of having 'workshops' had been from the outset one of the main goals of the 'Founding Fathers'. The concept of the conference was rejected as this formula does not enable those who attend to participate fully. The mode which was adopted was that of the small workshop, whose numbers were to be limited to no more than twenty, everyone having to present a paper which was to be discussed in the course of a four-day session.

The realization of the idea was difficult, as funds were too scarce and organizational initiatives too few to launch more than one or two workshops a year. At such a rate, the majority of scholars in member institutions would never be able to participate. The proposal made by Rudolf Wildenmann in 1973 to hold 'Joint Sessions' was therefore crucial: the principle was kept, but costs could be reduced by holding workshops in parallel; moreover the 'Joint Sessions' added the opportunity for a variety of other links to develop, as occurs normally during conferences. By having invented the 'Joint Sessions' (and indeed later by having invented, on a somewhat similar model, the Research Sessions), Rudolf Wildenmann ensured that most European political scientists could recognize the ECPR as their home. The move clearly boosted the demand for membership: even small departments found it difficult to resist internal demands to find the funds required to join the Consortium.

The ECPR has thus played a key part in the Europeanization of political science; it has also played a key part in professionalizing it. Yet it did not achieve all the goals which some founders at least had in mind, those who wished European political science to become, if not first, at least a very close second. To an extent, the ECPR has become an organization like any other, perhaps because of its very success. Warren Miller's view was that the ECPR should include like-minded political science departments only. I did not agree, as this would have kept the organization small and as, therefore, the ECPR would not have been able to fulfil its fundamental role, which was to professionalize and unify political science in a geographical area which was culturally – and linguistically – very diverse. Yet the very large growth of the organization (to 150 member departments or more) has meant, not just a dilution of this 'missionary role', but a certain bureaucratization. The ECPR sometimes floats above the various national political science schools of thought instead of helping them to merge or confront each other. So long as the organization is lively and innovative in its activities, it provides many other benefits, however. So far, there is no reason to believe that the ECPR will not remain lively and innovative for many years to come.

Comparative government: the effort to develop an empirical and general approach

Meanwhile, having a free hand at Essex in the second half of the 1960s was giving me the opportunity to work in my field, which was comparative government. I do not know why I became particularly interested in comparative government. Perhaps my move from France to Britain was in part the cause of this interest, as I was forced to reflect continuously on two types of political systems. Yet my emphasis quickly went beyond comparing two systems and came to focus on general comparisons among governments. If one is to look for a specific influence, the one which comes to mind, despite what are regarded by most (including myself) as its many defects, is the volume *The Politics of the Developing Areas* by Gabriel Almond and Jim Coleman, which appeared in that vintage year of 1960.

This volume made an impact on me both by what I thought – and still think – was positive and by what was less satisfactory. The book deserves major praise because it moved comparative government out of the corner in which it had, in effect, been not merely since 'Third World' countries had come on the scene, but, in reality, since Lenin had taken over power in Russia in 1918. As I have said elsewhere, comparative government was previously adapted to countries which practised liberal politics, since it was based on the theory and practice of constitutional government. This basis was potentially universal, but it was narrow: it left no place for non-constitutional systems. These were dismissed, before 1914, as having disappeared or being about to disappear: unfortunately, they returned after World War I. Inter-war texts dealt with the issue by devoting sections to 'dictatorships', but this meant that there was no longer a comprehensive model. What Almond and Coleman did was to change this perspective: they stressed that it was essential to take non-constitutional systems into account and that it was possible to do so. General comparative politics could proceed.

Objections against general comparative government remain voiced in some quarters. Yet comparative government has to be general as this is the only way to give the subject a genuine intellectual base. So long as one merely studies a number of countries, even in detail, the justification can only be on practical grounds. Such a justification is convincing with respect to one's own country: it seems sensible to study Britain if one lives in Britain, as it seems sensible to study Colorado if one lives in Colorado. But the case becomes much less strong if one describes a number of countries in sequence. It is, for instance, difficult to justify the suggestion that British students should study French politics in the context of a comparative government course. One can produce the argument of proximity, but this is not an intellectual argument and in any case Belgium is also close. One can make the case on grounds of importance, but then why not study Germany, let alone Japan or the United States? A 'special subject' on French politics does of course make sense, but it is a special analysis, not comparative government; nor can comparative government be constituted by the successive examination of several countries, typically 'important' ones such as France, Germany, Japan, the United States, the Soviet Union previously, as well as other, more 'exotic' nations, such as Brazil or Nigeria, in order to provide a kind of panorama of political systems. Comparative government analysis must go beyond such descriptions; it cannot be built in the way one puts together a set of beads to make a necklace. However difficult the undertaking and however great the challenge, the only intellectually acceptable answer to the problem raised by comparative government analysis is to follow a general approach. It is the only way to leave the plane of mere descriptions and to move to the plane of explanations.

I worked on the basis of these principles when I began preparing the comparative government course I taught at Essex, a course which eventually led to the publication of my *Introduction to Comparative Government* in 1969. Almond and Coleman had shown that it was possible to adopt a general framework and to locate all political systems within this framework: most of us, if not all of us, owe them a major debt as a result. What was needed was to go beyond the framework and to start amassing the facts. Few facts were available; how to proceed to collect the facts was not altogether clear. The authors seemed to have operated under the illusion – an illusion which may still be widespread among comparative government specialists – that facts are easy to collect and the building of theories and models is not only markedly more important but also appreciably more complex to elaborate. These views are wrong.

The belief that facts are either easy to collect or not terribly important has indeed been a major handicap with which comparative government has had to contend. It probably has two origins. One is probably the desire to be 'scientific', that is to say, to be able to develop in the way economics has done, in turn following physics. This move is premature: we just do not know enough about most aspects of political life to be able to develop useful theories, except in very limited areas. The second origin is less laudable: it stems from the insufficiently recognized and yet wholly unnerving point that facts are extremely difficult to collect in political science. Researchers are therefore naturally impatient when they are confronted with the need to obtain data. Yet the 'astonishing stones of the reality' are there, to use the expression of the twentieth century French poet Jacques Prévert: they cannot be set aside or circumvented.

The word 'astonishing' is indeed relevant here, as progress in comparative government must be based on 'astonishment': this has always been so in science, as Socrates indeed intimated long ago. The facts of government are 'astonishing': they should not be regarded as easily predictable. As comparative government specialists, we must be prepared to look for the unexpected. This is ultimately why the urge to elaborate theories before discovering the facts is at least premature, as to follow such a strategy means to refuse to be 'astonished'. In a deductive context, one is concerned to see whether facts prove or disprove hypotheses: but the reality may be on another plane altogether. To progress, comparative government must discover 'worlds' and 'universes' beyond these hypotheses, 'worlds' and 'universes' which these hypotheses cannot compass. Theory-building has thus to come afterwards, in a second phase. A hypothesis or 'law' may occasionally be found which turns out to be seminal: Downs's law about the tendency of the two parties in two-party systems where there is only one basic cleavage to look remarkably alike has this character, but it is an almost unique example in the field. Indeed, this 'law' has not meant that studies of parties and party systems could be confined to the testing of its applicability. In general, the most serious danger is the temptation to generalize too quickly: much of what is called 'theory-building' has often in reality the characteristics of hasty generalization.

If we are not to make hasty generalizations, we have to have a whole array of data at our disposal. Yet data collection is difficult for a number of reasons. One of these is secrecy, not just in dictatorial regimes, but in liberal democracies as well. Parties, for instance, are typically inclined to hide or falsify their membership figures, while the levels of effective participation of members can only be discovered by extremely long and painstaking exercises. Evidence for this desire for secrecy, or at least for the refusal to be truly open in the political realm, is shown by the absence of international organizations entrusted with the collection of political data while such organizations collect social and economic data. Yet an even greater problem stems from the limited number of political scientists, even in the West, let alone elsewhere. Only very recently have numbers begun to grow. Thus political science cannot progress as rapidly as economics or the natural sciences. It must be accepted by all concerned that comparative government is at a very early point of development and that only by painstaking and long efforts will our knowledge gradually expand.

What specialists of comparative government have to do is first to collect data. Perhaps the best parallel is with botany or zoology in the eighteenth and nineteenth centuries. As in the case of these two disciplines, there are large number of 'plants' and 'animals' in political science: these are groups, parties, governments, legislatures, bureaucracies, armies, courts. The characteristics and the life of these 'bodies' need to be monitored closely and systematically if we are to understand truly how they work. We cannot forecast their workings in advance: we have to be ready to be 'astonished'. Thus Lord Bryce was right when he called for 'facts, facts, facts again', not David Easton, who claimed, rather strangely, in his book *The Political System* (1953), that we suffered from 'hyperfactualism'. He was wrong – it was as if he did not realize (but he is not alone) how little was known in comparative government at the time (and little remains known at the end of the twentieth century despite the advances which have been made).

Thus comparative government has to have strong empirical roots: but it must also be general. It may seem impossible to accomplish both tasks, as we cannot hope to 'discover the facts' of political life all over the globe. Yet the same problem arose in other disciplines: eighteenth century botanists wanted to collect specimens of plants in order gradually to obtain a general knowledge in their field. To say that comparative government must be general does not mean that we must always collect data covering the whole world; it means only that there must not be compartmentalization as if ideas or problems which arise in one part of the world were held, a priori, not to be applicable in other parts. 'Culturalists' seem to hold the view that such compartments exist and that human beings were fundamentally diverse in different parts of the world, although their escape route appears often to be that the environment, in reality, is the cause of this 'fundamental' diversity. Such an approach is merely a hypothesis; it is also unhelpful as it restricts rather than increases the scope for investigation.

Of course, most studies will remain limited in geographical scope in order to be truly empirical: I have myself undertaken work primarily devoted to Western European governments during the decade I have been at Florence, an example being the volume *Governing Together* published in 1993 which I edited jointly with Ferdinand Müller-Rommel. The key point is that such studies can be replicated. In this way, we shall acquire an increasingly greater knowledge of all aspects of political life in all corners of the world.

Conclusion

I stated at the outset that this was not to be an autobiography. I felt it more valuable, if I was to write about my experience, to concentrate on the three aspects of my career which seem likely to have most resonance in the life of other scholars in the discipline of political science. Yet I would like to end by returning to a point which has often been made to me, namely to the fact that I 'decided' to move from France to teach in Britain. Indeed it is not so much the 'decision' itself that I wish to discuss further, but how valuable this move has been to me, in both practical and intellectual terms. The intellectual benefits have been great, in particular by forcing me to raise, and raise continuously, questions of comparison, as the Brazilian journey of a few years previously had already begun to induce me to. These changes of surroundings made me deeply aware of the *relative* character of political life. I am often struck by the narrowness of the horizon, of the framework of many political commentators or even many political scientists: what I call narrowness, perhaps a little unfairly, is the fact that most of those who have not lived for long periods in a country other than 'their own' simply find it conceptually impossible to get out of the structure of thought and of imagery which characterizes that country. Living in another country makes it simply impossible not to feel, at every moment, how correct Pascal's comment was about 'truth on this side of the Pyrenees, error on the other side'.

As an understanding of politics must mean a deep realization that values, rules, modes of behaviour vary from one country to another, indeed often from one region to another, I naturally conclude with the plea that political scientists be prepared, indeed be anxious, to move, not just from one department to another (which many still do not do, and not just in the smaller countries of Europe), but from one country to another:

this is one respect in which I feel that the ECPR has not been successful enough. I am making a plea for such moves as the future of political science depends on the ability of all of us to be 'astonished' by different systems and practices. 'Astonishment' will not come from within, but from without. Let it not be said by those who look at us from outside and perhaps come to judge us that the political scientists of today and tomorrow do not have the capacity or the will to be 'astonished'.

12 The art of writing about politics

Richard Rose

UNIVERSITY OF STRATHCLYDE

I have always wanted to be a writer. The only question was: what to write about? For anyone born in 1933, politics was a natural concern. My first political memory is listening to an eye-witness account of Hitler accepting the French surrender by Marshal Pétain in 1940. I was fortunate in having an ocean rather than a land border or a narrow Channel between my home and Hitler's forces.

Writing is an art, not a science; to be a good writer requires practice and discipline as well as inspiration. For two decades I trained myself to be a writer, turning my hand to everything from news bulletins and television scripts to a four-act play. To be a good writer one must also have something to say: that requires a good education, a wide experience of life, and empathy with the people one is writing about. These skills cannot be got in a few years of postgraduate education. But if one starts early, they can be acquired by the time one becomes a professor of comparative politics.

Learning how to write

My base was an extremely secure home in an extremely secure suburb of St Louis, Missouri. It had been under the French and Spanish flags but never under the British. It had boomed in the 1840s, thus attracting a large number of 1848 German liberals as immigrants. My father's family were South St Louis Dutch (that is, *Deutsch*). My father attended the University of Illinois, doing postgraduate work in engineering, and worked as a research chemist before deciding that a family business suited him better than bureaucracy. Later in life I realized that his interest in how things work is reflected in my curiosity as a social scientist. My mother's mother had been born in Kansas when Indians were around, and my mother was born on a farm in Macon County, Illinois, near where Abraham Lincoln is buried. She went to a small town high school with Harold Lasswell, and then to the University of Illinois, where she met my father. No one in the family had been to Europe or talked about it or even seen the Atlantic Ocean until I went to university.

St Louis was a border city in every sense. It was a slave state that stayed in the Union during the Civil War. T.S. Eliot's uncle had founded Washington University, and our

127

next door neighbours were friends of the Prufrocks. The city had a great many poor Southern whites and blacks. The school systems of the metropolitan area reflected classic Lipset/Rokkan divisions. Race was the primary division. Second came religion: the Catholic church financed a separate school system and so did the Lutherans. Class came a weak third. My suburb also had an urban/rural division.

When I was eight years old my father bought a typewriter and I soon taught myself to type. My first interest was baseball, and I spent many hours transcribing baseball statistics from books. I followed baseball news in the St Louis *Post-Dispatch*, founded by Joseph Pulitzer, the pioneer of investigative journalism. I decided to become a reporter on the *Post-Dispatch*. Crooked teeth required regular trips to an orthodontist with an office across the street from the local library; by the age of ten I had started reading H.L. Mencken, a critic and etymologist who stood for culture with a capital K and, as my introduction to England, Sherlock Holmes.

School was a problem for me, and for my teachers too. The philosophy of the school system was life adjustment, which meant adjusting advanced pupils downwards. To have something to do, I would take a book to school; my worst day in elementary school was the day I left my book at home. The teachers were hardly inspiring and some were fellow travellers, voting for Henry Wallace for President in 1948. To annoy my teachers, I read memoirs of anti-communist refugees, which complemented wartime books about Nazi atrocities. To escape the boredom of school, at the age of 14 I thought about entering the University of Chicago, which then admitted youths mired in the wasteland of American secondary school. However, the syllabus was dogmatic, requiring every student to read Mortimer Adler's choice of 100 great books. I preferred to stay home reading authors whose names were picked up from Mencken, such as Ibsen and O'Neill, plus classic American and English novelists.

Secondary school offered sophisticated classmates; my friends have gone on to write books about subjects as varied as Malcolm X, Janis Joplin and Henry James. We read Freud not Marx. By the time I was 16 teachers were encouraging me to stay away from class. Doing make-up on the school paper with printing craftsmen working in hot metal was good discipline in writing to fit a space. I was also very active in the school's public speaking programme.

Local radio stations introduced me to music. As a small boy I liked hillbilly music played by the local Jesuit station; the local Lutheran station played Bach, Beethoven and Brahms; and one white and one black station played jazz. For eight years I stood in the back of the school band and orchestra, playing the drums. This gave me a good ear for orchestrating musical instruments, a skill parallel to creating effects with words. At the age of 16 I got a driver's licence that enabled me to roam the city, listening to riverboat musicians and touring jazz stars. I will always remember seeing Charlie Parker play anguished solos at Jazz at the Philharmonic concerts and then sweat profusely on the sidelines in mute anguish. From my early upbringing I gained a lifelong love of music and a loathing of discrimination on grounds of race and religion.

The Democratic Party dominated the city. It was liberal in the German sense; there is a statue to Schiller in front of City Hall. No one spoke much about what happened in Washington, twenty hours away by train. When Harry Truman became President on the death of Franklin D. Roosevelt in 1945, Missouri politics and cronies moved onto the national stage. I am a Truman Democrat; the longer I write about the presidency the better he looks.

The education of a comparativist

I entered Johns Hopkins University in Baltimore in 1951. Hopkins allowed undergraduates to work for a degree at their own speed, and I wanted to learn as much as I could as fast as I could. Unlike the University of Chicago, Hopkins allowed students to select courses according to their own taste. To become a newspaper reporter I reckoned a good general education was necessary; on my application form I said that I wanted to study the humanities, and did so with lasting benefit.

Johns Hopkins in my day still evidenced its foundation as the first American research university, begun in 1876 on the German model. Its faculty had many refugees too. The Ph.D was the degree to which a student was meant to aspire, and there were relatively few undergraduates. The small size threw undergraduates into contact with graduate students and senior professors. In freshman orientation week my section was assigned as a speaker Professor Leo Spitzer, a great philologist, who knew more than two dozen languages and looked like Einstein. Spitzer read a paper about stylistics in Romanian poetry. I realized with wonder and pleasure that I had finally found a place of learning.

Hopkins taught on the historical method, thus giving me an excellent introduction to Europe in time and space. I did some architectural history, art history and history of music as well as standard topics. The stock of knowledge gained there has been of great practical use to me ever since, whether searching for a hotel in a distant country or for an apt example in comparative analysis. At that time, Hopkins had a Department of Writing, Speech and Drama; that was my major. Since I did not have the urge to write a novel or a play, I spent two years reading plays, starting with the Greeks and ending up with Arthur Miller and Tennessee Williams.

The literature seminars mixed American and European authors; I was particularly struck by Eliot, Proust, Kafka and William Faulkner. Among many images that captured my imagination was Proust's depiction of Bergotte transcending mortality by writing books. Aesthetic theories, starting with Aristotle and Longinus, were an integral part of my undergraduate education. The Greeks, especially Aeschylus and Sophocles, made a lasting impact; closer in space and time was William Faulkner's evocation of Yoknapatawpha County, Mississippi. For 'comic' relief, I read Chekhov. I wrote two BA dissertations. One contrasted the meaning of time in the novels of Marcel Proust and Thomas Wolfe, as Proust wrote about *Le Temps Retrouvé*, whereas Wolfe saw time as a river always surging forward. Concern with time keeps cropping up in my work (see e.g. Rose and Davies 1994). My second dissertation contrasted the evolution of T.S. Eliot from the disintegration of 'The Love Song of J. Alfred Prufrock' and 'The Waste-land' to the integration of *Four Quartets* with the evolution of jazz from the integration of New Orleans to the atonalities of bebop. I learned the importance of proportion from Jelly Roll Morton; his principle was, 'If you have half a glass of water, you can go up or down'.

If social scientists think about form, it is usually in terms of mathematics and closed deductive theories. To me, form is aesthetic, a creative discovery of what is behind or beneath what we see and count. It is the composition of objects of different qualities in a relationship that feels right in the hands of the maker. Issues raised in architecture – does form follow function or function follow form? – are relevant to writing about politics too.

Exploring the East Coast was an important part of my undergraduate education too. By trying all the newspaper offices in the phone book, I became a stringer for the Baltimore office of United Press, and covered my first murder trial at the age of 19. Washington was only an hour away. It was then a sleepy Southern town, but with plenty to see. I would walk out of Union Station and work my way westward, ending the day at the Lincoln or Jefferson Memorials, where the words chiselled on stone are as moving as anything I have ever read. New York City was the big magnet, for it had theatre, opera, museums, and jazz. I would go there to see at least one play a day and sometimes two on matinee days. In January 1953 I took a Greyhound bus trip south to New Orleans and Charleston. This gave me a better feel for the Deep South, which previously I had only read about. It felt like it read.

The Korean War was important, for I was of military service age, and initially expected to be in Korea rather than Baltimore. In my freshman year a law was enacted giving students temporary draft deferment on the basis of an intelligence test. My temporary deferment was later made permanent because of a knee injury acquired playing high school football. McCarthyism was especially important at Hopkins, for Alger Hiss was a Hopkins graduate and recipient of an honorary degree. A faculty member, Owen Lattimore, was indicted for alleged perjury in Congressional testimony. As a liberal in the nineteenth-century sense, I joined the American Civil Liberties Union, but did not became a liberal in the conventional Americans for Democratic Action sense. Among writers on political and social values, Reinhold Niebuhr impressed me most.

My encounter with political science was limited to the great seminars in American Constitutional Law and Jurisprudence of Carl Swisher, who had served in the Justice Department during the New Deal. Swisher was a man of great wisdom; I once naively thought one had to be as wise as he to earn a Ph.D! We took Supreme Court cases seriously, for many issues were open and contentious; for example, the landmark desegregation case, Brown vs. Board of Education, was then pending in the Supreme Court. I can remember being at the Court one Monday in Spring 1953, wondering what the many black lawyers there were looking for. A year later they received what they had long waited for, justice.

An unexpected consequence of voracious reading was that I was awarded a BA after two years of study instead of the conventional four. This posed the problem, what to do next? One of my drama instructors had worked at the British Museum on his thesis, and was full of stories about theatre in London. It sounded even better than New York. Studying abroad might also help me become a foreign correspondent. Hence I applied to the London School of Economics to do an MSc. in international relations. I had no knowledge of England or things English.

Discovering Europe

In September 1953, I sailed for England, thinking I could speak English. My first encounter with a Cockney taught me I was wrong. After Hopkins, the LSE was a shock, for it was then oriented towards undergraduates. I registered to write a thesis about Anglo-American relations, but abandoned my first two supervisors. Fortunately, my third was Robert T. McKenzie. Bob McKenzie was well grounded in the sociological classics; his big books were based on ideas of Michels and Bagehot. He was also worldly-wise about politics and politicians.

England was full of thought-provoking surprises. Rationing was still on and the effects of war were very evident. Many leading politicians came to the LSE to talk to political clubs, and theatre and music were in easy walking distance. There was much political talk in the student common room too. One evening I interrupted a discussion with a stranger to say: 'I have to see Martha Graham; would you like to come with me?' I knew nothing about Martha Graham, about dance or about the girl. Since then I have learned something about all three, as my companion of that occasion has long been my wife.

My guide for travelling around Europe was Sir Banister Fletcher's *A History of Architecture*, a great Victorian compendium that systematically analysed architectural styles across time and space. I walked the streets of London looking at buildings, and hitchhiked to medieval cathedral towns. In the month-long Christmas break I went to Italy; travelling alone meant I was talking to Italians or not at all. The architecture and mosaics of Ravenna opened my eyes to the world of which Constantinople is the capital. This has given me a perspective on European history very different from that taught in the Anglo-American tradition. At Easter I travelled around German-speaking lands before the *Wiederaufbau* had gained momentum. I saw my first Russian troops in Vienna, then under four-power occupation, and celebrated my twenty-first birthday in the only concert hall in Munich with a roof on it.

By chance, I learned in late spring that my MSc. thesis topic was covered in a book about to be published by Leon Epstein (1955). I decided there was no point searching for another topic; my Hopkins grounding made me feel that if ever I wrote a thesis, it should be to get a Ph.D. But at that time newspaper work was my calling. Hence I went back to America to look for a job as a reporter.

Becoming a social scientist

After six months of work in political advertising and public relations, in Spring 1955 I achieved my lifelong ambition of becoming a reporter on the St Louis *Post-Dispatch*, writing about everything from plane crashes to $50 robberies. When not sitting at a typewriter and telephone I covered such beats as police headquarters and the courts. Doing the rounds as a reporter was good training in developing empathy with all kinds of people whom one would not meet in university libraries. Elected politicians received little attention, except when there was a hint of corruption. To supplement my union minimum wage I wrote articles for the *Christian Science Monitor*, *The Reporter* and *The Nation*, and wrote for *The New Leader* for free. I also produced a series of programmes on civil liberties for the local educational television station.

Whereas the traditional academic reads written sources, a reporter creates written sources. The *Post-Dispatch* wasted no time on literary flourishes. The Pulitzer tradition emphasized the importance of knowing how to find information. Two reporters were ex-FBI men, and ten had worked on Pulitzer prize stories. The basic rule is simple: figure out who should know the relevant facts and go straight to the source by telephone, face-to-face, direct observation or careful indirection.

After two and a half years on the *Post-Dispatch* I had a trade in my hands as a general assignments reporter, but was dissatisfied. I had had too much education to enjoy day-to-day reporting and too little to be a scholar. Writing about the rising demand for higher education in Missouri in the years ahead made me realize that I might earn a living in a university. But first I had to get a doctorate. The choice in my mind was between Harvard and Oxford. The latter appealed because all one had to do was write a book-length thesis; it was also cheap and easy to get into. In 1957 I quit my job on the *Post-Dispatch* and headed for Oxford, thinking I was leaving journalism.

Writing and reading at Oxford

When people ask me where I was trained, the answer is, 'I am untrained; I have an Oxford D.Phil.'. The title of the degree emphasizes the Oxford desire to distance itself from German-American scholarship; its success in doing so was still evident in my time (Simpson 1983, pp.75ff). Dons preferred to wear the gown of a person who had been an Oxford undergraduate and some winced when addressed as 'Dr'. I matriculated at Lincoln, a typical undergraduate college founded in 1427. After a year I was elected a student of Nuffield, a postgraduate college; it paid.

My thesis topic reflected a Pulitzer-trained scepticism about what politicians said and did. It examined the contradiction between principles of socialist foreign policy outlined by the Labour Party in opposition and what the Labour Government did in office. The subject gave me an excellent grounding in the sources of British party politics. I derived socialist principles from annual conference debates and pamphlets from the period 1900–1945, and for the period of the Attlee government read through the daily press, *Hansard* and many books and documents. During vacations I worked in the Labour Party library at Transport House. I interviewed members and critics of the government from Attlee to Zilliacus, and ended up an admirer of Ernest Bevin. The standard British working week was then 44 hours, so this was the time that I devoted to my thesis.

My supervisor, Saul Rose of St Antony's College, had been Denis Healey's successor as International Secretary of the Labour Party. He was chary of ideas, but fastidious about the use of words, being literate in four alphabets plus Japanese. This was the heyday of linguistic philosophy. My contemporaries agonized with Wittgenstein and sought freshness with Ayer. While I had no desire to spend all my life pondering imponderables, the analytic approach increased my sensitivity to the traps and strengths of metaphor and allusions. Student plays, Union debates and common room talk gave great scope for making the most of words too.

I completed my D.Phil. after 21 months in the summer of 1959. By coincidence, a general election was due that autumn, and David Butler invited me to go along for the ride as he toured the constituencies. As preparation, I read all the British and American voting studies that had then been written. The biggest impact was made by the appendix of Berelson, Lazarsfeld and McPhee (1954, pp.327–47); it listed propositions about voting derived from American surveys and in principle applicable to Britain. The 1959 election saw the introduction of modern public relations and television techniques into campaigning. I volunteered to write a chapter and ended up as co-author (Butler and Rose 1960). My *Post-Dispatch* training enabled me to obtain accurate figures about spending on campaigning, which became the subject of a House of Commons debate.

Interviewing politicians made me realize that they did not know any more about what made British voters tick than did David Butler and myself. So I went straight to the source, two LSE Ph.Ds who were not academics but directors of public opinion firms, Mark Abrams, and Henry Durant of the Gallup Poll. Each was generous with time and information. Mark Abrams invited me to contribute chapters to a Penguin special, *Must Labour Lose?* (Abrams and Rose 1960). While writing it, I read *The American Voter* (Campbell *et al.* 1960); it made me appreciate how social, psychological and sociological approaches could complement each other. When my proud father offered to buy me the red and blue silk gown of an Oxford D.Phil. I asked instead for some Free Press books (e.g. Merton 1957; Weber 1947; Eulau, Eldersveld and Janowitz 1956). One lucky day the Warden of Nuffield's secretary enquired if I would like to meet a visiting Norwegian; it was Stein Rokkan.

In Autumn 1960, I had a doctorate, a wife and almost two children, but no job. David Butler told me that he did not think I was cut out for an academic career and advised me to go back to journalism. His judgement was supported by Oxford and the LSE. When I applied for posts there, each turned me down. At Manchester W.J.M. Mackenzie thought differently. One morning I opened an envelope with the offer of a job there. I had never studied or taught political science.

'Manchester made me'

I began to learn political science by teaching it as an assistant lecturer in the Department of Government at the University of Manchester in 1961. It was Europe's closest equivalent to the social science faculty of the University of Chicago in the 1930s. The setting was similar, an institution that attracted people who wanted to be professionals rather than dilettantes. The department was extraordinarily stimulating, for each of its ten members was well read, thoughtful and outspoken.

The central influence in the Manchester Department was W.J.M. Mackenzie, a classical philologist by training, a Scot, and a big man in every sense (see Chapman and Potter 1974). His published works give some sense of his wide interests (Mackenzie 1967), but many of his wisest and most memorable comments were scrawled on the margin of a manuscript or dropped in conversation in the hallways of Dover Street. Mackenzie had both depth and directness. A characteristic comment about some policy of government was: 'I can explain it but not justify it'. At Johns Hopkins I learned what scholarship was. From Bill Mackenzie and my colleagues at Manchester, I learned to become a political scientist.

A few months after joining the department Allen Potter asked if I would like to write a book about England for a new comparative politics series being edited by Gabriel Almond; he rightly sensed that he should not accept an invitation to contribute. Before saying yes, I tried applying the analytical framework from Almond and Coleman (1960) to England. The result was an outline better than the conventional Penguin textbook, so I happily signed a Little Brown contract for *Politics in England* (Rose 1964). To write the book I had to read widely across the social sciences. Because there were very few journal articles or books with relevant data, I used my reporter's training to dig out information directly from sources. Two readers on British politics and policy-making were a byproduct.

Bill Mackenzie's marginal comments opened up new directions and warned me off many pitfalls. For example: 'I never thought I would meet anyone who could write English, American and German-American; for god's sake, choose one language and stick to it'. After writing the first edition in American, I translated the book into English for the first London edition. By the 1970s this was no longer necessary. James Douglas, then working in the Conservative Research Department, engaged in an extended dialogue about the circumstances and the extent to which behavioural ideas illuminated politics in England. Gabriel Almond, a man of broad learning and interests (1970, pp.5ff), added a particularly helpful piece of advice: 'Never use culture in the active voice'.

Shortly after I arrived at Manchester, Mackenzie mentioned that once celibacy was abolished at Oxford in the late nineteenth century dons without a private income had turned to freelance journalism to finance a married lifestyle, and added that I might find this useful too. As usual, he was right. *New Society* was founded as a social science weekly in September 1962. Its format was congenial, as the idea for a journal article could be outlined in several thousand words. I also contributed unsigned leaders drawing on my research and political interests, and wrote short observations on the human comedy.

Out of the blue I was invited to become the by-lined Election Correspondent of *The Times* in 1964. This enabled me to meet a number of lobby correspondents of great wisdom and shrewdness who had left school at 14 and, by intelligence, sympathy and skill in writing, had risen to the top (cf. Tunstall 1970). David Wood of *The Times* was an excellent exemplar of that group; he taught me how to 'decode' the hints and allusions in which Cabinet ministers spoke in those days. A Fleet Street by-line and television exposure gave me visibility in British public life, and helped me keep a hand in American politics; as a journalist I covered five American Presidential conventions from 1964 onwards.

Choosing problems

When appointed Professor of Politics at the University of Strathclyde, Glasgow, in 1966, at the age of 33 I had a clear idea of what I wanted to do. One goal was to build a department that combined the best of both worlds, Manchester and Michigan. But I also wanted to continue writing. In England writing about politics usually meant 'contemporary history', an unreflective grubbing of facts or parade of precedents. Real historians were better than that. A second alternative was to choose one topic and stick to it. That sounded boring, abandoning the world of the *Kulturmensch* for what Max and Alfred Weber described as the world of the *Berufs– und Diplom–Mensch* (see Derlien 1991, pp.13ff).

Creating a good book is like diamond-cutting: the point is not how hard you hit the diamond, but how well. In selecting problems my first criterion – 'Make it new' – came from T.S. Eliot's mentor, Ezra Pound, a writer born in Idaho territory five years before it was admitted to the United States. Rudolf Wildenmann re-enforced this outlook in the first seminar I ever gave in Germany. Offered a choice between a polished article or a rough outline of emerging ideas, he said unhesitatingly: 'Give us the new idea' (the talk evolved into Rose and Mossawir 1967). A second rule is: 'Go for bear'. A social science problem requires concepts meaningful beyond a specific context or, in aesthetic terms, metaphors that sign something greater. The world of politics imposes constraints different from the world of art or mathematics, for what is written must not only be pleasing but also true to life. Rose's third law is: 'First, catch your dependent variable'. I try to find problems in life that can be related to problems in books. From Bill Mackenzie I learned to puzzle about what others took for granted or ignored.

Influencing Voters. A Study of Campaign Rationality (Rose 1967) was my first book for which the subject was not given. In the Spring of 1964 David Butler and Tony King urged me to write a book about political campaigning, since I had so many facts in hand. My immediate reaction was negative because so many thoughtless books had been published about the subject. On reflection, I saw this as a challenge to write something that went deeper. Using Robert Merton's (1957) distinction between manifest and latent functions, I produced a different book about campaigning.

After finishing *Politics in England*, I analysed the book to see what chapter was most important yet weakest; the winner was the chapter on legitimacy. Therefore, in 1965 I began a study of a partially legitimate political system, Northern Ireland. At the time friends thought it an odd thing to do; when I stayed with the subject after the gun came out this was thought odd for different reasons. I went to Stanford in its Almond/Verba heyday to get perspective on Northern Ireland. This produced a journal article (Rose 1969) about the dynamics of divided regimes and the draft of a questionnaire that took me eighteen months to write, pilot, rethink and revise. Fortunately, the survey posed the right questions.

I was at the Bogside rising of August 1969, and noted that while the tear-gas thrown at the 1968 Chicago presidential convention was nastier, Irish rocks were harder and more dangerous. The next morning I went into a local bookshop, since blown up, to start reading the history of riot and rebellion in Ireland. I reread Yeats, and realized that while he could be apt, he was also irresponsible. Mrs Boyle's lament at the end of O'Casey's *The Plough and the Stars* offers the ultimate word on Irish politics. The pictures as well as the tables of *Governing Without Consensus. An Irish Perspective* (1971) tell of a uniquely searing experience. The calm indifference of Whitehall to much that has happened there has taught me things that I would rather not have learned (cf. Rose 1976b). Once I went to see Shirley Williams to suggest that Labour might come out for proportional representation in local government elections there. She rejected the idea as politically infeasible. When I pointed out fiercely that people were being killed in Ulster, she said with surprise, 'Why Richard, you care'.

My work on comparative parties and elections was made possible by the Committee on Political Sociology, of which I was the most junior member, and exceptionally, an American in Europe rather than a European in America (cf. Rose 1990). Stein Rokkan's vision was matched by his scholarship and patience. Before meeting Marty Lipset I had already read three of his extraordinary books (1950, 1960; Lipset, Trow and Coleman, 1956). Mattei Dogan knew a lot about countries then very foreign to me (cf. Dogan and Rose 1970). Giovanni Sartori's concern with concept formation was congenial to my interest in words and meaning, while Karl Deutsch was full of immense knowledge and original ideas about how to quantify concepts. My memory of a good dinner would be a meal with Mattei, Karl and Stein, or latterly, reflecting with Juan Linz. The Committee confirmed my commitment to comparison.

Comparison first of all requires concepts. As the author of *Polimetrics*, Ted Gurr, once remarked to me, 'All the best variables are nominal'. Collecting numerical data for its own sake and pinning labels on it afterwards does not increase understanding. A *social* science must be about more than the logical manipulation of concepts in an abstract calculus; otherwise, it is an 'asocial' science, as neo-classical economics has become, a closed system in which society is treated as exogenous. Like Herbert Simon, whose writings I first read in Manchester, I am interested in understanding how societies and institutions actually work.

Whether writing about many countries or a single country, I use both qualitative and quantitative data as appropriate (see Rose 1991a). In *Electoral Behavior* (Rose 1974b), the table of contents names countries but the index is conceptual, so that a reader interested in following the influence of education or age on voting can read the book from back to front. Anyone wanting a synthesis can find it at p. 17, a single table summarizing the relative importance in fifteen countries of Lipset and Rokkan's (1967) cultural and economic cleavages. *The International Almanac of Electoral History* (Mackie and Rose 1974, 1991) required much more conceptualization than is apparent to the user, for we had to decide when free elections started and what constitutes a political party. It also required a great deal of digging for facts. Tom Mackie and I have preferred going back to source across four continents and sixteen languages rather than copy errors already in print. This has produced windfalls paid by other authors for breach of copyright, as people have copied our figures in the mistaken belief that data are spontaneously created and packaged.

My philosophy is to alternate broad comparative analysis and the intensive examination of key questions in a single nation. *The Problem of Party Government* (1974a) was inspired by first-hand knowledge of how members of the 1964 Labour Government were unprepared for the challenge of governing, and watching Conservatives make U-turns after 1970. *Do Parties Make a Difference?* (1984a) combined Pulitzer-trained scepticism and social science concepts and evidence. It also led me to reread Schumpeter (1942), whose answer to the question would have been: yes and no.

The emergence of public policy was very congenial, since I have always believed in joining the world of ideas and the world of practice (cf. Rose 1995b). I was fortunate to come into the field through the social indicators movement, which attracted a diverse number of very bright scholars such as Mancur Olson. Yet I knew that governors had got along for centuries without the theories of academics. To understand what happened when politicians met Ph.Ds, I began research in Washington in the Watergate summer of 1974. Using my reporter's training, within a few weeks I had acquired a large mass of unpublished exchanges between the Executive Office of the President and the agencies about presidential objectives. This was the start of my work on the Presidency (Rose 1976a; Rose and Suleiman 1980; Rose 1991b). It also brought me close to Aaron Wildavsky. His inimitable style not only reflected his Brooklyn upbringing but also a concern with the craft of writing; he could also use his wits and shoe leather to generate profound insights (e.g. Caiden and Wildavsky 1974, pp.i–xviii).

The unexpected 1975 downturn in the world economy created a lot of emotion about 'overloaded government'. Knowing why the gun came out in American politics in 1861 and in Northern Ireland in 1969 I was very sceptical about claims that marginal economic reversals would cause people to revolt. The answer to *Can Government Go Bankrupt?* (Rose and Peters, 1978) was: no, government just gets refinanced. The predicted worst response was *incivisme*. Writing this book taught me a lot of economics. I particularly appreciate its emphasis upon integrating concepts in models. Thinking about overloaded government made me wonder what was a normal load. This led to a major multi-book programme focusing on the question, what grows when government grows? The answer required books about public employment, government organizations, taxation, the role of law in public policy and public expenditure. Theories of big government could not be tested in the land that produced the most theories, the United States, for American government is small compared to such 'un-American' countries as Germany and Sweden (cf. Rose 1991c). In *Understanding Big Government* (Rose 1984b) and other writings I tested concepts across OECD countries.

An invitation from Wolfgang Zapf to spend the autumns of 1988, 1989 and 1990 at the *Wissenschaftszentrum Berlin* enabled me to think about lesson-drawing, a form of applied comparative politics that everyone usually does without thinking. The result was a trilogy of publications (Rose and Wignanek, 1990; Rose 1991d, 1993). Living in Berlin deepened my understanding of things German. Living in Charlottenburg made me conscious of my roots, for the street names – Schiller, Goethe, Ranke and Mommsen – were meaningful at Hopkins and in St Louis too. In the second autumn of our stay, the Wall fell. I keep a piece of the Berlin Wall in my study as a permanent reminder that even bad things have an end.

The fall of the Berlin Wall has faced social scientists everywhere with a people-friendly challenge to rethink many fundamentals about politics, society and economics. It took me a year to figure out what I might do. The idea of writing a book about the democratic reconstruction of Europe came to me at a bus-stop along the Landswehr Canal by the Stauffenberg monument, waiting to go back to a flat by Rathenau Platz. The result, *What Is Europe?* (Rose 1996), recognizes the achievements and the tragedies of European politics in my lifetime.

Communist regimes exemplified Karl Deutsch's point (1963, pp.105ff) that power is the ability to ignore feedback. Their distortion of information and institutions has left a corrupt legacy. The fall of the Wall has given hundreds of millions of people new opportunities, and the spur of necessity to act. Since the Communist Party was no longer around to tell people what to think, I decided to survey how ordinary people were coping with the transformation of political and economic regimes. The underlying concept was satisficing, or rather, escaping from absolute dissatisfaction (cf. Simon, 1979; Rose 1992).

Designing a questionnaire for exceptional circumstances requires listening to what people are talking about, observing what they are doing, and reflecting on its significance. If one does the job well, a questionnaire can turn anecdotes into data. I knew something about the 'rainbow-coloured' economies of communism and the hidden life of internal émigrés (see Katsenelinboigen 1977; Shlapentokh 1989). My motto in working with collaborators in post-communist countries has been: 'I don't want you to ask questions that you think are stupid'. In collaboration with the Paul Lazarsfeld Society, Vienna, led by a practical and non-academic idealist, Dr Heinz Kienzl, I started a programme of annual barometer surveys in post-Communist countries of Central and Eastern Europe and the former Soviet Union (see e.g. Rose and Haerpfer, 1994; Rose and Mishler, 1994). Very generous support from the Austrian Federal Ministry of Science and Research and the Austrian Central Bank makes it possible to repeat surveys each year. By 1996 there were more than 65 nationwide sample surveys in 15 countries. It has also given me an appreciation of Germanic culture *auf italienischer Art*.

I always think several books ahead. The changes that have transformed communist countries also transform its neighbours, most obviously the reunified Germany. The enlargement of the European Union is another visible example (Rose 1995a). So too is the travel log of Richard Rose. Presidential scholars speak of the President as a global leader, but describe his activities as if he lived in a solipsistic world. *The Post-Modern President* (Rose 1991b) treats the United States and its primary leader as part of a system of interdependent countries. Interdependence is relevant in Britain too. I am starting a study of the changing role of the Prime Minister in a changing world; an attention-grabbing title might be: *From First Among Equals to One Among Fifteen*.

Writing as a vocation

Even though I relied for years on journalism for a livelihood or to underwrite scholarly research, I have always regarded writing as a 'calling', living for writing rather than from it (cf. Weber 1948, pp.77ff). A test came in my Manchester days when a London literary agent asked if I would like to write a journalistic book. While the money and the *réclame* would have been welcome, I had no hesitation in declining.

My mind is always active, and when not at a keyboard I carry a pencil and paper to make notes in a shorthand that I taught myself when young. Most days of the year I write something, whether part of a book or journal article, or simply 'finger exercises'. A normal day's writing, which lasts from 10 a.m. to 10 p.m., produces 5,000 to 6,000 words in draft. After turning my mind to other things, I reread what I have written, and rewrite everything several times before publication. Nowadays I treat material in books, journal articles and daily papers as databases. My object is not to read to recycle information but to see what I can add to what is already known.

A lifetime of public speaking makes me write with a specific audience in mind. A lifetime of listening to jazz makes me enjoy improvising ideas for a specific audience and occasion and, as that sixteenth-century communication theorist Sir Philip Sidney advised, to combine delight and instruction. When I give a talk, the chair sometimes remarks with surprise that I enjoy public speaking. It surprises me that people would give talks that inflict suffering on themselves and their audience.

Newspaper work taught me to organize thoughts before phoning or keying in a story, for deadlines allow no time for second thoughts. I always write from an outline. I do not start writing a journal article until I have its end in mind. Titles are chosen with care in order to establish a theme in the mind of both readers and author. Outlining a journal article takes an hour or two; writing a first draft two or three days.

A book is a different challenge, needing an idea that can be elaborated at considerable length. Most books that I write are analytic; a beginning, middle and end are not given by chronology but must be created. Where do such ideas come from? Many start with an observation that something is not quite right, whether in life, in theory, or in a contradiction between the two. James Joyce scholars would describe such an observation as an epiphany. It is helpful if the puzzle can be turned into a question, for when the question is answered, the book is finished. Knowing what is required to answer a question is a job for a trained social scientist. Knowing how to get information can use the skills of a reporter, a historian, a data analyst or a mixture of all three. Knowing how to form materials into a book is a creative task. Disraeli, himself a novelist, viewed the creation of political ideas as requiring the imagination necessary to see 'the angel in the marble' (as quoted in McKenzie and Silver 1968).

A son once posed the riddle: 'What's the most boring sound in the world?' The answer was: 'A tape recording of Dad writing a book'. There is some truth in this, for writing about politics, like politics itself, can be described as the 'strong and slow boring of hard boards' (Weber 1948, p.128). Weber adds that such activity 'takes both passion and perspective'. The work is agreeable to me, for my education is based upon a very strong sense of *Bildung*, and I enjoy writing books to educate myself.

The result is that I can no longer read books for pleasure, nor do I go to the theatre, for plays are also verbal. But everyone needs what Denis Healey calls 'a hinterland'. Like him, I am fortunate in having a hinterland that is aesthetic. I cannot write four bars of music, but I find music fills the space around me when I write. I cannot draw an architectural sketch, but I enjoy exploring buildings. I cannot knot a rug, but I like Islamic arts in many forms and Coptic work, created where four cultures met in space and time.

The motto of *Politics in England*, 'only connect', comes from E.M. Forster's *Howard's End*. The full quotation stresses the need to connect prose and passion, symbolized by the Wilcoxes and the Schlegels. This is not a bad motto for someone who takes politics seriously. As I am more Schlegel than Wilcox, my taste has gravitated to German opera, especially the *Gesamtkunstwerk* of Richard Wagner (Magee 1988, pp.75ff) and the humane operas of Richard Strauss. From time to time my concern with form raises the question: which is more important, words or numbers, art or science? During the physical and moral disintegration of a central European state (Hartmann 1981, pp.253ff), Richard Strauss provided the answer to this question in the transcendent last scene of his last opera, *Capriccio*.

13 Between France and universality: from implicit to explicit comparison

Jack Hayward

ST ANTONY'S COLLEGE, OXFORD

Being born in 1931 in the International Concession in Shanghai, with its independent French Concession, might suggest that from the start I would be inclined towards comparative political economy, with a particular emphasis upon 'exceptional' yet universal France. However, these concerns took a long time to surface and were the result of far less personal influences than the accident of birth. Nevertheless, the cosmopolitan character of Shanghai must have exerted an important influence upon a young British boy of Jewish upbringing who spent the first fourteen years of his life in China, although three-and-a-half of my most mature years were spent interned in a Japanese camp. My stay in China was also marked by a move, at six years old, to Hong Kong for six months during the 1937 Japanese attack on the areas of Shanghai in the vicinity of the International Concession. War was a very present context for my generation, as it has been for most of recorded history, but in our case it had a global rather than parochial dimension.

I arrived in England to catch up on an education deemed to have suffered from the vicissitudes of war. In addition to continuing with the conventional school subjects I also – unusual in the 1940s – studied economics. This was of a rather simple and ideologically-oriented kind. I remember using a textbook called *The Economics of Private Enterprise* from which I derived the view (Thatcherism *avant la lettre*) that the laws of supply and demand were the be-all and end-all of economics. I also learnt about comparative economic advantage and believed as a simple act of rational conviction that free trade at all times and in all circumstances was the only sensible way of avoiding short-sighted, mutually impoverishing attempts to 'beggar one's neighbour'.

An LSE apprenticeship

After completing my pre-university education, I wished to study modern history but war precluded me from doing so through my not having acquired a qualification in Latin at school. This left me with a frustrated interest in history that I was able later in some measure to satisfy. Meanwhile, I therefore chose to study politics, or

'Government' as it was called, at the London School of Economics. My first act on entering that institution's celebrated library in 1949 was to ask for a copy of Keynes's 1926 essay *The End of Laissez-Faire*, of whose existence I had heard with some incredulity. As an ardent adept of *laissez-faire*, I was curious to discover what arguments the famous macro-economist had deployed against its canons. Having read his essay, I emerged with my conviction still intact. It would take several years of studying for the BSc.(Econ.) degree to shake what I took to be a demonstrable scientific basis for understanding economic activity.

At that stage of my academic development, even in an institution entitled, by its Fabian founder Sidney Webb, the London School of Economics and Political Science, it was not thought desirable to study politics in too specialized a way. So, for the first two years all students combined the study of politics and economics in their historical as well as contemporary dimensions. One was entitled to choose two optional subjects and I hesitated between French, Logic and Scientific Method and Sociology. I attended Karl Popper's first lecture in Logic, at which he explained that if one had chosen to do this course in the mistaken belief that it would help one to think more clearly, one should leave. This I did on the spot, for that – in my simple-minded way – was why I had been tempted to do it. Thereafter, I contented myself with reading Popper's *Open Society and its Enemies* (1945) and *The Poverty of Historicism* (1957) and ceased to attend his lectures on logic.

Harold Laski was then still the dominant personage at the LSE, not only in the study of politics but as the institution's intellectually emblematic figure (cf. Dahrendorf 1995, pp.223–32). I had the pleasure of hearing only a few lectures from him, as he died in February 1950, just before he was due to give an address to the inaugural meeting of the Political Studies Association of the UK. What remains in the memory (apart from the arresting manner of his delivery) was his concern to relate the principles he was discussing to current preoccupations, so that sheltered students were made aware that they were studying a subject whose relevance to the harsh world was part of its life's blood. The other memory was his uninhibited expression of his own views, coupled with the remark that as 'an antidote to my poison', students should read views diametrically opposed to his, for which he offered appropriate bibliographical suggestions. What a sound corrective to the dogmatic brand of economic liberalism I had imbibed, from one more renowned for his Marxism than for his authentic liberalism!

My first tutor was Ralph Miliband, Laski's most ardent disciple at the School. He gave me *Parliamentary Government in England* (1938) to read for the first essay he set and we argued inconclusively, as I expressed my refusal to regard this book as the accurate description of British politics it purported to be. I found the older book by Ramsay Muir *How Britain Is Governed* (1930), with all the reservations one might wish to make, or even Walter Bagehot's classic *The English Constitution* (1867), more instructive. What exercised more influence upon me were Laski's early pluralist writings, as well as the chapter in his *A Grammar of Politics* (1925) entitled 'Authority as Federal'. Providing a society- rather than state-based approach to politics, it surfaced later in my concern with interest or pressure groups, which were interpreted within a structured pluralist framework. I remember no course on Comparative Government, although we did study the governments of the USA and France. I found William Pickles's lectures on French political thought and on the Fourth Republic entertaining but they aroused my interest rather than offering the intellectual capacity to study France as a political scientist. Nevertheless, Pickles provided a welcome corrective to the excessively Anglocentric nature of the study of Government at the LSE.

An abortive attempt at a comparative history of an idea

As an undergraduate, I had become interested in the political thought of LSE's first Professor of Sociology, L.T. Hobhouse, especially his little book *Liberalism* (1911). I was working my way towards a liberal socialist standpoint during my undergraduate years from 1949 to 1952, when Britain was shifting in the opposite direction from the reforming postwar Labour Government back to the Conservatives. Having decided that I wanted to continue as a postgraduate student, I sought to discover if there was a sound foundation for the attempt to reconcile individualism and collectivism which I took to be the intellectual basis for the Welfare State that had been created, first by the Liberals after 1906 and then by Labour after 1945. Rather than work directly on those such as William Beveridge who were the most immediate progenitors of the Welfare State, I decided to investigate whether Hobhouse's political philosophy offered its rational justification. His surviving disciple at the School, Morris Ginsberg, on the verge of retirement, did not prove particularly encouraging, so, as I had – significantly – decided that in any case I wished to do a comparative, Franco-British study, I took up a one-year French Government scholarship in 1952 to see whether I could find in France a thinker comparable to Hobhouse who would enable me to ascertain whether the interventionist state had a firm normative foundation. I had come quite a long way from the uncritical enthusiast for classical micro-economics of 1949 but was groping in uncharted territory, unguided by my teachers and haphazardly allowed to go my own way in a fashion that would become much more difficult in the systematically organized world of postgraduate studies forty years later.

My interest in France derived practically from the fact that French was the only foreign language I had learnt at school and university, so that, if I were to undertake comparative work outside the English-speaking world, it was France that beckoned. My studies had already whetted my appetite for what was clearly going to offer some startling contrasts with much that was taken for granted in Britain. So, I initially went to search in the *Bibliothèque Nationale* for a French Hobhouse! My first candidate was the neo-Kantian Charles Renouvier, of a slightly earlier generation. He had affinities with the Englishman who, through the influence of T.H. Green, also borrowed indirectly from Kant. I then discovered the writings of Alfred Fouillée, who seemed closer to Hobhouse, but by this time I was becoming uneasy about dealing with my problem by comparing two thinkers.

Visiting a second-hand bookshop near Saint-Michel, I came across a book entitled *Solidarité*, whose author, a Third Republic Radical politician and ephemeral Prime Minister, had the unprepossessing name of Léon Bourgeois (1896). A quick glance suggested it merited further perusal, so I bought it. I did not realize that I had found an alternative direction for my research. I would study how the concept of interdependence or *solidarité* had been used in France to justify both state intervention and voluntary association during the post-Revolutionary reaction to liberal individualism. So a concept became the focus of my research and it quickly assumed such an extensive scale that I abandoned explicit for implicit comparison between France and Britain. When the French socialists returned to power in 1981, the concept of 'solidarity' achieved great prominence. It has also been invoked by the American political philosopher Richard Rorty (1989) but further discussion of it would be inappropriate here.

My doctoral thesis occupied four out of the six years between 1952 and 1958, two of those years being taken up by national service as an Education Officer in the Royal Air Force. My nominal supervisor, Michael Oakeshott, and I had little in common. He must have found my rationalist manner of thinking profoundly repugnant but he was tolerant enough to let me go my own way. This benign neglect meant that I worked virtually in a state of nature, with no guidance to speak of. The result was that I wrote an excessively long, exhausting history of an idea that allowed me to satisfy myself that no satisfactory foundation for the welfare state had been based upon attempts at the theoretical reconciliation of individualism and collectivism. Even if these two were connected, pragmatic improvization under the pressure of social forces, themselves driven by industrial and democratic developments, were of greater significance. Nevertheless, I remain convinced that basing one's welfare system on solidarity (France) as against social insurance (Britain) has been of enduring normative and political significance. Recognition of the implications of the fact that industrialization preceded democratization in Britain, whereas the reverse was the case in France, also helped to steer me towards concern with political economy, from which I had to some extent diverged in a normative direction. Having 'cannibalized' numerous articles from my thesis, I turned my attention to the empirical role of interest groups.

The comparative experience of economic planning

This switch of direction was connected with the move in 1963 from my first post at Sheffield University to Keele University, where Sammy Finer was the presiding genius. I had read with admiration his *Anonymous Empire* shortly after its publication in 1958. I was already inclined to follow this pluralistic path to an understanding of how decisions were taken in ways that were not specified in the standard textbooks I had used as an undergraduate, although pioneering American works had long since showed the way. Curiously enough, my first book, *Private Interests and Public Policy* (1965), a study of the French Economic and Social Council, had a superficially closer affinity with the book by Sammy Finer's elder brother, Herman Finer, on the German Economic Council of the Weimar Republic (Finer 1923). Although it took a functionally representative institution as its framework and anticipated in part the neo-corporatist line of argument developed in a more sweeping form by Philippe Schmitter in the 1970s, it was an exercise in the study of how French business, trade union, farm and other groups sought to influence public policy. Because of its consultative role in the process of national economic planning, I was naturally drawn into the study of *le Plan*, then in its heyday. I was also, following a reading of a pioneering article by Jean-Louis Quermonne (1963) on functional regionalism in France, prompted to study the activities of a Breton regional pressure group, the CELIB (Hayward 1969). Other work over the years followed – comparing French group activity, notably with that of

Britain, but a more ambitious comparative study was conceived at the end of the 1960s and only brought to completion in the mid-1970s.

From the mid-1960s I had been making a study of the French planning process, at a time when the pale British imitation was rapidly becoming a fiasco, having got off to an inauspicious start under the Conservative Chancellor of the Exchequer Selwyn Lloyd. As I wrote, like Christopher Columbus discovering America, when he set out he did not know where he was going; when he arrived, he did not know where he was; and when he returned, he did not know where he had been. This spectacular example of how failure to understand the most elementary principles of comparison leads to disastrous consequences encouraged me to launch, in partnership with Michael Watson, a tripartite comparative study *Planning, Politics and Public Policy* (1975), which compared the unsuccessful British and Italian experience with that of France. Most of the studies of planning had been written from an economic perspective, so the challenge was to try to provide a political understanding of the phenomenon. Andrew Shonfield's *Modern Capitalism* (1965) was an important influence, particularly because of its comparative approach, but it remained primarily the work of an economist. I was especially influenced conceptually by Charles Lindblom's 1959 article 'The Science of Muddling Through', because he provided a model of the opposite of planning – a short-term, piecemeal, improvised and incremental way of taking decisions that was inclined towards inertia, by contrast with a medium- to long-term, comprehensive and innovative approach which used forecasts of what would happen without voluntaristic intervention. From this contrast, I derived a distinction between humdrum and heroic styles of decision, the boldness characteristic of the latter being counterpoised to the drift associated with the former.

In retrospect, it is clear that before our findings were published in 1975, even French planning was in a prolonged crisis, from which it has survived but not recovered. Our team of researchers included some leading French planners as well as academics. Three preparatory workshops achieved a higher than usual degree of integration in the resultant studies, through a learning process that was mutually enriching. While, at this stage, emphasis was placed on contrasting national policy-making styles – politics makes policy – the sectoral studies of specific policy areas were laying the ground for a different emphasis that only emerged subsequently, predicated on the view that policies made politics. Cross-national convergence in particular sectors might be more significant than national cultural and institutional diversities. In a later edited book *Planning in Europe* (Hayward and Narkiewicz 1978), comparison was extended to Eastern as well as Western Europe, although in 1978 it was too soon to transcend the dichotomy between them. A more general attempt at a cross-European study of *State and Society in Contemporary Europe* (1979, edited with Robert Berki) also proved to be premature, involving two sets of comparisons: intra-Western and intra-Eastern Europe. A pan-European companion had to await the mid-1990s (Hayward 1995a).

Franco–French comparisons

The technique of implicit comparison, so superbly demonstrated by Tocqueville's *Democracy in America* (1968) had fascinated me for some time and I decided to write what in 1973 was published as *The One and Indivisible French Republic*. A decade before, Stanley Hoffmann and others had published an exciting book entitled *France. Change and Tradition* (1963), in which Hoffmann's long introductory essay had gripped my imagination. Covering in part the same ground as Michel Crozier's *The Bureaucratic Phenomenon* which appeared in 1964, they showed that France had been a stalemate society, but whereas Hoffmann was more voluntaristically optimistic about France having emerged from this immobilism, Crozier's more deterministic pessimism suggested that she was still locked into a paralysing centralism. My book drew upon the insight they offered, as well as those from Crozier's *Centre de Sociologie des Organizations* team of brilliant researchers, notably Pierre and Catherine Grémion, Erhard Friedberg, and Jean-Claude Thoenig (three of whom participated in the *Planning, Politics and Public Policy* project, Hayward and Watson 1975). The title was meant to mock the Revolutionary claim to a unity that was the more ardently desired because it was absent, a claim which all too many French and foreign scholars have too readily taken at face value. The book was a sustained, implicit comparison with a more liberal and pluralistic, Anglo-American style of politics. At the end of the chapter on public order and civil liberties, the portrayal of French authoritarianism (including an early account of telephone tapping) seemed to require a comparative corrective. So I wrote: 'whereas in Britain everything is permitted except what is forbidden, in the Soviet Union everything is forbidden including what is permitted, whilst in France everything is permitted including what is forbidden' (Hayward 1983, p.171). Humour is no substitute for systematic comparison but it can provide an insight that is sometimes buried by more laborious, data-based analyses.

In 1975, the year of the twenty-fifth anniversary of the Political Studies Association of the UK, I was part of a group of middle-aged colleagues who thought our association needed to be given a more committed, professional emphasis. Its annual conference had become more like the meeting of a social club, the pretext for a friendly get-together. The journal, *Political Studies*, had become rather staid and was not a source of financial support for the association, which we felt should promote collaborative and comparative research. For the first and, so far, only occasion a complete slate of candidates challenged the outgoing executive and somewhat to our surprise, we won all down the line. We had so little anticipated this result that we did not have a candidate for Chairman and it was rather to my amazement that I was elected to this position by the new executive. We proceeded rapidly to put our programme into action and I think it would generally be agreed that the PSA has never been the same since then. The annual conference has attracted many more people, a much wider range of papers has been discussed, specialist research groups proliferated and new financially advantageous arrangements were made for the journal. One of these was that no editor would in future serve for more than six years. So when I was appointed to this post in 1987, I happily gave it up in 1993 according to the rules I had myself helped to make.

In the 1980s, two major works appeared which related to past concerns but extended them in different ways. In *The State and the Market Economy. Industrial Patriotism and Economic Intervention in France* (1986), I applied the 'policy community' approach to the study of French industrial policy. This approach had been suggested in their book on the British Treasury, *The Private Government of Public Money* (1974), by Hugh Heclo and Aaron Wildavsky and was developed by Jeremy Richardson and Grant Jordan in their book *Governing Under Pressure: The Policy*

Process in a Part-Parliamentary Democracy (1979). Related to my earlier identification of a heroic style of policy-making, I formulated the view that there was an identifiable group of actors whose institutionalized relationships imparted to them a collective *capacity* for policy initiative, a *potential* to engage in far-sighted planning and a *propensity* to impose their will to attain public objectives. In addition to the overall French macro-economic policy community which excluded some groups, such as the trade unions – usually reduced to pressured rather than pressure groups – there were sectoral policy communities at the national, regional and local levels. These were studied over time as the planning of growth was replaced by the crisis management of collective impoverishment or the decline of traditionally powerful firms and industries, leading to the breakdown or transformation of some policy communities and the emergence of new ones. The impact of Europeanization and globalization was touched upon at this stage, but it was not until my return to the subject of industrial policy in the 1990s that French national champion firms were seen as fighting a rearguard battle in which competitiveness ruthlessly asserted a priority over community.

An invitation to give the Tagore Memorial Lectures in 1984 at Baroda University led me to return for longer than I had intended to my old interest in the history of ideas with *After the French Revolution* (1991). The subject of the nation as the basis of the political community and democracy as the manner in which its affairs were conducted had not played a significant part in my work on French and comparative political economy, where interlocking directorates of techno-bureaucracy and market-oriented businesses predominated. (Nation and democracy had naturally featured in their twentieth-century forms in *The One and Indivisible French Republic*, whose second edition appeared in 1983.) The implicit comparative dimension arose from the fact that in India the nation and democracy were fundamental norms of the state and so in addressing an Indian audience I was returning to their modern source in the French Revolution. Because my implicit point of reference was Britain, which had also exported many of its values to the Indian élites, there was a sustained Anglo-French comparison, unspoken but underlined by the influence of British liberal thought especially on writers like Benjamin Constant. Furthermore, by considering the criticisms of these norms from the Right, the Centre and the Left of the political spectrum, I was engaging in explicit comparison between the traditional (de Maistre) and the modernist (Saint-Simon) Right, between an individualist (Constant) and a communitarian (Tocqueville) liberalism, between an anarchist (Proudhon) and an authoritarian (Blanqui) Left, whose ideas have been influential far beyond France. The bicentenary of the French Revolution in 1989 was to see a remarkable resurgence of both liberal democracy and nationalism in East-Central Europe, even where these norms had shallow roots or virtually none at all.

Another exercise in intra-French comparison took the form of an investigation of the continuities and changes that had occurred in the nature of the presidential office between de Gaulle, Pompidou, Giscard and Mitterrand. This study of presidential power in France started with a comparison between the absolute and constitutional monarchies, as well as the First and Second Empire conceptions of the role of the head of state, with its subsequent domestication under the Third and Fourth Republics. This longitudinal comparison placed in historical perspective the Fifth Republic's revival of a notion of state power – to which attention had been drawn by the French political scientists Georges Burdeau (1959) and Jean-Louis Quermonne (1987) – distinct from partisan power, which acquired direct democratic legitimacy through the election of the president by universal suffrage. By comparing the letter and the practice of the constitution, it was possible to show that an unstable, ambiguous compromise had been struck between state and partisan power, with effective control shifting when there was a non-coincidence of party identity between the president and a parliamentary majority. It was also possible to show that state power was particularly evident in certain policy sectors, such as the 'high politics' of defence and foreign policy, whereas partisan power flourished especially in areas of 'low politics', subject to occasional incursions as dictated by circumstances or the personal predilections of the particular incumbent of presidential office (Burdeau 1959; Quermonne 1987, pp.187–9; Hayward 1993, pp.38–42).

Comparing within Western Europe and beyond

Such preoccupations with the practical politics of the state as a pivotal concept for the understanding of contemporary politics stood in sharp contrast with predominant American concentration upon political behaviour, to the neglect of the institutional and normative aspects of the political process. European political scientists rediscovered in the mid-1980s what should never have been contemptuously expelled from the study of politics. We felt that we did not need to 'bring the state back in' because our theoretical paradigms had always accepted that the organizational structures of the state could autonomously act upon society and were not simply a 'black box' for processing societal inputs and outputs. This was because, in our empirical work on European polities, we were constantly brought face to face with governments that were active not passive, even if they were acting within societal constraints. Given the international dominance of American political science, it was a welcome sign for European political scientists that methodological pressures and premises that threatened to distort research by the imposition of inappropriate paradigms would ease and the transatlantic divergence of presuppositions would decrease. By adapting rather than abandoning traditional approaches, European political science had provided a continuity of scholarship that would once again be recognized as within the mainstream of comparative politics.

In a world where interdependence if not solidarity was becoming an ever more present reality, it seemed indispensable to move on from implicit to explicit comparison. After one has resisted the trend towards rather superficial comparisons between over a hundred states based upon frequently misleading indicators, but sought also to avoid generalizing from the singular, there remains what Richard Rose has called 'analysing countries in parallel' in a situation where national boundaries have become increasingly permeable (Rose 1991a; Page 1995). In particular, following on earlier edited works drawing upon the specialist knowledge of a carefully selected team of contributors, I have engaged in the systematic comparison of a limited number of European countries. Initially, these were confined to Western Europe but after 1989, it has begun to be possible to extend one's comparative reach to Central and Eastern Europe as well.

However, in the early 1990s explicit comparison still meant narrowing the subject-matter both to a specific policy sector and to a limited number of West European states:

Britain, France, Germany and Italy. My concern was to investigate how national firms were adapting both to the globalization of the competitive economy and to the more specific effects of a single market within the European Community of which these countries were members. The organizing concept used was that of the national champion firm, which had achieved particular prominence in France but which took different forms in all four countries. Although it derived in part from centuries-old mercantilist, Colbertist, protectionist principles and practices, the national champion form was seen as an appropriate response to what Jean-Jacques Servan-Schreiber called *The American Challenge* (1968) and its agents, the multinational corporations. The problems posed by the loss of public control over the national wealth-producing process could be studied and the responses compared. The attempt to develop European champion firms by mergers or less integrated forms of joint action as a way of avoiding complete loss of national identity was investigated comparatively as between different industrial sectors as well as cross-nationally.

Just as the earlier study *Planning, Politics and Public Policy* (Hayward and Watson 1975) involved teams of contributors from the countries studied, *Industrial Enterprise and European Integration* (Hayward 1995a) necessitated drawing upon contributions by specialists from the four countries. Comparative work, as it seeks to derive lessons from cross-national analysis – in this case an assessment of the relative effectiveness with which countries and sectors have adapted to the competitive international market – generally requires teamwork. If the complex interactions that occur between firms and countries which find it increasingly difficult to preserve the integrity of their boundaries are to be documented and explained, it has become ever more indispensable to collaborate cross-nationally, the academic researchers being compelled to imitate their subjects. This poses severe problems as regards achieving agreed guidelines. To the extent that a meeting of minds is eventually achieved, this is usually the result of an extended iterative process of mutual socialization and friendly argument, without which the results of the collective work lack the minimum of consistency that is the prerequisite of attaining added comparative value. The seemingly endless proliferation of workshops and conferences that are such a marked feature of late twentieth century research lends itself all too readily to mockery, some of it well merited. However, that they are functionally indispensable, particularly to comparative research, accounts for their popularity with those who fund research as well as those who undertake it.

Much remains to be done by way of comparison between selected Western European countries. I shall myself be engaged with Vincent Wright in a collaborative project in the coming years to study the problems of co-ordination within the core executive of France, Germany, Italy and the Netherlands both in general and through case studies. This involves a focus (with a vengeance) upon the nucleus of the state, all the more necessary because of the rapid processes of change that have compelled governments to adapt their practices in recent years. However, the opportunities to overcome the dichotomy between research on West and East-Central Europe afforded by the end of the First World/Second World invite work, albeit exploratory and tentative, to compare across the Oder-Neisse line. Once again, the problems posed by the dichotomy-induced specificity of expertise necessitate collaboration to an even greater extent.

Governing The New Europe (1995b, edited with Edward Page, a colleague at the

University of Hull, which I left after twenty years in January 1993 for Oxford) has been an ambitious attempt at a comparative politics of Europe. It might have been safer to have waited until the new post-communist regimes of East-Central Europe had established themselves more firmly. It might also have been wiser to have postponed generic studies to await authoritative country-specific research on the less familiar states. Nevertheless, we decided to proceed as if it were possible to compare and chose as contributors specialists who were willing to extend their expertise either eastward or westward. Others will judge how far it has been a successful enterprise. Its pedagogic justification is that if students are to be encouraged intellectually to transcend the political barriers that no longer exist, their teachers need to have at their disposal the literature that will enable them to offer instruction on a pan-European scale. Despite its inevitable limitations, it is a venture that is intended to encourage the reconstruction of syllabuses in European politics to conform to the present and the future rather than anachronistically to perpetuate the past. It is destined to be modified and superseded as we have access to a better understanding of a rapidly evolving reality. Meanwhile, it should guard against the naive urge to transpose this or that institution or practice – French presidentialism or British privatization – without the comparativist's understanding of why they worked in their original habitat and how they will need to be modified if it is judged sensible to graft them on to a foreign body politic. Otherwise, they may be rejected, adding to the instability and conflict which they were intended to overcome.

Paying an intellectual debt

While I would not have had the boldness to undertake the comparative history of government over 5000 years upon which Sammy Finer embarked during the last ten years of his life, I cannot think of any other political scientist in my own lifetime who would have taken on such an intimidating task. I mention it for two reasons: because I have been closely involved in its preparation for posthumous publication and – much more important – because I believe it to be of immense importance in extending the range of examples available to the comparativist across time as well as space, and in the conceptual framework Finer developed to cope with such an ambitious project.

Finer's *History of Government from the Earliest Times* (1997) has five interrelated themes: state-building, military formats, religious belief systems, social stratification and time-span. He was an early and vigorous critic of the ahistorical approach to state-building characteristic of the behavioural 1960s in American political science. In his final work, he argued that only by generalizing from pre-European polities could we distinguish the territorial characteristics of states. Finer settled on two variables to clarify governmental forms: how far rulers had created a standardized central administration and the extent to which a homogeneous culture, language and law were established.

For most of history, Finer argued, military organization has been crucial to the founding of political regimes and their survival. The 'coercion–extraction' cycle has been central not merely to supporting armed forces but in the creation of a permanent civil service. He went on to argue that only when the prevailing belief system, social stratification and political institutions were congruent did political communities achieve enduring stability. Once the Reformation destroyed that congruity, European societies acquired a destabilizing political dynamism. Thus, whereas Pharaoh's Egypt lasted nearly 3000 years and the Chinese Empire over 2000 years, the Roman Republic and Empire together lasted less than a thousand years and the Venetian Republic 1112 years, while the British Empire survived a mere 190 years.

Finer's diachronic comparison of similarities and differences over and across time has four dimensions. The territorial dimension distinguished city, national and imperial regimes. Decision-making personnel provided the distinction between masses and élites and among élites. The level and nature of central relationships within central government and between it and local government provided the basis for contrasting constrained and unconstrained government. Lastly, the decision-implementing personnel dimension allows Finer to show how the increasing complexity and specialization of the governmental process is reflected in the shift from a community-in-arms with minimal bureaucracy to a standing army and large bureaucracy. This allows him to distinguish four pure types of polity – Palace, Forum, Nobility, and Church – and six hybrid types, and the vast bulk of his book is devoted to applying his conceptual framework to 5000 years of history. However, Finer is careful in his comparative history to avoid allowing his trajectory of governmental innovations with a future and dead-ends to degenerate into a teleology.

Unlike his contemporary political scientists, Sammy Finer had the self-confidence and breadth of vision single-handedly to take on an immense work and almost bring it to completion before death imposed its own premature conclusion. This leads us to question if one of the great disciplinary weaknesses, in a period which in quantitative terms has seen such an enormous expansion in the academic study of politics, has been a tendency to retreat in the face of complexity into collective projects where the imaginativeness of the individual scholar tends to be submerged. Overawed by the yawning gaps in our own knowledge, we seek security in the specialist haven, from which we emerge with circumspection for brief excursions into the unknown or unfamiliar. The extent to which specialist journals have increasingly displaced general journals as the focus of research interest is indicative of the increasing tendency towards disciplinary fragmentation which leads to a loss of any overall grasp of the subject. The attraction of special issues of even sub-disciplinary journals is a further indication of a process of narrowing down that was alien to those of an earlier generation. The activities of national political science associations, the European Consortium for Political Research and the International Political Science Association have all contributed to this process of fragmentation, even when they have sought to counteract it. Our agenda should have at its forefront the pursuit of countervailing professional practices that encourage the cultivation of the solitary tree rather than another row of lettuce, for which there is a place provided it does not become too pervasive, crowding out what is more elevated and more enduring. If for no other reason, that is the justification for the doctoral thesis, but this first apprenticeship to one's profession should not be the last time at which the political scientist recoils from the crowd and thinks as an individual.

Personal experience suggests that the comparative study of European politics should be firmly based upon the intimate knowledge of at least one foreign political system. In my case, it was France. There is the danger that one will become so absorbed in the peculiarities of one's adopted country that the implicit comparisons made with one's own country are unconsciously biased. A country like France also encourages the paradoxical view that one can attain generality through what is specific because French experience has been exemplary, a pretention to which few others lay claim. It therefore requires an exceptional effort to establish that there are comparisons to be made that neither retreat into insularity nor inflate into universality, with the concomitant need to make testably explicit what otherwise all too readily become unobtrusive but arbitrary judgements.

14 Seeking to understand European politics

Gordon Smith

LONDON SCHOOL OF ECONOMICS AND POLITICAL SCIENCE

A Europe on the move

European political scientists with a comparative bent are living in quite 'interesting times'. In the Europe created after 1945 it was easy to define and delimit their areas of interest. At least they were content enough with their assumptions about just what they were studying. There were those specializing in the countries practising liberal democracy, plus a few deviant cases. Alternatively, 'Western' Europe was defined by the international political divide, regardless of the political complexion of those in the Western camp. Others, the East Europeanists, largely concerned themselves with the theory and practice of Soviet-style socialism. It was a neat division with no troublesome demarcation disputes. Attempts to span the divide by, for instance, looking for signs of convergence at various levels in the two opposing systems appeared forced and unproductive.

These area specialists – and the present writer is one – lived in a comfortable world. It did not disturb them too much that others doubted whether true comparativists could restrict themselves to the confines of a selected group of states and still hope to establish comparative generalizations; and for West Europeanists it seemed altogether more productive to concentrate on the functioning and failures of liberal democracy within a fairly tight setting of historical experience and geographical concentration.

All that has changed over the past six years: these same comparativists may well have gone through a phase of intellectual vertigo. How is the new map of Europe to be defined? How do we cope with the 'rediscovery' of *Mitteleuropa*? What are the common characteristics of this new Europe? Which countries should be placed firmly beyond the pale? These questions need not detain us too long, if we are more excited by all the research possibilities that the vastly expanded new area of 'Europe' presents. To take one example: the subject of 'transition' alone has injected new life and already a substantial literature into European comparison. Not only that: transition has also come to resemble a kind of 'golden bridge' linking the theorizing devoted to liberal democracy and its institutions with the study of the post-communist order. Still, it may be asked, have we been perhaps too hasty in putting so much weight on this slender structure?

The sudden shock of disappearing boundaries is compounded with a more insidious disturbance to the old world of European comparison: the creeping advance of European integration towards an 'ever closer political union'. How should comparativists handle this phenomenon? Should they dust off and refashion their theories of nation- and state-building? Apply nationally-derived models to the emerging political institutions? Or should they rather treat the whole subject of European integration as a distinctive specialism, not really suitable for comparative analysis? Such doubts and problems confront European political scientists. Yet many will query whether the difficulties are real ones at all: European comparative politics and its frontiers have simply 'moved on'.

A chequered career

Rather late in my own career, I had to readjust my thinking about the nature of comparison in European politics. The label of a 'late developer' is no exaggeration in my case – not for an academic who had not published a single word until his fortieth year. I have always been in the unenviable position of trying to catch up, never seeming to have time to reflect. So it was with hesitation that I responded to the invitation to contribute to this volume. However, a few others – in their 'frustrated thirties' perhaps – may draw encouragement, providing their universities take a longer-term view, a doubtful prospect in the present British climate.

Being a latecomer is not entirely a handicap, and there were some unexpected benefits. I was a teenager during most of World War II, and I was only called up for military service in 1945. At the time it was a blow to my hopes of taking a science degree. Yet it was only during the three years in the army that I had second thoughts and discovered that there were other attractive subjects such as politics and economics. That was the extent of ignorance of a youth evacuated from London to a small country grammar school during the war years.

A second benefit was soon to be posted to Germany, and at that living in a half-bombed former school set in the middle of the ruins of a working-class district of Hamburg. The impact of the utter devastation and visible suffering of the people was at odds with all I had thought and felt about Germany not so long previously. Struggling to learn the language, meeting many ordinary Germans, trying to put myself in their place – apparently hopeless as it then appeared – were experiences that stayed with me. In retrospect it was a better education than any university could have provided. Nevertheless it would be idle to pretend that my comparative interests were then suddenly awakened: army life is not conducive to deep reflection.

Once out of the army, however, I knew what I wanted to do: study politics. At that time Britain was still in the throes of creating its 'brave new world' under a Labour government, and (though it may seem improbable to those who know me now) I wanted to be in the vanguard. I passed the entrance examination for the London School of Economics. Yet once I graduated, I put thoughts of an academic career behind me, and (misguidedly) opted for a career in personnel management. It proved to be a long, hard road back to the academic world. After British industry decided it could do rather better without my services, I had to try something else. I ended up in 1954 at Melton Mowbray College, probably the smallest college of further education in the country, teaching civics to a succession of day-release apprentices – plumbers, electricians, carpenters and others unclassified. Everyone has a nadir at some point in their working lives, and this was mine!

The 'road back' took several years and passed through a variety of institutions, all with an exclusive emphasis on teaching, and what now seems to have been an unbelievably demanding load – at one stage 32 hours a week. It was an effort in those circumstances, with my wife and two children, to embark on doctoral research as a part-time student at the LSE; in all I managed to see my supervisor on about four occasions. After completing the doctorate with a dissertation entitled *Party System and Party Structure in Western Germany* (1964), I realized my horizons were still very limited. Sociology at that time, in the 1960s, was an exciting subject, and I took a London University external degree as a private student. It is worth remarking how valuable this external service is in giving opportunities to students worldwide while maintaining rigorous standards.

The road was still there, however. I was then commuting from Bournemouth, 250 miles several days a week, to a polytechnic in London's East End. Strangely, though, those interminable hours jolted me to a desperate inspiration: I decided to write, and start then and there, on the train. It is always interesting to trace the genesis of an idea, but this one defeats me. I could have taken the subject of my Ph.D thesis, German politics, but maybe I needed an entirely new impetus. By the time I had reached my destination I had resolved to write a comparative text on European politics. It was a risky, even foolhardy enterprise to try something that, as far as I knew, had not been previously attempted, at least not on a strictly comparative basis, rather than just taking the major powers or dealing with individual countries one by one. Perhaps the pent-up frustration of teaching and yet more teaching drove me to find a fresh outlet. Anyway the eventual outcome was *Politics in Western Europe* (Smith 1972).

Kinds of influence

The influences on a 'lonely scholar' are rather different from those experienced by academics with the good fortune or judgement to stay on at university, work with figures of renown, and build up a stimulating network of academic relationships. In those earlier years the universities were very much 'closed shops', and British higher education reproduced a form of 'caste system'. My three years at the LSE had not been productive. 'Great professors' such as Harold Laski and Lionel Robbins were fascinating lecturers (there were dismal ones as well), but perhaps I was then not ready enough to follow up the leads they gave. Like many others, both then and now, I was too concerned with examinations to realize what a university education is meant to be about.

The most important influences came from books. In studying for my degree I naturally read the classical writers mainly of the nineteenth century, such as de Toqueville, John Stuart Mill, Hume, Hegel, Bryce, Green, Ostrogorski, Michels, Graham Wallas, Walter Bagehot, to name a few at random. There was little inspiration to be had of a genuinely comparative nature that focused on the post-1945 period. If only, say, Bagehot had reapplied his concept of the 'efficient secret' of the English Constitution on a comparative level, then developments would have been more rapid.

It was in later reading for a sociology degree that I found a refreshing extension: Max Weber, George Simmel, Wittfogel, Durkheim, Fromm, Pareto and Mosca. Admittedly, this all did not add up to a coherent intellectual whole, but it was a compensation for the earlier institutional bias in studying the government and politics of the leading powers.

For some years after the war there was not a great deal of academic interest in contemporary German politics or in its new institutions. Germany was rather treated as a 'problem'. Starting my research in the early 1960s on German politics and the developing party system meant working virtually from scratch. I have to admit that if now a student sought my advice on a similar threadbare basis, I should warn against trying anything so silly! On rare occasions, however, it may be that we are better off not asking for advice or being too influenced by others: we should follow where our inclination leads us. All the same, I underestimated just how extensive my voyage would have to be, for I soon found that I could not hope to understand the present without being inescapably led back through the convolutions of German history.

I suppose a measure of self-confidence came through the different kinds of reading over the years. Some books have an extraordinary influence at a particular juncture – like throwing wide open the shutters of a dark room – although at another time they may not have a strong effect. Indeed, a later rereading can be sobering: the once-treasured insights become 'obvious' and 'dated'. It should suffice to mention half a dozen that opened shutters at different times. On comparative politics, there was Sigmund Neumann's volume on political parties (Neumann 1956) and Jean Blondel's path-breaking 'introduction' to comparison (Blondel 1969); I was especially impressed by his liberal use of diagrams. Helping me to think more flexibly about politics was Dennis Pirages's examination of the different ways in which political conflict could be regarded (Pirages 1976), and the same applied to Rosenau analysing the many-sided nature of political adaptation (Rosenau 1981). Both the study by Hans Kohn of the development of German intellectual thought (Kohn 1960) and Ralf Dahrendorf's socio-historical interpretation of German democracy (Dahrendorf 1968) proved invaluable in relating history to contemporary politics. Perhaps they are not so significant in determining short-term policy outcomes, but they are certainly so in presenting and reflecting basic societal choices. This kind of experience, often quite isolated, puts all the necessary 'plodding' into perspective.

Books can stimulate, but there has also to be an active exchange of ideas. My rather chequered career had cut me off entirely from the academic mainstream. Besides having no personal contacts, I had no conception either of what gatherings of political scientists were all about. I well remember the first such meeting I attended: the 'joint workshop sessions' of the ECPR at Mannheim in 1973, and braving a paper entitled, 'A Model of the Bureaucratic Culture' which found its way into print (Smith 1974). A few years later a colleague remarked that an aspiring academic should have written at least one piece that others couldn't quite understand. My 'model' surely qualified, if for no other reason than that a printing error had made the main diagram meaningless, but possibly that had a desirable effect.

Mention of the ECPR is far from incidental. On the contrary, besides fostering research, it has made an inestimable contribution in forging a collegial awareness throughout Europe. Like myself, there are many whose work has benefited by participating. Its focus on week-long working sessions of specialist groups has ensured that it has not drifted into becoming a venue for speech-making or a glorified job-market. The ECPR provides what all 'networks' need if they are to flourish – a solid organizational infrastructure. It has given valuable opportunities to generations of younger political scientists. Three people should be named in this context: Jean Blondel, Hans Daalder and the late Rudolf Wildenmann. Besides their individual contributions, this trio – in establishing, with Stein Rokkan and others, the ECPR, and also in other ways – succeeded in overcoming national barriers and creating the feeling for a European political science. Perhaps my closest connection was with Rudolf Wildenmann. I knew him only in his later years, but I was impressed even then by his enormous enthusiasm and capability in bringing together academics from several countries in a joint enterprise, resulting, for instance, in the 'Future of Party Government' series (see Castles and Wildenmann 1986; Katz 1987). There must be many of us who have benefited from his 'entrepreneurial' spirit. Now such forms of collaboration have become almost routinized, but it is worth emphasizing that we were not so fortunate in the past.

The elusive charm of the LSE

There must be many who have felt disappointment on first visiting the London School of Economics and Political Science – to give the School its proper title. Tucked away behind the Aldwych and Kingsway, its jumble of buildings spreading into neighbouring streets follows no coherent plan. Like Lewis Carroll's Topsy, it simply 'grewed'. I used to wonder where its 'heart' was to be found (perhaps in the Senior Common Room?), but all I have become aware of is its restless pulse-beat. It is not difficult to understand why the LSE is a peculiar establishment: in small compass it spans the whole range of social sciences and more besides. It has to be highly pluralistic if it is to preserve its collective sanity. The centenary celebrations of the LSE in 1995 were marked by, among other ways, the publication of a volume of essays on the concept 'Freedom' as interpreted by a variety of social scientists at the School – a fitting way of showing the diversity of interests linked by a common concern (Barber 1995; Dahrendorf 1995).

Obviously the LSE is atypical in several respects, given its specialization in the social sciences and its very high proportion of postgraduate students. But it also epitomizes the strong qualities of the British university system: the balance between the needs of research and teaching; the open accessibility (at times too open) of academic staff to students – 'remote' professors are a rarity; teaching in relatively small groups; the high standards of scholarship expected, but a freedom to decide the kind of contribution to make. Thinking about this list of 'virtues' makes me aware that they are increasingly under strain and how dangerous it is to generalize about the university sector as a whole. The huge expansion of higher education, the mushrooming of new universities, the pressure to increase student numbers, the drive to generate research income, sometimes irrespective of the value of the research itself, the proliferation of administrative requirements, the competitive atmosphere as between universities – all these factors put the 'virtues' in a different light, and the LSE can not regard itself as a specially exempt case.

I was appointed as a Lecturer in the Department of Government in 1972, at the ripe age of 45, and it took some time to adjust to the quite different rhythms and demands of university life. Previously, no one had cared whether I was researching and publishing or not, just as long as I was present and teaching. It was not quite the other way round at the LSE, since for the first few years it seemed that no one was particularly bothered whether I was researching and publishing or not. In fact, there was the natural assumption that everyone was self-driven. The contrast with the present era is striking: the periodic 'Research Selectivity Exercise', well-intentioned as it may be, makes the university system more like a cruel game of 'snakes and ladders'.

Returning to the School after a lapse of about twenty years was a strange experience. Not too much had changed. I had missed Michael Oakeshott's long and stimulating reign over the Government Department entirely, but he and many of the 'old guard' (e.g. William Pickles, Richard Greaves, Willie Robson) were still around and influential. There is much to be said in favour of not disposing of retired academics too hastily (I declare an interest at this point!), since what helps to hold a Department together are its continuing links and traditions, not just the busy atmosphere of research and teaching.

To say that 'not much had changed' has a critical aspect as well. That particularly applied to the field of comparative politics. There was, it is true, a solitary two-year (compulsory) course in 'Comparative Political Institutions', although unloved by staff and students alike. In addition, there was a strong reliance on single-country courses; at the postgraduate level there was little option but to continue with research into British, French, German, American or Soviet politics. That took a few years to change. I well remember that in the course of the interview for the lectureship I sought to interest the selection committee in a comparative approach to European politics. Leonard Schapiro interrupted me crisply: 'Mr. Smith, we are interviewing you for a post in German politics.'

Much has altered in the intervening years. That particularly applies to postgraduate courses; it was anyway far easier to implement initiatives at this level than to do so for the highly structured first degree involving a number of departments. The results have been impressive: at present there are several comparative politics degrees for the MSc. including the interdepartmental courses with a home in the European Institute – itself a creation that could not have been envisaged a decade ago.

Earlier, I made a critical comment about the single-country bias in teaching politics at the LSE, but this needs qualification. I take the view that, on the contrary, a good knowledge of the history and politics of at least some foreign states is the only sound way of approaching comparison. Without such a grounding, generalization on the basis of a few selected features or quantitative indicators courts the danger of becoming superficial, just as it is to make a comparative journey armed with a selection of handy concepts without any real awareness of the context to which they are being applied. One of the problems with courses taking the European Union as the central point of reference is that they tend to operate at a level removed from the member states themselves and inevitably give a simplified and distorted view of European realities.

It is also true to say that the weight given to the study of other European countries in British universities is not matched by a corresponding interest on their part. Courses specifically focused on British politics are few and far between. The LSE may not be entirely representative, but its European coverage is indicative of a strong tradition: French, German, East European, Russian, Irish and Scandinavian politics, now with the addition of Spain. It is a little strange that in some quarters the British are regarded as 'insular' in their interests. Do typical French or German universities give their students comparable opportunities?

Editing journals

Keeping a balance between comparative/theoretical approaches and the analysis of individual political systems is essential. Meeting these two requirements is what we have sought to achieve from the outset with *West European Politics*, although in practice it is rather more eclectic – editors have to learn to be flexible. Back in 1978, when the first issue appeared, it was by no means certain that the venture would succeed; now it is firmly established with a wide readership. One of the journal's merits is that it has become a valuable resource for a range of European politics courses, especially with its numerous 'special issues'. At the same time our policy has been to encourage younger academics to publish accounts of their own research. With the proliferation of academic journals, they can have no complaint about the shortage of suitable outlets. An admission I recently heard from a postgraduate student, no less, that she no longer read books, only journal articles, is perhaps a disturbing insight into changing styles of study.

Vincent Wright and I conceived the idea of *WEP* shortly before he left the LSE in favour of 'another place' (under the fond illusion that there he would be free of students). At the time neither of us could have imagined that we should be still working together, relatively harmoniously, so many years later. Those who have themselves had the joy of editing a journal will know that an editor's lot is rarely a happy one, and certainly no one takes it on (or at least keeps at it) for fame or power – and certainly not fortune.

Co-editing has its rewards in the productive exchange of ideas and the inevitable arguments that are usually amicably resolved. But there are some problems that no amount of discussion can overcome, and they relate to the general direction that *West European Politics* should be taking. Of principal concern are the uncertainties I referred to at the beginning: the nature and definition of the new Europe. Thus, although in earlier years we took the decision that matters relating to European integration should be outside of the scope of *WEP*, we later realized – not least because of the increasing number of submissions we began to receive – that the subject could no longer be ignored. Immediately, however, the difficulty of achieving a fair balance became more acute.

More problematic for editorial policy is the 'definition' of Europe, and that is compounded by the journal's title: no sensible publisher will lightly consent to jettisoning an established trademark. So what is 'Western' Europe? One harsh option is to exclude *Mitteleuropa* and all points east, whatever the successes in anchoring liberal democracy – originally an essential qualification. A more subtle approach is to extend Western Europe eastwards, insensibly, and in the spirit of 'the inevitability of gradualism'. Of course one may conclude that these editorial disputes are, in the usual phrase, merely 'academic' issues ...

To edit one journal may be praiseworthy, but to become involved with a second one needs a good excuse. For many years in Britain we have had a lively group of academics concerned with contemporary German politics, and German reunification was not just an 'excuse' for starting a new journal, but something that had to be done if the much wider interest and the concerns about the new Germany and its role in Europe were to be satisfied. *German Politics* was launched in 1992, and to judge by reactions both in Britain and Germany (as well as our risk-enjoying publisher) it is proving a worthwhile venture. Yet inevitably – as many others have found – editing, whether of new editions of books or of journals, also has treadmill qualities, in the endless flow of manuscripts and the recurring deadlines. Then why not stop? But do good parents willingly abandon their children?

'Understanding Germany'?

Throughout my career, Germany and its politics has held a special place in my interests. Yet for all my pondering I remain unsure how far a foreign observer can ever hope really to 'get inside' the politics and the political culture of another country. The observer may be more knowledgeable – in terms of the history, the functioning of institutions, political personalities, results of opinion surveys, statistical data, and so on – than the average person born and living there. But the difficulty lies in making it all add up, and there is even the lurking feeling that one can 'know' too much! Possibly therein lies one of the fascinations: 'understanding' is a continuing quest.

I was helped along the way by the gentle prodding and encouragement of my late wife, Dorothea, who – as a *Berlinerin* with an adopted home in Bavaria – saved me from hasty judgements and gave me insights (perhaps unknowingly on her part) into German ways of thinking. I benefited, too, from her deep love of German history and culture. It was a good partnership. Dinner-table discussions, with a bottle of wine to share, often became open-ended seminars.

For me, as for many others specializing in German politics, the suddenness of reunification in 1990 caused a reassessment of almost all aspects of the Federal Republic. Is Germany now a 'normal' state, and for the first time in its history? But then can Germany ever be normal, considering its history and – for better or for worse – given its power and its position in Europe? The division of Germany only temporarily obscured the underlying realities, one might conclude, but can we be certain of what those realities are, and that they are unchanging?

Admittedly, these are all 'big' questions, and on one level it may not seem profitable to attempt answers and engage in speculation. Yet the alternative, concentrating solely on the 'nuts and bolts', the institutions and particular areas of policy, appears equally unsatisfactory. At the back of one's mind, the big questions should always be lurking, even though neither directly posed nor answered. I believe that is the case for my own writing; certainly it was so when I first wrote about 'democracy' in the old Federal Republic (Smith 1979), although inevitably the requirements of a textbook obscure those concerns. Moreover, the prime need is for readers to have information on which to base their own judgements. That has been our aim in bringing out successive editions studying developments in contemporary German politics (Smith, Paterson and Merkl 1989; Smith *et al.* 1992; Smith, Paterson and Padgett 1996). We were caught out badly when the first edition appeared just when the Berlin Wall was breached! Political scientists may be quite good on long-term trends, but should be careful about next week's news. Most of us have written a smaller piece that we think stands up well to later scrutiny; my nomination here is 'The German Volkspartei and the Career of the Catch-All Party' (Smith 1982), not least in arguing that Kirchheimer was right about Germany for the wrong reasons, and that is significant if his transformation thesis was largely an extrapolation from the Germany case (see Kirchheimer 1966a, 1966b).

Do the British have particular difficulties in understanding Germany and the Germans? In so many ways they think alike and have the same attitudes, but the similarities are deceptive, and that may lead to non-comprehension, even antagonism, on both sides. In fact, there are wide gulfs, highlighted, of course, by the decisions (or non-decisions) that have to be made about the future course of European integration. Quite apart from issues of national interest that may be involved, there is a deep cultural difference. That can be expressed in summary terms: the British (at least hitherto) are pragmatic because they have a sense of security. In contrast, German insecurity shows itself in a drive for 'certainty', and that is satisfied by having an overall plan, or as a former ambassador to Bonn well put it, the search for a *Gesamtkonzept*. But for all that, so many Germans are relaxed pragmatists, and perhaps it is the British turn to enter an era of self-doubt and uncertainty.

Confessions of an 'old-fashioned' comparativist

I find it particularly difficult to define my own approach to comparative politics. I have never felt at ease with 'grand theory' or with law-like generalizations, but happy enough to seek to clarify a concept, work out a satisfactory basis of classification, develop a typology, gather evidence of a general trend, in other words – and it is in the nature of all comparison – to reach a measure of generalization. But generalization is not the end of the process, since it rarely fits particular cases, and then the task is to explain the deviations and exceptions. That requires a 'turning back': to understanding the 'why not' in non-conforming cases, and for that matter the 'just why' in conforming ones. So, ultimately, I believe the use and the attraction of comparative politics lies not so much in arriving at generalizations, but rather in the sensitivity the process gives in properly comprehending the history, culture and politics of individual countries. Yet there is no single 'correct' comparative standpoint; as with Weldon's (1962) analogy in relation to a taste for ice-cream, we each choose the flavour we like best, and go on our way – it's only that I naturally think that my choice is more nutritious than others.

It would be pleasant to record that this 'credo' represents a long-held, coherent standpoint. I am not sure whether the lack of prior self-examination is a failing or not. I have always found it more stimulating to encounter a 'problem' (at least one for me) relating to a specific country or a concept. The very first article I wrote, with the title 'What is a Party System?' (Smith 1966) is indicative. My interest in political parties and party systems has persisted, because they are important. Perhaps they are not so significant in determining short-term policy outcomes, but they are certainly so in presenting and reflecting basic societal choices. Although some of the 'parties don't matter' school of thought may dismiss their study as resembling Hermann Hesse's *Glasperlenspiel*, there are few other branches of comparative analysis that have produced a comparable productive development of explanatory theory, initially with Lipset and Rokkan (1967), through Kirchheimer (1966a) and Sartori (1976), to Panebianco (1988), and most recently Katz and Mair (1992, 1994, 1995) with their concept of the 'cartel' party, as well as Kitschelt's contributions (1992, 1995) relating the concepts applied to the structuring of Western European party systems to the East European context.

That brings me to the problems facing those who have hitherto concentrated on Western Europe. They need to enlarge their area of interest, but they have to be careful about assuming that political institutions mean the same and work in a similar fashion in Eastern Europe. Nor should they assume that the process of transition, even in favourable circumstances, has only one outcome. I have ventured putting my toes in the water, but I am all too conscious of the fact that in these countries there are already many first-rate comparativists.

One last reflection: a reviewer of my *Politics in Western Europe*, when it first appeared, wrote that the approach was 'old-fashioned' (but added kindly that it was 'all the better for that'). Since the book has been in print, through successive editions, ever since, that may serve as a comment on the deceptive nature of 'fashion' in comparative politics. Nevertheless, I am quite aware that a project looming before me is a 'Politics in Europe' ... I still have some catching-up to do!

15 The path to hesitant comparison

Vincent Wright

NUFFIELD COLLEGE, OXFORD

Perhaps the easiest way to recount the tale of my development into a hesitant comparatist is to allow it to unfold chronologically – even at the risk of confirming my colleagues' firm impression that I am an ill-disguised historian posturing as a political scientist. Of course, no authentic historian would happily identify a definite starting point for any particular phenomenon or for any of the interconnected threads that constitute the phenomenon. In my own case the three major threads of my current hesitant comparison are history, single country specialism (France), comparative West European government and politics, with an emphasis on the former rather than the latter. But how to trace the origins of each of these constitutive elements? Did my future taste for continental Europe spring from my father's obsession with European politics – a politics which placed the British Tories on the same footing as the Germans as the enemies of humanity, and which created reassuring myths about the Popular Front in France, the Spanish Republicans and the Attlee Government of 1945? Or was it rooted in my mother's fervent ultramontane Catholicism which held the same view of Protestants as my discreetly agnostic and religiously indifferent Protestant father held of Germans and British Tories? Or was it nurtured in a Catholic primary school system in which, admittedly, catechism was taught with much less fervour than English or maths, but in which the odour of Rome was all-pervasive? The early debts are indelible but nebulous.

Less nebulous is the legacy of two other pre-university institutions: grammar school and the Royal Navy.

Early education: the seeds of doubt

Whitehaven Grammar School was a traditional northern English educational institution dedicated to élitism, learning and minor snobberies. Entrance was by the so-called 11-plus system – a barbaric examination system which filtered out the clever according to absurdly narrow criteria and which condemned the excluded – the vast majority – to a sub-standard education system (an obsession with the education of the élite at the expense of the population at large is a congenital and expensive failing of

162

the English ...). Learning was construed in the narrow sense of preparing the inmates for examination success. The names of pupils who succeeded in entering Oxbridge were given permanent and prominent place on boards which decorated the walls of the school assembly hall, recalling the long and sombre lists of the fallen of the 1914–18 War which are to be found in every French parish church. Although the school aimed at education (sport was abundant and a much welcome relief) it provided instruction. Much later, when I was told Clemenceau's celebrated description of the students of the *École Polytechnique* ('they know everything there is to know – but nothing more') my own school experiences came immediately to mind. I was taught to cope with foreign languages (including Latin, which was then required for university entry) and mathematics, rather than to understand them – let alone appreciate them. Whilst I came to perceive the aesthetic appeal of languages I remain totally untouched by the beauty of mathematics ('the closest thing to philosophy' according to a friend who was a Cambridge-trained mathematician). I recognize, with no sense of anguish, that lack of mathematical skills is an increasing handicap, given the current developments in political science.

I look back with singular lack of affection on Whitehaven Grammar School, with its self-conscious aping of the public school, its attachment to empty tribal rites, its explicit and largely unwarranted hierarchies, its sense of being apart from the local community (local accents were actively discouraged by well-meaning teachers blessed with the gift of 'received pronunciation'), and with its headmaster, a practising Methodist who raised priggishness and pomposity to a fine art. When a university student in London I resolutely refused to join the local group of Whitehaven Old Grammarians (or Wogs as they unsmilingly called themselves), and shed no tears when the school was abolished and transformed into a comprehensive school. Yet, perhaps my assessment of my school experience is unjust: it was undoubtedly an instrument of social mobility for the academically gifted, and individual teachers bestowed upon me two precious and enduring gifts: a love of the English language and, perhaps more significantly, of history. In truth, it was difficult to remain insensitive to history in a town such as Whitehaven with its famous and infamous past, a past forged by shipping and coalmining, and deeply marked by the opulence of one family and by the squalor of almost all the others. Despite the endeavours of municipal vandals who demolished some of the town's splendid houses (including my maternal grandparents' ...), Whitehaven still bears the marks of its invasion by John Paul Jones (an apprentice trained in Whitehaven who was to become the founder of the American Navy), its association with Washington and Swift, its Georgian heyday, its violent and tragic mining economy, its religious diversity. As a schoolboy, I spent prolonged periods in the local library (directed by a fine local historian) reading about the turbulent past of the town. I still have a tendency to romanticize about Whitehaven and about my hours spent pottering in the local port. But my overwhelming impression is relief about not having to live in its all-pervading atmosphere of geographical remoteness and of social and intellectual claustrophobia. I was almost certainly wedded to the big town before I left Whitehaven.

Before going to the LSE I spent two years in the Royal Navy – 'the university of life' to borrow a characteristically vacuous phrase of Prince Philip. It was in no sense a university. Indeed, at first sight, with its institutionalized and internalized unquestioning of orders – however fatuous – its basic principles ran counter to those which underpin the logic of the university. Yet my stay in the Royal Navy was an immensely rewarding one, and not only personally. I spent most of my two years on HMS *Bulwark* – an aircraft carrier – and travelled widely from the Baltic to the Mediterranean. I had also a great deal of spare time to read (in peace-time the military fight not the enemy but boredom). Happily, the ship's library numbered a plentiful supply of history books. Intellectually, my time on the Bulwark taught me the difference between intelligence and intellect, since some of the most intelligent (and interesting) people I encountered had little formal education whilst the obverse was even more apparent. I also learnt – though probably in retrospect – about the significance of institutions in shaping behaviour and in mediating conflicts, about the capacity of institutions to attract a deep loyalty which would rarely, if ever, be articulated, and about the vulnerability of even entrenched authority. Hierarchy on board ship was functional, but its efficacy was rooted in legitimacy, and it was highly dependent upon trust. Oddly enough, those notoriously slippery concepts of legitimacy and trust are at the heart of some of my current interests in regulation. Again, in retrospect, it is possible for me to identify on board HMS *Bulwark* the practical application of some of the insights of the political philosophers who provided part of my intellectual diet at the LSE. I have to admit that Hobbes, whose virtues I preach to my students, would not be the best guide to an understanding of the human society that made up a Royal Navy warship.

The LSE: the legacy of Oakeshott

My intellectual home was – and remains to a considerable extent – the London School of Economics *and* Political Science. Yet, in terms of my development as a comparatist, it is difficult to trace the source of the intellectual attachment. The School, as it is affectionately known, was a wonderful environment, in spite of its architectural drawbacks, its overcrowded and ill-swept classrooms, and its inadequate facilities (the student refectory produced food which was the stuff of legend, the library was a researcher's dream but a nightmare for the average undergraduate, and the sports ground was an eternity away by British Rail). Yet the School was unique, and I remain defensive and impatient of criticism of it. It is unmistakably metropolitan, situated as it is in the heart of one of the great cities of the world, and cosmopolitan. My student peer group was interesting and argumentative (one of the major criteria of any first-class academic establishment), and my teachers, when accessible, were friendly and helpful. Economics was dominated by Robbins, and Political Science – my apologies, Government – was under the benign if tenacious control of Michael Oakeshott. Uncharacteristic discretion prevents me from passing comment on the leadership of the Sociology and International Relations Departments. Hayek had already departed to the intellectually more congenial pastures of Chicago, although *The Road to Serfdom* remained compulsory reading for the LSE Government students. So, too, were the works of Karl Popper, another dignitary of the School, and one of the many out-standing teachers recruited from the ranks of the persecuted.

What was the standard diet in the Government Department of the LSE in the late 1950s and early 1960s? It was not formal theory. It was certainly not numerate. And it was not comparative – even though comparative government was a compulsory subject. Methodology? The very word would have elicited a gentle chuckle from Michael

Oakeshott and a calculated guffaw from some of his disciples who colonized the Department. Indicators? The idea would have been greeted with pure incredulity. The dominant ethos of the Department was dictated by Oakeshott who gently exorcized the spirit of Harold Laski, his predecessor as head of the Department. The key principles were enquiry, questioning and argument, and they were directed to the great texts in the history of political thought – those of Plato and Aristotle, of Saint Augustine and Saint Thomas Aquinas, of Machiavelli and Hobbes – the beloved Hobbes – Locke, Hume and Burke and Rousseau, Bentham and Mill, and ending in Hegel. Marx was rejected on the grounds that he had authored no worthy text. On the other hand, Marsilius of Padua (yes, Marsilius of Padua) was included because he had done so.

The intellectual tone of the Department was established and protected by Oakeshott and by the philosophers and historians he recruited. Oakeshott was a brilliant if elusive scholar. His lectures on Greek political thought, given to a capacity crowd of undergraduates, were magic, and provided, without question, the most memorable academic occasion of my entire career. That the lectures took place in the Old Theatre was entirely appropriate. Argument was conveyed with a deceptive gentility and simulated understatement which did nothing to mask the conviction of the central message. Yet conviction did not always signify clarity, for Oakeshott's fatal ease with language sometimes conveyed the impression of clarity about ideas characterized by opacity. My subsequent reading of Oakeshott leaves me uncertain about the degree of calculation in the obfuscation. Oakeshott's central message, powerfully conveyed in *Political Education*, his inaugural lecture which sent shock waves through the Laski-dominated Department, was simple and paradoxical: there was no message. A profound scepticism and pessimism pervade all his teachings, and his conservatism was both philosophical and historical: Margaret Thatcher would have appalled him (although, I suspect, also amused him in a wry sort of way). It takes little imagination, therefore, to conjure up his sentiments on the teaching of comparative government. Like the rest of the teaching of political institutions, it was formed and deformed by scepticism and history. The Department's strength lay in the teaching of individual countries – notably Britain, the USA, France, the USSR – which were taught by historians. Of particular note was Leonard Schapiro who, in that wonderfully gravelly voice, clearly conveyed his love of nineteenth-century Russia and his distaste for anything post-1917. Lecturing on France were a formidable couple, Dorothy and Bill Pickles: Dorothy, the hard-working and trenchant critic; Bill, the perceptive and witty, who could lecture for an hour on the most abstruse points of the French Constitution aided only by a few pencilled notes on the back of an envelope. It was Bill Pickles who triggered my interest in France and who was to convince me to pursue postgraduate work on France – and in France. Bill Pickles, Leonard Schapiro and all the other teachers of institutions at the LSE were not comparatists even though they were generally well-informed about politics outside the country of their speciality. And this was reflected in the type of examination questions set in the comparative politics paper: the rare invitations to compare and contrast had a horrible inevitability about them.

I have no regrets about my undergraduate education (I genuinely feel sorry for modern politics students who have little grounding in history and little occasion to read the great texts of political thought), but I have to recognize that it provided me with no training (another taboo word) for comparative work. If it led to my love of France, it also reinforced my love of history and my natural leanings to scepticism.

France: an abiding love affair

After the heady days of the LSE I initially found it difficult to adjust to the career-oriented atmosphere and formal rules of the *Institut d'Études Politiques* in Paris. The ethos of the place was shaped by the *concours* – particularly the highly competitive examination for entrance into the *École Nationale d'Administration*. I missed the intellectual rough and tumble and cosmopolitanism of the LSE, and the contact with teachers that the British system afforded. I was also unpleasantly surprised by the narrowness of the intellectual focus of *Sciences-Po*. Subjects were almost exclusively Franco-French and were taught in a Franco-French way, and a great deal of the education was technical in character and taught by high-ranking public officials who were recruited for part-time teaching purposes. The general air of formality even affected sport, and I can still recall the register being called on the Saturday morning compulsory sports session to a group of impeccably turned out if resentful young bourgeois. I discovered that playing rugby for *Sciences-Po* was an admirable way of making friends – although the team was viewed with either total indifference or disdain by most of the student body. Incidentally, playing rugby for teams of different nationality is a speedy recipe for learning about profound cultural differences ....

I spent my first six months in Paris reading nineteenth-century French anarchist thought, and even wrote a long and rambling essay on Elisée Reclus (whom I came to revisit when, in circumstances too complicated to relate, I had to supervise an Oxford thesis on Kropotkin). I found, however, that there was a mismatch between the unbridled idealism of the anarchists and my own ingrained scepticism. Perversely, I then turned to a study of nineteenth-century Catholic thought, but the anguished verbal acrobatics of the liberals trying to explain away the oppressive authoritarianism of Pius IX soon palled. So, too, did the acerbic and dogmatic defence of papal authority by the ultramontanes led by Louis Veuillot whose total lack of doubt was refreshing in only small doses. I abandoned my study of nineteenth-century Catholicism, but am still fascinated by certain aspects of it, and have written on its relationship with the state (Wright 1973a).

It was under the influence of René Rémond – a fine historian who constantly violates disciplinary borderlines – that I changed tack completely, and turned to electoral geography. However, I found the determinism of Siegfried, the father of the subject in France, unappealing. Perhaps unsurprisingly, I was more attracted to the approaches of Armengaud, of Dupeux and of Vigier, historians who had written highly detailed *thèses d'Etat* (those great monuments to the excellence of the French historical tradition) on particular localities and whose interests lay in placing elections in a much wider economic, political and social context (Armengaud 1961; Dupeux 1962; Vigier 1963). After discussion with René Rémond and François Goguel – already the grand old man of French elections – I chose the Basses-Pyrénées, a *département* characterized by geographical isolation and social and ethnic diversity. It was a singularly happy choice, and my two years in the local archives of Pau, the *cheflieu* of the *département*, anchored my love of provincial France, created close friendships, and proved an invaluable apprenticeship in dealing with French officialdom (the local archivist loved his archives so much that he was determined to reserve them for himself). Those two years were also intellectually challenging, for I had only sporadic contact with Bill Pickles, my official supervisor at the LSE. The period selected for my thesis covered the first twenty-five years of universal suffrage – a period of massive electoral mobilization and only incipient political parties. Two initial interconnected questions held together my thesis: how far did the elections in this area reflect the national situation? How were similarities and specificities to be explained? The two questions broadened into a wider issue of the political integration of a remote territory into the nation and the mechanisms (including electoral) deployed to facilitate it. It is an issue which continues to intrigue me. In the case of my own thesis, the role played by local *notables* and their relationship with the state-appointed prefects emerged as critical explanatory variables. This was true even during the period of the Second Empire – a constitutionally authoritarian and heavily centralized system in which the prefectoral administration acquired the reputation of being composed of brutal and insensitive *préfets à poigne* (defined as 'an official who would, if ordered, execute an opponent twice'). Behind the constitutional façade lay a practice of constant negotiated accommodation between Paris (represented by the prefects) and certain Basque and Béarnais *notables* whose position was strengthened by the conferment of state patronage. Electoral opposition to the regime – invariably expressed by a republican vote – could generally be attributed to the activities of local *notables* excluded from the negotiation and patronage process. Tracking down the correlation between attitude and activity of a particular *notable* and the voting in his *commune* as well as the integration of that disgruntled *notable* into a wider political movement required painstaking archival work in the national and local archives.

In writing my thesis I explored and even discovered themes which remain central to my intellectual interests. I also acquired a taste for detailed archival work which has never deserted me. Given the choice of listening to yet another lecture on rational choice or spending the time in the local archives I should not hesitate an instant.

On the completion of my thesis in 1965 I left France – but only after a great deal of soul-searching – and returned to Britain, to take up a post at the University of Newcastle upon Tyne. For both my personal and intellectual life the three years spent in Newcastle were to prove critical. Intellectually, I was forced to broaden my interests, since, in a tiny Department of three, I had to teach a range of subjects. I taught, among other things, socialist thought, Jean-Jacques Rousseau, British politics (I can still remember – not altogether fondly – some of those classes), the government and politics of the USSR and, of course, France. I also taught comparative government – or a rather timorous version of it. Perhaps more important than the broadening experience of teaching was the exposure to Hugh Berrington, the head of the Department, an implacable critic who would tolerate no limp reasoning and who would question any loose proposition. Berrington also had the uncanny knack of integrating theory and institutions, rendering immediately relevant the great texts – even those of Marsilius of Padua. Even at the time I had the impression of attending a prolonged and enriching seminar, and of accumulating a considerable intellectual debt. I was also acutely aware that, under Berrington's direction, the Newcastle Politics Department provided its students with a better grounding in the subject than anything I had received at the LSE or was initially to perceive in Oxford.

The return to the LSE: single country specialism and the beginnings of comparison

After a brief spell at St Antony's College, Oxford, I returned, in 1969, to my Alma Mater, the LSE, where I was to remain for seven years, first as a Lecturer, then as a Senior Lecturer and finally as Reader in Government. During this period I specialized in French government and politics, and wrote three books on France and took my first tentative steps in Franco-British comparison. The first of the three books – on the French prefects (Leclère and Wright 1973) – was an attempt to test some of the findings of my thesis. More specifically, it sought to explain how and why the prefects of the Second Empire, armed with all the resources of authoritarianism, increasingly locked themselves into a strategy of mediated accommodation. The second work – *Le Conseil d'État* of the same period (Wright 1972) – was embedded in the same set of intellectual problems – those connected with the relationship between individual ambitions, exogenous pressures and institutional structures, norms and memories. Both books relate and explain the subversion of imposed institutional roles by men (there were no women in either institution at the time) carefully recruited to perform them. Both books were based on extensive archival research and were the product of a typical country specialist. As such they elicited the approval of my LSE colleagues, including Michael Oakeshott himself who, despite official retirement, continued to haunt the corridors and the collective intellectual ethos of the Government Department.

My work on *Le Conseil d'État* and on the prefectoral administration brought me into contact with members of both corps. One of the more endearing qualities of many high-ranking civil servants in France is their interest in the past of their own institution (the contrast with their British counterparts could not be sharper ...). Through constant contact with these *hauts fonctionnaires*, notably Guy Thuillier of the *Cour des Comptes*, Guy Braibant and Louis Fougère of the *Conseil d'État*, I became interested in the contemporary French administration, and, very much under their influence, wrote an article which was considered to be iconoclastic at the time, but which was to become part of the received truth (Wright 1974). My third book, written at the LSE and commissioned by Professor William Robson, a mild left-winger with strong regal bearing and proclivities, *The Government and Politics of France*, was a textbook. Unfortunately, it sold well, and I have been the prisoner of its success since its first appearance in 1978, for I have been pressured into updating it on more occasions than I should have chosen.

My period as a teacher at the LSE was also marked by three factors which were to ease me into a comparative direction. The first was the constant stream of invitations to lecture in French universities on British politics, which forced me into constant, if largely implicit, Franco-British comparison. These invitations extended my contacts to that tiny band of French academics who were beginning to be interested in explicit comparison. This band included Jacques Lagroye at Bordeaux, with whom I was to edit a volume on local government in Britain and France (Lagroye and Wright 1979), and Yves Mény, then at the University of Rennes, who was to become a close friend and constant collaborator and who was rapidly transforming himself into a comparatist. The second factor was renewed acquaintance with Jack Hayward, a friend from Paris student days. Hayward was a French specialist, and we collaborated in a series of articles on French elections. He was keenly interested in issues of comparative political economy – and long before they became fashionable. I am forever grateful that he managed to infect me with his enthusiasm. It was thus a political scientist who rekindled my interest in economic issues which economists had singularly succeeded in extinguishing. Working initially on economic policy-making under the Mitterrand presidency (Wright 1984; Wright and Machin 1985) I was slowly to take the same comparative path as Hayward, particularly after I left the LSE in 1977 to take up a post at Nuffield College, Oxford.

The third factor which moved me at the LSE in a more comparative direction was the arrival in the Government Department of Gordon Smith, a German specialist but also the author of the about-to-be-published *Politics in Western Europe*. Personal and intellectual empathy was immediate. This empathy led to the creation of a jointly-organized Master's degree in *West European Politics* which became increasingly comparative in nature. It also led to the founding of the jointly-edited *West European Politics*, a journal which is soon to celebrate its twentieth birthday under the same joint editorship. Editing is an intellectually rewarding exercise, since the flood of manuscripts submitted to the journal exposes the editors to new subjects, new approaches, new ideas and a barrage of up-to-date information. Perhaps no less important is the link that it maintains with Gordon Smith, whose droll and tragi-comic attitude to life and whose mixture of protested innocence and deliberately provocative cynicism are a source of endless appeal. Smith and I have our disagreements about editorial policy, and these are often expressed in simulated rows which would alarm the ill-informed eavesdropper. They centre on the balance of the journal (the space accorded, for example, to the European Union) and the topics (I cast a bilious eye on political parties and elections while he is instinctively suspicious of manuscripts on public policy). The journal reflects the differences between the editors and the competing requirements of its readerships, but this does not appear to have impaired its apparent success. Indeed, while continuity of editorship may have helped to establish the profile of *West European Politics*, differences within the editorship may have spared it from becoming the vehicle of a narrow sect. *West European Politics* remains an object of some pride: its breadth, eclecticism and accessibility, its openness to young academics (and even to research students), convey, however unwittingly, a plea for pluralism and tolerance within the European comparative politics community.

The EUI and Nuffield College: comparison made explicit

It was at the LSE, which had initially made me into a sceptically-minded and historically-sensitive single country specialist, that I tentatively moved to Franco-British comparison and then to a direct interest in wider West European comparison. My comparative interests were further stimulated after my arrival at Nuffield College, Oxford, and even more so in 1980, after my appointment to a Chair at the European University Institute in Florence.

The EUI had many problems at the time: it lacked critical mass; it spent too much time reinventing its own memory; it was isolated from its own Florentine hinterland; its professors were transient; its teaching methods were ill-formed. It was also wracked by a number of personal enmities. and was unclear about its intellectual vocation. Yet the Institute was also aware of its defects, agonized about them, and, in spite of them, managed to produce some excellent students and research. Personally, my stay there represented a significant stage in my intellectual trajectory. Not only was I able to organize, with Yves Mény, a weekly comparative seminar on centre–periphery relations in Western Europe. I also co-directed, with Mény, a research project on the political management of the steel crisis in Western Europe. The project combined our interests in economic policy-making and centre–periphery relations. The subsequent book (Mény and Wright 1987) has the proportions and sometimes the meandering quality of a Gothic tale, and I personally prefer the shorter French version (Mény and Wright 1985). Yet it was an invaluable exercise in managing a large inter-disciplinary group, and taught me the need for modesty in structuring a comparative proposal.

The EUI also brought me into contact with Peter Flora, Rudolf Wildenmann and Hans Daalder. It was the last who most influenced my thinking – probably because his approach was most closely in sympathy with my own incipient comparative efforts. Daalder's comparative approach, forged by the Rokkan school, was tempered by his own historical sensitivity (his critique of Lijphart should be made compulsory reading), and it did not prevent him from considering the critical role of individuals in politics. Yet Daalder was a comparatist, and although his misgivings about my own timidity rarely surfaced (a growing friendship probably blunted his customary frankness) it was nevertheless clear. No less important in expressing my failings as a comparatist were two Young Turks at the Institute – Peter Mair and Stefano Bartolini. The first did so with a mixture of gentle condescension and good-humoured fatalism, the second with explicit and systematic precision. On more than one occasion, fuelled by a bottle of Chianti, Bartolini and I argued about the aim of comparison and the role of theory in structuring it. I was probably more convinced by Bartolini's arguments than I was prepared to admit at the time. In retrospect, my relatively brief time at the Institute proved crucial in forcing me to address the methodological problems involved in comparison as well as taking into consideration the need for some basic theorizing. It also convinced me that good comparative work probably required collaborative effort and provided me with contact with some of the scholars with whom I was to co-operate in the future.

Nuffield College, Oxford, my academic base since 1977, has many obvious advantages: excellent colleagues, a first-class library, friendly and effective secretarial facilities (indispensable for a Luddite like myself), and the means to finance a sustained seminar activity, a constant flow of visitors and collaborative research. It also recruits a small group of very good students whose demands have been a source of both constant irritation and intellectual stimulation. Philip Williams, a close friend and colleague at Nuffield, and a scholar of unimpeachable credentials, once confided that his ambition was to reach retirement before my bluff was finally called. I understood perfectly what he meant. Able and increasingly well-trained students oblige their supervisors to function on their own terrain, and it is not false modesty which provokes this claim. My research students at the LSE, the EUI and Oxford, and more recently at the Juan March Institute in Madrid (where I help to supervise some of the most talented students I have ever encountered), have represented a collective and persistent pressure on me to adjust to the exigencies of a changing political science. In that sense, they have trained me, and not the reverse. Several of my students have become friends and close collaborators.

Nuffield College has one final advantage for the scholar: it is imbued with an austere and remorseless work ethos, and its financial means help to insulate it from a wider

British university environment which is undergoing radical and damaging change. Even its relationship with the rest of Oxford University is a curiously distant one. The College makes a hefty financial contribution to the University, it has produced many of the social science teachers of the University, the lectures and seminars organized in Nuffield are open to all university students, the College Fellows supervise students from other Colleges. Yet the College cultivates its own sense of separateness, and is viewed with little warmth by much of the University. As a research environment, Nuffield could hardly be bettered. Not only has it exposed me to good students, but it has also enabled me to work with economists, has provided links with the College's methodologically exacting sociologists, and has provided the facilities for fostering collaborative comparative work. It accepted – not without a certain wariness and suspicion – the creation of the Centre for European Studies which, after some initial teething troubles due to insensitive management, now functions, in a modest way, to facilitate research and collaborative links with European and American colleagues. The Centre has active programmes for visitorships from Eastern Europe, Italy and France, and welcomes visitors from the USA and from other European countries. It has also now forged friendly and fruitful relations with the European Centres of St Antony's College and of the University, which is responsible for the running of a Master's degree in European Politics and Society.

Current interests and activities

Since my return to Nuffield from Florence my work has extended over several areas. My interest in nineteenth- and twentieth-century French history has in no way diminished. It remains the bedrock of my research activity, and I remain a constant and uncontrite visitor to Paris and provincial archives. My historical research focuses on the French administration, and has ranged from its relationship with Parliament, and the problems of the first *École Nationale d'Administration*, to the internal discussions in the War Ministry and the recruitment and role of *directeurs* in the central ministries (Wright 1973b, 1976a, 1976b, 1982, 1993a). However, most of this historical work continues to centre on the prefectoral corps and on the *Conseil d'État* – both as administrative machines and as élite institutions (Wright 1973c; for an example on the prefectoral administration see Wright 1978b). I have become increasingly interested in the role of the administration in the management of political systems under extreme stress (Wright 1975, 1976; Wright and Mazey 1992) and am completing a prolonged and self-indulgent period of research (involving work in every departmental archive in France) for a two-volume study of France during *l'année terrible* – 1870–71 – when the country experienced a change of regime, an aborted revolution, military defeat and occupation, separatist tendencies in some parts of the country, social turmoil, religious tensions, economic dislocation, and major administrative purges (resulting in the replacement of all the prefects and sub-prefects). My central questions are simple: what happens to an allegedly over-centralized political system when the centre is effectively destroyed? If the country was so weakened by military defeat and by intense internal divisions, what held it together? More generally, it will be addressing – rather critically – some of the larger questions arising out of the political science literature – on cleavages and integration.

I was stimulated by John Armstrong's *The European Administrative Élite* (an impressive work, and all the more so since it was written before the great outpouring of administrative history research which commenced in the mid-1970s; see Armstrong 1973), but it was not until the mid-1980s that my work on administrative history assumed a comparative dimension. Thus, I have completed a study of the development of the French *Conseil d'État* and the Italian *Consiglio di Stato*, in an attempt to explain why apparently similar institutions have taken such divergent paths (Wright 1994a).

My interest in the comparative dimension of administrative history has been sustained by my membership of the History Working Group of the International Institute of Administrative Sciences – a group which I have chaired since 1992. I was responsible for editing a comparative volume on the issue of representativity in public administration, which originated in the work of the group (Wright 1991). Further volumes emanating from the Working Group include one on the impact of the Napoleonic model on other European states (Wunder 1995) and one on the administrative entourage of the core executive in several countries (Raadschelders 1996).

My joint editorship of the *Yearbook of European Administrative History* which, by 1996, had helped to produce eight volumes, has also been a means of consolidating my interest in comparative administrative history. Overall editorial responsibility lies with Erk Heyen, a genial and long-suffering scholar, although the co-editors are charged with responsibility for particular volumes (my own dealt with the early administration of the European Community (Volume 2, 1992) and with public administrations in times of crisis (Volume 6, 1996)).

As Chairman of the History Group of the International Institute of Administrative Science and as joint editor of *The Yearbook* I have become increasingly and acutely aware of my own intellectual schizophrenia, for my view of history oscillates between two extremes: on the one hand, perceiving the study of history as intellectually fascinating in its own right, driven by its own intellectual imperatives and generating its own disciplinary dictates; on the other, seeing it as the best mode of political science explanation. The tensions on the perception of history within the History Group of the International Institute of Administrative Science are sometimes palpable. It is scarcely surprising, therefore, that I have been interested in the current unnecessarily acrimonious debate in sociological circles on the relationship between history and social science. Characteristically, my views are ambivalent. I am convinced of the need for history – based on detailed research and not on a culling of selected secondary sources – as the principal instrument of comparative explanation: most of the crucial 'why' questions demand resort to history. Yet I am unclear how far back into history we have to delve to find explanation, and I am queasy about imposing rigid social science frameworks or even exploiting contemporary questions as a method of structuring historical research (for two recent examples, see Torstendahl 1991 and Silberman 1994), since its much criticized random quality (a source of considerable inconvenience for the social scientist) has its own distinct intellectual advantages. I also share John Goldthorpe's misgivings about macro-historical sociology. However, I have yet to work out satisfactorily my view of the relationship between history and political science beyond a nebulous belief that they are indispensable bedmates. It is to be regretted that political scientists, unlike sociologists, have singularly failed to confront the methodological problems involved in the relationship.

My second current interest lies in contemporary public administration. Although I continue to publish on the French system (Wright 1989) I have become increasingly interested in the British civil service – probably because it has been so dramatically and damagingly reformed (Wright 1993b) – and in the reform movement in the rest of Western Europe (Mény and Wright 1994). My interests lie in essentially four directions: in the problems involved for national bureaucracies in adjusting to new modes of regulation (some of which are international or transnational in character, cf. Wright 1992, 1993c); in the national bureaucratic management of membership of the European Union (Kassim and Wright 1991); in the unintended and paradoxical consequences of the privatization of public administration (Wright 1993d); in the reasons why similar pressures for administrative reform are translated into ambitions which differ and into programmes which differ even more (Wright 1994b). This last concern naturally led me to the literature on institutionalism, to historical institutionalism and more especially to Peter Hall and to March and Olsen whose work I have come increasingly to admire and whose anti-rational choice bias strikes a responsive chord in my own readings of politics and history (Hall 1986; Olsen 1976; March and Olsen 1984; Olsen 1986). My work on bureaucratic reform tends to confirm the thrust of the historical institutionalist argument, although it might be becoming somewhat less valid in the area of economic reform – a point I shall touch upon later. Acquaintance with the work on bureaucracies by Patrick Dunleavy (1991) and by Christopher Hood (1976, 1983, 1986, 1991), a reading of a short comparative work by Ed Page (1985), and very recently my collaboration with Guy Peters from Pittsburgh have combined to strengthen – and widen – my comparative interests, and also to awaken a number of theoretical concerns. Thus I am currently engaged with Guy Peters on several projects, including a piece describing and explaining the attempts to dismantle, in certain bureaucracies, key features of the Weberian model. This has obliged me to go back to the texts (Oakeshott would be proud of me) – an exercise which has revealed that Weber was not entirely free from ambiguity and even contradiction. This may be highly reassuring, but it has rendered difficult the writing of the article.

The third area of my current interests lies in economic policy-making, and more especially in government–industry relations (Wright 1994c) and in privatization and regulation. A conference on privatization in Western Europe, organized with John Vickers, an economist from Nuffield, was transformed into a special issue of *West European Politics*. A later conference on the same subject, which I organized for the *Observatoire du Changement Social* in Poitiers, was published in French and English (Vickers and Wright 1989; Wright 1993e). Privatization is a gold mine for political scientists, for it raises profound philosophical and moral questions about property rights, about the concept of state and of the nature of public goods, and about the balance between state, market and society. For public policy specialists, it provides valuable material for analysing well-known phenomena, ranging from policy diffusion and policy reversal to policy slippage and policy fiasco, as well as enabling the testing of rational choice theory, theories of regulation, interest group theory, and approaches based on policy networks and policy communities. My own interest in privatization is twofold. Firstly, as with public-sector reform generally, I am interested in the unintended and paradoxical nature of the reform programmes. Secondly, as a comparatist, I am interested in explaining the differences in the different privatization programmes. Historical institutionalism is without doubt a good explanatory starting point, but my research suggests two caveats. The first is that in an area such as privatization institutionalism needs to be extended beyond the already broad category of political and governmental institutions, conventions, rules, customs, prejudices, instincts and culture, in order to embrace economic and financial institutions (the shape of domestic capitalism, the size of the financial markets, the structure of investors, the culture of investment). The second caveat relates to the growing impact of the cumulative and intense pressures of an economic, ideological, political, financial and technological nature – some international or European Union in character, others purely domestic – that are sweeping aside some of the impediments rooted in historically-embedded institutionalism.

From privatization I have, almost inevitably, moved to regulation – at both national and domestic level. Regulation is an intellectually more demanding and more exciting field than privatization. It requires a comparative, interdisciplinary and theoretical approach, since it raises clear questions for economists, international political economists, political scientists, sociologists, organizational theorists and even social anthropologists. It is certainly much too serious a subject to be left to pure economists (which was the theme of a lecture I gave in Harvard in 1994). It raises questions of authority, legitimacy and trust, questions which my days in the Royal Navy had already posed. The research of certain British applied economists and the pioneering work of Giandomenico Majone have greatly influenced my own thinking, and are surely pointing to developments which political scientists will ignore at their peril (Majone 1989, which should be read by all students of comparative public policy; for an example of his work on regulation see Majone 1994). Unlike corporatism, a geographically limited and conjectural phenomenon – even if it was sometimes imprudently presented otherwise – regulation is a permanent and structural feature of modern capitalism. Its nature is rapidly changing and becoming much more problematic. Together with administrative reform and privatization it is helping to reshape the nation state in Western Europe, which brings me to my fourth area of interest.

My intellectual preoccupations, combined with living through the unpalatable experience of Conservative Britain and witnessing the reaction of British political scientists to that experience, could not fail but to provoke questions about the alleged process of state demise or state retreat. Two joint-edited volumes – one with Wolfgang Müller of the University of Vienna, the other with Sabino Cassese of the University of Rome – take a very sceptical look at the allegation (Müller and Wright 1994; Cassese and Wright forthcoming). The major theme of both volumes is that there is a major process of state restructuring (not demise) at work, that the process is nationally differentiated, that countervailing pressures are evident (decline in one area, growth in another), that pressures on the nation state are sometimes exploited as opportunities, that within the state apparatus there are winners and losers resulting from the reshaping process, that decentralization and Europeanization should not be construed as zero sum games, that popular demand for state intervention remains high, and that the nation state, with all its problems, remains, for most citizens, the principal repository of legitimate authority. In arguing this case, I am aware that I lay myself open to the not entirely unjustifiable accusation of being an old-fashioned Jacobin, perverted by a nostalgia for the 1950s and 1960s, by a penchant for limited social democratic distributionalism, and by an admiration for the French prefectoral administration.

My instinctive and intellectual Jacobinism (which has survived the years of mindless centralization in my own country) informs my fifth area of interest, which is centre–periphery relations in Western Europe. The development of the interest reflects my general intellectual trajectory. The interest, born in French history and extended to Britain by requests to lecture and write on my own country, became more comparative under the influence of Sidney Tarrow (a valued friend whose *Between Center and Periphery* I continue to recommend to students as a model for two-country research; Tarrow 1977) and of Yves Mény when I collaborated with him at the European University Institute. I continue to write on French historical aspects of centre–periphery relations (Wright, forthcoming; Hazareesingh and Wright, forthcoming) and, in French, on Britain (Wright 1986). But comparison is now well entrenched in my academic agenda. In retaining this interest in centre–periphery relations I am acutely sensitive to the jibe that academics spend their lives rewriting their theses. I am conscious, too, that it is not always easy to escape the confines of one's academic past: we become prisoners of our colleagues' perceptions and invitations. I am no less aware of the siren calls of inertia and laziness, rationalized by claims for the need for experience: having taken years to accumulate an intellectual baggage is it desirable or wise to discard it? I can only plead a persistent fascination with centre–periphery relations, and enjoyed putting together, with Rod Rhodes (whose work on British intergovernmental relations should serve as the model for his continental counterparts), a comparative volume on the subject (Rhodes and Wright 1987). At the time of writing, I am preparing another volume on the subject with Ernesto Carrillo of the Josè Ortega y Gasset Institute in Madrid. I derive particular pleasure from witnessing the renovation of the field by a generation of younger scholars, whose ideas I shamelessly pillage and whose influence I readily acknowledge.

Last, but far from least, I am currently involved, with Jack Hayward, long-standing friend and collaborator, in a comparative project on core executives in Western Europe. This is part of a much wider research venture, directed by Rod Rhodes and financed by the British Economic and Social Research Council and which focuses on Whitehall. The Hayward–Wright project has mobilized a group of proven scholars, known for their expertise, reliability and collaborative skills, who are responsible for co-ordinating work on France, Germany, Italy, the Netherlands, Spain and Austria. The essential purpose of the project is to analyse and compare the co-ordinating capacity of the core executives in the above countries. Four sectors have been selected (immigration, European policy-making, budget-making, public sector reform and privatization) and a spectrum of policy types (ranging from the politicized emergency to the bureaucratic routinized) have been chosen. As with all comparative work, an apparently straightforward project, based on a relatively simple matrix, quickly ran into a methodological and definitional quagmire: what is meant by co-ordination? what constitutes a core executive? how to identify comparable case studies? And, endlessly, so on. Yet regular meetings of the team, organized at Nuffield, are slowly ironing out some of the difficulties.

Present uncertainties

Thirty years in British and French academia, punctuated by visits to other European and to American universities, have slowly transformed a historically-minded single-country specialist into a prudent and inadequate comparatist, and one who, under the pressure of institutional attachments and student pressure, is more sensitive to problems of methodology and the need for theory.

Why a hesitant comparatist? In part, it is simply a description of my intellectual development. In part, it is no doubt motivated by the charms of intellectual indolence: it is so much easier to remain a single-country specialist. But my hesitancy is also a reflection of my continued doubts and uncertainties, in spite of the recent and increasingly dogmatic pressures which I place on my students for rigorous methodology, for close attention to the nature of evidence, for the need for clear indicators, for a firm theoretical basis. But, what is the purpose of comparison? To test a theory (but why not a detailed case study?)? To reveal the similarities and differences amongst nation states (but at what level of analysis does the problem of plausibility in the choice of states begin to emerge?)? To highlight the specificities of a particular country (then how to select the other countries?)? As a heuristic exercise? In truth, I am unable to favour any one approach, for I do not know which of the purposes is superior. I admire the work of Stefano Bartolini and Peter Mair no more or no less than that of Rudy Andeweg and Wolfgang Müller – to mention four younger members of the profession who use comparison for different purposes. Clearly, the answer to the question determines the methodology employed. Unfortunately, I have sometimes the impression that methodology dictates the questions that are raised.

To reiterate a further point, I am also uncertain about the relationship between history and comparative politics. As an undergraduate I was shaken to discover my own intellectual attraction for Burke and Oakeshott and was torn between intuitive sympathy and political rejection. I confess that I am occasionally assailed by the uncomfortable thought that comparison and history are intrinsically ill-suited partners, and relegating each to different roles (the first to demonstrating differences, the second to explaining them) does not resolve the discomfort. Why should history be restricted to the role of elucidating the issues that exercise political scientists? – the rather tart rejoinder of a friendly historian to my lame plea for the interdependence of the two subjects (Wright 1990). More importantly, I suspect that the ingrained scepticism, the eye of detail and the sensitivity to individual action that are required by the good historian are likely to inhibit the comparatist. For historians, the concept of the model is anathema, and parsimony and elegance (two dangerous intellectual goals imported into political science from economics) are to be eschewed at all costs. Furthermore, simplification – the first step in comparison – is considered to be intellectual betrayal. A similar inhibiting effect on the kind of political comparison most admired by many non-political scientist springs from an intimate knowledge of one or two countries. In short, how does comparison incorporate the requirements of the historian and the country specialist? Can it? Such questions induce hesitation. However, I have to confess that this hesitation has never spilled over into anguish. I am happy to live with my intellectual schizophrenia – to preach the need for comparative method, to practise timid comparison, to close my door in Nuffield on occasions and write history, and to profit from the networks of colleagues and friends created and consolidated by both politics and history.

16 Encounter with power

Pierre Birnbaum

Université de Paris I

I

I was born at the end of the Phoney War at a time when the force of arms had already shaped the destiny of France. My early childhood was played out against the backdrop of a general military and political collapse, a time fraught with danger and marked by extreme violence. As a Jew I was born into a hostile world; both the Nazis and the Vichy French hunted my family who, on many occasions and in the most incredible circumstances, only just managed to evade deportation. During my time in hiding in the Hautes-Pyrenées, I became acquainted with stealth, the use of an alias, disguise, mistrust and an ever-present sense of danger. I was separated from my parents who came to see me from time to time under the most dangerous of circumstances. I fully embraced a peasant lifestyle, which was Catholic and tolerant, and close to the Resistance. It was here that I served my apprenticeship in the skills of restraint and marking time, and it was also here that the process of my socialization began. Through the medium of a new language, *Béarnais*, I learnt new ways of expressing myself. These early experiences linger to this day: my first memories are linked to the War: convoys of German soldiers surrounding a farm where my parents and I would later be hidden, shot-down aircraft, the feeling of potential threat.

I felt part of history, without being an actor in it. From 1940 to the present that would continue to be the case, as I observed the rows of striking workers in the streets of Paris from the early 1950s and the harsh police crackdown at the time, and as I followed the conflicts in Indo-China and Algeria day by day. I recall the shock of Stalin's death and later the invasion of Hungary. Violence lurked in the streets of Paris as I mingled on the Place du Colonel Fabien (the site of the headquarters of the French Communist Party) in the nightly confrontations which were characterized by an intolerable bitterness: I understood the logic of both the attackers and the attacked, and found myself physically exposed to the violence of both.

Being born in 1940 meant that, unlike so many other future French academics, I was far too young to belong to any of the successive generations of communists. The pattern was set by the start of my adolescence; I was not haunted by the spectre of appeasement before World War II (cf. Judt 1993; Nora 1987); I did not follow the lead of some guru or other, such as Althusser who fascinated so many young French intellectuals of my generation, who blindly followed his ahistorical and mechanistic theses; I was never a member of the Communist Party nor one of its political bedfellows. Standing back from the business of power, be it institutional or personal, I remained on the side, and took little part in innumerable student discussions in the Paris of the 1960s. During the Algerian crisis and in relation to Cuba I mixed nevertheless, at times quite closely, with those who subscribed to various utopian ideals; in July 1961 I boarded immediately an empty plane to Cuba from Miami, independent of any political organization. Linked to many of the militants by a genuine affection, I remained nevertheless there too, in the words of Raymond Aron, a *spectateur engagé* (Aron 1981).

Being a teenager in Paris, first at the *lycée* and later at university, meant a political socialization marked by violence and ideological struggles. From the war in French Indo-China to the war in Algeria, the process of decolonization provoked intense Franco-French struggles: communist mobilization led to mass demonstrations in the streets of Paris, which were brutally broken up; the establishment of the *Union et Fraternité Française* saw the relaunching of extreme right-wing nationalism; and frequent threats of a *coup d'état* created a stifling atmosphere. There were constant clashes between left-wing student societies and those linked to nationalist movements. For more than ten years, both at the *lycée* and later at university, I took part at the lowest possible level, as though at some distance, giving out leaflets, joining forbidden demonstrations or occupations in the *Quartier Latin* which turned ugly. Yet I did not become a professional militant, nor did I carve out a career with any political party or union. I didn't even manage to chant the ritual slogan of all student demonstrations: 'CRS = SS'. I was aware of how severe the crackdown had been, but I felt France was in no way a 'police state', 'a gaullist dictatorship' or 'a Fascist, totalitarian state', slogans shouted loudly at demonstrations in which I took part. I remained detached, like I did during the events of May 1968 when as a *maître assistant* in sociology I understood the dreams and the longings for freedom, but also sensed the risk of provocation and repression. I was still physically there, in the lecture theatres with the students, or in the streets of Paris where the barricades were aflame, but symbolically I refused to grasp torn-up paving stones, being convinced that the demonstrations were a naive, irrational act, a piece of collective theatre which provided fertile ground for the emergence of new forms of coercion by those still green who wanted to assert their authority in the name of their privileged relationship to the truth.

II

I was at the margin of society as much by my social background as by my cultural heritage. My parents were lower-middle-class Jews who had fled Pilsudski's Poland and later Hitler's Germany. In a Mertonian sense I felt more cosmopolitan than local; since my early student years I looked towards the United States, which I visited on many occasions. I was also constantly interested in the fate of Israel. At the age of 12, I spent several months in a Kibbutz under the auspices of a Jewish young socialist movement. Even there I witnessed once more the exercise of brute force when the feddayin came over the nearby border with Jordan and machine-gunned my group of young Jewish, song-singing, socialists. I was fascinated by stories of old-time Russia and Poland, and by the history of successive waves of Jewish emigration, including the most recent one of my family. My parents remained true to their past, both through observing a minimum of cultural practices and their desire to retain the many lively particularist linkages existing in an extended family. Yet, my own values are those of 1789 France which I acquired through a schooling in the republican tradition: emancipation, equality between men and universalism. If those years were marked by encounters with brute force, by the many degradations I suffered, for example in education and in day-to-day life, it was the meritocratic republican state that opened doors for me, allowing social mobility and an opening-up of public space. My socialization was marked entirely by republican ideology. In the 1950s the public school was still that of Jules Ferry. In a poor but central immigrant area of Paris I encountered committed teachers full of their mission to educate, devotees of discipline and hard work. One of them in particular, a no-nonsense character, as in an Épinal print of France under the Third Republic, was responsible for my going to the *lycée*. Since then I have been attached to the cult of the emancipating republican state in both body and soul, the former becoming later, in the jargon of political sociology, the *État fort*.

III

Having entered the *Institut d'Études Politiques* de Paris, I focused my attention on the public administration section which was the one most concerned with the institutional and judicial functioning of the state. Completing the courses for a Law degree at the same time in the *Faculté de Droit de Paris*, I found myself confronted with a difficult choice: should I prepare, yes or no, for entry to the *École Nationale d'Administration*, and in doing so become one of the high functionaries who symbolize with their intellect and their austerity the *État fort* in action?

After several weeks of preparation I abandoned this course of action, finding it impossible to imagine myself a high official in a system which implicitly requires one to be at ease in the most diverse social settings, from the provincial social circle to the rarefied heights of the upper class. Instead of serving this *État fort* I found myself observing it from the point of view of its sociology as well as the structuring of its power. I thus turned to political sociology.

As luck would have it Raymond Aron, the holder of the only chair of political sociology, agreed to act as my supervisor. Once enrolled for a doctorate I discovered the many facets of this discipline. Raymond Aron's teaching – pluralist, critical, sceptical of explanations which sought to offer simple justifications for the *État fort*, open to British and American theories – was for me decisive. From that time on the study of the élite, which was to be the salient feature of my long academic career, allowed me to focus on the working of influence and power within the *État fort*. In Raymond Aron's ambiance, I hesitated between several courses of research: I was first tempted by Pareto's élite theory, then by élite theories in the United States. My first study thus consisted of an examination of the American debate between pluralism and élitism. The study consisted of reconstructing the rival ideologies surrounding the idea of equality of opportunity, producing some first-hand research on the empirical distribution of resources held by the various élites, then moving on to their behaviour as a means to test the actual degree of pluralism amongst the élite. I extended this work with a study of 'community power structures' (Birnbaum 1970), in response to the celebrated work by Robert Dahl *Who Governs?*, which I co-translated into French. Around that time I also wrote a small book on Tocqueville (1969), which dealt particularly with the nature of ideologies and power and also stressed the comparative aspects of his work. And, being concerned with sociological theory, I also wrote several papers on Émile Durkheim's political sociology (1971b, 1976b). In 1971, in what was to herald the start of a long collaboration, François Chazel and I produced two textbooks on political sociology which became classics as they gave French readers translations of Erik Allardt, James Davies, Franz Neumann, David Apter, Stein Rokkan and others (Birnbaum and Chazel 1971a). Following the Anglo-Saxon model, in contrast to the traditional *manuels* used by French students, we offered a selection of texts which centred on questions such as system and power, élites and revolution, dealing also with ideologies, and using the most diverse historical and spatial examples.

IV

Appointed to the University of Paris I, I completed my doctorate in 1975 under the friendly supervision of François Bourricaud (himself a sociologist close to the thinking of Raymond Aron, who was also concerned with the problems of power in specific societies, from the United States to Latin American countries). My *doctorat ès lettres* dealt with the influence of the End of Ideology literature on American political theory, a perspective which within the most sophisticated models, such as the theories of Talcott Parsons, David Easton, Robert Dahl and even Peter Blau, implied a rehabilitation of the dominance of élites to the detriment of the much acclaimed democracy by consent (Birnbaum 1975, 1976a).

At the start of the 1970s I became involved in the newly established European Consortium of Political Research. I presented papers during successive joint sessions, and participated actively with Brian Barry, Jack Lively and Geraint Parry in animating a political theory group (Birnbaum *et al.* 1978). In this privileged circle I met a great number of researchers from several European countries. I became used to thinking comparatively and to debating throughout the year points of political theory, as well as problems of élites and power, with specialists concerned with other western societies. Once elected to the Executive Committee of the ECPR, I attended many of its meetings, restrictive in their nature, and thus came to be integrated, bit by bit, in a network with other European political scientists. Within this intimate circle there was a genuine warmth. I became close to Stein Rokkan, becoming increasingly interested in his acclaimed conceptual map of Europe which analyses the problems of state formation in a comparative manner.

During this time I completed a piece of research on the historical construction of the state in France with particular attention to the changing relationship between élites within the political-administrative power and outside it. In an academic world which was largely influenced by a variety of Marxist currents – and in which Nicos Poulantzas (who was to become a close friend) pushed many researchers into neglecting the role of political actors and the specificity of politics, which was reduced directly or indirectly to external socio-economic factors – I insisted, on the contrary, in an almost Weberian perspective, on the advances and retreats of the state through the creation of a unique political-administrative body of individuals, recruited on merit, at the heart of the political-administrative entity, with its own set of values, yet remaining impervious to the business world outside it. By implication I rejected in equal measure the usual Marxist interpretations and the perspective adopted by C. Wright Mills. In *The Heights of Power* (1981) I stress, from an implicitly comparative perspective, the homogeneity of political power stemming from the history of French society, with an emphasis on the careers of the main players at the heart of the state. At the same time I also consider the circumstances under which an authority is formed which operates through its ability to require others to act rather than through recourse to brute force; a comparison with oppressive power in both authoritarian and totalitarian guises provides a backdrop to this theme. In particular there is the question of whether a republican state like France can avoid exercizing the considerable force at its disposal. What are the foundations of legitimacy of such a power (close to Weber's concept of rational authority), which protects the liberty of its citizens thanks to a meritocratic élite while avoiding a concentration of power which inevitably leads to domination and exclusion?

This work was a turning-point in my career. For the first time, in an empirical study, I tried to reconcile history and sociology in order to consider politics. Without fully realizing this, I had taken a route which would lead me, just as it had led the many American scholars with whom I was quickly developing contacts, to a historical-comparative sociology of politics. Ever-present and supportive, Stein Rokkan, in a long critique of my book which he published in his *Newsletter*, provided enormous assistance to me in constructing a relational model of the political, administrative and economic élites throughout recent French history. Thanks to his intervention my work developed into a more elaborate model of exchange relationships à la Parsons. I was to return to this systematization, the product of Rokkan's insight, on many occasions.

At the end of the 1970s my contacts with British and American researchers had become particularly intense. I taught for one term at Oxford where I became close to Steven Lukes and took part in various seminars with Alessandro Pizzorno, which proved a decisive encounter. I also taught for one term in Chicago, where I met the left-of-centre Chicago Boys who would also become close friends of mine, open to comparative study and history, talented and interested in lively debate: they included Adam Przeworski, Philippe Schmitter, Ira Katznelson and Aristide Zolberg. With Stein Rokkan and Charles Tilly, whom I met a little later, they constituted the circle with whom I exchanged papers, attended conferences in the United States and elsewhere, and published a variety of articles. In one manner or other these scholars, who often came from a fairly Marxist sociological perspective, now directed their attention towards the history of political actors, their strategies and their values against a changing structural context. Far from the somewhat rigid Marxism that still existed in France, opposed also to the various structuralist and institutional approaches which so dominated French research at that time, it was here that I found space to breathe. In small but very lively discussion groups, historical examples were thrown around, giving birth to sociological imagination. My acceptance into this small, creative group of political sociologists continued, after its break-up, in New York under the auspices of the New School of Social Research, which Charles Tilly would join later as well. In contrast with a France which had fallen largely under the spell of the authoritarian right, in contrast also with left-wing Parisian Marxist circles who still heaped anathema on anathema, or retained political philosophy perspectives far removed from empirical research which was held in open contempt, I found here a critical source of innovation as well as an open environment full of friendship.

With Bertrand Badie, who had himself completed a critique of developmentalist perspectives, I wrote *Sociology of the State* (Badie and Birnbaum 1983), a comparative study on sociology and state structures which, whether directly or not, will be the seedcorn for our new respective orientations. This book met with strong criticism in France, given its diametrical opposition to the dominant philosophical, jurisprudential and Marxist stances. But it was favourably received by Georges Lavau and Jean Leca, who were receptive to the idea of historical comparisons and who assisted considerably in gaining legitimacy for it in academic circles. The book was translated into numerous languages and represented a genuine encounter with cultural norms. Each of us tried increasingly, in his own way, to reflect on the importance of values and cultural norms for political institutions and the behaviour of political actors. For my part I apply such comparative approaches in the limited environment of Western Europe. In what way do the trade unions, the political parties and the ethnic minorities behave differently as a consequence of the differing nature of the state, be it *fort* or *faible*? In what ways do both collective action and political mobilization take on different forms, in response to the sort of state which they confront? Does corporatism, the holy grail of so many researchers, find itself controlled by this sort of state?

For several years I was led to work on such types of comparison, starting with empirical and historical studies which were often novel. In spirit I became imperceptibly a man of the *État fort* and I asserted forcibly that this sort of state sometimes competes quite successfully with the classical democratic model of the *État faible*, while still reducing the risks inherent in the various totalitarian and authoritarian powers. It is true that in approaching the concept of the *État fort* from the perspective of the French example, and in wanting to legitimize the republican meritocratic state, which had been the source of my own intellectual and civic training, I run the risk of arriving at an analysis opposed to that of Tocqueville who was concerned with the inevitable dangers of despotism in the French bureaucratic state. The republican meritocratic state, with its universalist and emancipationist pretensions, had been responsible for my own intellectual development and acceptance in civic society and in the hierarchical and meritocratic world of academia, that essential symbol of the 'public space' so dominated by the state. Here again, then, an encounter of my personal history, bound so strongly to the heart of the republican state, and of my comparative work risks being an implicit validation of the *État fort*. And this in contrast with, on the one hand other societies more tolerant of pluralist and democratic forces, organized as *États faibles*, but with a strong one-religion establishment, and, on the other, the model of the oppressive, one-party state which claims emancipationist and utopian credentials, even though its *État fort* turns its back on republican universalism.

V

Without doubt my own background led me to pursue other research topics in political sociology with a clear personal leaning. I wanted to extend an earlier study concerned with the myth of the 'gros' (the 'fat cats') which had been a common thread in French political thought since the nineteenth century, unable to take account of the specificity of the state in France, and sliding towards a populism of either the far right or the far left, targeting the Jews as the supposed oppressors of upright, innocent French citizens (Birnbaum 1979, 1985c).

As the threats aroused by the posturing of the authoritarian Right receded, the defence of the Republic took less energy in the 1980s. I belonged at the time to a small group of left-wing intellectuals who met privately to discuss the future of French democratic socialism. Surprisingly enough, after some fiery pronouncements inspired by earlier revolutionary experiences, socialism in France went beyond basic ideologies and hopes of radical change in French society, to favour the flowering of an unexpected consensus which would hencefore somewhat dampen the internecine Franco-French struggles (Birnbaum and Vincent 1978; Birnbaum 1985a). Admittedly, the rise of Le Pen bore witness to a persisting, large nationalist populist force, with clear anti-Semitic accents, bringing into question once more the universalist values of the Republic. But the *grande première* of a successful transfer of power in 1981, integrating social forces into French society which had formerly been almost totally excluded, contributed enormously to laying conflicts to rest.

The retreat of the hopes of changing the world, both in France and abroad, favoured a more considered and empirical approach to comparative studies. Historical and comparative sociology developed in France all the more as ethnic cultures awakened. Differently from the mechanistic or institutional perspectives preferred so much in Anglo-Saxon systems approaches, differently even from the various developmentalist thinkers (including the different Marxist strands), the legitimacy of cultural norms has now become for many French social scientists a decisive element in constructing politics. France in the 1980s, more even than other western societies, rediscovered internal cultural pluralism and explored their parallel existence. Throughout western societies, but in France in particular, the presence of a large, recently arrived immigrant population, which frequently wants to preserve its cultural identity, relaunched the debate on the reasons for political integration, the issue of citizenship, and the coexistence of universalism and particularism. In the context of its own historical logic, each society now confronts the issue of multiculturalism. The question of the nature of the state is no longer a purely academic matter, but a decisive factor which may or may not help to resolve these internal cultural pluralisms. Comparative and historical sociology of politics thus acquires a new dimension; it offers views on how to resolve the burning questions at the heart of different types of state which vary geographically, but which are relatively constant in a temporal sense.

For my part I continued my earlier work on sociological theory (1982, 1985b, 1988). In collaboration with Jean Leca I published a collective work on methodo-logical individualism which brings together the methodological approach and the comparative history dimension, in a volume in which a great many American and British researchers participated (Birnbaum and Leca 1992a). I also wrote an article on Tocqueville and the state (1992c) and various other ones: on conflict (1993b), on the new social movements and on the theory of political mobilization (1993c).

VI

The change in my approach became manifest. To the considerable surprise of some of my colleagues I launched myself into lengthy preparation of a work on the specific nature of anti-Semitism in France. The approach was deliberately comparative: I set out to show the link between anti-Semitism in France and the nature of political power, citizenship, civil rights and, in the final analysis, the state. Rather than consider this phenomenon in an evolutionary perspective, or look at similar manifestations in other societies, I wished to show (true to the school of historical comparative sociology) that in France, as distinct from Germany, Britain or the USA, it was more or less the construction of the *État fort* which led to a new type of anti-Semitism, which I call 'political anti-Semitism'. Unlike religious, racial or even economic prejudices against Jews which exist to varying degrees in all societies, political anti-Semitism should be understood as a nationalist reaction to the appearance of the strong and universalist state, which favours a rapid integration of religious minorities and allows them to enter into public life and even into the heart of the state itself. The hypothesis signals the importance of the entry of Jews into the republican *État fort* on the basis of merit, in order to explain a hostile and anti-Semitic reaction which opposes the presence of the Jews (as of Protestants) in a state blessed for being a republic. This political anti-Semitism only minimally exists in societies which can be said to have an *État faible*, where there is a strong political-religious establishment, and where Jews have enjoyed only very limited access to political and administrative power prior to the twentieth century (1992b; Birnbaum and Katznelson 1995b).

At the forefront in the rapid granting of civil rights, already in the early nineteenth century France permitted the entry of Jews into the *Grandes Écoles*, which fostered the formation of a Jewish élite at the heart of the state (Birnbaum 1981; cf. 1980, 1987). These *Juifs d'État*, as I propose to call them, climbed the steps of the career ladder and became, particularly from the time of the Third Republic onwards, generals, prefects, High Court Judges, judges in the Court of Appeal, Privy Councillors, deputies, senators or ministers, without the need to convert. As a result they were found, especially in France, in the highest government offices.

Remaining true to my original interest in élite studies, I introduced the cultural factor which had really been neglected in this kind of work. I commenced empirical historical sociological studies. I looked at national and local archives and private records. I took a period which more or less covered the years 1850–1944, that is, the period which saw the entry of the first *Juifs d'État* into the political–administrative structure and which ends with their temporary exclusion by the Vichy régime, which barely missed having a decisive impact on my life. By implication this study was a consideration of my own experiences after Vichy and, without being conscious of it, true to the ideals of the *Juifs d'État*. I realized that I had employed all of my energies in the service of the *État fort* which had granted me my civil rights, yet which in the same breath distanced me from other forms of private social mobility as well as from the temptations of the radical change proclaimed by those ideologies which attacked the existing social order and which were equally indifferent to the very legitimacy of the scheme of the republican state. My starting point were the personnel files of 171 *Juifs d'État* who during this time had attained the highest offices among the political–administrative élite. I also relied on local archives which allowed me to study the attitude of the local populace towards them in their roles as sub-prefects, prefects, judges, senators or even deputies. I used church records and those of the *Alliance Israélite universelle* so as to gain a better understanding of the extent of their cultural involvements. Whilst undertaking this systematic study of their reasoning, relying on parliamentary records, or their books, articles and myriad publications, I tried to reconstruct in their entirety both the careers of these *Juifs d'État* and their cultural backgrounds.

The project was a sort of validation of the republican scheme to which I had remained true as a member of this set, yet I recognized a marked retreat from the emancipationist ideologies for which I was probably seeking a *raison d'être* in my comparative sociology of the state: a thesis which would be favourable to the logic of the *État fort*. This republican scheme alone, perhaps, would be capable of establishing a public secular space, thus allowing within the private domain the maintenance of specific beliefs and cultures which, for each individual, did not interfere with the role he or she played within the very institutionalized state structures. For many years I studied the values of these *Juifs d'État* who were attached to the Republic and who devoted all of their energies to its service. I examined their religious practices, their own form of endogamic marriage and their patronyms, as well as those of their forebears. I also looked at their careers with a view to taking a fresh look at any local anti-Semitic activity against them. I was hardly surprised to discover that a number of assumptions were made about them, usually anti-Semitic, within the state hierarchy. In the personnel files of these senior civil servants, a number of serious anti-Semitic comments had been written out by their superiors, long after the disestablishment of the Church from the state. On occasion the Jewish origins of these *Juifs d'État* were treated with open contempt. I was disturbed to discover that certain elements in the Vichy regime had emerged within the state, and not just in wider society, before the establishment of Vichy itself. My sociology of the *État fort* was somewhat turned on its head: the external strong dislike of Jews and prejudices against them permeated in no small measure the boundaries of the state, and it is for this reason that the degree of institutionalization of anti-Semitism was shown to be less of a break than one thought (Birnbaum 1992d, 1996). How could one begin to understand the mentality of these senior civil servants who showed themselves to be overtly racist?

Once more the questions that had been asked about the great crisis of the Vichy regime were being asked again. By studying certain corporatist practices or even the activities of political parties and clientelistic groups, one can discern processes of partial dedifferentiation in this *État fort*. This time, moreover, it was the very legitimacy of the state which was brought into question: the moving away of the state from its respect for universalist values, in respect of the Jews and other communal groups, had scarcely affected me, given the emphasis on the republican *État fort* within my political socialization. I now found constant examples of the extent of the slide towards racism, populism and nationalism which was evident at the heart of the state, for example in its prestigious universities. In this sense, the slogan 'France for the French', which many extreme militants now flaunt, can also be heard within the *État fort* (Birnbaum 1993a, 1994b, 1995a).

In being surprised by this discovery I partially lost, at the same time, my yardstick for a comparative study of the state, i.e. the strong state being in fact, in some crucial aspects, a weak state penetrated to its heart by non-universalist values.

17 Providing against certainties: the discreet charms of political comparison

Guy Hermet

FONDATION NATIONALE DES SCIENCES POLITIQUES, PARIS

Within a short interval, this is only the second time in my already extended professional life that I am faced with the arduous, or more exactly, narcissistic duty of discovering what kind of a political scientist I am. The first circumstance occurred when the editor of the *International Social Science Journal* asked me to contribute to an issue devoted to the ill-defined methods of historical sociology (1992a). However much I puzzled over it, it at least gave me the sensation of looking like a historical sociologist at the very moment when such an academic dedication was more and more considered an outright scientific extravagance. Now this book provides me with an unlimited opportunity to contrive another complementary, if not contradictory, hypothesis. Am I not joining the family of comparativists at a time when the comparative method seems all too frequently frowned upon as an obsolete frivolity?

I dare not judge myself. Nevertheless, in defence of my perplexing scientific vagueness, I will argue that I have never confused my self-conscious love of history with a systematic analytical device, that is with something which could provide proof of a theory. Without doubt, historical macro-sociology, as practised by de Tocqueville, Barrington Moore, Theda Skocpol or Charles Tilly, edges towards extensive metaphors that shed quite some uncertain amount of light on current situations which are ultimately inexplicable – in the strictest sense – by any method whatsoever. In my opinion, a familiarity with history is absolutely necessary for the political scientist, as a mere remedy for the ingenuousness of synchrony advocates. With respect to my comparativist propensity, which matters here, the point is that it stemmed gradually from the diversity of the political objects and the variety of the areas which successively attracted my attention. It was neither reflection nor a deliberate methodological choice. The comparative spirit came into me surreptitiously, not intentionally.

My roundabout approach to the academic world

To begin at the beginning, I must confess that I am not a natural born political scientist, nor even an academic. I rather expected to become a civil servant, with some dreams of exotic diplomatic splendour. That is the reason I studied at the *Institut d'Études*

Politiques de Paris, well known for being the sanctuary of would-be higher state bureaucrats in France. Then an accident struck me: the war in Algeria, where I had to stay almost three years as a rank and file draftee. I came back with a deep aversion to any institutional position. I then worked for a few months with the Unilever company, as a 'product manager', but dropped everything when I was offered an Assistantship in political science at the *Institut d'Études Politiques*, thanks to the extreme benevolence of one of my former professors. My salary was half as much as I earned before, but I considered it a marvellous stroke of luck which allowed me to fulfil my ideals at that time, i.e. those of disinterested scholarship.

Later on, I progressed normally along the road to higher academic responsibilities, though with some perplexity about the privileges and comforts I enjoyed in an ivory tower of sorts. It is probably because of this partial uneasiness that eventually I became more and more involved in the board of *Médecins sans Frontières,* a French medical NGO operating all over the world on behalf of populations facing civil wars or natural disasters. I am now its Vice-President.

Facing politics and peripheral political science

I must admit that I have always had scant regard for French politics – even as a citizen – perhaps because of its proximity. Conversely, what I could call 'strange politics' – *la politique étrange* – constantly fascinated me. Since I was not a fortunate anthropologist provided with generous funding for faraway missions, my first research works dealt for quite a number of years with Franco's dictatorship in Spain. During this initial Iberian stage of my academic life, I considered the Spanish Communist Party as an example of an underground political movement acting inside an authoritarian regime (1974a, 1977a), and I analysed intensively the role of the Church and the Catholic forces from 1936 to 1974 (1980–1, 1984a). At the same time, I indulged myself in some general articles (1976, 1977b) and a book (1974b), which tried to theorize about the Francoist regime as well as on the ways and means of its political fabric. The crucial issue, which is worth mentioning here, is that my Spanish commitment introduced me to the works of Juan Linz and opened my mind to political comparison. It was for this very reason that the idea of a comprehensive study of elections without choice (Hermet 1974c, 1978a, 1978b) occurred to me and was welcomed by Linz as well as by Richard Rose, Alain Rouquié and Philippe Schmitter. My assumption that authoritarian politics as 'strange politics' were not anti-politics was developing at last into an actual comparative project. As a first step, the fact that elections do not have the same meaning when they are without choice was not taken any longer as evidence that they had no meaning at all. And as a second step, this kind of professional orientation labelled me, surprisingly, also to myself, as an expert in authoritarian politics (1975, 1985).

Becoming a comparativist

This brings us to the 1980s. It was a time when I managed to set aside my prevailing obsession with authoritarianism in order to embrace issues involved in a wider perspective. It was also a period characterized, in my case, by new practical experiences. First, I was posted in 1980–1, as a foreign expert at the Colombian Ministry of External Affairs. Whether I liked it or not, this experience immersed me all of a sudden into the depth of day-to-day Latin-American internal rather than external politics. I became an observer as well as a sort of transplant, rapidly accustomed to the peccadilloes of clientelism and of topsy-turvy democratic practices. Since then, I have no longer been surprised to be classified additionally as a Latin-Americanist, even though I wrote only one serious article – more than ten years later – on the concept and reality of citizenship in this region (1992b). Moreover, a second stimulus struck me during the same period. I was confronted with the need to widen my understanding of the influence that religion had exerted, and was still exerting in general, on the formation of citizenship. I had some idea of this influence as concerns Spain, Mediterranean societies and Latin America, but I undoubtedly needed to go back to the fundamentals, and acquire a deeper knowledge of the sociological literature on this subject. Aristide Zolberg was living in Paris at this time. He lent me an invaluable hand. And the same can be said of Bertrand Badie. Badie introduced me to comparative politics as a theory. He became my permanent *confidant* for the years to come.

The first outcome of these encouragements appeared in my essay titled 'The Citizen-Individual in Western Christianity' (1990b). The same matter had already been treated more ambitiously in my book devoted to the cultural and economic origins of democracy (1986a). Moreover, I endeavoured to reconcile this broader scope with my previous interests in autocratic governments of all sorts, especially by editing a collective volume on the concepts and plural substances of totalitarianism (1984b). As dictatorships were beginning to collapse in Latin America and the Philippines, I availed myself of my knowledge of the Spanish return to democracy to join the ranks of a booming academic community; the community, that is, of those studiously commenting on the current so-called democratic transitions, the *transitologos* in Philippe Schmitter's terms. I began with a deliberately historical and retrospective book entitled *Aux frontières de la démocratie* (1983) – in my opinion my best work, if any good one is to be found – which analysed the various forms of the accidental emergence of modern political regimes in Western and Southern Europe as well as in America, not to mention a series of more or less repetitive publications on transitions which were occasioned by the circumstances of the time (1977c, 1982, 1984c, 1986b, 1987, 1988, 1990a). Looking back over this research experience, I find it influenced outright by Juan Linz's conceptualization as expressed in *The Breakdown of Democratic Regimes*, and very little by the numerous collective books published more recently.

Since then, things have changed in many respects. Due to Bertrand Badie's friendly insistence, I could no longer defer the co-writing with him of a postgraduate university manual in comparative politics, or more exactly, about what in our opinion comparative sociology should be for political science (Badie and Hermet 1990). It should not only be a formal method for restricted use by patented specialists, or still less a mere comparison of governments, but mainly a permanent disposition to question comparatively whatever topics the political scientist is working on, at least ideally. This does not necessarily imply displaying a hotch potch of crossed statistical data or apparently contrasting sets of institutions, but having in mind the intellectual resources needed for a really comprehensive understanding of any empirical object. Of course nobody can fully achieve such an aim. However, some progress in this direction is attainable. For instance, at the most basic level, it should be clear that the word 'state' has completely different values in, say, France, Britain, Spain, Switzerland and the United States. The same could be observed for concepts like the law, secularization or even democracy (which means mainly the left–right ideological cleavage for the French, and a mixture of populist gestures and electoral disappointments for the Latin Americans or the Bangladeshis, for example). In brief, I would argue that non-comparative sociology is in my opinion an uncritical version of political science, while the comparative effort indicated in this perspective is the critical one.

My concern about democracy

This statement leads me to the last, though as ever provisional, stage of my course as an all-purpose comparativist. It is twofold. On the one hand, I have been personally and deeply engrossed for five or six years in the consideration of what appears to me to be a disregard of the most crucial issue of politics, that is, the mysterious submission of the many to the everlasting authority of the few who govern (another way of expressing this puzzling question would emphasize the mystery of the persisting condition, in rational and democratic societies, of the subjective artefact called political legitimacy). I expressed this concern in a rather provocative essay entitled *Le peuple contre la démocratie* (1989), which tries to cover both comparatively and historically the wide range of popular reactions to the developments of democratic rule in Europe and America as well as in more exotic polities. I came back to this topic in 1991, although now more precisely concerned with the current, much lamented crisis of citizenship in the old democracies (1988b, 1991b, 1991c). This apparently new focus was not so different from the more fundamental scope of the previous study. In fact, today's crisis arises from the long-delayed but growing discovery that the legitimacy of democracy is based far less on the positive consent of the body politic than on its passive acceptance of a democratic government deprived of any conceivable alternative (a kind of legitimacy by default). The only novelty is that this passiveness has been spreading for some twenty years, due to the progress of education and in proportion to the age of the democracy concerned. With respect to the sources of this passivity, it is fair to point out that democracy has always been defined by its accessory features and instruments rather than by an active and direct practice of popular sovereignty.

Indeed, democracy is defined everywhere in terms of a set-up based exclusively on two of its purely instrumental modalities, that is majority decision-making and the representative mechanism held to be complementary legitimizing principles. The first problem with this position stems from the fact that majority rule rests on the fiction that the will of the majority should prevail, being the will of all the citizens, which it is not. The minority continues to exist, so that the amalgamation of the mere criterion of decision with more eminent principles of legitimacy – overall sovereignty or general consensus – is clearly wrong. And the second problem arises from the fact that, as the citizen is insufficiently informed, the decision of the majority is in its final outcome a matter of chance or manipulation.

As I have said before, the present stage of my course as a comparativist was twofold. My second centre of interest goes beyond the boundaries of any reasonable comparativeness. In the beginning, I applied my mind to the already complex situations involved in the process of democratization which was taking place in Latin America and Eastern or Central Europe; but I found myself confronted later on with a global world where everything was turning so topsy-turvy that one dared not use any longer the words 'transition to democracy'. Everybody agrees that a transition is understood to be an intermediate situation by nature, that the process of transition necessarily involves the inherent risk of a reversion to a dictatorship in case of failure, or of democratization being halted in an unfinished state (as in the case of Brazil, Argentina and Romania). Worse still, a whole range of concepts or frameworks of analysis so far applied to regime changes had to surrender at the beginning of the 1990s, faced with the convulsive reality emerging from the ruins of the deceased Soviet Union or from the collapse of African post-colonial political arrangements.

Since my previous background did not pass seriously beyond Western and Southern Europe, Latin America and the Philippines, I had to gain a more precise acquaintance with a series of countries, cultures, political traditions and forms of governments disseminated all over the world. I had, in particular, to alert my mind to what Eastern Europe and Sub-Saharan Africa really meant. It took me at least three years, for just an introductory initiation. Then, I discovered that the paradigms that had been used before both for the study of political change and for that of the democratic breakdowns of the past had lost their relevance in the current political jumble. I could no longer take advantage of the classical recipes of wise democratic engineering as listed, for instance, by Philippe Schmitter or Juan Linz. The vast amount of academic literature devoted to transitions in progress in Latin America was no more useful, as it referred to countries which were already provided with a civil society and did not need to be rebuilt from the start. In short, there was unfortunately no state of the art which could heal the uncertainty of the post-communist comparativist that I was; only an upsetting accumulation of facts and a great many very general writings dealing with the most uneasy co-ordination of political and economic reforms.

In the end, I had to swallow my pride as a political scientist. I laid down my arms and put a provisional stop to this despairingly difficult undertaking in the final form of a book, called after much hesitation *Les désenchantements de la liberté* (1993a; cf. 1990c, 1991c). Apart from being quite pessimistic with regard to the actual prospects of steady and meaningful democratization in a series of ex-communist as well as non-communist countries which make up the bulk of UNO's membership, this work was nothing more than a first glance at events which are still unfolding. It was also a demonstration of the limits of the comparative method or, more modestly, of my own prowess as a comparativist. I imagine, therefore, that its only importance to me in the future will be as a by-product to be used in further studies, though it could also provide a modest source of information to other scholars. With respect to myself again, the publication of this work allows me to engage now in a more classical comparative and collective project aimed at the new populist cleavages which are affecting party systems in Europe East and West. It also gives me some time to pay attention to the new factor linked with the emergence of humanitarian values in the face of the declining ideological or political ones (1992c).

In the intervening years, I took a kind of a holiday by writing an overtly historical study on the formation of the national spirit in Europe (1996), as well as a sort of guidebook, entitled *Culture et démocratie* (1993b) which I published at the request of UNESCO.

A general balance

I realize, in conclusion, that I cannot avoid adding some more substantial considerations about my general experience as a comparativist. First and foremost, my comparative perspective is more a personal methodological concern than a method in itself. Then, according to this previous assumption, I should point out that it provides me not only with the best tool for knowing something about other political arrangements but also with the unique means of rediscovering my own, in the light of peculiarities which would not appear otherwise. In my opinion, there is no other way to get free from ethnocentrism as well as from universalist simplifications or amalgamations. The comparative endeavour is the key to the understanding of any political object. In other words, even if it does not permit one to demonstrate anything with proof in hand, it allows the researcher to interpret what politics means or not in such a case, and what it means in another case. Any parliament, any party, any kind of popular mobilization is necessarily moulded by a particular history, a culture which makes it different from the same institutions or behaviours observed in other situations. The moving target of the comparativist must always be the documented identification of each political uniqueness.

Such a view might seem to jump over any systematic theoretical ambition. That is not exactly so. The truth is rather that it is promoting an endless, though systematic, oscillation between concepts and empirical observation. It is also a mainly relativist and auxiliary exercise, in the sense that it reinforces the analytical capacity of those who are really and deeply aware of one case or one country. The comparative method can only provide superficial outcomes when it wraps itself around as a self-sufficient and abstract field of study. One could even say that the comparative view is more critical than positive, and that the comparativist is performing a much better role as a spreader of doubt than as an assertive analyst. There is also no doubt that political science in general was born primarily from 'comparative curiosity'. There is no shame, therefore, in being a comparativist beset with immense methodological perplexities.

18 Exploring non-majoritarian democracy

Gerhard Lehmbruch

UNIVERSITY OF KONSTANZ

Political socialization: cultural cleavages and terrorist rule

In 1953 Theodor Eschenburg, a former public servant recently appointed to the new Chair of Political Science at the University of Tübingen, hired me as a research assistant. That is how I became a political scientist. The 'founding fathers' of the discipline in West Germany came mostly from public life and had an academic training in neighbouring disciplines: in law, in economics, or – in Eschenburg's case – in history.[1] The decisive political experience in their intellectual formation was most often the downfall of the Weimar Republic. They had grown up in a civilized polity and had experienced its crisis and final breakdown. Their central problem was the institutional reconstruction of democracy.

To recruit assistants the professors of this first generation turned to young academics who likewise had received their university education in another discipline. Joining this second cohort of German political scientists was thus a sort of 'late vocation' (*Spätberufung*). How did somebody with my background finally specialize in comparative politics? I suppose that this was due to a specific pattern of political socialization on the one hand, and to earlier (pre-political science) academic socialization on the other.

My political socialization took place in the shadow of terror. I was born in 1928, the son of a pastor, and had my first – and probably decisive – political experience when I was nine years old: two men in long dark leather coats searched the parsonage and then led away my father, who earnestly kissed us goodbye. After this farewell mother told us children that these men had taken our father to prison. However, they were not from the regular police (still perceived as a constitutive part of the legal order) but from the secret state police or Gestapo. If somebody was imprisoned by the Gestapo one did not have to be ashamed, but could be proud of him. I was, and boasted of it at school – just as I was proud of my father's distinguished World War I career from 1914: volunteer with the Potsdam rifle guards to airforce pilot. My father remained an overwhelming authority, stern and courageous, and I was – and certainly continue to be – strongly imbued by his political attitudes.

Since the preceding century, a remarkably high number of German scholars have descended from the protestant clergy. Still in my generation one finds a sizeable proportion of political scientists whose fathers were ministers. However, the firm political beliefs held by my own father were not often found in the – generally conservative – milieu of German protestantism of that time. A son and grandson of dedicated republicans of lower-middle-class origins who hated the authoritarian monarchy, my father remained proud all his life that in 1918, as an airforce officer, he was delegated to a revolutionary soldiers' council by the men of his squad. He was a member of the semi-legal leadership of the anti-Nazi 'Confessing Church' in our home province of East Prussia, and in one of his first Gestapo interrogations he learnt how his ecclesiastic superior had denounced him – a former soldier and German patriot – as an 'enemy of the state'. One of my father's closest friends from the times spent in the illegal postwar defence forces (the 'black *Reichswehr*') was a Jewish ex-officer and judge, and my parents remained loyal to him and his family and finally helped them to emigrate just before it was too late. They taught me that anti-Semitism was highly reprehensible, and that those who ruled our country were immoral people.

Another, but related element of early political socialization had to do with the particular local environment of my childhood and adolescence. I grew up in a rural region of East Germany, with a sizeable Polish minority, and my father's huge parish included Lutheran, Catholic and Mennonite villages. These highly visible cultural cleavages were one of the central elements in my early experience of social relations. Then the war broke out – a very vivid remembrance, since we lived close to the Polish border and the local militia company led by my father was among the first to receive the invasion order. My father later told me how, soon after crossing the border, he ticked off one of his men shouting 'A German soldier does not fire at civilians'; but, he added, 'soon I discovered that in this war such a rule did not count any more'.

Similar experiences did not remain hidden from an adolescent who grew up practically at the door of the slaughterhouse. When the deportations of our Jewish neighbours began I wondered what might happen to them. I remember well having read an article by Goebbels in his weekly *Das Reich* in which he wrote in ominous phrases that these 'enemies of the German people' would now receive the destiny they deserved – and having concluded from this that they would be murdered. When I recently rediscovered this article I was surprised to find that at the time I was only 13 years old. In early 1944, in a discussion at school, two of my classmates told us that the Jews were killed by gas. (They disagreed about the details.) I do not remember that any of us doubted the truth of this terrible information. One year earlier a peasant from the German minority, close to the Polish village of Sitno, near Sepolno, (his name was Erdmann), had led me and one of my classmates to the mass graves of the local Polish leadership executed by the SS in the autumn of 1939. After describing the hideous details of the massacre this daringly courageous man (he barely knew us!) added: 'I wanted you to see this so you may understand why I am ashamed of being a German.'

So I came to grasp, very early, that we were ruled by criminal terrorists. I even remember that at the age of 16 I reluctantly began to wish that our country might lose the war, that living in a victorious Germany might be much worse. It was not unexpected, neither by my parents nor by myself, that we had to flee from our home in 1945 at the approach of the Soviet army, and that we would never return. But the loss of our native country and the flood of extreme human misery which surrounded us in these months left traumatic memories.

After months of an odyssey of sorts I managed to find my family in a small town at the western border of the Soviet occupation zone, where my father had been appointed 'superintendent' to a larger church district. As refugees we were strangers in an unhospitable environment. I had very vividly experienced the remaining salience of regional cleavages in the Germany of that time during the weeks when I wandered throughout the country, asking for food and shelter every evening. A fundamental awareness of being a stranger in my environment is something which has never left me since. It may finally have led me to engage in cross-cultural comparativist social science.

I first worked as a lumberman, wishing to continue a career as trainee in the forest service, but then decided to finish high school and attend university. The discipline I chose was theology. This was not motivated by a desire to emulate my father: I found it difficult to empathize with his highly personal religiosity and moral rigour, and did not experience the 'vocation' he expected from me. Rather, mine was an intellectual attempt to make sense of the deeply disturbing political experiences of my youth, and of the forces of moral resistance of which I had become aware. From a contemporary historical perspective such a conclusion is of course easy to relate to the spiritual introversion that characterized even the progressive elements in German protestantism.

Academic socialization: interpretation of texts, culture and institutions

In my first semester at Berlin, in the summer of 1947, I wrote two seminar papers. The first was about the Church of England, for a seminar on the comparative study of Christian Churches. The second, from the Old Testament, treated the question of whether the curious Pentateuch text of Bileam's ass who talked to her master (Numbers 22: 21–35) derived from only one biblical author – as tradition and my professor pretended – or from two different original sources, as was assumed by most critical exegetes. As the latter seemed more plausible to me I tried to resolve my dilemma with a third original hypothesis which, unfortunately, was never accepted by the scientific community (nor by that professor).

During my years in theology, my interests remained largely confined to these two fields: the comparative history of ideas and institutions, and the critical exegesis of texts. Hence, theology was an important intellectual training ground for my later career. At Tübingen and Göttingen, I received the thorough scientific education that was the pride of the German theological faculties since the nineteenth century. It included introductions to the historical method, the philological exegesis of texts, the underlying problems of the theory of science, and the history of ancient and modern thought and institutions. It was here that I learnt the systematic interpretation of concepts in their historical context and became interested in the relationship between the development of belief systems and processes of institution-building. This served as an intellectual bridge to social science. I became familiar with Troeltsch's comparative typology of 'churches' and 'sects' (to mention one example), and it did not take me long to discover historical sociology and Max Weber.

In 1949 at Tübingen I took part in the launching of an organization labelled *Studentischer Arbeitskreis für Politik* ('study group for politics'). For a couple of years this group of students – mostly from philosophy, history and law – met every week to discuss and analyse political problems. The initiative came originally from the French military government's *officier de liaison* to the university, a young *agrégé* from the Touraine. Although he was a protestant his model was the *Conférence Olivaint*, an organization of progressive Catholic students at the *Institut d'Études Politiques* in Paris. We met them repeatedly for seminars in the Bavarian Alps or on the Côte d'Azur (where my path crossed that of Juan Linz) and came in contact with French political science. Through our selective procedures for admitting new members we endeavoured to become as élitist as our French model. In the mid-1950s, the *Arbeitskreis* split over the question of nuclear armament and disbanded; many of its former members later became professors of law or social science, senior bureaucrats, ambassadors, or business executives. Theodor Eschenburg was familiar with that group and turned to it in 1953 to recruit me as a research assistant.

After my final examinations in theology, I passed another year at Basle, in Switzerland, still officially matriculated in that discipline. My main emphasis, however, was on philosophy and sociology (with Edgar Salin and Karl Jaspers), but I also studied Russian language and literature and the history of political ideas in Russia. These lectures were given by Fritz Lieb, a maverick professor of theology who, as a left-socialist student, had been in personal contact with Lenin and helped to organize his transfer from his Swiss exile to Russia through Germany and Sweden in 1917. Later I considered specializing in Soviet politics, but was deterred from it by the political science literature which I read on the subject and found then pretty dull, and also by the consideration that it was impossible to travel in that country for research.

In my year at Basle I was still unaware of political science as an independent discipline, and my interest in Swiss domestic politics was rather limited. However, because of my biographical background I was very interested in religious institutions, and in Basle I discovered some intriguing 'consociational' practices in the Protestant state church which I came to remember a decade later (cf. Lehmbruch 1993).

My interest in social theory dates back to my last year of high school shortly after the war, in what was then the Soviet zone of occupied Germany. My teacher in history and philosophy was an old social democrat who introduced us to socialist thought, and the first social science texts which I read at that time were Marx's 'Wage Labour and Capital' and Engels's 'Development of Socialism from Utopism to Science'. As my special field for the *Abitur* I prepared the relationship of Marxism and Christian Socialism in nineteenth-century history. Of course I vaguely believed in socialism at that time, and joined the anti-fascist youth group that shortly after took the name *Freie Deutsche Jugend*. A year later, I resigned from it when its communist leadership revived the *Jugendweihe*, a traditional atheist initiation ceremony for adolescents. As a student of theology I remained strongly interested in the origins and development of Marxist theory. For some time I considered writing a theological dissertation on 'Marxist anthropology' – a subject that was then *en vogue* under the influence of existentialist philosophy. What finally came out of this was, however, not much more than a 'critical introduction to Soviet ideology', a little book with a *bibliographie raisonnée*. I think it was not bad at all. I also did the German translation of Alexandre Kojève's famous *Introduction à la lecture de Hegel*, lectures given at the *Collège de*

France by a Russian philosopher (formerly Prince Kojevnikov) in French prose, but with Russian syntax. Navigating in three languages and looking for equivalences and nuances of philosophical meaning was also a fascinating cross-cultural experience.

Party politics in the French Fourth Republic

When in 1953 I became Eschenburg's research assistant I formally enrolled in political science and Russian history. My first task was to investigate the institutional development of the chancellor's prerogative in the cabinet, and later I did research on the history of political expurgations in the German bureaucracy. To be sure, Eschenburg's lectures consisted largely of simple institutional descriptions, but – without having an institutional theory – his emphasis went beyond that. He was not only a former student of Fritz Hartung, Otto Hintze's most important disciple, but he came straight from the Lübeck of Thomas Mann's *Buddenbrooks* where his family was among those who governed this city republic, and later he was in close and continuous personal contact with important political leaders such as Gustav Stresemann. He then worked in the brains trust of the German engineering industry, became chief executive of a small business association in Berlin, and finally, after the war, served as a top civil servant in the small state of Südwürttemberg–Hohenzollern. This career resulted in a fascinating mix of concrete institutional experience and an analytical approach that was, to be sure, proto-theoretical rather than highly sophisticated. All of which helped me to understand that institutions define rules and duties and, hence, appropriate behaviour, and that institutional engineering is constrained by what today is called path dependency.

Of course I was soon aware that I needed further training in this new discipline. Given the embryonic state of political science in West Germany, many of us decided to pass some time and get experience at foreign universities. I successfully applied for a French government scholarship to study at the *Institut d'Études Politiques* in Paris and – for history and philosophy – the *Sorbonne*. My main interest originally was the politics of religious minorities in a democratic and secular state: first French protestantism, and then, increasingly, democratic catholicism. But my teachers in Paris, notably Maurice Duverger und René Rémond, directed my attention towards political parties and parliamentary institutions. So I embarked upon field research for a doctoral dissertation on the Christian-Democratic *Mouvement Républicain Populaire* in the Fourth Republic. Essentially, I focused on the strategic dilemma of party élites who had received their political socialization in progressive Catholic organizations (here I traced back the underlying history of ideas), but who had to woo voters traditionally tied to French 'clerical' conservatism. This led me then to analyse the problems of organizational cohesion and the ambiguities and changes in parliamentary coalition politics resulting from that dilemma. When I submitted that dissertation at Tübingen it was much too long for publication, and I postponed revision of it as I got interested in quite different research topics.

Consociational democracy

Since the early nineteenth century a German Ph.D aiming at an academic career is expected to write a second thesis (*Habilitation*). Therefore I began to search for a new subject, first on two quite different tracks. Finally, I discovered an interesting theoretical convergence of these seemingly unrelated topics. One was the cross-national study of the political management of ethnic and religious cleavages, a problem that was of course familiar to me from my childhood and adolescence; Bosnia before World War I was one of the important historical examples. The other field was coalition politics, particularly in parliamentary regimes. The crisis of Adenauer's rule in the last years of his chancellorship raised concerns about the project of an eventual 'great coalition' between Christian Democrats and Social Democrats. Some highly reputed political scientists, notably Ferdinand Hermens and Dolf Sternberger (but at that time also Eschenburg), rode the old battle-horse of electoral reform, where the replacement of PR by majority ballot was supposed to result in greater chances for 'alternative party government' and hence in greater stability and effectiveness of the regime. I was familiar with these theories since I attended Duverger's seminar, but – quite apart from doubts about the unintended consequences of such social engineering – they seemed inappropriate for coping with deep cleavages and the rights of minorities.

The 'black–red' coalition in Austria – at that time a favourite object of critique and derision in the West German press, but also of a penetrating analysis by Otto Kirchheimer (1957) – suggested the existence of an alternative strategy to achieve political stability. Of course, coalition politics in a parliamentary regime was a subject which I had already studied extensively in my doctoral dissertation on the French Fourth Republic, but the 'Proporz' practices of the Austrian coalition were obviously of a different nature. They reminded me, on the one hand, of what I knew about religious peace arrangements in modern German history. On the other hand, I discovered curious parallels with my observations in the protestant parishes of Basle a decade earlier. So I began research on Swiss as well as on Austrian politics and institutions with an eye on similarities and differences in the emergence and maintenance of party coalitions. Having learnt to pay attention to the historical processes of institution-building I talked about my observations to two historians each familiar with one of these countries. Hans Mommsen directed my attention to the parliamentary practices of Austria before World War I. And Erich Gruner in Berne pointed to the salience of the traditions of city government in Switzerland. I finally became convinced that coalition government in Austria as well as in Switzerland was a distinct 'pattern of conflict management' that had to be distinguished both from majority government based on the logic of party competition and from bureaucratic-hierarchical government. And I hypothesized that this pattern of conflict management was rooted in a process of institutional learning to cope with strong cultural – in particular ethnic or linguistic and religious or ideological – cleavages. The basic underlying norm – to be distinguished from the competitive logic of majoritarian parliamentarism – was *amicabilis compositio*, the 'amicable settlement' of conflicts between corporate groups, a formula I had discovered in the German and Swiss religious peace treaties of the seventeenth and eighteenth centuries (Lehmbruch 1966, 1967a).

At the same time, like other younger political scientists in West Germany of my generation I became increasingly aware of the developments in American political science since the 1950s. My interests in comparative research soon directed my attention to the work of the SSRC Committee on Comparative Politics, notably to Almond's adaption of structural–functional theory and his concept of 'political culture'. I felt that this approach might offer a useful framework for theoretical integration of my own research on patterns of conflict management. However, Almond's typological distinction between an 'Anglo-American' and a 'continental European' political culture appeared to me rather ethnocentric and not sufficiently informed about variations in the management of political cleavages in continental Europe. So, in a paper which I circulated in 1966 entitled *Amicabilis Compositio*, I questioned the 'unilinear' developmental perspective of that literature (Lehmbruch 1966; cf. 1967a). In my view, because of specific historical paths of cleavage management and institution building, political cultures differed by their dominant 'models of conflict regulation' – one of them the Anglo-American model of the 'political market' (with 'votes in exchange for policies'), another the bargaining model of the *Proporzsysteme* of some continental European countries (and Lebanon). These models were equifunctional in the sense that they were equally compatible with a development perspective emphasizing 'secularization' and increasing societal complexity. Comparing Switzerland and Austria I pointed out how the development of the political culture, the 'interest structure' and the 'government structure' of these two cases converged and where they differed, and discussed their consequences for system performance.

This paper one day fell into the hands of Stein Rokkan who was then involved in a project – together with Hans Daalder, Robert Dahl and Val Lorwin – on the politics of smaller European democracies. Rokkan passed the paper on to Hans Daalder, who invited me to present a paper on this subject during a session on recent research on typologies of political regimes and political development at the 1967 IPSA congress at Brussels (Lehmbruch 1967b), and thus introduced me to the international scientific community of comparativists. Before leaving for Brussels I read the other papers presented for Daalder's session, and I discovered that another paper-giver, Arend Lijphart, made a strikingly similar argument – including the critical discussion of Almond's typology of political cultures. To be sure he based much of his argument on the Dutch case, with which I was not very familiar at that time (see Lijphart 1968c). But his concept of 'consociational democracy' was clearly equivalent to what I first had described as *Proporzdemokratie* and later, with a term current in Switzerland, as *Konkordanzdemokratie*. (This has since become the German equivalent of Lijphart's English term.)

Lijphart and I had not known each other before meeting at Brussels. It was all the more striking that we developed largely similar theories – characterized moreover by a certain degree of complexity – in complete independence from each other. However, there were common points of departure: both of us had adopted a theory (namely Almond's) originally developed in what still was the hegemonic country in our discipline. But as Europeans familiar with smaller European countries both of us sensed an ethnocentric bias in the original theory, and tried to amend it through 'immanent criticism'. It was thus perhaps logical that – given a comparable observational basis – both of us arrived at similar theoretical conclusions. My main point of dissent from Lijphart's approach was his emphasis on the role of political élites in the emergence of consociational arrangements which I suspected of hidden voluntarism. My own formation led me to emphasize much more the importance of path-dependent institutional learning over long historical periods. Therefore I remained more sceptical about the chances to employ consociational arrangements in 'constitutional engineering' for the pacification of culturally divided societies. South Africa may become the test case regarding whether Lijphart's (relative) optimism or my pessimism (reinforced by personal observation in 1981) will be vindicated. I very much wish that Arend's theory – and South Africa – will win.

Federalism and the party system

After *Proporzdemokratie* I continued to direct my attention to similar 'bargaining systems', with a special emphasis on the role of the party system. Following my appointment as an associate professor at Heidelberg, in 1969, I taught the standard courses on West German government. However, with my previous experience in comparative politics, I viewed this subject matter in a comparativist framework, and that meant analysing German politics as I had done with Swiss and Austrian coalition politics, namely in a genetic perspective in which processes of institutional learning were important for understanding contemporary structures.

One focus in this comparative perspective were variations in party government. Although my critique of 'unilinear' concepts of political development in *Proporz-demokratie* was directed against the approach of the SSRC 'Committee', I had also current West German notions of party government in mind.[2] Early West German political science liked to define itself as the 'science of democracy' (*Demokratiewissen-schaft*). Its mission, hence, was the critique of anti-democratic thought, not least of the *Anti-Parteien-Affekt* considered as a traditional topic of German right-wing journalism and scholarship. Closely related to this trend was the strong emphasis placed on the virtues of a majoritarian competitive party system, considered as a superior mechanism of political control. The one Austrian, Schumpeter, was 'in', and the other Austrian, Kelsen, was 'out' because of his plea for proportional representation. Hence, if one investigated bargaining systems as I did in *Proporzdemokratie*, this raised implicitly the question of whether political parties and party competition really 'mattered'. For some time I wondered whether comparative policy analysis (as pioneered in American policy outcome research on the basis of inter-state comparison) might help to answer this question.[3] Finally, I felt personally more at ease with the configurative approach of my earlier research.

The West German parallel to Austrian coalition politics, the 'grand coalition' of Christian Democrats and Social Democrats (1966–69), was relatively short-lived and tends to be often neglected in accounts of the development of the Federal Republic. However, with its institutional innovations (particularly in the domain of federalism) it was an important watershed in the postwar history of West Germany. From my perspective, the polarization of the party system that set in with the demise of the 'grand coalition' and the formation of the 'social-liberal' coalition brought some of the institutional tensions between 'executive federalism' and competitive party government to the fore. This was the subject of a book I published in 1976 in which I placed the

German case in the comparative analytical perspective developed in *Proporzdemokratie* (Lehmbruch 1976, 1978).

In this book I pointed out that, as a result of the institutional development of German *Exekutivföderalismus* since Bismarck, federal-state relationships were dominated by practices of bargaining between autonomous bureaucracies.[4] After the introduction of parliamentary government in 1918, the executives of the *Reich* and of the *Länder* were dominated by largely overlapping centrist coalitions, but this situation changed in the Federal Republic, and the resulting institutional tensions between federalism and party government came into the open with the emergence of an opposition majority in the *Bundesrat* in 1969.[5]

'Liberal corporatism'

An additional analytical perspective which I learnt to introduce in these years was the political management of the economy. This led me straight from the theory of *Konkordanzdemokratie* to the discovery of the phenomenon of 'liberal corporatism'. Originally, this broadening of my research perspective was a reaction to the challenge of neo-Marxism that overwhelmed many universities beginning in the late 1960s. Heidelberg, where I taught from 1969 to 1973, was then a stronghold of student radicalism. For some time I was the only professor of political science who continued to give lectures, and in my seminars the diverse Marxist factions confronted not only me but also each other. Although I refused to compromise on the institutional foundations of academic freedom I considered it an intellectual duty of a university teacher to accept any challenge to established scientific thought as long as it was based on sufficiently articulated arguments. There were brilliant intellectuals among our radical students, and if one wanted to hold one's ground in these controversies a sufficient familiarity with Marxist theory and political economy was of course indispensable. One central theme in this context was of course the 'capitalist state', meaning in particular the problem of state intervention in a capitalist economy, and the recent (however belated) introduction of Keynesian economic policy in West Germany. Being familiar with comparative political research, and also not a novice to Marxist theory, I found that one of the most striking shortcomings of mainstream neo-Marxist political economy in those years was its neglect of the autonomy of politics which led it to overlook the importance of cross-national variations in the political management of capitalist economies.

I had already, in *Proporzdemokratie*, advanced the hypothesis that the occurrence of 'social pacts' between organized business and labour in Austria and Switzerland was related to their specific cultural heritage, the pattern of *amicabilis compositio*, that now appeared to 'spill over' to economic and social policy. In view of the recent discussion about similar developments in West Germany (the 'concerted action' of government, organized labour and business initiated by the Keynesian social democrat Karl Schiller),[6] and also informed by Andrew Shonfield's (1964) cross-national institutional analysis of the politics of interventionist 'modern capitalism', I concluded that those Austrian and Swiss observations should be placed in a broader comparative framework of the management of capitalist economies. In this context, phenomena like the Austrian 'social partnership' constituted a 'new' or 'liberal' corporatism (to be distinguished from the 'authoritarian corporatism' of the inter-war years). In a short paper presented in 1974 I related such 'participation of large organized social groups in public, especially economic policy-making' to the importance of co-ordination in Keynesian macro-economic policy (Lehmbruch 1974).

In 1975 I was invited to a workshop at Geneva, where I presented a slightly amended version of the paper just mentioned. At this occasion I met Philippe Schmitter, who had recently published 'Still the Century of Corporatism?'. We discovered the strong convergence of our research interests. For the 1976 IPSA congress in Edinburgh, Philippe Schmitter convened a panel on behalf of the Committee on Political Sociology, and two years later I organized a workshop for the ECPR Joint Sessions at Grenoble. From these meetings originated two collections of papers (Schmitter and Lehmbruch 1979b; Lehmbruch and Schmitter 1982). My principal contribution was a paper first presented at Edinburgh, 'Liberal Corporatism and Party Government', which returned to my earlier problem of the importance of party government, and discussed the 'symbiotic' relationship, in the process of policy formation, of corporatist arrangements and the party system (Lehmbruch 1977).

From the very beginning Philippe Schmitter's and my own work had each its specific profile. In my view the most important innovation in his seminal article of 1974 was the typological distinction between 'corporatism' and 'pluralism'[7]: it offered a basic conceptual framework for the comparative study of 'interest intermediation' at which the earlier efforts of the SSRC 'Committee' had not been able to arrive. The concept of 'interest systems' outlined in a later article (Schmitter 1977) presented a promising parallel to the existing typologies of party systems. Of course, in the field of interest intermediation the operational difficulties of organizing an extremely complex and variable reality with the aid of typological concepts were much bigger than in the field of party competition. However, the postulate of cross-national measurement could now at least be approximated.

Whereas Philippe Schmitter focused on organizational properties, I emphasized patterns of policy formation, and in adopting his typology I integrated these into this framework. Moreover, since I started with research on the role of organized interests in macro-economic policy formation, I focused on inter-organizational relations rather than organizational properties – hence my proposal to distinguish 'corporatism' and 'concertation' as two distinct dimensions of more complex phenomena.

From corporatism to comparative public policy

Edinburgh and Grenoble were the beginnings of a series of conferences and concerted research efforts across national borders. Later in 1978 another meeting on 'democratic corporatism', organized by Harold Wilensky, took place at the World Congress of Sociology at Uppsala. These experiences have taught me that large international congresses, with all their inevitable 'organizational slack', none the less serve as important forums for scientific communication. The 'Corporatist International', congregating at such occasions, became a meeting ground for social scientists from rather diverse theoretical and methodological persuasions, including Marxists as well as mainstream liberals, empirical researchers as well as speculative theorists. These exchanges soon transcended the focus on interest intermediation, and I think they contributed considerably to understanding of the policy dynamics of democratic industrial countries. In West Germany, an additional and important effect of the *Korporatismusdiskussion* was that it contributed much to bridge the political schisms that have divided the discipline since the late 1960s.

As I had placed my emphasis in corporatist theory on the 'concertation' of organized labour and business, I found myself immersed in an inter-disciplinary exchange at the intersection of several scientific sub-communities in comparative social research, most of them with a strong 'institutionalist' orientation. Apart from the established comparative politics and organizational sociology with its emerging interest in inter-organizational relations, this was, in particular, the industrial relations community which was dominated in Europe by sociologists. Here, I learnt most from my contacts with Wolfgang Streeck, but also from those with Marino Regini, Colin Crouch and others. Highly stimulating were also the discussions of a research group organized by John Goldthorpe on behalf of the SSRC Committee on Western Europe that led to the publication of *Order and Conflict in Contemporary Capitalism* (1984). An important link with public policy was provided by the contact with the group that, with Fritz Scharpf, specialized in labour market policy at the *Wissenschaftszentrum* in Berlin.

This growing interest in comparative public policy was linked to my appointment at Konstanz which I accepted in 1978 (after another four-year interlude at Tübingen). At this new university, Fritz Scharpf and others had, some years earlier, initiated an innovative curriculum in 'administrative science' with a strong focus on public policy. Since I was then fifty years old I felt it was time to move into an environment offering some new challenges.

The challenge to broaden the research perspective of comparative politics by integrating comparative public policy and political economy was the most important one.[8] Moreover, Konstanz offered a favourable environment for conducting larger research projects with the participation of highly qualified junior researchers. The first of these projects (with Klaus Armingeon, Roland Czada and others) investigated cross-national variations in corporatist concertation and their policy outcomes.[9] One guiding hypothesis was that corporatist arrangements were based upon a 'logic of exchange' between organizations, and that such exchange could include compensations across different policy sectors of the developed welfare state. Upon closer examination, this hypothesis was not sufficiently amenable to operationalization and therefore not really testable. However, it probably had some heuristic value and directed attention to the interdependencies between sectoral policies.

Today I would also not deny that the emphasis on patterns and processes of 'concertation' was somewhat too narrow as the basis for cross-national generalizations in comparative public policy research. Rather, it contributed – on a more general level – to a better understanding of the importance of particular institutional arrangements for patterns and outcomes of policy-making. On the other hand, the phenomenon of 'sectoral corporatism', which we distinguished from 'concertation', proved to be a fertile field for research that we had somewhat neglected: witness the important project 'The Organization of Business Interests' launched by Wolfgang Streeck and Philippe Schmitter.

Institutionalist perspectives on public policy

These efforts resulted in the strengthening of a research focus on the relationship of public policy and institutional arrangements. Of course it is true that the notion of a 'new institutionalism' covers a broad spectrum of approaches. For me, the central research perspective in the beginning resulted from the critique of neo-Marxist political economy mentioned above. The latter emphasized the importance of 'relations of production' as a determinant and restriction of policy formation in the 'capitalist state'; but in emphasizing the epochal character of an 'economic formation of society', it tended to neglect contingencies observed in cross-national comparison. Of course, variations in the 'relation of class forces' might have some explanatory power, but, I think, a rather limited one. By comparison, corporatist arrangements did have such explanatory power – and I think that our research confirmed this – but they did so as an element of complex, and historically contingent institutional configurations. In sum, starting from such an 'institutionalist' persuasion the variations of 'public policy profiles' of political systems are analysed as depending upon contingent institutional configurations at the interface of state and society.

Although for me this was one of the important insights obtained in the debate on 'corporatist arrangements', after more than one decade I would certainly admit that the focus on associations prevailing in the corporatist literature was too narrow for a systematic cross-national study of the institutional interface between the state and the economy. Broader conceptualizations which I have found useful for comparative research are, in particular, 'policy networks' and 'governance of the economy'.[10]

A second important conclusion from recent research in public policy and also from the project 'The Organization of Business Interests' was that, in the research perspective of a 'comparative political economy', it is particularly important to complement the study of cross-national by that of cross-sectoral variations. Both were important in the design of a comparative project on 'neo-conservative' policies from the late 1970s to the 1980s (with Marian Döhler, Edgar Grande and Otto Singer). When at that time the crisis of the social-democratic welfare state appeared to vindicate the belief in the superiority of markets for regulating social problems, it appeared tempting to apply cross-national approaches developed for research on the corporatist welfare state to the recent diffusion of 'neo-conservative' policies. The basic assumption of this project was that variations in the institutional configurations of the state–economy interface could explain why the assault on the welfare state finally went much further in Thatcher's Britain than, for example, in West Germany. Telecommunications reform and health policies proved particularly instructive cases (for a report on this project see Lehmbruch *et al.* 1988 and the articles by Döhler, Grande and Singer in Czada and Schmidt 1993).

Another 'institutionalist' perspective on interest intermediation followed when I was asked to participate in a larger, collaborative research effort at Konstanz on 'the changing public administration'. I proposed to invert the traditional perspective of 'pressure group' research and to investigate the importance of administrative strategies for cross-national variations in the patterns of interest intermediation (Lehmbruch 1991). Our research group investigated the role of bureaucracies in the development of national patterns of interest intermediation and the sectoral examples of the nuclear, telecommunications and pharmaceutical industries in periods when these industries became exposed to strong environmental challenges (on this project see the contributions by Ulrike Baumheier, Claudia Rose, Roland Czada and Frans van Waarden in Czada and Schmidt 1993).[11]

The institutional transformation of East Germany

The unexpected fall of the Berlin Wall and of the border between the two Germanies opened a new and unforeseen research perspective. Setting aside biographical motives, which in my case were important, German unification is a formidable challenge to a comparativist of the 'institutionalist' persuasion. The attempt to integrate a former socialist society and economy in the extremely complex framework of a highly developed democratic system with a ('mixed') market economy, and to simplify this formidable task by the 'transfer of institutions' (Lehmbruch 1990, 1992, 1994, 1995a), raises fundamental questions about the force of institutions and the resilience of markets. In particular the reconstruction of an administration based on the legal order certainly raises promising research questions. Moreover, how the united Germany will change will probably depend to a large degree on the developments of the institutional interface of the state and the economy. Hence the logical conclusion was to take up the analytical insights from our recent research and integrate them into new projects on the transformation of the East German political economy. The first results from this work not only point to strong and sometimes quite unanticipated cross-sectoral differences in the emerging governance structures (Lehmbruch 1995a; Lehmbruch and Mayer 1997), they also suggest that the united Germany may increasingly be characterized by structural heterogeneity in the spatial as well as in the cross-sectoral perspective.[12]

Notes

1. Among the most influential were: Wolfgang Abendroth, Arnold Bergsträßer, Theodor Eschenburg, Gerd von Eynern, Ernst Fraenkel, Ferdinand Hermens, Otto Stammer, Dolf Sternberger and Erich Voegelin. Some of these were emigrants who returned after 1945.
2. At that time, Ferdinand Hermens was particularly critical of my position.
3. This problem became the subject of important research by Manfred G. Schmidt, with whom I had worked since he was a student at Heidelberg.
4. At about the same time appeared Scharpf (1976), an analysis focusing on inter-administrative bargaining processes but fitting perfectly with my own interpretation of co-operative federalism.
5. Although I correctly predicted that a conservative government on the federal level would one day be confronted with a social-democratic opposition majority in the Federal Council, I overestimated at that time the destabilizing potential of such a situation because I still gave too much credit to the traditional theory of majoritarian party government (for a more recent analysis, see Lehmbruch 1989).
6. Despite my strong reservations about their narrow interpretation of 'union member interests', I found particularly suggestive the analysis of the development of the West German labour movement by a group of sociologists at Frankfurt (Bergmann, Jacobi and Müller-Jentsch 1975).

7. One should mention that the same distinction was already employed much earlier by Erich Gruner (Berne) in one of his important articles on the development of interest intermediation in Switzerland (Gruner 1959).
8. I employ the ambiguous concept of 'political economy' in the sense of an empirically-oriented (comparative) political theory of economic policy.
9. See the articles by Klaus Armingeon, Roland Czada, Walter Dittrich and Gerhard Lehmbruch on 'Neokorporatistische Politikentwicklung in Westeuropa', in *Journal für Sozialforschung*, vol. 23, no. 4, 1983.
10. For the first approach, Peter Katzenstein's typological efforts were particularly suggestive. For the second, see Campbell, Hollingsworth and Lindberg (1991) and Hollingsworth, Streeck and Schmitter (1994).
11. In the general framework of this project, the case of Japan on which I am presently working appears to be of particular salience (Lehmbruch 1995b).
12. Projects of my own research group include the energy sector, agriculture and banking.

19 Walking on two legs: comparative politics in East and West

Klaus von Beyme

University of Heidelberg

Personal background

In 1995, fifty years after the end of World War II, a typical abstract debate was launched in Germany about whether 1945 meant 'liberation' or 'collapse' to the Germans. I was only ten years old in 1945 and, at the time I certainly did not have a mature perception of what had happened. In spite of the disaster of being expelled from Silesia and the hardships of escaping to the West, the atmosphere for us youngsters was rather challenging as in a more serious game of 'cops and robbers' which we used to play. We were the robbers and the allied troops were the cops. Our fathers were in Siberia, so the youngsters had to organize food and timber for a mother with five children.

Comparative politics started for me in 1945: my mother gladly accepted coals stolen in a Russian camp, but she refused bread which I had obtained by breaking into a shelter of the American forces. Russians were considered as inferior and enemies; Americans were accepted as behaving on the whole correctly and offering prospects for a more civil and democratic life.

My interest in politics dated from the occupation years, as my zeal to learn Russian and Polish in the late school years was no doubt motivated by hatred. But hatred can grow into love. Only indifference is a poor motive for comparing nations.

Carl Joachim Friedrich, who came from Harvard University and accepted a part-time job at the University of Heidelberg, founded political science in Heidelberg. He became my teacher and he had certainly the deepest impact on my development, with the exception of Karl Deutsch whom I first met at MIT. Since the late 1950s I have divided my interests between East and West. Political science was almost inexistent in the winter term when Friedrich taught at Harvard. So I went to *Sciences-Po* in Paris, working mostly with Maurice Duverger and Raymond Aron. When Adenauer established diplomatic relations with Moscow he negotiated not only the return of the last German prisoners of war but also a cultural exchange of students. I went with the first crew of exchange students for one year to the Lomonossov University in Moscow. There was no political science and no possibility in 1959–60 to work on the Soviet system. I had to choose a topic on the history of political theory in Czarist Russia (von Beyme 1965). My Russian tutor was a professor of the history of economic ideas. Political scientists were sent to the Department of Economics, no doubt a useful experience for studying the Soviet system. Not only political theory (if it existed at all) was highly influenced by political economy; the whole system was determined by economic efforts. It is not by chance that my largest book on communist countries later dealt with *Economics and Politics within Socialist Systems* (von Beyme 1982). When I came back in 1960 Carl Friedrich recruited me for an academic career and organized a scholarship at the Russian Research Center of Harvard University.

Friedrich wanted me to become a specialist in Soviet affairs. He even invited me to work with him on a new edition of his seminal book *Totalitarian Dictatorship and Autocracy* (Friedrich and Brzezinski 1956, 1965). Soon our different views came between us: for one, I wanted to 'walk on two legs'. I refused to submit a book on Soviet federalism, which I wrote for his series on federalist systems, to the faculty as the 'second doctorate' (*Habilitation*) required of me to become a professor (von Beyme 1964a, 1964b). I turned instead to a comparative study, *Parliamentary Systems in Europe* (von Beyme 1970, 1973). We also had different perceptions concerning totalitarianism. Abundant travels in all the socialist countries had convinced me that there was a certain development in communist countries towards 'authoritarian rule with minimal pluralism'. Apparently Brzezinski, the co-author of the first edition of *Totalitarian Dictatorship*, also had views different from Friedrich's. The theory of totalitarianism involved the idea that 'one possibility should be excluded, except in the satellites: the likelihood of an overthrow of the regimes by revolutionary action from within' (Friedrich and Brzezinski 1956, p.375). Brzezinski pulled out, and the second edition of this book was revised by Friedrich alone. In his contribution to the Friedrich *Festschrift* Brzezinski wrote on 'Dysfunctional Totalitarianism'. Without attacking his former teacher he gave voice to his dissent on many details in the evaluation of totalitarian communist systems (von Beyme 1971a, pp.375–89).

Studies of western democracies

There was no chair on Soviet politics in Germany at that time, and I was advised to turn to comparative politics in East and West. After my *Habilitation*, with the work on *Parliamentary Systems in Europe* (von Beyme 1973), I accepted a chair in comparative politics at the University of Tübingen, where I stayed from 1967 to 1974, after which I returned to Heidelberg. At Heidelberg I was not the legal successor to Carl Friedrich, but to the second holder of the chair in the department, Dolf Sternberger. He induced me to engage in parliamentary studies, but not because I agreed with him. I was rather opposed to his devoted Anglophile views. Sternberger fought all his life for a 'British system' in Germany. Under the Grand Coalition (1966–69) in Bonn he even launched a campaign for the introduction of the British system of plurality vote. I was, instead, rather interested in disputing the ideology which was widespread after the war in Germany that 'true parliamentarianism' of the British type should be contrasted with the French type of *gouvernement d'assemblée*. The remnants of consociationalism in Germany, developed in a long tradition of religious pluralism which West Germany (excluding Prussia) shared with the Netherlands, Switzerland and Austria, led me to become more interested in non-majoritarian systems. The project on smaller European democracies, and contacts with Hans Daalder, Arend Lijphart, Stein Rokkan and Gerhard Lehmbruch, made the younger generation of political scientists in Germany more sceptical about the uncritical Anglomania of many scholars of the older generation. Only Carl Friedrich was free of it. He always had a strong interest in Switzerland, though he studied this country rather from the institutional point of view and hardly in the perspective of political sociology and political culture studies. In many historical studies on parliamentary systems since the French Revolution I discovered very different traditions of parliamentary government, especially in Scandinavia. A stay for several weeks in the library of the *Institut for Statskunskap* under Nils Stjernquist in Lund was very decisive for the pluralization of my views.

The methodological problem arising in these comparative studies was that Anglomania was in no way limited to German liberals. The British model was influential via diffusion of ideas in many other countries which lacked the social conditions for imitating the British model. A by-product of this kind of question was the study of competing models, especially the impact of the American model on European constitutionalism (von Beyme 1987c). The functionalist debate at that time made me alert to the fact that the old anthropological debate, whether institutions spread via *diffusion* or spring up as *functional equivalents* without direct impact from abroad, was pertinent to the development of political systems in political perspective. Semi-presidential systems and certain borrowings from the American model in Europe were frequently rather a search for the solution of a problem which created functional equivalents than a direct impact of a foreign device.

I had a parallel experience in another field of comparative politics, one which most political scientists left rather to sociologists: that of industrial relations. In Germany there was no tradition of studies on industrial relations, though the term *Arbeitsbeziehungen* was budding in political debate. The problem on the continent in the roaring late 1960s and early 1970s was that trade unions were mostly studied in an ideological way. After the failure of the students' rebellion the anarchical leaders of the movement turned into cadres for militant 'mini-parties'. They had no political success, but many of their leaders had some impact on the public debate. During the 'hot autumns', trade unions became for a while the hope for new forms of class struggles. In the mid-1970s I turned to comparative studies of labour relations. Again, I was fascinated by the plurality of systems, which had resisted the unifying impact of Marxist ideology in many countries. The model of German co-determination was criticized by the class-conscious researchers in the field. Scientific truth came rather to conclusions similar to those of a communist French trade unionist, a leading member of the CGT, who in a panel discussion complained:

> On Sunday, we fundamentally criticize the German trade unions for their course of integration and adaptation to the system. On Monday, however, we have to go back to our factories and dream of a position which the German trade unions have in their factories: being strong and united and being accepted by the employers' side and the government.

My study *Trade Unions and Industrial Relations* (von Beyme 1980) was the first attempt in Germany to evaluate the various systems and to study trade unions and their role in different political systems. With the smoothing down of ideological zeal more leftist researchers in Germany, too, slowly accepted my 'industrial relations perspective' on the topic.

The study of interest groups (von Beyme 1969) and trade unions (von Beyme 1980) was embedded in the activities of these organizations in the political system. The missing link between interest groups and the political systems were quite naturally political parties (von Beyme 1985). It was hardly possible to be original in the field of party studies, since parties were almost the only field which became exclusively the domain of political scientists. Only recently constitutional lawyers have begun to deal with this topic more frequently, at least in those countries where parties are mentioned in the constitution. The ideological debates on parties stirred my interest in the field. The German 'catch-all parties' were evaluated since Kirchheimer and others according to the old *Urpartei* SPD: strong organization, strong ideology, strong social links, strong leaderships under 'Kaiser' Bebel who led his 'attentive' revolutionaries like the emperor led the Prussian Army.

I opposed the nostalgia for parties of class struggles. Comparisons mostly relied on the major countries. I wanted to deal with party systems in a truly comparative perspective, including the smaller countries, including the results in the various national languages, largely neglected by the American literature, and avoiding doomsday scenarios about the decline of parties as a kind of reaction to the disappointments felt towards parties when they failed to transform the whole society.

A functionalist approach showed that certain functions of parties have declined, such as representation of segments of society and the mobilization of voters. Other functions, such as the recruitment function, are today more important than they used to be in the old days of the 'parties of notables' on the one hand and the 'mass parties' on the other.

In the early 1990s the critique of the party state in many European countries led to a global rejection of parties. The links between the political élite (denounced as 'the political class') and the party state had to be studied more thoroughly than former élite studies (including my own, von Beyme 1974a) had done. I came to the conclusion that there is hardly a decline of parties going on in most countries, as conservative populists (including even the former Federal President von Weisäcker) or Green leftists postulated. The Italian example had few consequences in the German party state, so often compared with Italy. The *lega* ideology, which claimed that the party nomenclatura of the old system would wither away as the nomenclatura did under Gorbachev in the communist countries, was hardly tenable (von Beyme 1993).

My attempt to walk on two legs seemed to have little in common with findings in Western and in communist systems. But the collapse of communism showed in East and West to what extent the scientific topics in comparative politics are shaped by historical events: trade unions were 'out' as a topic in the late 1980s. Parties – for a long time considered as a topic of 'grandpa's political science' by the progressivists – were 'in' again. Party developments in East and West have been compared since 1989. In retrospective, my East European leg had to be re-evaluated (von Beyme 1995).

My two areas of interest, Western democracy and communist autocracy, were not so unrelated as they may seem. Both areas were increasingly linked by a common outlook: the *policy approach*. As Chairman of the International Political Science Association (1982–85) I tried to promote a combination of institutional studies and the new policy approach so popular in America, but hardly internalized by most European scholars in the early 1980s (von Beyme 1986a). The policy approach was particularly fruitful in communist studies because it helped to avoid endless repetitions of the institutional setting of repression in totalitarian systems.

The *outcome* orientation could be practised even by a scholar in the field of international science policy involved in the activities of IPSA. Karl Deutsch and Candido Mendes, my predecessors, as well as my successors, K. Mushakoji and G. O'Donnell, have tried a common line in dealing with the conflicts in the world. Unlike other scientific organizations, IPSA, so close to the political conflicts, was never threatened by disruption, thanks to our course of mutually respecting the vital sphere of the respective powers. We have frequently been criticized for our 'appeasement policy'. In one case, that of China, it even failed. Without the co-operation of Georgii Shakhnazarov, who later became one of the chief advisers of Gorbachev and did a lot to 'social-democratize' the outlook of Soviet top leaders on world politics, this course might have failed more frequently. In the long run this policy and the agreement-oriented approach paid off.

Studies in communist systems and the transition to democracy

I have been involved in comparative communist studies since my studies in Moscow in 1959–60. The comparative perspective prevented a certain narrow-mindedness so characteristic of German studies on Eastern Europe which were completely absorbed by the competition of the two systems on German soil. My main criticism of the European Sovietologists was that they had lost touch with their discipline and the new approaches developed in comparative politics. The study was limited to official data – frequently distorted ones – and the informed guesswork of Kremlinology. A certain boredom attaching to Soviet studies could not be overlooked.

Friedrich was never a specialist in Soviet politics. As a matter of fact, impressive though his erudition in the North Atlantic area was, his bias against the under-development of Eastern Europe prevented him from gaining deeper insights into the particularities of the countries of the socialist camp. Though he was quite up to date with new approaches he was less interested in interest groups and élites than I was, as I had worked extensively on them (von Beyme 1974a, 1980). New approaches, as developed by Gordon Skilling in the United States, using an interest group approach in the context of socialist countries were applied by myself at the same time. The Nestors of German Sovietology, Boris Meissner and Richard Löwenthal, attacked me vehemently for abandoning the totalitarian paradigm and even deleted certain critical remarks in the written version of a presentation of 1966 on totalitarianism (von Beyme 1968).

The intellectual climate in West Germany, under the alleged constant threat of subversion from the GDR, was in the 1970s less tolerant towards those abandoning the totalitarian paradigm than that in the Anglo-Saxon countries. When I published a comparative and developmental comparison of communist countries (1982) the German *Ostforschung* was mostly hostile because of my 'positivism' in dealing with socialist countries and my criticism of normative anti-communist credos which were the norm for dealing with the communist phenomenon. I went too far even for Peter Ludz, the most enlightened specialist on the GDR.

These minor quarrels with Ludz did not prevent the perception from outside that both of us were 'embellishing the red system' with the assumption that the communist countries had developed towards '*consultative authoritarianism*'. Both of us got the unusual honour of an attack by the most conservative party leader of that time, Franz Josef Strauss, in a constitutional debate of 1976 in the German Bundestag. He read passages from the books of Ludz and mine and asked the Social Democrats: 'These are scholars not from East Berlin or Leipzig but from Munich and Heidelberg and they belong to your party. How do you dare to ask us why we state: "Freedom instead of socialism"?' (*Deutscher Bundestag*, 7; *Wahlperiode*, 11 June 1976, 1988c).

The positivistic attitude towards communism started from the assumption that the system works, that some of its underlying ideological premises are acceptable though probably in the long run not feasible, and that consensus in the population was increasingly 'organized' via 'Goulash' or 'Polski-Fiat "Communism"' and material benefits. Most of the Anglo-Saxon Sovietologists and some of the European specialists believed in the stability of the system. Most of us were, however, not as blind as the leading GDR specialist Gert-Joachim Glaessner, who in the month before the breakdown of the GDR published a book beginning with the introductory assumption that nobody doubted any longer that the GDR had become a legitimized system.

Fortunately, I could not be included in the 'gallery of scholars who failed in their predictions' (Hacker 1992) because they did not take seriously the fact that the majority of the East German population was still thinking in terms of one national state. I shared the assumption that the Soviet Union was in crisis. But, like most other scholars in the field, I did not anticipate its breakdown. In the German question I was a slightly deviant case because I assumed in the 1980s that the national question was not settled, as most intellectuals pretended and the surveys among the population suggested. I was convinced that the latent national issue would come up again as soon as the GDR system underwent a crisis, given the strong intellectual hegemony of the mass media in East Germany (von Beyme 1986b). But even a non-error in prognosis was but another proof for the extra-scientific beliefs that shape our hypotheses in the field of comparative politics. An old-fashioned patriotism prevented me from accepting the division of Germany for good. Wishful thinking this time was not wrong, but it was no proof of better scientific arguments in formulating predictive sentences.

Systems change in 1989 occurred while I was away on a conference of East European specialists in Australia. The colleagues lamented: 'We are ruined. We have got to apply for inclusion in the history department.' Turning to me, the only one working on East and West European systems, they added: 'You are in a good position. Not all of your books are made rubbish by history.' I was not so sure that my best-selling book on the German political system (for the English edition, see von Beyme 1983) would not be greatly affected by this systems change. It looked like the formation of a confederacy where new rules of the political game were negotiated by the two German states. Less than two years later I was able, however, to issue the book under the same title with added chapters on the impact of West German institutions and policies on East Germany. Again we did not anticipate how complete the collapse of the separate East German system would be (von Beyme 1996b).

Experiences of individual scholars are interesting only in the light of their consequences for the discipline of comparative politics. Looking back we have under-rated many developments in the East. Many of us writing on the Soviet Union were hopeful about the innovative capacity of socialist countries after the reforms of Khrushchev and the early Brezhnev. Gorbachev (1989) has fixed the moment of decline in the mid-1970s. The oil crisis of 1973 caused a deep crisis in the West. It overcame this astonishingly quickly, while the communist camp leaned back in a self-righteous attitude and hailed the final crisis of 'imperialism'. It overlooked that the satellites were increasingly affected by the oil crisis. The Soviet Union immediately prevented the imposition of new prices on its camp. But in the long run its resources got scarce and it had to hand over part of the prices on the world market to the Comecon countries (von Beyme 1987b).

The *perestroika* since 1985 led to a strange reversal of attitudes: conservative normativists in the field, such as Boris Meissner in Germany, hailed Gorbachev and believed enthusiastically in his success because they believed that 'men make history'. The 'positivists' like myself fell into pessimism for structural reasons and their knowledge of 'revolutions from above' that failed (von Beyme 1988b, 1989).

The collapse of communism in 1989 had quite a different impact on the scientific community: the conservatives fell into a mood of opening bottles of champagne. No self-criticism afflicted them that their assumptions of stability had been wrong. The more scientific positivists, on the other hand, experienced a crisis of the discipline: how was it that black Friday was possible? How was it possible that precise scientistic approaches (which emphasize a good prognosis, rather than a correct description of the situation; cf. Downs 1957, p.21) proved unable to predict the collapse of the socialist camp? How come non-scholars, such as Amalrik, with informed guesswork, came close to a correct prognosis even as far as the timing was concerned (1984, although this date had been chosen obviously only for linking this book to the tradition of Orwell's writings)? Even the conservative normativists shared the bias of positivism that prognosis had to be avoided. The extrapolation of trends in a scientific prognosis on the basis of quantitative studies of indicators was close to this type of scholarship. Though many specialists claimed to have seen the deep crisis in socialism, most of them still betted on stability. Mises's book on the unfeasibility of socialism even as a model was no longer taken seriously. Only after the collapse was his book reprinted.

There was only one school of social theory which in the 1980s developed an argument consistent with the autopoetic version of systems theory, which held that socialism was no longer feasible within a predominant world market society. But the circle around H.R. Maturana and F. J. Varela was certainly not taken seriously by comparative politics at this time.

Systems change fascinated me from the outset. My first study in this area was on Spain. Parallel developments in Western autocracies and Eastern dictatorships became an interesting topic for me very early (von Beyme 1974b). In the 1990s this is becoming a favourite focus of comparative politics, retrospectively.

The liberalization process, weak as it was in the era of Khrushchev, for me offered hope of new developments towards the more authentic participation and well-being of the citizens in East European countries. Khrushchev's attempt to liquidate Stalinism was halted half-way. It is obvious that even this author overrated the possibilities for liberalization in Eastern Europe given the backlash of Neo-Stalinism in the Soviet Union.

Comparisons between the consultative authoritarianism in Spain in the last years of the Franco regime and some peoples' democracies seemed to be fruitful. In Spain, many predictions of future developments towards liberalization and democratization proved to be correct (von Beyme 1971b). There were, however, errors in some details: I was in good company with Juan Linz, the scholar who did most to develop my interest in the transition from authoritarianism to democracy in general and my work on Spain in particular in wrongly predicting that a Christian Democratic Party might be the natural leading party after systems change in Spain.

Implications of political theory in the comparative perspective

I never dared to follow Friedrich on the path to becoming an all-round scholar, who combined political theory and comparative politics on an equal footing. But teaching in small departments in Europe involves a certain multifunctionalism. Friedrich succeeded in transmitting his theoretical interests also to those of his students who did not become professors of political philosophy. I started my critical reception of postmodern thought also only after the collapse of socialism (von Beyme 1991a, 1991b, 1992, pp.229ff.). I remained, however, rather critical of applying new paradigms from biology and physics to the breakdown of authoritarianism. The theory of fluctuations and chaos did not, so far, exceed a rather metaphorical application to the field of systems change. Moreover, useful predictions were no reason to accept wholesale the postmodern theories of the autopoetic version of systems theory. This new paradigm, which since Niklas Luhmann had begun to dominate large parts of macro-sociological theory in Germany as a kind of substitute for the structural assumptions of Neo-Marxism, which petered out in the 1980s, was extremely hostile towards theories of political action.

Political science – this is my hypothesis – will remain centred in the field of actors theories. Autopoetic systems theories do not deny that many processes are steered by political actors, or even 'the state'. But since theories start from the assumption that acting and steering are only possible within the code of various systems, they underrate political leadership. Processes influenced by political decision-makers are handed over to 'history', which only ex-post facto can translate influences from one system (e.g. the political one) to others (such as the economic or the cultural sphere). Political science specializes mainly in middle-range theories. On the level of restrictions it will have to take into consideration certain insights of macro-theoretical systems theories. But political science will stubbornly continue to work on theories which are centred on the actors' side.

Political science and comparative politics will, in the case of theories of systems change, also consider the first insights of theories of fluctuation and chaos so important for new approaches to systems theories, after political science's second change of paradigm. But it should not become too fashionable, by adopting metaphors from biology and physics which have not yet proved their usefulness in the context of the social sciences (von Beyme 1992, 1996a).

There are two traditions of comparative politics deriving from Weber and Durkheim (von Beyme 1992, pp.67ff.). The first tradition normally arrives in the end at historical typologies. The second is more theory-oriented, operationalizing indicators for quantitative measurement. The first method has been considered inferior in its intellectual status by quantification-minded scholars favouring correlational methods. Smelser (1973) called the Weberian type a 'method of systematic comparative illustration'. The number of cases compared tends to be small and the possibility of establishing systematic control over the sources of variation in social phenomena is reduced. Scientific generalizations seem hardly to be possible. But new approaches to comparative social research (Ragin 1989, pp.15ff.) have shown that the comparative method can be superior to the variable-oriented statistical methods in several ways: the statistical method is not combinatorial as each relevant condition is examined in a piecemeal manner with no access to holistic notions. The traditional comparative method reflects irregularities and deviant cases. The comparative method in the Weberian tradition forces the researcher to become familiar with the cases relevant to the analysis, whereas the statistical methods only disaggregate cases into variables without entering into the analysis of individual differences among them. The normal goal of a variable-oriented investigation is to produce generalizations about relationships among variables, not to understand specific historical outcomes. I have remained interested in both.

This schematic opposition of two investigative methods makes it clear that the study of systems change is mostly linked to the first approach. But the second approach will become more powerful in the new studies of East European changes as soon as there are reliable data on these countries. So far, the variable-oriented investigation is mostly concentrated on survey data, widely produced by trans-national co-operation in the ex-socialist countries also. The first experiences with transitions to democracy in Eastern Europe teach us that the historical differentiation of the area – artificially reduced for forty years by Soviet power – will progress, forcing the investigators to apply the case method predominantly (von Beyme 1996b).

Conclusion

Science is mortal: the more scientific a work, the quicker it seems to be dated. Even the exact natural sciences experience this every day. But political science is under a more serious threat: it is dated not only by new results but also by shifting fashions as regards the questions asked. The collapse of regimes leads to a situation in which scientific results are of only historical interest, mostly no longer able to compete with the results of historical studies. Once the archives are open, most political science assumptions and prognoses are exploded by shells of counter-evidence from sources so far unknown. Only jurisprudence has a still smaller life-expectancy as regards its findings. The proverb 'the act of the legislator can obliterate whole libraries every day' comes to mind. Some of my more historically-oriented early books had a longer life than later more theory-oriented works.

My excursions into architecture and politics and arts and politics (von Beyme 1987a) could be explained in terms of this methodological frustration. Actually this is not my reason for dealing with this topic. The history of art was one of my minor subjects as a student. Having started my life after school in a publishing house which published books on art and literature, my interest in the arts has been continuous. In this respect too I proved to be a disciple of Friedrich's. Dogan and Pahre (1990) mentioned the author of this essay as an exception of the rule that creativity normally develop at the intersections of various disciplines. I am afraid that there are hardly any exceptions to this rule. I felt most comfortable when intruding on other disciplines: history, economics, sociology, or even the history of art.

20 Four functions of comparison: an Austrian's tale

Peter Gerlich

UNIVERSITY OF VIENNA

So mußt du sein, dir kannst du nicht entfliehen . . .
(Goethe)

Introduction

To write about oneself, even to engage in the relatively innocent pursuit of sketching one's intellectual autobiography, is neither without its risks nor without its rewards. The rewards seem mostly for oneself: how interesting is it after all to reflect upon one's own past personal experiences, achievements and failures! The risks are for those who read these reflections. Could they really be of great relevance to anyone but the author?

Perhaps, a more general interest could be created by trying to place the experiences in a broader context of theoretical considerations and speculative interpretation. This cannot, of course, reduce the danger of another risk: the fact that it is certainly most difficult to be objective about oneself. Self-reflection, if taken seriously, is a rather arduous task. Karen Horney and other psychoanalysts have demonstrated this extensively (Horney 1970). On the other hand it may also be rewarding, leading not only to a better understanding of one's own character and personality but also, if one happens to be a scholar, to a discovery of why one set out on one's career, why one tackled certain themes, and why one did so in certain ways.

My aim in this paper is briefly to describe my intellectual development, starting with my historical and personal background, continuing with the academic training I received, and then dealing with my academic work as a professor and researcher. I will deal with certain specific questions in this context, and I also want to make some more general points (Gerlich 1993).

The questions I want to tackle first concern a search for causal factors. Why did I become a university person? How did I reach a position which in my country is still at the top of the pyramid of professional occupations in terms of status? Why, furthermore, did I become a political scientist? When I started my university studies the field as such did not yet exist in Austrian institutions of higher learning. How did I happen to become one of the pioneers in this discipline which, at least as far as the social sciences were concerned, was very much at the periphery? Next, why did I specialize in the area of government (and not in political theory or international relations – fields which I initially considered quite interesting)? And why, finally, did I become an empirical political scientist in a country and academic context where other approaches are traditionally more highly valued? Some of these questions may be more easily answered than others. In retrospect, I see myself in an environment of influences and opportunities. Some of these influences were of a rather psychological kind; others concerned specific circumstances of time and place. Some of the career choices I made probably followed unconsciously certain personal needs; others were responses to opportunities that offered themselves.

In a somewhat broader sense, what might be called comparison did play a large role in my personal development. I mean comparison in a sense very close to that used within the sub-field of political science known as comparative politics: comparison in the sense of experiencing and contrasting larger social entities – mainly nation states and their institutions, political cultures and similar forces.

From my personal perspective there are at least four functions or purposes of such comparisons, as far as both personal experience and scholarly research are concerned: identification, orientation, explanation and evaluation. One may compare, first, in order to become aware of the specifics of one's own entities or others' entities, that is, one may compare in order to identify. I am firmly convinced, and my own experiences bear this out, that one cannot understand any system, not even one's own, unless one uses the opportunity to confront and to compare them with others. Comparison in this way is a strategy to overcome one's own otherwise inevitable parochialism and ethnocentrism. Secondly, one may, of course, also compare in order to orient oneself in foreign environments and become aware of the cultural diversities existing elsewhere. The expansion of comparative politics in recent times is clearly a consequence of the increasing interdependence of nations. Indeed, if one thinks of the processes of European (or other) integration, comparison may even be a necessary precondition to make close co-operation possible. Thirdly, one may compare in order to explain. Since the social sciences cannot make use of experimentation, comparison of a qualitative or a quantitative variety may serve as a substitute, however inferior, for a more truly scientific model. Finally, one may compare in order to evaluate, in order to learn what is good and useful in the sense of functioning successfully elsewhere and what may in this way contribute to the discussions of institutional and other reforms which are a continuous side-show to any political activity or analysis. If one professes a somewhat more rigorous positivistic orientation, this fourth function of comparison may be considered not really proper for a scholar. However, the great transformations in particular which we are witnessing at the moment have once again shown of how much practical, if not theoretical, relevance considerations of political reform based on comparative evaluation may have.

Comparison may therefore be considered a multi-functional medium, which can promote intellectual activity on different levels and in different respects. One might even say that some of its functions of any given occasion may be manifest and others latent (Merton 1957). In the making of a political scientist and in his professional activities comparison might, for these reasons, be considered an impulse both for learning and for developing new insights. In describing my own intellectual development I shall come back to this point and thus demonstrate the meaning of these more general introductory arguments.

Background

I was born in Vienna in 1939, a few months after World War II began. My family was middle-class: it included civil servants and doctors, but also lower-middle-class artisans, teachers and the like. Towards the end of the war we had to leave Vienna for reasons of personal safety. We settled for a time in a rural area of the state of Upper Austria.

I consider myself very much a product of the so-called reconstruction period of Austria after its re-establishment as an independent country in 1945. Of the previous period, of war and Nazism, I have hardly any conscious memories, although, like the society out of which I came, I must have been, at least subconsciously, deeply affected. For my family the period of reconstruction was one of a new beginning. Living in a kind of emigration, even if a domestic one, must on the one hand have created a sense of lost opportunities, of downward mobility and frustrated ambitions, although at the time I did not personally experience any of this. On the other hand, the late 1940s and early 1950s were a period of restoration, economic growth and unprecedented optimism. And this spirit I remember very well.

My social development as a youngster took place in several steps. I can almost be said to have lived through the three subcultures of Almond's civic culture in succession (Almond and Verba 1963). First I grew up almost like a farm-boy in the very parochial setting of a small agrarian community where I attended primary school. I still remember, even if this was before I was actually admitted to school, how one day my father took me along to the next village and how surprised I was that there was more country and that there were more people beyond the area limited by the horizon – a first experience of the identification function of comparing one's own setting with that of others. The rural setting was that of a traditional society in which authorities loomed large, the teacher was entitled to absolute reverence, the church was very dominant, and the distant government made itself felt by its local representatives who were respected, but not loved.

To attend gymnasium I was sent to a boarding school in a small provincial town. This meant moving from a parochial to a subject culture. My teachers there were no longer openly authoritarian: they were far too flexible for that, having learned to adapt themselves to several changing regimes. But they were not enthusiastic supporters of democracy either. I think I was raised there in a centuries-old tradition of efficient bureaucratic authority, of a system in which the government knows best, in which individuals had to be loyal subjects and in which the main task of the school was to produce personalities useful in this respect. Incidentally, this provided the kind of socialization which fitted Austria's corporatist arrangements very well. Nazism was not approved of; it was treated as an aberration from the correct model, rather than as the almost unprecedented and inhuman political pathology it had been. The school was not intolerant. I remember one history teacher being rather fond of the French Revolution. This was considered strange but not impossible, but nobody took him seriously. It was only much later that I realized that one could consider the French

Revolution the starting point of the modern and democratic development in recent times. We were taught a great deal of history, but usually from an implicitly or explicitly very traditional perspective, extolling the achievements of the Habsburg monarchy. We also studied literature and languages intensively, but in a way which usually reinforced this traditional perspective. This was especially true of the study of Latin, which I had to take as a subject for six out of my eight years of secondary education. A somewhat different tone was introduced by the study of English (which I took for the full eight years) and the presence of the American occupation forces in the part of Austria where we were living. The US cultural centres especially – found even in such small towns as where I went to school – opened up an alternative perspective. I spent a great deal of time at the *Amerika-Haus* and I remember borrowing and reading a great many usually quite popular books from there, which allowed me to broaden my horizon a little.

Towards the end of my secondary school period the family moved back to Vienna. In a sense I now became a citizen of the capital city and old metropolis, entering, so to speak, the participant political culture. Or perhaps not, because not much changed in my intellectual environment. While the city offered many more cultural opportunities than the small town, the basic orientations of the gymnasium and of the University of Vienna did not really differ greatly. The latter was in a sense perhaps even worse. The French Revolution was definitely considered the most terrible of events, and even if the authoritarian traditions were more cleverly repressed, they nevertheless made themselves felt rather indirectly. Of course I must stress that these are very personal and specific memories. Some of my contemporaries may have had other experiences, but I do not think that mine were unusual. Only when I was able to travel outside Austria did my horizon widen.

I tend to trace back my ambition to become a university teacher, and even to deal with politics in some form, to the frustrated ambitions of my father, who was not given a chance to develop in these directions by the circumstances of the times. Incidentally, as the cultural historian Carl Schorske (1980) and others have pointed out, using scholarly pursuits as a substitute for political activity has a long tradition within Austrian society; this may earlier have decisively contributed to the intellectual achievements of *fin de siècle* Vienna. To have been concerned with politics without actively engaging in it must also have fulfilled some basic subconscious need within me. I grew intellectually by experiencing the functions of comparison, especially those of identification and orientation. My horizon, literally and figuratively, grew by my comparing my own environment, culture and country with others. But it did not grow much, because I had no opportunity to orient myself towards different environments before I spent some time abroad. In retrospect, I feel that I was rather hemmed in by my background and socialization. The opportunity to go abroad, which came towards the end of my university studies, really had a liberating effect upon me.

Academic training

After finishing secondary school and passing the final *Matura* exam with first-class honours (which proved, somewhat to my surprise, that my teachers did think rather highly of me), I was not at all certain which subject to study at university level. I remember being interested in taking up medical studies, but my parents talked me out of it. My father recommended the study of law, which had been his own subject, although he was now working as a businessman. In Austria, as in many continental European countries, legal studies provide a kind of generalist education: law graduates work in many different areas of public life and they generally enjoy a high social standing. Law studies are geared particularly to the needs of the civil service. The curriculum puts a heavy emphasis, first on legal history and Roman law, and later on public law. It also includes some social science, especially economics.

My legal studies at the University of Vienna were somewhat of a disappointment, in more than one respect, although I generally did very well in my exams. First, there was the method of instruction: one did not actually attend university lectures, but had to go to private cramming courses, which would prepare one for yearly university exams. At these one had to reproduce large amounts of legal provisions more or less by heart, literary thousands of pages of them. Second, there was the content: one learned a lot about legal norms, but even as far as the historical aspects were concerned, only those. One never knew or even learned whether these norms had or had had any practical relevance. That was simply outside the scope of strictly positivist 'scientific' legal teaching, as it was then understood. One would never visit a law court, to mention one example. That would happen only later, after graduation when one would become a sort of apprentice in practical legal life. This aspect especially of moving in a kind of unreal, even Kafkaesque, world started increasingly to trouble and frustrate me. Of course the orientation was also extremely ethnocentric. Intellectual curiosity or initiative was not really honoured. Fortunately there were some exceptions. A few professors impressed me, usually only those few younger ones who exhibited some enthusiasm for their subjects. Some of them invited me to their seminars and directly or indirectly motivated me to consider an academic career (Gerlich 1993).

A personal breakthrough, if not an intellectual rebirth, occurred only when I was offered the opportunity to study in the United States, more precisely to attend a one year LL M programme for foreign law graduates at Columbia Law School in New York in 1961–62. This experience proved to be a comparison on the grand scale with many side-effects of identification and orientation. I experienced a completely different academic culture which required intensive work with dedicated academic teachers and active involvement, including research. The completely different legal system placed much more emphasis on case law. Last but not least, and most surprising for me, one was encouraged to read. In Vienna we had had to learn the titles of important legal works by heart, but we were practically discouraged from studying them. For that we were considered not yet initiated enough. In New York I had actually to read partly the same books, which to my elation proved not only most enjoyable but also quite rewarding.

This positive culture shock went even further. The Law School also permitted us to audit courses in other departments. I discovered the social sciences. There existed disciplines, not found in Vienna, that tried to study systematically what was actually happening in the real social world. I remember attending some classes in political science. But of special importance to me were two consecutive courses on social psychology taught by Otto Klineberg (see Klineberg 1954), which made one aware of the empirical diversity and richness of human personalities and behaviour. This confrontation left an enduring impression. It was a great experience of widening horizons and expanding orientations. My American impressions were not limited to the university, however. I got to know a completely different political culture: traditions of constitutional government and participant democracy, a vibrant and active public discussion, a concern with reform and improvement, an open and cosmopolitan atmosphere (which I experienced especially during an internship at the UN Secretariat), and above all a spirit of optimism and belief in progress which was at that time still prevalent in American society.

Coming home caused a culture-shock in reverse. Having been away and having experienced a different culture helped me to identify my own, even if this was in several respects a painful process. The shock was somewhat abbreviated by my spending one more year outside Austria at two German universities, Saarbrücken and Munich. There I began systematically to attend political science courses, even if these were given by rather unempirical representatives of the discipline who stressed the German tradition of political philosophy. Among them were Eric Voegelin and Hans Maier. The German experience was a further opportunity to improve identification and orientation by comparison.

The beginning of an academic career

Back in Vienna in 1964 I was offered the opportunity to attend a two-year postgraduate programme in political science, and then to work another eight years as assistant and later as head of department at a newly founded institution, the *Institut für Höhere Studien*. This Institute for Advanced Studies was – as one can state in retrospect with some justification – a successful attempt to implant the modern social sciences upon a rather traditional academic culture (see Gerlich 1993). Not that this progress advanced smoothly, but ultimately, after thirty years of successful performance, one can maintain today that famous Austrian émigré scholars (above all Paul F. Lazarsfeld and Oskar Morgenstern) were absolutely right in talking the Ford Foundation into investing in this enterprise. Later on the Austrian authorities did take over. In my perspective, the establishment of the IHS proved to be a successful experiment in exporting a comparative perspective, and incidentally all four of its functions, to a foreign environment. However, there remained always some distance – to say the least – between the IHS established independently from the universities and the latter.

The idea at the IHS Department of Political Science was to train Austrian university graduates – who necessarily came from other fields, because political science was introduced at the university only ten years later, partly as an effect of the institute's activity – in this new discipline by inviting foreign (mostly American) visiting professors. The graduates of the department did receive a great deal of useful instruction at the Institute. Many of them are now teaching at Austrian universities.

The conception of political science which I myself and most of my colleagues developed at the IHS – in contrast, and sometimes in confrontation, with our previous studies and not always in a friendly academic environment – centred around three main conceptions: political science had to be empirical, comparative, and system-oriented (see also Gerlich 1982; Karlhofer and Pelinka 1991; Welan 1992).

The empirical emphasis I connect above all with two teachers who influenced us enormously, Paul F. Lazarsfeld and Heinz Eulau. Lazarsfeld was a most impressive teacher. He really gave systematic answers to the former frustrated law student who had never learned about reality. He convinced us that one could produce one's own evidence by the methods of social research and he taught us to interpret results with sensitivity and ingenuity (see Kendall 1982). Heinz Eulau spent almost a year in Vienna. He introduced us, perhaps somewhat dogmatically, to the behavioural approach in political science (see Eulau 1963). What was even more important, he conducted a study of the legislative behaviour of the Vienna legislature with us (Gerlich 1972; see also Gerlich and Kramer 1969). In a sense, his approach was anything but comparative. In fact, we had to take all kinds of aspects into consideration in the later interpretation of the survey results which afterwards corrected the lack of awareness of cultural differences in the original survey design. But partly because of this, the project proved to be a further comparative experience (Gerlich 1989).

The more specifically comparative emphasis was provided by two other guest professors, Gerhard Lehmbruch and Jean Blondel. Lehmbruch, who had previously published a revealing comparative study of the specific consociational political cultures of Austria and Switzerland (Lehmbruch 1967), helped us to understand ourselves better. He was also very helpful in a practical way, by introducing us, his young Austrian colleagues, to the German Political Science Association. Blondel, who taught a short but very intensive seminar at the IHS, which nobody who participated in will ever forget, introduced us to the systematic, general study of comparative politics (Blondel 1969). Referring to his own work as well as to that of, among others, S.M. Lipset and Stein Rokkan, he demonstrated the possible explanatory power of comparison to us (see Lipset 1960; Rokkan 1968a). He also invited us to the ECPR network and in this way opened up many possibilities for us to widen our experiences and to engage in research comparisons. I want to mention two more guests, who by their comparative approaches made me aware of the variability of political culture. Edward C. Banfield's study of a pre-modern, really amoral society (Banfield 1958), as well as Michel Crozier's analysis of the bureaucratic phenomenon (Crozier 1964), opened up additional avenues of insight and understanding.

One became at the same time aware that as a precondition for or as a result of comparative analysis one needed conceptual frameworks and theories of the context of political behaviour. Thus we studied the system theories of David Easton (1965), Karl W. Deutsch (1966), Gabriel Almond (Almond and Coleman 1960), and, finally, also Niklas Luhmann (1981), which we tried to apply and accommodate to our own scholarly needs and requirements.

Thus the mainstream of Austrian political science became empirical, comparative and system-oriented. It found its expression in the official curriculum of the university studies of political science in 1971 which in Austria requires parliamentary approval before one can pursue a subject at the university level. Now we had to try to accommodate the new approaches to existing traditions. I was ably assisted in this task by my colleagues Emmerich Talos and Karl Ucakar, as well as later by W.C. Müller. Our task was not always easy. But the professional success of the political science graduates of the universities later on proved that the attempt was not all in vain.

Why did I turn to government rather than to political theory or international relations? Partly by choice, partly by chance. Government seemed rather appropriate on the basis of my original law studies both in Vienna and in New York. I had then been interested especially in questions of constitutional law. At both universities it was the teachers in this field who had impressed me the most. The fact that the IHS tended to invite government specialists as visiting professors, rather than political theorists or experts on international relations, also played a role in this context. In comparison, theory – especially as practised in Europe at the time – seemed to me narrow-minded and unproductive (in this respect I am now having second thoughts). International relations appeared to be dominated by diplomats and people close to them, such as international civil servants. Somehow this did not appear an attractive crowd.

In which ways did comparison promote my intellectual development during my studies? As I pointed out previously all four functions did apply. Experiences abroad as well as foreign studies involving Austria had their effect on identification and opened up intellectual horizons. The opportunity to learn about the differentiation of systems and cultures both through experience and through literature served the purpose of orientation. From Blondel and others I learned to appreciate the explanatory power of comparison (see Gerlich 1971). Only the evaluative function of comparison remained somewhat neglected under the influence of positivistic thinking, both in my original legal studies and in my later ones in political science.

Academic practice

My further academic career was based on the intellectual foundations described above. I wrote my *Habilitation* thesis on the control functions of the Austrian parliament (Gerlich and Kramer 1969; Gerlich 1973a), which by the early 1970s had become quite an active institution once grand coalition government had been replaced by monotone one-party government faced by a more active opposition. In my book I tried to contrast and combine both the approaches I had learned during my studies, the legal and the political science one, and I treated the topic also in an implicitly comparative framework. The Law Faculty of the University of Vienna accepted my application, even if not without some misgivings. In 1973 I was granted permission to teach political science there. Shortly afterwards I was offered a position at the Technical University of Braunschweig in Germany, which also proved to be a comparative experience, this time of academic cultures. In 1975 I returned to Vienna, to a newly created chair of political science.

The role of a professor in Austria implies not only teaching and possibly research, but also a great deal of administrative work. Shortly after having been appointed I was elected Dean of the Faculty during a difficult time of university reorganization. This drained away a lot of my energies and unfortunately interrupted my research activities. Since then, I have been engaged in a number of other administrative responsibilities, which in a sense were consequences of the deanship. I spent six years at the Austrian Research Foundation being more or less in charge of all Austrian social science research applications. I was also appointed Director of the University of Vienna's International Summer Programme. Recently I was asked to return after twenty years to the Institute for Advanced Studies to direct the Politics and Sociology Departments. In a sense, taking on these administrative tasks did mean experiencing different subcultural environments, so they too have more or less also served some comparative function. Some of this has been quite explicitly comparative. I have participated in a number of OECD conferences on comparative university management and the Summer

School job implies taking responsibility for students from more than thirty countries each year, which obviously permits comparatively-induced insights of identification and orientation (see Gerlich 1994).

Comparative endeavours

My research work has been comparative in three respects. First, I have done, partly in conjunction with others, both some theoretical and some empirical work which was truly comparative, in that it attempted to follow the explanatory mode. This included a diachronic analysis of the institutionalization of European parliaments (Gerlich 1973b), an article on comparative corruption (Gerlich 1981), a collective effort on the politics of economic crisis in Europe, jointly with Jeremy Richardson and Eric Damgaard (Damgaard, Richardson and Gerlich 1989), and then comparative surveys of Eastern European political cultures jointly undertaken with Fritz Plasser and Peter Ulram (Gerlich, Plasser and Ulram 1992a). Although I am all too aware of the difficulties and limitations of these attempts, I have immensely enjoyed doing them. I always felt that I was really moving in the direction of actually grasping some potentially causal relationships.

Second, I have engaged in a number of international projects, most of which grew out of the ECPR context, in which I contributed pieces on my own country and engaged on this basis in a kind of comparative dialogue. Ideally all those undertakings should also lead to some truly comparative conclusions, but they rarely do, alas. But even when one exchanges views and information, the identification and orientation functions of comparison usually apply in this context. My international research experiences included among other topics the study of the processes of legislation (Gerlich 1986), political parties (Gerlich 1987) and cabinets. Much of this work was done in co-operation with Wolfgang C. Müller. Recently I have widened my organizational scope. Besides ECPR I have enjoyed participating in projects organized by Carlo Mongardini of the University of Rome and by Kurt Sontheimer of the University of Munich, and, with the assistance of Krzysztof Glass, in exchanges with colleagues from Poland and other Eastern European countries (see Gerlich and Glass 1992b).

Third, I have done a number of studies of my own political system put increasingly within conceptual and theoretical frameworks which imply a comparative perspective. This has included studies on the party system, the system of social partnership, institutional questions, and, more recently, different aspects and levels of political culture. Together with many of my Austrian colleagues I have published a bulky handbook on our political system in which much of this research has directly or indirectly been included (Dachs et al. 1992).

Aside from research, teaching has always very much interested me and I enjoy it (see Gerlich 1993). In this I have developed two personae who do not completely coincide. On the one hand I teach my Austrian students in German, mostly on questions of general political science and Austrian government. I also act as adviser for a great number of Master's and doctoral theses. In this the comparative perspective plays a role, even if a minor one. On the other hand I have also always taught foreign students, in English. These courses, taught in different contexts, have almost always been quite explicitly comparative. Besides the Summer School already mentioned, this has included a guest professorship at Stanford in 1981, where I met the most challenging group of graduate and undergraduate students of my career, as well as a number of international programmes in Vienna, such as Webster University and the Institute of European Studies. For reasons not yet really clear to myself, I rarely transfer these courses and topics to my German language students. Maybe there are subconscious limits to what one can do in the way of identification and orientation.

To sum up my academic practice I can say that my different activities are, as is to be expected, based on what I learnt before. The functions of comparison continue to be activated. Identification probably was pretty much concluded before I became a professional social scientist, but perhaps one should not be too sure. There could be possibilities for further growth. Orientation has slowly been extended to the four compass directions: first to the west and north, after earlier experiences mainly due to ECPR; later on also to the south in collaboration with my Italian friends; and now, after the miracle of 1989, also towards the east. Probably one should move further and not limit oneself to the European context. As I have mentioned above, I have engaged in explanation in some research projects. The strange effect is that one seems to understand some political developments better. Some of my always very tentative predictions about Austrian politics have become true, to my utmost surprise. This gives one a certain prestige and has even led to situations in which politicians ask my advice, and really seem to want to hear it, at least as far as one can trust their protestations. In a narrow sense evaluation has become a question of increasing concern to me. Partly because of my administrative responsibilities I am increasingly interested in questions of administrative (and academic) efficiency – something which also can be profitably analysed in a comparative perspective only. My friend Evert Vedung of Uppsala University, who teaches at the Vienna Summer School, has opened up new perspectives for me in this respect (Vedung 1991). More generally, I am fascinated by the question of how to evaluate and improve political systems, how to make them more democratic, more stable and more efficient. To compare national performances certainly seems a useful way to try to start contributing answers to these age-old problems.

Conclusion

Returning to my initial questions and assumptions I attempted to throw some light on a few influences that led to my present position and vocation. I also hope to have demonstrated how comparison, both in a scholarly as well as a personal sense, served the functions of identification, orientation, explanation and evaluation. In retrospect I feel I have been rather selective. So many other aspects – psychological experiences, influences of teachers, colleagues and students, books I read, conferences I attended, adult education programmes I organized, even projects which did not take off – might also have been included. Once one starts it is difficult to stop. One has to make a selection. In doing so one certainly constructs a life which, if one did not actually lead it, one would at least like to have led, or would like others to believe one had led. However that may be, I think one does, by telling one's story, open oneself to interpretation. If this should be a kind of confession, somebody more objective than I might and should be able to point out what really is implied by the aspects and themes

I chose and by those I left out. And maybe he might even provide me with some form of absolution.

Should I stop here? Not really. A scholar reaching an age at which some retrospection may be permissible should to my mind never stop being curious, willing to listen, or prepared to develop further. The possibilities of growing through the functions of comparison need not be exhausted. Scholarship is an unending quest. Indeed I see and engage in some activities, interests, contacts and experiences which may continue the attempts to improve identification, orientation, explanation and evaluation. Some of these developments may imply comparison in the sense our discipline involves; others imply borrowing from other disciplines or even applying comparisons to them.

So far as identification is concerned I have been increasingly intrigued by the question of how my scholarly research, which seems so objective and scientific, may be subconsciously influenced by basic personality traits and needs. Reading some psychoanalysis – including that quintessential Viennese professor Sigmund Freud (1974) himself, who has always been a kind of model for me, or some of his less orthodox followers like Karen Horney (1970) or Paul Parin (Parin and Parin-Matthey 1988) who stress cultural comparison – has opened up a vast and rather disturbing space for speculations and hypotheses in this respect. One colleague recommended Robert M. Pirsig (1974) to me. I must confess that reading him also proved somewhat disquieting, also instigating further self-reflection.

In spite of a certain satisfaction I expressed earlier about the expanding geographical scope of my attempts at orientation by comparison, I am increasingly aware of how very ethnocentric my understanding still is (see Blok 1985). All my research has been limited to Europe and to the industrialized world. I have never really tried to go beyond it, with one possible exception which proved to be a very educational one too, even if it did not really succeed. Jean Blondel recently attempted to organize an Institute of International Comparative Government conceived as a kind of worldwide ECPR. This brought me into contact with a number of Third World political scientists, who indeed baffled me by their intellectual brilliance. To extend comparison beyond the First World context remains therefore a task on the agenda. Eastern Europe provides obvious opportunities in this respect, but I have also tried to strike up some connections with colleagues from the Far East and from Latin America. A further area where orientation can be extended is interdisciplinary co-operation, involving at least the comparison of disciplinary cultures. I have engaged in joint teaching experiences, especially with representatives of history, economics, management science, sociology, theory of art, literature and ethnology. My students and I find the effects invariably stimulating and intellectually rewarding, even if truly interdisciplinary research is very difficult, not to say outright impossible. Finally, I have broadened my orientation by comparing my approaches with those of younger colleagues and students, who have chosen alternative theoretical positions. I feel that one can learn a great deal from feminist positions, even if one does not have to accept them completely. In this respect I have benefited greatly from one of my former students, Brigitte E. Steingruber (1989).

Even in the explanatory mode innovation is conceivable. The rise of the qualitative methods of social research has demonstrated that explanation may not only be provided by strictly quantitative comparisons – although I hasten to add that I still think this to be the royal road of empirical social science. Nevertheless I learned much from co-operation with my colleague Roland Girtler (1984), a cultural sociologist in Vienna, and from my former student Herbert Gottweis (1980), who have successfully applied qualitative methodology to a number of different fields of inquiry into society and politics.

Finally: evaluation. I have already hinted that, being socialized as a political scientist in an atmosphere of utter disdain for traditional political theory, it took me some time to reconsider that stand. Now I feel increasingly that political thinkers of the past, who worked very often on explicitly or implicitly comparative foundations, may be taken up again with considerable intellectual profit. One author among others, a quintessential intellectual, has recently especially fascinated me: Condorcet (1955), the representative of an unbounded and contagious, if ultimately unrealistic (but optimistic) belief in human progress and perfectability (see Gerlich 1990). With him I am back at the French Revolution, after all. But he too may be considered to have been a follower of the comparative approach, in a diachronic sense. Ultimately it seems to me that a political scientist who is only interested in the obviously imperfect empirical reality of contemporary politics may become a little shortsighted. I think there must also be time for reflection, at least a little, about the good community and the good polity, as Condorcet so enthusiastically showed.

I have put a quotation from Goethe, another authority who has accompanied me over the years, at the beginning of this essay (Goethe 1920). In a prismatic poem of his older days he summed up what constitutes and influences one's life: predetermination, as expressed in the quotation cited, necessity, chance, love – all these have played a role in my intellectual development. But at the end he mentions a further circumstance, which lifts us up into an ever more open future: hope. One has to stop telling one's story somewhere, but it is an encouraging thought that one is always able to carry on one's intellectual career beyond this point. Or so indeed one may hope.

21 A Smaller European's opening frontiers

Hans Daalder

LEIDEN UNIVERSITY

The beginning

I was born in 1928 into a family with strong, exclusivist values. Pacifism, vegetarianism, abstinence from alcohol and tobacco, an individualist kind of socialism, were the staple diet of my youth. But Hitler (my first political memory is the *Reichstag* fire), and more directly the German occupation of the Netherlands, put an end to expectations of a better world. Ever since, I have worried about both the merits and the fragilities of democratic government.

My gymnasium years fell almost entirely under the German occupation. Our teachers gave more to their work and pupils than they might have done in normal times. We reached very advanced levels in Latin and Greek, which I have since forgotten. If some say they learnt to 'think' reading Plato or Tacitus, I probably derived from the classics a tendency, rather, to write and think in parenthetical clauses: perhaps complex prose and qualifying sub-phrases serve a natural doubter well? I have reason to be lastingly grateful to a history teacher. He insisted on teaching us chronology and facts, and facts again. If many thought him a dreary schoolmaster, he gave me a grasp of historical material which has been a professional blessing ever since.

On my seventeenth birthday the Germans in the West of Holland capitulated. I started university in 1946. I had thought of studying either history or law, but then learnt that the University of Amsterdam was to start a new Faculty of Political and Social Sciences. This would group together a large number of disciplines including political science (not hitherto taught in the Netherlands), economics, modern history, sociology, communications and various parts of law, with a particular emphasis on comparative constitutional law. I studied history for one year, before I could enrol in the new faculty with some 300 or more of students in 1947. Less than 10 per cent of these would eventually obtain their degree, and it took those who did an average of nine years. Individual professors tended to insist that we become as good in their particular field as graduates in more specialized faculties or departments of economics, law, or history – while we still had to meet the requirements of professors in subjects more typical of a new social science faculty.

Elsewhere I have sought to portray the often remarkable professors in the Amsterdam faculty (Daalder 1994). From the German immigrant Kurt Baschwitz I learnt much about Nazi propaganda and mass psychology. The historian Jacques Presser (who spent fifteen traumatic years describing the destruction of Dutch Jewry; Presser, 1965, 1968) opened up American history to us. The sociologist A.N.J. den Hollander introduced us with considerable conviction to American social science approaches. After passing the *candidaats* degree as one of the first students in the faculty, I landed assistantships, first one with Baschwitz, then later, and for longer, with Jan Barents, the first holder of the new Chair of Political Science in the Netherlands (cf. Daalder 1991).

Barents (who combined great erudition with common sense and a highly critical mind) held doctorates in both philosophy and law. Before his professorship he had been a practising journalist and a director of the research bureau of the Dutch Labour Party, and he remained an active participant in public debate. He made us read some of the best work in the major subfields: political theory (I still treasure being forced through a rapid but thorough dissection of Sabine's *A History of Political Theory*); political ideologies (with a substantial reading of Marxist texts), modern political theory (centring on such authors as A.D. Lindsay, Ernest Barker, Charles Merriam and Robert McIver), Dutch politics, the political systems of a number of foreign countries, some international relations literature, and special topics, for example parties, bureaucracies, revolution, nationalism. Uniquely for those days, Barents charged me to teach my own courses, sometimes to large audiences. My first assignment was a course on political parties. In preparing this I was influenced much by the work of a well-known Dutch socialist and criminologist, W. A. Bonger, whose *Problemen der Demokratie* (1934) contained a powerful attack on Robert Michels and foreshadowed the later writings of Robert A. Dahl on élitism and polyarchy. There is, of course, no better way to learn than to teach.

Barents deliberately sought international contacts (cf. Barents 1961). He played a prominent role in the establishment of IPSA, for which he organized its Second World Congress in The Hague in 1952. I was drafted in as its 'publicity man', and saw some of the great men presenting papers, including Raymond Aron, Karl Loewenstein and Carl Friedrich.

As part of my studies I wrote papers on the institutional debate on the British political system, a comparison of the British and Dutch Prime Minister, and an analysis of policy shifts and stereotypes in Dutch foreign policy between 1940 and 1945 (both in occupied Holland and the London Government in exile) which became my first substantial publication (Daalder 1953, 1978a). But I worked above all in the field of Marxism and nationality. I saw this as one case which should show that major ideologies, including the various denominations of Christianity, had foundered on the reality of nationalism as the prime force in contemporary society. I submitted a paper on national self-determination (which made me read a great deal on differing conceptualizations of 'nation' as well as on attempts to protect minorities whom 'national' states inevitably reduced to secondary status). For a paper on Marxist theories of imperialism I dissected the works of classical neo-Marxists like Rosa Luxemburg, Rudolf Hilferding and Otto Bauer (see Daalder 1962b, 1968).

I had intended to write a dissertation on Marxism and the nation. But I dropped that idea when Barents insisted that I should first study Russian and other Slavonic languages as well as Yiddish, to do justice to the important debates on issues of nationality in Eastern Europe. Having spent much time already on many a turgid Marxist text, I did not wish to see that effort compounded by having to do so in another three or four unfamiliar languages. I might add that I turned down a job offer in the mid-1950s to become the second keeper of the Marx Archives in the International Institute of Social History in Amsterdam: when the scholar in charge, Werner Blumenberg, showed me the minute Gothic script and manifold papers to which he gave his life I could not but feel revulsion at the idea of following that example.

First foreign sojourns: Britain and a Round Table in Florence

Britain loomed large in postwar Western Europe. When the frontiers opened, I spent several months in Britain in 1946 and 1947. In 1950 my future wife Anneke and I attended a summer school on Western European Unity, organized as one of the last activities of a so-called German re-education programme by the University of Cambridge, directed by F.H. Hinsley. For that course I wrote one of my first papers on nationalism. I returned to that subject during the Salzburg Seminar in February 1951, where Hans Morgenthau was one of the most impressive lecturers I ever heard. His 'realism' was initially shocking, until one recognized (not without introspection) a desire not to fall victim again to the illusions of past idealism.

In 1954 we spent the full calendar year at the London School of Economics and Political Science. I wanted to work on comparative government. My supervisor was William A. Robson, Professor of Public Administration, a lawyer and a convinced Fabian, who was immersed in the problems of British government at central and local levels. Robson was an early participant in IPSA. He generously arranged for me to accompany him to two conferences which were to have a profound influence on my future development.

The first of these was the annual meeting of the British Political Studies Association. The association was then still small enough to see specialists from all branches of political science in action, including such luminaries as Isaiah Berlin, John Plamenatz, W.J.M. Mackenzie, Dennis Brogan and Max Beloff. I accepted with alacrity an invitation by Wilfrid Harrison, the first editor of *Political Studies*, to do an analytical article on Dutch politics, as one of a series he planned on smaller European democracies. The need to present one's country in English proved a valuable exercise in comparative politics: on the basis of concepts derived from another political system one had to portray one's own country stripped to its essence. Harrison turned out to be the strictest editor I ever encountered. He invited us over for a full weekend, in which he and I worked for some sixteen hours over what were to become some sixteen printed pages. He told me that he rewrote his own articles on average nine times. I remember telling this later to S.E. Finer, who reacted with a characteristic exclamation: 'What nonsense. If I can manage in five redrafts, he should be able to do so in seven!' The *Political Studies* article (Daalder 1955) was to bring me to the attention of at least three scholars who were to influence me greatly: the historian of France, Belgium and the working class, Val R. Lorwin; through him, Otto Kirchheimer; and then, Stein Rokkan.

The second conference Robson took me to was an IPSA Round Table on Comparative Government, held in Florence in April 1954. It brought together a number of scholars who had pronounced the need for revolutionary change in the study of comparative politics (e.g. Roy Macridis, Samuel Beer and Robert C. Ward, who had attended the Evanston Seminar in 1952; cf. Macridis and Cox 1953) along with some of the leading names in more traditional comparative government writing, including Carl J. Friedrich, S.E. Finer, Karl Loewenstein, Dolf Sternberger, Max Beloff, Maurice Duverger, Gunnar Heckscher, and others. As the new militants ran away with new paradigms all too easily for the taste of the more settled scholars, tempers often ran high. In Florence I met for the first time, Serge Hurtig who was an assistant to Jean Meynaud, the Secretary-General of IPSA, and I befriended Giovanni Sartori, who was in charge of much of the Round Table's organizational travail. A beginning scholar could hardly witness a more exciting introduction to the profession than that particular seminar (see Heckscher 1957). Although still at the lower end of the table, I was accepted by senior scholars who were to be very helpful to me later.

But first I had to write a dissertation. I had learnt from Barents the joy and the value of reading British memoirs and biographies long before I went to LSE. I married insights obtained from these sources with the more structurally-oriented teachings on British government and administration by Ivor Jennings, W.A. Robson, Norman Chester and others, in a doctoral dissertation on reform proposals in the British Cabinet structure. I finished the book in Dutch in 1960 (Daalder 1960), and later translated it for publication by Stanford and Oxford University Press (1963, 1964).

My first real jobs

When we returned to the Netherlands in 1955 after a year at LSE, I first did research for a study of the origin of a Dutch resistance newspaper, *Het Parool*. That research brought me into close contact with a self-made historian at the Dutch Institute of War Documentation, Ben A. Sijes. A confessed *Radencommunist*, Sijes became the acknowledged master of studies analysing the behaviour of workers under German repression. One of his works dealt with the February 1941 strikes in Amsterdam, in which workers threatened by a forced draft for work in Germany brought much of the Amsterdam population, Jew and non-Jew, together in a spontaneous protest against the Nazi handling of Jews (Sijes 1954). Another work of his contains a very exhaustive treatment of the forced draft policies themselves, and the various attempts of workers to elude a constantly more intimidating regime (Sijes 1966). No one understood the complex interaction between organizations and human beings in them better than Sijes. He was also, unselfconsciously, an inspiring methodologist who practised a rigorous form of oral history long before others were to proclaim its usefulness. I learnt much from him.

I have often wondered whether my study on the origins of *Het Parool*, and my contacts with Sijes and others at the Dutch War Documentation Institute, should not have led me to become a scholar of war and occupation. I was never formally asked to move into that area. Perhaps I shied away from it for fear of reliving totalitarianism in a scholarly life when there were also other choices. Have I been wrong? My most cherished essay is one on 'Dutch Jews in a Segmented Society' (1978b, 1995c). It stops in 1940. For the rest, my major academic efforts have been directed less on the German occupation itself than on the quality and conditions of democratic rule.

I worked one more year as junior lecturer in Amsterdam, in 1956–57. As a regular academic career did not then exist in the Netherlands I applied for jobs in the British Isles, but through the good offices of William A. Robson I landed an appointment at the International Institute of Social Studies in The Hague instead. The ISS was a graduate institute of development studies, formally established by all Dutch universities on the assumption that Dutch experience in colonial rule had much to offer to newly emerging states. It took some time before this claim was replaced by more modern interdisciplinary studies.

During the five years I spent in The Hague (from 1958 to 1963, with the important interlude of a post-doctoral fellowship in the USA in 1960–61), I learnt much. The Institute was to bring me into closer contacts with area specialists and the comparative development literature. The Institute did not have a political scientist on its staff at the time. My assignment was formally in public administration. But in the late 1950s the Institute had persuaded Sammy Finer to cross the North Sea every second week. He then went through two days of intensive lecturing, in an inimitable style of learning, hard thought, and mordant wit. He made me teach a large variety of subjects in tutoring classes to students who had degrees in economics or sociology, but no political science. I could not think of a more stimulating 'chief'.

Most 'students' at the ISS were civil servants from Third World countries who enrolled for short diploma courses. Their sometimes doubtful academic preparation was often compensated by a very real administrative experience. It made me aware of the importance of direct experience in government and administration for scholars in the field, which I had also noted in Robson and other British political scientists who had served in government during World War II. I have sometimes regretted having missed such an experience.

A post-doctoral year in the USA

A post-doctoral Rockefeller fellowship gave us a year in the USA, split between Harvard and Berkeley (1960–61). Harvard at that time was not the best place for someone who wished to retool in the area of comparative political development. But I did learn a great deal in courses and seminars taught by Carl J. Friedrich and Louis Hartz, and in a generous private tutorial by V.O. Key.

During transit from Harvard to Berkeley I visited in Chicago Edward Shils, whose work on the intellectuals in the new states I admired greatly (see his collected writings, Shils 1972). He was as powerful a scholar as any young man might ever meet and did much to broaden my outlook. Little did I then realize that processes of politicization and bureaucratization in the universities would bring us together later for joint work on university governance.

Seven months in Berkeley did not advance my socialization into comparative politics greatly either. I met area specialists like Robert Scalapino and Carl Rosberg, but felt more direct affinity with such scholars as Ernst Haas and Dwight Waldo. The real gain was free reading time, coupled with a growing wish to write a book on Dutch politics in a comparative perspective. I did indeed finish a draft of such a book in Berkeley, but it fell short of the standards I had in the meantime learned to set for 'real' work in comparative politics.

Why the change of heart? Exposure to the rich climate of American studies made me realize how much more we ought to know about our own countries. In transit from Harvard to Berkeley I had visited Ann Arbor, where I met Warren Miller for the first time (who like his other colleagues associated with *The American Voter* did not even have tenure in Michigan in 1960). It strengthened my awareness of how poorly developed electoral analysis still was in my own country. I was to have a share later in promoting electoral studies in the Netherlands, mainly in an organizational role. Not having ever gone through the hard school of methodology and statistics I have remained a dilettante in the area of survey research.

Furthermore, I was on leave from an Institute of development studies. The questions then asked by students of political development were rather different from the mainly institutional and historical approaches with which I had been familiar and which coloured my descriptive chapters of Dutch politics. I was also stimulated by a short visit to Harry Eckstein in Princeton, whose essay *The Theory of Stable Democracy* (1961) posed many a puzzle for those who saw Dutch society as showing at one and the same time hierarchical authority patterns and an inveterate pluralism of distinct subcultures with inherent rights.

But most influential was a growing realization that comparative politics required not so much isolated single-country studies, but a systematic analysis of the genesis and working of democracy in a number of European countries which were as yet insufficiently drawn into comparative study. A reading of the comparative politics literature made one feel that for all its universalist aspirations, its conceptualizations and preliminary theorizing sometimes showed remarkable parochialism.

The Smaller European Democracies and the Political Oppositions projects

Val Lorwin (who was working on Belgian politics at the time) and I then conceived a project on the smaller European democracies. Our initial intention was for a symposium volume, somewhat on the model of the Beer and Ulam book which covered larger states (Beer and Ulam 1958). But the project was immeasurely changed when we persuaded Stein Rokkan to join us. Rokkan put his sights much higher: he wished to develop a network of scholars who would write individual monographs rather than book chapters, and who would assemble a host of 'priority variables' for each country to allow for true comparative analysis. The list he drew up was a daunting one: to meet Rokkan's demanding list of data and queries I was eventually to engage in substantial, specialized research projects on different aspects of Dutch politics. I remember Basil Chubb suggesting that he be left out of the project, because there were no really adequate data for a Rokkan-type analysis of Ireland. Given the small group of scholars working in and on Irish politics, these were not likely to be collected in the near future either. In the event Chubb was the only author who was ever to finish a country volume in our project (Chubb 1970).

The SED group overlapped substantially with the well-known Political Oppositions in Western Democracies project initiated by Robert A. Dahl. Dahl and Lorwin were old friends (strengthened by the strong stand Dahl had taken when Lorwin nearly became a victim of McCarthyism in the 1950s). I first met Dahl through Lorwin in San Francisco in 1961: during an after-dinner walk he revealed his intention to follow up his theoretical work on democracy with a more empirically-oriented quest for the ways along which oppositions had become legitimate actors in different states. He invited me on the spot to join the project.

The interlude of 1961–63 and a Leiden appointment

We returned to Europe in the summer of 1961, via New York. I had been in touch with Otto Kirchheimer (whom we had hoped to persuade to become the author of a SED volume on Austria). Otto had just accepted a chair in Columbia. He had recommended me as a possible successor in the post he vacated at the New School for Social Research. Some inconclusive conversations took place. Anneke was reluctant to leave Europe. Yet returning with a young family on a half-empty ship to Europe in August 1961 during the building of Berlin Wall seemed like sailing on another 'Ship of Fools'.

I returned in 1961 for another two years to the Institute of Social Studies. For a public lecture I chose the subject 'The role of the military in the emerging countries'. I had undoubtedly come to this subject under the twin inspiration of Sammy Finer, who was working at the time on his *The Man on Horseback*, and Lucian W. Pye (whom I had read but not met; cf. Pye 1958, 1961). It was published as a separate booklet (Daalder 1962a) and became one of the best-distributed of my academic writings; it was stolen from a vitrine in the Library of the ISS and I later learnt about a pirate translation in Argentina! For a decennial volume of the ISS I reworked my Amsterdam thesis on Marxism and imperialism (1962b). Edward Shils was rather taken by it, and he asked me to write the article *Imperialism* for the new International Encyclopaedia of Social Science (Daalder 1968). My work at the ISS also led to 'Government and Opposition in the New States' (1966c), which analysed the many forces impairing the chances of democratic politics in the Third World.

In 1963 I was invited, much to my surprise, to occupy a new chair of political science in the Leiden Law Faculty. This put an end to any remaining ideas for an academic post in Britain or the USA. I retained some interest in the politics of the developing areas. I instigated a professorial *Dispuut* at Leiden, which has many area specialists. We held lively discussions on political developments in the 'Second' and 'Third' world. It ended when university conflicts turned participants inward to problems in their particular faculty, department or discipline. As a Leiden professor the brunt of my work was henceforth to centre on Europe, however, and on the Netherlands as one country within it.

For all its willingness to establish a chair in political science, the Leiden Law Faculty was not strongly interested in politics. In my inaugural lecture (1964) I sought to explain the traditional low salience of and interest in political life in the Netherlands. I threw out a number of hypotheses, including the heritage of particularist but collegial *Regent* rule of the Dutch Republic, the necessity of accommodating many minorities, the tendency towards deliberate depoliticization to overcome ideological divisions, the growth of what Finer (1958) had termed the new 'anonymous empire' of interest groups, and so on. It covered, in a few pages, many of the subjects which Lijphart was to treat more theoretically a few years later. He has gallantly acknowledged his indebtedness to that lecture for his analysis of the 'rules of the game' for a consociational polity (Lijphart 1968, p.123).

Intellectual fervour at Bellagio

Robert Dahl brought his research group on political oppositions to the Rockefeller Villa Serbelloni in Bellagio for two successive meetings. It resulted in the most high-powered intellectual interchanges among a small group of eminent scholars that it has been my privilege to see. Among the scholars Dahl collected were Alfred Grosser, Kirchheimer, Lorwin, Rokkan, Nils Stjernquist, and younger scholars like Samuel H. Barnes and myself (the still younger Ian Budge acted as *rapporteur*). Dahl proved a brilliant taskmaster, preparing meetings through theoretical papers with precise hypotheses, and making us write papers reacting to these on the basis of the experience of our countries. We then had discussions of a week or so, around a round table at the border of Lake Como, with a blackboard for anyone to draw up outlines, schemata, 'grids' or what not. To see the precise analytical statements of Dahl confronted by the bitter scepticism of Otto Kirchheimer, and the rich comparative insights of Stein Rokkan, all enlivened by the wit of Lorwin, was an intellectual delight. The book which was to result from these efforts was to have a long run (Dahl 1966). It was one of the few collective works where the editor laid the groundwork, saw it through and wrote seminal concluding chapters, making for more coherence than any later volume I have been involved in. I could not have written my chapter on the Netherlands (Daalder 1966a) in the manner I did had it not been for the searching questions put in a truly comparative perspective.

The Oppositions volume ran somewhat parallel in time with the LaPalombara and Weiner volume *Political Parties and Political Development* prepared under the auspices of the Committee on Comparative Politics. I was invited to contribute a chapter (but missed the crucial 1964 meeting at Frascati through illness). In it I sought to combine work I had done on parties with such comparative knowledge of European countries as I had acquired in the meantime. Among its main themes were the development of parties in processes of democratization, the rather different 'reach' or 'permeation' of parties over and against other agencies of government, the role of political cleavages, and what one might term an *Anti-Michels* (see Daalder 1966b). The LaPalombara and Weiner volume contains important articles by Kirchheimer (1966a), in which he spelt out his model of the catch-all party, by Sartori (1966a) on 'polarized pluralism', and by Rokkan (1966c) on numerical democracy and corporate pluralism in Norway. I became part of a distinguished circle of scholars who were greatly to influence each other's works in the following years.

A year at the Center

During my first years in Leiden, I had begun to set up some larger research projects. The (then four) Professors of Political Science in the Netherlands jointly approached the Dutch National Science Foundation for requests to finance larger research projects, including regular national election surveys (which was at first the responsibility of one university only, but which would soon follow the Michigan model of an all-university effort, with data becoming available for all interested scholars), and in my own case a study of the Dutch Parliament. An eminent parliamentary journalist, Nico Cramer, and I drew up plans for a three-pronged study: an oral survey, a biographical archive of

Dutch political élites since the advent of full parliamentary government in 1848, and a close analysis of the actual use of parliamentary powers in relation to government during the life of one entire parliament.

Before this study had reached the stage of actual fieldwork, I spent one full year at the Center for Advanced Study in the Behavioral Sciences in Palo Alto in 1966–67. That year had been arranged by Dahl, Rokkan and Lorwin, who were to join me for the second semester for a first attempt at joint analysis of the political experiences of the smaller European democracies. At the Center I was given my first introduction by David Peizer to the possibilities offered by a modern computer. It led me to undertake the building of three data-sets: one on Dutch ministers since 1848 (I had generously been given extensive data collected by a Dutch researcher in co-operation with Mattei Dogan), a second on political relations in Dutch city councils, and a third on the composition of cabinet coalitions since 1918 in the eleven countries of the SED project. Alas, the input for the first two data-sets was badly done by an American research assistant, so that the material proved to be too unreliable to analyse in detail. I was luckier with the latter data collection: for some six weeks I had the happy assistance of a young American methodologist recommended by Sidney Verba, John Ferejohn. The data were intended to throw light on the variety of political coalitions in different countries. I wrote a long draft for what had at one time been intended as part of our planned *Smaller European Democracies* book. I eventually presented a shortened version at an IPSA Round Table in Turin in 1969 at a panel I organized jointly with Klaus von Beyme. I published it in the Dutch journal *Acta Politica* (1971a), and it was picked up by the Bobbs Merrill reprint series. It foreshadowed many debates in the budding field of coalition theories, and would probably have made a greater impact if I had thought of a better place of publication. I remained active in this field for some time longer. As one of the first ventures of what was to become the ECPR I organized a workshop in 1971 in which I brought a number of younger coalition theorists (e.g. Eric Browne, Michael Taylor, Abram de Swaan, R.J. Mokken) together with more traditional specialists on government–parliament relations. That gap is still not fully bridged (but see Laver and Schofield 1991).

Once the three other 'horsemen' of the project arrived at the Center, writing and research moved into high gear. Lorwin wrote his seminal paper 'Segmented Societies' (Lorwin 1971), Rokkan his path-breaking 'The Structuring of Mass Politics in the Smaller European Democracies' (which at the behest of S.N. Eisenstadt he was later to amalgamate with a second paper (Rokkan and Lipset 1967a) in the famous Chapter 3, 'Nation-Building, Cleavage Formation and the Structuring of Mass Politics', of his *Citizens, Elections, Parties* (1970a, pp.72–144)). Rokkan and I collaborated also on what was intended as an opening chapter on the formation of states and nations; his knowledge and analytical skills soon proved so much ahead of me that I increasingly satisfied myself with the role of critic and admirer. To Dahl, one of the challenges of the SED project was the relative importance of size, which was to result in his book with Edward Tufte: *Size and Democracy* (1973).

Arend Lijphart and the consociational democracy model

When in Palo Alto I was asked by the University of California Press to read a manuscript on Dutch politics submitted by a young assistant professor at Berkeley, Arend Lijphart. I disagreed with some of the generalizations in the book and found it insufficiently historical, but I thought it breathtakingly original. I wholeheartedly recommended publication. My advice fortunately prevailed over that of another more sceptical reader. Neither I nor others fully realized at the time that *The Politics of Accommodation. Pluralism and Democracy in the Netherlands* (Lijphart 1968a) was to be the cornerstone of the 'consociational democracy' school. We had been contacted around that time also by some other scholars, working in the same direction (notably Gerhard Lehmbruch, whose *Proporzdemokratie* came out one year before Lijphart's book, and Jurg Steiner), and of course Lorwin's work on segmented societies was, to some extent, ahead of any of these writers in its comparative *circumspectus*. Still regarding it as a specific country study, I strongly recommended Lijphart's book also to a Dutch publisher. It was translated by Lijphart himself and published in the same year in the Netherlands as the original American edition. It was to have an overwhelming influence on future discussions on Dutch politics and society (the Dutch version went through as many as nine editions).

I tried all I could to lure Lijphart back to the Netherlands. An unforeseen opening arose at Leiden when a Chair in International Relations fell vacant, to which he was appointed in 1968. We became close colleagues and good friends, carrying on a running debate on the budding consociational democracy model and its applicability to the Dutch case over many a year (for my share, see Daalder 1971b, 1974, 1981, 1984b, 1987a, 1989b). During one intensive afternoon, we developed a full political science programme for Leiden, with comparative politics figuring prominently in it.

Years of turmoil

After our return to the Netherlands we did the fieldwork for the first parliament survey (1968). I played a role with Stein Rokkan in bringing SPSS to Europe. That package had been initially developed to cope with the problems of Sidney Verba's large-scale comparative survey work. We had undertaken to do the Dutch part of the study on political participation (cf. Verba, Nie and Kim 1978). As part of the project, Norman Nie worked at Leiden for over a year in our department, 'burning' much computing time at the Computing Centre, and strongly advancing the computing skills of many a social scientist at Leiden.

I was drawn also into other international studies: survey research on elections and political representation with Warren Miller and Philip Stouthard (which made us do a second parliament survey in 1972, cf. Kooiman 1976; Thomassen 1976); research on local élites (as part of the Verba project on political participation, we interviewed mayors, aldermen and councillors); a Dutch replication of the Michigan bureaucracies project (cf. Eldersveld, Kooiman and van der Tak 1981); and so on. All this implied the quest for funds and the finding of younger staff members. Having no earlier experience in directing large-scale projects, I underestimated the efforts involved. In the end, we gathered more data than we were able to analyse fully. A smaller number of studies might have brought a greater yield. But such projects did help younger research workers to work hand in glove with foreign scholars, and increased their methodological skill much beyond what I ever mastered.

My own work was greatly affected, however, by the university revolution of the late 1960s and early 1970s. Leiden itself did not experience the effects of the new politicization as much as other Dutch universities did. But when the student challenge came in 1969, polarization among professors, staff and students threatened even in Leiden. I found myself unexpectedly elected Dean of the Leiden Law Faculty in the summer of 1969, somewhat as a dark horse acceptable to staff members who hoped for a less subservient position, and to most professors who reckoned on me to resist demands for student power. I served as Dean only for the one crucial year of 1969–70, but long enough to lose my previous innocence in matters of university politics and administration for ever.

My involvement became greater when radical students and staff members came close to ousting my colleague, Hans Daudt, from his chair in political science in Amsterdam. Professors in other universities formed a common front in his defence, and for a few years we fought a difficult battle, eventually reaching the floor of Parliament. We formally won, but in day-to-day practice Daudt lost his control over the Amsterdam political science degree. I learnt a lot about actual politics, as well as about the opportunism of politicians, administrators and professors (for the full the story, see Daalder 1995d). At the request of Edward Shils and Giovanni Sartori, I undertook a larger research project on comparative processes of university politicization in Europe which eventually resulted in a solid tome *Universities, Politicians and Bureaucrats. Europe and the United States* (Daalder and Shils 1982). It was small compensation for lost time. Ill-considered 'democratization' soon led to increased bureaucratization and government intervention, as I had always expected. Too much of my life has since been spent in defending universities, and particularly our department, against continuously changing policy decisions from somewhere 'above'. If our department grew and flourished, I could not say the same of my own research and publications.

The ECPR and the European University Institute

The year 1970 saw the establishment of the European Consortium for Political Research, of which I was one of the eight founding fathers (see the chapters on Rokkan and Wildenmann and by Jean Blondel in this volume). Having organized the first two workshops, I became the Chairman of the ECPR Workshop Committee which decided on the programme of the Joint Sessions of Workshops, the fertile brainchild of Rudolf Wildenmann. There is no better look-out post if one wishes to know about international professional developments.

Once the ECPR Summer School, the *European Journal for Political Research* (successfully edited during its first years from Leiden by Arend Lijphart) and the joint sessions were established, the ECPR also moved into comparative research. A 1975 meeting at Bad Homburg led to a submission to the *Volkswagenstiftung* of four major projects, among them what was to be the last of Rokkan's major projects, *Territory, Economy and Identity* (Rokkan and Urwin 1983), and *Recent Changes in European Party Systems*, which was to be the responsibility of Wildenmann, Mogens N. Pedersen and myself.

Then, unexpectedly, came an offer for a professorship, and the chairmanship of the Department of Political and Social Sciences, at the European Institute in Florence, which was to open at the Badia in 1976. Sartori's unexpected departure for Almond's Chair at Stanford had left a gap, which at his suggestion I was asked to fill at short notice. It implied a sudden cut with my many responsibilities at Leiden, and as my wife and children correctly saw, a somewhat timely one at that.

The EUI offered many promises, but also immense problems. There was a fully-fledged Eurocratic administrative staff in place when the first professors arrived, but no agreed conception of the Institute's academic programme and procedures. We started work in the Badia building still under reconstruction, suffering considerable cold and other hardships. Decision-making within the small group of the President (Max Kohnstamm) and the initial eight professors was difficult by definition: to marry and merge the different traditions of what makes up a doctorate in European countries, to settle something of a research profile, to plan for one's succession almost from the beginning, demanded great efforts. To some extent, only my third and last year, when I had had substantial influence in the recruiting of doctoral candidates, proved really intellectually rewarding: it contained a number of brilliant younger scholars participating in my seminars on parties (including Stefano Bartolini and Peter Mair, who soon obtained junior positions at the Institute in their own right).

In December 1978 I organized a workshop to which virtually all prominent scholars in comparative party studies came, for a discussion of a number of puzzling problems in the comparative literature. It issued in the book (edited with Peter Mair), *Western European Party Systems. Continuity and Change* (1983), which remains something of a signpost in the field of comparative party studies. The *Recent Changes in European Party Systems* project also issued in a number of country studies (e.g., Finer 1980a; Farneti 1985; Mair 1987; Daalder 1987a; cf. Daalder 1984a, 1987b, 1992).

Another major adventure was the establishment, due to my prodding, of a programme of Summer Schools at the EUI, directed in principle towards university lecturers rather than graduate students. I was to direct four of these from 1979 to 1982. They differed from the more familiar methodological summer schools in being consciously directed towards a discussion of comparative theories and country findings.

Return to the Netherlands

I had spent much time on organization, both nationally and internationally (serving as Chairman of the ECPR in the same years as I was in Florence) in the 1970s. I found the Leiden Department in good shape on my return (although sadly Lijphart had decided to return to the USA in 1978). Chairs had been added in political theory, public administration, and (on a personal basis) political behaviour. Assistance from the Ford Foundation and similar grant-giving agencies had allowed some younger staff members to have at least one year abroad (notably in the United States). Many of them had begun building their own international contacts.

In a time of considerable economies, our department was to expand substantially in the 1980s. The abolition of the *licence*-type *candidaats* degree required us to open our gates to first-year students. At the same time, public administration began to develop rapidly, soon in a separate degree programme to which we contributed. Numbers of students rose in an unforeseen way, and we also had to meet the massive enrolment of students in the Law Faculty to whom, jointly with staff members of constitutional law, we taught a Dutch *Government I* course. More and more, I was given to teaching very large classes, made up, in the case of the Law Faculty, largely of students not very much interested in the realities of political life. I did not relish such tasks.

Even less welcome were the effects of increasing bureaucratization at all levels of higher education in the Netherlands, accompanied intermittently by often ill-considered and unsystematic new government measures. They required ever more bureaucratic reporting, and constant vigilance. One had to run hard to defend what one had. For all the talk of greater 'democracy' and professionalization of university governance, the fate of departments tended to rest largely on professorial prestige and action.

The supervision of doctoral candidates offered some intellectual compensation for the ensuing loss in political and administrative time. The Dutch doctorate presupposes a publishable book. It is generally very demanding on the supervisor, as he must take full responsibility towards both the faculty and the candidate for ensuring the quality of a published work. I saw some 33 dissertations through, about two-thirds of them since 1982. Many were on subjects once on the Rokkan list drawn up for the Smaller European Democracies project.

I cut down on involvement in collective research projects (whether national or international). I taught at the Summer School in Harvard for two years, and was appointed to a more prestigious, rotating chair (the Erasmus Lectureship in Dutch History and Civilization) at Harvard in 1989. At Harvard, I enjoyed great hospitality from Stanley Hoffmann and others at the Center for European Studies, a magnificent institution with highly individualist scholars, with a constant coming and going of all manner of politicians and social scientists (see also Hoffmann 1989). It was from there that we witnessed the crumbling of the communist regimes, which left even the most learned specialists as bewildered and excited as the rest of us.

Retirement to real work?

I laid down my chair in 1990, but I continued part-time, to oversee an inter-university network for graduate studies of political science in the Netherlands, which had been given a substantial seeding subsidy by the Minister of Education. There was goodwill all around, but to marry at least five different departments into a genuine alliance which, according to ministerial directives, should be a self-contained unit of advanced research, proved daunting. Dutch political science remains much too small to assume 'science'-oriented organizational forms, while the need to nurture separate sub-fields militates against the requirement of large-scale 'advanced collective research' (cf. Daalder 1991).

In 1993 I left my last responsibilities in Leiden behind me. I organized a workshop on 'The Intellectual Autobiography of Comparative European Politics' which laid the basis for this book. My major other commitment became the writing of the biography of Willem Drees, one of the Netherlands' most prominent socialist politicians who was Prime Minister from 1948 to 1958. He lived to be 101, and his political life spans virtually the whole of the twentieth century. He left a very substantial archive, much of it in shorthand, having been an accomplished and professional shorthand writer since the age of 16. What served him well proves a considerable handicap to a biographer.

A chronicle or a conclusion?

This paper is perhaps more of a chronicle of a professional life, than a true intellectual autobiography. It tells of happy accidents accounting for my moving outwards from the Netherlands to the intellectual and organizational companionship of some of the most interesting scholars in comparative politics. They made me analyse Dutch developments in a comparative perspective (for two volumes of collected papers, see Daalder 1990, 1995a). I have done my share in bringing the Netherlands on to the map of comparative politics (e.g. Daalder and Irwin 1989a), and in bringing out new generations of younger Dutch political scientists. To some degree, my share in comparative politics has remained ambiguous: for all my involvement in international projects, I may have remained too preoccupied with Dutch subjects for international specialists, whereas to many a Dutch 'local' I remained unnecessarily internationalist (but see Daalder 1993). If my best-known comparative work has been in party studies, it was motivated by a constant concern about legitimate democratic government, with an emphasis on the impact of historical differences in state formation and processes of democratization (e.g. 1966a, 1966b, 1981, 1987c). Élite-recruitment, the political role of bureaucracies (1995b) and the forces of nationalism have been other themes, more visible to myself than to others.

My continued *engagement* with the history of the Netherlands under German occupation and its aftermath (which also forms a leading theme in the political biography of Willem Drees) may seem somewhat removed from such areas of study. Seen in a more existential perspective, it is not.

22 About peripheries, centres and other autobiographical reflections

Arend Lijphart

UNIVERSITY OF CALIFORNIA, SAN DIEGO

Hans Daalder's idea of tracing the history of European comparative politics by examining the life stories of some of its prominent theorists and researchers has forced me, for the first time, to think systematically about the extent to which concepts, theories and approaches in this field (or any other field or discipline) can be explained in terms of personal background and experiences. In this chapter, I shall try to give an answer by reflecting on one case – my own. I shall first use a chronological approach to tell the story of my youth and early adulthood, from birth through graduate school; here my conclusion will be that some, but not all, of my interest in politics and the specific political science work that I have done can be explained in terms of personal background – but I shall come back to this question toward the end of my essay, where I shall give a dramatic instance of what seems to be a role of major importance played by my cultural background. Next, I shall give an account of the scholars and books that have had a strong influence on the development of my ideas; and finally, I shall take a bird's-eye view and self-critical look at the sum total of my scholarly work, its progression, its coherence, its strengths, and its weaknesses.

From periphery to centre

I was born and raised in the province of Gelderland, in the eastern part of the Netherlands. The city of my birth, in 1936, was Apeldoorn, but two years later my family moved to Heerde, a nearby small town in a largely rural area. During World War II and in the immediate postwar years, there was little opportunity for travel outside this area, let alone outside the Netherlands – I did not set foot on foreign soil (in nearby Belgium) until 1950 – so I grew up as a child of the cultural and political periphery of the Netherlands, the Dutch 'provinces'.

The impact of my upbringing in the periphery was reinforced by my father's strongly local orientation. He was a combination of businessman, industrialist and farmer, but also politically very engaged and active in a variety of community organizations – always at the local level. In the postwar era until his death in 1959, he was continuously a member of the town council, representing the Liberal Party[1] and he also headed the local dairy farmers' co-operative and other civic organizations for many years. Heerde was the place of his birth and where he spent most of his life; because he actually died in a hospital in nearby Zwolle, his tombstone inaccurately – but most appropriately – states Heerde as the place of his death as well as his birth. When he referred to 'Hollanders', the people of the two western provinces of North and South Holland which constitute the political and cultural centre of the Netherlands, it was usually in a pejorative sense.[2] Perhaps the fact that, in my professional career, my interests have moved rapidly from case studies of Dutch politics to a comparative European focus and then to a global orientation – that is, the study of democratic institutions and divided societies in all parts of the world – can be explained at least partly as a reaction to my peripheral background.

There is, however, an alternative explanation: my father's strong local roots and interests were counterbalanced by my mother's international background. She was born in Paramaribo in the Dutch colony of Surinam, South America, in 1907. Three years later, she moved with her parents to Zurich, Switzerland, where her father prepared for a Ph.D in biology. After he received his doctorate in 1914, and just before the outbreak of World War I, he moved with his wife and daughter to Java in the Netherlands East Indies. Hence, before my mother was seven years old, she had already lived in three different continents. As was the custom in those days, she was sent back to Europe to go to high school; in her case, this meant Geneva, Switzerland, where her grandmother lived. Her married years were spent in Heerde, but after my father's death, she soon went abroad again to live and work in the United States, Switzerland and Italy, and she only returned to Holland shortly before she died in 1979. As a Christian Scientist, she had a special interest in the United States – Christian Science being one of the two main religions (the other is the Mormon Church) that originated in the United States – which strongly influenced my decision to try to study at an American college after graduation from my Dutch high school.

World War II was an experience of enormous importance in my formative years. Although I was only about four years old when the war started and only nine years old when it ended, I remember it very well indeed. In fact, the beginning of the war is the very first vivid memory of my childhood. I remember the war – although many wars have occurred since then, to me World War II will always remain 'the' war – mainly as a painfully long period of great fear and insecurity. The Dutch periphery suffered less than the centre, but there was still plenty of military action – my home was located on the flight path of the allied bomber fleets heading for the Ruhr area, and German fighter planes and anti-aircraft artillery tried to bring them down before they reached Germany – as well as the continual threatening presence of and occasional arbitrary violence by the German occupation forces. One does not need to undergo this kind of experience in order to value the peaceful settlement of conflicts, human rights and democracy, but I believe that, in my case, it reinforced my commitment to these ideals and helped to make them a central concern in my scholarly work.

My high school years were relatively uneventful. The six-year gymnasium that I attended in my native city of Apeldoorn (1949–55), commuting from Heerde on a daily basis, gave me a solid and useful education but did not shape me in more fundamental ways. All students had to follow a fixed curriculum, except that in the last two years they could choose between a specialization in classical languages and one in mathematics and natural sciences. I opted for the latter, since I liked mathematics and physics better. No social sciences were included in the curriculum, although bits and pieces were taught indirectly via history and geography. I received a lot of old-fashioned training in foreign languages with an emphasis on translation (from the foreign language into Dutch) instead of speech and conversation: as much as six years of Latin and five years of ancient Greek (in spite of my specialization in mathematics and natural sciences!), six years of French, five years of English, and four years of German.

All these foreign-language classes did not make me into a linguistic prodigy, but they have turned out to be an important asset to me in my broadly comparative research. Later on, I picked up a basic, mainly passive, knowledge of Swedish as a result of my first marriage to a Swede. More recently, I made a special effort to learn some Spanish by attending an intensive Spanish-language programme in Costa Rica. And one of the few advantages of having Dutch as a mother tongue is that it automatically gives one a passive knowledge of Afrikaans. Although my knowledge of all these languages is far from fluent, I feel that, for research purposes, they have opened most parts of the world for me – something that I became especially aware of during recent research ventures into East Asia and Eastern Europe, where the native languages were truly 'foreign' to me and where, consequently, I was at a considerable comparative disadvantage.

My first introduction to political science occurred at Principia College (1955–58). Typical textbooks were Herman Finer's *Governments of Greater European Powers* (1956) for comparative government and Hans J. Morgenthau's *Politics Among Nations* (1954) for international relations. The behavioural revolution had started in the 1950s, but had not yet arrived at this small and isolated college in rural southern Illinois with its idyllically beautiful location overlooking the Mississippi river. My professors tended to be deductive in their approach to political science; Morgenthau, who was a traditionalist but who can also be regarded as an early rational-choice theorist, served as a prominent scholarly model. This approach tended to be reinforced by the fact that Principia was, and is, a Christian Science college, since the 'science' of Christian Science mainly means logical reasoning from a few fundamental axiomatic principles. In terms of its small size, geographical isolation and connection with a small religious sect, the college was an institution of the periphery, only partly counterbalanced by the fact that, also as a result of its religious character, it drew its students from all over the United States and many foreign countries. I had crossed the ocean, but without leaving the periphery.

Moving from a small and relatively little-known college to a major graduate school was not easy, but Yale was so kind to admit me – a very fortunate development for me since the Yale political science department was not only rated among the top graduate programmes but was the number-one centre of the new behavioural approach. I had finally moved from the periphery to the centre.

One of the first courses I took was statistics, which was a revelation to me not just in terms of the methods and techniques that were taught but also because it introduced me to probabilistic thinking. I found the inductive–probabilistic approach much more to my liking than the deductivism of my undergraduate days (and the recent, much more sophisticated, rational-choice approaches have not altered my scepticism about deductive reasoning). My principal mentors at Yale were Gabriel A. Almond, whose *The Politics of the Developing Areas* (1960, co-edited with James S. Coleman) was about to be published and who was working on *The Civic Culture* (1963, co-authored with Sidney Verba), and Karl W. Deutsch, whose *Nationalism and Social Communication* (1953) and recently published *Political Community and the North Atlantic Area* (1957) I read for his international relations seminar. I found Almond's structural–functional approach to comparative politics and Deutsch's treatment of groups as communication networks enlightening and highly congenial. Almond served as my dissertation supervisor, and Deutsch was a member of my dissertation committee. I also met Robert A. Dahl at Yale, of course, but I did not take his graduate seminar because my third field of study, in addition to comparative politics and international relations, was political theory rather than American politics; this was a choice that I regretted later on, but I was fortunate enough to get to know Dahl much better less than a decade later.

During the two years that I was in residence at Yale (1958–60) – I returned to Holland for my dissertation research in 1960–61, and wrote the dissertation while teaching at Elmira College in upstate New York (1961–63) – I also had the good fortune to meet three outstanding comparativists who were visiting professors at Yale for a semester or came down from the Boston area once a week to teach a graduate seminar: Lucian W. Pye (whose seminal 1958 article 'The Non-Western Political Process' had recently appeared), Alfred Diamant (comparativist and Europeanist, who had crossed swords with Pye on the nature of non-Western politics in a 1959 rebuttal), and Robert T. McKenzie. McKenzie had received high acclaim for his *British Political Parties* (1955), and he was very effective in transmitting his fascination with British politics to his students. Under his influence, I became a strong admirer of the elegant simplicity of the Westminster model and the excitement of the political game under its rules. Although I have become an advocate of the consensus model of democracy – the very opposite of the Westminster model – I still think that the British-style political game is the more attractive spectator sport.

After I received my Ph.D from Yale in 1963, I was appointed as an assistant professor at the University of California in Berkeley. Americans living on the East Coast think of California as a far periphery, of course, but in the world of political science, both Yale and Berkeley clearly belong to the centre; at the time, Yale was rated the number-one political science department and Berkeley the number-two department in the United States. After five years (1963–68) in Berkeley, which in 1964 also became a centre in an additional sense – the centre of the student revolution – I moved to the University of Leiden, where I stayed for ten years (1968–78). Leiden is not only the site of the oldest Dutch university but also located in the heartland of Holland between Amsterdam and The Hague – clearly another centre.

My move to the University of California, San Diego (UCSD) appears to be a move back to the periphery in two respects: San Diego is in a far corner (also an exceptionally beautiful corner) of the United States, and UCSD is a very new university, founded only about fifteen years before I joined its faculty in 1978. But it is also a remarkably successful university: I cannot think of any other example of a new university that has reached the top rank of universities in such a short time.

In terms of the two most vital statistics – the number of faculty members who belong to the prestigious National Academy of Sciences (NAS) and the amount of federal research funds received – UCSD has belonged to the top half-dozen American universities for many years. For instance, in 1992 (the most recent year for which these figures are available), UCSD had the fifth largest contingent of NAS members among its faculty; it was outranked by Harvard, MIT, Stanford and UC Berkeley – but was ahead of such old and famous universities as Yale, Princeton, Columbia, Cornell and Chicago, as well as all other state universities. UCSD was also the sixth largest recipient of federal research dollars, outranked by Johns Hopkins, Stanford, the University of Washington, MIT and the University of Michigan – but ahead of all Ivy League universities and many other prestigious institutions. Finally, only fifteen years after the UCSD graduate programme in political science was started in 1980, the National Research Council ranked it among the top ten (number nine, to be precise) together with such veteran top-ten programmes as Harvard, Yale, Chicago and Berkeley – an enormously impressive achievement in which I take special personal pride.

Influential scholars and books

At Berkeley, I was the colleague of eminent political scientists and sociologists like David E. Apter, Ernst B. Haas, William Kornhauser, Seymour Martin Lipset, Leslie Lipson and Neil J. Smelser. I was strongly influenced by many ideas in Lipset's *Political Man* (1960), especially his analysis of cross-cutting and mutually reinforcing social cleavages. *Comparative Politics: A Reader* (1963), edited by Harry Eckstein and David Apter, which defined the field of comparative politics in the early 1960s, was published shortly before I arrived in Berkeley, and I used it right away in my graduate comparative politics seminar. My articles on the comparative method in comparative politics were inspired by and drew on Smelser's (1967) work on the comparative method in sociology (Lijphart 1971, 1975a).

During my Berkeley years, I also met the leaders of the Smaller European Democracies project – Hans Daalder, Robert A. Dahl, Val R. Lorwin and Stein Rokkan – who were spending the year 1966–67 at the Center for Advanced Study in the Behavioral Sciences in Stanford – only about an hour's drive from Berkeley. I had already met Daalder briefly before, when I spent a few months in the Netherlands in 1964 to do research for *The Politics of Accommodation* (Lijphart 1968a). This book, as well as a number of articles on Dutch politics, drew heavily on ideas first formulated by Daalder. Daalder was also mainly responsible for 'drafting' me back to the Netherlands in 1968. An important consequence of this for me was that I was not only back in Holland but also back in Europe at the time when the European Consortium for Political Research, with Rokkan as chair and Jean Blondel as executive director, was founded. The Consortium was tremendously successful in promoting interaction and co-operation among European political scientists and creating a truly European comparative politics. From 1971 to 1975, I served as the founding editor of the Consortium's official journal, the *European Journal of Political Research*. It was largely in the context of my editorial responsibilities and other Consortium activities that I had a chance to meet and exchange ideas with just about all prominent political scientists in the different European countries.

Another group of scholars whose work strongly influenced mine were the comparativists who belonged to what Daalder in 1974 called the 'incipient school' of consociational analysis, which not much later became a well-established school. Especially important were the authors and books dealing with the European consociational systems other than the Netherlands: Gerhard Lehmbruch's path-breaking comparative study of Austria and Switzerland, *Proporzdemokratie*, already published in 1967 (Lehmbruch 1967a), Luc Huyse's case study of Belgium, *Passiviteit, pacificatie en verzuiling in de Belgische politiek* (1970), and Jürg Steiner's Swiss case study *Gewaltlose Politik und kulturelle Vielfalt* (1970; see also Steiner 1974). Other prominent members of the consociational school have been Daalder and Lorwin (both members of the Smaller European Democracies group mentioned above), German sociologist Theodor Hanf, Canadian political scientists Kenneth D. McRae and S.J.R. Noel, American political scientists Edward Dew, Robert H. Dix, Eric A. Nordlinger and G. Bingham Powell, Jr., South African social scientists Gerrit C. Olivier, F. van Zyl Slabbert, W.B. Vosloo and David Welsh, and Lebanon's Antoine N. Messarra.

The earliest consociationalist, although he did not use this term,[3] was Sir Arthur Lewis, whose masterful short book *Politics in West Africa* was published in 1965, two years before Lehmbruch's *Proporzdemokratie*. Lewis was different from the other consociationalists in two respects. First, he was not a political scientist or sociologist but an economist; he won a Nobel Prize for his outstanding work on international economics. Second, whereas the other consociationalists *discovered* consociational democracy in one or more countries, Lewis *invented* it. Lewis tried to explain the failure of democracy in one West African state after another, for whose governments he had been serving as an adviser; his diagnosis was that democratic failure was caused by the application of majority rule in ethnically plural societies and that the cure was a combination of broad multi-ethnic coalitions, proportional representation and federalism – in short, the equivalent of power-sharing or consociational democracy. He prescribed this cure without apparently being aware of empirical precedents. As a black scholar (a native of St Lucia in the Caribbean), advocating power-sharing for countries in Africa, he has been an important 'ally' for me in my efforts to get consociational solutions considered in divided countries outside of Europe. Lewis died in 1991; I never had the privilege of meeting him personally, which I deeply regret.

In addition to the general intellectual influence of scholars and particular books, I also received crucial advice in the form of very specific suggestions a few times. In my first draft of *The Politics of Accommodation*, the political apathy of the average Dutch citizen was a major explanatory variable – inspired by Daalder's emphasis on the *lijdelijkheid* of the Dutch masses. Ernst B. Haas, one of my senior colleagues in Berkeley, pointed out that I over-emphasized the importance of this factor; that, as Robert Michels (1915) had already pointed out half a century ago, political disinterest came closer to being a constant across different political systems than a variable on which the Netherlands happened to occupy an extreme position; and that, by treating the Netherlands as a special and unusual case, I was unnecessarily limiting the general explanatory power of consociational theory as well as its broad applicability as a normative model. As soon as he said this to me, I realized that he was right – a true *Aha Erlebnis*!

The second instance concerns my work in international relations theory and, in particular, my argument – using the terminology and theoretical framework of Thomas Kuhn's (1970) book on scientific revolutions – that the new approaches and theories developed from the 1950s on could be regarded as based on a common 'behavioural' paradigm that presented a revolutionary challenge to the centuries-old traditional paradigm of international anarchy. I first presented this idea in my inaugural lecture at the University of Leiden (Lijphart 1969), but I worked on it again while I was a Fellow in the Institute of Advanced Studies of the Australian National University in Canberra in 1972. During a conversation I had with Hedley Bull, who was then chair of the ANU Department of International Relations, he suggested to me that I should try to pinpoint the first 'revolutionary', and that his candidate for this title was Karl Deutsch. He was right, of course (see Lijphart 1974, 1981). Since Bull was the most prominent counter-revolutionary, it was perhaps relatively easy for him to recognize his principal theoretical enemy. Nevertheless, it is still difficult for me to understand that this point had escaped me before, since Deutsch had been one of my professors at Yale and since I not only knew his work very well but also had the greatest admiration for it. In fact, Deutsch and Dahl would be my nominees for any 'greatest political scientist that ever lived' award. (I am tempted to add Almond's name, but I fear that my nomination would then be regarded as having too much of a Yale bias.)

The third and last instance of this kind occurred while I was working on *Democracies* (Lijphart 1984), my own favourite among the several books that I have written. In the first draft, the concluding chapter was insufficiently conclusive; it failed to draw together the evidence of the preceding chapters into a coherent pattern – a classic example of not being able to see the wood for the trees. The 'wood' eventually became the two-dimensional conceptual map of democracy together with an explanation for the placement of individual democracies on the map. I needed several helpful nudges before I became aware of this overall pattern, and was fortunate to receive these from Powell (who served as the Yale University Press's referee), Adam Przeworski (while we attended a conference in Sao Paulo, Brazil), Robert G. Cushing (a sociologist and outstanding methodologist whom I have known since my days in Canberra), and my UC San Diego colleague Nathaniel L. Beck (also a methodologist).

Finally, let me turn to particular books that have had a great influence on my work. I have already referred to several of these in passing above. Two of them are so important that I should like to mention their titles again: Lewis's *Politics in West Africa* and Lehmbruch's *Proporzdemokratie*. Extremely important for my work on Dutch politics and consociational democracy generally were Daalder's 1964 inaugural lecture at the University of Leiden and his chapter on the Netherlands in Dahl's *Political Oppositions in Western Democracies* (1966) – as well as Lorwin's chapter on Belgium and Dahl's own three masterful concluding chapters – and Almond's seminal article 'Comparative Political Systems' (1956). My work on parliamentary vs. presidential government was strongly inspired by Douglas V. Verney's *The Analysis of Political Systems* (1959), to which I was introduced by means of the long excerpt included in Eckstein and Apter's *Comparative Politics. A Reader* (1963).

With two books I have developed strong love–hate relationships. When Douglas W. Rae's *The Political Consequences of Electoral Laws* appeared in 1967, I read it right away and was immensely impressed with the brilliance of its design and conception – but doubtful about several aspects of its empirical analysis. It took me more than twenty years to write a comprehensive critique of it, to reanalyse his data, and to show that several of his original conclusions were deeply flawed (Lijphart 1990, 1992b). Similarly, I have found Donald L. Horowitz's *A Democratic South Africa?* (1991) brilliant in his analysis of South Africa's ethnic divisions, but utterly wrong-headed in his recommendations for democratic institutions – presidentialism and majoritarian voting – for the new South Africa. I lost no time in pointing out the weaknesses in

Horowitz's arguments; my critique appeared in the South African political science journal *Politikon* only a few months after the publication of his book (Lijphart 1991a). I have felt relieved that the South Africans have not heeded his advice, and extremely pleased that they started their new democracy in 1994 with an interim constitution that is thoroughly consociational (Lijphart 1994b).

My *oeuvre*: progression and coherence

The development of my scholarly work can be partly explained in terms of background factors and partly in terms of how 'normal science' develops – moving from the solution of one puzzle to the next puzzle. My first two books, *The Trauma of Decolonization. The Dutch and West New Guinea* (Lijphart 1966) and *The Politics of Accommodation. Pluralism and Democracy in the Netherlands* (Lijphart 1968a; I am deliberately including the subtitles), would clearly not have been written if it had not been for my Dutch origins.

Trauma was a revised version of my Yale dissertation, defended in 1963. Dutch insistence on maintaining colonial control of West New Guinea, the last remnant of the Dutch East Indies empire, could not be explained in terms of economic motives, and was therefore a clear deviant case from the perspective of economic theories of imperialism such as V.I. Lenin's (1917) and John A. Hobson's (1902). Hence, selecting this deviant case as a dissertation topic had a perfectly valid scientific justification. However, truth to tell, a major reason for my choice of the subject was that, after five years in the United States, I wanted to return to the Netherlands and was eager to find a subject on which I could do the research in my native country. And the New Guinea question happened to be both Holland's major foreign policy issue and the main domestic political issue at the time. In fact, during my year of research (1960–61), the cold war between Indonesia and the Netherlands over this issue turned into a temporary and limited hot war; Holland surrendered its sovereignty over the area – after the United States stepped in as a 'big brother' saying 'enough is enough' – before I had completed the writing of my dissertation. (During the Vietnam war, I often wished that the United States could have received a similar big-brotherly shove out of an entanglement with many parallels to that of the Dutch in New Guinea. One of the disadvantages of being a superpower is that superpowers do not have big brothers ...)

After this case study, turning to a general treatment and interpretation of Dutch politics was a logical next step. I had the benefit of already having done extensive research on Dutch politics for the purposes of my dissertation, to which I added several months of additional interviewing and data collection, and of having a basic 'feel' for Dutch society as a result of having grown up in it. I worked on this project in Berkeley, which provided the extra advantage of physical distance from Dutch politics, making it easier to concentrate on the 'wood' and not be distracted by all the individual 'trees'. If I had tried to write the book while living in Holland, I wonder whether the book would have been written at all; at the very least, it would have been a very different book. Both the original version in English and the Dutch version (my own translation and adaptation, Lijphart 1968b) were published shortly before I moved from Berkeley to Leiden.[4]

My decision to move to San Diego ten years later had nothing to do with the facts that the Mexican border is only a half-hour drive away and that Spanish is San Diego's unofficial second language. But the geographical proximity to Latin America, combined with the democratization that started in this part of the world in the 1980s, stimulated my interest in Latin American developments and particularly in the problems of presidentialism – which is the standard form of democratic government in Latin America and which I have come to regard as one of the root causes of democratic instability and failure in the region (Lijphart 1992a).

A psychological explanation of my interest in electoral systems (Lijphart 1994a; Lijphart and Grofman 1984; Grofman and Lijphart 1986) could be that I was trying to compensate for the fact that, for many years, I was deprived of the right to vote. The current legal voting age in the Netherlands is 18, but when I grew up, it was 23. By the time I had reached this super-adult age, I was in the United States as a non-citizen and hence without the right to vote, and Holland did not give voting rights to its citizens who were not physically residing in the country. As a result, I did not have a chance to exercise this basic democratic right until 1970 when I was almost 34 years old. I have been a compulsive voter ever since, never failing to vote when I had the right to do so, including the casting of mail ballots (when these were finally introduced by the Dutch government) in Dutch and European Parliament elections and the filling out of the entire ballot in American elections after I became a United States citizen – which, since the typical California ballot has as many as fifty or sixty choices to make, is quite a chore!

So much for the accidents of birth and other personal circumstances. The development of my work can also be seen as a series of steps that follow each other naturally and logically. The early phases of my work consisted of a series of deviant case analyses. As I pointed out earlier, *The Trauma of Decolonization* (Lijphart 1966) was a deviant case study of colonialism. While I was working on it, I began to realize that, by being so uncompromising on this issue, Dutch politicians were deviating from their normal habits. It was logical, therefore, to turn to a general study of Dutch politics – stable and largely effective democracy in a religiously and ideologically divided country – which, in turn, could be seen as a deviant case in terms of the major theories concerning democratic stability like Almond's (1956) and Lipset's (1960).

The next phase entailed two major steps of generalization: first, from the Dutch case of consociational democracy to the formulation of the general theory of power-sharing, culminating in *Democracy in Plural Societies* (Lijphart 1977), and, second, the further broadening of the concepts of consociational vs. competitive democracy into the contrasting models of consensus vs. majoritarian democracy in *Democracies* (Lijphart 1984). This does not mean, incidentally, that I have given up consociationalism either as a theoretical concept or as a normative model. I now see consociational democracy as an exceptionally 'strong' or 'extreme' form of consensus democracy that can be particularly useful for the most deeply divided of plural societies.

Issues of democratic constitutional engineering naturally followed from my comparative studies of democratic institutions. A statement by Giovanni Sartori (1968c, p.273) that I have often cited with approval is that the electoral system is 'the most specific manipulative instrument of politics'. Similarly, the choice of presidential or parliamentary government is a strong instrument for constitutional reformers. Choosing proportional representation (PR) can steer a country in the direction of consensus democracy and choosing the plurality or another majoritarian election method can steer it toward majoritarian democracy. The relationship between presidentialism–parliamentarism and majoritarianism–consensus is more complex, but presidential government largely spells majoritarianism especially because of the concentration of power not just in the hands of one party but in the hands of one person. I have also acted as a formal or informal constitutional adviser for specific countries: especially and extensively for South Africa (Lijphart 1985, 1994b; Buthelezi Commission 1982), but also for Israel (Lijphart 1993), Northern Ireland (Lijphart 1982), New Zealand (Lijphart 1987), Lebanon, Angola, Chile and Fiji.

The above account of the substantive topics that I have treated shows that there is an underlying coherence to my work in spite of the variety of subjects, and my writings on comparative methodology complement the overall picture. I would even argue that my writings on international relations theory fit the same pattern (Lijphart 1969, 1974, 1981). The traditional international anarchy and security-dilemma paradigm is a competitive, adversarial paradigm, whereas the new paradigm is one of a more orderly, consensual world. My sympathies clearly lie with the consensual paradigms of both democracy and international politics. In this connection, it may also be worth noting that, while Deutsch was the modern scholar who first introduced the new paradigm, its roots can be traced back to Hugo Grotius – who happened to be a Dutchman. It may seem far-fetched to interpret this as another Dutch causal connection in my work, but I do not regard it as implausible myself.

My recent debate with Horowitz (1991) about South Africa has also made me wonder how much influence one's native background and culture may have not just on one's choice of subjects but also on one's substantive conclusions. Horowitz argues in favour of institutions similar to those of his native country, the United States: a presidential system of government and a majoritarian election system (although the specific form he favours, the alternative vote, is not in the American tradition). I have advocated PR and a parliamentary form of government (Lijphart 1991a, 1991b) – both characteristics of Dutch democracy. I have given this advice on what I believe to be strong theoretical grounds and persuasive comparative evidence, but who knows what role subconscious factors may be playing? The third element of Horowitz's advice is federalism, again consonant with his American background. With this I agree, in spite of the fact that the Netherlands is a unitary instead of a federal state. Or could I possibly be influenced by the earlier traditions of federalism of the United Provinces and the later informal practices of what Dahl has called 'sociological federalism' (quoted in Verba 1967, p.126) in the fields of education, health care and the mass media in the Netherlands?

Second thoughts

Autobiographical reflections should contain a section devoted to self-criticism; here it is. Leaving aside minor lapses, what major errors of fact and judgement have I committed in my scholarly work? I made two misjudgements in connection with the changes that took place in Dutch politics from the late 1960s on. One was that I exaggerated the degree of change. In the second edition of my *Politics of Accommodation* (Lijphart 1975b, p.vi), I wrote that 'revolutionary changes' had brought 'the politics of accommodation in the Netherlands ... to an end around 1967'. In fact, a great deal of consociationalism has survived in Holland to this day, and Holland is also still clearly among the consensus democracies and not a majoritarian democracy. A recent special issue of *West European Politics* about political change in the Netherlands, edited by Hans Daalder and Galen A. Irwin, has offered me a chance to correct this error and to try to gauge how much change actually has taken place – comparatively speaking, a rather modest amount (Lijphart 1989).

A second error of judgement is that, for a while, I subscribed to the constitutional reform of directly electing the prime minister, proposed by the new party Democrats '66 (D'66). This reform essentially meant the introduction of a presidential form of government; the term 'president' was not used because D'66 did not propose to abolish the monarchy. It seemed to me that the D'66 plan was a constructive way of introducing greater and more open competition in Dutch politics. I remember discussing these ideas with D'66 leader Hans van Mierlo when he visited Berkeley in 1967. I voted for D'66 in several elections. I have changed my mind and have become a strong foe of presidential government, but I did not write extensively about it when I was still more favourably inclined toward it – which means that, fortunately, I have not had to take too many of my words back.

In my book *Democracies* (Lijphart 1984), I made two errors. One is that I excluded India and Costa Rica, which, according to my own criteria, should have been included among the long-lasting democracies. This had the unfortunate consequence of making my universe of democracies more European, western, and wealthy, than it should have been. Secondly, if I had paid closer attention to the older theorists of federalism, I could have hypothesized that there would be two separate dimensions of the majoritarian–consensus contrast (to which I have since attached the labels of the 'executives–parties' and the 'federal–unitary' dimensions) in the introductory chapter instead of unexpectedly discovering it in the concluding chapter. I am planning to make the necessary corrections in the revised, updated and expanded version of *Democracies* which I hope to complete before too long.

My main regret, however, is that in my earlier writings I was much too apologetic and defensive about power-sharing. My argument was essentially that, while consociational democracy was qualitatively inferior to majoritarian–adversarial democracy, the latter was a luxury that deeply divided societies could not afford. This has enabled my critics, often citing me but vastly exaggerating my position, to undermine the power-sharing model as a normative model for plural societies. For instance, Pierre L. van den Berghe (1981a, p.82; 1981b, p.349) has called the democracy of the consociational model a 'façade', a 'pretense', and 'fiction', and Samuel P. Huntington (1981, p.14) has characterized consociational democracy as an 'élite conspiracy' and as at best consociational 'oligarchy'. This is utterly ridiculous, of course. The main European cases of consociational democracy – the Netherlands, Belgium, Switzerland and Austria – have been not only thoroughly and unambiguously democratic but among the most decent and humane of the world's democracies.

I have changed my mind in two ways. I no longer think that consociational and consensus democracies have anything to be ashamed of, but, in addition, I no longer think that majoritarian democracy is such a desirable luxury even for the homogeneous countries that are able to afford it. Instead, I now think of it more as a debilitating 'addiction' that English-speaking countries are prone to. I have ambivalent feelings about the 1993 decision by New Zealand's voters to adopt PR for parliamentary elections, which is likely to lead to a more consensual form of democracy. On the one hand, for scientific reasons, I hate to lose what has been the most perfect case of majoritarian democracy. On the other hand, had I been a New Zealand citizen and eligible to vote in the 1993 referendum, I would certainly have voted in favour of this major constitutional reform (see Royal Commission 1986; Lijphart 1987).

The 1990s and, in all probability, the early years of the twenty-first century, are the era of democratization but also the era of severe ethnic conflict. I am convinced that the only way to cope with the contradiction between these two developments is to promote consensus forms of democracy in those parts of the world which have not yet converted to democracy and which, by and large, have deeper internal divisions than the already existing democracies. Questions of democratic institutional design are, to my mind, of such crucial importance in today's and tomorrow's world that they are likely to demand most of my professional energies – both as a political researcher and a constitutional engineer – for many more years to come.

Notes

1. The Liberal Party, in the still strongly *verzuild* (pillarized) Dutch society of the 1940s and 1950s, was the party of upper-middle-class people with a secular or latitudinarian Protestant outlook. My mother belonged to the same subcultural 'tribe'. I inherited this political-ideological orientation from my parents and have felt basically comfortable with it ever since. I joined the same party in the 1970s when I lived in Holland; if I were to try to pinpoint my ideological position within the party, I would say that I was on the socio-economically more centrist side (that is, on the moderate right) but more liberal, even libertarian, on moral issues and matters of personal freedom. In the United States, I am a liberal or leftist Democrat – which may appear to indicate a sharp swing to the left. However, I do not think that I have changed at all: the explanation is that the entire political spectrum in the United States is skewed to the right, so that an old Dutch Liberal, remaining true to his convictions, finds himself unambiguously on the left in American politics.
2. Dutchmen have the annoying habit of trying to correct foreigners who use 'Holland' instead of 'the Netherlands' – completely disregarding the fact that, while the latter is the official name of the country, the former is very frequently used as a synonym by the Dutch themselves, too. However, 'Holland' also has the narrower meaning of the two western provinces that once formed a single province – the dominant province of the United Provinces that won independence from Spain in the Eighty Years' War (1568–1648).
3. The term 'consociational' is derived from Johannes Althusius's concept of *consociatio* in his *Politica Methodice Digesta* (1603). I first came across the term, and decided that it would be a good substitute for what I had been calling 'the politics of accommodation', in David E. Apter's *The Political Kingdom in Uganda* (1961, pp.24–5). Apter's own use of the term was consonant with but much broader than my definition, but he did not use it again in subsequent writings. At about the same time that I began using the term 'consociational', anthropologist M.G. Smith (1969a, 1969b) also hit upon the term – completely independently, as far as I know. In many of my later writings, I have preferred the term 'power-sharing' because it is less of a tongue-twister and more readily understandable for non-social scientists.
4. *The Politics of Accommodation* was favourably received in the United States and by the international political science community, but the Dutch version had even greater impact and success. Nine editions have been published – the last in 1992 – and it has become a standard textbook for Dutch political science students.

23 Present at the creation*

Mogens N. Pedersen

ODENSE UNIVERSITY

On my bulletin board I keep a faded photograph of a group meeting at the Villa Serbelloni in Bellagio in the summer of 1970. It is a picture of a number of political scientists, some famous, some who are no longer so well remembered, plus a few youngsters. I was the one with the most boyish face, even though I had already turned thirty years old. This conference, convened by Lewis Edinger, Mattei Dogan and Juan Linz, was supposed to start producing a major book about political élites and the effects of their varying backgrounds. The book never did materialize, but some, including myself, found in this capsized project a platform and a framework within which to work. When three years later I directed one of the first workshops in the ECPR Mannheim Sessions, some of the same scholars were present, and at least some of my own objectives had been accomplished. During a stay at Stanford University I laid the groundwork for a series of publications which appeared in print during the 1970s (e.g. Pedersen 1975, 1976, 1977a; Eliassen and Pedersen 1978). In the meantime I had been appointed professor at the new Odense University. The young man in the photo had 'made it', as some people say – and his hair and beard soon started greying.

It is my intention to tell something about a short phase in my career, namely the first crucial and formative years, roughly the time between my Freshman year in 1958 and the year of 1970, when I went to Bellagio, and later off to study and write at Stanford University.

The reason for concentrating on this short period is twofold. The first – unintended – one is the discovery to my chagrin that many of the ideas, many of the recurrent themes, and many of the weaknesses of my later work were already present at this early stage in embryonic form. This discovery has given me an excuse not to delve too deeply into the autobiographical quagmire. It also makes it possible to put some of my later work in context. Second, by my selecting this period the perspective becomes that

* The title of this chapter is – without any sense of shame – stolen from the memoirs of the late Dean Acheson. A somewhat longer version with a slightly different perspective can be found in *Scandinavian Political Studies*, vol. 19 (1996).

of the interplay between an emergent Danish political science and a young scholar who just happened to graduate as the first professionally trained political scientist in Denmark.

Other scholars have already told the story of the first years of Danish political science (Rasmussen 1978; Karup Pedersen 1980). Various attempts have even been made to present bits of the history to an English-speaking audience (Henningsen and Rasmussen 1966; Nannestad 1977; Rasmussen 1985). A major, unpublished, auto-biographical account by Erik Rasmussen is also available (Rasmussen 1991). What I can add is a personal memoir with a slightly egocentrical and 'bottom-up' bias. So much for warnings.

The pre-history

I entered Aarhus University in September 1958, intent on majoring in chemistry. Two weeks and an existential crisis later I enrolled in a political science programme that did not as yet exist with teachers and facilities, but was only a freshly signed Royal Decree.

Literally, there was no such thing as Danish political science in 1958. The Danes cannot boast of a century-old tradition for studying 'Rhetorics and Politics', 'Politices et Eloquentiae'. Although there had always been scholars who engaged in the study of political matters, there was no continuity and no institution-building.

In the 1950s a professor of law at the University of Copenhagen, who had written a couple of compendia on the history of political theory, also published an *Outline of Political Science*. He diagnosed the situation as follows:

> political science [never became] a traditional theme for thinking and scholarship by us, and most people don't even know what the term stands for. The plain fact is that political science in Denmark has to fulfil a demand that it first of all has to create. (Clausen 1956, p.11)

In saying so he also echoed what the Swedish scholar Elis Håstad had said in the early UNESCO survey (Håstad 1950, p.150).

When political science finally was introduced, it was not primarily in order to create a research discipline. The major objective was to train a new type of civil servant, a genuine generalist, who would combine law, economics and politics. The name of the new academic programme was *Statskundskab*, a name that rings a bell in Scandinavia – and with those who know of German *Staatslehre*. How this new degree programme and the related research might develop was anyone's guess. It could have turned into an abortive and by now long-forgotten attempt. It did not. Fortunately for me – because I was there at the time.

Students and professors at the frontier

My freshman year was spent digesting a heavy dose of public law and economics – plus some philosophy. The small group of foolhardy students had to wait a year before the ineffective university had selected the two first professors of political science.

Let us take a brief look at these two 'Founding Fathers' – Poul Meyer and Erik

Rasmussen. Their efforts were decisive and the effects were long-lasting, also in the sense of forming young minds – certainly my mind.

Poul Meyer (see Meyer 1992) was a legal historian and constitutional lawyer, who had moved away from dogmatic jurisprudence into public administration. His book *Administrative Organization* (1957) was acknowledged as a pioneering contribution. It was, strangely enough, also a genuinely comparative book. The author did, however, retain some of the habits of the legal scholar. Concepts and conceptual analysis were for him the cornerstones of all scientific activity, and God forgive the poor student who was sloppy in this respect. Or in any other respect for that matter ...

His companion – or counterweight – Erik Rasmussen was trained as a historian. He had drifted a bit away from his field by taking up a more systematic study of cabinet government and the principle of parliamentarism in Denmark – along the lines laid out by Swedish political scientists. From him one could, among other things, learn the principles of sound scholarship.

For a number of years these two – dare one say – 'outsiders' held the fate of Danish political science in their hands. They could easily have given the development an unfortunate turn. The truth is that one of them – if left alone – might have moved the infant Danish study of politics in a dogmatic direction and thus derailed it from mainstream political science. It is also true that their relationship was not always happy. But since they were scholars who had invested in a future in and for political science, they kept each other at bay and at the same time kept the field moving. First and foremost they delivered to Danish society the promised new type of civil servants – and in addition a considerable number of politicians as well. Thirty years later they could look back at an unqualified success.

What made this experiment become also an academic success story is not easy to tell. Maybe the simplest way to tell the story, and in the process to also provide a glimpse of the early socialization pattern, is by emphasizing the *eclecticism* of the new Danish political science. Fortunately neither of the new professors tried to invent the wheel anew. They borrowed and imported instead, from the old Swedish tradition as well as from the new Norwegian political science. They were also familiar with French and German scholarship. It was, however, the vivid Anglo-Saxon tradition that attracted them most. Their textbooks in Danish – of which they produced quite a few – introduced the students to the best of international scholarship, be it Scandinavian, European, or American (cf. Meyer 1959, 1962, 1965; Rasmussen 1968–69), and their students had to read the classics as well as the gurus of the day, Carl Joachim Friedrich, David Truman, Gabriel Almond, Harold Lasswell, Herbert Simon, Maurice Duverger, S.E. Finer, even the Norwegians Stein Rokkan and Henry Valen.

It was of crucial importance that political science was introduced in a coherent and systematic way, starting with the very basics. Later on it became fashionable to snigger at the disproportionate amount of time spent in defining the concept of *politics*. It could remind one a little of scholastic discussions in a medieval monastery, but it was probably a necessary step for an emergent academic discipline which had to carve its niche, lay out and defend its boundaries. The early David Easton (Easton 1953) was the hero of the day.

The search for identity also required a defensible normative position. The students became familiar early on with the important work of Gunnar Myrdal (e.g. Myrdal 1958). In Denmark three great scholars of international reknown, namely the economist Frederik Zeuthen (Zeuthen 1958), the legal philosopher Alf Ross (Ross 1953) and the sociologist Theodor Geiger (Geiger 1960), had discussed the value problem for years. First-year political science students had to master this discussion as well. Later on the reading list included Arnold Brecht's monumental compendium (Brecht 1959). The 'Logical Gulf Between Is and Ought' was thoroughly discussed, even to the point of indoctrination. I still do not see a valid alternative to the carefully reasoned scientific value relativism of Arnold Brecht (cf. Pedersen 1990). It was invaluable as a defence line during the skirmishes with Marxists in the 1970s.

The third problem discussed at length was the controversy between those who believed in 'grand theory' and those who could at most envisage partial, 'middle-range theory'. 'Mainstream' Danish political science adhered to the latter. What else could a bunch of novices do?

The story has been told in such a way that the 'frontier' atmosphere is emphasized. Maybe professors and students did not always get it right, when they immersed themselves in a literature that no one in Denmark had studied before. But they enjoyed studying together in a highly stimulating atmosphere – which unfortunately soon suffered, when students flooded the university around the mid-1960s. The spirit of the frontier disappeared for good during the tumults in 1968–9 (cf. Pedersen 1982, 1984a).

The reader may ask, was it all so rosy? Of course not. Below the quiet surface there was a current. The inherent structural problems only dawned on me when, upon graduation in 1964, I was hired as assistant (*amanuensis*) to Poul Meyer, a university position situated between apprentice and slave (cf. Pedersen 1984a). I then discovered the mixed blessing of having studied with two professors who were as different as night and day. Could one – and should one – choose between the primarily legalistic and conceptual, not to say highly personal, approach of Poul Meyer and the basically historical, somewhat more empirical and much more eclectic approach of Erik Rasmussen? What about other ways of practising political science? It is to these difficult questions that I now turn. It took me three to four difficult years to sort this out and choose a side.

One might say that the first couple of years of teaching and research was also a kind of graduate school. There was no school in physical terms, and there were certainly not many 'graduate' students around. The professors took some interest in one's research ideas, but there was no pressure, sometimes even a bit of benign indifference – like the atmosphere of many a real graduate school. My immediate boss, Poul Meyer, needed me primarily for teaching ever bigger classes of introductory political science according to his own ideas, which were laid out in a small, and somewhat idiosyncratic, textbook (Meyer 1962; cf. Pedersen 1984a).

This professor had high scientific standards, but he also harboured some indisputable ideas. In a blast of temper he once told me in no uncertain terms to lecture according to his understanding of the basic concepts, even if these – in my opinion – represented a complete mis-reading of the primary text. These were the conditions. No wonder that I had to create my own 'graduate' programme. Since this damned little textbook was based upon a very broad reading, these studies had to include important books from all the social sciences. I still remember immersing myself in the analysis of social norms (Newcomb, Rommetveit, Parsons); groups (Bentley, Truman); power (Lasswell and Kaplan); behavioural models (Simon, Shubik, Lipset, etc.); values (Myrdal, Ross, Zeuthen, Weber); philosophical/conceptual analysis (Ross, Hart, Ayer,

Hartnack); ethics (Toulmin, Løgstrup, Hare, Nowell-Smith); to say nothing of a lot of semantics (Hayakawa, Ogden). After having read and digested all this and more, and having made plenty of laborious excerpts, one was able to answer all sorts of simple-minded questions from students, who were not much younger than myself.

Early research

The next, unabashedly egocentric, pages will deal with my own research.

Let us suppose for the sake of argument that a research career is based upon rational decisions – and is not just a messy 'garbage-can' process. What is rational behaviour for a young scholar-to-be, who has been educated in the kind of milieu just described? That is, on the very 'frontier' of the national discipline, confronted with a vast virgin land? If the young man is neither an absolutely brilliant scholar nor the complete opposite, and if he is furthermore unsure about his intellectual powers – he is probably best advised to try to carve out a niche for himself, somewhat removed from the primary interests of his elders, but still within communication distance. If, at the same time, he also tries to build up what the negotiation theorists call a BATNA, a Best Alternative To a Negotiated Agreement (Fisher and Ury 1981), so much the better. This may sound a bit cynical, but I have to admit that this description fits my own situation much better than models that are based entirely on the nice idea that scholars are searching for The Scientific Truth from the very first day of their career. The crux of the matter is that one's academic career depends not only upon one's intellect, but certainly also upon timing, idiosyncracies, whom you meet and how you meet them, luck and mishaps. My early career contained all of these, but I have of course in the following tried to 'dress it up', as if I learned something all along the way.

The first choice was to decide upon a field of specialization. This decision, which happened over an extended period of time, may have contained an element of the unconscious, In the end, after having already invested a lot of time and energy studying parliaments and literature on this institution which was supposedly uninteresting and in decline, I decided to specialize on the Danish *Folketing*.

The second step, much more consequential for my future, consisted of picking the behavioural approach as the preferred 'paradigm'. Although I had never heard about Thomas Kuhn, I may have grasped his notion. The decision was made with my eyes wide open; in fact it was a quite deliberate act. Many of the books and articles that guided me into this new world had one name on the title page, Heinz Eulau (Eulau, Eldersveld and Janowitz 1956; Wahlke and Eulau 1959; Wahlke et al. 1962; Eulau 1963; plus many of the articles reprinted in Eulau 1969). I did not know this gentleman at the time, but I certainly admired his work for its elegant empirical analyses as well as its erudition. In a short time I decided that the behavioural persuasion was going to be my epistemological platform, not in its vulgar 'behaviouristic' form, but as a framework that would allow me to study political institutions in a somewhat broader perspective than I had been brought up with. I even defended my platform in public (Pedersen 1972b).

The third important decision that I am conscious of having made consisted of deciding to specialize in using primarily a certain type of data, 'process-produced', 'unobtrusive', and 'ecological' data. Again one can with hindsight see that this was a natural, maybe even necessary, choice given the place and the times. At the time no surveys had yet been conducted in Denmark. Without a strong organization and a department capable of backing up a major research project, one simply had to opt for 'cheap' data. Public research money was also scarce at this juncture. A good training in historical methodology and the conspicuous absence of training in 'quantitative' methods also supported this preference for 'process-produced' electoral statistics, roll-call data and other remnants from the legislative process, biographical information etc. It stuck. It is only in recent years that the less challenging survey data have become part of my daily life.

Some traumatic experiences

Looking back, it is easy to identify subjective experiences that were of importance, because they prompted the above-mentioned decisions and formed my thinking. I will mention some of these events.

The first was connected with my thesis for the *cand. scient. pol.* degree. I had been working like mad on a project on the internal border disputes in the Danish trade union movement. Archives had been rummaged. Data from every damned trade union – almost a hundred of them – had been collected and interpreted. This was before the invention of xeroxing. The research protocols were tomes of learning and piles of garbage in handwriting. After a while I became uneasy. I had vague ideas about how to generalize but could not find literature that could give me the crucial clue. An other-wise very fine discussion of the Danish labour movement by the American economist Walter Galenson (1952) was almost the only guidance at hand. All this work was done two years before Mancur Olson's *Logic of Collective Action* (1965) and eight years before Albert Hirschman published *Exit, Voice, and Loyalty* (1970). Neither had I heard about Thomas Schelling's work on bargaining theory (1960). I mention this because the nadir was reached when the thesis was graded. The grade was high, but not the top one. Apparently the work had not been seen to be a genuine political science thesis, but 'just' a piece of work that might as well have been written by an economist or a historian.

Apart from getting more confused about the proper character of political science within the family of social sciences, I also understood that I had better move on to new challenges and forget entirely about the study of the labour movement. It had been a great challenge to cross disciplinary borders, but it had not only been fun and easy. It is also risky business. Twenty-five years later I returned to the old data – and this time the going was much easier (Pedersen 1988).

The second traumatic experience happened in connection with my very first publi-cation, a little article on the political mobilization of women, which presented some time series of participation indices. It was published in an odd journal (Pedersen 1965), and the young author was infinitely pleased when the Association of Danish Women asked for permission to reprint it in a journal read mostly by middle-aged bourgeois ladies. The rest was silence. A few years later, when the feminists took over, it was of course completely forgotten. There is really nothing so depressing for a young scholar as lack of response. Especially if you sit in the middle of nowhere. The moral is that timing as well as a channel of publication is of vital importance, if one is keen to reach an audience.

Third, and the most traumatic experience: in an early description of Danish political science the reader may find a note in which two leading Danish professors were informing the English-speaking world that 'Mogens N. Pedersen is undertaking an analysis of the question hours of the Danish Folketing. His aim is to analyse the development of parliamentary questioning since its introduction in 1947, and to examine its function as a species of political control under the changing conditions of Parliament–Cabinet relations' (Henningsen and Rasmussen 1966, p.256).

This was an example of how the Danish professors at the time had to include even 'ongoing research' in their reporting, in order to make an impression on the outside world – in the process leaving in the annals an unintended trace of an abortive project, long forgotten.

The fact is that my first major attempt to do serious empirical research consisted in coding – by hand and all by myself – all parliamentary questions in the Danish *Folketing*, since this procedure had been introduced in 1947. Every question was coded according to an elaborate scheme, and a huge pile of coding sheets was accumulating, only waiting to be punched and analysed. And there it stopped!

Why did nothing come of all this labour? Apart from a number of explanations that are not flattering for the ego, the following comes to mind.

More exciting research options lured me away. But it also counted that it was difficult at the time to get the kind of professional advice which might have salvaged the project. And advice was necessary, since it gradually dawned upon the young scholar, first, that the project was perhaps theoretically as well as empirically unsound, and, second, that he himself needed training.

The international literature on parliamentary questions was small, traditionalist, and not very helpful (e.g. Chester and Bowring 1962; Ameller 1964). The tricky problem that I could not solve in a valid way was how to code the 'uses' or 'functions' of the parliamentary questions. Reading of Robert Merton's definitive analysis of the ambiguities of functional vocabulary in the social sciences founded a still lingering distrust in the 'functionalist' language, at least in its more vulgar appearances (cf. Pedersen 1993). The problem also became increasingly difficult the more I understood that the language of politicians, and the strategic use of it in connection with posing questions and with the evasion of questions, was far too complex and sophisticated to be treated by means of simple-minded punchcard-oriented coding. It is with some pleasure that I have recently noticed that the methodological problems that almost destroyed me back in 1965 still baffle not only thoughtful students of parliaments (Wiberg 1994), but social psychologists and linguistic scholars as well (cf. Wilson 1990, pp.131–78).

Equally important was the painful discovery that the formal political science curriculum had not equipped the novice with an adequate training, especially not if one drifted towards empirical work in the behavioural mode. It was of vital importance to read up some content analysis plus the most elementary statistics and general methodology. Soon one was into finite mathematics, game theory, econometrics, factor analysis, survey analysis techniques and – what later proved to be important – techniques for legislative roll-call analysis, some then not well-known in Europe.

Fortunately this disaster and waste of time and energy happened at a time when academic pressure was tolerable, and no one expected results here and now. Had it been today, I would have become a drop-out.

Another traumatic experience happened, when my first 'real' article on preferential voting had been accepted for publication (Pedersen 1966). It had been written in Danish. To have it translated into English was torture. To have it ruined by a Finnish printing company and only salvaged by chance in the final proofs was another memorable experience. I vowed that I would in the future write in English myself. My trust in editors was at an all-time low, from which it only slowly recovered.

A final experience was a *Metodenstreit* that took place in 1967. At the time a fragile tradition for ecological voting studies was developing along the lines laid out by Herbert Tingsten three decades earlier (Tingsten 1937). Poul Meyer (Jeppesen and Meyer 1964), as well as my slightly older colleagues Jan Stehouwer and Ole Borre (e.g. Stehouwer 1967; Borre and Stehouwer 1968) were breaking new ground. At this point a political journalist entered our circles. In an ambituous book he professed to understand the phenomenon of 'floating voters' in Denmark as well as in the neighbouring countries (Lassen 1967). The junior member of the department of political science recruited himself – or was prompted – to do the necessary job of hatchet-man. The unfortunate book was split into atoms and its author left bleeding (Pedersen 1967b). The notion of the ecological fallacy was spelled out in minute details for everyone to understand and avoid, and so devastating was the criticism that a historian fifteen years later could claim that I had paralysed ecological analysis in Denmark (Noack 1981). Fortunately it has recovered since then.

The lasting effect of this skirmish on the mind of the hatchet-man himself was a continuing interest in – phrased negatively – the underlying problem of logical fallacies in the social sciences, or – phrased positively – the great challenge of making inferences across analytical levels, especially in those parts of political science where data are not clean and nice. C. Wright Mills, Heinz Eulau, Erwin Scheuch, Stein Rokkan and Johan Galtung were the ones from whom one could learn about these epistemological problems. The 'level-of-analysis' problems and the 'micro-macro' problems are still among the most intriguing and exciting, and I have grappled with them ever since, in studies of political recruitment (e.g. Pedersen 1976, 1977a) as well as in discussions c f electoral volatility (Pedersen 1979, 1983). The linkages between the electorate, the party system, and the mechanisms of élite transformation are especially fascinating (Pedersen 1984b, 1994).

I have called these early experiences traumatic. Was I just naive? Before the reader makes his judgement, he should consider the times. The basic fact is that a Danish university in the 1960s was like the old American frontier. Fortunately one was allowed to learn by trial and error – and not shot at dawn.

Smaller European Democracies: joining a new network

By far the most decisive influence was the encounter with Stein Rokkan and his international friends, most notably Hans Daalder, but also many others. But it was Stein who just 'discovered' the young Dane, and suddenly everything was different.

The background was, probably, that the article on preferential voting (Pedersen 1966) had been noticed by the voracious Norwegian reader. For the First Nordic Congress of Political Science in Oslo, a more audacious paper had been concocted. The title was 'Consensus and Conflict in the Danish Folketing 1945–65'. It contained an analysis of all divisions and roll-calls in the Danish parliament over this long period. The analysis was done entirely by hand. The labour had been considerable, a fact which the reader would not notice since the analysis was parsimonious, not to say simplistic. According to a recent methodological treatise, 'investigators often take down the scaffolding after putting up their intellectual buildings, leaving little trace of the agony and uncertainty of construction' (King, Keohane and Verba 1994, p.13). For that reason I was also quite satisfied with the product. *En route* I had learned a lot about legislative behaviour methodology and about basic statistics and had read everything from Stuart Rice's classic book (1928) to the most recent scaling exercises. I had also invented my first descriptive gimmick, an 'index of distance', a measure that was later on used frequently by Danish scholars and also used and quoted widely for some time outside Denmark.

One of the first things that would impress one in Stein Rokkan's company was his tremendous breadth of knowledge. Stein would always tell you about the latest interesting book or article that he had read. And a minute later he would enquire if you had yourself read – or thought of – 'something'. I was deeply fascinated, primarily because I instantly liked the man, whose articles I had read with admiration. But, maybe, some deeper, 'Freudian' forces were at play here as well. I felt sort of 'adopted'. It may also have counted that Stein with his mixed background in history, philosophy, sociology and Scandinavian thinking in general might serve as a kind of mental 'bridge' between my more traditionally-oriented Danish mentors and the promised land of behavioural American political science. Who can tell?

This famous Norwegian professor, who at the time had only just been given a full chair in his own country, took an interest in the young Dane, as said. In quick succession this meant being hired as a sub-contractor, that is, part-time research assistant, to the great and hopeless Smaller European Democracies project. There was still a little money left at the time, and Stein Rokkan as well as Hans Daalder needed basic data about this strange little country, Denmark. They got some facts and analyses on the complicated electoral system and I also did my first pilot study of recruitment phenomena in connection with this engagement (Pedersen 1968).

A meeting of the entire SED group in The Hague in 1967 was a revelation and a boost. The core group, Dahl, Rokkan, Daalder and Lorwin, created a friendly and warm symposium, and if there were status differences between the project leaders and the younger scholars, they were not easily observable.

In this group of people one could learn a lot, just by sitting in. As a matter of fact one had of course to contribute as well. The very first lesson had to do with what was called the 'Zanzibar Ploy'. You could expect very tired faces in the group, if you objected to one of the many attempts at generalizing by suggesting that the Great Scheme did not work, because Zanzibar (read, Denmark) did not fit in. But if you suggested that some specific – but generalizable – characteristics (which you happened to know from back home) might be plausible and interesting to integrate into the scheme – then you could expect an instant response. When Przeworski and Teune some years later (in 1970) made their methodological point about treating particular social systems – like nations – as 'residua of theoretical variables', it certainly rang a bell.

For me the most intriguing observation was that the Danish political system did not play much of a role in the minds of this group. It could, in fact, be argued that Denmark was not at all on the map of comparative politics.

Denmark on the map of comparative politics c. 1965

If we go back to early comparative scholarship like the writings of James Bryce and Carl J. Friedrich, only fleeting and flimsy references to Danish politics can be found. Mostly the country was mentioned alongside Norway and Sweden as if differences did not exist – or at least did not matter. With the illustrious exception of Maurice Duverger's *Les Partis Politiques* (1951), it was only at the end of the 1950s that the proper name of this more than a thousand-year-old monarchy started to appear in the systematic literature.

Dankwart A. Rustow wrote a book about Sweden in 1955 (Rustow 1955), and a year later he contributed a chapter on Scandinavian parties to the influential Neumann volume *Modern Political Parties* (1956). In this he coined the catchy term 'Working Multiparty Systems' to describe the Scandinavian party systems – a phrase which stuck (cf. Pedersen 1987). This was about all that existed in print about Danish politics in the English language before 1960, at least if one searched the notes and references of the early American comparative politics literature. The doubtful reader is referred to the excellent bibliography by Miller (1968).

What struck me was the relative lack of references to solid scholarship on smaller European countries, my own in particular. In some cases, such as the work of Gabriel Almond, one could easily harbour the suspicion that the author knew very little about these political systems. The problem apparently was a simple one. Since these scholars did not know the more esoteric languages, and since the British have never cared much about the smaller countries on the so-called continent, the emergent comparativists had to rely on newspaper reading and whatever flimsy English-language documentation they could get hold of in the United States. The European scholars may have had a better 'feel' for the European situation and heritage, but they were, with the exception of Stein Rokkan and a few other specialists on electoral systems, as ignorant as the Americans. This point can be illustrated by a look at the documentation available to some of the major figures in the movement – as it appears in their own work, when they deal with Denmark.

One of the most prolific writers in the early days was Seymour Martin Lipset, whose *Political Man* (1960) was on the reading list also in Denmark. Lipset's primary source on Denmark was the already mentioned Walter Galenson, who, among other things, had summarized some thought-provoking hypotheses of the differential development patterns of labour movements in Scandinavia, put forward by the Norwegian historian Edvard Bull. This theme had first appeared in the book – with Bendix – on *Social Mobility in Industrial Society* (1959b), and it was replayed also in later books by the same author (e.g. Lipset 1963, 1968) Lipset's footnotes demonstrated considerable knowledge of the writings of Nordic scholars; he even quoted an unpublished dissertation in Danish from the University of Copenhagen.

Gabriel Almond, whose 'preliminary sorting operation' – as he has himself named his influential attempts at classifying political systems – started in the 1950s, without fuss placed Denmark and the other Scandinavian systems 'somewhere in between the Continental pattern and the Anglo-Saxon' (Almond 1956). His knowledge of Scandinavian politics was not profound.

Robert A. Dahl was no different. He was very conscious of the fact that knowledge of smaller European nations rarely entered into comparative political analysis, as witnessed already in the *Political Oppositions* volume from 1966 – an edited volume from which Denmark was conspicuously absent. In later writings (e.g. Dahl 1970, 1971) he sometimes hinted at the puzzling Danish political system, but he apparently had decided to let it stay at that.

One could go on like this for a while. Harry Eckstein based his very general statements about Scandinavian politics on a relatively brief 'field trip' to Norway (Eckstein 1966). Arend Lijphart, who did more than many others to come to grips theoretically with Denmark and the other Nordic countries, even as late as 1977 would rely on an unpublished American doctoral dissertation (McDaniel 1963), when he attempted to fit Danish politics into his well-known classification (Lijphart 1977, p.111).

My point is that this little political system was gladly, grandly and without much documentation characterized as possessing a stabilizing 'homogeneous and secularized culture' (Almond and Verba 1963). It was a 'consensus system' (Eckstein 1966). Its party system was a 'working' one (Rustow 1956) in which 'centripetal' forces were at play (Sartori 1966a). It also looked as if it was on its way to becoming a 'depoliticized democracy' (Lijphart 1968a).

Denmark: an interesting case?

Was there a better role to carve out for oneself, being a marginal young scholar from a marginal country, than to become a sub-contractor to this burgeoning movement, specializing in the 'translation' of Danish politics into the general lingo of modern comparative politics? No.

So said, so done.

It is, however, easier said than done. One may end up using the 'Zanzibar Ploy' for a lifetime. Fortunately the 'case-method' saved me – or, at least, provided peace in mind. This is how it worked.

The 1967 article 'Consensus and Conflict' (Pedersen 1967a) turned out to be a godsend. It was noticed by some of the greater minds within the exclusive legislative behaviour section of the political science profession, among them Samuel C. Patterson, John C. Wahlke and Heinz Eulau. An exchange of information started, and suddenly came the *accolade*, an invitation to present a paper at the 1969 Shambaugh Conference on Comparative Legislative Behavior Research at the University of Iowa.

This time I had learned what to do. First of all to present something that would be interesting, and, second, not to go beyond the limits set by my modest skills in statistics.

If you go to the United States for an important meeting, where you will meet the very top of the profession in your branch of enquiry, you had better do something that will interest the participants. I decided to do something bordering on the foolhardy, namely addressing one of the classical problems in political recruitment theory, and by doing so also criticizing the work of one of the prominent scholars, Heinz Eulau himself: *in casu*, the theory of professional convergence as proposed by Eulau and Sprague (1961). This conference paper was entitled 'Lawyers in Politics. The Danish Folketing and United States Legislatures' (Pedersen 1972a). As the title indicates, I was aware of the problem of 'stretching' of concepts that Giovanni Sartori (1970) has warned against – but thanks to Max Weber's analysis of *Die Juristen* I also knew how to handle the conceptual problem (Weber 1921, pp.396–450).

It is today difficult to remember exactly the timing and how the various ideas were intermingling. Arend Lijphart's influential 1971 article was not at my disposal in 1968–69 – it was presented for the first time at an IPSA conference in late 1969. His paper on political typologies (1968c) was, however, circulating, and it may have guided my first steps towards the sociological literature on cases, especially deviant cases as a methodological tool. The only thing about which I am absolutely certain is that the most important source for my own development in this field was a book which turned up all the time in Eulau's work, Cohen and Nagel's *An Introduction to Logic and Scientific Method* (1934). Its exposition of John Stuart Mills's methods of Agreement and Difference was most informative, when in the winter of 1968–69 I wrote my first truly comparative paper. The methodological possibilities and problems of case methodology have intrigued me ever since. Quite apart from an attempt to generalize the methodology of historical casework (Pedersen 1977b), considerable parts of my work since then have belonged to the categories of interpretative or hypothesis-generating case studies. Another long-term effect could be traced in my efforts as editor of the *European Journal of Political Research*. These efforts frequently consisted in convincing authors that they should reformulate their often a-theoretical one-country-focused research in terms of a theoretically interesting case study.

The reception of the 'Lawyer-in-Politics' paper was very favourable, even from the formidable and not always easy target of my attack. It resulted not only in publication, but also in an invitation to spend a year at Stanford in the department of Heinz Eulau and Gabriel Almond. In the meantime Stein Rokkan and Hans Daalder had been instrumental in acquiring a Ford Foundation Scholarship for me, and off I went into the wide world to learn more about comparative politics, about Danish politics – and – eventually – also about my own ego ...

Behind in Denmark I left the *Institut for Statskundskab*, which at the end of the 1960s had grown to the incredible size of four full professors, more than a dozen assistant and associate professors, and more than 500 students. The days of the Frontier were gone for good.

A postscript with a brief Jeremiad

On 1 January 1973, when I had just reached the ripe age of 33 years, the Queen of Denmark appointed me to the first chair in political science at the newly founded Odense University. For me this meant a temporary goodbye to research, since I quickly found myself embroiled in an almost five year long, nasty and – almost – unproductive ideological fight with students, who had apparently been waiting for an old professor against whom they could vent their frustrations. Fortunately I did not at the time know that in the future research time would be a very scarce commodity. In 1974 I was appointed member of the Danish Social Science Research Council, and I spent eight happy and busy years travelling back and forth between Odense and Copenhagen all the time. Serving on a number of government committees also lured me away from research, as did some international consultancy work. In 1980 I was appointed editor of the *European Journal of Political Research* for a period that lasted until 1994. In the mid-1980s I started another eight-year-long career as Dean of Social Sciences, and new stints in committees of the Ministry of Education and Research followed.

Some of these activities also led to scholarly contributions (e.g. Pedersen 1982; Eliassen and Pedersen 1985), and I published all along. In retrospect it is, however, evident that the stream of fresh and innovative research tended to dry up in the long run, partly because too little time was left for reading, digesting – and making risky long-term investments. A new productive period has only started quite recently with, among other things, studies of local politics (e.g. Elklit and Pedersen 1995). Since I have returned to the calm and free life of an ordinary professor I am daily comforted by the wisdom of Francis M. Cornford (1908), who ended his warning against academic politics by suggesting that it is never too late to give up an academic political career: 'If you have a spark of imagination and try very hard to remember what it was like to be young, there is no reason why your brains should ever get woolly, or anyone should wish you out of the way.'

Since I am starting to sound like an old man, I had better end this brief memoir, but let me do it by addressing an important problem for the political science profession. In the above-mentioned recent book by King, Keohane and Verba (1994, p.15) the authors recommend scholars to choose their research topics with great care. First, a research project should pose a question that is 'important' in the real world. Secondly, 'a research project should make a specific contribution to an identifiable scholarly literature by increasing our collective ability to construct verified scientific explanations of some aspect of the world'.

One of the many lessons from my own experience is that these may be necessary requirements for the young scholar who wishes to make a contribution and who wants to get ahead in academic life. But they are not always sufficient – and that is so for two very simple reasons.

First, our 'identifiable scholarly literature' may exist in libraries, but not always in the minds of the members of the profession. How many Americans follow regularly the European journals? Not many. How many of us will discover important work that is published in an esoteric language, like French or Dutch? Not many. How many scholars will recall – and use – contributions made ten years back in time? Who nowadays reads the great – and still important – texts of yesterday, like for example Carl Joachim Friedrich's *Man and His Government* (1963)? Years ago, Gunnar Sjöblom analysed these questions and put forward a strong plea for more cumulative efforts in political science (Sjöblom 1977). Not very many colleagues will remember this article any longer, but its message is as relevant now as it was then. In the light of the transformation, and the re-education going on in Central and East European social sciences, it becomes extraordinarily important that the best of yesterday's western – and European – political science is made available and not forgotten. It is not enough to preach rational choice theory 'over there'. After all, political development in a number of countries just now takes the institutions in these political systems through the same processes of institutionalization and professionalization, but also the same kind of turbulences, that our own countries went through more than 100 years ago – for which reason the work of (e.g.) Stein Rokkan and many of his friends and followers – maybe even including me? – becomes more important every day, because it deals not only with history, but also with problems that are significant in the real world.

Secondly, my own experience at least, plus observation of the profession, tell me that the two most important factors in understanding what happens to published research are networks and timing. If you are just lucky in presenting a simple and important idea at the right moment and in the right arena, you can spend the next many years counting citations. But a considerable risk exists that even your very best and most original work will end up unread and forgotten in a dusty library, if the idea is not ripe or fashionable, or if, because of lack of name-recognition or use of a sub-optimal form of publication, it goes unnoticed by senior scholars who, because they are too busy, have given up reading.

Given these concluding words I do hope that it is appropriate to dedicate this small essay to the memory of Stein Rokkan, one of the greatest European political sociologists of our time, and one of the founding fathers of an organized and professional political science in Europe. He read, and he cared.

24 Political sociology and comparative politics

Erik Allardt

University of Helsinki and Åbo Akademi University

Post–war challenges for young Scandinavian social scientists

Although I doubt that one can ever be completely honest in personal recollections, there is strength in the knowledge that most features in one's intellectual background are shared by others. Looking back I conceive a web of four intellectual debts being central to my development. They also reflect general predicaments for those who started their studies in the social sciences in the Nordic countries after World War II.

First, when the social sciences began to develop and expand as academic fields in Denmark, Finland, Norway, and Sweden after World War II, they did so in a milieu with a pronounced positivistic orientation. In the 1920s and 1930s some of the leading philosophers in these countries had studied in Vienna, and were strongly influenced by the Vienna circle. Yet it seems misleading to describe the orientations influencing the social sciences as simply positivistic. Partly from Vienna, but from Continental Europe generally, came other influences too. Notably, new approaches in studying the psychology of motivation, and the hidden forces of human behaviour had an impact. Important influences came from different branches of psychoanalysis, the dynamic psychology of Kurt Lewin, and the *Gestalt* psychology of Kurt Koffka and Wolfgang Köhler. Academic psychology had an important position in the postwar intellectual climate in Finland. There existed a tension between positivistic methodology and the interest in the irrational aspects of human behaviour. I experienced this tension during my early student years and it has followed me throughout my career.

Secondly, my main field of study was sociology. In order to find out what sociology is about it became important to read the great social theorists and thinkers. In my case the leading founding father was Émile Durkheim. A central factor in this Durkheimian leaning was that Durkheim's description and theory about societal development seemed to fit the postwar political development of the Finnish society. Although Durkheim presumably was the most sociologistic among the founding fathers of modern sociology and never wrote explicitly about politics, I came to regard him as a political sociologist (Allardt 1968, pp.1–16). His view of human consciousness as divided between egoistic demands and the moral, sacred demands of society had a special appeal for me. To follow Durkheim not only permitted a combination of the positivistic methodological orientation with an interest in the altruistic, non-utilitarian human motives, but it also made it possible to distinguish social forms created on the basis of more or less rational calculations from those that emerged out of more or less irrational sentiments. At any rate, I saw this as the central theme in Durkheim's leading work on the division of labour in society (Durkheim 1893).

Thirdly, during the decades after World War II it was a must for young Scandinavian social scientists to go the United States for studies and research at some of the great American graduate departments. This shared experience probably contributed to the tendency to look upon one's own society in a comparative context. Stein Rokkan, the leading Scandinavian scholar of comparative politics, tells in his collection of essays (1970a p.5) how different aspects of comparative analysis became his central interests already in 1948. Thanks to a post-doctoral Rockefeller fellowship I was able to spend the year 1954 at Columbia University and its Bureau of Applied Social Research. A stay at the Department of Sociology of Columbia University in the 1950s was far from unique for young social scientists from the Scandinavian countries: Stein Rokkan, Johan Galtung, Natalie Rogoff Ramsoy, Hans Zetterberg and Bo Anderson, to mention only some of them, spent some time in different capacities at Columbia. Politics and political behaviour were central research interests at the time in the Sociology Department. Paul Lazarsfeld, S.M. Lipset, Bernard Berelson, William McPhee, James Coleman, Martin Trow, Juan Linz and Immanuel Wallerstein, all of whom have made considerable contributions to political sociology, were to be found there in different capacities in the 1950s.

Although I have contemplated afterwards how much I fumbled and failed to use many wonderful learning opportunities, the year at Columbia was decisive for my career and development. It was Marty Lipset who directed my interest towards political phenomena and political sociology. He had already begun then to amass the data and thoughts which led to his major work *Political Man* (1960). Some of the ideas were already published in 1954 in a lengthy article in the then very influential *Handbook of Social Psychology* (Lipset *et al.* 1954). Lipset emphasized a comparative approach, and although I had only brief encounters with him, it was through his comments and also his requests for Finnish data that I learned to look upon my own society in a comparative perspective.

Thus, political sociology and comparative European politics, which were to become central interests in my academic work, fell upon me in a totally unplanned way. In the application for a Rockefeller fellowship I had emphasized sociological theory, the psychology of social norms, and attitude measurement. The word politics was not even mentioned. At Columbia I was also very much influenced by its general intellectual climate, with its double emphasis on Paul Lazarsfeld's survey research methodology and Robert Merton's focus on hidden and latent undercurrents in social life. In hindsight, the divided focus on rational research methodology and the latent irrationalities of human behaviour exerted a strong appeal.

Fourth, social scientists are invariably influenced and moulded both by their national background and their generational experiences. I come from and live in Finland, in Europe's northern periphery. I was born in 1925, and like other Europeans in my generation, I experienced World War II in my youth. Finland fought two wars against the Soviet Union: the Winter War in 1939–40 when Finland had to fight alone, and the so-called Continuation War in 1941–44 when Finland was cobelligerent with Nazi Germany but made a separate truce with the Soviet Union in 1944. Due to a combination of many different factors Finland succeeded in remaining unoccupied, and maintaining its system of market economy and parliamentary democracy. In this respect it was more fortunate than many other European countries. But Finnish soldiers suffered heavy casualties. In the Winter War of 1939–40 Finland was a garrison state heavily concentrated on defending itself. At the age of fourteen I volunteered for armed guard duty on the home front in case parachuted saboteurs would appear. In the Continuation War I was in the Finnish armed forces for about two years, including two months at the battle front. It was a crucial personal experience, but more important for my interest in political analysis was the national predicament of the first postwar decade. Finland had succeeded in preserving its independence, but it had to pay heavy war reparations and it had to resettle the population from the territories ceded to the Soviet Union. Finland was on a rapid path from an agrarian to an industrial society, and its internal politics was very conflict-ridden. During the first decades after the war Finland had a strong Communist Party which in the 1950s and 1960s was supported by almost a quarter of the total electorate. The predicament of Finnish society invited studies in political sociology, the need for which I began to comprehend under the influence of Marty Lipset during my year at Columbia University.

An additional and autobiographically relevant feature is my background in the Swedish-speaking population in Finland. The Swedish-speaking minority in Finland has populated the southern and western coasts of Finland since the Middle Ages. It does not as a rule have traceable roots in Sweden. Thus, the national identity of the Swedish-speaking Finns is not Swedish but Finnish. At one time, the upper strata in Finland were Swedish-speaking, but the main bulk of the Swedish-speaking population have been farmers, fishermen and workers. My socially mobile grandfather came from a Swedish-speaking family of farmworkers and smallholders. Comparatively speaking, the Swedish-speaking population is a well-treated minority. Both Finnish and Swedish are official languages in Finland. Like most Swedish Finns today I am bilingual in Swedish and Finnish. Yet bilingualism, a natural capacity to communicate in the Scandinavian languages, and a minority identity in all likelihood have contributed to my interest in comparative politics.

Political sociology and the sociology of politics

As is obvious from the description above, my background as political sociologist was not in political science but in sociology. Mainly due to what I had learned at Columbia University I became, in 1956, the sole professor of sociology at the University of Helsinki, initially in an acting appointment, at a relatively young age, in my early thirties. In my application for the professorship I could list as my main works studies of political participation and of the Finnish non-voter in a comparative context (Allardt 1956; Allardt and Pesonen, 1960, pp.27–39).

Until some companion professorships in sociology were established my first duty was to teach sociology, and to open the vistas of the main international currents in sociology to Helsinki students. Yet the dominant part of my research focused on politics. I was fortunate to become a member of the international Committee on

Political Sociology (CPS) when it was established in 1959, with S.M. Lipset as chairman and Stein Rokkan as secretary. It brought me many fruitful and wonderful international contacts, with many political scientists among them. Membership in the Committee gave me opportunities to participate in intellectual discussions on comparative politics. To look at the politics of one's own country in a comparative perspective became almost a way of life.

In a challenging and witty paper Giovanni Sartori (1969, pp.195–214) made a clear distinction between political sociology and the sociology of politics. He characterized political sociology as a genuine and almost autonomous hybrid of political science and sociology, wheras the sociology of politics was just a branch of sociology in which political phenomena are explained by sociological factors, such as social structure and culture. Referring to a well-known conceptualization by Robert Nisbet, in which community, authority, status, the sacred, and alienation are depicted as the basic ideas of sociology, Sartori (1969, p.199) dryly concludes that these are not fundamental units of political science. Admittedly, I have internalized the Nisbetian unit-ideas, but through the CPS I learned a great deal about political science, in particular what it tells about political parties, party systems, conflict regulation, and ideologies.

Around 1970 there was a reorientation in the focus of my research. One reason was that the communist and radical leftist vote started to decline all over Western Europe, but it had also personal causes. In 1969 a new chair in sociology was established, which made it possible for me to be appointed in 1970 a research professor, with conducting research as my major duty. Both intellectual reasons and external possibilities made me search for new research themes. New foci for my research became the state (especially the welfare state) and ethnicity (especially the fate of linguistic minorities). I stayed with comparative politics, but with different research objects. I will return to these after a description of my whole-hearted Durkheimian period.

Durkheim as a political sociologist

Apart from Durkheim's views about the tensions between the sacred and the profane in human life there were additional attractive features in his writings. Admittedly, his political ambivalence had a special appeal. Durkheim was interested in political phenomena but he avoided taking all-encompassing political stands. For a student who began his studies after World War II there was a special aversion against dogmatic and total political solutions. Of course, Durkheim took definite positions with firm conviction in the crucial questions of the Third French Republic. He was a Dreyfusard with all its republicanism, anti-clericalism and beliefs in political liberty as well as in the rule of law. Yet, it is significant that even in his paper 'L' individualisme et les intellectuels' (1898), in which he takes a definite stand in the Dreyfus trial, he appears as a theorist. He defends the individual's right to protest against any injustices on grounds which are related to the main themes in his work on the division of labour. Durkheim's political views have been characterized in various ways. He has sometimes been branded conservative on the basis of his preoccupation with solidarity and his stress on the rule of law, but this seems as misleading as to characterize him as leftist. Durkheim held firm views on particular political problems but he remained sceptical as regards total political movements. He advocated some socialist views but he was repelled by certain traits of the socialist movement. He was for abolishing the inheritance of private property, but he was also too much an adherer of peaceful social change to go along with the socialist movement. He had close ties with the Reformist Socialist Party led by Jaurès, but he never joined.

Durkheim's most explicit analysis of issues related to political theory is found in the book which appeared in English under the title *Professional Ethics and Civic Morals* (1957). Durkheim never wrote about politics with the same devotion as he wrote about religion and suicide (Durkheim 1897). His most important book for political sociology is undoubtedly the *Division of Labor in Society* (1893). This is also the work which, more than his other books, contains the kernel of his leading ideas, and which influenced my first work in comparative politics.

Political radicalism under conditions of coercion and conditions of uprootedness

During the 1950s and 1960s political sociology was strongly concerned with studies of political radicalism and extremism. The rise and fall of Nazism in Germany was still a recent phenomenon, and the Communist Party and its voting support were strong in many countries outside the Eastern bloc. In Western Europe, Finland was, together with France, Italy and Iceland, a country with a particularly heavy communist vote in the general elections. It was natural to study that phenomenon when one aimed at describing change and conflicts in Finnish society. In the literature, not only were political radicalism on the left and radical leftist voting interpreted as reflections of discontent and deprivation in the working class, but it was also assumed that a large communist vote in non-socialist countries was an indication of political instability. The differences in style and background of the moderate social-democrats and the extremist communists were emphasized. In addition to having a specific class background, the communist voters, like the original supporters of the Nazi movement, appeared to be uprooted and alienated, with tendencies to authoritarianism. Such views and results were presented both in Lipset's *Political Man* (1960, pp.87–126), and in the analyses of mass society (Kornhauser 1959, pp.77–193).

Finland provided an interesting case for the study of communist strength and voting support in non-socialist countries. The Finnish Communist Party had a backing in some heavily industrialized communities as well as in the backwoods of Northern and Eastern Finland. There existed both an industrial and a backwoods communism. The distinction amounted to much more than to just a geographical division. Ecological analyses (Allardt 1964a, pp.49–72) showed that the two types of communist support had a very different social and political background. The conditions associated with communist support in the developed communities reflected hindrances of movement, strong group ties and strong social pressures created by a rigid class structure. In the backward areas, on the other hand, almost the contrary was true. Communist support was strong in communities in which there had been rapid social change, uprootedness and a weakening of traditional group ties (Allardt 1971, pp.493–4). In organizing the results and combining them into a coherent presentation Émile Durkheim's basic distinction between mechanical and organic solidarity offered itself as a good explanatory tool. When aiming at societal consensus, backwoods communism was a deviant case and a negative alternative to mechanical solidarity, whereas industrial communism in the same vein was a deviant case from organic solidarity. The results suggested a simple model according to which strong social constraints in developed and differentiated communities are apt to lead to radical discontent, whereas in underdeveloped and undifferentiated communities, on the other hand, it is the loss of group ties and the weakening of social constraints which have similar effects (Allardt 1964b). Uprootedness and alienation exist when radicalism is about to emerge but they are not typical of an earlier established radicalism which had already become traditional.

The distinction between traditional and emerging radicalism inherent in the differences between industrial and backwoods communism was a typical feature in Finnish politics, but comparable cases have existed elsewhere. The pattern of traditional radicalism has often prevailed in industrialized communities dominated by one industrial plant, whereas the attributes of emerging radicalism has been observable in communities undergoing a rapid process of secularization. The distinction seemed also applicable to political currents in the Third World and in heavily underdeveloped areas. Some millenarian movements have a clear resemblance with backwoods communism (Allardt 1966, pp.1–10).

The interpretation offered in the explanations of industrial and backwoods communism is simple, but it nevertheless introduced a new aspect by pointing to both rational and irrational roots of political radicalism. There existed a clear difference in the conditions for traditional and emerging radicalism. It is interesting to note that the model was criticized, because it acknowledged that political radicalism may have irrational roots. The Swedish sociologist Walter Korpi (1971, pp.971–84) criticized both Lipset and me in the *American Sociological Review* for assuming that party choice among working-class communists is non-rational, in whole or in part. According to Korpi, a review of the data used failed to support Lipset's hypothesis that authoritarianism was an important feature of working-class communism. Korpi continued to say that data also failed to support 'Allardt's theory of anomie behind emerging communism'. As a conclusion Korpi maintained that it seems possible to interpret available data on communist sympathies among workers in Western Europe in terms of a model of rational, self-interested workers. In a comparison of Korpi's, Lipset's and my conclusions, it appears that the divergences reflect points of departure rather than strict empirical results. Korpi aimed at a combination of Marxism and rational choice theory, whereas I was, and still am, preoccupied with the relationship between rational and irrational forces in human life.

Whatever the correct interpretations of the results, the studies of communist voting support became obsolete for other reasons. Despite the strong interest of students in Marxism, communist support began to dwindle in the 1970s, not only in Finland but all over Europe. In the mid-1990s there prevails an unusual situation with no truly radical, viable political movement at all. In his small book on Eastern Europe Ralf Dahrendorf (1990, p.37) quotes a remark by the French historian François Furet that for the first time in 150 years no alternative view of society is on offer for a solution of the problems of the world. Dahrendorf sees this as a hopeful sign for the growth of an open society.

Dahrendorf's ideas (see Dahrendorf 1959) had had an impact on Finnish political discussions before. Together with some other political sociologists I introduced in the 1960s into the Finnish political debate his thesis that in order to reach political stability conflicts should be regulated rather than eliminated. Partly because such ideas fitted the political world of Finland's President Urho Kekkonen they received publicity, and were probably not without a certain political impact. The communists became more and more integrated into the Finnish political life and, presumably partly as a consequence of the attempts at conflict regulation, they began to lose their once strong voting support.

The return of the state

During the 1950s and 1960s sociological aspects were strongly emphasized in studies of political behaviour. One of the side-effects was that the state tended to be forgotten not only in sociology but also within political science. The once central objects of political science, the state and governmental institutions, became less appealing than the study of political behaviour, public opinion, political parties and the relationships between structural cleavages and political preferences. Such a neglect of the state as an object of study occurred not only in Finland but in other Nordic countries as well. An ironic feature of the situation was that during the same period the importance of the state in terms of the number of public employees, governmental organizations, state regulations and state-sponsored projects grew considerably. The state moved strongly into the lives of the individual citizens, who in contrast to earlier historical periods now have to face state regulations, governmental decisions and public servants practically all the time. This change could not remain unnoticed for long, and in the beginning of the 1970s the state came back in force, not only into political science but also into sociology.

In the Nordic countries a sign of the revival of the state as an object of study was a rapidly growing interest in analyses of the welfare state. In descriptions of the Scandinavian countries it became popular, in a direct reference to the welfare provisions, to speak about the Scandinavian model. Sometimes the term used was the Swedish model because Sweden had spearheaded Scandinavian social development. It was emphasized that the welfare state had roots and a firm background in the history of the Scandinavian countries. Yet historical research also showed that the idea of a Scandinavian type of the welfare state had definite continental roots, for example in the historical school of political economy of Gustav von Schmoller and others, and in the famous *Verein für Sozialpolitik* (Allardt 1995, pp.131–2). The actual provisions of the welfare state are of a comparatively recent origin. All the welfare provisions and institutions of welfare policy considered typical of the Scandinavian welfare state were created and developed after World War II. The large public welfare bureaucracies, which have been associated with Sweden and Denmark in particular, also are of a very late date. Since World War II the public sector has grown in every developed country. According to OECD statistics the percentage of public servants in the labour force had been lower in Sweden in 1960 than in the USA, the UK, France, Australia, and New Zealand, but by 1980 Sweden had moved up to first place among the OECD countries in its proportion of public employees. In 1985 the percentage of public servants in the labour force in Sweden exceeded 33 per cent. Denmark had the second-largest public sector, whereas both Norway and Finland were also above the average (Allardt 1990, pp.69–70). It would be wrong, however, to depict this as a historical heritage.

The new importance of the state in the Scandinavian countries gave rise to a host of government-sponsored studies of well-being, power, and the actual accomplishments of the welfare state institutions. The first studies initiated by the governments were

large-scale surveys of well-being and the level of living. They represented the
Scandinavian version of the social indicator movement, popular in the 1960s and 1970s
among social scientists elsewhere. Both economists, sociologists and political scientists
were at that time involved in constructing national indicators of economic, social and
political development. In Scandinavia this research tradition became institutionalized
with the Swedish standard of living study (Johansson 1970), which spread
subsequently to all the Nordic countries. I was also caught up by the movement, but I
tried to sustain the comparative approach of political sociology. Together with some
colleagues from the Research Group for Comparative Sociology at the University of
Helsinki I conducted, in the years 1970–75, a comparative study of the standard of
living and quality of life in Denmark, Finland, Norway and Sweden (Allardt 1975). In
addition to the comparative approach and the focus on all the Scandinavian countries
there were some interesting differences in political values which guided our study, as
distinct from the national Scandinavian surveys.

The Swedish research design had implied a focus on equality and citizen command
over resources in the form of money, possessions, knowledge, mental and physical
energy, social security and so on. The indicators and the criteria of well-being were
chosen on the basis of their political significance, and their presence in the Swedish
political debate. It meant that the criteria used and emphasized were mainly social-
democratic in their ideological content and origin. The choice and preference for
certain types of social indicators are generally clearly related to politics and ideologies.
The standard of living studies have as their points of departure conceptions of what is
good or bad in society.

The Swedish standard of living study emphasized strongly the importance of
tangible and objective goods, and at least non-personal resources. Although the
Swedish Study had been an inspiring model and provided a point of departure, my
predilections for also studying solidarities and non-utilitarian human motives led me to
use a different indicator system in the comparative Scandinavian survey. In addition to
non-personal, material conditions I wanted to study need-satisfaction related to social
ties and personal development. A need classification under the labels 'Having',
'Loving', and 'Being' was used in the Comparative Scandinavian study (Allardt 1993,
pp.88–94). Needless to say, the emphasis in the Swedish standard of living study was
strongly on 'Having'.

The emphasis on different values was not the only difference between our comparative study and the Swedish standard of living study. One important issue of debate
in studying well-being was whether one should measure wants, i.e. what people by
attitudinal expressions indicate that they want to possess and command, or whether
one should try to measure need satisfaction by more or less objective standards. Needs
point to things the lack of which make people suffer. Should one, for instance in
studying the level of housing and shelter, just ask people whether they are satisfied with
their living quarters, or should one try to define some objective standards both for the
size of the living quarters and the household goods available, and then measure
whether an acceptable level has been attained? The Swedish as well as the other
Scandinavian standard of living studies were based on the assumption that there exist
more or less objective criteria for what people need in order not to suffer. In the
comparative Scandinavian study it was assumed that both objective indicators of
factual conditions and subjective indicators of attitudes and individual preferences are

important. Accordingly, in the comparative study we tried to use both objective and subjective indicators, to measure both external conditions and attitudes. One reason for this double-headed approach was that the objective and subjective indicators often give different results. Those in possession of, objectively speaking, high-standard housing may in fact be dissatisfied, and vice versa. Actually, from the point of view of political analysis and political sociology the most revealing results are found when there exist discrepancies between objective conditions and subjective attitudes.

In all the Scandinavian studies, both in the national surveys and in our comparative survey, one important indicator was the measure of political resources available to the citizens. Our study contained measures of political activity, for instance the ability and willingness to contact decision-makers and politicians on different levels in society. On the whole, the indicator studies contained a great deal of politically relevant facts and results. In fact, the indicators constructed and selected are understandable only in a comparative politics context.

The ethnic revival

The political mobilization and assertion of cultural identities by ethnic groups was a conspicuous feature of the internal politics of many West European societies from the late 1960s and throughout the 1970s. This ethnic revival did not go unnoticed in the fields of political science and sociology. There was, in fact, an abundance of books and papers observing and analysing the rebirth of ethnic feelings. One may rightly speak of a revival and a rebirth. Suddenly at the end of the 1960s minority groups started to emphasize their special characteristics. Many of them had remained quiet and subdued for a long time, but became rapidly activated and mobilized. The renaissance of open ethnic feelings took a variety of forms. In some cases there was an actual rebirth of a minority regional language; in other cases it amounted to renewed or new demands for self-determination; and at a minimum there were claims for the right to use the minority language in schools, in the mass media, and in dealings with the government.

Like many political sociologists, I became interested in analysing the ethnic revival. During the second half of the 1970s I began a comparative study of the fifty or so historical, territorial linguistic minorities in Western Europe (Allardt 1979). In the study Western Europe was equated with the 'non-socialist' states. The delimitation was clearly related to the political situation. It was impossible in the 1970s to gather data for a comparative study of linguistic minorities in Eastern European states. Requests for data from the Soviet Union were often met by the argument that all problems related to ethnicity had been solved. My urge to study the linguistic minorities corresponded clearly to some factors in my background. I was now able to combine my academic interest in comparative research with a natural interest in ethnic minorities as a member of a linguistic minority.

Although my friend and colleague Stein Rokkan started to study the social and political consequences of the European ethnic and territorial identities about the same time (Rokkan and Urwin 1983), I was not directly influenced by him in my views and conceptualizations. The main intellectual influence came from one of his countrymen, the social anthropologist Frederik Barth (1969). One of Barth's main points is that ethnic groups cannot be defined on the basis of race, culture and language alone but that the existence of an ethnic group always presupposes categorizations, border-making mechanisms and a social organization. There is nothing inherent or necessary by nature in the birth of an ethnic group. It is a human construct dependent on the social definitions people use and constantly create. This is also the reason why ethnic and national groups seem to be in a state of constant flux. They come and go, they can vanish for centuries but they also rise again from the dust of history. Despite their moving borders they create solidarities and moral commitments far beyond the pure self-interest of their members. For analyses of the grounds for solidarities, and especially the tensions between egoism and altruism in social life, ethnic and linguistic minorities provide an intriguing object of study.

In a great number of studies the occurrence of ethnic mobilization among the minorities was explained in the terms of the social structure and the culture of the country in which they were located. A structural, cultural approach tended to render very incomplete explanations, however. Active mobilization, even militancy, was observable among both economically rich and poor minorities (Allardt 1981). Many important explanatory factors were directly related to the political traditions and patterns in each country (Allardt and Miemois 1982).

Political elements were highly conspicuous in the attributes of the revival movements. Despite the fact that the West European territorial and linguistic minorities have very different histories, having experienced different kinds of grievances, and expressed different demands, there were clear similarities of a political nature in the revival movements of the 1960s and 1970s. At least four general traits in the 'new' ethnicity were clearly observable: (1) the ethnic categorizations were not performed by the majority populations but by the minorities themselves; (2) a coincidence of timing of the revivals indicated a pattern of a rapid diffusion of political ideas; (3) there was a definite professionalization of the ethnic activists; and (4) governments showed an increased willingness and ability to manage conflict (Allardt 1979, pp.16–26).

Despite the recrudescence of conflicts of ethnic origin in today's Western Europe a scrutiny of the cases of revival indicate an increase in governmental responsiveness. Many examples of the willingness either to grant autonomy or to organize plebiscites in order to gauge the support for autonomy can be given. An interesting example is France, in which a Jacobin conception of a totally unified culture had long prevailed but in which, after the report of the so-called Giordan Commission in 1981, a governmental acceptance of the existence of ethnic minorities became visible (Allardt 1992). To an increasing extent, the minorities in Western Europe have been able to speak about their rights in terms of accepted policy goals. Resistance to increased rights and autonomy by minorities often comes from other minority groups, not from governments. The ethnic conflicts have not disappeared, but they have changed character. Before World War II the categorizations and definitions of the minorities were performed by governments representing the national majority populations. Today, the categorizations are most actively pursued by the minorities themselves. At any rate, the study of the ethnic revivals and conflicts is indeed a topic and a theme for comparative political sociology. The political element is central; the political factors have an active role and cannot be reduced to structural and cultural factors.

The continuing riddle of the balance between reason and sentiment

Despite many aberrations and transient preoccupations with administrative tasks associated with being full-time President of the Finnish National Science Council in 1986–91 and Chancellor of the Åbo Akademi University in 1992–94, both Durkheim and comparative political sociology have remained with me strongly. Two intellectual riddles I feel to be particularly pressing. The first and more recent one concerns a preoccupation with civil society – which has proliferated because of the revolution of 1989 in the former socialist states in Eastern Europe. Civil society can be defined in many ways. A useful definition reads that the civil society is 'the totality of social institutions and associations, both formal and informal, that are not strictly production-related, nor governmental or familial in character' (Rueschemeyer, Stephens and Stephens 1992, p.6). One way to describe the difficulties in recon-structing the former socialist societies has been to say that intermediary groups which are not production-related, governmental or familial are largely lacking. Émile Durkheim's insistence on solidary relations, on moral commitments, and on forms which are felt sacred have suddenly a great actuality again. The question is whether societies can survive without social bonds which go beyond both the interest of the state and simple self-interest (Seligman 1992, pp.119–26). It would be a mistake to assume that a weakening or lack of a civil society is a problem facing former socialist states only. The problem is also pertinent to the Scandinavian countries, in which voluntary associations and popular movements used to have considerable effects on both political views and the social integration of the citizens. To an increasing extent, political standpoints are influenced and created by political debates and presentations in the electronic mass media. Communication between citizens occurs more and more through electronic devices, internet programmes and e-mail. The political effects of these changes are not as yet well understood.

There is another long-standing reason for my interest in Durkheim. I have always been preoccupied by a general, and I think important, theoretical problem that I have not been able to solve and develop very clearly. In all good societies, organizations, and even social groups, there exists a kind of balance between rational and emotional elements. In social science parlance one may speak about the balance between instrumental and expressive tendencies. Societies, organizations, and communities which lean too much towards either the instrumental or expressive extremes produce bad consequences for human beings. In present-day Western Europe there is in my opinion too strong a tendency to instrumentalism. In his studies of science policy the Swedish political scientist Bjorn Wittrock (1993, pp.214–15) has spoken about 'radical rationalism' or the tendency to believe that administrative and political activities can be more or less completely steered by decision-makers who possess the methods of systems analysis. The tendency towards radical rationalism may be proliferating because there are an increasing number of international civil servants with weak social bonds but with many methods and tools for monitoring, controlling and steering human activities. A scrutiny of radical rationalism is becoming an important topic in today's political sociology.

25 *The Civic Culture* and beyond: citizens, subjects and survey research in comparative politics

Sidney Verba

HARVARD UNIVERSITY

It is appropriate to begin an intellectual autobiography by situating it at the time of its writing. I will do so in relation to an article in the *New York Times* I happened to read on the day I started to jot down notes for this account of my involvement with the study of comparative politics. It was on 26 June 1993 and it dealt with the World Conference on Human Rights that was taking place in Vienna at that time. The debate at the Conference was over the development of general principles to govern human rights. The issue discussed was the attempt of a number of nations, mainly Asian, to 'challenge the universality of human rights by arguing that they existed as a function of a country's history, level of development, cultural tradition, and religion'. The alternative position, pressed by the American delegation among others, was that human rights were universal, 'regardless of the political, economic, and cultural systems'.

Here was the fundamental dilemma of comparative politics still with us after all these years. This was the issue for comparative politics when I first became involved with the subject in the late 1950s and early 1960s – at the beginning of what might be called the new systematic study of comparative politics. In Vienna it was being raised in connection with the deepest of moral issues: what standards does one use to evaluate state action in relation to the state's own citizens? Are they universal or nation-specific? In Princeton, New Jersey, where I first encountered the new comparative politics, the question was raised as an intellectual issue: what models and methods do we use to understand political systems? But the issue even then had a deep normative component: was Western democracy the appropriate goal for all nations, East and West? Or, even more parochially, was US democracy the appropriate system for other democracies, especially those of the West?

The organizers of the Vienna conference, according to the *New York Times* account, overcame the intense disputes and managed to maintain a commitment to universality. '[T]he conference closed in a flurry of self-congratulatory speeches, however, experts said its success could only be measured by how many of its recommendations were eventually carried out.' I remember many heady meetings and conferences about comparative politics in that earlier era that ended in a flurry of self-congratulations about the new ways in which we had to understand the world. But the measure of success is what happened eventually.

Early influences

My entry into comparative politics was accidental. I came to the Woodrow Wilson School at Princeton with no particular leaning towards political science or comparative politics. At the time, my career goal was the US Foreign Service. Luckily, Senator Joseph McCarthy turned my mind elsewhere. Nor did I have any deep political agenda. I came to graduate school with left political views but found myself uneasy with many of my student colleagues whose politics I shared. They seemed political rather than analytical, and I soon became more enamoured with the intellectual puzzles of politics than with any particular political agenda. I later found out that this was a common syndrome among many of my background – though I like to think I kept my political views more intact than did many others. One could be of the left and analytical at the same time, though the latter takes the edge off the former (many would say the 'cutting edge' – but that is all right).

I was unusual as a student of comparative politics in that I had no 'country'. Comparative politics in those days was tightly linked to particular locations. People in the field were specialists on one place or another. Without quite realizing what it meant, I entered the field as a 'comparativist' somewhat before the recognition of that genre (if it is yet recognized). Over the years, I have often experienced 'comparativist's anxiety'; this is the syndrome that hits the comparativist in a discussion with a specialist on one of the areas the comparativist compares. Try as we may to read and learn about the places we compare, our knowledge of language and culture and internal variation is never enough to deal with the country specialist's inevitable question: 'But what about X?' – with X being a particular region of the country or a particular person or event. The anxiety is only made greater by the fact that the questions are very often right on the mark. It is the inevitable price of comparison. It is also, I believe, why I have devoted about half of my research efforts over the years to the study of American politics – but always with comparative questions in mind. Incidentally, I advise my students who find themselves faced with obscure issues of regional variation to invoke the generalization that applies to that topic in every country: 'It's very different in the South'.

If I were to list the figures who influenced me in my early years as a student of comparative politics, I would list Gabriel Almond, V.O. Key, Robert Dahl, Stein Rokkan and Harry Eckstein, as well as the members of the SSRC Committee on Comparative Politics. It would be hard to do better.

Almond was my mentor at Princeton both in the usual sense in which mentoring takes place – as a dissertation adviser – and in many other ways. I was a floundering graduate student looking for a new dissertation topic after I found that the one on which I was working (in the area of constitutional law) was deeply boring and unrewarding. I had an interest in social psychology and he was willing to supervise a dissertation on small groups in politics about which neither he nor I knew very much. In an era when much of political science was quite traditional, I was lucky to find someone willing to allow me to explore relatively uncharted waters. My work on small groups led to a dissertation and then a book (Verba 1961) that introduced political science to a relevant parallel body of material, and began my continuing interest in the relationship between leaders and ordinary members of a collectivity.

In addition, he offered me a job as a research assistant on a project he had just begun comparing the political cultures of several nations. It was the best offer anyone ever

made to me, though I did not quite realize it at the time. I had no real grasp of the
project, certainly no sense that the research would lead to *The Civic Culture* (Almond
and Verba 1963) and certainly no expectation that I would be a co-author. Indeed, my
main reason for welcoming the offer was that I needed the money since my wife who
had been supporting me through graduate school by teaching elementary school had
become pregnant. (By the time *The Civic Culture* was published our daughter was old
enough to read her name in the preface.)

It was a time when Almond was beginning to reshape the study of comparative
politics through his efforts with the SSRC Committee on Comparative Politics. Though
many of the approaches developed by the Committee have been replaced by new
approaches, the Committee played a seminal role in making comparative politics truly
comparative. I learned from Gabriel and the other members of the Committee how to
think comparatively – to seek generalizations out of the vast complexity of politics
within each nation. The fact that Almond was both a visionary, filled with large
schemes for understanding politics at all places at all times (as seen in the broad
functional schemes he developed with James Coleman and others; Almond and
Coleman 1960) and an empirical researcher who believed in gathering systematic
information (as in his works *The Appeals of Communism* (1954) and *The Civic
Culture*), had a big impact on me. Much of the comparative politics of the day
consisted in the development of grand schemes; they needed to be grounded in reality.
The interaction with Almond during the writing of *The Civic Culture* and the work
with the Committee on Comparative Politics represented an induction into the
discipline that was hard to match.

My early view of how one goes about studying politics (comparative or otherwise)
was also shaped by two books I read early in my career. One was V.O. Key's *Southern
Politics* (1949) and another Robert Dahl's *Who Governs?* (1961a). Both were on
American politics but had broad implications, both theoretically and substantively.
They represented a style of social science analysis that I have long found attractive. The
books raise big questions but deal with the issues with very solid 'feet-on-the-ground'
empirical methods. And they have a clarity of logic in terms of what they are trying to
explain. I found a parallel to this work in the comparative field in the works of Stein
Rokkan. Rokkan belonged to no particular school: he encompassed them all. His work
was micro and macro, quantitative and historical, richly detailed and grounded in data
while taking on the biggest questions. Many of his themes are ones I have pursued in
subsequent work.

Lastly, I was lucky to have Harry Eckstein as a colleague during my first few teaching
years. As with the others in my panoply of mentors, he was one of the early true
comparativists who saw the range of nations as testing places for general ideas but who
also stressed that one could not ignore the complexities of context.

The study of comparative politics had a number of features at the time I first encountered it. It was heavily country-centred (one studied country X followed by Y
followed by Z), the countries were usually European, they were usually the big powers
(the basic comparative politics seminars in the Princeton Politics Department covered
Britain and the USSR in the first semester and Germany, France, and Italy in the
second), and the subject matter was heavily institutional. Much of the concern of the
field centred on two big issues: the issue of stable democracy and the issue of
totalitarianism. Both issues were on the agenda because of events in Europe: the rise of

Nazism and Stalinism and the seemingly uncertain future of a number of the European democracies. The behavioural revolution had begun, but it was seen as an approach (and a controversial approach) to American politics.

It was a time of great ferment in comparative politics. New theoretical orientations were emerging, structural functionalism and systems analysis being the most noticeable. The non-Western nations and political development had come on to the agenda, though they were often seen as a special and not comparable part of the world. I remember, as a young and somewhat brash assistant professor, suggesting a course on democracy that would include some of the usual European nations but Japan as well. The senior department member who specialized in Japan scotched the idea, arguing that one could not compare Japan to these other countries and, furthermore, suggesting that Verba did not know much about Japan anyway. (He was wrong on the first point, but probably not off the mark on the second.)

One thing that was missing and that did not emerge for a while was a serious concern about the logic of the comparative method. The emerging theories raised big issues and focused attention on real comparison. But how did one, in fact, compare among nations. Stein Rokkan (1968a) and Harry Eckstein (1963) had valuable things to say on this. I found that the work I had done on experimental techniques (Verba 1961) provided a useful framework that was reinforced by my introduction to the works of Donald T. Campbell (especially, Campbell and Stanley 1963).

My own orientation towards comparative politics (and the study of politics more generally) grew out of these multiple sources. I have approached the subject as a middle-range theorist-cum-empirical researcher. I was exposed to the grand schemes of the day, from Almond's functionalism to Easton's systems approach to Deutsch's cybernetic-communications models, and found them useful in framing the issues to be studied. But I was always more comfortable in research that asked general but answerable questions. And I have always had an interest in answering social science questions with as precise and reliable data as one can find.

The Committee on Comparative Politics

I was particularly fortunate to have become a member of the Social Science Research Council's Committee on Comparative Politics quite early in my career. The impact of the Committee on the study of Comparative Politics cannot be overstated. It approached the subject, as I have said, from a truly comparative point of view. Though the Committee is often identified with the functional approach to comparative politics, its activities were much broader. The many volumes in the Princeton Series on Political Development contained various essays on theoretical issues. These were often of the middle range – about parties, or political culture, or bureaucracy. And all volumes contained essays with serious substantive content.

The work of the Committee expanded the scope of comparative politics to include the use of methodologies such as surveys. The participation on the Committee of Herbert Hyman and, later, Philip Converse and myself, helped connect survey work and comparative studies. In addition, the Committee sponsored a close association with historical studies. One of the volumes in the Princeton Series, *Crises and Sequences in Political Development* (Binder et al. 1971) represented a major attempt to work closely with historians in developing a model of the sequences of political development. The plans for the book involved numerous political scientists as well as historians. It was a good example of the value and difficulty of cross-fertilization. For some historians, the sequence and crisis model was too abstract as a guide to research and did not fit what they believed were the main issues in the development of the nation state. In addition to the book by Binder *et al.*, another volume was produced by a number of the historians who participated in the process; a volume that raised a number of other issues not encompassable in the crisis and sequence framework (Tilly 1975). The result was a good example of the way in which many flowers could bloom under the Committee on Comparative Politics umbrella. (For a critique of the crisis and sequence framework from a political science rather than historical perspective, see my essay in the Binder *et al.* volume.)

The Civic Culture and comparative politics

I would not presume to give an account of the evolution of comparative politics from those earlier years to today. Since I believe that the field of comparative politics is more or less conterminous with politics – with the exception of purely theoretical and philosophical exercises and some narrowly construed studies in international relations – it would be difficult to make such a characterization. I will rather look at how my own work has evolved in comparative politics, starting with *The Civic Culture*.

The Civic Culture had a number of unusual features for its time. It was systematically comparative in its framework; it was based on cross-national survey research; it proposed a general explanation of a complex phenomenon, stable democracy; and it proposed a cultural explanation. Since any one of these features would have been both innovative and difficult to accomplish, the combination of them all in a single study indicates how bold (or foolhardy) the enterprise was. The book did have a major impact on the field. The impact was at least fourfold.

For one thing, the particular argument and conclusions as to the role of citizen beliefs entered the literature as an explanation of stable democracy. It is not so much that the argument was new, but rather that it was now developed systematically with data to support it that gave it its potency. Though the field has come a long way and our understanding of the role of cultural beliefs is more nuanced today, one certainly hears echoes of *The Civic Culture* in the discussions of the prospects for democracy in newly democratizing states. Indeed, since 1989, I have received numerous enquiries about replications of *The Civic Culture* from newly 'liberated' social scientists in Eastern Europe. I usually recommend against a straight replication; we have learned too much to make that fruitful. But I do suggest using some of the same questions since there will be comparable data from many other places and we do find that many of the themes remain significant.

Second, the interest in cultural explanations of politics, coupled with the use of survey techniques in a comparative context, triggered off a continuing series of cross-cultural survey studies. These include many replications of *The Civic Culture* study in other settings, but include as well other comparative surveys. I do not mean to trace the worldwide comparative survey 'industry' to *The Civic Culture*. It was but one of the sources. Even more important, probably, were the later role of the Michigan election studies and the training and networks that emanated from Ann Arbor; the international development of polling institutions; and such regularized polls as the Eurobarometer. But the role of *The Civic Culture* was significant.

Third was the general impact of the focus on systematic comparison among nations using quantitative techniques. The methods used in *The Civic Culture* were relatively simple: a straightforward random population sample, questions that were rather rigidly parallel, and relatively simple tabular statistical techniques. Given the state of cross-national research and computer technology at the time, these were not so simple. More important, they helped open the way for many later works that used parallel approaches. The advantage of systematic survey techniques is not that they measure more precisely or solve the complex issues of measurement within differing contexts. Surveys, and especially cross-national surveys, are replete with random and systematic measurement error – as are all observations of human activity. But one is forced to explicate these measurement problems within the context of survey techniques. This develops a self-consciousness about measurement that is important for all kinds of research.

Perhaps, the most important contribution of *The Civic Culture* was that it excited the field. Not all those who were excited were positive about the book. Indeed, I think the most fruitful contribution of the book was that it motivated a variety of responses. Some people liked it enough to replicate it elsewhere. That is an important contribution to continuities in research. Others used the basic set of ideas and techniques to extend its reach to other domains, also a contribution to continuities. In the process the approach and the techniques were refined. Other scholars were unsatisfied with the approach and were motivated to refute it or go beyond it in various ways. That may be the most useful of all. Pareto says (somewhere) 'Give me fruitful error, bursting with the seeds of its own correction. You can keep your sterile truth.'

The 'goings-beyond' took many forms. Some found that the work, by being so generally comparative, did not do full justice to one or another of the nations studied. They argued for closer analysis of particular places. One cannot disagree with the need for awareness of and sensitivity to the complexities of particular places. If that awareness can be in a comparative framework rather than a retreat to pure contextualism and uniqueness, research can only improve.

Others criticized the use of surveys for macro-analyses of such issues as the stability of democracy. The arguments here are several, and of great importance. One strand of the argument – part of the more general argument that much work in the 'behavioural' tradition downplayed the role of state institutions – was that the values and attitudes observed in *The Civic Culture* were only partial explanations; the structure of institutions was equally important. The aggregation of individual attitudes as done in the five-nation study to the level of independent variables that 'explain' an outcome such as stable democracy did represent a rather large leap. For one thing, it mattered whose attitudes were at stake; not all citizens are equal in their centrality to governmental functioning. The argument was made that the study took too little account of class and other variations within the several nations. Lastly, the causal arrow was uncertain. Attitudes to democracy may affect the functioning of democracy; but the effective functioning of democracy also shapes attitudes.

From the perspective of the study of European politics, the effect of *The Civic Culture* was, I believe, large but mixed. (For this evaluation, I draw on the essays in

Almond and Verba 1989, especially the essays by Kavanagh, Conradt, Sani and Wiatr.)
The key countries in relation to its reception were, of course, the three European
countries included in the study: Germany, Italy and Britain. In each, the reaction was
muted, and for similar reasons. For one thing, the approach to political study through
surveys was unfamiliar in these countries and many scholars were suspicious of what
seemed to be American technology imported into the social sciences. Critics felt that
there ought to have been more historical and institutional grounding for the cultural
patterns the book attempted to uncover. This, of course, fitted the more traditional
research approaches of that time. The reaction to the quantitative survey approach, to
be sure, was not limited to those who were unfamiliar with it. The study received
serious criticism from some sophisticated quarters (Scheuch 1968). In addition, critics
felt the study focused too heavily on an Anglo-American model of democracy. (In
Britain, the complaint was that it was an American model: Kavanagh, in Almond and
Verba 1989.) Interestingly, the features that were felt to be missing in *The Civic Culture*
were ideology and class – both features of society that appear less salient in the
American context than elsewhere. The absence of class analysis, according to Wiatr (in
Almond and Verba 1989) was responsible for its relative neglect in Eastern Europe.
Lastly, each nation seemed to find that the cross-national perspective produced results
that did not pay sufficient attention to the special features of the local nation.

The *Civic Culture* may have had the largest effect on the study of European
comparative politics in the United States. In the United States, the quantitative,
behavioural revolution was well under way, and students were open to the new
approach. In addition, the somewhat US centred flavour of the book that limited its
appeal in Europe was less of a deterrent in the United States.

The work spawned a lot of follow-up work on Europe. Putnam (1972) used ideas
from *The Civic Culture* in his pioneering work on élite culture in Italy and Britain;
Nordlinger (1967) studied working-class Tories in Britain; Di Palma reanalysed *The
Civic Culture* data and put them into a more historical context; and Dennis *et al.*
(1968, 1971) used some of the ideas in analyses of political socialization. In addition,
scholars studied the political culture of communist countries from a similar perspective
(Brown and Gray 1977). More than anything, I think, it provided a focus for a concern
for political beliefs as a significant aspect of political analysis in the United States and
Europe. As an aside, it is interesting that *The Civic Culture* had its largest effect in the
United States on the study of comparative politics. It had less of an effect – at least
early on – on the study of American politics. Apparently country specialists all over are
uneasy with comparisons.

The *Civic Culture* study contributed to the general study of comparative politics in
one other significant way. The data from the study were deposited in the databank of
the Inter-University Consortium for Political and Social Research at the University of
Michigan and were then used by students and scholars in the United States and in
many parts of the world. Other studies, such as the American Election Studies, were
also made available in that way and widely used, but it was the depositing of *The Civic
Culture* data that, I believe, brought comparative survey research to students of
comparative politics.

Beyond *The Civic Culture*

To a large extent, my own work in comparative politics since *The Civic Culture* has been a response to these themes. *The Civic Culture* was a good base on which to build other works. My continuing work in comparative politics has focused on themes close to those in the five-nation study: the relationship between the citizen and the state in democratic societies. And it has remained highly empirical, within (I hope) a more general theoretical framework.

I have always been sensitive to the problem of the comparativist who knows something about lots of places but not enough about any. Though much of my work has been boldly comparative, it has involved close collaboration with scholars who are specialists in that area (Verba, Ahmed and Bhatt 1969; Verba, Nie and Kim 1978; Verba et al. 1985). Collaborative, cross-national teams have become common in the discipline. They represent an important and reasonable institutional approach to the complexities of comparative research. In addition, I have devoted approximately half of my scholarly activity to studies of my own area, the United States – often work that overlaps with the comparative work (Verba and Nie 1972; Schlozman and Verba 1979; Verba and Orren 1985; Verba, Schlozman and Brady 1995).

Though my more recent work has dealt with the role of citizens in a democracy, the focus has been less on democratic stability than on issues within functioning democratic regimes. The turn away from the issue of stable democracy was partially historical. The issue of the post-World War II era was the stability of democracy in the western world, a focus that was natural, given the terrible consequences of democratic collapse in the period between the two world wars. As it became apparent that most of the European democracies were here to stay, the issue faded somewhat.

The issue that has concerned me in recent work has had less to do with whether or not the pattern of values and attitudes within the citizenry is conducive to the survival of democracy than it has been with the question of the relationship between citizen activity and the policies pursued by governments. Equality in political output and equality in governmental response are the two main foci of this work. The main questions have to do with citizen activity, its various forms, the process by which citizens come to be active, and, above all, the degree of inequality in political activity across the citizenry. If participation is the main mechanism by which citizens communicate their preferences to the government and pressure the government to respond, it matters a good deal who is active, and who is not.

The research focuses on two aspects of politics that European researchers (cf. Wiatr and Sani in Almond and Verba 1980) found missing in *The Civic Culture*: the role of class and the relationship between the economic system and the political system. Equality in the political system means something quite different from equality in the economic system. In the former, a more substantive notion of equality reigns (symbolized by the notion of one person one vote), while in the economy equality is more a matter of equality of opportunity (Verba and Orren 1985; Verba 1987). The result is that citizens with different resources derived from their economic circumstances can use those resources in politics, undercutting the norms of political equality (Verba and Nie 1972; Verba, Nie and Kim 1978; Verba, Schlozman and Brady 1995).

There are several features of this change in direction which have, I believe, implications for the agenda and methods of comparative analysis. For one thing, there is a closer relationship between that which is explained and the variables that explain it. Citizen attitudes of the sort measured in *The Civic Culture* are quite distant from the outcome they were supposed to explain – the nature and stability of the democratic regime in each country. The relationship between the level and type of activity of citizens and the resultant representativeness of the participant population is much closer.

In addition, the more recent work has relied less on cultural variables than on measures of citizen activity and of the positions of citizens in the stratification hierarchy. This has both a substantive and methodological advantage. From a substantive point of view, it focuses attention on characteristics of individuals that are of great political significance since politics is usually about advantage and disadvantage. The issue is not whether democracy survives but rather who gets what within democratic regimes. From a methodological point of view, the focus on citizen behaviour and citizen location in stratification hierarchies has the advantage of being more reliably and validly measurable. Our ability to measure values or beliefs – such things as civic values and political efficacy – is severely limited within a single culture. Their measurement in a cross-cultural context is much harder. On the other hand, questions about actual activity or about social circumstances – though by no means simple – are a lot more straightforward. Though I do not believe, as economists often argue, that cultural explanations are of little value or validity, I do admit to a good deal of bafflement as to how in fact they can be made.

Lastly, this focus allows one to bring social structures more directly into the analysis. In my cross-national work on political participation I have focused on the impact of the configuration of parties and organizations in a nation on the equality of participation, in particular on the extent to which the patterns of cleavage as reflected in institutions affect the likelihood that an individual will be mobilized to political activity. This has, I believe, been especially fruitful in comparisons across nations that differ in the 'strength' of their political institutions; differences that have significant effects on whose voice is heard in the political process (Verba, Nie and Kim 1978).

Social scientists are always dissatisfied. They were when I was a graduate student, and they still are now. Paradigms come and go; we never seem to know what we need to know as new issues and problems emerge. But as I look back on the past three or four decades of comparative politics, I am impressed by what has been accomplished. New ideas have flourished. Comparative politics transcends national boundaries both in terms of subject matter and in terms of who studies what in collaboration with whom. We have a long way to go – but we will always have a long way to go. The comparative study of politics will always be a journey, not a destination.

26 Autobiographical reflections: or how to live with a conceptual albatross around one's neck

Philippe C. Schmitter

STANFORD UNIVERSITY

Comparativists tend to be blessed (or cursed) by their association with a single country or region of the world. The burden I have had to bear as a student of comparative politics has been somewhat different. For I have been identified, not with a country, a region or even a theory, but with a single concept and a controversial one at that! Try to imagine how you would feel if people that you were meeting for the first time professionally addressed you as 'Mister Corporatism'.

In these brief reflections, I propose to concentrate on how and why I came into contact with this concept. I apologize to those mentors, colleagues and friends who have inspired and helped me to work on other things, for I have worked on topics other than corporatism. Indeed, I have occasionally met younger scholars for the first time who believed that there must be other Philippe C. Schmitters than the Mr Corporatism in front of them – for example, a mysterious Mr Neo-Functionalist who wrote some articles with Ernst B. Haas beginning in the 1960s; an even more obscure Mr Comparative Public Policy Analyst who crunched a lot of Latin American aggregate data during the 1970s; and, most recently, a Mr Democratization who wanders from continent to continent and collaborates periodically with Guillermo O'Donnell and Terry Karl. The other day, in a seminar in Paris, I was asked publicly whether I really was all those personae and what, if any, link could there conceivably be among them. I admit that I was hard pressed to give an answer.

Returning to the past

I did not just stumble upon corporatism unassisted. Several scholars during my graduate career at Berkeley prepared me to discover it – without knowing it. No doubt the example of Ernst B. Haas had surreptitiously planted in my embryonic professional consciousness the idea that imaginative use of an appropriately catchy concept – spill-over, in his case – could serve to focus the attention of scholars when one had something novel to say (Haas 1958; cf. Haas and Schmitter 1964). He also must have been the one who taught me that established theories are never changed by facts, but only by alternative conceptualizations of them – long before I read Thomas Kuhn on paradigmatic revolutions. Seymour Martin Lipset got me started on the subject of representation and the role of intermediaries – even if he tried unsuccessfully to convince me that political parties were where the action was (Schmitter 1992). But the scholar who may have influenced my discovery the most was Sheldon Wolin. Taking his magisterial Political Science 118A & B (required of all graduate students at Berkeley at the time) instilled in me an enduring respect for the contemporary relevance of the classics of political theory (Wolin 1960). I owe to him (I believe) a strong re-enforcement of my conviction that little, if anything, about politics has not been thought of long ago, and probably published somewhere. Whenever I have been faced with an apparent puzzle or anomaly in my work, I have always found it profitable to *reculer pour mieux sauter*, to return to the past in order to gain inspiration about the present. For example, when I desperately needed inspiration about the problem of democratization and could find precious little among contemporary democratic theorists, I quite literally became a devoted disciple of Niccolò Machiavelli for some time – a conversion made perhaps easier by my association with the Istituto Universitario Europeo in Florence! (See Schmitter 1980b, 1985a.)

Finding and labelling the albatross

Looking back over my research experience since writing my dissertation on Brazil in the early 1970s, I now regret having used the term 'corporatism': first, to describe a distinctive mode of interest intermediation; later, to analyse a particular pattern of policy-making. The confusion this has caused was driven home to me when I met, for the first time, Norberto Bobbio, the *doyen* of Italian political philosophy. We were introduced by a mutual acquaintance in a spectacular frescoed room of a Milanese *palazzo*. Bobbio literally grabbed the lapels of my jacket, shook me and said, 'Ah! Alora, lei è Schmitter. Interessante, la sua opera, molto interessante. Ma, perché lo ha fatto chiamare *corporativismo?*' Bobbio, of course, had lived through and struggled against an earlier version of corporatism, *lo stato corporativo* of Mussolini, and its memory was too entrenched in his memory for him to be able to use it as anything but a term of opprobrium. To apply it to contemporary polities where it had not been imposed by an authoritarian ruler, but had emerged from the independent calculations of self-organized classes, sectors and professions and survived side-by-side with a competitive party system and full respect for civic and human rights, must have seemed to Bobbio to have been stretching the concept beyond all recognition.

On occasion, I have been credited with the 'wisdom' (or 'shame') of having distorted the spelling of the word in order to cleanse it of its unfortunate past associations, that is, by changing it from *corporativism* or *corporativismo* or *Korporativismus* to *corporatism* or *corporatismo* or *Korporatismus*. That missing 'iv' was supposed to be sufficient to convert the old into the new and to make it palatable for contemporary scholarly usage. I must confess, however, that my choice of spelling was not so clever or deliberate. The language of my earliest childhood was French and much of my first exposure to writings on the subject was in French. All I really did was to drop the 'e' from the end of *corporatisme*!

What I did not do, unfortunately, was to invent a completely new term for what I (re)discovered in the early 1970s. For I should be quite candid, I was not alone at the time. A number of authors of different nationalities and disciplines had come independently to the conclusion that the dominant paradigm for analysing the interest politics of advanced industrial democracies, *pluralism*, was inadequate. Theodore Lowi (1971) and Stein Rokkan (1966), for example, were aware of this – although neither attempted to develop a full-blown, competing conceptualization of the generic problem. Among Latin Americanists, the idea had arisen that the countries of this part of the world suffered from a distinctive 'Iberian' mentality, part of which consisted of an anti-liberal, collectivist tradition. Frederick B. Pike, Ronald C. Newton, Glen Dealey and, most of all, Howard Wiarda were using the term 'corporatist' to describe this (alleged) characteristic of the region's political culture.

Saved by a strange habit

My initial encounter with corporatism, however, came from a different source. I arrived in Brazil in 1966 with an impeccably pluralist design for writing a dissertation about the role of interest associations in relation to that country's economic and political development. Based on my reading of the existing literature and influenced by my mentors at Berkeley, especially Ernst B. Haas, Seymour Martin Lipset, William Kornhauser, Reinhard Bendix and David Apter, I fully expected to find evidence for a proliferation of autonomous, overlapping, competing and dispersed organizations representing a diverse set of interests – all the more since Brazil had supposedly shed authoritarian rule from 1945 to 1964, enjoyed (then) exceptionally high rates of industrialization and urbanization, and clearly had a multiplicity of potential cleavages based on class, status, regional location, national origin, ethnicity, religion, gender, etc. I knew, of course, that the country had had a different system of interest representation during the *Estado Novo*, but I assumed that democratization and development had subsequently undermined that – and that the authoritarian rulers who had seized power in 1964 had neither the time nor the will to impose a return to the past. Very soon after my arrival, I became aware, not only that the *ancien régime* had never really been dismantled after 1945, but that it had even been strengthened. Far from destroying the basis of hierarchical, monopolistic, state-sponsored and controlled interest associability, development was being used as an excuse for continuing and even extending it!

From this state of 'paradigm confusion', I was saved by an old habit of mine: that of haunting used bookstores. Since I was a student in Geneva and during trips to Paris and London, and then again at Berkeley, I simply could not pass in front of a used bookstore without entering and browsing. If asked to justify this seemingly irrational passion, I suppose it has something to do with the aforementioned suspicion that nothing in politics is really new, that every notion has already been published somewhere. The only problem is finding out who first articulated it, when it was said, in what language it was recorded, and where to find it now. In many countries, used bookstores allow one easier access to the past than libraries.

There, in Rio de Janeiro on the shelf of an obscure shop, I found a beautiful, leather-bound copy of Mihaïl Manoïlesco's *Le siècle du corporatisme* in its original (1934) edition – admiringly annotated by some (unknown) Brazilian fascist intellectual. For the equivalent of $5, I bought it, took it home and read it. That book not only gave me the central concept I needed, but it contained a very complex argument linking this mode of interest representation to the specific conditions of delayed, peripheral, capitalist development. Manoïlesco's case was based primarily on his native Romania (with a substantial boost from Mussolini's experiment with the *stato corporativo* in Italy after 1928), but the parallels with Brazil were striking. Moreover, in very considerable detail, he anticipated most of the arguments of what later became known as the ECLA Doctrine. My indebtedness to Manoïlesco should be evident to anyone reading my article: 'Still the Century of Corporatism?' (1974; cf. 1978b).

Before leaving Brazil, I ravaged the bookstores of Rio, Sao Paulo, Belo Horizonte and Bahia for items on corporat(iv)ism, and was richly rewarded. The topic was not fashionable and the death of so many of the leading figures from the 1930s meant that their libraries were being unloaded on the used market. I must have returned to the States in 1967 with forty to fifty books and pamphlets in Italian (especially), Spanish, French, German and Portuguese – none, needless to say, in English.

From this experience, I came away with four firm conclusions about corporat(iv)ism:

1. It was not native to Latin America, but had been imported to it from, and imposed upon it by, Europe, where both its ideology and practice had originated.
2. It was inextricably linked to the role of the state and would not have emerged without its sponsorship and coercive support.
3. It was also closely involved with the peculiar dynamics of capitalist development and both reflected and affected its patterns of class and sectoral conflict.
4. It was a much more important and pervasive phenomenon than had been recognized.
5. It was, moreover, neither dead nor dying.

I cannot claim, even in retrospect, to have imagined how rapidly the concept would spread and, least of all, that it would come to have such an impact upon the study of Western European politics and society, but I did know from the beginning that I had hold of a topic worth pursuing further. (Looking back at my first book (Schmitter 1971a), I note with some embarrassment that I did not even mention Mihaïl Manoïlesco in it. I suppose that for a young scholar just beginning his career, I thought it too risky to admit that some of my best ideas had come from an obscure, 'fascistoid' Romanian! I did, however, cite several Brazilian 'authoritarian corporatists' such as Oliveira Viana and Azevedo Amaral who were influenced by Manoïlesco.)

In 1969, I spent some six months in Argentina trying to make sense of the Peronist version of corporatism. I conducted a large number of interviews with trade union and business association leaders, assembled even more documentary material than in Brazil, and ravaged the used bookstores again – without as much success. Somehow, the pieces did not fit together as they had in Brazil and I never wrote a word on Argentina.

At this point, I hesitated. Maybe this approach to the problem of political development, regime change and policy outcomes was not the 'Open Sesame' that I had presumed. I began to drift away from the subject of the mode of interest associability, and to use other techniques of analysis for exploring such topics as the impact of military rule and the importance of various forms of *dependencia* (Schmitter 1971b, 1971c, 1973).

Going to the heartland

But I simply could not let go of corporat(iv)ism and decided in 1971 to go to its heartland – to the country where it had been preached and practised for the longest period of time and where it had been applied to the widest range of interests: Portugal! There, I not only found used bookstores crammed full of missing books from the 1920s and 1930s, but an intellectual-cum-ideological tradition that continued well into the 1950s and 1960s. The interviews I conducted with the leaders of official *grémios*, *sindicatos* and *confederaçoes*, and even more the contacts I developed with those who were trying to organize interests outside the *corporativismo integral* that Salazar had gradually put together since the early 1930s, were immensely useful (Schmitter 1975a, 1978a, 1979a, 1980a). I was especially impressed by the following factors:

1. The enormous 'negative significance' of the Portuguese experience, the fact that its most important impact could only be measured by what had not happened, by the way that its institutions did not really function as they were supposed to, but were successful in effectively filling the space between the interests of social groups and the agencies of the state, thereby pre-empting more autonomous and conflictual forms of associability.
2. Portugal's extraordinary ability to survive the demise of fascism and National Socialism and to accommodate itself to the external pressures of a newly democratized Europe and the internal demands of an increasingly complex (if still very backward) social and economic structure.
3. The virtually complete dependence of the whole organizational apparatus upon the coercive power of the state and the absence of supportive roots for it in Portuguese civil society or political culture – despite an ideology that stressed just that.

After this fieldwork in Portugal, I thought I was finished with the subject of corporat(iv)ism. I had observed its most venerable and extreme manifestation. I had no inkling that it would collapse in Portugal, because that clearly depended on the prior collapse of the authoritarian regime and state apparatus that had created and sustained it, and that certainly did not seem imminent – despite the fact that the country was fighting a hopeless war to defend its overseas empire. Moreover, at a normative level, I had never liked the corporat(iv)isms I had studied – although I tried to disguise this judgement and to present as 'objective' a view as possible of their accomplishments and failures. It seemed time to get rid of my obsession with autocratic regimes and institutions, and to start working on something I could admire for a change.

Saved by an odd coincidence

All this changed in a single day in Geneva. I had accepted a position as visiting professor in the Department of Political Science of the University of Geneva for the 1973–74 academic year. Nothing could have been intended to place me further from any preoccupation with corporat(iv)ism. There, I received a polite letter from Frederick Pike who reminded me that I had long since promised to contribute an article to a special issue of *The Review of Politics* to be devoted to ... corporatism in Latin

America! I still remember the sense of panic. I had left all my books and notes back in Chicago. Nothing was further from my mind. What could I possibly say?

In my consternation, I happened to look down at that day's issue of the *Tribune de Genève*. It was open at the business section and there was an article about the annual price-fixing mechanism for milk and the role that the *Association Suisse des Producteurs de Lait* had played in it. I thought: how corporatist! Glancing at other articles, I became more and more aware that certain specified, monopolistic interest associations in Switzerland had been directly incorporated within the public policy-making process (at both the federal and cantonal levels) and made co-responsible for the implementation of these very same policies. All this in a highly developed, thoroughly democratic European country with a strong reputation for liberalism and bourgeois hegemony! Excited by this shocking discovery, I literally ran across the street to the *Bibliothéque Publique et Universitaire* and headed for the card catalogue. There, at the back of an entire drawer full of items on corporat(iv)ism was what I was really searching for: 20 to 30 books, pamphlets and even a dissertation or two on '*corporatisme, suisse*' – all written during the 1930s and 1940s. I had the central theme for my article: corporat(iv)ism was not dead; it was alive and well within some advanced Western democracies – only it was societal and voluntary in its origins, not statist and compulsory as it was in Brazil and Portugal! In three, very intensive, weeks of writing I dashed off the article that I called 'Still the Century of Corporatism?' (1974) in remembrance of my former inspiration, Mihaïl Manoïlesco.

What I did not know then was that several other scholars were independently coming up with a somewhat similar set of observations and giving them the same label. Within a few months of each other, two articles in addition to mine in *The Review of Politics* were published or given at conferences: Ray Pahl and Jack Winkler's 'The Coming Corporatism' (1975) and Gerhard Lehmbruch's 'Liberal Corporatism and Party Government' (1977). The latter's conception was much closer to mine than the formers' and we subsequently teamed up to edit two major compilations that served, at least initially, to define the emerging field (Schmitter and Lehmbruch, 1979b; Lehmbruch and Schmitter, 1982).

Coping with an (unexpected) growth industry

The rest is, as they say, (academic) history. The concept spread during the second half of the 1970s with extraordinary rapidity. It became immediately clear that students of European politics, in particular, had long desired to break with the orthodox pluralist interpretation of 'their' democracies and that the neo-corporatist label gave them a licence to do so. It began to be discovered everywhere – especially in Northern Europe. Dozens of different (and not always compatible) definitions cropped up – divided largely between those who considered it just another way of organizing interests and those who saw it as a whole new form of the state. Observers from conflicting ideological vantage points praised it for incorporating trade unions more integrally into the policy process, or condemned it as a capitalist trick for diverting workers from their true revolutionary goals.

Frankly, I was astonished by the reaction and more than a little bit wary of becoming too associated with the concept. It was difficult enough to study corporat(iv)ism without being accused of being a corporatist; it was impossible to defend all the multiple uses to which the concept was being put. The moment of saturation (for me) was reached when I received an article by an eminent Sovietologist accusing Brezhnev of being the ultimate 'corporatist'!

Realizing, however, that I was stuck for the foreseeable future with corporat(iv)ism, I decided quite consciously not to spend much effort in responding to the (multiple and varied) attacks levelled against it as a concept, but to concentrate on applying it to major substantive and normative issues. On the grounds that 'attack is the best defence', I plunged myself into the task of demonstrating that corporat(iv)ism was not just a descriptive label or an isolated term, but only the most visible part of a broader theoretical perspective which analysed relations between society and the state in novel ways, which allowed one to see variations in the nature and role of representation – hence, my introduction of the concept of intermediation – and which provided critical insights into changes in the practice of modern democracy. In the years from 1981 to 1985, I wrote essays on the four issues that I judged most important:

1. The (variable) impact of different forms of intermediation upon the governability of advanced capitalist democracies (Schmitter 1981a).
2. The (dubious) relation between the practice of neo-corporatism and prevailing theories of liberal democracy (Schmitter 1983).
3. The (ambiguous and contingent) role that the state has played historically in encouraging and supporting such arrangements (Schmitter 1985b).
4. Finally, the (precarious) viability of existing neo-corporatist arrangements faced with a changing domestic and international economy (Schmitter 1982).

Exploring some missing links

As the result of a close collaboration with Wolfgang Streeck, then at the *Wissenschaftszentrum* in Berlin, I subsequently became convinced that the missing link in our understanding of how this mode of interest intermediation does or does not work was the organization of business interests. Wolfgang and I set up an international working group on this subject, which produced a large volume of theoretical and empirical work stressing the problems that capitalists face in engaging in collective action and, especially, the difficulty that trade and employer associations have in entering into concertation arrangements and governing the subsequent behaviour of their members (Schmitter and Streeck 1981b; Schmitter 1981c; Streeck and Schmitter 1985a; Lanzalaco and Schmitter 1989; Coleman and Jacek 1989; Martinelli 1991).

Almost all of my work since 1979 has relied on comparisons between advanced capitalist societies. Sometime during these years, I set aside my previous interest in Latin America and its statist-authoritarian forms of corporat(iv)ism and devoted my attention exclusively to Europe. More or less at the same time, I moved physically from Chicago to Florence where my position at the European University Institute placed me in a different network of personal and professional relations.

Switching to another topic

Not until the topic of democratization began to displace that of neo-corporatism in my mind – again, Portugal was instrumental in focusing my attention (Schmitter 1975b) – and not until I renewed a collaboration with my friend and colleague Guillermo O'Donnell, did I return (at least partially) to the geographic-cultural area in which I began my work in comparative politics. An attentive reader would note, however, that in the volume that Guillermo and I wrote, *Tentative Conclusions about Uncertain Democracies* (1986), summarizing the results of a Woodrow Wilson Center Working Group on transitions from authoritarian rule, the word corporat(iv)ism barely appears.

This does not mean that I have given up on the phenomenon. By the late 1970s, virtually all 'real-existing' corporatist systems were in difficulty, thereby vindicating the scurrilous accusation that social scientists only manage to discover, label and analyse phenomena that are in decline or *en voie de disparition*. While agreeing that technological change, shifts in the structure of employment and, especially, burgeoning international interdependence have all undermined the viability of comprehensive national systems of concertation, I argued that it would be premature to announce the death of corporat(iv)ism. Not only could they be expected to survive and even thrive at the meso-level of industrial sectors or sub-national regions, but there were reasons to suspect that macro-level arrangements will eventually make a cyclical comeback.

In a quite different direction, Wolfgang Streeck and I have extended the earlier concern with interest intermediation into the more remote domain of interest governance, that is to say, into a discussion of the multiplicity of institutions that contribute to reproducing capitalism and ensuring international competitiveness. We even went so far as to suggest the possibility that an 'associative order' may be gaining in importance relative to the classical trio of 'community, market and state' – protestations by neo-liberals to the contrary notwithstanding (Streeck and Schmitter 1985b). My subsequent essay 'Sectors in Modern Capitalism' takes that argument further and asks how differences in the way industries and professions are organized and govern their affairs may have a long-term impact on economic performance (Schmitter 1990).

The process of European integration is another substantive area where the neo-corporatist approach has continued to produce important insights. Wolfgang Streeck and I examined the repeated efforts of the founding fathers of the European Community and, more recently, of Jacques Delors to create something like a Euro-corporatism, in effect transcending unsuccessful national experiences with a 'social dialogue' at the level of Europe as a whole. We concluded that this effort was doomed to fail and that the emerging interest system surrounding the EC was much more likely to be pluralist than corporatist (Schmitter and Streeck 1991a). With the entry into effect of the Single European Act and the negotiation of the Maastricht Treaty, the entire complex of national institutions for private interest governance – price fixing, standard setting, quota restrictions, sectoral regulation, professional licensing, quality control, vocational training, and so forth – are in jeopardy. Whether they will be dismantled in the name of mutual recognition and neo-liberal deregulation or whether they will be reassembled and transposed to the EC level remains to be seen. Whatever the outcome, it will be highly significant for the future competitiveness of European goods and services and for the future configuration of the European polity.

Even when I managed momentarily to set aside my obsession with interest associations and take up issues involved in the democratization of Southern and Eastern Europe and Central and South America, I could not completely turn my back on corporat(iv)ism for long. Not surprisingly, I found myself arguing that, while political parties may be the crucial actors determining the immediate outcome of the transition and the success or failure of consolidation, the emerging system of interest intermediation may be the more important determinant of what type of democracy will eventually assert itself, as well as of the quality of that democracy (Schmitter 1991b, 1992, 1995).

Focusing on the quality of democracy

Finally, the albatross around my neck kept reminding me of my discontent with the quality of theorizing about how democracy actually works in modern societies. Most particularly, it convinced me of the need to come to terms – empirically and normatively – with the fact that the effective citizenry of these democracies consists not of individuals but of organizations, and that most public policies are produced by negotiations between self-regarding collectivities, not by voting among civic-minded persons. To address this issue adequately would require nothing less than a 'post-liberal' theory of democracy, and that is the long-term goal I have set for myself. In the first of the two articles, I have suggested a specific set of policy changes that I believe could substantially (but consensually) transform the basis of associability by distributing the ability to engage in collective action more equally in society and make its practice more responsive to long-range public goals (Schmitter 1988). In the second essay, I addressed some of the criticisms that have already been made (and others that I anticipate will be made) of my reform proposal (Schmitter 1991c). With this, I have moved almost full circle. Having started out with someone else's normatively loaded concept, I have come around to my own normatively loaded proposal.

Concluding with some rules of prudence

I conclude this essay by offering some *rules of prudence* gleaned (alas, retrospectively) from my experience as a comparativist and, most particularly, from my experience as a comparativist who settled into a concept rather than a country or region. Had I come across these lessons at an early stage of my career, I probably would have ignored them – even rejected them. None the less, I offer them to those younger scholars who might wish to take more time to reflect on their future than I did. Perhaps they will be better able to exploit the opportunities (and avoid the pitfalls) than I was:

1. Do not imagine that comparative politics is something invented by North Americans in the 1950s. It has a long and honourable history, and the further back in it that you can ground your research, the more you will be protected against ethnocentrisms and presentisms of limited and fleeting importance.
2. Do not be afraid to take 'natives' and 'practitioners' seriously, even when they write in strange languages, come from backward (*sic*) countries and profess

political values that are anathema to you. You may learn more from such exotic sources than from all your *collègues*, *camarades*, *concitoyens* and *compagnons de route*.

3. Pick for your dissertation committee scholars who know nothing (or relatively little) about the country or countries you have chosen to work on, but who know a lot about social and political theory, have strong paradigms of their own, and are nevertheless still willing to take you seriously.

4. Do not be embarrassed by the fact that your initial research is likely to be on a single country and be prepared to offer to the discipline 'models' and 'concepts' that have been generated by that single case – provided that you are confident of having captured its most generic properties and are willing to spend a lot of subsequent effort defending that assumption.

5. If, heaven forbid, you find yourself with a conceptual albatross around your neck, make sure it is a big and important one that your colleagues and rivals cannot afford to overlook and then make yourself a moving target – but try, at all costs, to avoid concepts that have too many unpleasant associations with the past or whose current usage is too far removed from the connotation you wish to give it. To invert the immortal saying of De Lampedusa, learn 'to change without appearing to change' by defending the essential of your insights while modifying their applications and implications in response to your critics. Typologies, fourfold tables and periodizations are especially useful in this regard.

6. Move back and forth between *théorie* and *empirie*, between the library and the field, between deduction and induction, between abstract concepts and concrete observations without allowing yourself to imagine that only one side of this dialectical process of inquiry will produce truth or, worse, science. This is another way of presenting a moving target – and of adapting your insights to the real world faster than your critics.

7. Be prepared to accept invitations to give talks and attend conferences on obscure topics in obscure places. You never know when you might learn something quite unexpected and you are much more likely to do so 'out in the bush' than in the more predictable confines of your national political science or area studies association. If you really wish to be a comparativist, you must be prepared to live a comparative life (although it doesn't hurt to select your longer research stays carefully for climatic, cultural and human comforts).

8. Try to learn as many languages as possible, preferably without wasting a lot of time in the classroom. Not only will this facilitate your being invited to obscure places, but you can never tell when the political jargon spoken by the actors in weird and remote systems will alert you to some relationship that you might otherwise have ignored.

9. Co-authorship is a good idea, especially when it crosses national and disciplinary lines. Never, however, agree to write anything with a scholar whom you do not regard as your intellectual equal and never try to resolve your (inevitable) disputes with him or her by opting for a lowest common denominator solution. After a truly successful collaboration, it should be impossible for either of you to tell who contributed the best ideas. In any case, readers will impute the not-so-good ideas to you.

10. Forging close personal links with other scholars across national and even continental divides can be an important component in the 'design' of comparative research. It permits one not only to include more cases and to capture a wider range of variation, but also to control for idiosyncratic or ethnocentric perspectives. However, never 'network' for its own sake and never join a working group unless you know what its substantive agenda is.

11. If you must become a political scientist, think protractedly and carefully before choosing to specialize in comparative politics. It is by far the most demanding (and most rewarding) of the sub-disciplines.

27 Conflict and political order

Ted Robert Gurr

University of Maryland, College Park

Inspiration

The summer of 1964 was hot and humid in Ann Arbor, where the Inter-University Consortium for Political Research offered, then as now, an intensive programme on empirical political enquiry. I had a subject, the decolonization of Africa, but recently had lost out in competition for a fellowship that would have supported my plans for fieldwork on the emerging – and, as it proved, short-lived – East African Federation. So I was relearning methods of research that I had studied when taking my first degree in psychology at Reed College (1957) and attending lectures by Fred Frey and others about political development. Most of all, I was shopping for a new dissertation idea.

On a July weekend we fled the cramped student quarters at the University of Michigan, my wife Erika and year-old daughter Lisa and I, invited by a relative to spend a weekend on his cabin cruiser moored at a Detroit marina. While I was watching the sun set from the boat's afterdeck, a set of ideas about conflict and development in newly independent countries suddenly gelled. In ten minutes of inspiration, probably less, I conceived the initial argument and research design that motivated the *Why Men Rebel* argument and 15 years' efforts to test it empirically.

The basic insight, which in retrospect seems simple and not entirely original, was this: the process of social mobilization, as conceived by Karl Deutsch (1961), was paralleled by a psychological process of rising expectations, especially among educated urban people. Failure to attain those expectations due to lack of economic and political opportunities increased the likelihood of political violence, following John Dollard's frustration–aggression argument (Dollard *et al.*, 1939). My plan was to explain aggregate political phenomena based on insights from a well-studied psychological argument. The first challenge was to overcome the problem of reductionism by identifying the variables or processes that intervened between the psychological and the political levels of analysis. Leonard Berkowitz's overview of social-psychological research on aggression (1962) was especially helpful on this point, undoubtedly the most influential psychological study I read while working on the dissertation. The second challenge was to test whether differences in rates of mobilization and growth of opportunities – 'capabilities' was the term I used – helped explain why political violence had erupted in the early 1960s in some but not all newly independent African states.

The criteria for good empirical theory were more or less commonly understood by young American political scientists of my cohort who were exposed to research on voting behaviour and public opinion. Social science was supposed to proceed by formulating sets of statements (hypotheses) about the relations between independent and dependent variables. These concepts were to be defined precisely and measured using quantitative data for a number of cases – respondents, counties, or countries. The strength and direction of statistical relationship among the variables was the empirical test of the argument.

There were many variations on this methodological prescription. I knew more than most of my peers about the actual conduct of social research through my work for the journal *Political Research: Organization and Design*, which Alfred de Grazia founded in 1957 to promote empirical approaches to political science. Almost every month between 1958 and 1961 it was my task to identify and abstract the empirical articles related to political topics that appeared in more than 100 social science journals. I also learned early about, and shared, the enthusiasm of other doctoral students at the Consortium for the new collections of aggregate data and conflict-event data that were being published and analysed by Bruce Russett and Rudolph Rummel at Yale University (Russett *et al.*, 1964). And one of my fellow graduate students at New York University, William Ellis, now a senior official at the US Library of Congress, introduced me to the use of multiple regression analysis for testing theories that identified many different causal variables.

There were significant theoretical influences on my work also, most notably the work of Harold Lasswell. His conceptual framework for political inquiry, *Power and Society* (Lasswell and Kaplan 1950), had a great impact on my thinking during graduate studies, and provided a set of concepts and a model for how to frame a general theoretical argument about political conflict. His work also provided encouragement for taking a psychological approach to explaining political phenomena, although I was not persuaded by the tenets of his arguments about *Psychopathology and Politics* (1930).

The dissertation that was later revised and published as *Why Men Rebel* (1970) outgrew its original concern with political violence in Africa. The basic argument was elaborated into a general structure that incorporated, or offered interpretations of, evidence on the dynamics of riots, coups, and revolutions in Western as well as postcolonial societies. Each hypothesis was justified at two levels of analysis, following my initial plan: it was shown to be plausible in terms of psychological theory, and consistent with observations about social and political behaviour.

Second thoughts

Two formative experiences occurred between the dissertation's completion in 1965 and the book's publication in 1970. One was personal and intellectual: Harry Eckstein invited me to work on the empirical testing of the arguments at Princeton's Center for International Studies. He had recently completed the 'Internal War' project, the first serious effort by American social scientists to deal conceptually with the challenge of

Third World insurgencies (1966). He widened my understanding of comparative politics and taught me, by example and gentle persuasion, how to think through and express clearly the intricacies of verbal theory in comparative politics. Whereas Lasswell's work had a formative influence on my dissertation research, Harry Eckstein's development of congruence theory was an exemplar of how to go about developing and testing the plausibility of 'strong theory'. But I have always sensed that I fell well short of meeting his criteria of parsimony and elegance in theory formulation.

The other formative experience was a political one: the eruption of widespread violent protest by urban African-Americans in 1965 and the demands of public officials, journalists, and the American public for explanations and for ideas about what should be done. By mid-1968 I had published papers on a theory that looked promising and had just submitted a book-length account of the research to an editor at Princeton University Press (Gurr 1967). The theory offered a plausible social-psychological accounting of the expressive rage of rioters, its key hypotheses seemed to be supported by cross-national tests using aggregate data (Gurr 1968; Gurr and Ruttenberg 1969), and it appealed to the liberal imagination by implying that violence was best restrained by improving the status and opportunities of minorities. So I was eager to accept an invitation to join the staff of the National Commission on the Causes and Prevention of Violence, which President Lyndon Johnson established shortly after the assassinations of Dr Martin Luther King and Robert Kennedy in spring 1968.

During my year with the Commission I was teamed with a young historian from Johns Hopkins University, Hugh Davis Graham. We were tasked with preparing a background report that summarized the insights of social scientists and historians on the origins of American violence. It was a year of total immersion – an intensive seminar in American history, dialogues with expert consultants, critical exchanges with the staff directors – sociologist James F. Short and criminologist Marvin E. Wolfgang – and the Commissioners themselves, a mixed lot of public figures and politicians headed by Dr Milton S. Eisenhower. The report we prepared, *Violence in America. Historical and Comparative Perspectives* (Graham and Gurr 1969), was an intellectual collage: its contents were commissioned, reviewed and published in less than twelve months. The report challenged Americans' 'historical amnesia' about their violent past and diagnosed a number of its sources and implications. We also were at pains to relate the American experience to that of Europe. Charles Tilly contributed the lead chapter on 'Collective Violence in European Perspective' which persuasively argued his political interpretation of collective violence – a useful antidote to prevailing North American views that collective violence was anomic and irrational. I provided comparative evidence on more than 80 contemporary societies, suggesting that protest and rebellion in the United States in the 1960s was somewhat more extensive but not fundamentally different in kind from collective action in other large democratic societies.

The report's scope and novelty probably justified the ensuing media attention, favourable reviews in leading newspapers as well as scholarly journals, and the sale of some 300,000 paperback copies. In 1979 Hugh Graham and I put together a vastly revised edition that incorporated the best of a decade's new scholarship in political science, sociology and history (Graham and Gurr 1979). But by then the climacteric of American violence was long past, the subject was no longer topical, and the book attracted virtually no attention except from students.

By 1970 I had two well-reviewed books on my account and had resigned my temporary post at Princeton to take a tenure track position at Northwestern University. I was 34 years old. I also had begun to question the narrowly behavioural approach to political conflict. The research for *Violence in America* (1989) had convinced me that to understand conflict behaviour one also needed to examine its historical antecedents and cultural context. Thoughtful criticisms of the *Why Men Rebel* argument by Mancur Olson, Jr., Charles Tilly, Terry Nardin, Edward N. Muller and others stretched my conceptual frame of reference. They helped persuade me to take seriously the rational calculations of rebels as well as their anger, the effects of group context in shaping rebels' grievances and actions, and the proactive role of the state in many conflicts. I sought to incorporate these new perspectives in empirical and theoretical papers done by and with Ph.D students at Northwestern, especially Michael Stohl, Raymond Duvall and Mark Irving Lichbach, all of whom later went on to make their own autonomous contributions to the study of civil and international conflict (a recent example is Lichbach 1995).

My methodological preferences also had broadened. Aggregate analysis was only one means for evaluating theoretical arguments about conflict. Such analyses should be complemented by studies that looked directly at the attitudes motivating political action, of the kinds that were being pioneered by Edward N. Muller.[1] And the plausibility of theories should be probed using comparative case studies of specific types of conflict, as Harry Eckstein was advocating. Some of my students carried out case studies, but I did not participate in such a project until the 1980s, when I helped plan and compare ten conflicts examined in *Revolutions of the Late Twentieth Century* (Goldstone, Gurr and Moshiri 1991).

Diversions

During the 1970s most of my time and resources were given to the pursuit of several new projects that struck off at tangents from the work on political violence. One was the comparative study of the performance and stability of political institutions, originally conceived as part of Harry Eckstein's study *Patterns of Authority* (Eckstein and Gurr 1975). The idea was to ascertain which kinds of regime authority patterns were most stable and free of violent challenges by tracing the historical sequences of institutional change. My contribution to the project began in 1968 with in-depth studies of political performance in twelve countries during 1927–36 and 1957–66. Seven of the countries were European: France, Germany, Italy, the Netherlands, Spain, Sweden and Yugoslavia. This rather eclectic set of choices was dictated by decisions of doctoral students in Harry Eckstein's Workshop on Comparative Politics about their dissertation fieldwork sites. Analysis supported a general causal argument that efficacy of political decision-making enhanced regime legitimacy and reduced civil strife, and that both conditions in turn contributed to regime durability (Gurr and McClelland 1971).

At about the same time I decided to develop the data needed for a global test of the essential arguments about regime durability. In the Polity study, as it became known, data were coded on political institutions for all internationally recognized states beginning in 1800. My late wife, Erika Gurr, did much of the coding for the first-generation study. We found, consistent with one of Harry Eckstein's basic hypotheses, that regimes with coherent (internally consistent) democratic or authoritarian patterns were more persistent than systems that mixed elements of both kinds of patterns (Gurr 1974). When the study was expanded and updated in the 1980s (the Polity II study) the data were used to track the ascendance of democratic regimes and the decline of authoritarian ones in Europe and Latin America (Gurr, Jaggers and Moore 1990). The Polity studies were mainly descriptive, but on a large scale, and their data have been used extensively by scholars doing longitudinal studies of conflict and change in the world system. They have recently been updated once again, to 1994, and are being used to trace the fate of the 'third wave of democracy' (Jaggers and Gurr 1995).

The other main tangent was also historical: I embarked on a comparative enquiry into the records of crime and group conflict in nineteenth and twentieth century London, Stockholm, Sydney and Calcutta (Gurr, Grabosky and Hula 1977). The objective was to examine the impact of individual and collective disorder on the evolution of the institutions that define and maintain public order. The capital cities of the three western societies showed similar dynamics: from the early nineteenth century to the middle of the twentieth century they experienced periods of widespread public disorder, especially collective violence, that led with some regularity to reforms in criminal law, policing and treatment of offenders. Most of these reforms had the intended effect of improving public order: serious crimes against persons and property declined over the long run, and collective violence became less common. After the 1950s, however, the dynamics changed. Public disorder, especially crime, began to move sharply upwards but institutional adjustments had little effect on the trends. The 'reversing U-curve' of public disorder documented in this study has been accepted as one of the landmark regularities in historical criminology (see Gurr 1989, especially Chs 1–3). European as well as North American scholars have tested it against the experience of a number of societies. I have some ambivalence about the outcomes of this study. The movement of violent crime over time attracts enduring attention; I continue to get reprints, and calls from journalists, about trends in violent crime. But my initial intellectual concern was with the political and institutional context in which disorder is defined and recorded, and this is a topic that remains underdeveloped.

At Northwestern during the 1970s I met Eric Jones, a British economic historian who was in transition from detailed inquiries into prices and wages in early modern England to a vastly more ambitious study of the sources of the 'European economic miracle', which contrasted Asian and European economic histories across a thousand years. Eric had no influence on my choice of subjects or methods, but he offered an explanation for his shift of focus that had the ring of generalizable truth. Tenure, he suggested, was for him a licence to take intellectual risks by exploring big subjects. The worst that might happen was to be told that he was wrong. I have chosen to follow that principle, or perhaps have used it to rationalize a pre-existing disposition. Fear of failure or criticism has never inhibited me from starting off in a new direction. There is, however, something worse than critical rejection and that is being ignored for work one thinks is path-breaking. It is salutary for a successful senior scholar to be ignored occasionally, if for no other reason than to generate empathy for other scholars, junior and senior, who do good work for years or decades yet gain little recognition.

One thread that links virtually all the studies I did from the 1960s to the present is a general concern with the interplay between conflict and order, or between people's pursuit of their own interests against the efforts of élites to establish stable patterns of rule. This was the underlying theme of the *State and the City* project, a new intellectual venture that I began in the late 1970s with Desmond King and completed in the early 1980s (Gurr and King 1987). Influenced by scholarship on the 'new institutionalism' and the relative autonomy of states, we began by specifying the hierarchy of interests pursued by the local and national states in contemporary Western societies. Then we compared the policies of national states towards declining cities in contemporary Britain and the United States, concluding that the 'urban decline' of Margaret Thatcher's Britain and Ronald Reagan's United States was not only or mainly a consequence of inexorable economic change, but the result of weakness of the local state and of deliberate policies of national governments in both countries. Though I have given up this line of enquiry, Desmond King (now at Oxford) has gone on to do a series of incisive comparative studies of social policy in Western Europe and the United States, most recently on labour market policy (King 1995).

Renewal

In the 1980s my interests shifted again, away from the tedium of analysing public policy and back to more fundamental questions of conflict between citizens and states. A year's leave in Australia in 1981–82 was formative in several respects, more so than previous research leaves spent in London and Cambridge (UK) in 1970 and 1976. I was escaping from the trauma of my first wife's unexpected death, in 1980, which left me largely incapable of caring for two teenage daughters. Within a year I was remarried to Barbara Harff, a 'returning student' who had recently completed her doctorate at Northwestern University. Her first position was at LaTrobe University in Melbourne, where I soon followed with support in the form of a senior Fulbright research fellowship. We were accompanied by my stepson and my second daughter Andrea; her elder sister chose to go her own way, eventually to become a cultural anthropologist who studies industrial relations in contemporary Poland.

My immediate source of new intellectual inspiration was Barbara Harff's comparative work on the causes of genocides and mass political murder, and her examination of the international doctrine of humanitarian intervention in such conflicts (Harff 1984, 1987). These gross violations of human rights pose three intellectual puzzles (at least), two of which I had either dealt with or explained away in my earlier work. The first is why some civil conflicts, especially those involving communal groups, become so intense and protracted that they result in humanitarian disasters. This suggested a much closer look at a subject given passing attention in the *Why Men Rebel* studies: the role of group status and inequalities in the genesis of civil conflict. I had learned much about discrimination and political action among African-Americans from the *Violence in America* research. Moreover I used the year in Australia to study the politics of Aboriginal protest (Gurr 1983). The challenge was to generalize from such case specifics.

The second puzzle posed by Harff's studies of genocide and politicide (political mass murder) is why state élites should resort to extreme forms of coercion to maintain their authority. There were no explicit answers to this question either in *Why Men Rebel* or my later writings on state theory, both of which argued that rational élites ordinarily prefer strategies of accommodation and reform, because reliance on violence is costly and risky. The third question concerns the emergence of supranational authorities, global and regional, that assume responsibilities for responding to and managing conflicts within states. This question – the focus of Barbara Harff's work – is outside the customary domain of comparative politics but is of the greatest relevance for contemporary Europeans (see Harff's exploration of this issue in Gurr and Harff 1994, Chs 8 and 9).

The comparative project that embodies my present theoretical, empirical and policy concerns is the *Minorities at Risk* study (Gurr 1993a). The theoretical heart of the work is a loosely specified model of the processes of conflict between ethnic groups and states. Unlike *Why Men Rebel*, which deals mainly with causal relations affecting individuals and governments, the *Minorities at Risk* study is explicitly group-centred. The analysis begins with the sources and salience of ethnic identities, and the status and grievances of communal minorities and nationalities *vis-à-vis* dominant groups. Then it shows how disadvantaged communal groups mobilize to assert their interests, and how macro-processes such as development, democratization, and international circum- stances shape people's choices of protest or rebellion. The conflicts to be explained are not country-wide aggregates but the political actions of specific groups. My main policy concern is not the explanation of communal conflict *per se*, but rather an inventory and assessment of various strategies for accommodating communal and state interests.

To study these kinds of questions systematically I found it necessary to turn again to the kinds of data collection and coding procedures used in earlier projects. This meant, first, defining the universe of politically active communal groups. Some 230 were identified, summarily described, and profiled on a number of variables: their size, cultural traits, economic and political status *vis-à-vis* dominant groups, the grievances they articulated in the 1980s, and their involvement in conflicts with the state and with other groups from 1945 to 1989. The initial reports on this research include quantitative analyses of the correlates of inequalities, grievances and conflict (Gurr 1993b), plus region-by-region assessments of the patterns and dynamics of ethnopolitical conflict (Gurr 1993a, Chs 6–9).

Minorities at Risk concludes with a comparative assessment, based on case study materials, of the strategies and outcomes of communal conflict. I have been particularly struck by the number and diversity of accommodations that have been reached between peoples and states. These examples provide models for conflict management that are being used to dampen the sharp but temporary increase in ethnopolitical conflict that characterized most world regions in the early 1990s.

I am too close to the *Minorities at Risk* project to be able to judge its larger significance. The quantitative data on which it is based are novel: no previous study has attempted to codify or analyse the universe of politically active ethnic groups. The study's interpretations and comparisons also rely heavily on what are, in effect, mini- case studies (mostly unpublished) of the groups. In other words the study bridges and incorporates both quantitative and case study information. On the other hand the theoretical arguments of *Minorities at Risk* lack the formal definitions and specifications of hypotheses that I would have said twenty years ago were a *sine qua non* for good empirical research in comparative politics. I have relied more on *Verstehen* and less on *science* to communicate the essential arguments. I could have formalized the theory, and might still do so, but thus far have been too impatient to proceed with matters of substance.

A reprise: the empirical studies of civil conflict I began in 1965 went through three cycles, each starting with theorizing followed by data collection, empirical analysis, and ending with respecification of the problem and the theory that prompted a further cycle of research. The Polity study also has had three iterations. And the Minorities project is in its third phase, with substantial support from the National Science Foundation and the United States Institute of Peace. The collection of information was completed in mid-1996. This time around – my assistants and I call it Phase III – we have coded more detailed profiles of 268 groups and have used new information technologies to prepare more informative 1990s chronologies for all groups, concluding each with a risk assessment of future conflict. These mini-studies are significantly better than those we constructed for the 1980s. In 1996–97 I have a visiting research professorship at Uppsala University's Department of Peace and Conflict Research, where I am completing a book manuscript on *States vs. Peoples: Managing Ethnopolitical Conflict in the 1990s*. The challenge in writing this manuscript is to synthesize the analysis of the coded data with the richness of information from 268 case studies.

Beginning in October 1996 the mini-case studies have been accessible to all Internet users through a World Wide Web site at the University of Maryland. Since the 1960s empirical social scientists have made their datasets and codebooks available to other scholars by depositing them with the Inter-University Consortium for Political and Social Research at Ann Arbor; I have archived half-a-dozen datasets there, and will do so with Phase III of the Minorities codings. But I do not know of larger bodies of research text such as our case studies that have been made publically available electronically. One major future task for the Minorities project is to continue to update and improve the information on our Web site.

There is also a further question, which is what directions or tangents of ethnopolitical conflict to explore next. I have long thought that the ultimate test of empirical theories of conflict was whether they enable us to anticipate future episodes. The logic of forecasting is inherent in many of our research designs, including those used in the *Why Men Rebel* and *Minorities at Risk* studies. If independent variables measured at past time t_1 enable us to postdict magnitudes of conflict at past time t_2 with some statistical reliability, then real-time observation of the independent variables should enable us to forecast future magnitudes of conflict. Mark Lichbach and I carried out several empirical experiments of this sort (Gurr and Lichbach 1979; Lichbach and Gurr 1986) which suggested that theory-based forecasts of magnitudes of conflict were at least better than forecasts derived by projecting trends (though not nearly as accurate as, say, weather forecasts).

Ethnopolitical conflict is amenable to the same kind of analysis, using the data and results of the *Minorities at Risk* study as a point of departure. There also are compelling policy reasons for the renewal of forecasting research. In the 1970s and 1980s forecasts of political conflict were mainly of interest to US foreign policy and defence planners who were concerned with responding to insurgencies. In the 1990s a much broader international constituency needs to anticipate ethnopolitical conflicts in order to initiate peacemaking diplomacy, prepare for refugee assistance, and plan peacekeeping operations. These concerns are shared in overlapping ways among the United Nations, the UN High Commission for Refugees, regional organizations, governments that supply humanitarian aid, and NGOs like the Watch organizations and International Alert (London). The current catch-phrase for this kind of forecasting is 'early warning'. Early-warning efforts thus far are limited mainly to monitoring trends in rights violations, and to assessing reports from field observers. The next phase is to develop and apply predictive models of political crises and ethnopolitical conflicts to high-risk peoples and regions. In a first effort of this kind, Barbara Harff and I juxtaposed our datasets on geno/politicides and minorities at risk in the 1980s and identified the groups that were most at risk of future victimization by the state (Harff and Gurr 1989). We recently completed an updated version of this study that makes use of mid-1990s data from the Minorities study to establish a 'watch list' of 97 communal groups at risk of rights violations and intensified conflict in the late 1990s (Harff and Gurr, 1996).

The 'Victims of the State' papers provide global assessments that are too general for most organizations and people who must deal in a practical way with humanitarian crises. So each of us has gone one step further toward developing and applying working early-warning models. I have used the Phase III data from the Minorities project to identify and measure factors that dispose communal groups in the 22 largest Asian countries to rebel, and that provoke states to respond to ethnic challenges with accommodation or repression. The result is a theoretically and empirically grounded 'watch list' of Asian communal groups that are at various levels of risk of rebellion and repression. Barbara Harff has focused more tightly on four recent cases of genocide and near genocide (including Rwanda and Burundi) with two objectives: first to test her sequential model of the international and internal causes of genocide and politicide; second examine the trends in eight categories of 'accelerators' during the twelve months preceding each episode. The results of this kind of empirically grounded early-warning research are proving of considerable interest to national and international policy-makers and NGOs concerned with humanitarian issues (Davies and Gurr 1998).

Reprise

Let me return, in conclusion, to a few of the many unresolved questions in the analysis of civil conflict that have been implied and passed over in the preceding sketch.

There is, first, a cluster of conceptual questions about how best to approach the explanation of conflict. For example, I have always thought that explanations of human action that begin and remain at the structural or macro level are fundamentally flawed. Political challenges and responses are the deliberate actions of collectivities of people, responding to situations as they perceive and experience them. The psychological and cultural levels of analysis are an integral part of the explanation of conflict. Structures shape the situations of conflict; but within those constraints, people make choices about how to deal with them, including making concerted efforts to reshape structures.

A second general conceptual issue concerns the social psychological processes by which people become engaged in open conflict. It is widely debated whether they are responding mainly in an expressive way to frustrations, as I argued in *Why Men Rebel*, or to the normative incentives and constraints of their collectivities, or to calculations of costs and opportunities. The advocates of rational-actor theories and models of political behaviour, including conflict, are now in the ascendant. Twenty years ago, when I first rethought the arguments of *Why Men Rebel*, I concluded that it is misleading to think that any one motivational system is a priori more important than another. People join risky political action for a mix of reasons: expressive, normative and instrumental. The challenge for the theorist is to specify the mix that is present in any given type of situation. I am persuaded by my research on ethnopolitical conflict, for example, that historically rooted grievances as well as normative factors play a major role for most participants in this kind of conflict – but they are invoked and channelled by the instrumental planning of their leaders. The most serious intellectual error that can be made by a scholar who studies these issues is to assume, a priori, that one source of motivation is *ab initio* more fundamental than another. I made this kind of error when I wrote *Why Men Rebel* and I see rational-choice theorists making the same kind of error now.

Another kind of question concerns the most appropriate methodologies for studying civil conflict. Over time I have become increasingly dissatisfied with formal and purely quantitative approaches, and more attuned to interpretive and historicist approaches. At the same time I am acutely aware of the dangers of generalizing from one's understanding of particular situations. My conclusion is that this is not a tension that can be or should be resolved. We should pursue multiple strategies of enquiry on conflict and then contrast and synthesize the results of each. My own choices should be clear from the foregoing account: I alternate back and forth between aggregate analysis and case studies of conflict situations. My sense that I have understood the phenomena is sharpest when the results of both kinds of analysis converge.

The third general puzzle, the last to be mentioned here, concerns the uses and misuses of knowledge gained through the analysis of conflict. This is both a normative and a practical question that surfaces repeatedly among practitioners of peace and conflict research. Almost all of us were drawn to our subjects from a desire to improve the human condition, not merely to understand it in abstract categories. That implies that we intend our knowledge to be useful to someone, somehow. The question is who, and by what means. The modelling and forecasting of conflict that I did in the 1960s and 1970s was open to the criticism that it framed the questions and answers in ways that strengthened the hands of authorities to deal with their opponents. The counter-challenge was to use knowledge to empower less advantaged parties to conflict. Even if one argues that scholarly knowledge is neutral, states and their agents are more likely to acquire knowledge and to have the means to make use of it than those who challenge power. The same critique has been made of the new flurry of interest in early warning of communal conflicts: Johan Galtung posed just such an 'Early Warning to Early Warners' at the Kyoto meeting of the International Peace Research Association in August 1992.

Each researcher must reach his or her own decisions on these matters. My own view is that research on the sources and accommodation of communal conflict, or any other kind of conflict, is unlikely to have more than marginal effects on any of the protagonists. To the extent that it does have a potential effect, it is to give participants and observers a more general understanding of the likely consequences of their actions and inaction. And 'early warnings', if they are credible, should help international organizations to plan and justify preventive diplomacy and humanitarian assistance. I hope, but am not convinced, that 'early warnings' will contribute to the kinds of intervention needed to end practices such as political massacres and ethnic cleansing. These events are the result of unheeded early warnings – many observers anticipated the course of events in Bosnia, many others are pointing to similar potentialities in the Caucasus and the Greater Horn of Africa. The interventions needed to forestall mass murder and genocide are shaped by political will, a sense of collective responsibility, and the enforcement capabilities of the UN and regional organizations. Academic research may help heighten awareness of crises and clarify understandings of their causes and possible responses, but it cannot create the will or means to act (see Harff 1995; Gurr and Harff 1996, Ch. 4).

Notes

1. Edward N. Muller was the most prolific of all North American authors working empirically on violent political conflict from the 1970s through the early 1990s. Much of his work aimed at testing the relative significance of normative and rational factors versus discontent as determinants of aggressive political behaviour (see for example Muller 1979). His research on violent political participation in West Germany with Germany collaborators is well known. He died in a riding accident in Spring 1995, leaving unfinished a book-length study of the intricate relations between material inequality and rebellion.

28 A journey through the social sciences*

Harold L. Wilensky

UNIVERSITY OF CALIFORNIA, BERKELEY

The classical scholars who most influenced my work – Durkheim, Weber, Marx, Veblen – were too busy with their substantive studies to bother writing even a line of autobiography, intellectual or personal. That fact gives me doubts about this effort. But I cannot resist the temptation to put into print, however briefly, my reflections about the social-science enterprise, interdisciplinary work within it, the effect of social science on public policy, and the subversive effect of overspecialization, methodological ideologies, and the politicization of academic institutions. These are themes I have sounded for more than four decades in classrooms in three universities and in more than one discipline.

The major sources of intellectual inspiration since I was 17 have been jobs in and around the American labour movement and studies and academic positions at the University of Chicago 1947–54, the University of Michigan 1954–62, and the University of California, Berkeley from 1963 to the present. Two stimulating years at the Center for Advanced Study in the Behavioral Sciences (1956–57, 1962–63) were intellectual feasts; they were also crucial as opportunities to write and to plan research, especially two large projects that have occupied most of my time since 1956. The first was the 'labor–leisure' project at Michigan designed to test mass society theory. The second was the 'welfare state and equality' project at Berkeley – a continuing programme of research on the politics of taxing and spending in nineteen rich democracies, designed to play convergence theory against other theories of society and politics.

Political education in the labour movement

Staff jobs in unions doing 'research and education' taught me much about the politics of the left, the nature and variety of work experience, and the problem of the interplay of knowledge and power. I came to graduate work at the University of Chicago after several jobs in and around the American labour movement – some of them obtained through the work-study programmes of Goddard College (1940–42) and Antioch

---

* I am grateful to the Center for German and European Studies and the Institute of Governmental Studies, University of California, for support.

College (1942, 1945–47), some of them on my own. The union jobs that shaped my early intellectual and political interests include the following:

1. *National Maritime Union* (1941) Here I wrote a background history of the merchant seaman's role in wars from the Revolution up until World War I for the editor of the union newspaper. Intermittently, I hung around the union hiring hall in awe of what the NMU had done to eliminate the corrupt shape-up system on the New York waterfront that had preceded the union.
2. *The United Autoworkers* (UAW-CIO) (1942) Before I was admitted to aviation cadet training, I spent several exciting months in the United Autoworkers (UAW) headquarters in Detroit as a research assistant. It was here that the anti-communist left headed by Vice-President Walter Reuther was battling against the Communist Party and its fellow-travellers for control of one of the best-run unions in the USA. I found myself assigned to the CP-dominated Research Department. Beyond general lessons in left politics and sectarian enthusiasms, the CP's clumsy effort to recruit me in Detroit reinforced my already-sceptical attitude towards ideologues.[1] The hypocritical cynicism of the CP activists as they tortuously followed the Soviet foreign policy line shocked my youthful sensibilities and gave me a lifelong inoculation against sectarian politics.
3. *Voters' Research Institute* (1945–46) This was a 'liberal-labour' political consulting firm. I was assigned to interview almost all Democratic county chairmen, some Republican chairmen, and many Congressional candidates, labour leaders, and newspaper editors in twelve marginal Congressional districts in Ohio, Indiana and Pennsylvania, while gathering precinct election statistics for several past elections. The ultimate clients were the Democratic National Committee and labour unions. The aim: to gauge the prospects for Democratic Congressional candidates in 1946 as a basis for allocating aid to campaigns. This practical analysis of voting behaviour gave me my first understanding of the need to combine quantitative and qualitative data in a political and economic context, something I later put to use in my cross-national research.
4. *Ohio CIO Council* (1947) Here I worked for a labour lobbyist, spending much time covering hearings in the Ohio state legislature, watching how a legislature works and how labour tried to shape legislation.

In retrospect, I believe that these labour and political research jobs – as well as summer jobs in a factory, a construction gang, and in sales and truck-driving – were crucial in shaping my work in comparative political economy and public policy. For my later academic research, they constituted a continual source of reality checks. They inspired a lifelong interest in the role of intellectuals and experts and the interplay of labour, management and the state. One cannot talk usefully about 'American exceptionalism' without a deeper knowledge of American politics and society than most academics have a chance to acquire. And without some immersion in the practical details of labour and politics, it is easy to write abstract generalizations about both that miss the essentials. This is no crude equivalent of the businessman's complaint about academics, 'They never met a payroll'. It *is* a recommendation against the kind of insular education that characterizes some leading intellectuals.

Education: a lucky drift into Chicago graduate work and a lively sociological cohort

The story of how I came to sociology and political science is a story of the accidental in career development. Like many labour intellectuals, I drifted into academic institutions because I was searching for a place where ideas could be cultivated and communicated more freely than in unions, and because I felt the limits of my understanding of politics and society, especially of the upheavals in Europe and America that had shaped my life in the years before and during World War II. My interest in these issues was heightened by reading Franz Neumann's *Behemoth* (1942) while I was flying B-17s in Florida and Cuba.[2] However, I came to the University of Chicago not for a degree in any discipline but for a full-time job as a staff member of the Union Leadership Training Project that was lodged there. I thought that I might influence the labour movement and American society from a university base where ideas would count. For three years I prepared teaching materials for local and regional union leaders on union administration, labour and politics, labour and the community, etc. I went on the road to train rank-and-file activists as workers' education leaders, spending a week at each of twenty-odd union-sponsored institutes, an experience that cured me from ever speaking of 'the' labour movement. (The variety of unions and occupational groups I encountered was astounding.)

When I first entered the Chicago job in 1947, a friend suggested that I get a degree in my spare time. Because I had majored in economics and political science at Antioch College, I made an appointment with the graduate adviser and another young member of the economics department, Milton Friedman. They asked me what I had been reading in my Antioch major. 'Thorstein Veblen, Karl Mannheim, Karl Marx, Harold Laski, J.S. Mill, Adam Smith, Max Weber, Joseph Schumpeter, and Franz Neumann', I replied. 'Oh', they said. 'You are not an economist, you are a sociologist' – and sent me to Herbert Goldhamer and Albert J. Reiss, Jr. of the Sociology Department, where I recited the same list and was welcomed with open arms. So, while I worked with the union leadership training project, I got degrees in sociology, gradually becoming more interested in the subject. It was a lucky drift into a graduate cohort that included Erving Goffman (with whom I exchanged dissertation drafts), William Kornhauser, Kurt and Gladys Lang, Joe Gusfield, Howard Becker, and assorted poets and authors on the periphery of the Social Science Division. Among the younger Chicago faculty I got to know well were the two scholars who recruited me to Michigan in 1954 after my three years as an assistant professor at Chicago – political sociologist Morris Janowitz and social psychologist Guy E. Swanson – as well as labour economist Albert Rees and labour historians Val Lorwin and Joel Seidman.

Chicago social science – interdisciplinary in the best sense

The Chicago school of sociology, like its school of political science, defies easy labelling, but the characteristic strengths of both have been an accent on first-hand observation; an abiding interest in the interplay of theory, empirical observation, and public policy; a continual search for the shape of modern urban-industrial society; attention to the social, economic and political structures within which individuals act out their strivings; and a conviction that the choice of methods depends upon the substantive problems to be solved, not the other way round.[3]

The Social Science Division was permeated with the idea that Chicago was a laboratory for testing theory and exploring big issues. It developed a style of urban ethnography evident in a spate of monographs from Louis Wirth's *The Ghetto* (1928) to Gosnell's *Machine Politics: Chicago Model* (1937). The message was 'Put yourself in touch with the lives of people you study; continually make forays beyond the intellectual fraternity to anchor yourself in social and political realities' – a message obviously congenial to an activist fresh from the labour movement.

The second strength of Chicago was that it was interdisciplinary not in the sense of those awful meetings where representatives of disciplines negotiate a lowest common denominator but of intellectuals thoroughly anchored in their disciplines who are guided by the demands of their research questions rather than the constraints of their discipline. It was mainly at Chicago that I was exposed to exemplars of 'inter-disciplinary-thought-in-one-head' as in Schumpeter's *Capitalism, Socialism, and Democracy* (1942), especially his treatment of classical versus other forms of democracy. I was also introduced to Dahl and Lindblom's *Politics, Economics, and Welfare* (1953), and the work of Roberto Michels, Harold Lasswell, Hannah Arendt, Robert Merton, Edward Shils (whose classes and essays in social theory taught me much) and of course the classics by Durkheim, Weber and Marx. (I had already read Veblen's *The Theory of the Leisure Class* (1934) as a college freshman; I later learned that this institutional economist had influenced a great many other sociologists.)

By inclination and training I was attracted to such interdisciplinary scholars. Their work is 'basic' and yet 'policy-oriented' in the broad sense that it addresses the persistent problems of the human condition – hierarchy and equality, consensus and conflict, security and efficiency, participation and political legitimacy, the causes and consequences of the wealth of nations. It also addresses recurrent problems of modern society: the breakdown and regeneration of democracy, social rights and individual liberties, public interests and private troubles. To develop knowledge of these basic problems and dilemmas and their resolution is to provide a framework for shaping the public agenda.

My later research on the role of intellectuals and experts shows that the character of social science research and its effects on the public agenda and public policy depend upon the structure of the political economy in which it is financed and used. Hence, in the short run of, say, a generation or two, American social scientists have less steady influence on policy than their counterparts in several rich democracies where there is a tighter relationship between knowledge and power (Wilensky 1983, pp.61–8). But I also show that the long-term impact of ideas in the social sciences is substantial, even where a populist anti-intellectual spirit is most developed, as in the USA (Wilensky, 1967, Ch. 5). Social science theories are implicit in major policies and approaches of many political leaders.

I put this lesson about the policy relevance of basic interdisciplinary research to use in the early 1950s while I was administering a new Master's degree in Social Science and Industrial Relations at Chicago and writing *Industrial Relations: A Guide to Reading and Research* (Wilensky 1954). It was an effort to show how economists, political scientists and sociologists viewed the labour problem. At the time I was sharing an office at the Industrial Relations Center with labour economist Albert Rees and then labour historian Val Lorwin. These two friends took my ignorance of their fields as a challenge and ran the equivalent of Oxford tutorials for me. From Rees I learned that economics was not all foolish and I began some serious reading of economic theory and labour economics. From Lorwin I learned that history could be thematic and connect with social science. As the recent US labour attaché in France, Lorwin also shared with me his knowledge of France and Belgium. (When I later interviewed the *Chef de Cabinet du Roi* in Brussels he told me that there was only one English-speaking scholar who truly understood Belgium, Val Lorwin.)

This early exposure to comparative labour movements, comparative industrial relations, and, more generally, political economy was a felicitous entry point to the comparative research I did from the late 1960s on. For if anything is clear from my current study of nineteen rich democracies it is that the structure, function, and behaviour of a nation's labour movement mightily shape its path of political and economic development.

This initial journey through the social sciences gave me insight into the limitations of the disciplines as practised in American universities. In contrast to both classical nineteenth-century scholars and many European colleagues of our time (e.g. Hans Daalder, Arend Lijphart, Stein Rokkan and Fritz Scharpf), most American sociologists were narrowly specialized; they knew little about political structures, electoral systems, and behaviour. And most political scientists thought little about the social bases of behaviour. Although American political scientists talked much about social class and minority groups, many did not read sociological and anthropological literature on social structure and change. This is why they often adopted atomistic versions of group life in general and social and political structures in particular. (Today, under the label 'rational choice theory', a growing number of political scientists write of 'institutions', but conceive of them as no more than an aggregate of individual preferences, interests and goals, a conception diametrically opposed to the sociological tradition, a conception that misses what is most useful for analysing societies, communities, parties, interest groups, governments, nation states and their interaction.) For their part, economists were becoming more technical and narrow in their grasp of the political and social contexts of economic behaviour or were oblivious to these contexts.

These disciplinary prisons have opened up somewhat in the last twenty years or so. Because much of sociology penetrated political science in the postwar period there is now much more sophistication in conceptualizing social structure as a source of politics, as in the work of my colleagues in the political science department at Berkeley – including Nelson Polsby, Aaron Wildavsky, Ray Wolfinger, Robert Kagan, Herbert McClosky, Henry Brady, Andrew Janos, and David and Ruth Collier. Reinhard Bendix, of course, was a sociologist who, like me, migrated to the political science department. Similarly the postwar generation of economists in labour economics, public finance, economic history, and international economics were often open to sociological and political science perspectives.

At Chicago I was coming to appreciate the necessity of a careful mapping of social structure – economic organization, political organization and social organization. There was no shortage of theories about the direction of social change or assertions about the engines of change (technology, great men, culture, etc.) but there was a real shortage of useful classifications of structure. The crude dichotomies – status to contract, *Gemeinschaft* to *Gesellschaft*, primary to secondary – struck me as only a beginning. One cannot say anything about the causes, direction, rate, or amount of change without first describing the structures that are changing. For this task the advantages of interdisciplinary thinking at Chicago were substantial. Political sociologists who combine the perspectives of sociology and political science (like the late Morris Janowitz and Edward Shils, and Edward Banfield, Juan Linz and S.M. Lipset) are especially good at mapping and classifying attributes of social structure and culture that shape politics. Political economists such as Charles Lindblom who combine the perspectives of political science and economics and focus on the interplay of markets and politics are, in turn, especially good at generating hypotheses about the effects of different types of political economy on system performance. It is often in the interstices between the disciplines that we can find some of the most lively research questions, as the work of Weber, Durkheim and Schumpeter had amply demonstrated. After Chicago, my own work was increasingly an effort to combine the perspectives of political sociology and political economy in a continuing search for the shape of modern society.

Survey research at Michigan: tests of mass society theory

At Chicago I learned the valuable lesson that the search for problems worth studying, research questions worth exploring, and theories worth testing was more important than disciplinary boundaries, methods, techniques, or even answers. At Michigan for eight years I learned that with a little imagination almost any concept could be measured, almost any proposition could be tested. It was there that I launched my study of 'Work, Careers, and Social Integration' (1960) (the labour–leisure project), designed to test mass society theory – another effort that made me realize the necessity of cross-national comparison of institutions and the limits and uses of survey research for institutional analysis.

Mass society theory is a general theory of modern society inspired by a vision of the breakdown of social order or democracy or both. From de Tocqueville to Mannheim (1940) and other refugees from the Nazis, traditional mass society theorists have concentrated on two problems: (1) the debilitation of culture-bearing élites (and of the core values they sustain) brought on by their diminishing insulation from popular pressures; (2) the rise of the masses, who, for various reasons, are increasingly susceptible to demagogues and extremist movements, the carriers of fanatical faiths of race, nation and class. Although they vary in their depiction of the generating forces, these scholars tend to accent either the atrophy of primary and informal relations or the atrophy of self-governing secondary groups and associations. They also believe that the mass society develops a mass culture in which cultural and political values and beliefs tend to be homogeneous and fluid. In the middle and at the bottom – in the atomized mass – people think and feel alike; but thoughts and feelings, not being firmly anchored anywhere, are susceptible to fads and fashions. At the top, poorly-organized élites, themselves mass-oriented, become political and managerial manipulators responding to short-term pressures; they fail to maintain standards and thereby encourage the spread of populism in politics, mass tastes in culture – in short, a 'sovereignty of the unqualified' (see Selznick 1951; Kornhauser 1959; Wilensky 1964a).

Although I had doubts about the generalizability of this theory, I thought that two research tasks should be pursued: (1) development of a discriminating typology of social relations and organizations focused on their integrative or disintegrative potential; (2) location of the sources of the vulnerability of even stable democracies to mass society tendencies.

The research design aimed not only to gauge the degree of standardization of attitudes and behaviour across social groups and classes but also to permit projections of social-political trends based on comparisons of vanguard and rearguard groups at the same stage of the life cycle and the same social level: for example, college graduates of growing mass institutions vs. graduates of élite colleges, which produce a declining percentage of the educated. On the basis of 1,354 long survey interviews in the Detroit metropolitan area with a cross-section of what I defined as the 'middle mass' (lower middle class and upper working class), selected professional groups (professors, lawyers, engineers) in various work settings, and two samples of the underclass (down-and-out whites and blacks) I was able to test the relative importance of various forms of social differentiation as sources of social solidarity, personal identity and political behaviour. The data covered the entire daily round. I asked the Durkheimian question: as sources of ties to the larger community and society, how important is the vitality of participation in primary groups and mediating groups of various kinds relative to workplace, occupational and religious communities, and other forms of social differentiation? Could these variations in the vitality of participation explain patterns of alienation from or attachment to the political and economic institutions?

From twenty-six articles of mine (a typical one is 'Mass Society and Mass Culture', 1964a) and from the findings of several dissertations and articles by my students, I concluded: (1) As predictors of lifestyle, cultural tastes, ideology and politics, sex, age, and class are far weaker than variables that represent positions in organized groups, namely religion, types of education, work, and career. (2) As sources of social and political behaviour all of these older forms of social differentiation (churches, schools, workplaces and career patterns) remain important. But they are slowly giving way to stronger forces of the centralized state, mass communications, mass education, and mobility. (3) In 1960 there was already a striking standardization of culture: American television, the most 'massified' of the mass media, had become central to the leisure routines of majorities at every educational level. Although some differences in media exposure and response remained – reflecting an occupation supported by an occupational community, a religion buttressed by a religious community – the main story was the small size of those differences. The General Motors executive, his foreman in an auto plant, the clerk in the front office, the worker on the assembly line, and the unemployed underdog in the slum, I found, were bound together by the common culture of the TV network news, advertising slogans, situation comedies, and detective-police-adventure shows. (4) This cross-sectional snapshot reflected a paradox of the simultaneous growth of structural differentiation – the increasing specialization by occupation, industry, and workplace noted by all students of modernization – and cultural uniformity. I speculated that the former would give way to the latter. (5) For those concerned about the vitality of modern democracy, the most interesting and seldom-noted finding of this 'mass society' study was as follows:

What takes place in the economy and locality – work, consumption, and participation in formal associations – forms coherent styles of life, one of which I have come to label 'Happy Good Citizen-Consumer'. The style includes these pluralist-industrial traits: strong attachment to the community (supporting increased school taxes, contributing generously to churches and charity, thinking of the neighborhood as one's 'real home', voting in elections); consumer enthusiasm (planning to buy or to replace many luxury possessions); optimism about national crises; a strong belief that distributive justice prevails (feeling that jobs are distributed fairly). It also involves long hours at gratifying work, little or no leisure malaise; wide-ranging, stable secondary ties and, to some extent, wide-ranging, stable primary ties – the very model of a modern pluralist citizen. But this benign pattern of work, consumption, and participation is independent of participation in and feelings about mass culture. And both happy good citizenry and the uses of the mass media are more or less independent of approaches to national politics – or at least go together in ways not anticipated in received theory. Thus, the good citizen-consumers tend to be unusually prone to personality voting (party-switching, ticket-splitting), dependent on the media for opinions on issues, susceptible to advertising and to mass behavior generally (e.g. they score high on a measure of susceptibility to manipulation by the media in politics and consumption). Men who have confidence in the major institutions of American society distrust 'TV and radio networks'; men who trust the media distrust other institutions. Finally, men whose social relations are stable tend to have fluid party loyalties. *To be socially integrated in America is to accept propaganda, advertising, and speedy obsolescence in consumption.* The fact is that those who fit the image of pluralist man in the pluralist society also fit the image of mass man in the mass society. Any accurate picture of the shape of modern society must accommodate these ambiguities. (Wilensky 1964a, pp.195–6)

This attempt to test mass society theory and arrive at some reformulation of industrial society and mass society theories inspired my shift to more thoroughly cross-national research. I realized that data on individuals in one metropolis – however hard one tried to situate them in the groups and organizations they belong to and however hard one tried to embed them in analysis of big social trends – could not substitute for systematic cross-national comparison and actual data on time trends focused on the institutions and organizations themselves. I spent the next decades gathering such data on nineteen rich democracies – the universe of democracies that have a million or more population and are in the upper sixth of countries ranked by per capita GNP.[4]

Testing four theories of modern society: convergence, mass society, democratic corporatism and post-industrialism

In my research and teaching through all those Michigan and Berkeley years I was continually searching for the shape of modern society. I asked these questions: As rich countries get richer do they become more alike in social structure, culture, and politics? Do the changes labelled industrialism overcome the differences among societies labelled authoritarian, totalitarian and democratic? If there is convergence, what specific attributes of structure, culture, and politics are becoming more alike? If they are *not* converging, if rich countries are following different paths of economic and political development, what are the differences and do the differences remain stable or become larger? Can we specify the divergent paths? My first book on this subject was *Industrial Society and Social Welfare* with C.N. Lebeaux (1958, enlarged 1965); it tried to push convergence theory as far as possible while taking some account of American exceptionalism.

For specifying the *divergent* paths of development and accounting for the remaining differences among countries equally rich I have found parts of mass society theory and a theory of democratic corporatism useful.[5] In so far as 'post-industrial' theory deals with the role of experts and intellectuals it poses good questions but is very limited as a picture of general economic, political and cultural change. For instance, the idea that modern populations embrace 'post-materialist' values in a post-industrial society (Inglehart 1977, 1990; Huntington 1974) is dubious; they remain overwhelmingly and consistently concerned with job and social security, equality of opportunity, family income, and safety that is, protection against crime (Wilensky 1981a, pp.255–62). My current research confirms those themes.

In recent decades I have been playing convergence theory against mass society theory and theories of corporatism in an effort to explain similarities and differences among rich countries as they became richer. My aim is to synthesize these theories and arrive at a valid picture of modern society and politics.

In 1970, from a base in Sweden, I began the nineteen-country project that has occupied me since, *Tax and Spend: The Political Economy and Performance of Rich Democracies* (the title of the current book I am writing). Over the next twenty years I assembled a database bearing on these three theories: I completed interviews with over 400 politicians, government health and welfare officials, experts in budgeting and taxation, and labour and employer negotiators in fifteen of the nineteen rich democracies, meeting informants from the other four as I participated in international conferences and gathered quantitative data and documents covering the period 1950–90, with some historical data going further back.

Although theorists of corporatist democracy (Philippe Schmitter, Gerhard Lehmbruch, Peter Katzenstein) or more generally of various types of bargaining structures are not addressing a new problem, they have done much to revitalize an older tradition in political science – that is, the analysis of the interaction of parties, interest groups, public bureaucracies, and political élites (see Almond 1990, Ch. 7 on the work of Ehrmann, Dahl, Rokkan and others). Just as sociology has neglected a basic task for students of group life – a taxonomy of types of social groups that is useful for explaining the behaviour of groups (Wilensky 1961b) – so political science needs a more effective mapping of types of interest groups, political parties, nation states, and bureaucracies that comprise the polity. Students of corporatism have begun the difficult task of cross-national comparison of the structure, functions, and behaviour of trade associations and employer associations, professional associations, farm organizations and labour federations.

In an early empirical test of corporatist theory going beyond a few countries (1976), I focused on 'tax-welfare backlash' – national public resistance to the welfare state indicated by social-political movements and parties that express anti-taxing, anti-social spending, anti-bureaucratic sentiments; achieve electoral success; and persist for substantial periods. I found that corporatist bargaining arrangements dampen tax-welfare backlash because they produce balanced tax systems and spend in consensual ways: they avoid too much reliance on highly visible taxes (income taxes and property taxes on households) and highly visible spending (means-tested benefits targeted to the 'undeserving poor') and instead move toward mass-based consumption taxes, social security taxes, and universal categorical benefits. It is not the *level* of taxes and spending that provokes strong tax revolts but their structure. In subsequent research I explored the ideological and structural sources of corporatism and its effects. I showed that its three main roots were proportional representation, cumulative Catholic party power and to a lesser extent, left party power (e.g. 1976, p.37; 1981b) although the effect of late industrialization on industrial and union structures also plays a part. Regarding real welfare outputs, I find that democratic corporatism (and the policies these negotiated economies typically produce) fosters good economic performance, political legitimacy, income equality, reduced poverty, and increased safety and security with only limited tax-welfare backlash (e.g. 1981b, 1983, 1993; Wilensky and Turner 1987; and work in progress).

The mass society model has the great merit of focusing on these questions: Under what conditions do various types of social relations – primary, informal, or secondary – effectively mediate between the person and the larger community and society? How do variations in density of organization, types of organization, and the vitality of participation in them, affect alienation from or attachment to major institutions? How do these things affect the prospects for social order and political democracy? Unfortunately, before a discriminating typology of social relations and organizations focused on their integrative or disintegrative potential was developed, interest in mass society theory waned. Discussions of corporatism have revived these classic questions to good effect.

At the level of the nation state, all independent self-governing organizations – so central as mediating forces in mass society theory – cannot function equally well as either buffers against state coercion and manipulation or as bases for aggregating and expressing interests and facilitating accommodation among warring parties. As a structural base for social consensus and democracy, political parties, churches and unions, with their broad mass bases, representing enduring divisions of values and interests, doubtless have an edge over bird-watchers' societies, gay rights organizations, or groups organized against pornography, because they are great mixers of age grades, genders, ethnic groups and classes. (Even unions, because they everywhere move toward multi-industrial, multi-craft models, are mixers of classes and occupational groups.) More important, local and national unions of the United States or the United Kingdom, even where they are strong and well-organized, have less integrative potential than more inclusive unions with tighter ties to a central labour federation characteristic of corporatist democracies. It is this failure to present an adequate account of the structure and mediating potential of churches, unions, employer associations, and voluntary associations that limits mass society theory's capacity to understand social change and public policy among rich democracies. Its accent on the rising power of the media in politics and culture, however, remains valid. Indeed, political science has recently resurrected mass society theory under the labels 'party decomposition' or 'party decline', giving proper weight to the atrophy of mediating associations and the ascendance of the media.

The model of corporatist democracy is complementary to the mass society model: it enables us to pinpoint countries most and least vulnerable to tendencies predicted by mass society theory. The decline of political parties as consensus-builders is not yet a universal trend among modern democracies. In fact, corporatist bargaining structures may reduce the rate of decline of political parties or even reverse the trend. When I first applied a model of democratic corporatism in my research, I shared the view that a negotiated economy was an end run around the seeming chaos of multi-party systems (Wilensky 1976, p.37) – functional blocs substituting for weak and fluid parties in parliamentary systems with proportional representation. But as more cross-national data became available on party decomposition, I have since concluded that the reverse process is more likely, with corporatism in symbiotic relationship to parties. In corporatist countries the constituency base for major parties and coalitions includes strong and relatively disciplined, co-ordinated unions, employer federations, farm organizations and churches, whose relations to parties are tight and whose consultation with government bureaucracies is frequent and easy. In turn, the quasi-public associations find parties helpful in mobilizing support for peak bargains. Together both parties and economic power blocs help governing parties or coalitions control the policy agenda, framing media content and containing single-issue groups and other particularistic pressures. By contrast, the more numerous, fragmented and decentralized interest groups of least-corporatist democracies open the way for dominance by the media in symbiotic relation to single-issue movements and political demagogues, thereby hastening the decline of parties and the development of a mass society (Wilensky 1983). In the absence of alternative conflict resolution mechanisms, lawyers and judges, as they try to redress injustice and uphold the law, also enter the vacuum, creating a pattern of adversary legalism, adding to political polarization.[6]

The comparative data on party decline or party dealignment (as opposed to mere realignment) are still quite limited, but what we have confirm my theme (see e.g. Reiter's 1989 summary of eleven measures of dealignment in six countries and Franklin, Mackie and Valen's 1992 analysis of electoral change in sixteen countries). With few exceptions, from the 1960s through the 1980s corporatist democracies experienced later and less party decomposition than other democracies (e.g. West Germany, Norway, and France, little or no decline; Sweden and the Netherlands, some decline; the USA and the UK, the most decline).

Although types of political economy – corporatist, corporatist-without-labour, and fragmented and decentralized (and therefore more vulnerable to massification) – explain diverse policy mixes and political responses to the common problems of rich democracies (e.g. tax structures, social policies, protest movements) as well as variations in real welfare outputs, there is considerable convergence in their structures and the values rooted in those structures. At the top of the agenda for comparative research on advanced industrial societies in my view is the integration of the theories I have sketched. My own strategy is to see how far you can go with convergence theory and then use the other two theories to explain the remaining differences. This led me to the following conclusions.

What is truly modern about modern society are seven major structural and demographic shifts rooted in industrialization, especially at a level of economic development where about three-quarters of the labour force is no longer in agriculture and 40 per cent or 50 per cent of adult women are at work in non-domestic settings. (In 1910 the USA still had almost a third of its labour force in farming, about where France was in 1946, Japan in the 1950s, and the USSR in the mid-1960s.) With some variation in timing, these convergent tendencies among the currently rich democracies include the following:

1. *Changes in the kinship system* – an accent on the nuclear household, an increase in female non-agricultural labour-force participation, a decline in fertility rates and family size, a push for gender equality, increasing family breakup rates, and strong government responses in the form of family policies. Several of my articles dealt with these developments (e.g. 1961b, 1968, 1981a). My current work explains national differences and similarities in government responses to the common problem of family change (e.g. Wilensky 1990).

2. *The push for equality among minority groups*, especially those based on descent and early socialization (race, religion, ethnicity-language). If there were once large differences among affluent countries, because of the social homogeneity of some, these differences slowly diminish with the postwar migrations of economic and political refugees. Ethnic resurgence is a recurrent phenomenon (Allardt 1979) but the organization of minorities and openness to ethnic claims have probably increased in modern democracies and government responses have become similar – affirmative action of one kind or another. A series of articles tests the theory of structural and cultural integration (e.g. Wilensky and Ladinsky 1967; Wilensky and Lawrence 1979). Typical was 'From Religious Community to Occupational Group: Structural Assimilation among Professors, Lawyers, and Engineers' (Wilensky and Ladinsky 1967), followed by further publications by my students on Canada and the USA. The theory of consociational democracy, closely related to corporatist theory, explains some of the variations in government response to minority/majority cleavage (Lijphart 1968a; Daalder 1974); but among rich democracies, the differences in public policy, I think, are lessening.

3. *The rise of mass higher education and the increasing dominance of mass media of communication and entertainment in culture and politics.* My labour–leisure project analysed the impact of these trends (e.g. 1960, 1961d, 1964a, 1964b). Although large national differences in media dominance persist because of differences in the control, financing and organization of the media, here again the differences, rooted in types of political economy, have recently diminished.

The national differences include marked contrasts in the role of public broadcasting networks and their financial base (the licence fee for a TV set in Japan and most of Europe buys a large public-interest presence) and related variation in cultural, educational and news content of television and radio, in hours of broadcasting (non-stop in the USA) and in the amount and kind of advertising. Similar differences appear in restrictions on the media role in campaigns; almost all rich democracies prohibit or limit paid political advertising and have much shorter election campaigns than the USA; France even bans stage props and other gimmicks. However, the recent commercialization of large segments of broadcasting in several countries; the decline of licence-fee revenue; the increase in cross-national access that comes with the new cable and satellite technology and multi-channel expansion; the earlier development and technological edge of American producers of film, television, music, and press services (AP and UP) – all of these combine to reduce the national differences. The cultural mission, assurance and pride of public broadcasting authorities in Europe are fading; the prestige newspapers are in some measure aping the tabloids. The media are indeed becoming American.

Regarding education, convergence is pervasive. Despite remaining national differences in access, standards and performance, as well as degree of centralization, teacher participation and unionization, and vocational emphasis, schools have moved toward a common mould, while diversified mass higher education, pioneered in America, is spreading, driven by both the skill demands of a modern economy and rising mass aspirations (Wilensky and Lawrence 1979).

4. *The increasing number and perhaps influence of experts and intellectuals.* Men of knowledge have always interacted with men of power, as Machiavelli's classic, *The Prince*, reminds us. But in modern society the demand for their services is more widespread and their impact more obvious. My work here is mainly in three books, from *Intellectuals in Labor Unions* (1956b) to *Organizational Intelligence. Knowledge and Policy in Government and Industry* (1967) and *The Uses of Sociology* (with Lazarsfeld and Sewell, 1967). They applied organizational theory to the problem of the role of experts with only a couple of chapters on the effect of national variations in political, economic, and cultural context. Through more systematically-comparative research on nineteen countries (Wilensky 1983; Wilensky *et al.* 1985) I have concluded that types of political economy powerfully shape the interplay of intellectuals and politicians. More corporatist democracies encourage stronger links between knowledge and power – a dialectic of expertise, a rational-responsible bias which itself is a force for accommodation among competing interest groups. It is ironic that a general theory of post-industrialism accenting the rise of experts in command of theoretical knowledge (Bell 1973), derived largely from US data, applies least well to the United States and other decentralized and fragmented political economies (Australia, the UK, Canada, New Zealand) and best to such corporatist democracies as Sweden, Norway, Austria, Belgium, the Netherlands and Germany. In the latter, experts and intellectuals are located in national policy networks of centralized labour federations, employer federations and at least moderately centralized governments with effective channels for steady policy deliberation and implementation. Japan accomplishes the same linkage of experts to policy without including labour. In contrast, while the USA has an abundance of experts and intellectuals, their voices are typically cast to the winds – or drowned out by the media noise; the relation of knowledge to power is erratic, a factor in the wilder swings of policy, as in the frequent reversals of tax policy in the USA and UK in recent decades.

5. *The changing organization of work and the class structure.* There is solid evidence of convergence in the occupational and industrial composition of the labour force and even in some of the ways in which work is organized and work incentives are structured. Social scientists have built elaborate theories of class struggle and class realignments from data on such trends. For instance, patterns of industrial conflict evidence some convergence. A finding that has stood up is Kerr and Siegel's discovery, in their 1954 cross-national comparison of the inter-industry propensity to strike, that workers who are socially and geographically isolated from the containing society and given unpleasant work to do – miners, longshoremen, loggers, lumbermen, maritime workers – have relatively high strike rates whatever the political-cultural context (Kerr and Siegel 1954). If by technological and social change they become less isolated and their work improves – the current case – their strike rates decline. On the other hand, large national differences persist: industrial conflict varies greatly according to whether the locus of conflict is the local industrial level or national politics (Hibbs 1978), as in the tripartite bargaining arrangements of corporatist democracies. In short, the total

volume of strikes varies by type of political economy but occupational rates vary by the nature of the work and hence the level of economic development.

In the postwar period, perhaps a third of published sociology consisted of the analysis of social stratification. My own research by 1960 concluded: that 'class', 'class consciousness' and 'class conflict' were among the vaguest and most misleading concepts in social science; that whether we analyse social class in Marxian or non-Marxian terms, a clearly defined 'middle class' or 'working class' in the USA and increasingly in other countries no longer existed, if it ever did; and that 'much behavior and many attitudes said to be rooted in class are instead a matter of race, religion, and ethnic origin, education, age, and stage in the family life cycle ... Almost any of these [categories] display more homogeneity of behavior and belief' than does social class (Wilensky 1966a, pp.12–13; cf. 1960, 1961a, 1961b, 1961c, 1964c, 1966b). To scholars who closely study occupational groups and workplaces and trends in the labour force these ideas were easy to understand, but for decades they were ignored by sociologists and many others who write about class conflict.

My work in this area accented the persistence, importance and discrete social-political character of self-employment and its contrast with bureaucratic employment; and the continued importance of such distinctions as orderly careers vs. chaotic work histories and blocked mobility (types of cumulative work experience that cut across classes) as sources of attachment to or estrangement from society, community and politics (e.g. 1961a, 1966b). I also emphasized the emergence of a 'middle mass' brought about by the increasing similarity of behaviour, attitudes, and lifestyles of lower middle and upper working classes (and their difference from college-educated upper middle strata above and the poor below) as a potential source of institutional estrangement and political disaffection (e.g. 1961a, 1975, pp.116–18). The outcomes – sustained tax revolts and xenophobic movements vs. brief outbursts – again depend on national variations in mobilizing structures (e.g. national differences in the structure, functions and interaction of labour federations, employer associations, professions, political parties and governments).

By the end of the 1980s, cross-national research on party decline and political behaviour had abundantly confirmed the declining significance of social class. Scattered data on tax revolts and the rise of populist demagogues confirmed the idea of the revolt of the 'middle mass'. For instance, Perot voters in the USA in 1992 were concentrated in the lower middle and upper working classes, as were voters for Le Pen in France, the *Lega Lombarda* in Italy and the xenophobic anti-immigrant parties in Germany, who evidence similar anxieties and fears. While they share a common social base, such protest movements, of course, are channelled differently in different types of political economy.

6. *The welfare state.* In three books (Wilensky and Lebeaux 1958; Wilensky 1975, 1985) and other publications, I analysed the development, content and effects of the welfare state. The social science reception of these books was pleasant but puzzling. What I argue in all three is that the welfare state 'is at once one of the great structural uniformities of modern society and, paradoxically, one of its most striking diversities'. Convergence theory can explain the presence of 'seven or eight health and welfare programmes with similar content and expanded funding – even some convergence in methods of financing and administration' (1975, pp.2–3); economic level and related

demographic and organizational correlates account for these similarities whatever the regime type or élite ideologies (collectivistic, individualistic, etc.), but:

> To understand major *differences* in welfare-state effort, administration, and output ... we must look not to these broad, self-cancelling, ideological themes but to more concrete, sharper contrasts in social, political, and economic organization. For at the level of affluence achieved by the twenty-two richest countries in the world, we find both convergence and divergence, unexplained by a model covering the time span of a century and embracing Sweden and Tunisia, Denmark and Bulgaria, the USSR and India. (1975, p.49)

In the rest of the same book – and in twenty years of subsequent research testing hypotheses presented therein – I spelled out theories (including corporatist theory and mass society theory) that explain the specific differences. Yet this 1975 book is still repeatedly cited as a case of 'the logic-of-industrialism theory' counterposed to the work of theorists who are 'bringing the state back in', showing the importance of political forces. I attribute this distortion to three recent developments. First, we see the intensification of product differentiation in a large and growing social science professoriate; some of the more ambitious young scholars, confronting a burgeoning literature, are moved to announce that their elders have missed the boat. Second, some departments in some universities, even leading ones, have succumbed to politicization of their recruitment and evaluation processes and curriculum content. That tendency reduces the hold of universalistic scholarly standards, so remaining true to the text of those you cite, which takes time, is a less compelling strategy for achieving success. The final reason for the distortion of the work of scholars who embrace more than one theory at a time is a strange incapacity to tolerate the obvious: a theory of convergence that might explain big differences in social expenditures by economic level when comparing sixty-four countries cannot explain differences among nineteen equally rich democracies. This requires complementary theories, which the same author might entertain. Comparative research on the welfare state, like comparative politics generally, suffers from misleading controversies over 'political' vs. 'economic' theories that reflect the impulse to demolish straw men – a great waste of time and journal space.

What research on the welfare state in fact shows is that convergence theory is a powerful explanation of levels of social expenditure; that regime type and social mobilization better explain the timing of initiation of welfare-state programmes in industrial societies from Bismarck to World War I (although no one has taken the trouble to examine age distribution in those years as an added explanation of programme demand), but once in place these programmes expand and converge. Remaining differences in programme content, generosity, administration, political and economic impact, can be explained by the interaction of electoral systems, cumulative Catholic party power and, to a lesser extent, left party power, which are the main determinants of corporatist bargaining arrangements; in turn, type of political economy (corporatist, corporatist-without-labour, and fragmented and decentralized) explains policy and political responses and real welfare outputs, including national differences in the rate of poverty and inequality.

7. *Polity.* Given the contrast between authoritarian, totalitarian and democratic regimes and the variety within each type, the polity at first glance may be the area of

least convergence; a high level of economic development may not be a decisive determinant of political systems. But the areas of most convergence – increased family break-up and gender equality, the push for equality among minority groups, the rise of mass education, the increasing number of intellectuals and experts, changes in social stratification and the organization of work, and rising social expenditures – may very well foster some convergence in politics. Students of comparative politics have already established that all democracies are market economies (Lindblom 1977 and others), and that at high levels of economic development internal collective political violence decreases (Gurr and Ruttenberg 1969; Gurr (ed.) 1980). More recently, modernization theory is being revived with a burgeoning literature on the democratic transition. It took the collapse of the Soviet empire – and the obvious shift of many NICs toward pluralism if not democracy and free markets – to turn social science attention to the older work on convergence theory. Much politically-inspired nonsense was written in the late 1960s and 1970s about the ethnocentrism of modernization theory or the conservatism of 'structural functional analysis' or the capitalist bias of theories of industrialism. Only part of this froth can be explained by the penetration of neo-Marxism in the academy, especially in the humanities and sociology. For with the politicization of academic life there was also a speed-up in the swings of intellectual fashion and moods. In the 1960s we saw an obsessive condemnation of the sickness and oppression of modern society or 'capitalism' and in the 1980s a wild exaggeration of the joys of the unfettered free market – both reminiscent of the nineteenth-century indictment and defence of the industrial revolution. Now we are witnessing a more fruitful revival of older theories of the roots of democracy and its alternatives and a more discriminating discussion of what markets do well or badly, what governments do well or badly, and what voluntary associations do well or badly. Fortunately, through it all a good many scholars continued to pursue their work, guided by the interaction of their theories and data, undeterred by intellectual fashion (e.g. Alex Inkeles, Arend Lijphart, Robert Dahl, Peter Katzenstein, Samuel Huntington and Peter Flora). As they analyse national paths of development, all these scholars continue to assess the relative importance of social, economic and political forces that shape the variety of system outcomes.

Lessons from my journey

On the basis of my research successes and failures and my observation of barriers to graduate-student learning in the social sciences, I would distil a few lessons others might find useful. Ignoring complexities I shall state them as aphorisms.

1. *Avoid two misleading dichotomies, 'quantitative vs. qualitative' and 'positivist vs. humanist'.* They get us nowhere. When I was writing a book on intelligence (1967) based on historical documents, case studies of intelligence failures, and a few conversations with intelligence agency managers, I obviously could not quantify much. When I studied the structure of taxes and spending in nineteen countries over time, there was no alternative to quantification. And to make sense of the numbers it was important to add interviews, case studies and comparative historical context. Methodological ideologies that counterpose qualitative and quantitative, etc. are an

excuse for remaining ignorant of relevant research using methods different from your own. As for the virtues of humanism and the vices of positivism – often rendered as left-humanist and right-positivist – these are not only gross oversimplifications but miss the point about values and social science. While all social science contains an element of ideology, especially in the choice of problems and even research questions, it is only an element. Systematic comparative research requires detachment from the passions of the moment; it demands the discipline to specify comparisons that can disconfirm your favourite propositions.

2. *When dealing with internal strains within various systems* – 'democratic corporatism is collapsing', 'American democracy is polarized and paralysed' – *do the job of systematic comparison*. Because all complex social-political systems evidence internal strains and in modern society consensus is difficult to achieve, the issue is which internal strains lead to most and least change, to most and least conflict, at what rate of change, in what direction, and why. Or in other words: What conditions foster sufficient social consensus to permit the public interest effective expression?

3. *Follow the problem; transcend disciplinary and sub-field boundaries.* As an itinerant academic I have repeatedly observed the conceptual confusion and loss that results from a reluctance to reach out for the best work in an adjacent field, as in the cases I have discussed – the counterposition of democratic corporatism and pluralism; the casual misapplication of 'social class' and 'class conflict'. In America such segmentation within and between disciplines is only partly a product of the sheer size of the academic establishment. Individual academics can and do roam across the lines, gaining analytical power in the process. More of them should feel free to do so, as our European colleagues typically have. Although it is safer and more comfortable to stay at home in one's discipline or sub-field, it is more invigorating to mix it up intellectually.

4. *Develop an immunity to intellectual fads and fashions.* Spend some time with the history of ideas; it will provide an anchor. It will prevent your pronouncing, with an air of breathless discovery, propositions embedded in the literature of 30 or 100 years ago. Nine-tenths of originality is bad memory; much of genius is hard work.

The best social science is produced by intellectuals working within traditions of social and political thought who steadily pursue their research interests over very long periods, broadening their comparisons over space and time.

Notes

1. This questioning stance of a 19-year-old had many sources but two, I think, were most important. The first was my family background: my parents were fiercely independent entrepreneurs (they owned a small mom-and-pop grocery store that went bankrupt in the Great Depression) and my mother had a highly-developed sense of irony. As American Jews they and I had the advantages and disadvantages of marginality, always between cultures and therefore able to see them with some detachment. The second source of my independence was my freshman-sophomore reading at Goddard College of Arthur Koestler and such iconoclasts as Thorstein Veblen, H.L. Mencken and George Orwell (among the favourite authors of my English literature professor), as well as numerous accounts of the failures of secular utopian communities.

2. Cuba because an officer on our base was supplying rum to officers' clubs in the Southeast. We would fly to Cuba on practice gunnery and bombing missions, park the plane at Batista

airfield and, when the weekend was over, find the B-17 filled with cases of rum for which I signed – my contribution to victory through air power. This had a direct effect on my later work: Air Force experience inspired the section of *Organizational Intelligence* (1967) on 'the power of preconceptions', an account of how the doctrine of precision bombing seized the minds of the American high command and persisted through the Vietnam war despite evidence of its ineffectiveness and the huge cost.

3. Robert Park, Chairman of Sociology, and his contemporary of the 1920s and 1930s, Charles Merriam, Chairman of Political Science, were the pre-war builders of these extraordinary departments.

4. This excludes tiny countries (Iceland, Luxembourg) and includes New Zealand with more than 3 million. In 1966, Israel and Ireland were the poorest of the nineteen rich democracies and still are. It is a common mistake in both the press and social science research to lump Greece, Portugal, Spain and Turkey together with these nineteen as 'OECD countries' and use averages that obscure the great range of development and behaviour within the category. In 1990, even after much catch-up, all but Spain were much poorer and had a much larger percentage of the labour force in agriculture than any of the nineteen modern affluent democracies. For studying similarities and differences among similarly rich democracies, the nineteen are the most appropriate universe. And for analysis of system performance the universe yields much more valid generalizations than any subset. For instance, if you conclude that lavish spending on the welfare state is a drag on postwar economic performance on the basis of comparison of Italy and Denmark with Japan and Switzerland, you have selected the four deviant cases: Italy and Denmark are big spenders with poor performance, the other two are lean spenders with good performance. The subset thus obscures the central tendency, a positive correlation for all nineteen rich democracies before 1974 and a mixed picture thereafter (big spenders after the two oil shocks retained an edge in growth and did no worse in controlling inflation and unemployment).

5. My model of corporatist democracy accents four interrelated tendencies in several modern political economies: (1) Bargaining channels develop for the interplay of strongly organized, usually centralized economic blocs, especially labour, employer, and professional associations with a centralized or moderately-centralized government obliged to consider their advice. (2) The peak bargains struck by such federations reflect and further a blurring of old distinctions between the public and the private. (3) These quasi-public peak associations bargain in the broadest national context rather than focusing only on labour market issues. (4) Consequently, social policy is absorbed into general economic policy, and chances for social consensus are enhanced. A variant is corporatism without full integration of labour – epitomized by Japan and France, with Switzerland as a marginal case (Wilensky 1976, 1983). And, of course, these types are sharply contrasted with the authoritarian corporatism of Mussolini, Franco or Perón. In much of the literature on democratic corporatism there is much conceptual muddiness and too little effort to frame propositions for systematic tests. First, there is a strong tendency to mix up attributes of structures (e.g. degrees of centralization or bureaucratization or oligarchy); processes of policy-making (e.g. stages of decision-making); the content of particular policies and programmes (e.g. incomes policies); policy implementation (effective or ineffective implementation) or effects (good or poor economic performance, more or less equality). The result: it is impossible to relate corporatism as structural attributes of political economy to policy processes, content, implementation and impact.

The second conceptual confusion is the recent tendency to counterpose democratic corporatism (or 'liberal corporatism') and 'pluralism', now lodged in the literature of comparative political economy. Students of American government and political behaviour who developed theories of pluralism would hardly recognize their work as rendered by scholars who see pluralism and corporatism as polar opposites. 'Pluralism' is a system in which many relatively autonomous groups representing a real division of values and interests compete for power within a nation state. Democracy is a system in which the people choose leaders through competitive elections made possible by a rule of law and freedom of association and related civil liberties. It follows that all democracies are pluralist and democratic corporatism is a sub-class of pluralist democracy. Comparativists could reread Robert Dahl and Stein Rokkan with profit. These conceptual confusions intensify the already severe difficulties of data collection and cross-national comparability familiar to everyone. They account for a few disagreements about which countries qualify as 'corporatist' although there is agreement about most. In my scheme the nineteen rich democracies are classified as follows: corporatist (Sweden, Norway, Austria, the Netherlands, Belgium, Finland and, in lesser degree, Denmark, Italy, Israel and, marginally, West Germany). A variant is corporatist without the full integration of labour (Japan, France and, marginally, Switzerland). Least corporatist democracies are the USA, the UK, Canada, Australia, New Zealand and Ireland.

6. In the early 1980s the top eight (of nineteen) democracies in lawyers as a percentage of the civilian labour force were Israel, the USA, Finland, Canada, the UK, New Zealand, Australia and Ireland; six of them are classified as least corporatist.

Bibliography

This bibliography lists references given in the text, and provides some further bibliographic references to major writings of authors who are treated in, or who have contributed to this volume.

Abrams, M. and Rose, R. (1960) *Must Labour Lose?* Harmondsworth: Penguin.

Alker, H.A. Jr., and Deutsch, K.W. (eds) (1973) *Mathematical Approaches to Politics.* Amsterdam: Elsevier.

Allardt, E. (1956) *Social struktur och politisk aktivitet.* Borgå: Söderströms.

Allardt, E. and Pesonen, P. (1960) 'Citizen Participation in Political Life: Finland', *International Social Science Journal*, vol. 12, pp.27–39.

Allardt, E. and Littunen, Y. (eds) (1964) *Cleavages, Ideologies, and Party Systems. Contributions to Comparative Political Sociology.* Helsinki/Turku: Transactions of the Westermarck Society/ Academic Bookstore.

Allardt, E. (1964a) 'Social Sources of Finnish Communism. Traditional and Emerging Radicalism', *International Journal of Comparative Sociology*, vol. 5, pp.49–72.

Allardt, E. (1964b) 'A Theory on Solidarity and Legitimacy Conflicts', in Allardt and Littunen, pp.78–96.

Allardt, E. (1966) 'Reactions to Social and Political Change in a Developing Society', *International Journal of Comparative Sociology*, vol. 7, pp.3–10.

Allardt, E. (1968) 'Emile Durkheim sein Beitrag zur politischen Soziologie', *Kölner Zeitschrift für Soziologie und Sozialpsychologie*, vol. 20, pp.1–16; also (1971) 'Emile Durkheim et la sociologie politique', in Birnbaum and Chazel, vol. 1, pp.15–37.

Allardt, E. and Rokkan, S. (eds) (1970) *Mass-Politics. Studies in Political Sociology.* New York: The Free Press.

Allardt, E. (1971) 'The Radical Vote and the Social Context. Traditional and Emerging Radicalism', in Eisenstadt, pp.490–7.

Allardt, E. (1975) *Att ha, att älska, att vara. Om välfärd i Norden.* Lund: Argos.

Allardt, E. (1979) *Implications of the Ethnic Revival in Modern, Industrialized Society.* Helsinki-Helsingfors: Societas Scientiarum Fennica.

Allardt, E. and Valen, H. (1981) 'Stein Rokkan. An Intellectual Profile', in Torsvik (ed.), pp.11–38.

Allardt, E. (1981) 'Ethnic Mobilization and Minority Resources', *Zeitschrift für Soziologie*, vol. 10, pp.427–37.

Allardt, E. and Miemois, K.J. (1982) 'A Minority in Both Centre and Periphery. An Account of the Swedish-speaking Finns', *European Journal of Political Research*, vol. 10, pp.265–92.

Allardt, E. (1990) 'Social Structure and Social Change in the Nordic Countries', in K. Härnqvist and N.E. Svensson, *Swedish Research in a Changing Society*. Hedemora: Gidlunds, pp.66–85.

Allardt, E. (1992) 'Qu'est-ce qu'une minorité linguistique?', in H. Giordan, *Les minorités en Europe. Droits linguistiques et droits de l'homme*. Paris: Éditions Kimé, pp.45–54.

Allardt, E. (1993) 'Having, Loving, Being. An Alternative to the Swedish Model of Welfare Research', in M.C. Nussbaum and A. Sen, *The Quality of Life*. Oxford: Clarendon Press, pp.88–94.

Allardt, E. (1995) 'The Europe of Scandinavia and Scandinavians', in Chehabi and Stepan (eds), pp.131–40.

Almond, G.A. (1938) *Wealth and Politics in New York City*. Ph.D dissertation, University of Chicago.

Almond, G.A. (1947) 'The Resistance and the Political Parties of Western Europe', *Political Science Quarterly*, vol. 62, pp.27–61.

Almond, G.A. (1948a) 'The Christian Parties of Western Europe', *World Politics*, vol. 1, pp.30–58.

Almond, G.A. (1948b) 'The Political Ideas of Christian Democracy', *Journal of Politics*, vol. 10.

Almond, G.A. (ed.) (1949) *The Struggle for Democracy in Germany*. Chapel Hill: University of North Carolina Press.

Almond, G.A. (1954) *The Appeals of Communism*. Princeton: Princeton University Press.

Almond, G.A. (1956) 'Comparative Political Systems', *Journal of Politics*, vol. 18, pp.391–409.

Almond, G.A. and Coleman, J.S. (eds) (1960) *The Politics of the Developing Areas*. Princeton: Princeton University Press.

Almond, G.A. and Verba, S. (1963) *The Civic Culture. Political Attitudes and Democracy in Five Nations*. Princeton: Princeton University Press.

Almond, G.A. and Bingham Powell, G. (1966) *Comparative Politics. A Developmental Approach*. Boston: Little, Brown.

Almond, G.A. (1970) *Political Development*. Boston: Little, Brown.

Almond, G.A., Flanagan, S. and Mundt, R. (eds) (1973) *Crisis, Choice, and Change: Historical Stories of Political Development*. Boston: Little, Brown.

Almond, G.A. (ed.) (1974) *Comparative Politics Today*. Boston: Little, Brown.

Almond, G.A. and Bingham Powell, G. (1978) *Comparative Politics. System, Process, and Policy*. Boston: Little, Brown.

Almond, G.A. and Verba, S. (eds) (1980) *The Civic Culture Revisited. An Analytical Study*. Boston: Little, Brown.

Almond, G.A., Chodorow, M. and Pearce, R.H. (eds) (1980) *Progress and Its Discontents*. Berkeley: University of California Press.

Almond, G.A. (1990) *A Discipline Divided. Schools and Sects in Political Science*. Newbury Park: Sage.

Almond, G.A., Sivan, E. and Appleby, S. (1995) 'Fundamentalism: Genus and Species', in G.A. Almond, E. Sivan and S. Appleby (eds) *Fundamentalism Comprehended*. Chicago: University of Chicago Press, pp.399–405.

Althusius, J. (1603) *Politica Methodice Digesta* (1st edn; 3rd edn 1614, with an introduction by C.J. Friedrich. Cambridge Mass.: Harvard University Press, 1932).

Ameller, M. (1964) *Les Questions. Instrument du Contrôle Parlementaire*. Paris: Librairie Générale de Droit et de Jurisprudence.

Andrews, W.G. (ed.) (1981) *International Handbook of Political Science*. London: Greenwood Press.

Apter, D.E. (1961) *The Political Kingdom in Uganda. A Study in Bureaucratic Nationalism*. Princeton: Princeton University Press.

Armengaud, A. (1961) *Les Populations de l'Est-Aquitaine au Début de l'Époque Contemporaine*. Paris: Mouton.

Armstrong, J. (1973) *The European Administrative Elite*. Princeton: Princeton University Press.

Aron, R. (1981) *Le spectateur engagé*. Paris: Julliard.

Arrow, K. (1951) *Social Choice and Individual Values*. New Haven: Yale University Press.

Arrow, K. (1967) 'Values and Collective Decision-making', in P. Laslett and G.W. Runciman (eds), *Philosophy, Politics, and Society*, 3rd series. New York: Barnes and Noble.

Badie, B. and Birnbaum, P. (eds) (1983) *Sociology of the State*. Chicago: University of Chicago Press.

Badie B. and Hermet, G. (1990) *Politique comparée*. Paris: Presses Universitaires de France.

Baer, M. *et al.* (eds) (1991) *Political Science in America. Oral Histories of a Discipline*. Lexington: University Press of Kentucky.

Banfield, E.C. (1958) *The Moral Basis of a Backward Society*. New York: The Free Press.

Barber, E. (ed.) (1995) *LSE on Freedom*. London: LSE Books.

Barents, J. (1961) *Political Science in Western Europe. A Trend Report*. London: Stevens.

Barth, F. (1969) *Ethnic Groups and Boundaries. The Social Organization of Culture Differences*. Oslo: Universitetsforlaget.

Beer, S.H. and Ulam, A. (eds) (1958) *Patterns of Government. The Major Political Systems of Europe*. New York: Random House.

Beer, S.H. (1965) *British Politics in the Collectivist Age*. New York: Knopf.

Bell, D. (1973) *The Coming of Industrial Society*. New York: Basic Books.

Berelson, B.R., Lazarsfeld, P.F. and McPhee, W.N. (1954) *Voting*. Chicago: University of Chicago Press.

Berg-Schlosser, D. and de Meur, G. (1994) 'Conditions of Democracy in Interwar Europe. A Boolean Test of Major Hypothesis', *Comparative Politics*, vol. 26, pp.253–79.

Berg-Schlosser, D. and Mitchell, J. (eds) (forthcoming) Vol. 1: *Conditions of Democracy in Europe 1919–1939: Systematic Case Studies*, Vol. 2: *Authoritarianism and Democracy in Europe 1919–1939: Comparative Analyses*. London: Macmillan.

Berger S. (ed.) (1981) *Organizing Interests in Western Europe. Pluralism, Corporatism and the Transformation of Politics*. Cambridge: Cambridge University Press.

Bergmann, J., Jacobi, O. and Müller-Jentsch, W. (1975) *Gewerkschaften in der Bundesrepublik. Gewerkschaftliche Lohnpolitik zwischen Mitgliederinteressen und Systemzwängen*. Frankfurt: Europäische Verlagsanstalt.

Berkowitz, L. (1962) *Aggression. A Social Psychological Analysis*. New York: McGraw-Hill.

Binder, L. *et al.* (1971) *Crises and Sequences in Political Development*. Princeton: Princeton University Press.

Birnbaum, P. (1969) *Sociologie de Tocqueville*. Paris: Presses Universitaires de France.

Birnbaum, P. (1970) *Le structure du pouvoir aux États-Unis*. Paris: Presses Universitaires de France.

Birnbaum, P. and Chazel, F. (1971a) *Sociologie politique*. Paris: Armand Colin, 2 vols.

Birnbaum, P. (1971b) 'Préface à la première réédition', E. Durkheim, *Le Socialisme*. Paris: Presses Universitaires de France.

Birnbaum, P. (1975) *La fin du politique*. Paris: Le Seuil.

Birnbaum, P. (1976a) 'Power Divorced from its Sources. A Critique of the Exchange Theory of Power', in B. Barry (ed.) *Power and Political Theory*. London: Wiley, pp.15–33.

Birnbaum, P. (1976b) 'La conception durkheimienne de l'État. L'apolitisme des fonctionnaires', *Revue Française de Sociologie*, vol. 17, pp.247–59.

Birnbaum, P., Lively, J. and Parry, G. (eds) (1978) *Democracy, Consensus and Social Contract*. London: Sage.

Birnbaum, P. and Vincent, J.M. (eds) (1978) *Critiques des pratiques politiques*. Paris: Galilée.

Birnbaum, P. (1979) *Le peuple et les gros. Histoire d'un mythe*. Paris: Grasset.

Birnbaum, P. (1980) 'The State in Contemporary France', in R. Scase (ed.) *The State in Western Europe*. London: Croom Helm, pp.94–114.

Birnbaum, P. (1981) *The Heights of Power*. Chicago: University of Chicago Press.

Birnbaum, P. (1982) *La logique de l'État*. Paris: Fayard.

Birnbaum, P. (1985a) *Les élites socialistes au pouvoir*. Paris: Presses Universitaires de France.

Birnbaum, P. (1985b) *Dimensions du pouvoir*. Paris: Presses Universitaires de France.

Birnbaum, P. (1985c) 'Anti-Semitism and Anti-Capitalism in Modern France', in F. Malino and B. Wasserstein (eds) *The Jews in Modern France*. Hanover: Brandeis University Press, pp.214–23.

Birnbaum, P. (1987) 'France. Polity with a Strong State', in M. Heper (ed.) *The State and Public Bureaucracies*. New York: Greenwood, pp.73–88.

Birnbaum, P. (1988) *States and Collective Action*. Cambridge: Cambridge University Press.

Birnbaum, P. and Leca, J. (eds) (1992a) *On Individualism, Theories and Methods*. Oxford: Clarendon Press.

Birnbaum, P. (1992b) *Antisemitism in Modern France*. Oxford: Blackwell.

Birnbaum, P. (1992c) 'Tocqueville and the Historical Sociology of the State', in E. Nolla (ed.) *Liberty, Equality, Democracy*. New York: New York University Press, pp.91–102.

Birnbaum, P. (1992d) 'Particularism versus Universalism within a Strong State. The Case of the French Civil Servant', in R. Tostendahl (ed.) *State Theory and State History*. London: Sage, pp.223–37.

Birnbaum, P. (1993a) *'La France aux Français'. Histoire des haines nationalistes*. Paris: Le Seuil.

Birnbaum, P. (1993b) 'Conflit', in R. Boudon (ed.) *Traité de Sociologie*. Paris: Presses Universitaires de France, pp.227–61.

Birnbaum, P. (1993c) 'Nouveaux mouvements sociaux et types d'États', in F. Chazel (ed.) *Action collective et changement social*. Paris: Presses Universitaires de France, pp.163–76.

Birnbaum, P. (ed.) (1994a) *La France de l'Affaire Dreyfus*. Paris: Gallimard.

Birnbaum, P. (1994b) *L'Affaire Dreyfus. La République en péril*. Paris: La Découverte/Gallimard.

Birnbaum, P. (1995a) *Destins Juifs. De la Révolution française à Carpentras*. Paris: Calmann-Lévy.

Birnbaum, P. and Katznelson, I. (eds) (1995b) *Paths of Emancipation. Jews, States and Citizenship*. Princeton: Princeton University Press.

Birnbaum, P. (1996) *Jews of the Republic. A Political History of State Jews from Gambetta to Vichy*. Stanford: Stanford University Press.

Blok, A. (1985) *Anthropologische Perspektiven*. Stuttgart: Klett-Cotta.

Blondel, J. (1955) *As condicoes da vida politica no estado de Paraiba (Brazil)*. Fond: Vargas.

Blondel, J. (1963) *Voters, Parties, and Leaders*. Harmondsworth: Penguin.

Blondel, J. and Ridley, F. (1964) *Public Administration in France*. London: Routledge & Kegan Paul.

Blondel, J. (1969) *An Introduction to Comparative Government*. London: Weidenfeld & Nicolson.

Blondel, J. (1973) *Comparative Legislatures*. Englewood-Cliffs: Prentice-Hall.

Blondel, J. (1978) *Political Parties*. London: Wildwood.

Blondel, J. (1980) *World Leaders*. London: Sage.

Blondel, J. (1981) *The Discipline of Politics*. London: Butterworth.

Blondel, J. (1982) *The Organization of Governments*. London and Los Angeles: Sage.

Blondel, J. (1985) *Government Ministers in the Contemporary World*. London: Sage.

Blondel, J. (1987) *Political Leadership*. London: Sage.

Blondel, J. (1990) *Comparative Government*. Oxford: Allan.

Blondel, J. and Thiebault, J.L. (eds) (1991) *The Profession of Government Minister in Western Europe*. London: Macmillan.

Blondel, J. and Müller-Rommel, F. (1993) *Governing Together. The Extent and Limits of Joint Decision-Making in Western European Cabinets*. London: Macmillan.

Blondel, J. (1993) 'Rudolf Wildenmann', *ECPR News*, 5. Colchester: University of Essex, 2.

Blondel, J. (1996) 'The Government of France', in M. Curtis (ed.) *Comparative Politics*. New York: Harper and Row, 4th edn.

Bonger, W.A. (1934) *Problemen der Demokratie*. Amsterdam: Arbeiderspers.

Borre, O. and Stehouwer, J. (1968) *Partistyrke og social struktur 1960*. Aarhus: Akademisk Boghandel.

Bourgeois, L. (1896) *Solidarité*. Paris: A. Colin.

Bowie, R.R. and Friedrich, C.J. (eds) (1954) *Studies in Federalism*. Boston: Little, Brown.

Bracher, K.D. (1952) 'Auflösung einer Demokratie. Das Ende der Weimarer Republik als Forschungsproblem', *Faktoren der Machtbildung, Wissenschaftliche Studien zur Politik*. Berlin: Schriften des Instituts für Politische Wissenschaft.

Bracher, K.D. (1957) *Die Auflösung der Weimarer Republik. Eine Studie zum Problem des Machtverfalls in der Demokratie*. Stuttgart: Ring Verlag.

Brecht, A. (1959) *Political Theory. The Foundations of Twentieth-Century Political Thought*. Princeton: Princeton University Press.

Brown, A. and Gray, J. (1977) *Political Culture and Political Change in Communist States*. New York: Holmes & Meier.

Bryce, J. (1921), *Modern Democracies*. London: Macmillan, 2 vols.

Brzezinski, Z. and Huntington, S. (1963), *Political Power: USA/USSR*. New York: The Viking Press.

Burdeau, G. (1959) 'La conception du pouvoir selon la Constitution du 4 Octobre 1958', *Revue Française de Science Politique*, vol. 9, pp.88–99.

Buthelezi Commission (1982) *The Requirements for Stability and Development in KwaZulu and Natal*. Durban: H and H Publications.

Butler, D.E. and Rose, R. (1960) *The British General Election of 1959*. London: Macmillan.

Caiden, N. and Wildavsky, A. (1974) *Planning and Budgeting in Poor Countries*. New York: John Wiley.

Cambó, F. (1982) *Meditacions. Dietari (1936–1940)*. Barcelona: Alpha.

Campbell, A., Converse, P.E., Miller, W.E. and Stokes, D.E. (1960) *The American Voter*. New York: John Wiley.

Campbell, D.T. and Stanley, J. (1963) *Experimental and Quasi-Experimental Design*. Boston: Houghton-Mifflin.

Campbell, J.L., Hollingsworth, J.R. and Lindberg, L. (eds) (1991) *Governance of the American Economy*. Cambridge: Cambridge University Press.

Cassese, S. and Wright, V. (forthcoming) *La Restructuration de l'État en Europe*. Paris: La Découverte.

Castles, F.G. and Wildenmann, R. (eds) (1986) *Vision and Realities of Party Government*. Berlin: De Gruyter.

Chapman, B. and Potter, A. (1974) *W.J.M.M.: Political Questions. Essays in Honour of W.J.M. Mackenzie*. London: Manchester University Press.

Chehabi, H.E. and Stepan, A. (eds) (1995) *Politics, Society and Democracy. Comparative Studies: Essays in Honor of Juan J. Linz*. Boulder, Col.: Westview Press.

Chester, D.N. and Bowring, N. (1962) *Questions in Parliament*. Oxford: Clarendon Press.

Chester, D.N. (1975) 'Political Studies in Britain: Recollections and Comments', *Political Studies*, vol. 23, pp.48–75.

Chubb, B. (1970) *The Government and Politics of Ireland*. Stanford: Stanford University Press.

Clausen, S. (1956) *Omrids af Statskundskab*. Copenhagen: Gyldendal.

Clay, L.D. (1950) *Decision in Germany*. Garden City: Doubleday.

Cohen, M.R. and Nagel, E. (1934) *An Introduction to Logic and Scientific Method*. New York: Harcourt and Brace.

Coker, F.W. (1934) *Recent Political Thought*. New York: Appleton-Century.

Coleman, J. (1965) *Education and Political Development*. Princeton: Princeton University Press.

Coleman, W. and Jacek, H. (eds) (1989) *Regionalism, Business Interests and Public Policy*. London: Sage.

Coppedge, M. and Reinicke, W. (1988), 'A Scale of Polyarchy', in R.D. Gastil (ed.) *Freedom in the World. Political Rights and Liberties, 1987–1988*. Lanham: University Press of America, pp.101–25.

Coppedge, M. and Reinicke, W. (1990), 'Measuring Polyarchy', in *Studies in Comparative International Development*, vol. 25, pp.51–72.

Cornford, F.M. (1908) [1964] *Microcosmographia Academica. Being a Guide for the Young Academic Politician*. London: Bowes & Bowes.

Coser, L.A. (1965) 'The Stranger in the Academy', in L.A. Coser (ed.) *Georg Simmel*. Englewood Cliffs: Prentice Hall, pp.29–39.

Crick, B. (1959) *The American Science of Politics*. Berkeley: University of California Press.

Crozier, M. (1964) *The Bureaucratic Phenomenon*. Chicago: University of Chicago Press. London: Tavistock.

Czada, R. and Schmidt, M. (eds) (1993) *Verhandlungsdemokratie, Interessenvermittlung, Regierbarkeit. Festschrift für Gerhard Lehmbruch*. Opladen: Westdeutscher Verlag.

Daalder, H. (1953) 'Nederland en de Wereld 1940–1945', *Tijdschrift voor Geschiedenis*, vol. 66, pp.170–200.

Daalder, H. (1955) 'Parties and Politics in the Netherlands', *Political Studies*, vol. 3, pp.1–16.

Daalder, H. (1960) *Organisatie en Reorganisatie van de Britse Regering 1914–1958*. Assen: Van Gorcum.

Daalder, H. (1962a) *The Role of the Military in the Emerging Countries*. The Hague: Mouton.

Daalder, H. (1962b) 'Capitalism, Colonialism and the Underdeveloped Areas. The Political Economy of (Anti-)Imperialism', in E. de Vries (ed.) *Essays on Unbalanced Growth. A Century of Disparity and Convergence*. The Hague: Mouton, pp.133–65.

Daalder, H. (1963) *Cabinet Reform in Britain 1914–1963*. Stanford: Stanford University Press. Oxford: Oxford University Press, 1964.

Daalder, H. (1964) *Leiding en lijdelijkheid in de Nederlandse politiek*. Assen: Van Gorcum.

Daalder, H. (1966a) 'The Netherlands. Opposition in a Segmented Society', in Dahl (ed.), pp.188–236.

Daalder, H. (1966b) 'Parties, Elites and Political Developments in Western Europe', in LaPalombara and Weiner (eds), pp.43–77.

Daalder, H. (1966c) 'Government and Opposition in the New States', *Government and Opposition*, vol. 1, pp.205–26.

Daalder, H. (1968) 'Imperialism', *Encyclopedia of the Social Sciences*. New York: Macmillan and The Free Press, vol. 7, pp.101–7.

Daalder, H. (1971a) 'Cabinets and Party Systems in Ten Smaller European Democracies', *Acta Politica*, vol. 6, pp.282–303.

Daalder, H. (1971b) 'On Building Consociational Nations. The Cases of the Netherlands and Switzerland', *International Social Science Journal*, vol. 23, pp.355–70; also in Eisenstadt and Rokkan (eds) 1973, vol. 2, pp. 14–31.

Daalder, H. (1974) 'The Consociational Democracy Theme', *World Politics*, vol. 26, pp.604–21.

Daalder, H. (1978a) 'The Netherlands and the World 1940–1945', in J.H. Leurdijk (ed.) *The Foreign Policy of the Netherlands*. Alphen: Sijthoff, pp.49–116.

Daalder, H. (1978b), 'Dutch Jews in a Segmented Society', *Acta Historiae Neerlandicae. Studies on the History of the Netherlands*, vol. 10, pp.175–94.

Daalder, H. (1981) 'Consociationalism, Center and Periphery in the Netherlands', in Torsvik (ed.), pp.181–240.

Daalder, H. and Shils, E. (eds) (1982) *Universities, Politicians and Bureaucrats: Europe and America*. Cambridge: Cambridge University Press.

Daalder, H. and Mair, P. (eds) (1983) *Western European Party Systems. Continuity and Change*. London: Sage.

Daalder, H. (1984a) 'In Search of the Center of European Party Systems', *The American Political Science Review*, vol. 78, pp.92–109.

Daalder, H. (1984b) 'On the Origins of the Consociational Democracy Model', *Acta Politica*, vol. 19, pp.97–116.

Daalder, H. (ed.) (1987a) *Party Systems in Denmark, Austria, Switzerland, the Netherlands and Belgium*. London: Pinter.

Daalder, H. (1987b) 'Countries in Comparative European Politics', *European Journal of Political Research*, vol. 15, pp.3–21.

Daalder, H. (1987c) 'European Political Traditions and Processes of Modernization. Groups, the Individual and the State', in Eisenstadt (ed.), vol. 1, pp.22–43.

Daalder, H. and Irwin, G.A. (eds) (1989a) *Politics in the Netherlands: How Much Change?* London: Frank Cass.

Daalder, H. (1989b) *Ancient and Modern Pluralism in the Netherlands*. The 1989 Erasmus Lectures at Harvard University: Center for European Studies, Working Paper Series No. 22.

Daalder, H. (1990) *Politiek en Historie. Opstellen over Nederlandse Politiek en Vergelijkende Politieke Wetenschap*. Amsterdam: Bert Bakker.

Daalder, H. (1991) 'Political Science in the Netherlands', in Vallès and Newton (eds), pp.279–300.

Daalder, H. (1992) 'A Crisis of Party?', *Scandinavian Political Studies*, vol. 14, pp.269–88.

Daalder, H. (1993) 'The Development of the Study of Comparative Politics', in H. Keman (ed.) *Comparative Politics. New Directions in Theory and Method*. Amsterdam: VU Press, pp.11–30.

Daalder, H. (1994) 'Universitair Panopticum I: Studeren in de Zevende Faculteit', *Maatstaf*, vol. 42, pp.59–68.

Daalder, H. (1995a) *Van Oude en Nieuwe Regenten. Politiek in Nederland*. Amsterdam: Bert Bakker.

Daalder, H. (1995b) 'Paths towards State Formation in Europe. Democratization, Bureaucratization, and Politicization', in Chehabi and Stepan (eds), pp.113–30.

Daalder, H. (1995c) 'Dutch Jews in a Segmented Society', in Birnbaum and Katznelson (eds), pp.37–58.

Daalder, H. (1995d) 'Over standvastigheid en lafhartigheid in de Academie. Een geschiedenis van de zaak-Daudt', in H. Daudt *Echte Politicologie. Opstellen over Politicologie, Democratie en de Nederlandse Politiek*. Amsterdam: Bert Bakker, pp.40–86.

Dachs, H. *et al.* (eds) (1992) *Handbuch des politischen Systems Österreichs*. 2. Aufl., Vienna: Manz.

Dahl, R.A. (1940) 'On the Theory of Democratic Socialism', *Plan Age*, vol. 6, pp.325–56.

Dahl, R.A. (1947a) 'The Science of Public Administration: Three Problems', *Public Administration Review*, vol. 7, pp.1–11.

Dahl, R.A. (1947b) 'Workers' Control of Industry and the British Labor Party', *American Political Science Review*, vol. 41, pp.875–900.

Dahl, R.A. (1947c) 'Marxism and Free Parties', *The Journal of Politics*, vol. 10, pp.787–813.

Dahl, R.A. and Lindblom, C.E. (1953) *Politics, Economics and Welfare*. New York: Harper & Row; with a new preface, Chicago: University of Chicago Press, 1976.

Dahl, R.A. (1956) *A Preface to Democratic Theory*. Chicago: University of Chicago Press.

Dahl, R.A. (1957) 'The Concept of Power', *Behavioral Science*, vol. 2, pp.201–15.

Dahl, R.A. (1961a) *Who Governs? Democracy and Power in an American City*. New Haven: Yale University Press.

Dahl, R.A. (1961b) 'The Behavioral Approach in Political Science. Epitaph for a Monument to a Successful Protest', *American Political Science Review*, vol. 55, pp.763–72.

Dahl, R.A. (1963) *Modern Political Analysis*. Englewood Cliffs: Prentice-Hall; 5th edn. 1991.

Dahl, R.A. (ed.) (1966) *Political Oppositions in Western Democracies*. New Haven: Yale University Press.

Dahl, R.A. (1967) 'The City in the Future of Democracy', *American Political Science Review*, vol. 61, pp.953–70.

Dahl, R.A. (1970) *After the Revolution? Authority in a Good Society*. New Haven: Yale University Press.

Dahl, R.A. (1971) *Polyarchy. Participation and Opposition*. New Haven: Yale University Press.

Dahl, R.A. (ed.) (1973) *Regimes and Oppositions*. New Haven: Yale University Press.

Dahl, R.A. and E.R. Tufte (1973) *Size and Democracy*. Stanford: Stanford University Press.

Dahl, R.A. (1979) 'Procedural Democracy', in Laslett and Fishkin (eds), pp.97–133.

Dahl, R.A. (1982) *Dilemmas of Pluralist Democracy. Autonomy versus Control*. New Haven: Yale University Press.

Dahl, R.A. (1983) 'Federalism and the Democratic Process', *Nomos*, vol. 25: *Liberal Democracy*. New York: New York University Press, pp.95–108.

Dahl, R.A. (1984) 'Polyarchy, Pluralism, and Scale', *Scandinavian Political Studies*, vol. 7, pp.225–40.

Dahl, R.A. (1985) *A Preface to Economic Democracy*. Berkeley: University of California Press.

Dahl, R.A. (1986) *Democracy, Liberty, and Equality*. Oslo: Norwegian University Press.

Dahl, R. A. (1987) 'Dilemmas of Pluralist Democracy: the Public Good of Which Public?', in Peter Koslowski (ed.) *Individual Liberty and Democratic Decision-Making*. Tübingen: Mohr, pp.201–14.

Dahl, R.A. (1989) *Democracy and Its Critics*. New Haven: Yale University Press.

Dahl, R.A. (1992a) 'Reflections on *A Preface to Democratic Theory*', *Government and Opposition*, vol. 26, pp.293–301.

Dahl, R.A. (1992b) 'Why Free Markets Are Not Enough', *Journal of Democracy*, vol. 3, pp.82–9.

Dahl, R.A. (1994a) 'A Democratic Dilemma. System Effectiveness versus Citizen Participation', *Political Science Quarterly*, vol. 109, pp.23–34.

Dahl, R.A. (1994b) *The New American Political (Dis)Order*. Berkeley: Institute of Governmental Studies Press.

Dahl, R.A. (1995) 'Justifying Democracy', *Society*, vol. 32, pp.43–9.

Dahl, R.A. (1997) *Toward Democracy: A Journey. Reflections: 1940–1997*. Berkeley: Institute of Governmental Studies Press, University of California.

Dahrendorf, R. (1959) *Class and Class Conflict in Industrial Society*. Stanford: Stanford University Press.

Dahrendorf, R. (1968) *Society and Democracy in Germany*. London: Weidenfeld & Nicolson.

Dahrendorf, R. (1990) *Reflections on the Revolution in Europe*. London: Chatto & Windus.

Dahrendorf, R. (1995) *LSE. A History of the London School of Economics and Political Science*. Oxford: Oxford University Press.

Damgaard, E., Gerlich, P. and Richardson, J.J. (1989) *The Politics of Economic Crisis*. London: Avebury.

Davies, J.L. and Gurr, T.R. (eds) (1998) *Preventive Measures. Building Risk Assessment and Crisis Early Warning Systems*. Boulder, CO: Rowman and Littlefield.

De Condorcet, A.N. (1955) *Sketch for a Historical Picture of the Progress of the Human Mind*. Westport: Greenwood.

De Madariaga, I. (1994) 'Introduction', *Government and Opposition*, vol. 29, pp.567–71.

Dennis, J. *et al.* (1968) 'Political Socialization to Democratic Orientations in Four Nations', *Comparative Political Studies*, vol. 1, pp.71–101.

Dennis, J. *et al.* (1971) 'Support for Nation and Government Among English Children', *British Journal of Political Science*, vol. 1, pp.25–48.

Derlien, H.U. (1991) 'Bureaucracy in Art and Analysis. Kafka and Weber', *Journal of the Kafka Society of America*, vol. 15, pp.4–20.

Deutsch, K.W. (1953) *Nationalism and Social Communication. An Inquiry into the Foundations of Nationality*. Cambridge, Mass.: MIT Press.

Deutsch, K.W. (1957) *Political Community and the North Atlantic Area. International Organization in the Light of Historical Experience*. Princeton: Princeton University Press.

Deutsch, K.W. (1961) 'Social Mobilization and Political Development', *American Political Science Review*, vol. 51, pp.494–514.

Deutsch, K.W. (1963) *The Nerves of Government*. New York: The Free Press; 2nd edn. Glencoe: The Free Press, 1966.

Deutsch, K.W. and Wildenmann, R. (eds) (1976) '*Mathematical Political Analysis. From Methods to Substance*', *Sozialwissenschaftliches Jahrbuch für Politik*, vol. 5. Munich: Günter Olzog Verlag.

Deutsch, K.W. (1980) 'A Voyage of the Mind 1930–1980', in Ionescu (ed.), pp.323–45.

Deutsch, K.W. (1989) 'A Path among the Social Sciences', in Kruzel and Rosenau (eds), pp.15–26.

Di Palma, G. (1970) *Apathy and Participation*. New York: The Free Press.

Di Palma, G. (ed.) (1972) *Mass Politics in Industrial Societies. A Reader in Comparative Politics*. Chicago: Markham.

Diamant, A. (1959) 'Is There a Non-Western Political Process?' *Journal of Politics*, vol. 21, pp.123–27.

Diamond, L., Linz, J.J. and Lipset, S.M. (eds) (1988) *Democracy in Developing Countries*. Boulder, Col.: Westview, 4 vols.

Dogan, M. and Rokkan, S. (eds) (1969) *Quantitative Ecological Analysis in the Social Sciences*. Cambridge, Mass.: MIT Press.

Dogan, M. and Rose, R. (eds) (1970) *European Politics. A Reader*. Boston: Little, Brown.

Dogan, M. and Pahre, R. (1990) *Creative Marginality. Innovation at the Intersections of Social Sciences*. Boulder, Col.: Westview.

Dollard, J. *et al.* (1939) *Frustration and Aggression*. New Haven: Yale University Press.

Downs, A. (1957) *An Economic Theory of Democracy*. New York: Harper.

Duguit, L. (1919) *Law in the Modern State* (trans. F. and H. Laski). New York: Huebsch.

Dunleavy, P. (1991) *Democracy, Bureaucracy and Public Choice*. Hemel Hempstead: Harvester Wheatsheaf.

Dupeux, G. (1962) *Aspects de l'Histoire Sociale et Politique du Loir-et-Cher, 1848–1914*. Paris: Mouton.

Durkheim, É. (1897) *Le Suicide. Étude de sociologie*. Paris: Alcan.

Durkheim, É. (1898) 'L'Individualisme et les intellectuels', *Revue Bleu*, vol. 4, pp.7–13.

Durkheim, É. (1893) *De la division du travail social. Étude sur l'organization des sociétés supérieures*. Paris: Alcan.

Durkheim, É. (1957) *Professional Ethics and Civic Morals*. London: Routledge; original French version *Leçons de sociologie, physique des moeurs et du droit*. Paris: Presses Universitaires de France, 1950.

Duverger, M. (1951) *Les Partis Politiques*. Paris: A. Colin.

Duverger, M. (1954) *Political Parties. Their Organization and Activity in the Modern State*. London: Methuen.

Easton, D. (1953) *The Political System. An Enquiry into the State of Political Science*. New York: Knopf.

Easton, D. (1965) *A Systems Analysis of Political Life*. New York: Wiley.

Eckstein, H. (1961) *A Theory of Stable Democracy*. Research Monograph No. 10, Center of International Studies, Princeton University; reprinted as Appendix B in Eckstein (1966), pp.225–88.

Eckstein, H. (1963) 'A Perspective on Comparative Politics, Past and Present', in Eckstein and Apter (eds), pp.3–32.

Eckstein, H. and Apter, D.E. (eds) (1963) *Comparative Politics. A Reader.* Glencoe: The Free Press.

Eckstein, H. (1966) *Division and Cohesion in Democracy. A Study of Norway.* Princeton: Princeton University Press.

Eckstein, H. and Gurr, T.R. (1975) *Patterns of Authority. A Structural Basis for Political Inquiry.* New York: Wiley.

Ehrmann, H. (1957) *Organized Business in France.* Princeton: Princeton University Press.

Ehrmann, H. (ed.) (1958) *Interest Groups on Four Continents.* Pittsburgh: University of Pittsburgh Press.

Eisenstadt, S.N. (1953) *The Absorption of Immigrants.* New York: The Free Press.

Eisenstadt, S.N. (1961) *Essays on Sociological Aspects of Political and Economic Development.* The Hague: Mouton.

Eisenstadt, S.N. (1963) *The Political Systems of Empires.* New York: The Free Press.

Eisenstadt, S.N. (1964) 'Institutionalization and Change', *American Sociological Review*, vol. 29, pp.235–97.

Eisenstadt, S.N. (1966) *Modernization, Protest and Change.* Englewood Heights: Prentice-Hall.

Eisenstadt, S.N. (1967) *Israeli Society.* London: Weidenfeld & Nicolson.

Eisenstadt, S.N. (1968a) 'Charisma and Institution Building', Introduction to S.N. Eisenstadt (ed.) *Max Weber on Charisma and Institution Building.* Chicago: Chicago University Press, pp.ix–lvi.

Eisenstadt, S.N. (1968b) 'Prestige, Stratification and Center Formation', in J.A. Jackson (ed.) *Social Stratification.* Cambridge: Cambridge University Press, pp.62–103.

Eisenstadt, S.N. (1969a) *The Political Systems of Empires.* New York: The Free Press (paperback edition).

Eisenstadt, S.N. (1969b) 'Social Change Differentiation and Evolution', *American Sociological Review*, vol. 29, pp.375–86.

Eisenstadt, S.N. (1971) *Political Sociology.* New York: Basic Books

Eisenstadt, S.N. (1972) (ed.) *Post-Traditional Societies.* New York: Norton.

Eisenstadt, S.N. and Rokkan, S. (eds) (1973) *Building States and Nations.* Beverly Hills: Sage, 2 vols.

Eisenstadt, S.N. (1973a) *Tradition, Change and Modernity.* New York: Wiley.

Eisenstadt, S.N. (1973b), 'Traditional Patrimonialism and Modern New Patrimonialism', *Sage Research Papers in the Social Sciences.* Vol. 1. Beverly Hills: Sage.

Eisenstadt, S.N. and Azmon, Y. (eds) (1975) *Socialism and Tradition.* Jerusalem: The Van Leer Jerusalem Institute.

Eisenstadt, S.N. (1977) 'Sociological Characteristics and Problems of Small States. A Research Note', *Jerusalem Journal of International Relations*, vol. 2, pp.35–50.

Eisenstadt, S.N. and Roniger, L. (1984a) *Patrons, Clients and Friends.* Cambridge: Cambridge University Press.

Eisenstadt, S.N. (1984b) 'Die Paradoxie von Zivilisationen mit auserweltlichen Orientierungen', in W. Schluchter (ed.) *Max Webers Studie über Hinduismus und Buddhismus.* Frankfurt: Suhrkamp, pp.333–59.

Eisenstadt, S.N. (1985a) *The Transformation of Israeli Society.* London: Weidenfeld & Nicolson.

Eisenstadt, S.N. (1985b) 'Max Webers Sicht des frühen Christentums und die Entstehung der westlichen Zivilisation. Einige vergleichende Überlegungen', in W. Schluchter (ed.) *Max Webers Sicht des Antiken Christentums.* Frankfurt: Suhrkamp, pp.509–25.

Eisenstadt, S.N. (ed.) (1986) *The Origins and Diversity of Axial Civilizations.* Albany, New York: SUNY Press.

Eisenstadt, S.N. (ed.) (1987a) *Patterns of Modernity.* London: Pinter, 2 vols.

Eisenstadt, S.N. (1987b) *European Civilisation in a Comparative Perspective*. Oslo: Norwegian University Press.

Eisenstadt, S.N. (1987c) 'Reflections on Center–Periphery Relations and Small European States', in Eisenstadt (1987b), pp.65–74.

Eisenstadt, S.N. (1987d) 'Webers Analyse des Islams und die Gestalt der Islamischen Zivilization', in W. Schluchter (ed.) *Max Webers Sicht des Islams*. Frankfurt: Suhrkamp, pp.342–59.

Eisenstadt, S.N. (1988a) 'State Formation in Africa. Conclusions', in S.N. Eisenstadt, M. Abitol and N. Chazan (eds) *The Early State in Africa*. Leiden: Brill, pp.168–200.

Eisenstadt, S.N. (1988b) 'Max Webers Überlegungen zum Westlichen Christentums', in W. Schluchter (ed.) *Max Webers Sicht des Okzidentalen Christentums*. Frankfurt: Suhrkamp, pp.554–85.

Eisenstadt, S.N. (ed.) (1991) *Kulturen der Achsenzeit*. Frankfurt: Suhrkamp, 3 vols.

Eisenstadt, S.N. (ed.) (1992a) *Martin Buber. On Intersubjectivity and Cultural Identity*. Chicago: Chicago University Press.

Eisenstadt, S.N. (1992b) 'The Breakdown of Communist Regimes and the Vicissitudes of Modernity', *Daedalus*, vol. 121, pp.27–41.

Eisenstadt, S.N. (1992c) *The Political Systems of Empires*. New Brunswick: Transaction Publishers.

Eisenstadt, S.N. (1992d) 'A Reappraisal of Theories of Social Change and Modernization', in H. Haferkamp and N.J. Smelser (eds) *Social Change and Modernity*. Berkeley: University of California Press, pp.412–29.

Eisenstadt, S.N. (1993) 'Small States in the "Post-Modern" Era', in A. Waschkuhn (Hrsg.) *Kleinstaat: Grundsätzliche und aktuelle Probleme*, Liechtenstein Politische Schriften, vol. 16.

Eisenstadt, S.N. (1995) *Barbarism and Modernity*. Paper given at the meeting of the Theory Section of the German Sociological Society, Hamburg.

Eisenstadt, S.N. (1996) *Power, Trust and Meaning*. Chicago: University of Chicago Press.

Eldersveld, S.J., Kooiman, J. and van der Tak, T. (1981) *Elite Images of Dutch Politics. Accommodation and Conflict*. Ann Arbor: University of Michigan Press.

Eliassen, K. and Pedersen, M.N. (1978) 'Professionalization of Legislatures. Long-Term Change in Political Recruitment in Denmark and Norway', *Comparative Studies in Society and History*, vol. 20, pp.286–318.

Eliassen, K.A. and Pedersen, M.N. (1985) *Nordiske politiske fakta/Nordic Political Facts*. Oslo: Tiden Norsk Forlag.

Elklit, J. and Pedersen, M.N. (eds) (1995) *Kampen om kommunen – ni fortællinger om kommunalvalget 1993*. Odense: Odense University Press.

Epstein, L. (1955) *Britain. Uneasy Ally*. Chicago: University of Chicago Press.

Erikson, R., Hansen, E.J., Ringen, S. and Hannu, U. (1987) *The Scandinavian Model. Welfare States and Welfare Research*. New York: Sharpe.

Eulau, H., Eldersveld, S.J. and Janowitz, M. (eds) (1956) *Political Behavior. A Reader in Theory and Research*. Glencoe: The Free Press.

Eulau, H. and Sprague, J.D. (1961) *Lawyers in Politics. A Study in Professional Convergence*. Indianapolis: Bobbs-Merrill.

Eulau, H. (1963) *The Behavioral Persuasion in Politics*. New York: Random House.

Eulau, H. (1969) *Micro-Macro Political Analysis. Accents of Enquiry*. Chicago: Aldine.

Farneti, P. (1985) *The Italian Party System (1945–1980)*. Ed. S.E. Finer and A. Mastropaolo. London: Pinter.

Finer, H. (1923) *Representative Government and a Parliament of Industry. A Study of the German Federal Economic Council*. London: Allen & Unwin.

Finer, H. (1932) *The Theory and Practice of Modern Government*. London: Methuen, 2 vols.

Finer, H. (1949) *The Theory and Practice of Modern Government*. 2nd edn. New York: Holt.

Finer, H. (1956) *Governments of Greater European Powers*. New York: Holt.

Finer, S.E. (1952) *The Life and Times of Sir Edwin Chadwick*. London: Methuen.

Finer, S.E. (1956) 'The Individual Responsibility of Ministers', *Public Administration*, vol. 34, pp.377–96.

Finer, S.E. (1958) *Anonymous Empire. A Study of the Lobby in Great Britain*. London: Pall Mall.

Finer, S.E., Bartholomew, D. and Berrington, H. (1961) *Backbench Opinion in the House of Commons*. Oxford: Pergamon.

Finer, S.E. (1962) *The Man on Horseback. The Role of the Military in Politics*. London: Pall Mall.

Finer, S.E. (ed.) (1966) *Vilfredo Pareto. Sociological Writings*. London: Pall Mall.

Finer, S.E. (1969) 'Almond's Concept of the "Political System". A Textual Critique', *Government and Opposition*, vol. 5, pp.3–21.

Finer, S.E. (1970) *Comparative Government*. Harmondsworth: Penguin.

Finer, S.E. (1972) 'The Transmission of Benthamite Ideas', in G. Sutherland (ed.) *Studies in the Growth of Nineteenth Century Government*. London: Allen & Unwin, pp.11–32.

Finer, S.E. (1975a) 'State- and Nation-Building in Europe. The Role of the Military', in Tilly (ed.), pp.84–163.

Finer, S.E. (ed.) (1975b) *Adversary Politics and Electoral Reform*. London: Anthony Wigram.

Finer, S.E. (ed.) (1979) *Five Constitutions*. Harmondsworth: Penguin.

Finer, S.E. (1980a) *The Changing British Party System (1945–79)*. Washington DC: American Enterprise Institute.

Finer, S.E. (1980b) 'Political Science. An Idiosyncratic Retrospect of a Putative Discipline', *Government and Opposition*, vol. 15, pp. 346–63.

Finer, S.E. (1983) 'Perspectives in the World History of Government', *Government and Opposition*, vol. 18, pp.3–22.

Finer, S.E. (1997) *History of Government from the Earliest Times*. Oxford: Oxford University Press.

Fisher, R. and Ury, W. (1981) *Getting to Yes. Negotiating Agreement Without Giving In*. Boston: Houghton Mifflin.

Flora, P. (ed.) (1986–), *Growth to Limits. The Western European Welfare States since World War II*. Berlin: De Gruyter, 4 vols.

Franklin, M., Mackie, T., Valen, H. *et al.* (1992) *Electoral Change. Responses to Evolving Social and Attitudinal Structures in Western Countries*. Cambridge: Cambridge University Press.

Freud, S. (1974) *Das Unbehagen in der Kultur*. Studienausgabe. Band 9. Frankfurt: Fischer.

Friedrich, C.J. (1937) *Constitutional Government and Politics*. New York: Blaisdell.

Friedrich, C.J. (1938) *Foreign Policy in the Making*. New York: Norton.

Friedrich, C.J. (1940) *Controlling Broadcasting in Wartime*. Cambridge, Mass.: Littauer Center.

Friedrich, C.J. (1942) *The New Belief in the Common Man*. Boston; later edition: *The New Image of the Common Man*. Brattleboro: Vermont Printing 1949.

Friedrich, C.J. (1946) *Constitutional Government and Democracy*. Boston: Ginn; 4th edn. New York: Blaisdell, 1968.

Friedrich, C.J. (1948) *Inevitable Peace*. Cambridge, Mass.: Harvard University Press.

Friedrich, C.J. (1949) 'Rebuilding the German Constitution', *American Political Science Review*, vol. 43, June, pp.461–82 and August, pp.704–20.

Friedrich, C.J. (1952) *The Age of Baroque*. New York: Norton.

Friedrich, C.J. and Brzezinski, Z. (1956) *Totalitarian Dictatorship and Autocracy*. Cambridge, Mass.: Harvard University Press; 2nd edn by C.J. Friedrich, 1965.

Friedrich, C.J. (1957) *Constitutional Reason of State. The Survival of the Constitutional Order*. Providence: Brown University Press.

Friedrich, C.J. (1958) *The Philosophy of Law in Historical Perspective*. Chicago: University of Chicago Press.

Friedrich, C.J. (1959) *Puerto Rico. Middle Road to Freedom*. New York: Rinehart.

Friedrich, C.J. (1963) *Man and his Government. An Empirical Theory of Politics*. New York: McGraw-Hill.

Friedrich, C.J. (1967) *The Impact of American Constitutionalism Abroad*. Boston: Boston University Press.

Friedrich, C.J. (1969) *Europe: An Emergent Nation?* New York: Harper and Row.

Friedrich, C.J. (1972) *The Pathology of Politics*. New York: Harper and Row.

Galenson, W. (1952) *The Danish System of Labor Relations*. Cambridge, Mass.: Harvard University Press.

Galtung, J. (1971) 'A Structural Theory of Imperialism', *Journal of Peace Research*, vol. 8, pp.81–118.

Gastil, R.D. (ed.) (1988) *Freedom in the World. Political Rights and Liberties, 1987–1988*. Lanham: University Press of America.

Geiger, T. (1960) *Die Gesellschaft zwischen Pathos und Nüchternheit*. Aarhus: Acta Jutlandica.

Gerlich, P. and Kramer, H. (1969) *Abgeordnete in der Parteiendemokratie*. Vienna: Geschichte und Politik.

Gerlich, P. (1971) 'Allgemeine Ansätze der neueren vergleichenden Politikwissenschaft. Möglichkeiten und Grenzen', *Österreichische Zeitschrift für Aussenpolitik*, vol. 11, pp.322–36.

Gerlich, P. (1972) 'Orientations to Decision-Making in the Vienna City Council', in Patterson and Wahlke (eds), pp.87–106.

Gerlich, P. (1973a) *Parliamentarische Kontrolle im Politischen System*. Vienna: Springer.

Gerlich, P. (1973b) 'The Institutionalization of European Parliaments', in A. Kornberg (ed.) *Legislatures in Comparative Perspective*. New York: McKay, pp.94–111.

Gerlich, P. (1981) 'Korruption im Systemvergleich', in C. Brünner (ed.) *Korruption und Kontrolle*. Vienna: Böhlau, pp.165–81.

Gerlich, P., Talos, E. and Ucakar, K. (1982) 'Austria', in Andrews (ed.), pp.85–92.

Gerlich, P. (ed.) (1986) 'Cause and Consequence in Legislation', Special Issue, *European Journal of Political Research*, vol. 14, pp.265–368.

Gerlich, P. (1987) 'Consociationalism to Competition: The Austrian Party System since 1945', in Daalder (ed.) (1987a), pp.61–106.

Gerlich, P. (1989) 'Some Reflections on Latent Functions', in C. Mongardini and S. Tabboni (eds) *L'Opera di R.K. Merton*. Geneva, pp.199–208.

Gerlich, P. (1990) 'Revolution and Political Culture, or: Should Condorcet Have Ordered a Smaller Omelette?', in C. Mongardini and M.L. Maniscalco (eds) *L'Europa moderna e l' idea di revoluzione*. Roma: Bulzoni, pp.71–82.

Gerlich, P., Plasser F. and Ulram, P.A. (eds) (1992a) *Regimewechsel, Demokratisierung und politische Kultur in Ost–Mitteleuropa*. Vienna: Böhlau.

Gerlich, P. and Glass, K. (eds) (1992b) *Zwischen den Zeiten*. Vienna: Notring.

Gerlich, P. (1993) 'Die ersten zehn Jahre. Anfänge der Politikwissenschaft', in B. Felderer (ed.) *Wirtschafts- und Sozialwissenschaften zwischen Theorie und Praxis. Dreißig Jahre Institut für Höhere Studien*. Heidelberg: Physica, pp.139–62.

Gerlich, P. (1994) *Hochschule und Effizienz*. Vienna: Passagen Verlag.

Germino, D. (1959) *The Italian Fascist Party in Power*. Minneapolis: University of Minnesota Press.

Girtler, R. (1984) *Methoden der qualitativen Sozialforschung*. Vienna: Böhlau.

Goethe, W. (1920) 'Urworte. Orphisch', *Lyrische und epische Dichtungen*. Leipzig: Insel.

Goldstone, J.A., Gurr, T.R. and Moshiri, F. (eds) (1991) *Revolutions of the Late Twentieth Century*. Boulder, Col.: Westview Press.

Goldthorpe, J.H. (ed.) (1980) *Order and Conflict in Contemporary Capitalism*. Oxford: Clarendon Press.

Gorbachev, M. (1989) 'Sotsialisticheskaya idea i revolyutsionnaya perestroika', *Pravda*, 26 November.

Gosnell, H.F. (1937) *Machine Politics. Chicago Model*. Chicago: University of Chicago Press.

Gottweis, H. (1980) *Die Welt der Gesetzgebung*. Vienna: Böhlau.

Gould, J. (1994) 'Sammy Finer. Scholar and Human Being', *Government and Opposition*, vol. 29, pp.587–600.

Graham, H.D. and Gurr, T.R. (eds) (1969) *Violence in America. Historical and Comparative Perspectives*. A Report to the National Commission on the Causes and Prevention of Violence. Washington DC: US Government Printing Office (also editions by Bantam Books, Signet Books, and Praeger).

Graham, H.D. and Gurr, T.R. (eds) (1979) *Violence in America. Historical and Comparative Perspectives*. rev. edn. Beverly Hills: Sage.

Graziano, L. (ed.) (1985), 'Dove va la scienza politica', in *La Scienza Politica in Italia*. Milan: Angeli, pp.98–114.

Grew, R. *et al.* (1978) *Crises and Political Development in Europe and the United States*. Princeton: Princeton University Press.

Grofman, B. and Lijphart, A. (eds) (1986) *Electoral Laws and Their Political Consequences*. New York: Agathon Press.

Gruner, E. (1959) 'Der Einbau der organizierten Interessen in den Staat', *Schweizerische Zeitschrift für Volkswirtschaft und Statistik*, vol. 95, pp.59–79.

Gunther, R. (ed.) (1993) *Politics, Society and Democracy. The Case of Spain. Essays in Honor of Juan J. Linz*. Boulder, Col.: Westview.

Gurr, T.R. (1967) 'Psychological Factors in Civil Violence', *World Politics*, vol. 20, pp.245–78.

Gurr, T.R. (1968) 'A Causal Model of Civil Strife. A Comparative Analysis Using New Indices', *American Political Science Review*, vol. 62, pp.1104–24.

Gurr, T.R. and Ruttenberg, C. (1969) *Cross-National Studies of Civil Violence*. Washington, DC: Center for Research in Social Systems, American University.

Gurr, T.R. (1970) *Why Men Rebel*. Princeton: Princeton University Press.

Gurr, T.R. and McClelland, M. (1971) *Political Performance. A Twelve-Nation Study*. Beverly Hills: Sage.

Gurr, T.R. and Duvall, R. (1973) 'Civil Conflict in the 1960s. A Reciprocal Theoretical System with Parameter Estimates', *Comparative Political Studies*, vol. 6, pp.135–71.

Gurr, T.R. (1974) 'Political Persistence and Change in Political Systems, 1800–1971', *American Political Science Review*, vol. 69, pp.1482–504.

Gurr, T.R., Grabosky, P.N. and Hula, R.C. (1977) *The Politics of Urban Crime and Conflict. A Comparative History of Four Cities*. Beverly Hills: Sage.

Gurr, T.R. and Lichbach, M.I. (1979) 'A Forecasting Model for Political Conflict Within Nations', in J.D. Singer and M.D. Wallace (eds) *To Augur Well: Early Warning Indicators in World Politics*. Beverly Hills: Sage, pp.153–93.

Gurr, T.R. (ed.) (1980) *Handbook of Political Conflict. Theory and Research*. New York: The Free Press.

Gurr, T.R. (1983) 'Outcomes of Public Protest Among Australia's Aborigines', *American Behavioral Scientist*, vol. 26, pp.353–74.

Gurr, T.R. and King, D.S. (1987) *The State and the City*. Chicago: University of Chicago Press.

Gurr, T.R. (ed.) (1989) *Violence in America. The History of Crime*. Newbury Park: Sage.

Gurr, T.R., Jaggers, K. and Moore, W.H. (1990) 'The Transformation of the Western State. The Growth of Democracy, Autocracy, and State Power since 1800', *Studies in Comparative International Development*, vol. 25, pp.73–108.

Gurr, T.R. (1993a) *Minorities at Risk. A Global View of Ethnopolitical Conflict* (with chapters by B. Harff, M. Marshall and J. R. Scarritt). Washington DC: United States Institute of Peace Press.

Gurr, T.R. (1993b) 'Why Minorities Rebel. A Global Analysis of Ethnopolitical Conflict', *International Political Science Review*, vol. 14, pp.161–201.

Gurr, T.R. and Harff, B. (1994) *Ethnic Conflict in World Politics*. Boulder, Col.: Westview.

Gurr, T.R. and Harff, B. (1996) *Early Warning of Communal Conflicts and Genocide. Linking Empirical Research to International Responses*. Tokyo: UN University Press.

Haas, E.B. (1958) *The Uniting of Europe*. Stanford: Stanford University Press.

Haas, E.B. and Schmitter P.C. (1964) 'Economics and Differential Patterns of Political Integration. Projections about Unity in Latin America', *International Organization*, vol. 18, pp.705–37.

Hacker, J. (1992) *Deutsche Irrtümer. Schönfärber und Hilfershelfer der SED–Diktatur im Westen*. Berlin: Ullstein.

Hagtvet, B. (ed.) (1992) *Politikk mellom økonomi og kultur. Stein Rokkan som politisk sosiolog og forsningsinspirator*. Oslo: Gyldendal.

Hall, P. (1986) *Governing the Economy*. Oxford: Oxford University Press.

Harff, B. (1984) *Genocide and Human Rights: International Legal and Political Issues*. Denver: University of Denver Monograph Series in World Affairs.

Harff, B. (1987) 'The Etiology of Genocide', in M.N. Dobkowski and I. Wallimann (eds) *The Age of Genocide*. Wesport, Conn.: Greenwood Press, pp.41–59.

Harff, B. and Gurr, T.R. (1989–90) 'Victims of the State. Genocides, Politicides, and Group Repression since 1945', *International Review of Victimology*, vol. 1, pp.23–41.

Harff, B. (1995) 'Rescuing Endangered Peoples: Missed Opportunities', *Social Research*, vol. 62, pp.23–40.

Harff, B. and Gurr, T.R. (1996) 'Victims of the State. Genocides, Politicides, and Group Repression from 1945 to 1995', in A.J. Jongman (ed.) *Contemporary Genocides: Causes, Cases, Consequences*. The Hague: Interdisciplinary Program on Root Causes of Human Rights Violations (PIOOM), pp.33–58.

Hartmann, R. (1981) *Richard Strauss. The Staging of His Operas and Ballets*. New York: Oxford University Press.

Håstad, E. (1950) 'Swedish Political Science', in UNESCO 1950, pp.150ff.

Hayward, J. (1965) *Private Interests and Public Policy. The Experience of the French Economic and Social Council*. London: Longman.

Hayward, J. (1969) 'From Functional Regionalism to Functional Representation in France. The Battle of Brittany', *Political Studies*, vol. 17, pp.48–75.

Hayward, J. (1973) *The One and Indivisible French Republic*. London: Weidenfeld & Nicolson.

Hayward, J. and Watson, M. (eds) (1975) *Planning, Politics and Public Policy. The British, French and Italian Experience*. Cambridge: Cambridge University Press.

Hayward, J. and Narkiewicz, O. (eds) (1978) *Planning in Europe*. London: Croom Helm.

Hayward, J. and Berki, R.N. (eds) (1979) *State and Society in Contemporary Europe*. Oxford: Martin Robertson.

Hayward, J. (1983) *Governing France*. London: Weidenfeld & Nicolson.

Hayward, J. (1986) *The State and the Market Economy. Industrial Patriotism and Economic Intervention in France*. Brighton: Harvester Wheatsheaf.

Hayward, J. (1991) *After the French Revolution. Six Critics of Democracy and Nationalism*. Brighton: Harvester Wheatsheaf.

Hayward, J. (1991) 'Cultural and Contextual Constraints on the Development of Political Science in Great Britain', in D. Easton, J. Gunnell and L. Graziano *The Development of Political Science*. London: Routledge, pp.93–107.

Hayward, J. (ed.) (1993) *De Gaulle to Mitterrand. Presidential Power in France*. New York: Hurst and New York University Press.

Hayward, J. (ed.) (1995a) *Industrial Enterprise and European Integration. From National to International Champions in Western Europe*. Oxford: Oxford University Press.

Hayward, J. and Page, E. (eds) (1995b) *Governing the New Europe*. Oxford: Polity Press.

Hayward, J. (1995c) 'Finer's Comparative History of Government', Keele Research Paper 14, University of Keele: Department of Politics.

Hazareesingh, S. and Wright, V. (forthcoming) 'La Commune sous le Second Empire', in *Histoire des Communes en France*. Paris: CNRS.

Heckscher, G. (1957) *The Study of Comparative Government and Politics*. London: Allen & Unwin.

Heclo, H. and Wildavsky, A. (1974) *The Private Government of Public Money*. Berkeley: University of California Press.

Hennessy, P. (1974) 'Charismatic Dandy', *Times Higher Educational Supplement*, 15 February.

Henningsen, S. and Rasmussen, E. (1966) 'Political Research in Scandinavia 1960–65: Denmark', *Scandinavian Political Studies*, vol. 1, pp.254–57.

Hermet, G. (1974a) *The Communists in Spain. Study of an Underground Political Movement*. Farnborough: Saxon House.

Hermet, G. (1974b) *L'Espagne de Franco*. Paris: A. Colin.

Hermet, G. (1974c) 'Electoral Trends in Spain', *Iberian Studies*, vol. 3, pp.11–15.

Hermet, G. (1975) 'Dictature bourgeoise et modernisation conservatrice. Problèmes méthodologiques de l'analyse des situations autoritaires', *Revue Française de Science Politique*, vol. 25, pp.1029–61.

Hermet, G. (1976) 'Spain under Franco. The Changing Character of an Authoritarian Regime', *European Journal of Political Research*, vol. 4, pp.311–27.

Hermet, G. (1977a) 'Die Kommunistische Partei Spaniens', in A. Kimmel (ed.) *Eurokommunismus*. Cologne: Bölhau, pp.214–34.

Hermet, G. (1977b) 'Espana: cambio social y estrategias politicas', *Arbor*, vol. 97, pp.7–22.

Hermet, G. (1977c) 'Espagne: changement de la société, modernisation autoritaire et démocratie octroyée', *Revue Française de Science Politique*, vol. 27, pp.582–600.

Hermet, G., Rose R. and Rouquié, A. (eds) (1978a) *Elections without Choice*. London: Macmillan.

Hermet, G., Linz, J.J. and Rouquié, A. (eds) (1978b) *Des élections pas comme les autres*. Paris: Presses de la Fondation Nationale des Sciences Politiques.

Hermet, G. (1980–81) *Les catholiques dans l'Espagne franquiste*. Paris: Presses de la Fondation Nationale des Sciences Politiques, 2 vols.

Hermet, G. (1982) 'L'Espagne. Une tentative de démocratie octroyée', in L. Hamon (ed.) *Mort des dictatures?* Paris: Economica, pp.129–55.

Hermet, G. (1983) *Aux frontières de la démocratie*. Paris: Presses Universitaires de France.

Hermet, G. (1984a) 'Die katholische Kirche im franquistischen System', in P. Waldmann, W.L. Bernecker and F. Lopez-Casero (eds) *Sozialer Wandel und Herrschaft in Spanien Francos*. Paderborn: Ferdinand Schöningh, pp.237–8.

Hermet, G. (1984b) *Totalitarismes*. Paris: Economica.

Hermet, G. (1984c) 'La democracia. Predestinación o accidente?', *Arbor*, vol. 119, pp.9–28.

Hermet, G. (1985) 'L'autoritarisme', in M. Grawitz and J. Leca (eds) *Traité de science politique*. Paris: Presses Universitaires de France, vol. 2, pp.269–312.

Hermet, G. (1986a) *Sociologie de la construction démocratique*. Paris: Economica.

Hermet, G. (1986b) 'Riflessioni per lo studio della democrazia "octroyée"', *Teoria Politica*, vol. 2, pp.49–71.

Hermet, G. (1987) 'De la démocratie en Amérique latine', *Politique internationale*, vol. 34, pp.271–79.

Hermet, G. (1988a) 'Emerging from Dictatorship. The Role of the Constitution in Spain and Portugal', in V. Bogdanor (ed.) *Constitutions in Democratic Politics*. Aldershot: Gower, pp.257–73.

Hermet, G. and Trindade, H. (eds) (1988b) *The Paradoxes of Democracy*. Delhi: Gian.

Hermet, G. (1989) *Le peuple contre la démocratie*. Paris: Fayard.

Hermet, G. (1990a) 'From one Europe to the other. From Liberal Authoritarianism to Authoritarian Democratization', in D. Ethier (ed.) *Democratic Transition and Consolidation in Southern Europe, Latin America and Southern Asia*. London: Macmillan, pp.25–44.

Hermet, G. (1990b) 'The Citizen-Individual in Western Christianity', in Birnbaum and Leca (eds), pp.116–40.

Hermet, G. (1990c) 'La démocratisation à l'amiable. De l'Espagne à la Pologne', *Commentaire*, vol. 13, pp.279–86.

Hermet, G. (1991a) 'The Age of Democracy', *International Social Science Journal*, vol. 128, pp.265–74.

Hermet, G. (1991b) 'L'éducation des gouvernants par les gouvernés', *Cosmopolitiques*, vol. 9, pp.47–53.

Hermet, G. (1991c) 'The Disenchantment of the Old Democracies', *International Social Science Journal*, vol. 129, pp.265–74.

Hermet, G. (1992a) 'On Historical Obstinacy', *International Social Science Journal*, vol. 133, pp.344–50.

Hermet, G. (1992b) 'Citoyenneté et nationalité en Amérique latine', *Commentaire*, vol. 58, pp.341–50.

Hermet, G. (1992c) 'Humanitarian Aid versus Politics', in F. Jean (ed.) *Populations in Danger*. London: John Libbey, pp.107–11.

Hermet, G. (1993a) *Les désenchantements de la liberté*. Paris: Fayard.

Hermet, G. (1993b) *Culture et démocratie*. Paris: UNESCO/Albin Michel.

Hermet, G. (1996) *Histoire des nations et du nationalisme en Europe*. Paris: Le Seuil.

Hibbs, D.A. Jr. (1978) 'On the Political Economy of Long-Run Trends in Strike Activity', *British Journal of Political Science*, vol. 8, pp.153–75.

Hintze, O. (1975) *The Historical Essays of Otto Hintze*, trans. by F. Gilbert. New York: Oxford University Press.

Hirschman, A.O. (1970) *Exit, Voice, and Loyalty*. Cambridge, Mass.: Harvard University Press.

Hobhouse, L.T. (1911) *Liberalism*. London: Williams & Norgate.

Hobson, J.A. (1902) *Imperialism. A Study*. London: Nisbet.

Hoffmann, S. et al. (1963) *France. Change and Tradition*. London: Gollancz.

Hoffmann, S. (1989) 'A Retrospective', in Kruzel and Rosenau (eds), pp.263–78.

Hoffmann-Lange, U. (1992) *Eliten, Macht und Konflikt in der Bundesrepublik*. Opladen: Leske and Budrich.

Hollingsworth, J.R., Streeck, W. and Schmitter, P. (eds) (1994) *Governing Capitalist Economies. Performance and Control of Economic Sectors*. Oxford: Oxford University Press.

Hood, C. (1976) *The Limits of Administration*. New York: Wiley.

Hood, C. (1983) *The Tools of Government*. London: Macmillan.

Hood, C. (1986) *Administrative Analysis*. Hemel Hempstead: Harvester Wheatsheaf.

Hood. C. (1991) *Administrative Argument*. Aldershot: Dartmouth.

Horney, K. (1970) *Self Analysis*. London: Routledge.

Horowitz, D.L. (1991) *A Democratic South Africa? Constitutional Engineering in a Divided Society*. Berkeley: University of California Press.

Huntington, S.P. (1957) *The Soldier and the State. The Theory and Politics of Civil-Military Relations*. Cambridge, Mass.: Harvard University Press.

Huntington, S.P. (1967) *Political Order in Changing Societies*. New Haven: Yale University Press.

Huntington, S.P. (1974) 'Post-Industrial Society. How Benign Will It Be?', *Comparative Politics*, vol. 6, pp.163–91.

Huntington, S.P. (1981) 'Reform and Stability in a Modernizing, Multi-Ethnic Society', *Politikon*, vol. 8, pp.8–26.

Huyse, L. (1970) *Passiviteit, Pacificatie en Verzuiling in de Belgische Politiek*. Antwerp: Standaard.

Inglehart, R. (1977) *Silent Revolution. Changing Values and Political Styles among Western Publics*. Princeton: Princeton University Press.

Inglehart, R. (1990) *Culture Shift in Advanced Industrial Society*. Princeton: Princeton University Press.

Inkeles, A. (1981) 'Convergence and Divergence in Industrial Societies', in Z. Suda and B. Holzner (eds) *Directions of Change. Essays on Modernization Theory and Research*. Boulder, Col.: Westview Press, pp.3–39.

Ionescu, G. (ed.) (1980) *A Generation of Political Thought*. Special issue of *Government and Opposition*, vol. 15, pp.257–566.

Ionescu, G. (1994) 'New and Old Perspectives on Government', *Government and Opposition*, vol. 29, pp.601–22.

Jaggers, K. and Gurr, T.R. (1995) 'Tracking Democracy's Third Wave with Polity III Data', *Journal of Peace Research*, vol. 32, pp.469–82.

Jeppesen, J. and Meyer, P. (1964) *Sofavælgerne*. Copenhagen: Nyt Nordisk Forlag.

Johansson, S. (1970) *Om levnadsnivåundersökningen*. Stockholm: Allmänna förlaget.

Jones-Finer, C. (1994) 'S.E. Finer. A Memoir', *Government and Opposition*, vol. 29, pp.572–86.

Judt, T. (1993) *Un passé imparfait*. Paris: Fayard.

Kaase, M. and Klingemann, H.D. (1994) 'Electoral Research in the Federal Republic of Germany', in Thomassen (ed.), pp.343–66.

Kaase, M. (1995) 'Nachwort', in E. Jahn and R. Wildenmann (eds) *Stabilität in Ostmitteleuropa? Studien zur gesellschaftlichen Entwicklung*, 13, Baden-Baden: Nomos, pp.208–12.

Karl, B. (1974) *Charles E. Merriam and The Study of Politics*. Chicago: University of Chicago Press.

Karlhofer, F. and Pelinka, A. (1991) 'Austrian Political Science. The State of the Art', *European Journal of Politcal Research*, vol. 20, pp.399–411.

Karup Pedersen, O. (1980) 'Samfundsfag', *Kobenhavns Universitet 1479–1979*, vol. 10, pp.527–68.

Kassim, H. and Wright, V. (1991) 'The Role of National Administrations in the European Community Decision-making Process', *Rivista Trimestrale di Diritto Pubblico*, vol. 2, pp.31–54.

Katsenelinboigen, A. (1977) 'Coloured Markets in the Soviet Union', *Soviet Studies*, vol. 29, pp.62–85.

Katz, R.S. (ed.) (1987) *Party Governments. European and American Experiences*. Berlin: De Gruyter.

Katz, R.S. and Mair, P. (eds) (1992) *Party Organizations in Western Democracies*. London: Sage.

Katz, R.S. and Mair, P. (eds) (1994) *How Parties Organize. Change and Adaptation in Party Organizations in Western Democracies*. London: Sage.

Katz, R.S. and Mair, P. (1995) 'Changing Models of Party Organization and Party Democracy. The Emergence of the Cartel Party', *Party Politics*, vol. 1, pp.5–28.

Katzenstein, P.J. (1985) *Small States in World Markets. Industrial Policy in Europe*. Ithaca: Cornell University Press.

Kavanagh, D. and Peele, G. (eds) (1984) *Comparative Government and Politics. Essays in Honour of S.E. Finer*. London: Heinemann.

Kendall, P.L. (ed.) (1982) *The Varied Sociology of Paul F. Lazarsfeld*. New York: Columbia University Press.

Kerr, C. and Siegel, A. (1954) 'The Interindustry Propensity to Strike. An International Comparison', in A. Kornhauser *et al.* (eds) *Industrial Conflict*. New York: McGraw-Hill, pp.189–212.

Kerr., C. *et al.* (1960) *Industrialism and Industrial Man.* Cambridge, Mass.: Harvard University Press.

Key, V.O. Jr. (1949) *Southern Politics in State and Nation.* New York: Knopf.

King, G., Keohane, R.O. and Verba, S. (1994) *Designing Social Inquiry.* Princeton: Princeton University Press.

King, D. (1995) *Actively Seeking Work? The Politics of Unemployment and Welfare Policy in the United States and Great Britain.* Chicago: University of Chicago Press.

Kirchheimer, O. (1957) 'The Waning of Opposition in Parliamentary Regimes', *Social Research*, vol. 24, pp.1128–56.

Kirchheimer, O. (1966a) 'The Transformation of the Western European Party System', in LaPalombara and Weiner (eds), pp.177–200.

Kirchheimer, O. (1966b) 'Germany. The Vanishing Oppostion', in Dahl (ed.), pp.237–60.

Kitschelt, H. (1992) 'The Formation of Party Systems in East Central Europe', *Politics and Society*, vol. 20, pp.7–50.

Kitschelt, H. (1995) 'Formation of Party Cleavages in Post-Communist Democracies', *Party Politics*, vol. 1, pp.447–72.

Kohn, H. (1960) *The Mind of Germany. The Education of a Nation.* London: Macmillan.

Klineberg, O. (1954) *Social Psychology.* 2nd edn. New York: Holt.

Kooiman, J. (1976) *Over de Kamer gesproken.* The Hague: Staatsuitgeverij.

Kornhauser, W. (1959) *The Politics of Mass Society.* Glencoe: The Free Press.

Korpi, W. (1971) 'Working Class Communism in Western Europe. Rational or Nonrational', *American Sociological Review*, vol. 36, pp.971–84.

Korpi, W. (1983) *The Democratic Class Struggle.* London: Routledge.

Kruzel, J. and Rosenau, J.N. (eds) (1989) *Journeys through World Politics. Autobiographical Reflections of Thirty-Four Academic Travelers.* Lexington: Heath.

Kuhn, T.S. (1970) *The Structure of Scientific Revolutions.* Chicago: University of Chicago Press.

Kuznets, S. (1958) *The Challenge of Development.* A Symposium held in Jerusalem 26–27 June 1957. Jerusalem: Eliezer Kaplan School of Economics and Social Sciences, Hebrew University of Jerusalem, pp. 9–27.

Lagroye, J. and Wright, V. (eds) (1979) *Local Government in Britain and France. Problems and Prospects.* London: Allen & Unwin.

Lanzalaco, L. and Schmitter, P.C. (1989), 'Regions and the Organization of Business Interests', in Coleman and Jacek (eds), pp.201–30.

LaPalombara, J. (ed.) (1963) *Bureaucracy and Political Development.* Princeton: Princeton University Press.

LaPalombara, J. (1964) *Interest Groups in Italian Politics.* Princeton: Princeton University Press.

LaPalombara, J. and Weiner, M. (eds) (1966) *Political Parties and Political Development.* Princeton: Princeton University Press.

Larsen, S.U., Hagtvet, B. and Myklebust, J.P. (eds) (1980) *Who Were the Fascists?* Bergen: Universitetsforlaget.

Laski, H.J. (1925) *A Grammar of Politics.* London: Allen & Unwin.

Laski, H.J. (1938) *Parliamentary Government in England.* London: Allen & Unwin.

Laslett, P. and Runciman, L.W. (eds) (1967) *Philosophy, Politics and Society.* New York: Barnes and Noble.

Laslett, P. and Fishkin, J.S. (eds) (1979) *Philosophy, Politics and Society.* New Haven: Yale University Press.

Lassen, A. (1967) *Vælgere på vandring.* Aarhus: Universitetsforlaget.

Lasswell, H.D. (1930) *Psychopathology and Politics.* New York: Viking.

Lasswell, H.D. and Kaplan, A. (1950) *Power and Society. A Framework for Political Inquiry.* New Haven: Yale University Press.

Laver, M. and Schofield, N. (1991) *Multiparty Government. The Politics of Coalition in Europe.* Oxford: Oxford University Press.

Lazarsfeld, P.F., Sewell, W.H. and Wilensky, H.L. (eds) (1967) *The Uses of Sociology.* New York: Basic Books.

Leclère, B. and Wright, V. (1973) *Les Préfets du Second Empire.* Paris: A. Colin.

Lehmbruch, G. (1966) 'Amicabilis compositio' (unpublished paper).

Lehmbruch, G. (1967a) *Proporzdemokratie. Politisches System und politische Kultur in der Schweiz und in Österreich.* Tübingen: Mohr-Siebeck.

Lehmbruch, G. (1967b) 'A Non-competitive Pattern of Conflict Management in Liberal Democracies. The Case of Switzerland, Austria, and Lebanon'. Paper presented to Seventh World Congress of the International Political Science Association, Brussels 1967; published in McRae (ed.), 1974, pp.90–7.

Lehmbruch, G. (1974) 'Consociational Democracy, Class Conflict, and the New Corporatism'. Paper presented to Round Table of the International Political Science Association on Political Integration, Jerusalem; published in Schmitter and Lehmbruch, 1979, pp.53–61.

Lehmbruch, G. (1976) *Parteienwettbewerb im Bundesstaat.* Stuttgart: Kohlhammer Verlag.

Lehmbruch, G. (1977) 'Liberal Corporatism and Party Government', *Comparative Political Studies*, vol. 10, 91–126.

Lehmbruch, G. (1978) 'Party and Federation in Germany: A Developmental Dilemma', *Government and Opposition*, vol. 13, pp.151–77.

Lehmbruch, G. and Schmitter, P.C. (eds) (1982) *Patterns of Corporatist Policy-Making.* London: Sage.

Lehmbruch, G., Döhler, M., Grande, E. and Singer, O. (1988) 'Institutionelle Bedingungen ordnungspolitischen Strategiewechsels im internationalen Vergleich', in M.G. Schmidt (ed.) *Staatstätigkeit.* Opladen: Westdeutscher Verlag, pp.251–83.

Lehmbruch, G. (1989) 'Institutional Linkages and Policy Networks in the Federal System of West Germany', *PUBLIUS*, vol. 19, pp.221–35.

Lehmbruch, G. (1990) 'Die improvisierte Vereinigung. Die dritte deutsche Republik', *Leviathan*, vol. 18, pp.462–86.

Lehmbruch, G. (1991) 'The Organization of Society, Administrative Strategies, and Policy Networks', in R. Czada and A. Windhoff-Héritier (eds) *Political Choice. Institutions, Rules and the Limits of Rationality.* Frankfurt: Campus, pp.121–58.

Lehmbruch, G. (1992) 'Institutionentransfer im Prozeß der Vereinigung. Zur politischen Logik der Verwaltungsintegration in Deutschland', in W. Seibel *et al.* (eds) *Verwaltungsintegration und Verwaltungspolitik im Prozeß der deutschen Einigung.* Baden-Baden: Nomos.

Lehmbruch, G. (1993) 'Consociational Democracy and Corporatism in Switzerland', *PUBLIUS*, vol. 23, pp.43–60.

Lehmbruch, G. (1994) 'Dilemmata verbandlicher Einflußlogik im Prozeß der deutschen Vereinigung', in W. Streeck (ed.) *Staat und Verbände.* Opladen: Westdeutscher Verlag, pp.370–92.

Lehmbruch, G. (1995a) 'Sektorale Variationen in der Transformationsdynamik der politischen Ökonomie Ostdeutschlands', in W. Seibel and A. Benz (eds) *Regierungssystem und Verwaltungspolitik. Beiträge zu Ehren von Thomas Ellwein.* Opladen: Westdeutscher Verlag, pp.180–215.

Lehmbruch, G. (1995b) 'Ressortautonomie und die Konstitution sektoraler Politiknetzwerke. Administrative Interessenvermittlung in Japan', in K. Bentele *et al.* (eds) *Die Reformfähigkeit von Industriegesellschaften.* Frankfurt: Campus Verlag, pp.64–100.

Lehmbruch, G. and Mayer, J. (1997) 'Die Transformation des Agrarsektors', in R. Czada and G. Lehmbruch (eds) *Sektorale Transformationsprozesse.* Frankfurt: Campus Verlag.

Lenin, V.I. (1917) *Imperialism. The Last Stage of Capitalism.* London: Communist Party of Great Britain.

Lerner, D. (1958) *The Passing of Traditional Society. Modernization in the Middle East.* Glencoe: The Free Press.

Lewis, W.A. (1965) *Politics in West Africa.* London: Allen & Unwin.

Lichbach, M.I. and Gurr, T.R. (1986) 'Forecasting Internal Conflict. A Competitive Evaluation of Empirical Theories', *Comparative Political Studies*, vol. 19, pp.3–38.

Lichbach, M.I. (1995) *The Rebel's Dilemma.* Ann Arbor: University of Michigan Press.

Lijphart, A. (1966) *The Trauma of Decolonization. The Dutch and West New Guinea.* New Haven: Yale University Press.

Lijphart, A. (1968a) *The Politics of Accommodation. Pluralism and Democracy in the Netherlands.* Berkeley: University of California Press.

Lijphart, A. (1968b) *Verzuiling, pacificatie en kentering in de Nederlandse politiek.* Amsterdam: De Bussy.

Lijphart, A. (1968c) 'Typologies of Democratic Systems', *Comparative Political Studies*, vol. 1, pp.3–44.

Lijphart, A. (1969) *Paradigmata in de leer der international betrekkingen.* Amsterdam: De Bussy.

Lijphart, A. (1971) 'Comparative Politics and the Comparative Method', *American Political Science Review*, vol. 65, pp.682–93.

Lijphart, A. (1974) 'The Structure of the Theoretical Revolution in International Relations', *International Studies Quarterly*, vol. 18, pp.41–74.

Lijphart, A. (1975a) 'The Comparable-Cases Strategy in Comparative Research', *Comparative Political Studies*, vol. 8, pp.158–77.

Lijphart, A. (1975b) *The Politics of Accommodation. Pluralism and Democracy in the Netherlands.* 2nd edn. Berkeley: University of California Press.

Lijphart, A. (1977) *Democracy in Plural Societies. A Comparative Exploration.* New Haven: Yale University Press.

Lijphart, A. (1981). 'Karl W. Deutsch and the New Paradigm in International Relations', in R.L. Merritt and B.M. Russett (eds) *From National Development to Global Community. Essays in Honor of Karl W. Deutsch.* London: Allen & Unwin, pp.233–51.

Lijphart, A. (1982) 'Consociation: The Model and Its Applications in Divided Societies', in D. Rea (ed.) *Political Co-operation in Divided Societies. A Series of Papers Relevant to the Conflict in Northern Ireland.* Dublin: Gill & Macmillan, pp.166–86.

Lijphart, A. and Grofman, B. (eds) (1984) *Choosing an Electoral System. Issues and Alternatives.* New York: Praeger.

Lijphart, A. (1984) *Democracies. Patterns of Majoritarian and Consensus Government in Twenty-one Countries.* New Haven: Yale University Press.

Lijphart, A. (1985) *Power-sharing in South Africa.* Policy Papers in International Affairs, No. 24, Berkeley: Institute of International Studies, University of California.

Lijphart, A. (1987) 'The Demise of the Last Westminster System? Comments on the Report of New Zealand's Royal Commission on the Electoral System', *Electoral Studies*, vol. 6, pp.97–103.

Lijphart, A. (1989) 'From the Politics of Accommodation to Adversarial Politics in the Netherlands. A Reassessment', *West European Politics*, vol. 12, pp.139–53.

Lijphart, A. (1990) 'The Political Consequences of Electoral Laws, 1945–85', *American Political Science Review*, vol. 84, pp.481–96.

Lijphart, A. (1991a) 'The Alternative Vote. A Realistic Alternative for South Africa?' *Politikon*, vol. 18, pp.91–101.

Lijphart, A. (1991b) 'Constitutional Choices for New Democracies', *Journal of Democracy*, vol. 2, pp.72–84.

Lijphart, A. (ed.) (1992a) *Parliamentary Versus Presidential Government.* Oxford: Oxford University Press.

Lijphart, A. (1992b) 'The Electoral Systems Researcher as Detective. Probing Rae's Suspect "Differential Proposition" on List Proportional Representation', in D. Kavanagh (ed.) *Electoral Politics*. Oxford: Clarendon Press, pp.234–46.

Lijphart, A. (1993) 'Israeli Democracy and Democratic Reform in Comparative Perspective', in E. Sprinzak and L. Diamond (eds) *Israeli Democracy Under Stress*. Boulder, Col.: Lynne Rienner, pp.107–23.

Lijphart, A. (1994a) *Electoral Systems and Party Systems. A Study of Twenty-seven Democracies, 1945–90*. Oxford: Oxford University Press.

Lijphart, A. (1994b) 'Prospects for Power-sharing in the New South Africa', in A. Reynolds (ed.) *Election '94 South Africa. The Campaigns, Results and Future Prospects*. New York: St Martin's Press, pp.221–31.

Lindblom, C.E. (1959) 'The Science of Muddling Through', *Public Administration Review*, vol. 19, pp.79–99.

Lindblom, C.E. (1977) *Politics and Markets. The World's Political-Economic Systems*. New York: Basic Books.

Lindzey, G. (1954) *Handbook of Social Psychology*. Cambridge, Mass.: Addison-Wesley.

Linz, J.J. and Lipset, S.M. (1956) *The Social Bases of Political Diversity in Western Democracies*. Stanford: Center for Advanced Study in the Behavioral Sciences, unpublished manuscript.

Linz, J.J. (1963) *The Social Bases of West German Politics*. Ann Arbor: University Microfilms C.C. card N. Mic 59–4075, 2 vols.

Linz, J.J. (1964) 'An Authoritarian Regime. The Case of Spain', in Allardt and Littunen, pp.291–341.

Linz, J.J. (1966a) 'Michels e il suo contributo alla sociologia politica', introductory essay to Roberto Michels, *La sociologia del partito politico nella democrazia moderna*. Bologna: Il Mulino, pp.vii–cxix.

Linz, J.J. and de Miguel, A. (1966b) *Los Empresarios ante el Poder Público. El Liderazgo y los Grupos de Intereses en el Empresariado Español*. Madrid: Instituto de Estudios Políticos.

Linz, J.J. and de Miguel, A. (1966c) 'Within Nation Differences and Comparisons: The Eight Spains', in Merritt and Rokkan (eds), pp.267–319.

Linz, J.J. (1967) 'The Party System of Spain. Past and Future', in Lipset and Rokkan (eds), pp.197–282.

Linz, J.J. and de Miguel, A. (1968) 'La élite funcionarial española ante le reforma administrativa', *Anales de Moral Social y Economica*, vol. 17, pp.199–249.

Linz, J.J. (1969) 'Ecological Analysis and Survey Research', in Dogan and Rokkan (eds), pp.91–131.

Linz, J.J. (1970a) 'An Authoritarian Regime. The Case of Spain', in Allardt and Rokkan (eds), pp.251–53; 374–81.

Linz, J.J. (1970b) 'From Falange to Movimiento-Organización. The Spanish Single Party and the Franco Regime, 1936–1968', in S.P. Huntington and C.H. Moore (eds) *Authoritarian Politics in Modern Societies. The Dynamics of Established One Party Systems*. New York: Basic Books, pp.128–303.

Linz, J.J. (1971) *Elites Locales y cambio social en la Andalucia rural. Estudio socio-económico de Andalucía*, vol. 2. Madrid: Estudios del Instituto de Desarrollo Económico.

Linz, J.J. (1972a) 'Five Centuries of Spanish History. Quantification and Comparison', in V.R. Lorwin and J.M. Pierce (eds) *The Dimensions of the Past. Materials, Problems, and Opportunities for Quantitative Work in History*. New Haven: Yale University Press, pp.177–261.

Linz, J.J. (1972b) 'Intellectual Roles in Sixteenth and Seventeenth Century Spain', *Daedalus*, vol. 101, pp.59–108.

Linz, J.J. (1972c) 'Continuidad y discontinuidad en la élite política española. De la Restauración al régimen actual', *Estudios de ciencia política y sociología. Homenaje al profesor Carlos Ollero*, pp.361–423.

Linz, J.J. (1973a) 'Early State-Building and Late Peripheral Nationalisms against the State', in Eisenstadt and Rokkan (eds), vol. 2, pp.32–116.

Linz, J.J. (1973b) 'The Future of an Authoritarian Situation or the Institutionalization of an Authoritarian Regime. The Case of Brazil', in A. Stepan (ed.) *Authoritarian Brazil. Origins, Policies and Future*. New Haven: Yale University Press, pp.233–54.

Linz, J.J. (1973c) 'Opposition to and under an Authoritarian Regime. The Case of Spain', in Dahl (ed.), pp.171–259.

Linz, J.J. and de Miguel, A. (1974) 'Founders, Heirs, and Managers of Spanish Firms', *International Studies of Management and Organization*, vol. 4, pp.7–40.

Linz, J.J. (1975a) 'Totalitarian and Authoritarian Regimes', in N. Polsby and F. Greenstein (eds) *Handbook of Political Science*. vol. 3, Reading, Mass.: Addison Wesley Press, pp.175–411.

Linz, J.J. (1975b) 'Politics in a Multilingual Society with a Dominant World Language', in J.-G. Savard and R. Vigneault (eds) *Les états multilingues. Problèmes et Solutions/Multilingual States. Problems and Solutions*. Québec: Presses de l'Université Laval, pp.367–444.

Linz, J.J. (1976) 'Some Notes Toward a Comparative Study of Fascism in Sociological Historical Perspective', in W. Laqueur (ed.) *Fascism. A Reader's Guide*. Berkeley: University of California Press, pp.3–121.

Linz, J.J. (1977a) 'Spain and Portugal. Critical Choices', in D.S. Landes (ed.) *Western Europe. The Trials of Partnership*. Lexington: D.C. Heath, pp.237–96.

Linz, J.J. (1977b) *Tradición y Modernización en España*. Discurso en el acto de Investidura de Doctor 'Honoris Causa', Universidad de Granada.

Linz, J.J. (1978a) *The Breakdown of Democratic Regimes. Crisis, Breakdown, and Reequilibration*. Baltimore: Johns Hopkins University Press.

Linz, J.J., (1978b) 'Fonctions et dysfonctions des élections non concurentielles. Les systèmes autoritaires et totalitaires', *Des élections pas comme les autres*, in Hermet, Linz and Rouquié (eds), pp.101–67.

Linz, J.J. (1978c) 'From Great Hopes to Civil War. The Breakdown of Democracy in Spain', in J.J. Linz and A. Stepan (eds) *The Breakdown of Democratic Regimes. Europe*. Baltimore: Johns Hopkins University Press, pp.142–215.

Linz, J.J. and DATA (1980a) 'The New Spanish Party System', in R. Rose (ed.) *Electoral Participation. A Comparative Analysis*. London: Sage, pp.101–89.

Linz, J.J. (1980b) 'Political Space and Fascism as a Late-Comer', in Larsen *et al.* (eds), pp.153–89.

Linz, J.J., Gómez-Reino, M., Orizo, F.A. and Vila, D. (1981a) *Informe sociológico sobre el cambio político en España, 1975–1981*. Fundacion Foessa, IV Informe Foessa, vol. 1, Madrid: Euramérica.

Linz, J.J. (1981b) 'Some Comparative Thoughts on the Transition to Democracy in Portugal and Spain', in J. Braga de Macedo and S. Serfaty (eds) *Portugal Since the Revolution. Economic and Political Perspectives*. Boulder, Col.: Westview Press.

Linz, J.J. (1981c) 'A Sociological Look at Spanish Communism', in G. Schwab (ed.) *Eurocommunism: The Ideological and Political-Theoretical Foundations*. Westport, Conn.: Greenwood Press, pp.217–69.

Linz, J.J. (1981d) 'Peripheries within the Periphery?', in Torsvik (ed.), pp.335–89.

Linz, J.J. and Stepan, A. (1984) 'Political Crafting of Democratic Consolidation. European and South American Comparisons', in R.A. Pastor (ed.) *Democracy in the Americas. Stopping the Pendulum*. New York: Holmes & Meier, pp.41–61.

Linz, J.J. (1985a) 'Los Jóvenes en una España multilingüe y de nacionalidades', in F. Andrés Orizo *et al.* (ed.) *Juventud española, 1984*. Madrid: Ediciones SM, pp.325–436.

Linz, J.J. (1985b) 'From Primordialism to Nationalism', in E.A. Tiryakian and R. Rogowski (eds) *New Nationalisms of the Developed West. Toward Explanation*. Boston: Allen & Unwin, pp.203–53.

Linz, J.J. (1985c) 'De la crisis de un Estado unitario al Estado de las Autonomías', in F.F. Rodríguez (ed.) *La España de las Autonomías*. Madrid: Instituto de Estudios de Administración Local, pp.527–672.

Linz, J.J. (with the collaboration of M. Gómez-Reino Orizo, A. Francisco and D. Vila) (1986a) *Conflicto en Euskadi*. Madrid: Espasa-Calpe.

Linz, J.J. (1986b) 'Il fattore tempo nei mutamenti di regime', *Teoria Politica*, vol. 2, pp.3–47.

Linz, J.J. and Montero, J.R. (eds) (1986c) *Crisis y cambio. Electores y partidos en la España de los años ochenta*. Madrid: Centro de Estudios Constitucionales.

Linz, J.J. (1988) 'Legitimacy of Democracy and the Socioeconomic System', in M. Dogan (ed.) *Comparing Pluralist Democracies, Strains on Legitimacy*. Boulder, Col.: Westview Press, pp.65–113.

Linz, J.J. (1989) 'Spanish Democracy and the Estado de las Autonomías', in R.A. Goldwin, A. Kaufman and W.A. Schambra (eds) *Forging Unity out of Diversity: The Approaches of Eight Nations*. Washington DC: American Enterprise Institute for Public Policy Research, pp.260–303.

Linz, J.J. (1991) 'Types of Political Regimes and Respect for Human Rights. Historical Cross-National Perspectives', in A. Heide and B. Hagtvet (eds) *Human Rights in Perspective. A Global Assessment*. Oxford: Blackwell, pp.177–222.

Linz, J.J. (1992) 'Stein Rokkan – venn og forskningspirator', in Hagtvet, pp.415–20.

Linz, J.J. (1993a) 'Innovative Leadership in the Transition to Democracy and a New Democracy. The Case of Spain', in G. Sheffer (ed.) *Innovative Leadership in International Politics*. Albany: State University of New York Press, pp.141–86.

Linz, J.J. (1993b) 'Religión y política en España', in R. Díaz Salazar and S. Giner (eds) *Religión y sociedad en España*. Madrid: Centro de Investigaciones Sociológicos, pp.1–50.

Linz, J.J. (1993c) 'State Building and Nation Building'. *European Review*, vol. 1, No 4, pp.355–69.

Linz, J.J. (1994) 'Presidential or Parliamentary Democracy. Does it Make a Difference?', in J.J. Linz and A. Valenzuela (eds) *The Failure of Presidential Democracy*. Baltimore: Johns Hopkins University Press, pp.3–87.

Linz, J.J. (1995a) 'Der religiöse Gebrauch Politik und/oder der politische Gebrauch der Religion', in H. Maier (ed.) *'Totalitarismus' und 'Politische Religionen'. Konzepte des Diktaturvergleichs*. Paderborn: Ferdinand Schüningh, pp.129–54.

Linz, J.J., (with the collaboration of Rocío de Terán) (1995b) 'La sociedad', in J. Andrés-Gallego et al. (eds) *Historia de España. España actual. España y el Mundo 1939–1975*. Madrid: Gredos, pp.117–231.

Linz, J.J. (1995c) 'Plurinazionalismo e democrazia', *Rivista Italiana di Scienza Politica*, vol. 25, pp.21–50.

Linz, J.J. and Stepan, A. (1996) *Problems of Democratic Transition and Consolidation. Southern Europe, South America and Post-Communist Europe*. Baltimore: Johns Hopkins University Press.

Lipset, S.M. (1950) *Agrarian Socialism*. Berkeley: University of California Press.

Lipset, S.M., Lazarsfeld, P.F., Barton, A.H. and Linz, J.J. (1954) 'The Psychology of Voting. An Analysis of Political Behavior', in Lindzey, vol. 2, pp.1124–75.

Lipset, S.M., Trow, M. and Coleman, J. (1956) *Union Democracy*, Glencoe: The Free Press.

Lipset, S.M. (1959a) 'Some Social Requisites of Democracy', *American Political Science Review*, vol. 53, pp.69–105.

Lipset, S.M. and Bendix, R. (1959b) *Social Mobility in Industrial Society*. Berkeley: University of California Press.

Lipset, S.M. (1960) *Political Man. The Social Bases of Politics*. New York City: Doubleday.

Lipset, S.M. (1963) *The First New Nation*. New York: Basic Books.

Lipset, S.M. and Rokkan, S. (eds) (1967) *Party Systems and Voter Alignments*. New York: The Free Press.

Lipset, S.M. (1968) *Revolution and Counter-revolution*. New York: Basic Books.

Lipset, S.M. (1994) 'Some Social Requisites of Democracy Revisited', *American Sociological Review*, vol. 59, pp.1–22.

Lipset, S.M. (1995) 'Juan Linz: Student–Colleague–Friend' in Chehabi and Stepan (eds), pp.3–12.

Loewenstein, K. (1957) *Political Power and the Governmental Process*. Chicago: University of Chicago Press.

Lorwin, V.R. (1966) 'Belgium: Religion, Class, and Language in National Politics', in Dahl (ed.) pp.147–87.

Lorwin, V.R. (1971) 'Segmented Pluralism, Ideological Cleavages and Political Cohesion in the Smaller European Democracies', *Comparative Politics*, vol. 3, pp.141–75.

Lowi, T. (1971) *The End of Liberalism. Ideology, Policy and the Crisis of Public Authority*. New York: Norton.

Lowell, A.L. (1896), *Government and Parties in Continental Europe*. London: Longmans.

Lucci, Y. and Rokkan, S. (eds) (1957) *A Library Center of Survey Research Data*. New York: Columbia University School of Library Services.

Luhmann, N. (1981) *Politische Theorie im Wohlfahrtsstaat*. Munich: Olzog.

MacKay, A.F. (1980) *Arrow's Theorem. The Paradox of Social Choice*. New Haven: Yale University Press.

Mackenzie, W.J.M. (1967) *Politics and Social Science*. Harmondsworth: Penguin.

Mackie, T.T. and Rose, R. (1974) *The International Almanac of Electoral History*. London: Macmillan.

Macridis, R.C. and Cox, R. (1953) 'Research in Comparative Politics'. Report of the SSRC Interuniversity Research Seminar on Comparative Politics, Evanston 1952. *American Political Science Review*, vol. 47, pp.641–75.

Macridis, R.C. (1955) *The Study of Comparative Government*. Garden City: Doubleday.

Magee, B. (1988) *Aspects of Wagner*, 2nd edn. Oxford: Oxford University Press.

Mair, P. (1987) *The Changing Irish Party System. Organization, Ideology and Electoral Competition*. London: Pinter.

Majone, G. (1989) *Evidence, Argument and Persuasion in the Policy Process*. New Haven: Yale University Press.

Majone, G. (1994) 'The Rise of the Regulatory State in Europe', *West European Politics*, vol. 17, pp.77–101.

Mannheim, K. (1940) *Man and Society in an Age of Reconstruction*. London: Routledge & Kegan Paul.

Mannheim, K. (1952) 'The Problem of Generations', *Essays on the Sociology of Knowledge*. New York: Oxford University Press, pp.276–320.

Manoïlesco, M. (1934) *Le Siècle du Corporatisme*. Paris: Alcan.

March, G. and Olsen, J. (1984) 'The New Institutionalism. Organizational Factors in Political Life', *American Political Science Review*, vol. 78, pp.734–49.

Marshall, T.H. (1964) *Class, Citizenship and Social Development*. New York: Doubleday.

Martinelli, A. (ed.) (1991) *International Markets and Global Firms*. London: Sage.

McDaniel, G.R. (1963) *The Danish Unicameral Parliament*. Ph.D dissertation, University of California, Berkeley.

McKenzie, R.T. (1955) *British Political Parties. The Distribution of Power Within the Conservative and Labour Parties*. London: Heinemann.

McKenzie, R.T. and Silver, A. (1968) *Angels in Marble*. London: Heinemann.

McKeon, R. and Rokkan, S. (eds) (1951) *Democracy in a World of Tensions. A Symposium Prepared by UNESCO*. Chicago: University of Chicago Press.

McRae, K.D. (ed.) (1974) *Consociational Democracy. Conflict Accommodation in Segmented Societies*. Toronto: McClelland & Stewart.

Mény, Y. and Wright, V. (eds) (1985) *La Crise de la Sidérurgie Européenne 1974–1984*. Paris: Presses Universitaires de France.

Mény, Y. and Wright, V. (eds) (1987) *The Politics of Steel. Western Europe and the Steel Industry in the Crisis Years (1974–1984)*. Berlin: De Gruyter.

Mény, Y. and Wright, V. (eds) (1994) *La Riforma Amministrativa in Europa*. Bologna: Il Mulino.

Merriam, C.E. (1931) *The Making of Citizens. A Comparative Study of Civic Training*. Chicago: University of Chicago Press.

Merritt, R. and Rokkan, S. (eds) (1966) *Comparing Nations*. New Haven: Yale University Press.

Merton, R.K. (1957) *Social Structure and Social Theory*. Glencoe: The Free Press; revised and enlarged edition.

Meyer, P. (1957) *Administrative Organization. A Comparative Study of the Organization of Public Administration*. London: Stevens.

Meyer, P. (1959) *Politik*. Copenhagen: Nyt Nordisk Forlag.

Meyer, P. (1962) *Politisk videnskab*. Copenhagen: Gyldendal.

Meyer, P. (1965) *Politiske partier*. Copenhagen: Nyt Nordisk Forlag.

Meyer, P. (1992) *Nederlag. Politiske erindringer 1932–1947* (edited and introduced by M.N. Pedersen). Odense: Odense Universitetsforlag.

Michels, R. (1915) *Political Parties*. New York: Dovers.

Miguel, A. de (1975) *Sociología del Franquismo. Análisis Ideológico de los Ministros del Régimen*. Barcelona: Euros.

Miller, K. (1968) *Government and Politics in Denmark*. Boston: Houghton Mifflin Company.

Miller, W. (1994) 'An Organizational History of the Intellectual Origins of the American National Election Studies', in Thomassen (ed.) pp.247–65.

Moore, B. (1966) *Social Origins of Dictatorship and Democracy. Lord and Peasant in the Making of the Modern World*. Boston: Beacon Press.

Morgenthau, H.J. (1954) *Politics Among Nations. The Struggle for Power and Peace*. New York: Knopf.

Muir, R. (1930) *How Britain Is Governed*. London: Constable.

Muller, E.N. (1979) *Aggressive Political Participation*. Princeton: Princeton University Press.

Müller, W. and Wright, V. (eds) (1994) *The State in Western Europe. Retreat or Redefinition?* London: Cass.

Myrdal, G. (1958) *Values in Social Theory. A Selection of Essays on Methodology*. Paul Streeten (ed.) New York: Harper & Row.

Nannestad, P. (1977) 'The Growth of a Profession. Political Science in Denmark 1960–1975' and 'Political Science in Denmark: Trends of Research 1960–1975. Some Footnotes to a Bibliography', *Scandinavian Political Studies*, vol. 12, pp.13–27, pp.85–104.

Neumann, F.L. (1942) *Behemoth. The Structure and Practice of National Socialism*. New York: Oxford University Press.

Neumann, S. (ed.) (1956) *Modern Political Parties. Approaches to Comparative Politics*. Chicago: Chicago University Press.

Newton, K. (1980) *Balancing the Books. Financial Problems of Local Government in Western Europe*. London: Sage.

Noack, J.P. (1981) 'Aktuelle vælgerundersögelser i historisk belysning. Tre böger om danske valg 1960–1975', *Historie. Jyske Samlinger*, Ny række, vol. 13, pp.251–84.

Nora, P. (ed.) (1987) *Essais d'égo-histoire*. Paris: Gallimard.

Nordlinger, E. (1967) *The Working Class Tories*. Princeton: Princeton University Press.

O'Donnell, G. and Schmitter, P.C. (1986) *Tentative Conclusions about Uncertain Democracies*.

Vol. 4 of *Transitions from Authoritarian Rule*, G. O'Donnell, P.C. Schmitter and L. Whitehead (eds). Baltimore: Johns Hopkins University Press.

Olsen, J. (1976) *Ambiguity and Choice in Organizations*. Bergen: Universitetforlaget.

Olsen, J. (1986) *Organised Bureaucracy*. Oslo: Universitetforlaget.

Olson Jr., M. (1965) *The Logic of Collective Action*. Cambridge, Mass.: Harvard University Press.

Page, E. (1985) *Political Authority and Bureaucratic Power*. Hemel Hempstead: Harvester Wheatsheaf.

Pahl, R. and Winkler, J. (1975) 'The Coming Corporatism', *Challenge*, pp.28–35.

Panebianco, A. (1988). *Political Parties. Organization and Power*. Cambridge: Cambridge University Press.

Pareto, V. (1965) [1902–03] 'Les Systèmes Socialistes', *Oeuvres Complètes*, vol. 5. Geneva: Droz.

Parin, P. and Parin-Matthey, G. (1988) *Subjekt im Widerspruch*. Frankfurt: Athenäum.

Parry, G. (1994) 'Finer's Sixth Constitution. The Continuing Debate about the Written Document for Britain', *Government and Opposition*, vol. 29, pp.652–75.

Parsons, T. and Shils, E. (1951) *Toward A Theory of Action*. Cambridge Mass.: Harvard University Press.

Patterson, S.C. and Wahlke, J.C. (eds) (1972) *Comparative Legislative Behavior. Frontiers of Research*. New York: Wiley.

Pedersen, M.N. (1965) 'Kvindernes mobilisering i dansk politik', *Danske Ökonomer*, vol. 12, pp.531–9.

Pedersen, M.N. (1966) 'Preferential Voting in Denmark. The Voter's Influence on the Election of Folketing Candidates', *Scandinavian Political Studies*, vol. 1, pp.167–87.

Pedersen, M.N. (1967a) 'Consensus and Conflict in the Danish Folketing 1945–65', *Scandinavian Political Studies*, vol. 2, pp.143–66.

Pedersen, M.N. (1967b) 'Valgforklaringer. Kommentarer til Aksel Lassen: Vælgere på vandring', *Historie. Jyske Samlinger*, Ny række 7, pp.595–614.

Pedersen, M.N. (1968) 'Rekrutteringen af danske folketingsmænd'. Paper read at Second Nordic Conference of Political Science, Helsinki.

Pedersen, M.N. (1972a) 'Lawyers in Politics. The Danish Folketing and United States Legislatures', in Patterson and Wahlke (eds), pp.25–63.

Pedersen, M.N. (1972b) 'Nogle forskningspolitiske fodnoter til beretningen om behavioralismens gennembrud i statskundskaben', *Politica*, vol. 5, pp.13–33.

Pedersen, M.N. (1975) 'The Geographical Matrix of Parliamentary Representation: A Spatial Model of Political Recruitment', *European Journal of Political Research*, vol. 3, pp.1–19.

Pedersen, M.N. (1976) *Political Development and Elite Transformation in Denmark*. London: Sage.

Pedersen, M.N. (1977a) 'The Personal Circulation of a Legislature: The Danish Folketing, 1849–1968', in W.O. Aydelotte (ed.) *The History of Parliamentary Behavior*. Princeton: Princeton University Press, pp.63–101.

Pedersen, M.N. (1977b) 'Om den rette brug af historiske materialer i statskundskaben: Nogle didaktiske overvejelser', *Festskrift til Erik Rasmussen*. Aarhus: Politica, pp.235–71.

Pedersen, M.N. (1979) 'The Dynamics of European Party Systems. Changing Patterns of Electoral Volatility', *European Journal of Political Research*, vol. 7, pp.1–26.

Pedersen, M.N. (1982) 'State and University in Denmark: From Coexistence to Collision Course' in Daalder and Shils (eds), pp.233–74.

Pedersen, M.N. (1983) 'Changing Patterns of Electoral Volatility in European Party Systems 1948–1977. Explorations in Explanation', in Daalder and Mair (eds), pp.29–66.

Pedersen, M.N. (1984a) 'En forsinket boganmeldelse – eller hvorfor amanuensisoprøret startede og sluttede', *Medarbejderbladet. Meddelelsesorgan for medarbejderne ved Institut for Statskundskab*, vol. 144, pp.27–32.

Pedersen, M.N. (1984b) 'Vælgerbevægelighed og politisk rekruttering. nogle spekulationer og nogle foreløbige resultater', in O. Berg and A. Underdal (eds) *Fra valg til vedtak*. Oslo: Aschehoug, pp.60–85.

Pedersen, M.N. (1987) 'The Danish "Working Multiparty System": Breakdown or Adaptation?' in Daalder (ed.), pp.1–60.

Pedersen, M.N. (1988) 'Lyngsie som taktiker – Allerupsagen og fagbevægelsens strukturproblemer för förste verdenskrig', in H.C. Johansen, M.N. Pedersen and J. Thomsen (eds) *Om Danmarks historie 1900–1920*. Odense: Odense Universitetsforlag, pp.221–44.

Pedersen, M.N. (1990) 'Politologen som konsulent – Tanker om en rolle under udvikling', *Statsvetenskaplig Tidskrift*, vol. 93, pp.317–28.

Pedersen, M.N. (1993) 'Eine kurzgefasste Übersicht über die Entwicklung des Dänischen Parteiensystems', in F.U. Pappi and H. Schmitt (eds) *Parteien, Parlamente und Wahlen in Skandinavien*. Frankfurt: Campus Verlag, pp.91–108.

Pedersen, M.N. (1994) 'Incumbency Success and Defeat in Times of Electoral Turbulences. Patterns of Legislative Recruitment in Denmark 1945–1990', in A. Somit, R. Wildenmann, B. Boll and A. Römmele (eds) *The Victorious Incumbent. A Threat to Democracy?* Aldershot: Dartmouth, pp.218–50.

Pike, F.B. (ed.) (1974) *The New Corporatism. Social and Political Structures in the Iberian World*. Special issue of *Review of Politics*, vol. 36, pp.1–170.

Pirages, D. (1976) *Managing Political Conflict*. Sunbury-on-Thames: Nelson.

Pirsig, R.M. (1974) *Zen and the Art of Motorcycle Maintenance*. London: Bodley Head.

Popkin, S.L. (1991) *The Reasoning Voter. Communication and Persuasion in Presidential Campaigns*. Chicago: The University of Chicago Press.

Popper, K. (1945) *The Open Society and its Enemies*. London: Routledge & Kegan Paul.

Popper, K. (1957) *The Poverty of Historicism*. London: Routledge & Kegan Paul.

Presser, J. (1965) *Ondergang. De vervolging en verdelging van het Nederlandse Jodendom 1940–1945*. The Hague: Staatsuitgeverij, 2 vols.

Presser, J. (1968) *Ashes in the Wind. The Destruction of Dutch Jewry*. Abridged by Louis de Jong. London: Souvenir Press.

Przeworski, A. and Teune, H. (1970) *The Logic of Comparative Inquiry*. New York: Wiley.

Putnam, R. (1973) *The Beliefs of Politicians*. New Haven: Yale University Press.

Putnam, R. (1993) *Making Democracy Work*. Princeton: Princeton University Press.

Pye, L.W. (1958) 'The Non-Western Political Process', *Journal of Politics*, vol. 20, pp.468–86.

Pye, L.W. (1961) 'Armies in the Process of Political Modernization'. *European Journal of Sociology*, vol. 2, pp.82–92.

Pye, L.W. (1962) *Politics, Personality and Nation Building*. New Haven: Yale University Press.

Pye, L.W. (ed.) (1963) *Communication and Political Development*. Princeton: Princeton University Press.

Pye, L.W. and Verba, S. (eds) (1965) *Political Culture and Political Development*. Princeton: Princeton University Press.

Pye, L.W. (1966) *Aspects of Political Development*. Boston: Little, Brown.

Quermonne, J-L. (1963) 'Vers un régionalisme "fonctionnel"?', *Revue Française de Science Politique*, vol. 13, pp.849–76.

Quermonne, J-L. (1987) *Le Gouvernement de la France sous la Vᵉ République*. Paris: Dalloz.

Raadschelders, J.C.R. (ed.) (1996) *Administering the Summit*. Brussels: International Institute of Administrative Science.

Rae, D.W. (1967) *The Political Consequences of Electoral Laws*. New Haven: Yale University Press.

Ragin, C.C. (1989) *The Comparative Method*. Berkeley: University of California Press.

Rasmussen, E. (1968–69) *Komparativ Politik*. 1–2, Copenhagen: Gyldendal.

Rasmussen, E. (1978) 'Statskundskab', in G. Albeck (ed.) *Aarhus Universitet 1928–78*. Aarhus: Universitetsforlaget, pp.341–57.

Rasmussen, E. (1985) 'A Periphery Looks at its Centres. The Case of Danish Political Science', *Scandinavian Political Studies*, vol. 8, pp.319–28.

Rasmussen, E. (1991) 'Min Manddoms Muse. Statskundskaben'. Department of Political Science, Aarhus University: unpublished manuscript.

Reiter, H.L. (1989) 'Party Decline in the West. A Skeptic's View', *Journal of Theoretical Politics*, vol. 1, pp.325–48.

Rhodes, R. and Wright, V. (1987) *Tensions in the Territorial Politics of Western Europe*. London: Cass.

Rice, S. (1928) *Quantitative Methods in Politics*. New York: Alfred A. Knopf.

Richardson, J. and Jordan, G. (1979) *Governing under Pressure. The Policy Process in a Part-Parliamentary Democracy*. Oxford: Martin Robertson.

Riesman, D. (1950) (in collaboration with R. Denny and N. Glazer) *The Lonely Crowd. A Study of the Changing American Character*. New Haven: Yale University Press.

Rinde, E. and Rokkan, S. (eds) (1951) *International Working Conference on Social Stratification and Social Mobility. Vol 1. Preliminary Papers and Proposals*. Oslo: International Sociological Association.

Rokkan, S. (1952) 'Afterdsteoretiske Synspunter i Politisk Tenknings Historie', *Statsøkonomisk Tidsskrift*, vol. 66, pp.40–63; reprinted with an introductory note by the author in S.U. Larsen, *Problemer i samfunnsvitenskapelig metode*. Oslo: Universitetsforlaget, 1976, pp.238–64.

Rokkan, S. (1959) 'Electoral Activity, Party Membership and Organizational Influence', *Acta Sociologica*, vol. 4, pp.25–37.

Rokkan, S. and Torsvik, P. (1960a) 'Der Wähler, der Leser und die Parteipresse', *Kölner Zeitschrift fur Soziologie*, vol. 12, pp.278–301.

Rokkan, S. and Valen, H. (1960b) 'Parties, Elections and Political Behaviour in the Northern Countries. A Review of Recent Research', in O. Stammer (ed.) *Politische Forschung*. Cologne: Westdeutscher Verlag, pp.103–36.

Rokkan, S. (1961) 'Mass Suffrage, Secret Voting and Political Participation', *European Journal of Political Sociology*, vol. 9, pp.132–52.

Rokkan, S. (ed.) (1962a) *Approaches to the Study of Political Participation*. Bergen: Chr. Michelsen Institute.

Rokkan, S. and Valen, H. (1962b) 'The Mobilization of the Periphery. Data on Turnout, Membership and Candidate Recruitment', in Rokkan 1962a, pp.111–58.

Rokkan, S. and Valen, H. (1964) 'Regional Contrasts in Norwegian Politics', in Allardt and Littunen, pp.162–238.

Rokkan, S. (1965) 'Zur entwicklungssoziologischen Analyse von Parteisystemen', in J. Fijalkowski (ed.) *Politologie und Soziologie*. Cologne and Opladen: Westdeutscher Verlag, pp.275–300.

Rokkan, S. (ed.) (1966a) *Data Archives for the Social Sciences*. Paris: Mouton.

Rokkan, S. (1966b) 'Electoral Mobilization, Party Competition and National Integration', in LaPalombara and Weiner (eds), pp.241–65.

Rokkan, S. (1966c) 'Norway: Numerical Democracy and Corporate Pluralism', in Dahl (ed.), pp.70–115.

Rokkan, S. and Lipset, S.M. (1967a) 'Cleavage Structures, Party Systems and Voter Alignments. An Introduction', in Lipset and Rokkan (eds) (1967), pp.1–64.

Rokkan, S. (1967b) 'Geography, Religion and Social Class. Cross-cutting Cleavages in Norwegian Politics', in Lipset and Rokkan (eds) (1967), pp.367–444.

Rokkan, S. (ed.) (1968a) *Comparative Research Across Cultures and Nations*. Paris: Mouton.

Rokkan, S. (1968b) 'The Structuring of Mass Politics in the Smaller European Democracies', *Comparative Studies in Society and History*, vol. 10, pp.173–210.

Rokkan, S. (1968c) 'Electoral Systems', *International Encyclopedia of the Social Sciences*. New York: Macmillan and The Free Press, vol. 5, pp.6–21.

Rokkan, S. and Meyriat, J. (eds) (1969) *International Guide to Electoral Statistics*. Paris: Mouton.

Rokkan, S., Verba, S., Viet, J. and Almasy, E. (1969) *Comparative Survey Analysis*. Paris: Mouton.

Rokkan, S. (1969a) 'Methods and Models in the Comparative Study of Nation-building', *Acta Sociologica*, vol. 12, pp.53–73.

Rokkan, S. (1969b) 'Data Confrontation Seminars', *Scandinavian Political Studies*, vol. 4, pp.22–9.

Rokkan, S. (1970a) *Citizens, Elections, Parties. Approaches to the Comparative Study of the Processes of Development*. Oslo: Universitesforlaget.

Rokkan, S. (1970b) 'Cross-cultural, Cross-societal and Cross-national Research', in UNESCO, *Main Trends of Research in the Social and Human Sciences*. Paris: Mouton, pp.645–89.

Rokkan, S. (1970c) 'The Growth and Structuring of Mass Politics in Western Europe. Reflections on Possible Models of Explanation', *Scandinavian Political Studies*, vol. 5, pp.65–83.

Rokkan, S. (1971a) 'A Conceptual Map of Europe', in J. Burchard (ed.) *Thoughts from the Lake of Time*. New York: Josiah Macy Jr. Foundation, pp.49–79.

Rokkan, S. (1971b) 'Nation-building', *Current Sociology*, vol. 19, pp.3–86.

Rokkan, S. (1974) 'Entries, Voices, Exits. Toward a Possible Generalization of the Hirschman Model', *Social Science Information*, vol. 13, pp.39–53.

Rokkan, S. (1975a) 'Dimensions of State Formation and Nation-building', in Tilly (ed.), pp.562–600.

Rokkan, S. (1975b) 'Votes Count, Resources Decide', *Makt og motiv. Et festskrift til Jens Arup Seip*. Oslo: Gyldendalpp, pp.216–24.

Rokkan, S. (1976a) 'Introduction: une famille de modèles pour l'histoire comparée de l'Europe', *Journée d'études, Association Française de Science Politique*.

Rokkan, S. (1976b) 'A Geoeconomic–Geopolitical Model of Sources of Variations Across the Territories of Western Europe'. Paper, ISSC-MSH *Symposium on Wallerstein and Anderson*, Bellagio.

Rokkan, S., Szalai, A., Petrella, R. and Scheuch, E.K. (eds) (1977a) *Cross-National Comparative Survey Research. Theory and Practice*. Oxford: Pergamon.

Rokkan, S. (1977b) 'Towards a Generalized Concept of Verzuiling', *Political Studies*, vol. 25, pp.563–70.

Rokkan, S. and Svåsand, L. (1978) 'Zur Soziologie der Wahlen und der Massenpolitik', in R. König (ed.) *Handbuch der empirischen Sozialforschung*, vol. 12. Stuttgart: Enke, pp.1–72.

Rokkan, S. (1981) 'The Growth and Structuring of Mass Politics', in F. Wisti (ed.) *Nordic Democracy. Ideas, Issues and Institutions in Politics, Economy, Education, Social and Cultural Affairs of Denmark, Finland, Iceland, Norway and Sweden*. Copenhagen: Det Danske Selskab, pp.53–79.

Rokkan, S. and Urwin, D.W. (eds) (1982) *The Politics of Territorial Identity. Studies in European Regionalism*. London: Sage.

Rokkan, S. and Urwin, D.W. (1983) *Economy, Territory, Identity. Politics of West European Peripheries*. London: Sage.

Rokkan, S. (forthcoming) *State Formation, Nation-Building and Mass Politics in Europe. The Theory of Stein Rokkan* (based on his collected works, selected and rearranged by Peter Flora, Stein Kuhnle and Derek Urwin). Oxford: Oxford University Press.

Rorty, R. (1989) *Contingency, Irony and Solidarity*. Cambridge: Cambridge University Press.

Rose, R. (1964) *Politics in England*. Boston: Little, Brown.

Rose, R. (1967) *Influencing Voters. A Study of Campaign Rationality*. London: Faber & Faber.

Rose, R. and Mossawir, H. (1967) 'Voting and Elections. A Functional Analysis', *Political Studies*, vol. 15, pp.173–201.

Rose, R. (1969) 'Dynamic Tendencies in the Authority of Regimes', *World Politics*, vol. 21, pp.612–28.

Rose, R. (1970) *Governing Without Consensus. An Irish Perspective*. London: Faber & Faber.

Rose, R. (1974a) *The Problem of Party Government*. London: Macmillan.

Rose, R. (ed.) (1974b) *Electoral Behavior. A Comparative Analysis*. New York: The Free Press.

Rose, R. (1976a) *Managing Presidential Objectives*. New York: The Free Press.

Rose, R. (1976b) 'On the Priorities of Citizenship in the Deep South and Northern Ireland', *Journal of Politics*, vol. 38, pp.247–91.

Rose, R. and Peters, B.G. (1978) *Can Government Go Bankrupt?* New York: Basic Books.

Rose, R. and Suleiman, E. (eds) (1980) *Presidents and Prime Ministers*. Washington DC: American Enterprise Institute.

Rose, R. (ed.) (1980) *Challenge to Governance. Studies in Overloaded Polities*. Beverly Hills and London: Sage.

Rose, R. (1984a) *Do Parties Make a Difference?* 2nd edn. London: Macmillan.

Rose, R. (1984b) *Understanding Big Government. The Programmeme Approach*. London: Sage.

Rose, R. (1990) 'Institutionalizing Professional Political Science in Europe. A Dynamic Model', *European Journal of Political Research*, vol. 18, pp.581–603.

Rose, R. and Wignanek, G. (1990) *Training Without Trainers? How Germany Avoids Britain's Supply-side Bottleneck*. London: Anglo-German Foundation.

Rose, R. (1991a) 'Comparing Forms of Comparative Analysis', *Political Studies*, vol. 39, pp.446–62.

Rose, R. (1991b) *The Postmodern President*. 2nd edn. Chatham, NJ: Chatham House.

Rose, R. (1991c) 'Is American Public Policy Exceptional?', in B. Shafer (ed.) *Is America Different?* New York: Oxford University Press, pp.187–229.

Rose, R. (ed.) (1991d) 'Lesson-Drawing Across Nations', a special issue of the *Journal of Public Policy*, vol. 11, pp.1–131.

Rose, R. (1992) 'Escaping from Absolute Dissatisfaction. A Trial-and-Error Model of Change in Eastern Europe', *Journal of Theoretical Politics*, vol. 4, pp.371–93.

Rose, R. (1993) *Lesson-Drawing in Public Policy. A Guide to Learning Across Time and Space*. Chatham, NJ: Chatham House.

Rose, R. and Mishler, W. (1994) 'Mass Reaction to Regime Change in Eastern Europe. Polarization or Leaders and Laggards?', *British Journal of Political Science*, vol. 24, pp.159–82.

Rose, R. and Davies, P. (1994) *Inheritance in Public Policy. Change Without Choice in Britain*. New Haven: Yale University Press.

Rose, R. and Haerpfer, C. (1994) 'Mass Response to Transformation in Post-Communist Societies', *Europe–Asia Studies*, vol. 46, pp.3–28.

Rose, R. (1995a) 'Democracy and Enlarging the European Union Eastwards', *Journal of Common Market Studies*, vol. 33, pp.427–50.

Rose, R. (1995b) 'The Academic as Policy Analyst', in P. Day, D. Fox, R. Maxwell and E. Scrivens (eds) *The State, Politics and Health. Essays for Rudolf Klein*. Oxford: Blackwell.

Rose, R. (1996) *What Is Europe?* New York and London: Longmans.

Rosenau, J. (1981) *The Study of Political Adaptation*. London: Pinter.

Ross, A. (1953) *Om ret og retfærdighed*. Copenhagen: Nyt Nordisk Forlag – Arnold Busck.

Royal Commission on the Electoral System (1986) *Report of the Royal Commission on the Electoral System. Towards a Better Democracy*. Wellington: V.R. Ward, Government Printer.

Rueschemeyer, D., Huber Stephens, E. and Stephens, J.D. (1992) *Capitalist Development and Democracy*. Oxford: Polity Press.

Russett, B.M., Alker, H.R., Deutsch, K.W. and Lasswell, H.D. (1964) *World Handbook of Political and Social Indicators*. New Haven: Yale University Press.

Rustow, D.A. (1955) *The Politics of Compromise*. Princeton: Princeton University Press.

Rustow, D.A. (1956) 'Scandinavia: Working Multiparty Systems', in Neumann (ed.), pp.169–93.

Saelen, K.T. (1981) 'Stein Rokkan. A Bibliography', in Torsvik (1981), pp.525–53.

Sani, G. and Sartori, G. (1983) 'Polarization, Fragmentation and Competition in Western Democracies', in Daalder and Mair (eds), pp.307–40.

Sartori, G. (1957) *Democrazia e Definizioni*. Bologna: Il Mulino.

Sartori, G. (1962a) *Democratic Theory*. Detroit: Wayne University Press; New York: Praeger (1965).

Sartori, G. (1962b) 'Constitutionalism. A Preliminary Discussion', *American Political Science Review*, vol. 56, pp.853–64.

Sartori, G. (1966a), 'European Political Parties. The Case of Polarized Pluralism', in LaPalombara and Weiner (eds), pp.137–76.

Sartori, G. (1966b) *Stato e Politica nel Pensiero di Benedetto Croce*. Napoli: Morano.

Sartori, G. (1968a) 'Democracy', *International Encyclopedia of the Social Science*. New York: Macmillan/The Free Press, vol. 4, pp.112–21.

Sartori, G. (1968b) 'Representational Systems', *International Encyclopedia of the Social Sciences*. New York: Macmillan/The Free Press, vol. 13, pp.465–74.

Sartori, G. (1968c) 'Political Development and Political Engineering', in J.D. Montgomery and A.O. Hirschman (eds) *Public Policy*, vol. 17. Cambridge, Mass.: Harvard University Press, pp.261–98.

Sartori, G. (1969) 'From the Sociology of Politics to Political Sociology', in S.M. Lipset (ed.) *Politics and the Social Sciences*. Oxford and New York: Oxford University Press, pp.65–100.

Sartori, G. (1970a) 'Concept Misformation in Comparative Politics', *American Political Science Review*, vol. 64, pp.1033–53.

Sartori, G. (1970b) 'The Typology of Party Systems', in Allardt and Rokkan (eds), pp.322–52.

Sartori, G. (1971) 'La Politica Comparata: Premesse e Problemi', *Rivista Italiana di Scienza Politica*, vol. 1, pp.7–66.

Sartori, G. (1974) 'Philosophy, Theory and Science of Politics', *Political Theory*, vol. 2, May, pp.133–62.

Sartori, G. (1975) 'Will Democracy Kill Democracy? Decision Making by Majorities and by Committees', *Government and Opposition*, vol. 10, pp.131–158.

Sartori, G. (1976) *Parties and Party Systems. A Framework for Analysis*. New York: Cambridge University Press.

Sartori, G. (1979) *La Politica: Logica e Metodo in Scienze Sociali*. Milano: Sugarco.

Sartori, G. (1984) 'Guidelines for Concept Analysis', in G. Sartori (ed.) *Social Science Concepts. A Systematic Analysis*. Beverly Hills: Sage, pp.15–85.

Sartori, G. (1985) 'Dova va la Scienza Politica', in L. Graziamo (ed.) *La Scienza Politica in Italia*. Milan: Angelí, pp.98–114.

Sartori, G. (1987a) *The Theory of Democracy Revisited*. Chatham, NJ: Chatham House, 2 vols.

Sartori, G. (1987b) *Elementi di Teoria Politica*. Bologna: Il Mulino.

Sartori, G. (1991a) 'Comparing and Miscomparing', *Journal of Theoretical Politics*, vol. 3, pp.243–57.

Sartori, G. (1991b) 'Rethinking Democracy: Bad Polity and Bad Politics', *International Social Science Journal*, vol. 63, pp.437–50.

Sartori, G. (1992) 'Democrazia', *Enciclopedia delle Scienze Sociali*. Rome: Istituto della Enciclopedia Italiana, vol. 2, pp.742–58.

Sartori, G. (1993) 'Totalitarianism, Model Mania and Learning from Error', *Journal of Theoretical Politics*, vol. 5, pp.5–22.

Sartori, G. (1994a) *Comparative Constitutional Engineering. An Inquiry into Structures, Incentives and Outcomes.* London: Macmillan; New York: New York University Press.

Sartori, G. (1994b) 'Compare Why and How. Comparing, Miscomparing and the Comparative Method', in M. Dogan and A. Kazancigil (eds) *Comparing Nations. Concepts, Strategies, Substance.* Oxford: Blackwell, pp.14–34.

Sartori, G. (1995) 'How Far Can Free Government Travel?', *Journal of Democracy*, vol. 6, pp.101–11.

Sartori, G. (1996a) *Croce Filosofo Practico.* Bologna: Il Mulino.

Sartori, G. (1996b) *Croce Etico-Politico e Filosofo della Libertá.* Bologna: Il Mulino.

Scharpf, F. *et al.* (1976) *Politikverflechtung: Theorie und Empirie des kooperativen Föderalismus in der Bundesrepublik.* Kronberg: Scriptor.

Schelling. T.C. (1960) *The Strategy of Conflict.* Cambridge, Mass.: Harvard University Press.

Scheuch, E.K. and Wildenmann, R. (eds) (1965) *Zur Soziologie der Wahl*; special issue of the *Kölner Zeitschrift für Soziologie und Sozialpsychologie*, Cologne and Opladen: Westdeutscher Verlag.

Scheuch, E.K. (1968) 'The Cross-Cultural Use of Sample Surveys: Problems of Comparability', in Rokkan (ed.), pp.176–209.

Schlozman, K.L. and Verba, S. (1980) *Injury to Insult.* Cambridge, Mass.: Harvard University Press.

Schmitter, P.C. (1971a) *Interest Conflict and Political Change in Brazil.* Stanford: Stanford University Press.

Schmitter, P.C. (1971b) 'Military Intervention, Political Competitiveness and Public Policy in Latin America. 1950–1967', in M. Janowitz and J. van Doorn (eds) *On Military Intervention.* Rotterdam: Rotterdam University Press, pp.425–506.

Schmitter, P.C. (1971c) 'Desarrollo retrasado, dependencia externa y cambio político en América Latina', *Foro Internacional*, vol. 12, pp.135–74.

Schmitter, P.C. (1973) 'Foreign Military Assistance, National Military Spending and Military Rule in Latin America. 1945–1970', in P.C. Schmitter (ed.) *Military Rule in Latin America. Functions, Consequences and Prospectives.* Beverly Hills: Sage, pp.117–87.

Schmitter, P.C. (1974) 'Still the Century of Corporatism?', in F.B. Pike and T. Stritch (eds) *The New Corporatism. Social-Political Structures in the Iberian World.* Notre Dame: University of Notre Dame Press, pp.85–131.

Schmitter, P.C. (1975a) *Corporatism and Public Policy in Authoritarian Portugal.* Contemporary Political Sociology Series, Beverly Hills: Sage.

Schmitter, P.C. (1975b) 'Liberation by *Golpe.* Retrospective Thoughts on the Demise of Authoritarian Rule in Portugal', *Armed Forces and Society*, vol. 2, pp.5–33.

Schmitter, P. (1977) 'Models of Interest Intermediation and Models of Societal Change in Western Europe', *Comparative Political Studies*, vol. 10, pp.7–38.

Schmitter, P.C. (1978a) 'The Impact and Meaning of Authoritarian Portugal, 1933–1974', in Hermet, Rose and Rouquié (eds), pp.145–68.

Schmitter, P.C. (1978b) 'Reflections on Mihaïl Manoïlescu and the Political Consequences of Delayed-Dependent Development on the Periphery of Western Europe', in K. Jowitt (ed.) *Social Change in Romania 1860–1940.* Berkeley: Institute of International Studies, University of California, pp.111–39.

Schmitter, P.C. (1979a) 'The "Régime d'Exception" that Became the Rule. Forty-Eight Years of Authoritarian Domination in Portugal', in L.S. Graham and H.M. Makler (eds) *Contemporary Portugal.* Austin: University of Texas Press, pp.3–46.

Schmitter, P.C. and Lehmbruch, G. (eds) (1979b) *Trends Toward Corporatist Intermediation.* London: Sage.

Schmitter, P.C. (1980a) 'The Social Origins, Economic Bases and Political Imperatives of Authoritarian Rule in Portugal', in Larsen *et al.* (eds), pp.435–66.

Schmitter, P.C. (1980b) 'Speculations about the Prospective Demise of Authoritarian Regimes and its Possible Consequences', *Working Paper 60*, The Woodrow Wilson Center, Latin American Programme.

Schmitter, P.C. (1981a) 'Interest Intermediation and Regime Governability in Advanced Industrial-Capitalist Polities', in S. Berger (ed.) *Organizing Interests in Western Europe*. New York: Cambridge University Press, pp.285–327.

Schmitter, P.C. and Streeck, W. (1981b) 'The Organization of Business Interests', *Discussion Paper*, IIM/LMP 81–13, Wissenschaftszentrum Berlin.

Schmitter, P.C. (1981c) 'Needs, Interests, Concerns, Actions, Associations and Modes of Intermediation. Toward a Theory of Interest Politics in Contemporary Society', Wissenschaftszentrum Berlin, mimeo, March.

Schmitter, P.C. (1982) 'Reflections on Where the Theory of Neo-Corporatism Has Gone and Where the Praxis of Neo-Corporatism May be Going', in Lehmbruch and Schmitter (eds), pp.258–80.

Schmitter, P.C. (1983) 'Democratic Theory and Neocorporatist Practice', *Social Research*, vol. 50, pp.885–928.

Schmitter, P.C. (1985a) 'Speculations about the Prospective Demise of Authoritarian Regimes and its Possible Consequences', *Revista de Ciência Politica*, vol. 1, pp.83–102 and vol. 1, pp.125–44.

Schmitter, P.C. (1985b) 'Neo-Corporatism and the State', in W. Grant (ed.) *The Political Economy of Corporatism*. London: Macmillan, pp.32–62.

Schmitter, P.C. (1988) *Corporative Democracy. Oxymoronic? Just Plain Moronic? Or a Promising Way Out of the Present Impasse*. Paper presented at Conference on Politische Institutionen und Interessenvermittlung, Universität Konstanz.

Schmitter, P.C. (1989a) 'Regions and the Organization of Business Interests', in W.D. Coleman and H. Jacek (eds) *Regionalism, Business Interests and Public Policy*. London: Sage, pp.201–30.

Schmitter, P.C. (1989b) 'Corporatism is Dead! Long Live Corporatism! Reflections on Andrew Shonfield's *Modern Capitalism*', *Government and Opposition*, vol. 24, pp.54–73.

Schmitter, P.C. (1990) 'Sectors in Modern Capitalism. Modes of Governance and Variations in Performance' in R. Brunetta and C. dell'Aringa (eds) *Labour Relations and Economic Performance*. London: Macmillan, pp.3–39.

Schmitter, P.C. and. Streeck, W (1991a) 'Organized Interests and the Europe of 1992', in N.J. Ornstein and M. Perlman (eds) *Political Power and Social Change. The United States Faces the United Europe*. Washington DC: American Enterprise Institute, pp.46–67.

Schmitter, P.C. (1991b) 'Public Opinion and the Quality of Democracy in Portugal', in Chehabi and Stepan (eds), pp.345–59.

Schmitter, P.C. (1991c) 'Some Second Thoughts about Corporative Democracy. Oxymoronic or Moronic, Promising or Problematic?'. Paper presented at the conference on Competing Theories of Post-Liberal Democracy, University of Texas, Austin, 8–10 February.

Schmitter, P.C. (1992) 'The Consolidation of Democracy and Representation of Social Groups', *American Behavioral Scientist*, vol. 35, pp.422–49.

Schmitter, P.C. (1995) 'Organized Interests and Democratic Consolidation in Southern Europe', in N. Diamandorous, R. Gunther and H.J. Puhle (eds) *The Politics of Democratic Consolidation in Southern Europe in Comparative Perspective*. Baltimore: Johns Hopkins Press, pp.284–314.

Schorske, C. (1980) *Fin de Siècle Vienna, Politics and Culture*. New York: Knopf.

Schumpeter, J.A. (1942) *Capitalism, Socialism, and Democracy*. New York: Harper & Brothers.

Seeley, J.R. (1888) *An Introduction to Political Science*. London: Macmillan.

Seligman, A. (1992) *The Idea of Civil Society*. New York: The Free Press.

Selznick, P. (1951) 'Institutional Vulnerability in Mass Society', *American Journal of Sociology*, vol. 56, pp.320–31.

Servan-Schreiber, J-J. (1968) *The American Challenge*. London: Hamish Hamilton.

Shain, Y. and Linz, J.J. (eds) (1995) *Between States. Interim Governments and Democratic Transitions*. Cambridge: Cambridge University Press.

Shils, E. (1960) *Political Development in The New States*. The Hague: Mouton.

Shils, E. (1972) *The Intellectuals and the Powers and Other Essays*. Chicago: University of Chicago Press.

Shils, E. (1975) *Center and Periphery. Essays in Macrosociology*. Chicago: University of Chicago Press.

Shlapentokh, V. (1989) *Public and Private Life of the Soviet People*. New York: Oxford University Press.

Shonfield, A. (1965) *Modern Capitalism. The Changing Balance of Public and Private Power*. Oxford: Oxford University Press.

Sijes, B.A. (1954) *De Februaristaking 25–26 Februari; 1941*. The Hague: Nijhoff.

Sijes, B.A. (1966) *De Arbeidsinzet. De Gedwongen Arbeid van Nederlanders in Duitsland 1940–1945*. The Hague: Nijhoff.

Silberman, B.S. (1994) *Cages of Reason. The Rise of the Rational State in France, Japan, the United States, and Great Britain*. Chicago: University of Chicago Press.

Simon, H.A. (1979) 'Rational Decision Making in Business Organizations', *American Economic Review*, vol. 69, pp.493–513.

Simpson, R. (1983) *How the Ph.D. Came to Britain*. Guildford, Surrey: Society for Research into Higher Education.

Sjöblom, G. (1977) 'The Cumulation Problem in Political Science. An Essay on Research Strategies', *European Journal of Political Research*, vol. 5, pp.1–32.

Smelser, N.J. (1967) 'Notes on the Methodology of Comparative Analysis of Economic Activity', *Transactions of the Sixth World Congress of Sociology*, vol. 2. Evian: International Sociological Association.

Smelser, N.J. (1973) 'The Methodology of Comparative Analysis', in D. Warwick and S. Osherson (eds) *Comparative Research Methods*. Englewood Cliffs: Prentice-Hall, pp.101–17.

Smith, G. (1966) 'What is a Party System?', *Parliamentary Affairs*, vol. 19, pp.351–62.

Smith, G. (1972) *Politics in Western Europe*. London: Heinemann. 5th edn. Aldershot: Gower, 1989.

Smith, G. (1974) 'A Model of the Bureaucratic Culture', *Political Studies*, vol. 22, pp.31–43.

Smith, G. (1979) *Democracy in Western Germany*. London: Heinemann, 1979.

Smith, G. (1982), 'The German Volkspartei and the Career of the Catch-All Concept', in H. Döring and G. Smith (eds) *Party Government and Political Culture in Western Germany*. London: Macmillan.

Smith, G., Paterson, W. and Merkl, P. (eds) (1989) *Developments in West German Politics*. London: Macmillan.

Smith, G., Paterson, W., Merkl, P. and Padgett, S. (eds) (1992) *Developments in German Politics*. London: Macmillan.

Smith, G., Paterson, W. and Padgett, S. (eds) (1996) *Developments in German Politics*. London: Macmillan.

Smith, M.G. (1969a) 'Pluralism in Precolonial African Societies', in L. Kuper and M.G. Smith (eds) *Pluralism in Africa*. Berkeley: University of California Press, pp.91–151.

Smith, M.G. (1969b) 'Some Developments in the Analytic Framework of Pluralism', in L. Kuper and M.G. Smith (eds) *Pluralism in Africa*. Berkeley: University of California Press, pp.415–58.

Somit, A. and Tannenhaus, J. (1964) *American Political Science. A Profile of a Discipline*. New York: Atherton.

Stehouwer, J. (1967) 'Long Term Ecological Analysis of Electoral Statistics in Denmark' *Scandinavian Political Studies*, vol. 2, pp.94–116.

Stein Rokkan Committee (1980) *Stein Rokkan 1921–1979*. University of Bergen: Universitetsforlaget.

Steiner, J. (1970) *Gewaltlose Politik und kulturelle Vielfalt. Hypothesen entwickelt am Beispiel der Schweiz*. Berne: Paul Haupt.

Steiner, J. (1974) *Amicable Agreement versus Majority Rule. Conflict Resolution in Switzerland*. Chapel Hill: University of North Carolina Press:

Steiner, J. (1986) *European Democracies*. New York: Longmans.

Steingruber, B.E. (1989) *Wissenschaft als Selbsterfahrung- Selbsterfahrung als Wissenschaft*. Vienna: Böhlau.

Streeck, W. and Schmitter, P.C. (eds) (1985a) *Private Interest Governments. Beyond Market and State*. London: Sage.

Streeck, W. and Schmitter, P.C. (1985b) 'Community, Market, State – and Associations? The Prospective Contribution of Interest Governance to Social Order', in Streeck and Schmitter (eds), pp.1–35.

Szymanski, A. (1978) *The Capitalist State and the Politics of Class*. Cambridge, Mass.: Winthrop.

Tarrow, S. (1977) *Between Center and Periphery. Grassroots Politicians in Italy and France*. New Haven: Yale University Press.

Thomassen, J.J.A. (1976) *Kiezers en Gekozenen in een Parlementaire Democratie*. Alphen: Sijthoff.

Thomassen, J.J.A. (ed.) (1994) *The Intellectual History of Election Studies*. Special Issue of the *European Journal of Political Research*, vol. 25, pp.239–385.

Tilly, C. (ed.) (1975) *The Formation of National States in Western Europe*. Princeton: Princeton University Press.

Tingsten, H. (1937) *Political Behaviour. Studies in Election Statistics*. London: King.

Tocqueville, A. de (1968) [1835, 1840] *Democracy in America*. London: Fontana.

Torstendahl, R. (1991) *Bureaucratisation in North Western Europe*. London: Routledge.

Torsvik, P. (ed.) (1981) *Mobilization, Center-Periphery Structures and Nation-Building. A Volume in Commemoration of Stein Rokkan*. Bergen: Universitetsforlaget.

Tunstall, J. (1970) *The Westminster Lobby Correspondents*. London: Routledge.

UNESCO (1950) *Contemporary Political Science. A Survey of Methods, Research and Teaching*. Paris: Unesco.

Valen, H. and Rokkan, S. (1974) 'Conflict Structure and Mass Politics in a European Periphery', in Rose (ed.), pp.315–70.

Vallès, J.M. and Newton, K. (eds) (1991) *Political Science in Western Europe 1960–1990*. Special issue of *European Journal of Political Research*, vol. 20, pp.225–466.

Van den Berghe, P.L. (1981a) *The Ethnic Phenomenon*. New York: Elsevier.

Van den Berghe, P.L. (1981b) 'Protection of Ethnic Minorities. A Critical Appraisal', in R.G. Wirsing (ed.) *Protection of Ethnic Minorities. Comparative Perspectives*. New York: Pergamon Press, pp.343–55.

Veblen, T. (1934) *The Theory of the Leisure Class. An Economic Study in the Evolution of Institutions*. New York: The Modern Library.

Vedung, E. (1991) *Utvädering i politik och förvaltning*. Lund: Studentlitteratur.

Verba, S. (1961) *Small Groups and Political Behavior. A Study of Leadership*. Princeton: Princeton University Press.

Verba, S. (1967) 'Some Dilemmas in Comparative Research', *World Politics*, vol. 20, pp.111–27.

Verba, S., Ahmed, B. and Bhatt, A. (1971) *Caste, Race, and Politics. A Comparison of India and the United States*. Beverly Hills: Sage.

Verba, S. and Nie, N.H. (1972) *Participation in America*. New York: Harper & Row.

Verba, S., Nie, N.H. and Kim, J. (1978) *Participation and Political Equality. A Seven Nation Study.* New York: Cambridge University Press.

Verba, S. and Orren, G. (1985) *Equality in America. The View from the Top.* Cambridge, Mass.: Harvard University Press.

Verba, S., Orren G., Kelman, S., Kabashima, I., Miyake, I. and Watanuki, J. (1987) *Elites and the Idea of Equality.* Cambridge, Mass.: Harvard University Press.

Verba, S., Lehman Schlozman, K. and Brady, H.E. (1995) *Voice and Equality. Civic Voluntarism in American Politics.* Cambridge, Mass.: Harvard University Press.

Verney, D.V. (1959) *The Analysis of Political Systems.* London: Routledge & Kegan Paul.

Vickers, J. and Wright, V. (eds) (1989) *The Politics of Privatization in Western Europe.* London: Cass.

Vig, N.J. and Stiefbold, R. (eds) (1974) *Politics in Advanced Societies. Modernization, Development and Contemporary Change.* Englewood Cliffs: Prentice-Hall.

Von Beyme, K. (1964a) *Der Föderalismus in der Sowjetunion.* Heidelberg: Quelle & Meyer.

Von Beyme, K. (1964b) 'Federal Theory and Party Reality in the Soviet Union', *Public Policy*, vol. 13, pp.395–412.

Von Beyme, K. (1965) *Politische Soziologie im zaristischen Rußland.* Wiesbaden: Harrassowitz.

Von Beyme, K. (1968) 'Gesellschaftliche Organization und Interessenpluralismus in der Sowjetunion', in R. Löwenthal and B. Meissner (eds) *Sowjetische Innenpolitik.* Stuttgart: Kohlhammer, pp.39–48.

Von Beyme, K. (1969) *Interessengruppen in der Demokratie.* Munich: Piper.

Von Beyme, K. (1970, 1973) *Die parlamentarischen Regierungssysteme in Europa.* Munich: Piper.

Von Beyme, K. (ed.) (1971a) *Theory and Politics / Theorie und Politik. Festschrift zum 70. Geburtstag für Carl Joachim Friedrich.* The Hague: Nijhoff.

Von Beyme, K. (1971b) *Vom Faschismus zur Entwicklungsdiktatur. Machtélite und Opposition in Spanien.* Munich: Piper.

Von Beyme, K. (1974a) *Die politische Elite in der Bundesrepublik Deutschland.* 2nd edn. Munich: Piper.

Von Beyme, K. (1974b) 'Authoritarian Regimes: Developing Open Societies?', in D. Germino and K. von Beyme (eds) *The Open Society in Theory and Practice.* The Hague: Nijhoff, pp.109–20.

Von Beyme, K. (1980) *Challenge of Power. Trade Unions and Industrial Relations in Capitalist Countries.* London: Sage (original German edition 1977).

Von Beyme, K. (1982) *Economics and Politics within Socialist Systems.* New York: Praeger (German editions 1975, 1977).

Von Beyme, K. (1983) *The Political System of the Federal Republic of Germany.* New York: St Martin's Press.

Von Beyme, K. (1985) *Political Parties in Western Democracies.* New York: St Martin's Press (German editions 1982, 1984).

Von Beyme, K. (1986a) 'Plea for Policy Analysis', *Policy Studies Journal*, vol. 4, pp.540–4.

Von Beyme, K. (1986b) 'Attitudes of German Youth Toward Relations between the Two German States', *West Germany, East Germany and the German Question.* Baltimore: American Institute for Contemporary German studies, Johns Hopkins University, pp.33–43.

Von Beyme, K. (1987a) *Der Wiederaufbau. Architektur und Städtebaupolitik in beiden deutschen Staaten.* Munich: Piper.

Von Beyme, K. (1987b) *The Soviet Union in World Politics.* New York: St Martin's Press (German editions 1983, 1985).

Von Beyme, K. (1987c) *America as a Model. The Impact of American Democracy in the World.* New York: St Martin's Press (German edition 1976).

Von Beyme, K. (1988a) *Der Vergleich in der Politikwissenschaft.* Munich: Piper.

Von Beyme, K. (1988b) *Reformpolitik und sozialer Wandel in der Sowjetunion.* Baden-Baden: Nomos.

Von Beyme, K. (1989) 'Reform and Regional Policies in the Soviet Union', *The Journal of Communist Studies*, pp.267–84.

Von Beyme, K. (1991a) 'The Modernization of Socialism. Glasnost versus Perestroika?' in D.A. Rustow and K.P. Erikson (eds) *Comparative Political Dynamics*. New York: Harper Collins, pp.262–91.

Von Beyme, K. (1991b) 'Postmodernity, Postmaterialism and Political Theory', in K. Reif and R. Inglehart (eds) *Eurobarometer. The Dynamics of European Public Opinion*. London: Macmillan, pp.309–33.

Von Beyme, K. (1992) *Theorie der Politik im 20. Jahrhundert. Von der Moderne zur Postmoderne*. 2nd edn. Frankfurt: Suhrkamp.

Von Beyme, K. (1993) *Die politische Klasse im Parteienstaat*. Frankfurt: Suhrkamp.

Von Beyme, K. (1996a) *Das politische System der Bundesrepublik Deutschland nach der Vereinigung*. 8th edn. Munich: Piper.

Von Beyme, K. (1996b) *Transition to Democracy in Eastern Europe*. London: Macmillan (German edition 1994).

Wahlke, J.C. and Eulau, H. (eds) (1959) *Legislative Behavior. A Reader in Theory and Research*. Glencoe: The Free Press.

Wahlke, J.C., Eulau, H., Buchanan, W. and Ferguson, L.C. (1962) *The Legislative System. Explorations in Legislative Behavior*. New York: Wiley.

Wallerstein, I. (1974–1989), *The Modern World System*. New York: Academic Press, 3 vols.

Ward, R. and Rustow, D. (1964) *Political Development in Japan and Turkey*. Princeton: Princeton University Press.

Weber, M. (1921) *Gesammelte Politische Schriften*. Munich: Drei Masken Verlag.

Weber, M. (1922) *Wirtschaft und Gesellschaft*. Tubingen: J.C.B. Mohr.

Weber, M. (1947) *The Theory of Social and Economic Organization*. Glencoe: The Free Press.

Weber, M. (1948) *From Max Weber*. H.H. Gerth and C. Wright Mills (eds) London: Routledge.

Weber, M. (1958) 'Politik als Beruf', *Gesammelte Politische Schriften*. Tubingen: J.C.B. Mohr.

Weiner, M. (1962) *The Politics of Scarcity. Public Pressure and Political Response in India*. Chicago: University of Chicago Press.

Welan, M. (1992) 'Die österreichische Politikwissenschaft von innen und außen, wie ich sie sehe', *Österreichische Zeitschrift für Politikwissenschaft*, vol. 21, pp.445–52.

Weldon, T.D. (1962) *States and Morals. A Study in Political Conflict*. London: Murray.

Wiberg, M. (ed.) (1994) *Parliamentary Control in the Nordic Countries. Forms of Questioning and Behavioural Trends*. Jyväskylä: The Finnish Political Science Association.

Wildenmann, R. (1954) *Partei und Fraktion*. Meisenheim: Anton Hain.

Wildenmann, R. (1963) *Macht und Konsens als Problem der Innen- und Außenpolitik*. Frankfurt: Athenäum.

Wildenmann, R. (1985) 'Institutionalisierter Altruismus oder: Zehn Jahre ZUMA', in M. Kaase and M. Küchler (eds) *Herausforderungen der Empirischen Sozialforschung. Beiträge aus Anlaß des zehnjährigen Bestehens des Zentrums für Umfragen, Methoden und Analysen*. Mannheim: ZUMA, pp.18–23.

Wildenmann, R. (1986) 'The Problematic of Party Government' in Castles and Wildenmann (eds), pp.1–30.

Wildenmann, R. (1989) *Volksparteien. Ratlose Riesen?* Baden-Baden: Nomos.

Wildenmann, R. (1992) *Wahlforschung*. Mannheim: B.I.-Taschenbuchverlag.

Wilensky, H.L. (1954) *Industrial Relations. A Guide to Reading and Research*. Chicago: University of Chicago Press, Syllabus Division.

Wilensky, H.L. (1956) *Intellectuals in Labor Unions. Organizational Pressures on Professional Roles*. Glencoe: The Free Press.

Wilensky, H.L. and Lebeaux C.N. (1958) *Industrial Society and Social Welfare*. New York: The Free Press/Macmillan; enlarged edn 1965.

Wilensky, H.L. (1960) 'Work, Careers, and Social Integration', *International Social Science Journal*, vol. 12, pp.543–60.

Wilensky, H.L. (1961a) 'Orderly Careers and Social Participation. The Impact of Work History on Social Integration in the Middle Mass', *American Sociological Review*, vol. 26, pp.521–39.

Wilensky, H.L. (1961b) 'Life Cycle, Work Situation, and Participation in Formal Associations', in R.W. Kleemeier (ed.) *Aging and Leisure. Research Perspectives on the Meaningful Use of Time*. New York: Oxford University Press, pp.213–42.

Wilensky, H.L. (1961c) 'The Uneven Distribution of Leisure. The Impact of Economic Growth on "Free time"', *Social Problems*, vol. 9, pp.32–56.

Wilensky, H.L. (1961d) 'Social Structure, Popular Culture and Mass Behavior', *Studies in Public Communication*, vol. 3, pp.15–22.

Wilensky, H.L. (1964a) 'Mass Society and Mass Culture. Interdependence or Independence?' *American Sociological Review*, vol. 29, pp.173–97.

Wilensky, H.L. (1964b) 'The Professionalization of Everyone?' *American Journal of Sociology*, vol. 70, pp.137–58.

Wilensky, H.L. (1964c) 'Varieties of Work Experience', in H. Borow (ed.) *Man in a World at Work*. Boston: Houghton Mifflin, pp.125–54.

Wilensky, H.L. (1966a) 'Class, Class Consciousness, and American Workers', in W. Haber (ed.) *Labor in a Changing America*. New York: Basic Books, pp.12–44.

Wilensky, H.L. (1966b) 'Measures and Effects of Social Mobility', in N.J. Smelser and S.M. Lipset (eds) *Social Structure, Social Mobility and Economic Development*. Chicago: Aldine Press, pp.98–140.

Wilensky, H.L. (1967) *Organizational Intelligence. Knowledge and Policy in Government and Industry*. New York: Basic Books.

Wilensky, H.L. and Ladinsky, J. (1967) 'From Religious Community to Occupational Group. Structural Assimilation among Professors, Lawyers, and Engineers', *American Sociological Review*, vol. 32, pp.541–61.

Wilensky, H.L. (1968) 'Women's Work. Economic Growth, Ideology, and Social Structure', *Industrial Relations. A Journal of Economy and Society*, vol. 7, pp.235–48.

Wilensky, H.L. (1975) *The Welfare State and Equality. Structural and Ideological Roots of Public Expenditures*. Berkeley: University of California Press.

Wilensky, H.L. (1976) *The 'New Corporatism', Centralization, and the Welfare State*. Beverly Hills: Sage.

Wilensky, H.L. and Lawrence, A.T. (1979) 'Job Assignment in Modern Societies. A Re-examination of the Ascription-Achievement Hypothesis', in A.H. Hawley (ed.) *Societal Growth. Processes and Implications*. New York: The Free Press/Macmillan, pp.202–48.

Wilensky, H.L. (1981a) 'Family Life Cycle, Work, and the Quality of Life. Reflections on the Roots of Happiness, Despair and Indifference in Modern Society', in B.B. Gardell and G. Johansson (eds) *Working Life. A Social Science Contribution to Work Reform*. London: Wiley, pp.235–65.

Wilensky, H.L. (1981b) 'Leftism, Catholicism and Democratic Corporatism. The Role of Political Parties in Recent Welfare State Development', in P. Flora and A.J. Heidenheimer (eds) *The Development of Welfare States in Europe and America*. New Brunswick: Transaction Books, pp.345–82.

Wilensky, H.L. (1983) 'Political Legitimacy and Consensus. Missing Variables in the Assessment of Social Policy', in S.E. Spiro and E. Yuchtman-Yaar (eds) *Evaluating the Welfare State. Social and Political Perspectives*. New York: Academic Press, pp.51–74.

Wilensky, H.L., Luebbert, G.M., Hahn, S.R. and Jamieson, A.M. (1985) *Comparative Social Policy. Theories, Methods, Findings*. Berkeley: Institute of International Studies, University of California.

Wilensky, H.L. and Turner, L. (1987) *Democratic Corporatism and Policy Linkages. The*

Interdependence of Industrial, Labor-Market, Incomes, and Social Policies in Eight Countries. Berkeley: Institute of International Studies, University of California.

Wilensky, H.L. (1990) 'Common Problems, Divergent Policies. An 18-Nation Study of Family Policy', *Public Affairs Report*, vol. 31, pp.1–3. University of California at Berkeley: Institute of Governmental Studies.

Wilensky, H.L. (1993) 'The Nation-State, Social Policy, and Economic Performance', in M. Ferrara (ed.) *Globalizzazione e sistemi di welfare.* Torino, Italy: Edizioni della Fondazione G. Agnelli, pp.41–63.

Wilson, J. (1990) *Politically Speaking.* Oxford: Blackwell.

Wirth, L. (1928) *The Ghetto.* Chicago: University of Chicago Press.

Wittrock, B. (1993) 'The Modern University. The Three Transformations', in S. Rothblatt and B. Wittrock *The European and American University Since 1800. Historical and Sociological Essays.* Cambridge: Cambridge University Press.

Wolin, S. (1960) *Politics and Vision.* Boston: Little, Brown.

Wood, B. (1971) Committee on Comparative Politics, *A Report on The Activities of The Committee.* New York: Social Science Research Council.

Wright, V. (1972) *Le Conseil d'État sous le Second Empire.* Paris: A. Colin.

Wright, V. (1973a) 'L'archevêque d'Aix devant le Conseil d'État', *Revue d'Histoire de l'Eglise de France*, vol. 30, pp.259–89.

Wright, V. (1973b) 'Administration et Politique sous le Second Empire', *Procès Verbaux de l'Académie des Sciences Morales et Politiques, Institut de France*, May, pp.259–89.

Wright, V. (1973c) 'La réorganization du Conseil d'État en 1872', in *Études et Documents 1972*, Paris: Documentation Française, pp.21–64.

Wright, V. (1974) 'Politics and Administration under the Fifth French Republic', *Political Studies*, vol. 22, pp.44–65.

Wright, V. (1975) 'Politique et administration en temps de guerre', *Bulletin de la Société d'Histoire Moderne et Contemporaine*, vol. 15, pp.16–25.

Wright, V. (1976a) 'L'École d'Administration de 1848. Un échec révélateur', *Revue Historique*, vol. 260, pp.21–42.

Wright, V. (1976b) 'Les secrétaires généraux et les directeurs des administrations centrales: pouvoirs et pouvoir', in *Les Directeurs de Ministère en France.* Geneva: Droz, pp.38–78.

Wright, V. (1976c) 'L'administration du Ministère de l'Intérieur en temps de crise', *Administration*, autumn, pp.71–94.

Wright, V. (1978a) *The Government and Politics of France.* London: Macmillan.

Wright, V. (1978b) 'La vision interne du corps préfectoral', in *Les Préfets en France (1800–1940).* Geneva: Droz, pp.143–56.

Wright, V. (1982) 'Parlement et Administration aux débuts de la Troisième République: la crise', in *Parlement et Administration.* Geneva: Droz, pp.49–57.

Wright, V. (1984) 'Socialism and the Interdependent Economy. Industrial Policy Making Under the Mitterrand Presidency', *Government and Opposition*, vol. 19, pp.278–303.

Wright, V. and Machin, H. (eds) (1985) *Economic Policy and Policy Making Under the Mitterrand Presidency.* London: Pinter.

Wright, V. (1986) 'L'Administration locale sous le Gouvernement Thatcher. Problèmes et Paradoxes', *Revue Française d'Administration Publique*, vol. 38, pp.123–32.

Wright, V. (1989) 'The French Administration. Old Dilemmas and New Problems', in P. Hall, J. Hayward and H. Machin *Developments in French Politics.* London: Macmillan, pp.114–32.

Wright, V. (1990) 'The History of French Mayors. Lessons and Problems', *The Yearbook of European Administrative History*, vol. 2, pp.269–80.

Wright, V. (ed.) (1991) *The Representativity of Public Administration.* Brussels: International Institute of Administrative Science.

Wright, V. and Mazey, S. (1992) 'Les préfets de Vichy', in J. Azéma and F. Bédarida (eds) *Le régime de Vichy et les Français*. Paris: Fayard, pp.267–86.

Wright, V. (1992) 'The Administrative System and Market Regulation in Western Europe. Continuities, Exceptionalism and Convergence', *Rivista Trimestrale di Diritto Pubblico*, vol. 4, pp.1026–41.

Wright, V. (1993a) 'Les bureaux du Ministère de la Guerre', *Revue Historique des Armées*, vol. 3, pp.70–83.

Wright, V. (1993b) 'Whitehall et le local government à l'épreuve du thatchérisme', *L'Administration Territoriale en Europe*. Paris: Documentation Française, pp.94–117.

Wright, V. (1993c) 'Public Administration, Regulation, Deregulation and Reregulation', in K. Eliassen and J. Kooiman (eds) *Managing Public Organizations. Lessons from Contemporary European Experience*. London: Sage, pp.244–62

Wright, V. (1993d) 'Public Administration in the Nineties. Trends and Innovations', in *Public Administration in the Nineties*. Brussels: International Institute of Administrative Science, pp.33–48.

Wright, V. (1993e) *Les Privatisations en Europe. Programmes et problèmes*. Paris: Actes Sud (revised English edition: *Privatization in Western Europe*. London: Pinter).

Wright, V. (1994a), 'Conseil d'État and Consiglio di Stato. Le radici storiche della loro diversita', in Y. Mény (ed.) *Il Consiglio di Stato in Francia e in Italia*. Bologna: Il Mulino.

Wright, V. (1994b) 'Reshaping the State. The Implications for Public Administration', *West European Politics*, vol. 17, pp.102–34.

Wright, V. (1994c) 'The State and Major Enterprises. Persistent Complexity', in J. Hayward, *National Champions in an International Environment*. Oxford: Oxford University Press, pp.334–59.

Wright, V. (forthcoming), 'Le système territoriale en période de crise', in *L'Administration territoriale de la France, 1750–1940*. Paris: Fayard.

Wunder, B. (1995) *The Influences of the Napoleonic Model of Administration on the Administrative Organization of other Countries*. Brussels: International Institute of Administrative Sciences.

Zaller, J.R. (1992) *The Nature and Origins of Mass Opinion*. Cambridge: Cambridge University Press.

Zeuthen, F. (1958) *Videnskab og Velfærd i Ökonomisk Politik*. Copenhagen: Gads Forlag.

Name index

Crick, B. 55
Croce, B. 93
Crouch, C. 202
Crozier, M. 145, 221
Cushing, R. G. 247
Czada, R. 202, 204, 205

Daalder, H. 31, 32, 40, 52, 60, 73, 74, 82, 95, 105, 119, 120, 156, 170, 198, 208, 227–40, 245, 246, 251, 260, 261, 264, 313, 320
Dachs, H. 223
Dahl, R. A. 3, 10–11, 31–2, 60, 68–78, 80, 98, 104–6, 109, 116, 180, 198, 228, 232–3, 234, 235, 244, 245, 247, 261, 262, 279, 280, 312, 324
Dahrendorf, R. 141, 155, 156, 272–3
Damgaard, E. 223
Daudt, H. 237
Davies, J. 180
Davies, P. 129
Davis, K. 103
de Grazia, A. 299
de Janosi, P. 33, 119–20
de Madariaga, I. 15, 22
de Meur, G. 108
de Swaan, A. 235
Dealey, G. 289
den Hollander, A. N. J. 228
Dennis, J. 284
Derlien, H. U. 134
Deutsch, K. W. 6, 8, 9, 14, 35, 45, 49, 60, 82, 98, 116, 135, 137, 206, 210, 221, 244, 247, 250, 298
Dew, E. 246
Di Palma, G. 284
Diamant, A. 244
Diamond, L. 106
Dicey, A. V. 22
Dittrich, W. 205
Dix, R. H. 73, 246
Dogan, M. 31, 95, 105, 112, 135–6, 214, 235, 253
Döhler, M. 203
Dollard, C. 58
Dollard, J. 298
Douglas, J. 134
Downs, A. 212
Drees, W. 239–40
Duguit, L. 71
Dunleavy, P. 173
Dupeux, G. 166
Durant, H. 133
Durkheim, E. 57, 62, 104, 155, 180, 213, 267–8, 270–1, 277, 309, 312, 314
Duvall, R. 301
Duverger, M. 6, 97, 196, 206, 230, 255, 263

Easton, D. 16, 20, 62, 124, 180, 221, 255

Eckstein, H. 5, 9, 232, 245, 247, 262, 279, 280, 281, 299–300, 301, 302
Edinger, L. J. 253
Ehrmann, H. W. 6, 56, 58, 59
Eisenstadt, S. N. 30, 33, 79–92, 95, 235
Eldersveld, S. J. 133, 236, 257
Eliassen, K. A. 265
Elklit, J. 265
Ellis, W. 299
Engelmann, F. C. 73
Engels, F. 195
Epstein, L. D. 131
Erhard, L. 9
Erikson, E. H. 62
Eschenburg, T. 192, 195, 196, 197, 204
Eulau, H. 8, 133, 220, 221, 257, 260, 262, 264
Evans Pritchard, E. E. 80
Eynern, G. 204

Farneti, P. 52, 238
Ferejohn, J. 235
Festinger, L. 27
Fetcher, I. 103
Figgis, J. N. 71
Finer, C. J. 15, 18, 20, 24
Finer, H. 6, 16–17, 18, 54, 57, 143, 243
Finer, S. E. 15–25, 45, 52, 97, 115, 143, 149–50, 229, 231, 233, 238, 255
Firth, R. W. 80
Fisher, R. 257
Fisichella, D. 100
Flanagan, S. C. 63, 66–7
Flanigan, W. 78
Flora, P. 39, 170, 324
Follett, M. P. 71
Foltz, W. J. 73, 78
Forsthoff, E. 44
Fortes, M. 80
Fougère, L. 168
Fouillée, A. 142
Fraenkel, E. 204
Franklin, M. 319
Freud, S. 56, 57, 225
Friedberg, E. 145
Friedman, M. 311
Friedrich, C. J. 5, 7–14, 16, 18, 57, 97, 98, 206, 207, 208, 210, 213, 214, 228, 230, 231, 255, 263, 265

Galenson, W. 258, 263
Galtung, J. 29, 260, 268
Garceau, O. 58
Gardner, J. 58
Gastil, R. D. 78
Geiger, T. 256
Gentile, G. 93
Gerlich, P. 215–26
Ginsberg, M. 80, 142
Girtler, R. 226
Glaessner, G.-J. 211

Glass, K. 223
Gluckman, M. 80
Goethe, W. 215, 226
Goguel, F. 166
Goldhammer, H. 80, 311
Goldstone, J. A.
Goldthorpe, J. H. 172, 202
Gómez-Reino, M. 112
Gorbachev, M. 212
Gosnell, H. F. 54, 55, 57, 62, 66, 312
Gottweis, H. 226
Grabosky, P. N. 302
Graham, H. D. 300
Grande, E. 203
Gray, J. 284
Graziano, L. 99
Greaves, H. R. G. 157
Green, T. H. 142, 154
Greenstein, F. I. 106
Grémion, C. 145
Grémion, P. 145
Grew, R. 59
Grofman, B. 249
Grosser, A. 73, 234
Gruner, E. 197, 205
Guetzkow, H. S. 27
Gunther, R. 106
Gurr, T. R. 136, 298–308, 324
Gusfield, J. R. 311
Guyot, J. 78

Haas, E. B. 14, 231, 245, 246, 287, 289
Hacker, J. 211
Haerpfer, C. 138
Hagtvet, B. 39
Hall, P. A. 173
Hanf, T. 246
Harff, B. 303–4, 306, 308
Harper, S. N. 54
Harrison, W. 229
Hartmann, R. 139
Hartling, F. 196
Hartz, L. 231
Håstad, E. 254
Hayward, J. S. 15, 19, 24, 25, 140–51, 168–9, 175
Headrick, T. 64
Healey, D. W. 139
Heckscher, G. 230
Heclo, H. 145
Hegel, G. W. F. 93, 154, 165
Heller, H. 104
Hempel, C. G. 72
Hennessy, P. 17
Henningsen, S. 254, 259
Hermens, F. A. 44–5, 47, 197, 204
Hermet, G. 106, 186–91
Herring, P. 57, 58
Heyen, E. V. 172
Hibbs, D. A. Jr. 321
Hilferding, R. 228
Hinsley, F. H. 229
Hintze, O. 64
Hirschman, A. O. 35, 104, 258

Subject index